A NEWSPAPER HISTORY OF ENGLAND
1792–1793

A NEWSPAPER HISTORY
OF ENGLAND
1792–1793

by

LUCYLE WERKMEISTER

UNIVERSITY OF NEBRASKA PRESS · LINCOLN

Publishers on the Plains

UNP

Copyright © 1967 by the University of Nebraska Press
Library of Congress Catalog Card Number 67–13209

Manufactured in the United States of America

To

Mother

with

many grateful thoughts

Preface

The purpose of this volume is to view the world of 1792–1793 through the eyes of a contemporary reader of the London daily press. It will be followed by two other such volumes, each covering an additional two years, so that the study will finally encompass the period 1792–1797. Since I am attempting a new kind of history, contemptuous of documents and generally unconcerned with the accuracy and importance of its material, something should perhaps be said in its defense. Most obviously, I hope that it will prove useful to critics, biographers, and other scholars of the late eighteenth century, who might like to know something about the temper of the age in which they are working. To represent a Coleridge, a Wordsworth, and even a Burke as reacting to some imaginative construct, based on documents which they themselves never saw, has the disadvantage of being unrealistic. The documents to which they did react were in the main printed materials and especially, as Coleridge often enough lamented, newspapers; and the very fact that the information which they derived from these sources was frequently too trivial to become matter of formal history and in many instances unreliable besides would seem to make it all the more significant. In some instances the data may also prove helpful, supplying information not otherwise available. That I have myself found it helpful will be evident from two companion volumes, now in preparation: *Coleridge and the London Newspapers 1790–1797* and *Boswell and the London Newspapers 1790–1795*. I hope in addition that a detailed study of a period, different from and yet in some respects remarkably similar to our own, may have some interest in itself. The newspapers should in any event have interest for historians, for what was going on in the press during these years was at least as crucial politically as anything which was going on in Parliament.

If the chapters which follow are tediously detailed, it is partly because, to producers and readers of newspapers, every story is important for the moment, partly because each of them contributes its bit to the panorama. Since whatever has interested the newspapers has interested me, I have been much concerned with the Parliamentary debates, and I have delved into other matters insofar as they were newsworthy. I wish I could say that I have been an impartial reader. I have been impartial in the sense that I have not peeked behind the scenes. If Fox emerges from these chronicles a nobler figure than Pitt or Burke, it is not because of personal bias, for I have searched no correspondence, read no diaries, and except in rare instances have consulted no extra-newspaper sources for the purpose of ferreting out motives or even assessing the accuracy of newspaper accounts. But, since the newspapers were themselves violently partial, I have had to take a point of view, and the point of view I have taken coincides generally with that of the *Morning Chronicle*, the *Chronicle* being the most mature newspaper of the group, its evaluations the most reasonable, and its position, from all I can ascertain, the most representative of the country at large. More important, perhaps, I have had to be interested in the newspapers themselves, for the significance of a newspaper story always depends in part on the character of the newspaper which publishes it, and, when the press is as corrupt as it was in England during the 1790's, the character is all-important. Whatever I could learn about these newspapers has therefore been included, and, since I have had to reach outside the newspapers for much of this material, it would not have been common knowledge to readers of the time. Here I can say only that the corruption itself was common knowledge, so that, although Coleridge and Lamb might for example have been shocked to discover that one of their masters at Christ's Hospital was a paid propagandist for the Government, they did know that there were such propagandists and that almost all the newspapers they were reading were in the pay of one political faction or another. They, as for that matter we today, edited what they read and came to much the same conclusions, I like to think, as those here represented.

The newspapers consulted have been those in the Burney collection of the British Museum. If I have cited some newspapers more often than others, it is partly because the files of some newspapers are more complete than others, partly because some newspapers are simply more important. I have also tried to avoid duplication, and, since *The Times* and the *Gazetteer* have already been thoroughly studied, I have referred to them only when I can supplement the studies or reinterpret the material by bringing it into context. So far as quotations are concerned, the newspapers speak for themselves. In the most desperate cases, I have inserted a *sic*, but I have not destroyed the flavor of any paragraph by tampering with its syntax or orthography. Identifications of newspaper sources are indicated parenthetically in the text; identifications of extra-newspaper sources are indicated in notes. Sources are included in the introductory part, however, only when the material is new or when, alas, it corrects something I have previously said. Readers are otherwise referred to my earlier book, *The London Daily Press, 1772–1792* (Lincoln: University of Nebraska Press, 1963), on which this first part leans. The Bibliographical Note is in fact reprinted from that book. Presentation of the material has posed a major problem. Since no part of it is significant except in context, a strictly chronological presentation on a day-by-day basis might seem to have been indicated. But the material is much too complex for such treatment. I have therefore chosen to present it under loose topical headings, thus imposing some degree of order on the chaos. Factual background has been supplied from time to time for reasons of orientation, and readers who are still bewildered may consult the chronological table. Similarly, I have added to the index an identification of names in the hope of diminishing confusion on that score. Although I cannot, even so, promise that what follows will be easy reading, I can hope that it will not prove formidable.

Foremost among my creditors are the American Philosophical Society, which financed the research, and the staff of the British Museum, which made the research a delight. I cannot be sufficiently grateful to either. I am almost as indebted to the reference staff of Doheny Library, University of Southern California, without whose assistance the list of unidentified names would be considerably longer than it presently is. Permissions to quote have been graciously granted by Ernest Benn Ltd., successor to Home & Van Thal, publishers of Arthur Aspinall's *Politics and the Press c. 1780–1850* (London, 1949); by Hutchinson & Co., publishers of *The Farington Diary by Joseph Farington, R.A.* (London, 1922); by Arthur Barker Ltd., publisher of *Mrs. Jordan and Her Family*, ed. Arthur Aspinall (London, 1951); by *The Times*, publisher of *The History of The Times 1785–1841* (London, 1935); and by the Cambridge University Press, publisher of *The Later Correspondence of George III*, ed. Arthur Aspinall (Cambridge, 1963). Since no one can write a book of this sort without friends, I am bound to add that I have been blessed with some very knowledgeable ones, who know much more about specific aspects of the subject than I and have been extremely generous with their assistance. To Dr. David Erdman, to Dr. Cecil Oldman, to Professor Lewis Patton, to Professor Burton Pollin, to Professor Peter Stanlis, and to Professor Paul Zall, I can say only—thank you, gentlemen.

Contents

Preface   vii

I. PERSPECTIVE: 1 JANUARY, 1792

The Court, the Cabinet, and the Character of the Opposition   3
The Royal Dukes   11
Character of Newspapers: The Ministerial Press   19
The *Daily Advertiser* and the Opposition Press   30
The Theaters   42
    Notes for Part I   44

II. ANNUS ANTE BELLUM: 1792

The Opening of Parliament   49
The *Oracle*, the Prince of Wales, and Trouble in the Post Office   55
The *Morning Post* and the Westminster Election of 1788   63
The Friends of the People   72
The Proclamation Against Seditious Writings   79
The Theaters   85
Some Aftermaths of the Prorogation   96
Death of the Earl of Guilford   104
Will Pitt Resign?   111
Pitt Will Not Resign Willingly   119
Newspaper Reactions to a Fox-Pitt Coalition   125
The Insurrection Which Wasn't   134
The Convocation of Parliament   142
The Alien Act   151
    Notes for Part II   158

III. THE FIRST YEAR OF THE WAR: 1793

Character of the Newspapers: The Opposition Press   163
The Ministerial Press   169
Passage of the Alien Act   179

A Time for Conjectures 187
The Government and the Friends of the Liberty of the Press 194
A Message and a Postponement 202
Debate on the King's Message and the Declaration of War 209
Early Reactions to the War 218
The Government and the Reformers 228
Elections, the War, and Mr. Fox 238
The Traitorous Correspondence Bill 248
Passage of the Traitorous Correspondence Act 259
The Battle for Election Reforms 266
Immediate Aftermaths of Grey's Motion 275
The Government and Lord Rawdon; the Government and Mr. Burke 285
Patronage, Politics, and the War 293
Fox, the War, and the "Ingratitude" of Mr. Burges 302
The Finer Arts and Artists 311
State of the Theaters During the Parliamentary Recess 318
Fads and Fashions of 1793 328
Expiration of the Tattersall–Weltje Lease 332
The First Prorogation: Punishments 341
The First Prorogation: Rewards 349
The First Prorogation: State of the War 359
The Second Prorogation: On to Dunkirk! 368
The Second Prorogation: Demise of the *Diary* 378
Catastrophe at Dunkirk 389
First Alarm of an Invasion 401
The Third Prorogation 412
"Pitt's Manifesto" 420
Legal and Prison Reforms; The Death of Lord George Gordon 432
Prosecution of the *Morning Chronicle* 443
The Alarm Postponed 453
The First Preparations for the Opening of Parliament 465
    Notes for Part III 472

Chronological Table 477

Bibliographical Note 488

Index 493

A picture section follows page 212

I

PERSPECTIVE: 1 JANUARY, 1792

Although this chronicle is concerned with the London daily press and the world as it was represented by that press only during the years 1792–1793, it would have little meaning without a preliminary glance at the events which preceded, at the people who were responsible for those events, and at the newspapers themselves. The present survey therefore takes as its vantage point the beginning of the year 1792, which it attempts to understand in terms of its immediate past.

The Court, the Cabinet and the Character of the Opposition

The King was the Hanoverian, George III, who had succeeded to the throne in 1760. He was conservative in every respect. His convictions were strongly religious, and his interests, other than politics, were generally simple, running to agriculture, the hunt, and music, especially Handel. His marriage had not been a love match, but it had turned out well, for Queen Charlotte, also a German, was quite as conservative as he, and their tastes were at least compatible. Although the King liked people, he preferred to meet them casually, while the Queen was content with the society of her daughters and her companion, the dowdy Madame Schwellenberg, whom she had brought with her from Germany. Their entertaining was usually informal: a few friends assembled to hear the King read a sermon, to listen to some Handel, to play cards with the Queen, or to engage in an hour's dancing. State entertaining was reduced to a minimum, it was done on an almost miserly scale, and the Queen and Princesses were likely to appear in gowns of their own making. When their presence was not demanded in London, the King and Queen were usually at Windsor Castle, and even during the season they tended to take up residence at the Queen's palace, Buckingham House, rather than at the more formal St. James's Palace. But, although the Court was in no sense brilliant, the newspapers liked to think that it represented something more important: domestic values. Hence they had rejoiced at the birth of every one of the fifteen children, thirteen of whom were still living, and they were even prepared to rejoice at the birth of a sixteenth, when, on 31 July, 1792, the *Star* announced: "It is most confidently [although, as it turned out, erroneously] reported in the upper circles, that her MAJESTY is in a fair way to give an increase of happiness to the loyal subjects of this country, by an additional security to the Protestant succession of British Sovereigns."

In fact, the Royal Family was far from harmonious. By 1792 only the six Princesses were living at home. Ranging in age from nine to twenty-six, they appeared regularly with their parents in public, but the newspapers could never think of anything to say about them except that they were present and as usual were dressed alike. They were not even identified by name. Of the seven Princes, the four youngest were traveling abroad, and the three oldest—George, Prince of Wales, Frederick, Duke of York, and William, Duke of Clarence—had establishments of their own. Not one of them had demonstrated the slightest

3

affection for his parents, and the Prince of Wales and the Duke of York, with the occasional connivance of the Duke of Clarence, had long been in open conflict with them. At first, the newspapers had been sympathetic with the King and Queen, but Charlotte's conduct during her husband's illness of 1788–1789 had altered that situation. The spectacle of a mother engaged in a power struggle against the interests of her sons and seemingly applauding a man (Colonel Charles Lennox) who had just wounded one of them (the Duke of York) in a duel was too much for the press. The Queen was severely censured at the time, and, although these events were now apparently forgotten, she was still an object of suspicion. It was sometimes hinted that she was amassing a personal fortune in diamonds at her subjects' expense, and there was considerable disapproval of her lavish gifts to Madame Schwellenberg, especially since all of them were promptly transported to Germany.

The newspapers continued to be sympathetic with George, whose character as a parent, far from being impugned by the estrangement from his sons, was made only the more poignant. Since no newspaper could resist him in the rôle of a grieving father, subject to attacks of dementia besides, there was a tendency to regard him as a grieving monarch as well, utterly devoted to his subjects and as distressed as they were at the numerous injustices. Such an opinion required an immense amount of forgetfulness, for George had commenced his reign as a thoroughgoing autocrat, and, since he had had a large patronage at his disposal for the purchase of "friends," he had set out to manage the political affairs of the country himself. He had succeeded nicely until 1780, when the Commons had taken the first step toward regaining its integrity by resolving that "the influence of the Crown has increased, is increasing, and ought to be diminished." It had taken a second step in early 1782 by ousting Frederick Lord North (after 1790 the second Earl of Guilford), whose government had been in effect only a government from the Throne. After a two-year battle with the Commons, George had rallied his forces at the end of 1783 and, overriding the will of the lower House, had appointed as First Minister the young William Pitt. He had also managed on Pitt's behalf the crucial elections of 1784. Since these activities had greatly alarmed the country, his popularity, by the time the elections were over, was at a very low ebb, but Pitt was secure. At this point George supposedly retired from politics, and by 1792 all his sins had been forgiven. Not only did the Opposition newspapers hold Pitt singly responsible for the maneuver of late 1783, but most of them seriously believed that the King, now represented as a great humanitarian, himself disapproved of the Pitt Government. The *Morning Chronicle* had reservations on both accounts. It did not believe that George had retired, and it could not remember one single instance in which he had supported the interests of the people against those of William Pitt.

For George's purposes Pitt was in any event ideal. Although he had previously been identified with the cause of reform, he had promptly found reason to oppose it and to support instead everything which George had supported. He was also much shrewder than George. He was craftier in the management of people, wilier in the management of elections; and, by ignoring a law here and slipping through a loophole there, he had by now succeeded in subverting every due process and converting the vast machinery of state into a simple instrument for keeping himself in power. In addition, he was fashioned by nature to be a scapegoat, for one had only to look at him to dislike him. According to Cyrus Redding,[1] whose description is more charitable than most, "the sight of Pitt's person was not calculated to strengthen his cause. . . . His countenance, forbidding and arrogant, was repellant of affection and not made to be loved, full of disdain, of self will, and as a whole destitute of massiveness; his forhead alone was lofty and good." Evidently few of his contemporaries were susceptible to "foreheads," for, from 1783 on, Pitt was blamed for everything which happened, the King being therefore absolved altogether. The feeling about Pitt was strong. Inside Parliament the small opposition which had somehow survived the elections was extremely bitter, and even the Members who supported his measures often did so apologetically. Outside Parliament he was sarcastically known as "Our Heaven-born Minister" and "The Immaculate Boy" or more directly as "The Arch Apostate." A demonstration for him was unheard of, and, to avoid demonstrations against him, he avoided crowds, even to the point at times of lingering at a state dinner until the other guests had departed and the assembled throng dispersed. The newspapers also disliked him, for, although the Government paid lavishly for newspaper support and prosecuted lavishly for newspaper criticism, Pitt could rarely count on more than half of the dailies.

To begin with, Pitt's closest associate was his Secretary of the Treasury, George Rose. Rose was in charge of public relations: that is, he subsidized newspapers, engaged writers, contracted for pamphlets, handbills, hatbills, and ballads, purchased votes, and hired bludgeoners, all with Treasury money. He was very able and very enthusiastic. He was in fact too enthusiastic, for his management of the elections of 1788 was still an embarrassment to the Government, especially since it had been repeatedly demonstrated that he had acted under the direct supervision of Pitt. Although Rose was still Secretary of the Treasury in 1792, the second Secretary being Charles Long, and was still engaged in the same activities, he was now a distinct liability, and other arrangements would have to be made soon. Pitt had already taken a step in this direction by excluding him from the inner council, which by this time consisted only of himself, Henry Dundas, and William Wyndham Grenville.

Dundas, who had been Treasurer of the Navy since 1783 and Secretary of State for the Home Department since June, 1791, had been generally regarded as a fool. Blindly devoted to Pitt, he had thus far done his cause more harm than good. His speeches had been delivered in a thick Scots accent, and he had been likely to trip over a sentence, furnishing the Opposition with an hilarious phrase, which it could quote to bantering advantage in subsequent speeches. In his zeal to support the Government's cause, he had also been likely to blurt out one of its secrets. The speeches had been all the more ridiculous because they had been sprinkled with boasts of his popularity in Scotland, where he was notoriously unpopular. But Dundas had responded to the laughter and to the numerous jokes about his "modesty" and "popularity" with such great good humor that the Opposition had found itself liking him; or at least it could hardly dislike anyone as frankly unprincipled and openly prostitute as he. Pitt also liked him. In fact, to everyone's astonishment he had preferred the company of Dundas to that of anyone else. Journalists and cartoonists, who were at a loss to account for the intimacy on any other terms, had for years attributed it to a common fondness for red port. "[PITT] is a six-bottle man," the spurious *Star* had confided for example on 27 April, 1789. "The MINISTER will yield the Bacchanalian palm to none but DUNDAS." To everyone's even greater astonishment, Pitt respected him, for, not only had he made him Home Secretary, but he was gradually assigning to him the responsibilities which had previously been assigned to George Rose. But the real surprise was yet to come, for the Henry Dundas of 1792 was quite different from the Henry Dundas of even 1791. This Henry Dundas was not harmless.

The third member of the triumvirate was Pitt's cousin. There was no fun in Grenville, and neither were there any surprises. Always closely associated with the Government, he had in 1783 been appointed Paymaster General, in 1789 Speaker, and the same year Home Secretary. In 1790 he had been made President of the Board of Control, which position he still held, and also created Baron Grenville, so that he could manage the Government's affairs in the House of Lords. Since June, 1791, when he had quit the Home Department in favor of Dundas, he had functioned as Foreign Secretary.

Many of Pitt's other followers were early defectors. Principal among this group were perhaps William Eden and the Duke of Richmond. Originally a follower of Lord North, Eden had defected in 1785, and, since he had a talent for intrigue, he had been extremely useful to Pitt during his early struggles with the Opposition and especially during the Regency crisis of 1788–1789. But, once these were over, Pitt had had no employment for him at home, and Eden had therefore been rewarded with the Irish title of Baron Auckland and dispatched to the Continent on various diplomatic missions, all of an intriguing nature. The Duke of Richmond had defected in late 1783, just in time to become Pitt's Master General of Ordnance. His only qualification for that post was that he was a general in the Army, the Rockingham Whigs having got him the commission in 1782; and his only qualification for the generalship was that he was "thought" to have been Aide-de-Camp to Prince Ferdinand of Brunswick at the Battle of Minden in 1759. By 1792 he regarded himself as an authority on all military matters and also an authority on politics, his own being as far to the right as they had once been to the left; and he was sufficiently impulsive, sensitive, and hot-headed to fight anyone who thought otherwise.

As an alarmist the Duke of Richmond was equaled only by Edmund Burke, a more recent defector. Although Burke was too passionate and self-willed to conform with the principles of any party, he had previously allied himself with the Whigs because he had been personally attached to their leader, Charles James Fox, and because he had shared their alarm about the activities of the King. During those years he had opposed the war with the American colonies, had advocated certain economic reforms, and, more important in the present context, had busied himself with the affairs of the East India Company, especially with those of its Governor General, Warren Hastings, against whom he had initiated an impeachment proceeding. Although the King and hence the Government were strongly opposed to it and Hastings's agent, Major John Scott, had invested a fortune in newspaper abuse of Burke in order to prevent it, Pitt had finally found it expedient to support the impeachment; and in 1788 the trial of Hastings had begun, with Burke as principal prosecutor and the House of Lords in the rôle of jury. Pitt had had no reason for concern about the outcome of this trial, for the Lords could be counted on to acquit as soon as they had an opportunity; but he had had reason for concern about the evidence, which was as damaging to the King and the Government as it was to Hastings. Hence, although the trial might have been concluded within a few months, the hearings had been spaced so widely apart that it had dragged on and on, while the Ministerial newspapers, with the continued assistance of Major Scott, had tried desperately to rouse public feeling against it on the ground that it was expensive, tedious, time-consuming, and of consequence only to Burke, as in fact it was.

By 1792 Burke, still a zealot with respect to the prosecution of Hastings, had acquired a second zeal: the prosecution of "Jacobinism." The French Revolution had been acclaimed by the English as a triumph of freedom over despotism, comparable to their own Revolution of 1688, and there had been a surge of enthusiasm in 1790, as various societies celebrated its first anniversary. But there was no enthusiasm in Burke, who had seen in that event the end of religion, the annihilation of rights, and the destruction of the whole social order. On 1 November of that year, he had published his *Reflections on the Revolution in France*. Although Burke had no personal following, he was a man of stature, force, ability, and, it was thought, independence and integrity: at least, so far as anyone presently knew, he had accepted no sinecure or pension as reward for his long service to the Whigs. Hence, although the work had made no converts, it had attracted a great deal of attention, as so had some of the numerous replies, especially James Mackintosh's *Vindiciae Gallicae* and Part I of Thomas Paine's *Rights of Man* (both 1791).

The *Reflections* had marked no change in Burke's political philosophy, for Burke had always regarded the British state as an equilibrium of forces, but it had marked a radical change in his politics, for, whereas he had previously thought that the equilibrium was threatened by the Crown, he now thought that it was threatened by the people. This view had accorded nicely with that of Pitt, who depended on a strong King and a weak populace to keep himself in office, and of course it had accorded beautifully with that of the King himself. Although no newspaper had suggested that the *Reflections* was commissioned by the Government, the work had been interpreted as a defection, and it had therefore been agreed that Burke was in a fine bargaining position respecting the trial of Hastings. Rumors of negotiations between him and Pitt or between him and Rose had appeared in the press as early as June, 1790. But, as time went on, with no evident concession on the Government's part, the Opposition newspapers concluded that Burke had been duped, and by 1792 they were regarding him as primarily a tool of William Pitt. There was a great deal of evidence to support this conclusion.

As a politician Burke had always been naïve, for he had no understanding of people, and his passionate convictions made him easy prey for anyone who appeared to be sympathetic. Pitt, on the other hand, was a shrewd judge of people, a thoroughgoing opportunist, and by 1790 an adept at the political game, so that, if he had not undertaken the management of Burke, it would have been strange indeed. The first evidence that he had done so involved the reformers. The issue prior to 1790 had been the power of the Crown versus the power of the people, and, with the appearance of the *Reflections*, Burke and Pitt had agreed that the power of the people should be held in abeyance. But there were several ways of achieving this: by strengthening the power of the Crown, by confining the suffrage to its present narrow sphere, and by preserving corruptions, thus enabling the Government to control the outcome of elections. The *Reflections* was concerned only with an extension of the suffrage: it was therefore opposed only to any alteration in the Constitution and so only to radical reform and radical reformers. Pitt was concerned only with the eradication of corruptions, for, so long as the corruptions existed, it made no difference to him how many people voted or how frequently they voted. From 1791 on, Burke was just as opposed to the eradication of corruptions as he was to changes in the Constitution, and like Pitt he was stoutly defending the influence of the Crown.

There was also the matter of war. As a means, the Opposition press thought, of diverting attention from the corruptions, Pitt had in 1790 tried to involve the country in a war with Spain, and, having failed, had subsequently tried to start a war with Russia. Although the *Reflections* had not mentioned a war, Burke was by 1791 advocating a war with France as essential to the preservation of the British Constitution, and he was being supported by the Ministerial newspapers. Finally, there was the matter of political allegiance. After 1790 Burke always voted with the Government, and in mid-1791 he had broken with Fox. But, instead of resigning from "The Party," he had maintained his membership in the Whig Club, had continued to sit with the Whigs, and, on the ground that the Whigs had deserted him, not he them, had published in August, 1791, his *Appeal from the Old to the New Whigs*. He was still sitting with the Whigs at the beginning of 1792, was still making speeches in support of the Government, and was still representing himself in every one of them as "an old man," cruelly "deserted" by his "friends." This tactic must certainly have been suggested by Pitt.

Although no one responded to the *Appeal*, the Opposition was vulnerable, partly because, with Pitt's management of the elections, it had no hope of coming into power or even getting a bill through Parliament, principally because it consisted only of a collection of factions. The factions had combined in early 1783 for the purpose of ousting the King-supported Shelburne Government and had subsequently formed a government of their own, which had lasted from April to December of that year. The head of this coalition had been the Duke of Portland, with Lord North (second Earl of Guilford) as Home Secretary, Charles James Fox as Foreign Secretary, and Richard Brinsley Sheridan as Secretary of the Treasury. Since the four were ideologically at variance, nothing much was accomplished while they were in office, and the combination might well have dissolved upon their relinquishing it, had it not been for the "secret influence" of the King and the consequent "backstairs" entrance of William Pitt. Thereafter they were at least united in animosity toward Pitt. During the years which followed, the leadership of the group had quietly shifted from the Duke of Portland to Fox, whose personality and mediations had not only held the heterogeneous elements together, but had even unified them, albeit on a personal rather than an ideological basis; and, since Fox was a Whig, the whole Opposition had come to be known as Whigs or simply "The Party."

Fox had all the personal qualifications for leadership which Pitt lacked, for he inspired confidence, and he evoked loyalty even from those who disagreed with him. Outside Parliament he was enormously popular. Every year a host of devoted friends and ecstatic admirers celebrated his birthday and the anniversary of his election as Member for Westminster at one of the local taverns, the attendance sometimes being so large that an additional tavern had to be engaged for the overflow. Everything he said mattered to the people, who idolized him both as a man and as a statesman, for, although he was always scandalously in debt, the debts never interfered with his conviviality, and his conviviality never interfered with his political duties. Fox was called "The Man of the People," and he regarded himself as precisely that, a representative of the people's interests in Parliament against the Government, which represented the interests of the Crown. This was the import of all his speeches. On the people's behalf he had fought for peace, for a free press, and for the repeal of discriminatory laws. On the other hand he was no democrat. He was opposed to a Constitutional extension of the suffrage, and, although he felt that the people had a right to be heard, he liked to tell them when to speak and what to say. It was greatly to his credit that he had never used his influence to further his ambitions, to assist The Party, or to encourage sedition of any sort.

To the right of Fox in all respects were the Duke of Portland and Lord Guilford. Politically they were sympathetic with the Government, but thus far their contempt for Pitt and their admiration of Fox had outweighed their convictions. Both of them had followers. Among the Duke of Portland's followers were Earl Fitzwilliam, Earl Spencer, Lord Robert Spencer (brother of the fourth Duke of Marlborough), William Windham of Norfolk, and the Duke of Portland's son, presently called the Marquess of Titchfield. Lord Guilford's followers included the Earl of Carlisle, Viscount Stormont, Baron Loughborough (since 1780 Lord Chief Justice of the Common Pleas), Sir Gilbert Elliot, William Adam, and Lord Guilford's son, George Augustus North. In addition, there was the Earl of Shelburne, now (since 1784) the Marquess of Lansdowne. Lord Lansdowne disliked the Opposition, having been undone by it in 1783, but he was compelled to support it, since he detested Pitt.

Also no part of the Opposition, although voting with it, was Pitt's brother-in-law, Earl Stanhope. Stanhope, who was as much of a Jacobin as Thomas Paine, constituted a faction of his own, but, despite his outspoken radicalism, he had been ignored by the newspapers, probably out of deference to Pitt. Between Lord Stanhope and Fox was a large group, dedicated to peace and favoring reform to some degree, but, since this group was lacking a program, organization, and leadership, it was a collection of individuals rather than a faction. In the Lords there were the Duke of Bedford, the Duke of Norfolk, and the Earl of Lauderdale. The Dukes of Bedford and Norfolk were as yet politically inconspicuous, the Duke of Norfolk figuring in the news principally because he happened to be one of the wealthiest, the most slovenly, and the most convivial men in England. The conspicuous member of the trio was the Earl of Lauderdale, who was himself a man of considerable substance. When he succeeded to his title in 1789, he was already well-to-do, having married a daughter of Anthony Todd, Secretary of the General Post Office, seven years earlier. With her he had got a dowry of £50,000, along with the promise of an additional £10,000 at the birth of every child. As a politician, according to Lord Holland,[2] he "[possessed] two slight defects, viz. a restlessness of disposition, and a studied contempt of general opinion. The one, in spite of his disinterested conduct, led strangers to distrust his political integrity, and to attribute his active and friendly exertions to a love of intrigue and selfish designs; the other impressed all persons at that period with a very false notion, that his principles and designs were as extravagant and mischievous as his exertions for his party were active and, perhaps, factious. His attachment to Mr. Fox was invariable. . . ." Lord Lauderdale led the Opposition in the Lords, and, although he "spoke broad Scotch, and was not remarkable for correct grammar even in that dialect,"[3] he was much admired by the people, in England as well as in Scotland. The real problem in this case was the title, for, since it was Scotch, he was one of the elected peers and hence potentially removable.

In the Commons there were Samuel Whitbread, Philip Francis, William Henry Lambton, Charles Grey, Thomas Erskine, Michael Angelo Taylor, and Sheridan. Although all of them were well known to readers of newspapers,

Erskine was especially familiar, since he was defender of Whig interests in the courts, as well as Attorney General to the Prince of Wales. Taylor was perhaps even more familiar, for, since the Government had been trying to get rid of him ever since he first entered Parliament in 1784, he had been one of the principal butts of the Ministerial press. In 1785 Taylor had acquired the epithet of "The Chicken" because of his protest that he was "but a chicken in the profession [of the law]." He was still called "The Chicken" in 1792, but the *World* had evidently forgotten why, for on 11 January, 1793, it suggested that the nickname was owing to "the circumstance of his grandfather having been a Poulterer— which, in the Clare-market classics, signifies a Chicken Butcher." Most familiar was, however, Sheridan, for, although he had no personal following, he had a great deal of influence, being principal proprietor of Drury Lane, manager of the press for the Opposition, and intimate of the Prince of Wales. Unlike Lord Lauderdale, Sheridan was notoriously ambitious, and he was usually engaged in some kind of intrigue for the furthering of his own interests. That all of his intrigues had hitherto failed is less marvelous than that only one or two of them had aroused Fox's suspicions. Fox evidently had a very trusting nature, or he did not read the newspapers.

The Royal Dukes

Most of Sheridan's intrigues had involved the Prince of Wales, who also had a penchant for intrigue whenever money was concerned. The Prince was born in 1762 and had been in conflict with his father almost constantly since. With the birth of Frederick (Duke of York) in 1763 and William (Duke of Clarence) in 1765, the advantage was on his side, for, since both of them supported him, the three constituted a cabal, which by 1776 had become unmanageable. In 1780 the Prince had reached the age of eighteen. Despite a tendency toward corpulence, he was handsome, and he was also intelligent and accomplished, with a rich voice, elegant manners, sensitive tastes, and a fondness for music, literature, theater, and dress. In addition, he was amoral. He had no respect for truth, no loyalty to anyone except himself, and he had acquired an expensive passion for older women, his current mistress being the actress, poet, and novelist, Mary Robinson. By virtue of being born Duke of Cornwall, he had come into an immediate inheritance of £12,000 a year, and, since he was now traditionally entitled to an establishment of his own, he was looking forward to a considerable augmentation. But on this occasion he had been outwitted by the King, who had not only declined to recommend the establishment, but had taken steps to dissolve the junto by sending Frederick to Hanover for a lengthy military education and William to sea.

Hence the Prince had remained at home for an additional three years, but the results had been far from happy, for, at the end of that period, he had been substantially in debt. The settlement with Mrs. Robinson had itself been costly enough. In 1781 the King had paid her £5,000 to suppress publication of letters, and the Prince had been obliged to add a £600 lifetime annuity, plus a £200 lifetime annuity for her daughter as survivor, in order to recover a promissory note for £20,000. Other fortunes had meanwhile been lavished on further romantic adventures, on disreputable companions, and on wine, to which he was now addicted, with no evident concern for the future. But, in fact, the Prince had been greatly concerned, and, with an eye on political developments, he had craftily prepared for the settlement of his affairs by establishing an intimacy with Fox. This time the coup had been his, for, when he reached his majority, as he did in 1783, the Fox-North Coalition was in power, and the Duke of Portland had immediately asked Parliament for a settlement of £100,000 a year. Taken aback, the King had extravagantly revised his own recommendation, suggesting £50,000 a year, plus an additional £50,000 to liquidate debts and renovate Carlton House, which he himself donated as residence. The annuity was to be paid from the civil list. With the £12,000 from the Duchy of Cornwall, the Prince therefore had £62,000 a year, which was an adequate income and certainly a much larger one than he would have had without the Whigs' assistance. Since the Whigs had provided the assistance at considerable jeopardy to themselves, the Ministerial newspapers had expected the Prince to repay them by playing an active rôle in the crucial elections of 1784; but they had greatly overestimated his sense of honor. Except for some token support of Fox in the Westminster contest, his only contribution had been a noisy celebration party for Fox at the close, which had embarrassed the King without in any respect assisting the Whigs.

Carlton House, which had been built in 1709, was in a state of dilapidation, but the Prince had moved in during the summer of 1783 and, engaging the architect, Henry Holland, had immediately commenced alterations. The alterations had proved to be expensive, especially when their cost was added to the cost of mistresses, jewelry, race horses, plate, dress, and the numerous other objects upon which he was intent, so that by December, 1785, his debts had been estimated by the newspapers at upwards of £200,000. At this point he had married Mrs. Fitzherbert, she having refused to live with him on any other terms. This marriage he could certainly not afford. Six years older than he and already twice-widowed, Mrs. Fitzherbert was so wonderfully understanding of his mistresses and other peccadilloes that he had been able to live his life as before, with the sole difference that he now had a wife who was very fond of jewelry. There were other considerations. At the time of the marriage, he had been twenty-three, and, since as Heir Apparent he could not marry without the

King's consent until he was twenty-five, the marriage had been invalid. But the fact that Mrs. Fitzherbert was a Roman Catholic had introduced a complication, for, had the marriage been valid, it would have barred him from the Throne, and even an invalid marriage was occasion for alarm. Although the Prince had never indicated any concern for his reputation, his debts were another matter, and he had therefore attempted to conceal the marriage until they at least had been paid. The result had been another expense, for the newspapers, always alert to possibilities of extortion, had found him lucrative prey.

By 1786 the situation had become desperate, and, since this time the Whigs were not in office, they could only advise a retrenchment, followed by an appeal to the King. The Prince, who did nothing in moderation, had accordingly sold his horses, dismissed his servants, closed Carlton House, and, in a fine flourish of poverty, set off in a hired carriage for Brighton, supposedly to live out his days in a rented farmhouse. But the King had not been moved, and, since the Prince had taken with him Mrs. Fitzherbert, whom the Queen intensely disliked, neither had she. Hence in 1787 the Whigs had reluctantly submitted the debts to Parliament. A spokesman for the Government had at once raised an inquiry concerning the status of Mrs. Fitzherbert, but, on the basis of Fox's assurance that no marriage had occurred, the inquiry had been dropped, and Parliament had provided £160,000 for payment of the debts, plus £60,000 for completing the renovations of Carlton House. To this the King had surprisingly added £10,000 to the Prince's income, so that it now totaled £72,000 a year. The Prince in turn had solemnly promised that his debts would never again become a Parliamentary issue. The repercussions of all this had been numerous.

To begin with, there had been the sacrifice of Fox. The year 1787 was an awkward one for the Prince, for Mrs. Fitzherbert liked to be regarded as a respectable married woman, and, by repeating the ceremony of 1785, the Prince might have made her one, he being then twenty-five years old. But this he would not do, and her respectability had therefore depended on the acknowledgment of the earlier ceremony. That Fox should have denied it, even though he had done so as an act of devotion to the Prince, had upset her a great deal; and, in order to restore domestic harmony, the Prince had therefore terminated the friendship. Now that he had the money, the friendship was not very useful anyway. Fox's successor as Carlton House favorite had been Sheridan, who at the Prince's request had undertaken to salvage her reputation without actually calling her a wife; and, since Sheridan was already managing the press for the Opposition, he had henceforth managed it for the Prince and Mrs. Fitzherbert as well.

The Prince had otherwise reacted to the settlement with a recklessness which obscured in a flash everything he had done in the past. He had at once reopened Carlton House, resumed the improvements, re-engaged the servants, bought back the horses, and set about building a lavish house for Mrs. Fitzherbert in Pall Mall. He had also bought the farmhouse in which they had lived in

Brighton and again with the assistance of Holland, had commenced the process of transforming it into an Oriental pavilion, with a separate villa for Mrs. Fitzherbert on the grounds. There had meanwhile been celebrations, for that summer the peace of Brighton had been shattered by some of the most scandalous orgies in history. Among the bacchants had been the Duke of York, who, having completed his education, had returned from Germany to command the Coldstream Guards. Although the reunion had been joyful, it had also proved costly, for the Duke had introduced the Prince to gambling and had in turn been introduced to horse racing, with the result that by 1788 they were both in financial straits. At this point they seem to have commenced negotiations for a loan through Dutch banks of approximately one million pounds, bearing interest of 6 per cent and repayable at the death of George III; but, before the negotiations could be completed, it looked as if the loan might not be necessary after all.

The King's illness had been announced by the newspapers on 10 November, 1788, but advance symptoms of the disease had been apparent early in the summer, and the struggle for power had therefore begun at that time. Basically, the struggle had been one between the Prince of Wales, who was fighting for an immediate and unfettered Regency, and the Queen, who was opposed to any Regency whatever or at least to a Regency dominated by her son, the Prince being supported by the Duke of York and the Duke of Clarence, who, according to The Times (5 May, 1789), had returned to England without permission of the Commissioners of the Admiralty for the purpose, and the Queen being supported by the King's brothers, especially the Duke of Gloucester. In addition, the Queen had been supported by the Government, Pitt holding office only by grace of the King, and the Prince had been supported by the Opposition, he being their sole hope of coming into office. But in this case there had been complications, for Sheridan had had ambitions of his own, and he had happened to be in an advantageous position to realize them, since he was an intimate of Carlton House and of Major Edward Topham, proprietor of a powerful newspaper, the World. Sheridan had been secretly involved in this newspaper since 1787, and Topham had been quite willing to let him manage the political department altogether, provided he was adequately reimbursed. The first reimbursement had come from the Treasury.

Unlike his predecessors Sheridan did not make the mistake of trusting the Prince. Hence, although the Prince had supposedly broken with Fox, Sheridan had regarded Fox as his principal rival, and, during the elections of July, 1788, the World had therefore tried hard to get rid of him by defeating him as Member for Westminster. This tactic having failed, Sheridan had severed connections with the Treasury and, by publishing (6 Sept., 1788) a query as to Mrs. Fitzherbert's status, had extorted a subsidy from Carlton House instead, probably in the amount of £400 a year. Having thus satisfied, he thought, Topham, he had then dedicated the paper to the "New Whigs," who, it appeared, consisted of Burke, William Windham, and Lord Loughborough, with himself as leader of the group, and who, it further appeared, were distinguished from the "Old Whigs" by their utter devotion to the Prince's cause, it being their contention that the Prince had a Constitutional right to succeed as soon as the King was pronounced incompetent, that is, without an intervening act of Parliament. This tactic had been interrupted by Topham, who on 25 December had leased the *World* to the Treasury for £600 a year, thus evicting the "New Whigs" in favor of the Government. Although Sheridan never forgave him, the "New Whigs" were not homeless, for on 2 January, 1789, Carlton House had acquired a controlling interest in the *Morning Post*, its conductor, John Benjafield, having learned something about extortion from the *World*; and, since Sheridan always managed the press in its interests, he had moved the "New Whigs" to that newspaper. But a Regency bill had already been formulated, and, with its introduction on 5 February, the "New Whigs" had faded into history, and all Whigs were again apparently one. This was perhaps not quite the case, for Sheridan had continued to fight on long after the Whigs themselves had given up, moving finally to the spurious *Star* for the purpose. Although the King's recovery had been officially announced on 10 March and by 12 March newspapers had been warned that further references to his *"derangement"* or suggestions that he was unable to perform his duties would be regarded as "TREASON," the spurious *Star* had shifted its position only to the point of demanding a "New Regency Bill," so that the King could retire to Germany for a long "convalescence." The demands had continued throughout May.

Except for the King, who had been necessarily *hors de combat*, no one emerged from the Regency struggle unscathed, but the reputation of the Prince of Wales had probably suffered the most. The Ministerial newspapers had been greatly alarmed about his activities, and there had been special alarm when, on 11 February, the Irish Parliament had offered him the Regency of that country independently. The Prince's popularity in Ireland was still a matter of anxiety in 1792. Faring perhaps the best had been the Duke of Clarence, who was understood to have involved himself only out of loyalty to his brothers and whose subsequent conduct had been at least politically immaculate. Having already spent over eight years at sea, he had been placed on inactive duty at the end of 1789, with the subsequent rank of Rear Admiral; and, by the end of 1790, he had settled down with the actress, Mrs. Dorothy Jordan, to a quiet, although certainly procreative, life. Ten children have been traced to this union by biographers;[4] it appears from the newspapers that there were more. According to biographers, too,[5] Mrs. Jordan had already had four children—one fathered by Richard Daly, three by Richard Ford, and three of the four were still living in 1792, being cared for by her sister Hester Bland at No. 14, Somerset Street, Portman Square; according to the newspapers, four of them were still living and were frequently in the company of the Duke. No one was as yet offended by the arrangement, and the Queen herself seems to have approved of it, regarding Mrs. Jordan as a good influence on her son. She was certainly a safe one, for

unlike Mrs. Fitzherbert she was quite content to remain a mistress. Some time
during this period, the Duke had performed a final service for his brothers by
becoming a party to the Dutch loan, but, since the three realized only about
£12,500 apiece from the enterprise, owing to the war, and since the loan never
became a newspaper scandal, it figures only incidentally in these chronicles.

The Duke of Clarence had had the advantage of being financially solvent. The
Prince of Wales and the Duke of York had had no such advantage, and, at the
time of the King's recovery, their situation had been worse than it had been at
the onset of his illness. If either of them had been willing to marry, provision for
payment of the debts would have been part of the marriage settlement; but,
since neither of them was, the debts could properly speaking be paid only by the
King, from whom both Princes were now almost totally estranged. As early as
May, 1789, the Opposition newspapers had apologized for the extravagances of
the elder Prince by reminding their readers that he had introduced "elegance"
into England, that much of the money had been lavished on friends and servants,
and that his "generosity" had stimulated national "commerce." The Princes
themselves had evidently sought the mediation of Pitt, for, during the last six
months of the year, there had been reports of conferences and rumors of
attempted reconciliations between them and the King. But, since the King was
also, it appeared, insisting on marriage, negotiations had dragged on into 1790.
By 9 February, 1790, according to the Ministerial *World*, the Prince of Wales
had been presented with an ultimatum:

ROYAL ARRANGEMENT.

The following *Plan* is talked of with much confidence in the higher circles of
fashion: That a proposal has been made to a young *Personage* to marry.—The
PRINCESS of PRUSSIA is the Lady mentioned as the intended consort: in which case,
the sum of 5,000*l.* a year is to be settled on *another Lady* [Mrs. Fitzherbert]—
an addition is to be made to the income of the young PERSONAGE—and his Debts
are immediately to be paid.

Some short time has been asked for deliberation on this proposal.

On 10 February the *World* had added that the "*certain Lady*, besides a pension,
is to be created a Peeress. MUNSTER is mentioned as the title." Although the
Prince had been desperate, he had evidently not been quite this desperate. The
Duke of York evidently had been, for in 1791 Fredericka Charlotte Ulrica,
oldest daughter of Frederick II of Prussia, became the Duchess of York, the
marriage being celebrated in Berlin on 29 September and in London on 23
November. Settlement of their affairs was on the Parliamentary calendar for
early 1792. The Duchess, a very pious woman, who devoted her time to charities,
was much admired by the newspapers, although unfortunately not by her
husband.

For the Prince of Wales, the Ministerial newspapers were now suggesting
either the Queen's niece, Princess Louise of Mecklenburg-Strelitz, or the King's

niece, Princess Caroline of Brunswick; but no negotiations were in progress, and, as his debts increased, his reputation further declined. Since it was generally supposed that short of marrying he would do anything for the sake of money, he was sometimes accused of doing more than he actually did. One instance of this seems to have been the Newmarket scandal of late 1791. The Prince's stud had for some time been regarded as the finest in Europe, and, among the best of the horses, was one called Escape, which had been entered in the Newmarket events of 20 and 21 October. But, although Escape had won handily on the second day, it had been badly beaten on the first; and, since a great deal of money had been lost on these races, rumors had been rampant. According to one of them, the Prince had deliberately winded the horse on 20 October by giving him a pail of water just before the race began; according to another, the outcomes had been manipulated by the jockey, Samuel Chifney, on the Prince's instructions. The Jockey Club, which ruled on such matters, had undertaken an investigation by questioning Chifney at length, and, although two of the stewards had indicated satisfaction with his answers, the third, Sir Charles Bunbury, had not. He had even remarked that, if Chifney ever rode for the Prince again, no "gentleman" would enter a horse against him. The Prince, who had gone to Cambridge in pursuit of his most recent love, the singer, Mrs. Elizabeth Billington, had heard of this remark on his return and, sending for Bunbury, had told him that, since he was as convinced of Chifney's innocence as he was of his own, he would sell the horses and quit the turf rather than dismiss him.[6] Everyone had thought the sale was advisable, but it had not yet occurred, and the Ministerial newspapers were beginning to wonder if it ever would occur.

The Prince was still regarded as a Whig, not because he was doing anything for the Whigs, but because his intimates were generally of the Whig, or at least of the anti-Pitt, persuasion. Several of them were simply adventurers. Among this group were the Lades, Sir John and Lady Letitia. Although well known in sporting circles, Sir John seems to have had no official position in the household, but he was usually involved in its affairs: especially those of a somewhat shady order. His wife, noted principally for her obscenity, had once been the mistress of John Rann, the highwayman, now safely executed, and more recently the mistress of the Duke of York. She was born Letitia Darby, but until her marriage, probably in late 1787, she had called herself Mrs. Smith. Louis Weltje, the Prince's maître d'hôtel, was a German immigrant, almost completely illiterate and even ludicrous, but devoted to the Prince, who rewarded him handsomely for various services of a confidential sort. Weltje already owned a large house in London, used by the Prince and his friends as a gambling casino, and one wing of the Brighton pavilion, and, according to the newspapers, he had been the recipient of cash gifts amounting to an extremely sizable sum. On the reputable side, there was John Willett Payne, a veteran of the American war, a captain in the Navy since 1780, and a Member of Parliament since 1787. Long an intimate of the Prince, Captain Payne had been appointed Secretary and Keeper of Papers in 1788, had acted as intermediary during the Regency crisis of 1788–1789, and since 1791 had been Auditor and Secretary of the Duchy of Cornwall. Another long-time intimate was Samuel Hulse, Colonel of the First Footguards and for many years the Prince's Treasurer and Receiver General. Still another was Gerard Lake, since 1790 Major General in the Army and Member of Parliament for Aylesbury and since 1787 First Equerry and Commissioner of the Stables in the household. His brother Warwick Lake looked after the Prince's racing stables. There were also Mrs. Fitzherbert and the Duke of York, but not the Duchess.

Politically more conspicuous were Thomas Erskine, the Prince's Attorney General, and Francis Rawdon Hastings, first Baron Rawdon of Rawdon, a veteran of the American war; and there was Edward first Baron Thurlow of Ashfield. Lord Rawdon had been attracted to the Prince by a congeniality of tastes, he himself being somewhat of a libertine, Lord Thurlow, it was supposed, for political reasons. Lord Thurlow had come into office in late 1783 as a friend of the King and as Lord Chancellor had served the King's interests so well that in 1786 he had been rewarded with the Tellership of the Exchequer, a sinecure which he held for life, and by 1787 with provisions for his relations, the rich Bishopric of Durham having been given to his brother Thomas. He had cultivated the friendship of the Prince of Wales during the King's illness in the hope, the newspapers had then thought, of securing his position against the ambitious Lord Loughborough in the event of a Regency, and, since he had therefore opposed the Queen and the Government, the newspapers had expected him to be dismissed as soon as the King recovered. But the King had held no grudge, he had approved of his continuing friendship with his son, and he had liked the way he was presiding over the trial of Hastings, and so Lord Thurlow had remained. Pitt, who had never been fond of Lord Thurlow anyway, had not shared the King's confidence, and in 1790 he had sent Grenville to the Lords to block any possible maneuver on his part. Thus far there had been no maneuver. In addition there was Louis-Phillipe Joseph, Duke of Orleans and a thoroughgoing Jacobin, who even signed his name *Phillipe Égalité*. Having supported the rebels during the early months of the French Revolution, he had returned to England in 1790, had taken a house in Brighton, and had again attached himself to the Prince. Finally there was that journalist, poet, dramatist, wit, orator, drunkard, gamester, and rake, Sheridan, always very much a part of Carlton House affairs.

Character of Newspapers: The Ministerial Press

The situation respecting the newspapers was even more complicated than that respecting the politicians, since the newspapers reflected all political intrigues and added some intrigues of their own. At the beginning of 1792, there were fourteen dailies, each consisting of four pages, four columns to a page. The important news appeared on page 3, although news might splash over to pages 2 and 4; page 1 was usually reserved for advertisements, provided there were enough to fill it. Since a newspaper's prosperity was likely to be estimated by the number of these advertisements, they were sometimes copied or even invented. The coverage was broader than it is in the newspaper of today, but the presentation of the "intelligence" left something to be desired. The leading article tended to be a series of disjointed items, in which reports were intermixed with editorial comment, the comment itself being backed by letters from supposed readers. There was always a column devoted to the activities of the Royal Family, and during the season much space was taken up by the debates, which had been twisted and edited to serve the newspaper's purpose. What appeared otherwise depended on what had happened and on the policy of the individual newspaper, but readers could usually count on several columns of "paragraphs," one- or two-sentence items with "point." These were often indelicate, if not obscene, and their subjects were almost invariably personal. As James Grant put it,[7] "Much appeared in the journalism of those times which no lady of delicate mind would read aloud, and which no gentleman, however gay . . . , would dare to read in the hearing of a lady." In the main the paragraphs were abusive, in which instance they were likely to rely upon innuendo for their barb, but they might be complimentary, in which case they were fulsomely so.

There was also poetry. Since almost every poet sent occasional contributions to the newspapers, some of the poetry was very good; some of it was also very bad, consisting of jingles and epigrams and a maudlin sort of lovesick verse, generally described as "Della Cruscan." Della Cruscan verse had come into its own in 1787, when the *World* had published the lovesick correspondence of "Della Crusca" (Robert Merry) and "Anna Matilda" (Mrs. Hannah Cowley). Readers had been so infatuated with it that, for the next several years, all newspapers had been crammed with imitations. The infatuation was now on the wane. Although no newspaper was averse to an occasional effusion of "Albert" or "Emma" and the *World* still purported to specialize in the genre, only the *Oracle* retained Della Cruscans on its staff, and even it retained only such outstanding Della Cruscans as "Arno" (Miles Peter Andrews), "Laura" and "Laura

Maria" (both the Prince of Wales's ex-mistress, Mrs. Mary Robinson), and "Lorenzo." William Gifford liked to think that his *The Baviad*, published anonymously at the end of 1791, was responsible for the wane, but by that time the wane was so far advanced that his work was hardly noticed. In mid-January, 1792, the *Morning Chronicle* printed some excerpts with evident approval, on 23 January the *Oracle* denied that "Edwin" was Thomas Vaughan, as *The Baviad* had said, and on 25 January it added an identification of the author: "The MISGUIDED MAN, who has lately bespattered nearly all POETICAL EMINENCE of the day, is a Being by the name of GIFFARD. It is a very abusive piece of folly indeed!" Other newspapers said nothing.

On the face of it, the newspapers seemed to be very badly off. The average sale of a newspaper was probably less than 1,000 copies a day, and several dailies sold only a few hundred, the maximum price being 4*d*., of which 2*d*. was tax. The charge for advertisements, according to Trusler,[8] was 6*s*. for eighteen lines on page 1, 4*s*. on other pages, additional lines averaging about 1*d*. each, but for every advertisement accepted the newspaper paid a 3*s*. tax. "Letters or Essays" were published at the rate of a guinea and a half a column, 16*s*. a half-column, and 10*s*. 6*d*. a quarter-column; but these were evidently also subject to the advertisement tax, for editors frequently advised a "correspondent" that his "communication will interest the Stamp Office and must therefore be paid for in advance of publication." The expense of getting out a newspaper was meanwhile sizable, especially during the sitting of Parliament, when, in addition to an editor, a staff of printers, compositors, and clerks, a writer of "paragraphs," and a translator of foreign newspapers, there had to be a drama critic, a legal reporter, a reporter to cover the Government offices, and several reporters to attend the debates in Parliament, the trial of Hastings, meetings of the Board of the East India Company, public dinners, and such. There also had to be "correspondents" in Edinburgh, Dublin, Windsor, and Brighton, and some newspapers even had a "correspondent" on the Continent. By contemporary standards salaries were not low, and, if one adds to them only the cost of type, presses, paper, rent, and candles, it would seem clear that every newspaper was losing money. In the ledgers most of them were. Yet enormous prices were paid for a share in a newspaper or for the lease of a newspaper, and except in extraordinary cases the investor profited. The reason was that, in addition to its legitimate income, a newspaper could count on certain extralegitimate revenues, and these were not entered in the ledgers.

One of the several hidden sources of revenue was puffs. On 11 February, 1797, the *Telegraph* named forty-two persons who regularly "pay to have themselves puffed in the Newspapers," the list including Lord Grenville, Earl Spencer, Lord Hawkesbury, Henry Dundas, the Prince of Wales, the Duke of Richmond, the Duke of Portland, George Rose, John Wilkes, the Duchess of Gordon, Mrs. Mary Robinson, Lord Mountmorres, Mrs. Fitzherbert, the Duke of York, Madame Schwellenberg, William Pitt, and William Windham.

Almost everyone of prominence bought puffs if he was involved or likely to be involved in a scandal or if he had reason to call himself to the Government's attention. The theaters bought puffs as a matter of course, sometimes paying for them piecemeal, more often paying for them at a set annual rate. Other organizations, such as the Royal Academy and the East India Company, bought puffs on occasion.

A second source of revenue was abusive material. "[The] grand mover, money, can procure the insertion of the most villainous personal paragraphs, letters, inuendoes [*sic*], advertisements, &c.," said James Savage,[9] ". . . [just as] any man, for half a guinea, may puff his own writings, inventions, and fame, in a paragraph in any of the papers." Nor was the material merely printed. In the case of *The Times*,[10] for example:

> [the] subject was often informed previously by the journal's agent that a paragraph was in type, and it was hinted to him that the paragraph need not appear if a sum, known as the suppression fee, were paid. If the subject of the paragraph had not been reached before publication, a cutting was sent to him with a hint that room could be found for any "statement." Inclusion of the second paragraph was delayed until a payment, known as the "contradiction fee," was forthcoming. The person who officiated in the capacity of an editor managed these important business matters on behalf of his paper. Hence the personal paragraph was regarded by journalists as an essential concomitant of the liberty of the press.

At least three-fourths of the London dailies engaged in these practices, and they were still a commonplace in 1833, by which time the fees were known as "hush-money."[11] In many instances the newspaper knew nothing which was damaging to the victim's character, but it bombarded him with general ridicule until he paid for silence. In addition to the income from puffs, personal abuse, and private extortions, newspapers could count on an income from politics.

When it came to the management of newspapers, every advantage was on the side of the Government. Since it had the national treasury to draw on, it could pay more than the Opposition could, and it could reward loyalties with places and pensions. It could also provide priority of information, buy up issues of newspapers for free distribution, and frustrate attempts to prosecute for libel. Similarly, it could punish a recalcitrant newspaper by forcing it or its editor into bankruptcy, by blocking its sources of information, by interfering with its distribution through the Post Office, by increasing taxes, or by harassing its printer and editor with prosecutions, heavy fines, and long prison sentences, followed by "guarantees" of "good behavior" for another seven years. Since Pitt had already employed every one of these means to rid himself of criticism, the marvel is that the Opposition press still existed. That it did was owing entirely to his unpopularity, for a newspaper not paid for its services always supported the Opposition, and many a newspaper supported the Opposition for a much smaller subsidy than it could have got from the Government. Also he could go only so far with his harassments, for public opinion, hostile to him in any event, stiffened sharply at attacks on the press. Almost anyone became a hero when he was under prosecution. All of this had hampered Pitt considerably. He had had to be sparing with indictments ex officio, dealing with his enemies when possible in circuitous ways, and, even when indictments were issued, he had found it wiser to deal with the culprit out of court. His most outspoken critic, the *Morning Chronicle*, he had thus far been afraid to molest at all, since it represented that "Man of the People," Fox. That the Government had not even been able to manage its own newspapers was owing principally to muddled control; for, although George Rose was officially responsible for the press, he could do nothing without the approval of Pitt, whereas other members of the Government interfered without consulting anyone. The result was that even those newspapers which could be counted as Ministerial were so divided in their loyalties that they dissipated much of their energy quarreling among themselves.

Of the fourteen dailies in existence on 1 January, 1792, seven were or purported to be defenders of the Government: the *Diary*, the *Morning Herald*, the *Oracle*, the *Public Advertiser*, the *Public Ledger*, *The Times*, and the *World*.

The *Diary, or Woodfall's Register* was printed, conducted, and owned by William Woodfall and was located at No. 62, Dorset Street, Salisbury Square. Woodfall had begun the newspaper on 30 March, 1789, with the encouragement of George Rose, and the Treasury subsidized it throughout its existence in the amount of £400 a year. Woodfall was assisted in the conduct by his son William Woodfall, Jr., who was otherwise a lawyer. The only clue to other personnel is an advertisement for a publisher, a compositor, and a clerk, which appeared on 17 November, 1792, applicants being advised to ask for "Mr. BRETT,/ at the PRINTING OFFICE of this PAPER." A "Mr. BRETT" was later (1809–1810) connected with the bookselling trade, possibly with the firm of "Messrs. Longman & Co." [12] The *Diary* had always been a vehicle for Ministerial propaganda, and during 1789 and 1790 much of it had been supplied by James Bland Burges, Under Secretary of State for Foreign Affairs, his contributions having been reissued (1790) in pamphlet form, under the title, *Letters Lately Published in The Diary, on the Subject of the Present Dispute with Spain, under the Signature of Verus*. Aside from Ministerial propaganda, the *Diary* specialized in reports of Parliamentary debates and in reviews of theatrical performances. Its "paragraphs" were usually puffs, and it was a militant defender of Charles Dibdin, currently entertaining at "Sans Souci" in the Strand, from whom it was evidently receiving a particularly large stipend. As a newspaper, the *Diary* was more respectable than most, since it was not obsessively abusive and it was only rarely quarrelsome.

The *Morning Herald* was begun on 1 November, 1780, by the Rev. Henry Bate Dudley, who was still its sole proprietor in 1792. Its address was No. 18, Catherine Street, Strand. Dudley, a friend of the Prince of Wales and most of the Whig leaders, had conducted the *Herald* in their interests from 1784 to 1 June,

1790; but, confronted with a choice between going to prison for libel or leasing the paper to the Government, he had chosen the latter course. The Treasury paid him £600 a year for control of the paper, which it managed itself, Dudley having had nothing to do with it since the leasing. In October, 1790, the editor was Thomas Y. Hurlstone, who was perhaps still editor in 1792, the remainder of the staff being Treasury hirelings. By 2 March, 1792, the printer was H. Roaf. The *Morning Herald* had been noted for gossip of a scandalous sort, and it still was, but the "paragraphs," which had once been witty, were now coarse and heavy-handed. The circulation had correspondingly dropped from between three and four thousand in mid-1790 to possibly fifteen hundred at the beginning of 1792.

The *Oracle*. *Bell's New World* (by 3 June, 1791, retitled the *Oracle, or Bell's World*) was begun by the bookseller John Bell on 1 June, 1789, as an advertising medium for his British Library. Like the old *World*, on which it was modeled, it specialized in Della Cruscan poetry, literary titbits, theatrical gossip, and personal abuse on a particularly coarse level. Since early 1790 it had also specialized in foreign news, having engaged as correspondent the Rev. William Jackson, who was living on the Continent to escape his creditors. Except for advertisements and one or two "Addresses to the Readers," Bell himself seems to have written nothing for the paper, but he still owned and printed it and probably supervised the business management. The editors, for the preceding two years, had been James Boaden, whose interests were centered in the theater, he being himself a playwright, and Peter Stuart, whose interests were mainly literary; the printer had always been Buchanan Millan, and the paper's address had always been the British Library in the Strand. In 1790 the Treasury had given Bell £200 for the newspaper, and in 1791 it had raised the allotment to £250, allotting the same amount in 1792. But the *Oracle* had caused the Government more trouble than almost any one of the Opposition newspapers. Since its business was primarily extortion, much of its space was devoted to extortionary material, and it was an invariable participant in every personal misunderstanding, its support always going to the highest bidder, regardless of his politics. It could also be counted on to laud Peter Stuart's brother-in-law, the Whiggish James Mackintosh, and, because of an old grudge of Bell's, to beleaguer the Ministerial *World*. In addition, it was susceptible to subversion by Sheridan, who had previously been associated with both Stuart and Boaden on the spurious *Star*.

The *Public Advertiser*, which sold for only 3½d. instead of the usual 4d., could trace its ancestry back to 1734 and its title back to 1752. It had long been printed and conducted by Henry Sampson Woodfall at No. 1, corner of Ivy Lane, Paternoster Row. Woodfall was also one of the proprietors and by 1792 perhaps the sole proprietor. The paper was subsidized by the Treasury, but the amount of the subsidy is not recorded. Since Henry Woodfall was a brother of William Woodfall, the same stories were likely to appear in the *Public Advertiser* and the *Diary* simultaneously, and like the *Diary* the *Public Advertiser* was a champion of

Charles Dibdin. But the character of the two papers was quite different. The *Public Advertiser* was hysterical in its politics and abusive in its paragraphs, and it had little interest in the theater or the debates. Its interest was literature, but here it differed from the *Oracle* and the *World* in that it specialized in material relating to literary figures of the past. It was particularly fond of unknown poems, new anecdotes, and unpublished letters. The *Public Advertiser* also had some interest in history. Of its contributors the most persistent during 1791 and 1792 was perhaps James Boswell.[13]

The *Public Ledger* was founded on 12 January, 1760, as a shipping journal, and it was still specializing in shipping news in 1792. Otherwise it had little to recommend it. In return for a Treasury subsidy of £100 a year, it printed whatever propaganda was sent it, devoting the remainder of its space to scandal. For many years it had been printed and managed by John Crowder at No. 12, Warwick Court. Crowder was also a proprietor, although probably not the only one, as will be indicated later. The editor was most likely Alexander Chalmers.

The *Times* was a newcomer, compared with the *Public Advertiser* and the *Public Ledger*, but by 1792 it was outstripping its Ministerial rivals in circulation. The paper was founded on I January, 1785, as an advertising medium for the Logographic Press. Although it was still printed by the Logographic Press in Printing House Square, Blackfriars, it and its adjunct, the *Evening Mail*, were now almost the only things which were. On 20 March, 1792, the printer was A. Anderson. The founder and present managing director was John Walter, the assistant conductor was his son William Walter, and the editor was William Finey, the three being referred to by other newspapers as "Old Log," "Young Log," and "The Irish Monster," respectively. *The Times*, which had always supported the Government, had, for a number of years, been regarded as Pitt's special "Gazette," but it was currently superintended by Charles Long, the second Secretary of the Treasury. Its contributors included at least two Treasury writers, William Augustus Miles and William Combe, Combe being part of the regular staff. As payment for his services, the Government had appointed John Walter Printer of the Customs, had provided him with a £300 subsidy, had given the newspaper priority in releases of information, and had quashed those prosecutions for libel which were bound to result from its blackmailing activities. There had been some unpleasantness in the relationship between Walter and Pitt when, during the King's illness, Walter had perversely supported the Prince of Wales along with the Government. But Pitt had solved the problem by imprisoning him until the crisis was passed. Although Walter had emerged from prison a very angry man, the Government had paid his fines, reimbursed him for his sufferings, and evidently promised to wreak vengeance on one of his enemies, John King; the pacified Walter had in turn helped the Government demolish the *Argus*. By the beginning of 1792, all had therefore been forgiven, and *The Times* was again the favored Ministerial newspaper. It took its responsibilities seriously. Partly because of its status with the Government and partly because of its circulation, which at 2,500 topped that of any other Ministerial newspaper, it regarded itself as a scourge. But its flailing attempts to keep other newspapers in line, however much appreciated by the Government, were not welcomed by the newspapers themselves, so that no newspaper was so thoroughly hated by other newspapers as this one.

The seventh of the Treasury newspapers, the *World*, could truthfully boast that it had introduced "elegance" into journalism, had popularized boxing, and had made newspaper readers aware of poetry. For these achievements the reading public was indebted to Major Edward Topham. The *World* was begun by Topham and Bell on 1 January, 1787, Bell functioning as printer and Topham as conductor, with the assistance of his mistress, the actress, Mary Wells, and by late 1787 with the additional assistance of the Rev. Charles Este. The paper was an immediate success, and, since much of the success was owing to the poetry of "Della Crusca" and "Anna Matilda," it soon became known as "The Paper of Poetry." While it was at the peak of its glory, Topham, then sole proprietor, sold the political interests to the Treasury for £600 a year. Negotiations were completed at the end of 1788, and the money was still being paid in 1792. Since the prime mover of the *World*'s politics was George Rose, the paper was known as "Rose's Gazette."

But trouble had started as soon as Rose acquired the paper. Mrs. Wells, whose antics had always provided entertaining copy for the press, began a scandalous liaison with the playwright Frederick Reynolds; and the whole personnel of the *World*, Topham, Este, Mrs. Wells, "Della Crusca," "Anna Matilda," and "Arno," were made a laughingstock by an upstart print, the spurious *Star*. "Della Crusca's" adoration of "Anna Matilda" had meanwhile failed to survive a personal meeting, and on 16 March, 1789, the *World* had accordingly published "DELLA CRUSCA'S FAREWELL to ANNA MATILDA." Although Mrs. Cowley was leaving for Paris at the time, the poem was no *bon voyage*. Upon her return in late May, she penned some heartbroken verses "To DELLA CRUSCA," which appeared in the *World* on 2 June; but Merry was unmoved, and so that correspondence ended. On the previous day (1 June), Bell, having been dismissed as printer, had retaliated by beginning the *Oracle*, the first number of which was a blistering attack on Topham. By the end of the year, the *Oracle* had stripped the *World* of all its remaining Della Cruscans except "Arno," "Arno" defecting in June, 1791. There was further trouble in 1790, when the heirs of the third Earl Cowper had sued the newspaper for libel. Although the action was dismissed on 29 January, 1791, the result was only additional trouble, for Este, who had fled to the country to avoid prosecution, thereupon returned to file a suit in Chancery for collection of a lifetime "pension" of £400, which, he alleged, Topham had promised him in return for the use of some "valuable MSS." This action was still pending.

By 1792 the *World* had so deteriorated that it was of no use to Rose except as scapegoat for the Government's intrigues respecting Burke and the trial of

Hastings. But for Topham it was still a profitable business, since, in addition to the £600 subsidy from the Treasury, he was collecting £300 from theaters and whatever he could wrest from individuals who had something to hide. It was now printed by Robert Bostock at No. 335, Strand, opposite Somerset House; and Topham was assisted in the conduct by the Treasury writer, John Heriot, by Isaac Swan, who was also writing for the *Observer*, and by Warren Hastings's agent, Major John Scott. "Simkin" (Ralph Broome), whose speciality was epistolary verses ridiculing Burke, was a regular contributor; so, too, was Topham's friend, Miles Peter Andrews, although at the same time he was writing poetry for the *Oracle* under his pseudonym, "Arno." Mrs. Wells, who was supposedly part of the staff, was apparently writing very little, partly because she was engaged at Covent Garden, partly because she was convalescing from one of her numerous illnesses. Her brother-in-law Emanuel Samuel, who had previously reported the Parliamentary debates, had quit the paper and, having spent some time in prison for debts, was now on his way to Madras.

In addition to the seven dailies, the Government controlled almost all of the triweekly and biweekly newspapers and a few of the weeklies. The triweeklies and biweeklies were circulated mainly in the country, the dailies and weeklies mainly in London. A nondaily newspaper was likely to be linked with one of the dailies, sharing proprietors and copy, although not necessarily address, editor, or printer; but the linkage is not always evident. Among the triweeklies was the *Evening Mail*, an adjunct of *The Times*. It was printed by John Walter in Printing House Square, Blackfriars and was subsidized by the Treasury in the amount of £200 a year, so that Walter received £500 in all. The *London Packet, or New Lloyd's Evening Post* was an adjunct of the *Public Ledger* and like it was printed by John Crowder at No. 12, Warwick Court. On 11 December, 1792, the proprietors of the *London Packet* were, according to Boswell,[14] "[Charles] Dilly, little Davies [Charles Davis] (the son of Lockyer [Davis, who had died on 23 April, 1791]), [William] Lowndes (Bookseller), [John] Crowder (printer), and [Alexander] Chalmers (their former Editor)." This group probably owned the *Public Ledger* as well. In addition, there was *Lloyd's Evening Post, and British Chronicle*, printed by Thomas Spilsbury and Son, No. 57, Snowhill. Spilsbury seems to have been a chemist, since the paper was filled with advertisements for Spilsbury's drops, supposedly effective in the treatment of scorbutic fever. There were also the *London Evening Post*, printed by James Barker at No. 6, in the Old Bailey and subsidized by the Treasury in the amount of £200 a year; the *St. James's Chronicle, or British Evening Post*, printed by Henry Baldwin at the Britannia Printing Office, Blackfriars and similarly subsidized in the amount of £200 a year; and the *Whitehall Evening Post*, printed at No. 4, Peterborough Court and on the Treasury's payroll for £100 a year. Finally, on 21 April, 1793, a "Mr. Mathews" collected £100 from the Treasury as "late Editor" of the *London Mercury*,[15] but nothing is known of this paper or of "Mr. Mathews."

The official state newspaper, the *London Gazette*, appeared on Tuesdays and Saturdays.

Every Ministerial newspaper relied in part on material provided by the Treasury; some Ministerial newspapers relied on it almost entirely. Yet newspapers were themselves only one product of the Government's propagandistic machine, which also turned out handbills, posters, pamphlets, journals, and even ballads for street-singers. Since a great deal of material had constantly to be dumped into the hopper, most of the principals of Government, not excluding Pitt, Rose, and Dundas, helped out on occasion, as so did many of the placemen, pensioners, and other sympathizers. Their contributions were almost invariably unsigned, and, journalism of any sort being regarded as a disreputable employment,[16] the author rarely acknowledged his work later. One notable exception was James Bland Burges, who, having published anonymously in the newspapers, reissued the more important contributions in pamphlet form under his own name. Another was Lord Mountmorres, who wrote at least a dozen pamphlets for the Government during the course of his life and seems to have contributed to the daily press until the year of his death. Although his work was usually unsigned, he inserted statements in newspapers, identifying himself as author and praising himself highly for his "patriotic" labors. The Government was never allowed to forget what Lord Mountmorres had done for it. Another and even more notable exception was Edmund Burke, whose pamphlets were invariably signed. Burke, who had edited and in part written the *Annual Register* from 1758 to 1790, does not, strangely enough, seem to have contributed to the newspapers, although he was very much concerned about them, telling Charles Long on one occasion[17] "that eventually newspapers would govern the Country."

But, however much the Government appreciated and even expected such assistance, it did not rely upon it alone, for the Treasury retained a staff of writers to supply what was lacking, paying them an annual salary of approximately £200 each and often adding a bonus, such as a place, a pension, a sinecure, or a share in a newspaper. From everything one can learn, these writers represented a variety of talents and performed a variety of services. On the Treasury's payroll at the beginning of 1792 were the Rev. George Bathie, John Bowles, Joseph Cawthorne, William Combe, William Cook, Matthew Feilde, John Heriot, William Hewardine, William Augustus Miles, Arthur Murphy, the Rev. Robert Nares, James Sayers, John Taylor, and a "Mr. L. Wolfe." Bathie, who seems to have written only for the newspapers, also functioned as paymaster for the Treasury, as so did Thomas Harris, manager of Covent Garden and a personal friend of George Rose. Bowles specialized in pamphlets. Since he was obligated to average one every quarter, a pamphlet by Bowles usually preceded every important debate in Parliament, excerpts being published by the Ministerial newspapers until the issue was settled. He was still remembered[18] as "the celebrated Anti-Jacobin writer" as late as 1809.

Joseph Cawthorne had originally written for the Bute Government, but his recompense was evidently slight, for, in December, 1764, he was a bankrupt. During the early 1780's he had written for the North Government, signing his letters and pamphlets "Cincinnatus" and "Coriolanus," and this time he had fared better, since, when that government resigned, he had a "pension" of £100. His labors for Pitt commenced in late 1783, and he was still writing pamphlets on his behalf in 1796. If, however, he was the "Mr. Cawthorne" who, according to the *Gazetteer* of 18 May, the *Star* of 25 November, and the *Public Advertiser* of 26 November, 1791, was sued for libel by a Captain Larkens of the East India Company, then the labors were interrupted, inasmuch as he was in King's Bench Prison from 24 November, 1791, to 24 May, 1792. William Combe, later well known for *The Tour of Dr. Syntax in Search of the Picturesque* (1809–1811), was sent over to *The Times* in 1787 by Charles Long. There he was "to obey such instructions as were given me, and when I had no instructions, to act from myself and my judgment as occasion offered. £200 a year was the stipulated salary." He was sporadically connected with *The Times* until 1803, his salary being paid by the Government until Pitt resigned in 1801. From 1803 to 1810, he was acting editor of the paper.[19]

William Cook, an Irish dramatist and miscellaneous writer, had migrated to London in 1766, where, according to Taylor,[20] he wrote many political pamphlets "under the patronage of the Duke of Richmond and Lord Shelburne, later Lord Lansdowne," "was employed in reporting the debates in the House of Lords, and in the India House, for the public journals," and also "became proprietor in a daily newspaper." Although the pamphlets have not been identified, the "daily newspaper" was the *General Advertiser*, which he helped establish in 1776, and one of the "public journals" was probably the *Gazetteer*. One supposes at least that he was the "Mr. Cooke" and "W- C-," paid by that newspaper during 1781–1782 for "East India Intelligence."[21] In 1775 he had also published (London) his *Elements of Dramatic Criticism* and in 1777 had been called to the bar. He continued to write about the theater—his most notable work being *The Memoirs of Samuel Foote, Esq.*, which appeared in 1805—and evidently about politics, but the nature of these writings is not known. Matthew Feilde was the Rev. Matthew Feilde, Master of the Lower Grammar School at Christ's Hospital from 1776 to 1796. He had once distinguished himself as a dramatist, his *Vertumnus and Pomona. A Pastoral* having been performed at Covent Garden on 21 February, 1782; and he still regarded himself as a playwright, although he had not, to anyone's knowledge, written a play since. As a teacher, he was considered by Lamb[22] an adequate scholar, but a lax disciplinarian, mainly because he spent most of the time in his room.

John Heriot, a Scotsman and for a short time a student at the University of Edinburgh, had migrated to London to join the Marines and was in active service from 1778 to 1783. Retiring as a captain on half pay, he had turned his attention to fiction and had published two novels: *The Sorrows of the Heart*

(1787) and *The Half-Pay Officer* (1789). At the beginning of 1789, the Regency struggle being then in progress, he was "engaged" by the Treasury "to answer, by pamphlets and in the newspapers, some of the arguments [against the Government]" and to function generally, it appears, as trouble shooter. He had failed in every instance. Having tried ineffectually to reclaim *The Times*, then perversely supporting the Prince of Wales along with the Government, he had inserted some libels in the paper, thereby enabling Pitt to send John Walter to prison for the duration. His subsequent labors with the *Oracle* had resulted only in a bitter quarrel with John Bell, and he had moved on to the *World*, which he was commissioned to "redeem" from its state of decline. He was still attached to the *World* at the beginning of 1792, being paid "2g. a week" as reporter by Topham, in addition to the £200 a year he was being paid by the Treasury, and there was still no indication of a "redemption," but the Treasury was nevertheless pleased with him.

William Hewardine was remembered by Taylor[23] as a frequenter of Turk's Coffee House: a "buffoon" of little learning, but marvelous talent, especially in the use of "slang." His contributions would probably have been posters, ballads for street-singers, and other such miscellanea. William Augustus Miles, evidently the most valued of the Treasury writers, was receiving £500 a year, in addition to expenses. Miles had begun his work for the Treasury in 1784, when, as author of the "Neptune" letters in the *Morning Post*, he had helped the Government through the embarrassing "Scrutiny" which followed the Westminster election. Since that time he had been constantly active, both as pamphleteer and writer for the newspapers, working under the direction of Charles Long, and Pitt had even sent him on foreign missions. Arthur Murphy had migrated to London from Ireland in 1735, and, during the 1750's, 1760's, and 1770's, he had been associated with various newspapers and journals. He had also been trained in the law and, as an intimate of Lord Loughborough, had been appointed Commissioner of Bankrupts in 1783, Lord Loughborough then being Chancellor. When Lord Loughborough was forced out of office, Murphy had been forced out as well, and in 1788 he had retired from the courts altogether. By 1792 he was known only for his plays, of which there were many. His comedies were especially prized. The Rev. Robert Nares, later Archdeacon, Prebendary of Lincoln, and Keeper of Manuscripts for the British Museum, was a distinguished philologist and theologian. His labors to bring religion to the journalistic support of the Government were highly regarded by the conservatives of his day.

James Sayers, lawyer, caricaturist, satirical poet, and steady supporter of George III, had been made Marshal of the Court of the Exchequer at the end of 1783, which sinecure he still held. He seems to have worked principally in the field of caricature. John Taylor, described by a contemporary[24] as "lively and agreeable . . . and a thorough *bon vivant*," was a relative newcomer, having been added to the Treasury payroll in 1791, and he was paid only £160 a year, rather than the usual £200. His employment, as indicated in the Treasury ledgers, was "[writing] in the Papers," but he also helped the Government as pamphleteer. Although he was starting at the bottom of the ladder, he was loyal to the point of fanaticism: there was almost nothing he would not do for money. "Mr. L. Wolfe's" employment was reporting the debates in the Commons. His accounts, biased in favor of the Government, were sent to various Ministerial newspapers, which were therefore spared the expense of employing reporters themselves. In June, 1792, his bill for this service amounted to £359 2s.[25]

Although this is by no means a complete list of Treasury journalists, additional names being supplied by the Opposition newspapers from time to time, it seems to be a representative one. There was another corps of writers in Ireland and still another in Scotland. Among the group in Scotland was a "Revd. Dr. Grant," who, according to Farington,[26] "in some way was employed by government [during Mr. Pitt's administration], probably as a writer in periodical publications for which he was handsomely paid, as, when Mr. Pitt resigned in 1801 Dr. Grant sd. *He* lost half his income."

The Daily Advertiser
and the Opposition Press

Of the remaining seven dailies, one, the *Daily Advertiser*, was nonpolitical, being only an advertising sheet with a little "intelligence" added. Founded in 1730, it had inaugurated the age of the advertisers, and, although it was now a relic of the past, the age of advertisers having long since given way to the age of the scandal sheet, it was still outselling every other newspaper. Daniel Stuart's explanation,[27] which relates to the period prior to 1789, was still relevant in 1792:

> [Numerous] and various advertisements interest numerous and various readers, looking out for employment, servants, sales and purchases, &c. &c. Advertisements act and re-act. They attract readers, promote circulation, and circulation attracts advertisements. The Daily Advertiser, which sold to the public for twopence halfpenny, after paying a stamp duty of three halfpence [in 1792 it sold for 3*d*. after paying a tax of 2*d*.], never had more than half a column of news; it never noticed Parliament. . . . The Daily Advertiser lost by its publication, but it gained largely by its advertisements, with which it was crammed full. Shares in it sold by auction at twenty years' purchase. I recollect my brother Peter saying, that on proposing to a tradesman to take shares in a new paper [probably the *Star* in 1788], he was answered by a sneer and a shake of the head,—"Ah!

none of you can touch the Daily." It was the paper of business filled with miscellaneous advertisements, conducted at little expense, very profitable, and taken in by all public-houses, coffee-houses, &c., but by scarcely any private families.

The value of the property in 1792 was indicated by a notice in *The Times* of 23 March that "a twentieth share of the Daily Advertiser which has netted for the last seven years about 62*l*. per annum, was [yesterday] sold [at auction] by Mr. Robbins, at Garraway's Coffee House for 1040 guineas." The *Oracle*'s later (21 Apr.) statement that the share was sold "at the rate of Twenty-five Thousand Pounds for the whole Property" was an exaggeration, the actual "rate" being £21,840; and the price paid was too high, investors in newspapers usually expecting a better return than 5.7 per cent. Still no other newspaper was worth £21,840; nor did any other newspaper have a legitimate income of £1,240. Always conducted by the Jenour family, the *Daily Advertiser* was currently printed by Joshua Jenour at No. 33, Fleet Street, opposite St. Dunstan's Church.

The other six dailies, the *Argus*, the *Cabinet*, the *Gazetteer*, the *Morning Chronicle*, the *Morning Post*, and the *Star*, generally supported the Opposition. The *modus operandi* of the Opposition respecting newspapers was identical with that of the Government, except that the Opposition had no legalistic or legislative apparatus and no national treasury. Its newspapers were therefore always at the mercy of the courts, as they were the intended victims of every new law. If the law did not discriminate against them, it was not enforced. In 1789, for example, Parliament prohibited the renting of newspapers under penalty of a £5 fine. At this point every newspaper sold had, it was estimated, thirty readers, some of whom rented it for a penny or even a halfpenny; but there was little point in renting Treasury newspapers, since, when there was anything important at stake, the Government distributed one of them gratis. The supposition that only the Opposition papers would be injured turned out, however, to be wrong. The sales of all newspapers declined, the Treasury newspapers protested, and the law was quietly forgotten. Another law, passed in 1790, required the licensing of presses. This law was rigidly enforced, for it identified Opposition printers without affecting Treasury printers, of whose identity the Government was already aware. The Opposition papers were also the special victims of increases in taxes, for their financing was unsteady at best, and, unlike the Ministerial papers, they could not look to their party for compensation. The treasurer for the Opposition press was William Adam; and, of the several subsidizers, the two principals had for some time been Earl Fitzwilliam and Lord Robert Spencer, with the Duke of Portland a somewhat distant third. But, since this group was gambling on the Whigs' coming into office, its generosity had tended to flag as the chances worsened. There had already been some retrenchment, for writers could no longer count on "pensions" as rewards for past services, and, after

April, 1791, said Earl Fitzwilliam,[28] editors could decide whether they wanted payment for their work or rewards for their loyalty, but they could no longer have both. Although the newspapers were generally supervised by Sheridan, each of them had its own editor and its own point of view.

The *Argus* was devoted to radical reform. Founded on 7 March, 1789, by Sampson Perry, the *Argus* had always represented the point of view of Thomas Paine, and by mid-1790 it had become a scathing critic of Pitt. Pitt, who was always nettled by criticism, had endured this state of affairs until 5 November, when the Government indicted Perry for publishing "a scandalous libel" on the "Administration, and particularly Mr. Pitt." But, having commenced this action, the Government had indicated no eagerness to pursue it, for to imprison Perry on such grounds would seem to the people an act of personal vengeance: Perry had to be removed from the scene without involving the Government at all. The elaborate way in which Pitt had handled this matter is clear from the events which ensued. As it happened, the *Argus* had also been critical of *The Times*, which, it charged, was indulging in unethical practices even in the unethical business of extortion; and, in December, 1790, a subeditor of the *Argus*, the banker, John ("Jew") King, had filed suit against John Walter, as printer and publisher of *The Times*, for indulging in such practices with him. Both actions were tried on 23 February, 1791, Perry and Walter being alike convicted. Walter was still at this point in prison for having supported the Prince of Wales during the Regency battle, and the Government did not as yet entirely trust him. But on 9 March he was released with a full pardon, the Treasury having not only paid his fines, but even added some recompense for his sufferings, and he was supposedly free to go his way. He was in fact not, for the Government could return him to prison at any time by the simple expedient of allowing King to press for judgment. Walter gave the Government no provocation. Not only was *The Times* a steady supporter of Pitt, but Walter and his son, who had hitherto fought their battles in the newspapers, not in the courts, filed an action against Pitt's enemy, Perry, for libels on their newspaper, published by the *Argus* on 8 October and 30 December, 1790, and on 7 January, 1791. Perry was convicted of these offenses on 15 June and on 9 July was sentenced to six months in King's Bench Prison because of them. At the same time, he was indicted for publishing a libel on Lady Anne Fitzgibbon, wife of Pitt's friend, the Lord Chancellor of Ireland; and, having pleaded guilty, he was on 12 July sentenced to another six months in King's Bench and fined £200 on her account. Since he was now incarcerated until 9 July, 1792, anyway, the Government delayed action on its own grievance until 26 November, 1791, when, with a lavish show of mercy, much admired by the Ministerial newspapers, the Court ruled that a fine of £100 was adequate. Not only was Walter never sentenced, but King was later punished for his "audacity" in petitioning for a sentence and in filing the suit in the first place.

By 29 February, 1792, the *Argus* was calling itself the *Argus of the Constitution*. It was printed by J. Powell at No. 5, Catherine Street, Strand, and, although it was dedicated to Thomas Paine and the newly formed (25 Jan.) London Corresponding Society, it was silent on the subject of Pitt. Among its contributors were Daniel Stuart[29] and probably John Horne Tooke, and it was temporarily conducted by John King. John King, usually called "Jew" King, was, according to Taylor,[30] a moneylender, specializing in loans to "young Irish noblemen, not much renowned for rectitude." He was married to Lady Jane Isabella Lanesborough, widow of the second Earl of Lanesborough, who had died in 1779; and the two frequently entertained at musicales at their home in Duke Street, Westminster. Taylor remembered meeting Lord Falkland and his sister Mrs. Lucia Grattan at these gatherings, her husband, Major John Grattan, being in India at the time, and it seemed to him that everything was quite in order and quite "respectable." The group itself was certainly not "respectable," for both Lady Lanesborough and Mrs. Grattan were prominent in faro circles, and the unmarried Lord Falkland operated a faro table himself, being otherwise noted for obscenity, whoremonging, and bullying. King, whose origin is not known, had been educated at the Jews' Charity School and had been an early protégé of Thomas Paine, who mentioned[31] having first met him as "a child, without fortune or friends" and having "discussed" with him "those political notions" which later (London, 1783) became the basis for King's *Thoughts on the Difficulties and Distresses in which the Peace of 1783 Has Involved the People of England* and still later (1791) for Paine's own *Rights of Man*.

King had also engaged in other activities. As soon as Mrs. Robinson settled with the Prince of Wales, he, as an earlier seducer, had tried to settle with her. But Mrs. Robinson, who had demonstrated so little regard for virtue, demonstrated a great deal of regard for money. Having failed to extort a shilling from her, King had accordingly published (London, 1781) their correspondence, under the title, *Letters from Perdita to a Certain Israelite, and His Answers to Them*. At this time he was married to a Deborah Lara, whom he later divorced in order to marry Lady Lanesborough. The marriage to Lady Lanesborough had occurred in Paris sometime before 1787, and, since he was a Jew and she a Roman Catholic, there was a question as to its validity. There was also a question as to the paternity of the two infants she brought along to the match, but she was at least well connected, being the sister and heir of the Earl of Belvidere. Her connections were evidently helpful, for, although King had previously spent much of his time in prison for debt, he was now in a state of solvency. Not only was he a silent partner in the Liverpool banking firm of "Sir Michael Cromie, Bart., [Philemon] Pownoll and [Isaac] Hartman," but he was associated with Viscount Falkland, Henry Speed, and the fourth Earl of Sandwich in other money lending enterprises. Politically he was still a follower of Thomas Paine.

The *Cabinet* did not survive long enough to specialize. It was begun on 2 January, 1792, and expired a few days later. The printer was C. Macrae, the conductor was the Rev. Charles Este, and its office was located in Charing Cross. No one had a good word to say for the enterprise. "When first we heard of a CABINET," remarked the Opposition *Observer* on 8 January, "we expected

Curiosities, but, a-lack, we find ourselves miserably disappointed—it is the emptiest piece of such household furniture we ever remember to have looked into." In September the paper was recommenced by the same proprietors and possibly at the same address, but this time as an evening paper with a new title, the *Courier*.

The *Gazetteer, and New Daily Advertiser* represented the Constitutional Society. This society had been organized in 1780 as a middle-class Whig club, and, although it was now almost as radical as the Corresponding Society, it was still middle-class and hence somewhat better regarded. The *Gazetteer* itself had been founded in 1735. Having for many years been a leading Opposition newspaper, it was currently in a state of decline, but its circulation was still above average, and it was still a vigorous champion of peace and reform. The editor was William Radcliffe, the printer Mary Say, and the address No. 10, Ave Maria Lane, Ludgate Street. That the Government had not molested this paper was probably owing less to Pitt's gallantry respecting women than to the paper's own discretion respecting Pitt.

The *Morning Chronicle* was devoted to the interests of Fox. Like Fox, it advocated peace and moderate reform and was therefore opposed in principle to both extremes, although it was sometimes carried away by its zeal for freedom of the press to defend even Paine. Begun in 1769, the *Chronicle* had been purchased by James Perry and James Gray in 1790, the two of them still functioning as conductors, and it was presently printed by John Lambert at No. 1, Great Shire Lane, Temple Bar, being otherwise housed at No. 474, Strand, the corner of Lancaster Court. The house had been furnished by the Duke of Norfolk, and "a few" of Fox's other friends were providing a £300 subsidy. Gray, who had once been a teacher at Charter House, was, according to Taylor:[32]

> a learned, sensible man, and an able writer. . . . He, according to report, had a right to half the property of the paper while he lived, and his share was subject to a provision for his sisters in case of his death. . . . It is not understood that Mr. Perry wrote much in the paper himself, but, mixing with the Whig party . . . at Debrett's, he obtained all the intelligence they could afford him, as well as many able productions from the literary members of that party. Whatever were his qualities as a writer or a man, he had at least the merit of political consistency.

The slighting reference to Perry's "qualities as . . . a man" was probably inspired by the scandal of 1781, which resulted in his dismissal from the *General Advertiser*, but there is no indication that Perry was himself guilty of anything more than loyalty to an acquaintance. In general, his "qualities" both as "writer" and as "man" were highly regarded. Born in Aberdeen in 1756, he had had considerable experience with the London press before he acquired the *Morning Chronicle*, and he was one of the few professional journalists accepted in polite society. It was sometimes suggested that he underpaid his staff, but even this suggestion was repudiated by Lord Campbell, who was at one time a member of that staff. "Mr. Perry," he said,[33] "always behaved to me with great kindness and liberality. . . . He invited me to his house, where he splendidly entertained the best company. . . . For his political consistency and honourable conduct he stood high with all the leaders of the Whig party in both Houses." The *Morning Chronicle* had in fact almost no interests other than politics. It rarely noticed sports, science, or the arts, and its society column consisted of a few brief paragraphs, headed

THE MIRROR OF FASHION.
—To shew—
THE VERY AGE AND BODY OF THE TIME ITS FORM AND PRESSURE.—

As a concession to the period, it included occasional verses by Charlotte Smith, who wrote for other papers as well, and it had a poet of its own, John Towill Rutt, who signed his work "J. T. R." Although professionally a drug merchant, Rutt contributed copiously to journals, usually in defense of Unitarianism. But its principal concern was the Parliamentary debates, the activities of Charles James Fox, and the machinations of William Pitt. If Pitt had had reason to silence Sampson Perry, he had had better reason to silence James Perry, for the *Argus* had merely called him a liar, whereas the *Chronicle* assumed that he was a liar and concerned itself with his motives. Although the "character" of Pitt which emerged was much more devastating than any invective, the Government had thus far refrained from prosecuting, the *Chronicle* being too intimately associated with the popular idol, Fox.

The *Morning Post, and Daily Advertiser* represented the liberal wing of the Opposition; hence it was somewhat to the right of the *Gazetteer* and somewhat to the left of the *Morning Chronicle*. Founded in 1772, the *Post* had inaugurated the age of the scandal sheet, and its character had not changed since. In 1792, according to Aspinall,[34] the shareholders, listed in order of the extent of their holdings, were Richard Tattersall, Alderman Thomas Skinner, a Mr. Hicks, a Mr. Furlonger, Louis Weltje, James Christie, Jeremiah Hargrave, Rob Mitchell, a Mr. Weatherby, and a Mr. Davis. Of this group, Tattersall, Skinner, Christie, Hargrave, and Mitchell were original proprietors of the paper. Tattersall was a friend of the Prince of Wales and a good judge of horses, which he bought and sold professionally, but he had no education, and his "interfering" in the newspaper's "literary department" had been much resented by editors. Skinner was an auctioneer and once a vigorous supporter of Fox and Sheridan. Although he still represented the Opposition's interests in the London government, his enthusiasm had somewhat subsided. Christie, the most prominent of the London auctioneers, had, like Tattersall, a "very good head for scheming but [wanted] education."[35] Fortunately, he paid little attention to the *Post*, using it only as an advertising medium. Jeremiah Hargrave owned the Rainbow Coffee House in Cornhill, and Mitchell was a lawyer. Weatherby, a proprietor since at least 1780, was possibly J. Weatherby, for many years printer of the *Racing Calendar*, as well as Clerk of the Jockey Club. Except for Weltje, the other proprietors, all newcomers, have not been identified. Davis received a little publicity in 1792, when he sued a Mr. Riddell for damages, Riddell having refused to surrender a cane Davis had dropped. The case was heard in the Court of King's Bench on 4 December. But the *Public Advertiser*, which recorded (6 Dec.) the event, referred to the plaintiff only as "Mr. Davis, proprietor of the Morning Post."

The affairs of the *Morning Post* were much more complicated than a list of the proprietors would, however, indicate. On 3 July, 1786,[36] Richard Tattersall, the principal proprietor, and John Benjafield, who then owned two of the twenty-four shares, had leased the newspaper for a period of seven years at a rental of £1,400 a year, with the stipulation that, at the end of this period, "the lessees [would *indemnify*] the other proprietors against any depreciation of shares below £350, for each 24th." On 4 July they had signed a collateral contract, which gave Tattersall control of the finances and Benjafield control of the "literary department." But, on 2 January, 1789, Carlton House, concerned for the reputation of Mrs. Fitzherbert, had purchased all of Benjafield's interests, his half-share in the lease as well as his two shares in the newspaper, through the agency of Louis Weltje. For the shares in the newspaper, the Prince of Wales had paid "1000 guineas"; for "the lease and controul over the Morning Post," he had promised to pay Benjafield £350 a year for life, providing "real security" for the payment within a reasonable time. He had paid the annuity during 1789 and 1790, but the "real security" had not been provided. Hence in late 1790 Benjafield had threatened to sue Weltje for violation of contract. In order to keep the transaction out of the courts and the story out of the newspapers, Tattersall had immediately contracted to pay the annuity on the Prince's behalf and, by 1 January, 1793, to furnish securities "on his real estates, in the counties of *Cambridge* or *Lincoln*." He had paid the annuity during 1791, and he also paid it during 1792, but he did not provide the security.

The lease was due to expire on 3 July, 1793, at which point the matter of "indemnification" would assume real importance. Despite its blackmailing activities, the *Morning Post* was not in a thriving state, but the paper had at least escaped prosecutions, for the Government had indicated a reluctance to sue or to permit anyone to sue a newspaper in which the Prince of Wales was involved, thereby risking an exposure of the involvement to the consequent embarrassment of the Royal Family. The Prince himself had paid no attention to the paper since the purchase, and, since Weltje was hardly able to write his name, Sheridan had undertaken the management, and the *Post* had therefore supported his faction. Among the numerous contributors were James Mackintosh, Robert Merry, and Daniel Stuart. The printer, at the beginning of 1792, was William Williams, Blake Court, Catherine Street, Strand, and the editor was probably D. E. MacDonnell.

The *Star, and Evening Advertiser*, begun in 1788, was the first and still the only afternoon daily. The original thirteen proprietors, most of them somehow connected with publishing, had included John Mac Murray, William Lane, John Hall (the engraver), T. Preston, and Peter Stuart. In February, 1789, Stuart, who had also printed and edited the paper, had been replaced in all his capacities by the poet-journalist, John Mayne. Otherwise the proprietary seems to have persisted, for, on 15 November, 1792, the paper stated that it was then in the hands of the "same Persons by whom it has been conducted for more than three years." The *Star* was still printed and edited by John Mayne in Temple Bar. Although its political position was usually moderately liberal, it was given to fluctuations, for all the proprietors played an active rôle in the management, and some of them, notably Mac Murray, Lane, and Hall, were friends of the Government.

Of the triweekly newspapers, the Opposition controlled only the *English Chronicle, and Universal Evening Post*, an adjunct of the *Morning Post*, printed by John Vint at the *Post*'s address; the *General Evening Post*, an adjunct of the *Gazetteer*, printed by Mary Say at the *Gazetteer*'s address and evidently (*Courier*, 28 Jan., 1795) edited by Charles Rathband; and the *London Chronicle*, "Sold by T. Wilkie, the Bible, St. Paul's Churchyard," no printer being named. But it controlled most of the weekly papers. One of them, the Saturday *Craftsman, or Say's Weekly Journal*, was another adjunct of the *Gazetteer* and was also printed by Mary Say at the *Gazetteer*'s address. There were also *Ayre's Sunday London Gazettee, and Weekly Monitor*, printed by Richard Ayre, No. 705, Bridge Street, to which Abraham Raimbach had been a contributor in 1790;[37] *E. Johnson's British Gazette, and Sunday Monitor*, printed by E. Johnson, Ludgate Place; the *London Recorder, or Sunday Gazette*, printed by H. Macleish, No. 12, Duke's Court, Drury Lane; and the Saturday *Westminster Journal, and London Political Miscellany. By Simon Gentletouch of Pall Mall, Esq.*, published by G. Redmayne, No. 9, Creed Lane. In addition to these newspapers, all of them old and well established, the Opposition acquired a new one on 4 December, 1791: the *Observer, and Sunday Advertiser*. The paper was founded and originally edited by Frederick Bourne, who had previously worked for the *World*, it numbered among its contributors Isaac Swan, another employee of the *World*, and it was printed by William Locke, at No. 283, Strand. But by 23 September, 1792, there had been some changes, the printer now being C. Mollenir at No. 17, Holywell Street and the principal proprietor and conductor being William S. Bourne, an employee of the Post Office.

Although the Opposition press had been subsidized almost exclusively by the right wing of the party, the journalists had come almost exclusively from the left. There is at least no evidence that Lord Guilford, the Duke of Portland, and their respective followers wrote anything for the newspapers, and Fox seems to have had little interest in them. But Sheridan was a heavy contributor, especially to those papers which supported his faction, and he wrote numerous pamphlets. Erskine, too, was a contributor to newspapers and a pamphleteer, as so apparently were George Tierney, Francis, "Chicken" Taylor, and others. The Opposition also retained a corps of professional journalists, but, so far as anyone knows, only conductors of newspapers were regularly salaried, and not all of them. James Perry received £300 a year for his conduct of the *Morning Chronicle*, the money being supplied by friends of Fox, and John Almon had received £200 a year, with the promise of an additional £100, for his conduct of the *General Advertiser*, the money in this case being supplied by Lord Robert Spencer. When the *General Advertiser* expired in 1790, Almon had a claim against the Whigs of £900. He still had the claim in 1792, but there was little possibility that the Whigs would honor it. Like Sampson Perry, Almon had made the mistake of criticizing Pitt; but, unlike Sampson Perry, Almon was no hero. Having been convicted of publishing a libel on the King, inserted, as it happened, by one of the Government's own agents, he had absconded to the country to write an apology, which he had published (London, 1790) under the title, *Memoirs of a Late Eminent Bookseller*. To this he was adding a laudatory account of Pitt's father, the two-volume *Anecdotes of the Life of the Right Hon. William Pitt, Earl of Chatham*, due to appear at the beginning of 1792. This kind of behavior endeared him to no one. Except in such instances as these, payment seems to have been made in a flat sum or when possible by patronage, and much of it came from outside the party proper. The Whig Club probably contributed at times, the *Gazetteer* would have been rewarded by the Constitutional Society for its vigorous defense of that organization, and during 1792 the *Argus* must have received financial assistance from the Corresponding Society. One of the heaviest investors in the Opposition press was the Prince of Wales, even though he was providing the money under duress.

By 1792 the corps of Opposition writers was comparatively small. Of the Rev. Thomas Lewis O'Beirne, once a vigorous pamphleteer for the Opposition, nothing had been heard for some time. While the Rockingham Whigs were in office (1782), he had been private secretary to the Duke of Portland as Lord Lieutenant of Ireland; while the Coalition was in office (1783), he had been private secretary to the Duke as First Minister. What he had done thereafter was a matter of some conjecture, for in late 1784 he was suddenly presented with two valuable livings.[38] Although he protested (*Morning Post*, 15 Jan., 1785) that the one in Cumberland was given to him by Lord Thurlow, to whom he had dedicated a volume of sermons, and the one in Northumberland was given to him by the Duke of Northumberland "in consequence . . . of old patronage and family connections," the newspapers strongly suspected that they were given to him by Pitt as reward for services during the elections of 1784. But by 1785 he was back in the Opposition fold, supposedly as author of *A Gleam of Comfort to This Distracted Empire*. He was evidently the author of a great deal of such material, for in 1791 he had relinquished the livings in Cumberland and Northumberland to accept the richer benefices of Temple-Michael and Mohill, which he had got through the influence of the Duke of Portland. He was still firmly attached to the Duke of Portland's faction. Another Irishman, Dennis O'Bryen, had begun his career as a surgeon, but had long since shifted to journalism and was currently connected with the *Morning Post*, possibly even as subeditor. O'Bryen was an intimate of Sheridan.

William Hamilton Reid was a relative newcomer. He had been one of the authors of *Criticisms on The Rolliad. Being a More Faithful Portraiture of the Present Immaculate Young Minister and His Friends, than Any Extant*, which Ridgway had published in 1784; and in 1786 he had made his debut in the *Gazetteer*.[39] Since then he had written prose and verse for a number of newspapers, but, since he was contributing to the Ministerial *Public Advertiser* as late as December, 1789, he probably did not become regularly allied with the Whigs until 1790. His work appeared in the *Gazetteer* throughout its existence and for many years in the *Morning Chronicle* as well. He also wrote ballads for street-singers, one of them, *Hum! Hum! A New Song* (1793), being listed in the *Catalogue* of the British Museum. Dr. John Wolcot, whose verse and prose had appeared in Opposition newspapers for years, under the signature, "Peter Pindar," was inactive during much of 1792, owing, it appears, to a libel action brought against him by Lord Lonsdale.

The four most prominent Opposition journalists were probably Robert Merry, James Mackintosh, and the Stuart brothers, Daniel and Charles. Although it is difficult to trace the activities of any one of them, it does seem clear that they were all allied with Sheridan and all somehow connected with the *Morning Post*. Robert Merry had discarded the pseudonym, "Della Crusca," in late 1789 and had quit the Ministerial *World* at approximately the same time to travel in France. He had returned an enthusiast for the French Revolution. As a favor to his friend, Major Topham, he had helped the *World* through the elections of 1790, but, since he was opposed to the newspaper's politics, he had done little thereafter, and in November he had quit again, this time forever. By the end of the year, he had moved to the *Morning Post*, and, since perhaps August, 1791, he had been one of its principal contributors. He had himself figured in the news on 3 June, 1791, when he helped organize the Friends of the Liberty of the Press, on 26 June, when he married the actress Elizabeth Brunton, and on 14 July, when he provided the "Ode" for the anniversary celebration of the French Revolution at the Crown and Anchor. As a person, Merry seems to have been warmhearted and charming with a child's disregard for reputation and a fine sense of humor, which expressed itself best in satire.

Mackintosh was a brother-in-law of the three Stuarts, Peter, Daniel, and Charles, having married Catherine Stuart in 1789. As an intimate of the family, he had helped Peter and Charles on the original *Star* in 1788 and on the spurious *Star* in 1789 and had written for other newspapers thereafter as a confederate of

Sheridan. In mid-1791 he had published an answer to Burke's *Reflections*, entitled *Vindiciae Gallicae*. Since the work was executed with urgency, Mackintosh retiring to the country, where he would not be disturbed, and feeding pages to the press as he finished them, it would appear to have been written on commission, he being in the pay of the Opposition at the time. But the Opposition could not have anticipated the result. Paine's *Rights of Man*, Part I of which had already appeared, was a Bible to the radicals, but it was not acceptable to the moderate reformers. The *Vindiciae* was acceptable to everyone as a dignified, well-reasoned, well-written, and thoroughly proper answer to Burke. The Whigs were ecstatic, and Mackintosh, who yearned for respectability, was now trying to divorce himself from his somewhat unsavory past. Having been an active member of the radical Constitutional Society, he was now identifying himself only with the Friends of the Liberty of the Press, which he had helped to organize; and he was going to great lengths to separate himself from the French extremists. Since he now aspired to a career in politics, he was also going to great lengths to conceal his journalistic activities.

Equally concerned for his reputation, although in a different way, was Daniel Stuart. According to one observer,[40] Stuart was "a rather stilted pompous sort of man, . . . a Scotchman by birth, and he had been originally a tailor in the neighbourhood of Covent-garden. . . . He was a discreet managing man, full of worldly shrewdness; but though I spent scores of evenings in his society, I never discovered that he possessed any portion of scholarship or talent." Stuart had never been a tailor, but the persistence of the fiction indicates how plausible it seemed to his acquaintances. Coleridge remembered him[41] as "a very knowing person," with a "knowledge of *men*," but little "knowledge of *man*;" and still another biographer[42] was impressed by his "inviolable secrecy." Stuart was certainly canny, he had an excellent head for business, he was not saddled with principles, and he had a genius for keeping quiet, or, if it served his interests to talk, a comparable genius for lying. He had no intimates, and, although he turned out to be a tycoon in the newspaper industry, he seems always to be lurking in the shadows, hiding from whatever the light might reveal. It is clear, however, that he was born in Scotland, that he had migrated to London in 1778, that he had learned printing from his brothers, and that, from 1782 to 1 May, 1789, he had been connected with the *Morning Post*. But, by at least November of that year, he and a "Duncan" Stuart had become partners in the "Peterborough-House Press," located in Peterborough Court, Fleet Street; and, "being provided with an ENTIRELY NEW, EXTENSIVE and ELEGANT ASSORTMENT of the most approved MATERIALS," were soliciting patronage from "a LIBERAL and DISCERNING PUBLIC." Since they wanted the patronage only of those concerned for "the Cause of LIBERTY—the true Principles of which [the art of printing] has with so much Success disseminated through the Nation," they had sent a copy of the prospectus,[43] dated "30ᵗʰ NOVEMBER, 1789," to "Sir Joseph Banks, Soho Square," he being at the time sympathetic with the cause.

Banks did not respond, and neither, it appears, did anyone else, for nothing whatever has been traced to this press. According to the *Universal British Directory of Trade and Commerce*, "Stuart, D. and D. Printers, Peterborough Ct. Fleet St." were nevertheless still active in 1790 and 1791, but not in 1792. And, according to Mary Stuart,[44] Daniel was throughout this period also writing for the *Morning Post* and the *Argus*. Except for mentioning[45] that he had attended "a contested election for Exeter in 1791," Daniel himself said nothing.

"Duncan" Stuart, one may suppose, was an alias for Charles Stuart: at least, "Duncan" invariably appears when Charles himself disappears. In the early 1780's, Charles Stuart and a "Mr. Stevenson" had been reporters for the *Gazetteer*.[46] Charles had quit that newspaper to work for the *Morning Post*, and, from 16 May, 1782, to the end of 1783, his name had appeared in the colophon of the *Post* as printer. In late 1786 he had joined the staff of the *Morning Herald*. Although his activities during the intervening years are accounted for only in terms of some theatrical trifles, "A List of the Letter-Press Printers in London, Westminster, and Southwark"[47] indicates that by 1785 a "Duncan" Stuart and a James Stevenson were conducting a printing business at "No. 2, Martlett-court, Bow-street." During the elections of 1788, Charles was employed by the Treasury. Having finished this assignment, he "assisted" his brother, Peter, with the conduct of the *Star* and was largely responsible for his leaving that paper in early 1789 to begin the spurious *Star*. A short time later he was in prison, but not necessarily under his own name, for, according to a document in the Public Records Office,[48] a "Duncan" Stuart and a James Stevenson had appeared in the Court of King's Bench during Trinity term, 1789, as defendants in an action for debt, the plaintiff, John Graham Phillipson, being awarded the £40 due him, plus 62s. costs. Charles was at any rate rescued by Sheridan, who restored him to the spurious *Star*, so that he could publish some exposés of Rose and Pitt, who, he maintained, had failed to pay him for his services in the 1788 elections. By the time the Government had silenced this newspaper, Charles's debts totaled "near twelve hundred pounds," and, in order to escape another imprisonment, he was supposedly living in the country from June, 1789, to July, 1791. But during this period he somehow paid off all but "£50 or £60" of the amount, and the Peterborough-House Press was evidently only one means, for on 22 November, 1790, he mentioned that his only "dependance" at the moment was an "engagement" with the *Morning Post*. He was in fact returned to the *Morning Post* in July, 1791, and was subsequently responsible for that newspaper's campaign against George Rose. He was still writing for the *Post* in 1792. Unlike most of his colleagues, Charles became emotionally involved in the cause he was paid to defend, supporting it even to the point of violence; hence he was always less a rogue than a hired assassin.

The Theaters

Almost as intimate a part of the Londoner's life as the newspapers were the theaters. Newspapers and theaters were in fact inseparable, for much of the material presented on the stage was supplied by journalists, and a considerable part of the material published in newspapers was supplied by actors and playwrights. Most of the plays also had political overtones, and, in addition, one gathers from the newspapers, actors, especially comedians, were inclined to insert their own political commentary. Like the newspapers, the winter playhouses were divided into two camps. The Ministerial playhouse was Covent Garden. This one was managed by Rose's friend, Thomas Harris, and its actors included Miss Brunton (now Mrs. Merry), Mrs. Esten, Mrs. Pope, Mrs. Wells, Mr. Bannister, Mr. Farren, Mr. Holman, Mr. Lewis, Mr. Quick, and Mr. Wilson. The Opposition playhouse was Drury Lane, supervised and principally owned by Sheridan and managed by John Philip Kemble; its actors included Mrs. Bland, Mrs. Crouch, Miss Farren, Mrs. Goodall, Mrs. Jordan, Mrs. Powell, Mrs. Siddons, Mrs. Ward, Mr. Dignum, Mr. Palmer, Mr. Parsons, and Mr. Kemble himself. Although the actors were usually not politically active, they were expected to be sympathetic with the point of view of their theater; and, except for the Royal Family, which was expected to divide its patronage equally, the audiences were invariably so. The playwrights were another matter, for, since good ones were difficult to find, Thomas Harris was inclined to ignore their political shortcomings, provided the plays themselves conformed with the theater's position. One of Covent Garden's most popular playwrights was, for example, Godwin's friend, Thomas Holcroft, but, since Holcroft's comedies seemed to be ridiculing the Prince of Wales and hence by indirection the Opposition, there was no protest from the Ministerial newspapers.

A third theater, the Haymarket, long managed by the elder George Colman and currently managed by his son George Colman, the younger, was a summer playhouse, limited by patent to the season between 15 May and 15 September. Because it had to rely on the winter playhouses for its actors, the elder Colman had adopted a policy of political neutrality. Everyone had been offended. Unable to count on the support of either the Ministerial or the Opposition press, he had had to be active in the newspapers himself, usually owning a share of one or two of them. In addition, there was the Opera House, also located in the Haymarket. This one was often called the King's Haymarket to distinguish it from Colman's theater, which was called the Little Haymarket. The lessee of the Opera House was William Taylor, and the theater had been devoted to Italian opera, introduced to London audiences many years earlier. But in 1790 the Opera House had been rebuilt, and the opera company had therefore moved to the Pantheon, where it still was. Finally there were the concerts in Hanover Square rooms, planned and directed by Salomon. London had in fact become one of the musical capitals of the world. Mozart had been there in 1764–1765; Haydn was there at the moment, having arrived on 1 January, 1791, to leave on 23 June, 1792. Foremost among the singers were Miss Storace, Madame Mara, and Elizabeth Billington, whose voices were regarded at the time as the sweetest ever heard.

Reports of the Italian operas, the oratorios, and the concerts were usually unbiased, but the three playhouses—Covent Garden, Drury Lane, and the Haymarket—had for many years been a political battleground. Reviews of performances had been violently partisan, and scandals at Drury Lane had been widely publicized by the Ministerial press, as scandals at Covent Garden had been widely publicized by the Opposition newspapers. Such publicity could be devastating, for, although the public was not offended by an actress's extra-marital affairs, an actor's desertion of his wife and children or any show of temperament on the part of actor or actress, especially if it resulted in failure to appear in an announced rôle, was likely to provoke a riot. In order to preserve the building, the manager therefore had no choice but to remove the offender from the scene, at least until public indignation had subsided. Although the actors were the principal victims of these tactics, the ultimate object was to damage the theater, and, in the case of Drury Lane, these were only two of the means employed. Having tried for years to rid itself of this playhouse, the Government had in 1791 given it what appeared to be a push into the abyss. The occasion was an announcement of the renovation of Covent Garden. The Ministerial press had immediately demanded a renovation of Drury Lane as well, and, before the year was over, the building had been condemned. Since Drury Lane was always reeling on the verge of bankruptcy anyway and the cost of rebuilding was estimated at £140,000, this seemed to be the end; but thus far the company had survived, Sheridan having contracted for the Opera House, now completed and as yet unlicensed for operas. Although the Ministerial newspapers had been greatly upset by this development, there had been con-solations, for the Opera House was much too large for drama, and the "bargain" was understood to be ruinous. John Taylor had said so in a pamphlet, entitled *A Statement of Transactions Respecting the King's Theatre at the Haymarket* (London, 1791).

The Government had also concerned itself with the Haymarket. While the elder Colman was active, it had been unable to jar this theater loose from its political neutrality; but in 1789 he had been legally declared a "lunatic" and removed to a Paddington asylum to spend the rest of his life. His affairs had accordingly become a court matter, to be decided, as it turned out, by Sir James Eyre, Lord Chief Baron of the Exchequer. This was evidently the opportunity the Government had been waiting for; although Eyre had appointed the younger Colman "Committee," he had allowed him only £200 a year for managing the theater and a comparable amount for supporting his father. The amounts had been justified as a necessary economy, the "lunatic's" debts already amounting to £7,000. Colman, who was not at all naïve in such matters, had brought the Haymarket into the Ministerial camp and, at the end of 1791, had employed the *World* to assure the Administration of his continuing loyalty and to protest the inadequacy of his provisions.

Notes for Part I

1. Cyrus Redding, *Fifty Years' Recollections, Literary and Personal, with Observations on Men and Things* (London, 1858), I, 20.

2. *Memoirs of the Whig Party during My Time. By Henry Richard Lord Holland*, ed. Henry Edward Lord Holland (London, 1852), I, 33.

3. *Memoirs of the Whig Party*, I, 80.

4. See, for example, *Mrs. Jordan and Her Family*, ed. Arthur Aspinall (London: Arthur Barker, 1951), p. xi.

5. *Mrs. Jordan and Her Family*, pp. xii, 4, note.

6. For Chifney's explanation, see *Genius Genuine . . . : A Fine Part in Riding a Race Known Only to the Author* (London, [1795?]).

7. James Grant, *The Newspaper Press: Its Origin—Progress—and Present Position* (London, 1871), I, 229–230.

8. Rev. Dr. [John] Trusler, *The London Advertiser and Guide* (London, 1790), p. 137.

9. James Savage, *An Account of the London Daily Newspapers, and the Manner in which They are Conducted* (London, [1811]), pp. 13–14.

10. [Stanley Morison,] *The History of The Times 1785–1841* (London: The Times, 1935), p. 49.

11. "The Newspapers, Reporting, Editing, Speculating, and Proprietorships," *Metropolitan Magazine*, VI (1833), 57.

12. *Collected Letters of Samuel Taylor Coleridge*, ed. Earl Leslie Griggs (Oxford: Oxford University Press, 1959), III, 267, note, 268, 269.

13. For some of Boswell's contributions, see Lucyle Werkmeister, *Jemmie Boswell and the London Daily Press, 1785–1795* (New York: New York Public Library, 1963); other contributions will be noted in forthcoming papers. Material relating to previous literary figures has been and will be presented separately.

14. *Private Papers of James Boswell from Malahide Castle*, eds. Geoffrey Scott and F. A. Pottle (Mount Vernon: McGraw-Hill, 1928–1934), XVIII, 185.

15. PRO 30/ GD 8/ 333–34.

16. See Arthur Aspinall, "The Social Status of Journalists at the Beginning of the Nineteenth Century," *Review of English Studies*, XXI (1945), 216–232; *History of The Times*, p. 16.

17. *The Farington Diary by Joseph Farington, R. A.*, ed. James Greig (London: Hutchinson and Co., 1922–1928), V, 196.

18. *The Farington Diary*, V, 142.

19. *History of The Times*, pp. 132–133.

20. John Taylor, *Records of My Life* (London, 1832), II, 365–367.

21. Robert L. Haig, *The Gazetteer 1735–1797* (Carbondale: Southern Illinois University Press, 1960), p. 179.

22. Charles Lamb, "Christ's Hospital Five and Thirty Years Ago."

23. Taylor, I, 249–252.

24. "Editors and Newspaper Writers of the Last Generation. By An Old Apprentice of the Law," *Fraser's Magazine*, LXV (1862), 173–174.

25. PRO 30/ GD 8/ 333–334, 355–357.

26. *The Farington Diary*, V, 209.

27. "The Late Mr. Coleridge, the Poet," *Gentleman's Magazine*, n.s., X (1838), 25.

28. Arthur Aspinall, *Politics and the Press c. 1780–1850* (London: Ernest Benn Ltd., 1949), p. 448.

29. *Letters from the Lake Poets . . . to Daniel Stuart*, ed. Mary Stuart (London, 1889), p. x.

30. Taylor, II, 341–345.

31. *Mr. King's Speech, at Egham, with Thomas Paine's Letter to Him on It* (London, 1793), pp. 8–9. For the account which follows, see *Notes and Queries*, 11th ser., VI (1912), 229, XI (1915), 333–334, 437–438; *Complete Baronetage*, ed. George Edward Cokayne (Exeter: W. Pollard and Co. Ltd., 1906), V, 386; and *Oppression Deemed No Injustice toward Some Individuals. Illustrated in the Late Treatment of Mr. John King, Under a Commission for Bankruptcy* (London, 1798), *passim*.

32. Taylor, I, 242.

33. Mary C. Hardcastle, *Life of John Lord Campbell, Lord High Chancellor of Great Britain* (London, 1881), I, 179. For a confirmation of Lord Campbell's opinion, see *Metropolitan Magazine*, VI, 65.

34. *Politics and the Press*, p. 279.

35. *The Farington Diary*, I, 227–228.

36. Having re-evaluated documents presented by Aspinall (*Politics and the Press*, pp. 278–279), I have redated the lease, which I had previously supposed was executed at the beginning of the year. See my *The London Daily Press, 1772–1792* (Lincoln: University of Nebraska Press, 1963), p. 88.

37. *Memoirs and Recollections of the Late Abraham Raimbach, Esq., Engraver*, ed. M. T. S. Raimbach (London, 1834), p. 34.

38. The recipient of these gifts was not the Rev. William Jackson, as I previously stated. See *London Daily Press*, p. 86.

39. Haig, p. 205.

40. *Fraser's Magazine*, LXV, 174.

41. *Table Talk* (London, 1835), 1 May, 1832; *Letters from the Lake Poets*, p. 257.

42. *Gentleman's Magazine*, XXVIII (1847), 323.

43. The original is in the British Museum.

44. *Letters from the Lake Poets*, p. x.

45. Daniel Stuart, *Peace and Reform, against War and Corruption* (London, 1794), p. 89, note.

46. Haig, p. 179.

47. See *John Pendred. The Earliest Directory of the Book Trade* (1785), ed. Graham Pollard (London: Bibliographical Society Transactions, No. 14, 1955).

48. Ind. 6272.

II

ANNUS ANTE BELLUM: 1792

The Opening of Parliament

The opening of Parliament having been fixed for 31 January, the Ministerial newspapers prepared for the event with the usual ridicule of "Chicken" Taylor and some denunciations of Lord Lauderdale, who had left Paris on 1 January, in the company of his brother, Thomas Maitland, Major of the 62nd Foot Regiment, and Colonel Gordon, to return to England (*Morning Chronicle*, 3 Jan., 1792). Although the Ministerial newspapers did not know what he had been doing there, they liked to think that he had been conspiring with the Jacobins. There was also the usual abuse of Burke and the trial of Hastings, concentrated in the *World*, but splashing over into the other Treasury newspapers, and there were the usual pamphlets by Bowles. One of them, entitled *Dialogues on the Rights of Britons, between a Farmer, a Sailor, and a Manufacturer. Dialogue the Second* (*Dialogue the First* having appeared the previous year), was simply opposed to reformers. Another, entitled *A Second Letter to Charles James Fox, upon the Matter of Libel*, was opposed to Fox's bill, which empowered juries to make the whole decision in actions for libel. This decision had previously been made by judges, juries considering only the fact of publication. Bowles had opposed the bill right along, having in 1791 published *A Letter to the Right Hon. Charles James Fox: Occasioned by his Late Motion in the House of Commons respecting Libels* and *Considerations on the Respective Rights of Judge and Jury: Particularly upon Trials for Libel*; and, since he always spoke for the Government, the Opposition newspapers had been astonished when the Government permitted the bill to pass the Commons. The appearance of a third pamphlet on the subject indicated that it would not pass the Lords.

The Opposition newspapers were adding their own abuse of Burke, and the *Morning Post* was demanding an inquiry into the Government's management of the Westminster election of 1788, in preparation for a motion which was planned on that subject.[1] With the demise of the spurious *Star* in 1789, this issue had lain dormant for over two years, but, the Treasury being a notoriously slow pay-master, it had been revived in 1791 by a series of lawsuits. The first and most important of these was an action brought by George Smith, a publican, against George Rose, who, Smith charged, still owed him £110 5s. for "services rendered" in connection with the election. Although the Government had evidently hoped to keep this litigation out of the newspapers, Sheridan had somehow heard of it and on 19 July had paid the remaining debts of Charles Stuart and returned him to the *Morning Post*, so that he could deal with the matter. Stuart was an authority on the subject, having been in the employ of the Treasury himself at the time and having been responsible for the earlier exposés of Rose and Pitt in the spurious *Star*. Everything had turned out well. The trial had occurred on 21 July, Smith had been awarded the full amount of his claim, and Pitt had emerged smelling almost as bad as Rose. As the *Morning Chronicle* had put it on 23 July: "It was before sufficiently known that persons connected with the Treasury took an active part in the Westminster Elections; but that Mr. PITT was ever one of a Committee to engage publicans and bludgeon-men, was not suspected, till Mr. SECRETARY ROSE contrived to have it sworn to in a Court of Justice." The *Morning Post* had carried every word of the testimony and a great deal of commentary besides. A second action had promised to be equally rewarding. John Frost, a lawyer and now a disciple of Thomas Paine, had filed suit against the Ministerial candidate, Lord Hood, for the recovery of £12,168, which, he maintained, Lord Hood had owed him since 1788 for his various services as "agent." But this time there was little to be learned, for, instead of hearing the evidence itself, the Court of King's Bench had referred it to "three Gentlemen," and all the *Morning Post* knew was that, on 6 August, Frost had been awarded £9,238 10s. of the claim. On 19 November Frost had sued for the amount of the award, but, Lord Hood having promised to deliver the money immediately, the action had been dropped.

Having arranged this campaign for the *Morning Post*, Sheridan had quietly moved over to the Ministerial *Oracle*, where he could count on the co-operation of John Bell and Peter Stuart in another plot, provided of course they were paid for it. As usual[2] he planned to get the money by extortion, principally, it appeared, from the Duke of York. The Duke was gratifyingly vulnerable, for, since the settlement of his affairs was one of the first items of Parliamentary business, he would need to appear at the best possible advantage, and the only advantage he could muster depended on his command of the Coldstream Guards. On 5 January the *Oracle* had something to say on this subject: "Certain Scoundrels, wearing the Uniform of that most execrable of all nuisances, the Guards, with the butt-ends of their firelocks, beat several persons about the head so effectually, as to fell them to the ground. The Majesty of the people suffered all this; but after they bear to be driven into their own highways by the wretches they supply with daily bread, what will they bear?" There was more on 7 January:

THE GUARDS.
"Let the gall'd Jade wince, our Withers are unwrung."

From the *Conductors* of the *Oracle*, it could never be expected that we should in general, censure but upon sure ground.—OBLOQUY, when it is poured down by pure hands upon the heads of any, falls heavily indeed.

The OFFICERS of these Troops are in every sense of the word GENTLEMEN— Gentlemen of FAMILY, of FORTUNE—Men of the nicest HONOUR—If example had its proper influence, the PRIVATES could not be bad. The pay of these depraved People, it is true, is but *small*, but then does not COMMERCE, do not MANUFACTURES throw open their thousand arms to welcome the industry of those so able to labour?

When the Colonel of one of the Regiments arrived, what was his enquiry, from conviction of their unworthiness—

"Are all my Rascals hanged?"

They are conspiring to arrive at the summit of atrocity, and to their accustomed vices of plunder and desertion, now add the detestable Cowardice of ARMED BRUTALITY.

On 12 January the *Oracle*, always more grateful than discreet, thanked Sheridan in effect for what he was doing for it. The thanks consisted of a puff, which concluded with the protest: "Though, God knows, far enough removed from any connection with the PARTY, yet we should blush to be thought for an instant combined with Men who assail the *private* Character of this Gentleman."

On 25 January there was another paragraph, this one implying that the Duke of York's stud was mortgaged to the notorious Phillipe Égalité: "Should the PRINCE of WALES's Stud come under the hammer, as is at present intended," said the *Oracle*, "the Horses of the *Duke*, or more properly *Mr*. ORLEANS, will be sold at the same time." The last paragraph of the series appeared on 28 January and was again concerned with the Guards: "COLDSTREAM GUARDS./ On Monday [23 Jan.] one *Elliot*, a private of very flagitious character, received *one hundred and fifty* lashes—the DUKE of YORK remitting the other half of the sentence./ The man had it seems been flogged frequently before this—he was thought obdurate and regardless; however, the fact was otherwise, for the fellow *shot* himself on Thursday morning. The adjutant reported that he was not dead yesterday." By this time Sheridan was also practicing his arts on the Prince of Wales, who was to figure more directly in his plans.

The sale of the Prince's stud had originally been scheduled for December, 1791; it was now positively scheduled for January, 1792. But the *Public Advertiser*, which reported this information on 5 January, itself reacted with "hope" rather than confidence:

THE PRINCE OF WALES.

His Royal Highness, it is confidently said, [has] made up his mind, (we hope finally) to forsake the turf.

He has signified this determination to his most intimate friends, and has ordered Col. Hulse to sell all the running horses immediately.

His Highness, it is further said, goes to Newcastle no more.

He meditates a more generous use of his fortune—the protection of Arts, the encouragement of Manufactures, the splendor that is useful as well as brilliant.

We hope it may be true, as has been stated, that an illustrious Personage intends to quit the Turf, and dispose of his Stud; —it is also to be hoped that when disposed of, no advice or inducement will occasion a *third* purchase.

On 14 January the *Morning Post* denied that the Prince was unmindful of "[useful] splendor": "The state-carriage building for the PRINCE of WALES, will be the most sumptuous and tasteful thing of the sort ever seen in this country. In this and other expenditures, encouraging the arts, [the nation] will eventually derive riches from the disbursement." On 18 January the *Star* further denied that he was squandering his "fortune" on residences: "The PRINCE of WALES has purchased the house lately belonging to [his Master of the Robes] General CONWAY and [his wife] the Countess of AYLESBURY, in Warwick-street, behind Carlton-House. The price given for it was 10,000*l.* ready money. The Margrave of ANSPACH [who had recently sold his principality to the King of Prussia and was now settled in England] was in treaty for the house, but the PRINCE perhaps not wishing to have so opulent a neighbour to overlook his gardens, desired a preference, which was granted." Nothing further was said of the horses until 25 January, when the *Oracle* referred to the sale as "at present intended," although evidently no longer determined upon. The Prince had been encouraged by someone from the *Oracle* to hope that it might be avoided.

But the *Oracle* clearly meant to be paid for its services, for on 28 January it mentioned casually that "The PRINCE, it is said, has given 1000 guineas for a Ring. —If it had been the *Nuptial* Hoop thus dearly purchased, few would have lamented it." The possibility that his bachelorhood might become a newspaper issue always alarmed the Prince, and, to add to the alarm, the *Oracle* of 30 January indicated its awareness of the "ONE MILLION Sterling," which he and his brothers were borrowing through Dutch banks. At the same time it commenced the campaign for which all these negotiations had been but preparation by publishing the following dialogue:

AN IMPORTANT CONVERSATION.

GREAT PERSONAGE.

I have a subject of much moment to speak with you about. Thus it is: My SON and I have no longer a difference between us; the most perfect reconciliation has taken place, and I have determined that his DEBTS shall be paid.

HIS MINISTER.

Sir, your SON owes the sum of ONE MILLION Sterling.

GREAT PERSONAGE.

Well Sir—be it so. I would have their liquidation proposed to Parliament immediately.

HIS MINISTER.

YOUR MAJESTY is to use your Royal pleasure.—But in the present position of Affairs, it would be *dangerous* for a MINISTER to venture such a step.—Such is my opinion.

GREAT PERSONAGE.

Then, Sir, *you decline* the RECOMMENDATION of it to Parliament?

HIS MINISTER.

As far as my single Vote may go, I shall not oppose it; but it is not my advice.

GREAT PERSONAGE.
Then, Sir, I shall apply to the House MYSELF by Message.
HIS MINISTER.
Unquestionably YOUR MAJESTY is free to do so.

The *Oracle*'s purpose was to drive a wedge in the public mind between the King and Pitt, and, since Pitt depended on the King's supposed confidence in him for whatever confidence he in turn commanded from the people, he could not ignore this kind of thing. But the first one to respond was apparently the Prince of Wales, for on 31 January the *Oracle* digressed to applaud Captain Payne for "his enlightened services" on behalf of the Heir Apparent, Payne being no doubt the intermediary. On the same day the King journeyed down to the House of Lords to open the second session of the Seventeenth Parliament.

The King's report on the state of the nation was extremely bright. Whatever external problems the country had had were settling themselves nicely. Thanks to some timely intervention on the part of the British, there was no longer danger of a war with Russia, and there was reason to hope that, "under the able conduct of Lord Cornwallis," even the war in India would soon "be brought to an honourable conclusion." The "continuance of [the] present tranquillity" seeming thus assured, the King was "induced to think that some immediate reduction may safely be made in our naval and military establishments." He was also "induced to think" that "a system" for reducing "some part of the existing taxes, at the same time giving additional efficacy to the plan for the reduction of the national debt," might be in order. But the greatest stroke of good fortune was the marriage of the Duke of York to "the eldest daughter of my good brother and ally, the King of Prussia." Certain that both Houses must share his own "satisfaction" in this "happy event," the King "[expected their] cheerful concurrence in enabling me to make a suitable provision for their establishment." Except for the continuation of the Indian war, the Opposition could hardly object to this report, and the Addresses of Thanks were therefore passed as moved.

The only issue at this point seemed to be the Government's recent interference in the affairs of Russia, but, although there were a few motions on the subject, none of them succeeded. Among Pitt's numerous defenders was Robert Banks Jenkinson, who delivered his maiden speech on 29 February. The Government had brought Jenkinson into Parliament in 1790 as Member for Appleby, but he was not then seated, being still underage; he had now been brought back as Member for Rye. The Ministerial newspapers thought he was great; the Opposition papers thought that George Canning, a friend of Fox and Sheridan, was greater, and there was a small polemic as to who would out-debate whom when Canning was also brought in. For once the *World* had no opinion. "CANNING *versus* JENKINSON," it said on 15 March. "—The OPPOSITION, we understand, shortly mean to start a young man who was a *Brother Etonian* with

JENKINSON, against him. His Name is CANNING; he was the joint author of the MICRO-COSM, a paper written by him and other *Eton Boys*. They say he was, in those days and since, JENKINSON's superior at every thing. All we can say, is—/ 'NOUS VERRONS.'" What finally went awry in the Opposition's plans for Canning, no newspaper seems to have known.

Although the King had not touched on the possibility of a war with France, everything indicated that this possibility had been ruled out as well. Burke, who had previously advocated such a war, now said not a word, and Pitt seemed to be concerned only with preparations for "tranquillity." His "sinking fund," established in 1786, was, with certain augmentations and modifications, finally, it appeared, going to justify its existence. The expectation now was that the national debt, long a matter of great anxiety, would be eradicated by 1808 and that the country would meanwhile be insured against the accumulation of any new debt and almost insured against a rise in taxes. Taxes for the moment would even be decreased. A cut in the Army budget of £51,403 would, it was understood, be only the first of many, and the Navy budget would be comparably slashed. France was in fact relatively quiet. In June, 1791, the Royal Family had tried to escape to the protection of Marie Antoinette's brother, Leopold II of Austria, and had been returned to Paris, where in September Louis XVI had subscribed to the new constitution. Since then the government had been generally dominated by the Girondists, under the leadership of Brissot, and, although the Girondists were not monarchists, the government appeared to be stable. There was only one discordant note, for, while Pitt was posing as a lover of peace, his newspapers were beating the war drums harder than ever. It seemed to the Opposition press, therefore, that all the talk of "tranquillity" was a hoax, to be exploded as soon as the proper "incident" presented itself.

There were two "incidents" in early 1792. The first was the death on 1 March of Leopold II. The news reached England on 10 March, and, since Leopold had been so conspicuously involved in French affairs and since he had died under somewhat mysterious circumstances, the Ministerial newspapers at once suggested that he had been poisoned by the Jacobins. The Opposition newspapers were distraught, and the *Morning Chronicle* exhorted its readers not to submit to war on his account. But on 16 March the *World*, which had been particularly certain of the poisoning, suddenly changed its mind. The Emperor had not been poisoned, it said: "He had been dropsical some time: but the immediate cause of his death was the too frequent use of a *certain stimulus* to force passion. The ENGLISH who were there knew this perfectly well; and alluding to the name of his attachment, used to say, '*He is finding work for the* COOPER.'" Since in 1790 the *World* had been sued for libel by Lady Cowper and other heirs of her husband, this paragraph was obviously an act of spite; but any explanation which exonerated the Jacobins was welcome to the Opposition newspapers. Lady Cowper accordingly became the culprit, and the *World*'s hope of 21 March that "Lady COWPER, from the death of the EMPEROR, will [now] perhaps become *devote*, and sink into a quiet widow" was echoed by most of the Opposition papers. Only the *Morning Chronicle* dissented. While subscribing to the thesis in general, it was unwilling to blame Lady Cowper exclusively, for, as it pointed out on 12 April, Leopold had had numerous mistresses at the time of his death, the "declared" one being the Countess of Wolkenstein. There was a more frightening development on 29 March, when news arrived of the assassination on 16 March of Gustavus III of Sweden. Since this time there was no doubt that the Jacobins were responsible, the Opposition papers reported the event with foreboding. But the Ministerial papers said nothing at all.

The Oracle, the Prince of Wales, and Trouble in the Post Office

The second item on the Parliamentary calendar, a "suitable provision" for the Duke and Duchess of York, was not in itself a political issue, especially since the King was apparently inclined toward generosity; but it was already evident that it was going to entail one. The Prince of Wales, it appeared, had finally agreed to the financial demands of the *Oracle*, for on 2 February that newspaper added to its notice, "The PRINCE of WALES and the DUKE of YORK were in the House of Commons during the debate on Tuesday [31 Jan.]; and afterwards his Royal Highness the PRINCE gave a dinner to his Friends at Carlton House," the seemingly irrelevant comment, "*Mieux tard que jamais.*" Following this comment was a series of paragraphs, all obviously penned by Sheridan, charging that the King had ordered Pitt to request payment of the Prince's debts, as well as provision for the Duke and Duchess of York, and that Pitt had refused. The charge was repeated daily, and by 7 February Pitt himself had acted, his friend, the extremely wealthy and politically powerful Lord Lonsdale, having filed actions for libel against James Evans, bookseller, and John Bell, printer, Evans for having published a pamphlet, entitled *A Commiserating Epistle to James Lowther, Earl of Lonsdale and Lowther. By Peter Pindar*, and Bell for having stated in his newspaper, the *Oracle*: "The Painters are much perplexed about the *Likeness* of the *Devil*. To obviate this difficulty concerning his *Infernal Majesty*, the humorous PETER PINDAR has recommended to his friend [JOHN] OPIE the countenance of Lord Lonsdale." Both libels were many weeks old, the pamphlet having appeared in early December, the paragraph on 17 December. On 7 February Dr. Wolcot appeared in court to ask that his name be substituted for that of Evans, and Bell appeared to ask that Peter Stuart's name be substituted for his, Stuart being, he said, the author of the libel. Neither request was granted; nor did these actions have any effect on the *Oracle*.

On 8 February the Ministerial *World* took the first notice of what was going on. "The OPPOSITION," it remarked, "are boldly advancing a story, 'that the KING thinks less favourably of Mr. PITT than heretofore: that his MAJESTY much wishes the embarrassments of the PRINCE to be discharged; and that the MINISTER resists the measure.' Should such a thing be possible, some hopes are entertained by them—*for themselves.*" On 13 February it stated again: "The OPPOSITION are affecting to play a very *cunning Game* with Mr. PITT. The PEOPLE are, it seems, to be called upon for a *second* [actually a *third*] *payment* of certain ROYAL DEBTS, which, if the MINISTER will not favour, a resentment is to be worked up against him from a quarter where it may be most formidable." On the same day, Lord Lonsdale filed additional actions for libel against Wolcot and Stuart.³ By this time the *Oracle* was pretending that the "story" had originated in other newspapers and that it itself had never believed it. As it said on 13 February, including in this instance another reference to the Dutch loan, the Prince being almost a lax a paymaster as the Treasury: "Those who insinuate a *shyness* between a GREAT PERSONAGE and the MINISTER, in consequence of the [latter's] reluctance to apply to the Parliament on a *certain account*, do the highest injustice to the honourable feelings of both.—The EXALTED CHARACTER alluded to, must admire the *patriotism* of the MINISTER; for he must know, he is the ONLY man in the Kingdom with whom such an enforcement could be ineffectual. Would Mr. Fox hesitate to ask this MILLION? Assuredly he would *not.*" There was more of this on 17 February: "It has been confidently affirmed by the base Opponents of the Minister, that it is not the grant of Money he wishes to prevent, but the PERSON receiving [it] is not the object he regards with complacency.—More infamous calumny than this never disgraced the worst of Prints in the worst of times.—It would be extremely indecent to presume to assign the reasons for such dissent on the part of so great a Personage [as Pitt], either officially or mentally considered; yet they may be sufficiently obvious." At approximately this point (the newspapers do not record the exact date), Bell was indicted ex officio for having published two libels on the Guards. The paragraphs cited were those of 5 and 7 January, the first clearly the work of Sheridan, the second clearly the work of Stuart.

With the paragraph of 17 February, the *Oracle* abandoned this particular "*Game,*" and on 21 February it announced that the "Stud of His Royal Highness the PRINCE of WALES, we rejoice to hear, is immediately to be disposed of by Public Auction." But the Prince had no intention of selling the stud unless he had to, and by now the Opposition was at least obliged to mention his "embarrassments." The possibility of Parliament's responding, gloomy enough to begin with, was rendered gloomier by the appearance on 27 February of Part I of Charles Pigott's *The Jockey Club: or, A Sketch of the Manners of the Age.* Published anonymously, the work consisted of a collection of characters: the subject of the first one being the Prince, whose extravagances, debts, and licentious habits were detailed at devastating length; the subjects of the others being his friends, who were generally categorized as "the very *lees* of society, creatures, with whom a person of morality, or even common decency, could not associate." Although the pamphlet hardly needed any publicity, one of the "creatures," Sir John Lade, supplied it by threatening to sue, so that by 7 March probably everyone in the House had read it.

It was under these circumstances that Fox rose to present the case for the Princes. Although his point of departure was the provision for the Duke and Duchess of York, he went on to say that, as a matter of "solid principle," all of "His Majesty's numerous family" should be adequately provided for to begin with and that, if subsequent "adjustments" were necessary, they should be made by the King, not by humiliating appeals to Parliament. The provision for the Duke of York had, he thought, been grossly inadequate and the provision for the Prince of Wales disgracefully so. Parliament now had the power to rectify the first, and he could not, he admitted, understand why the King had not rectified the second, especially since he had been granted huge increases in both the privy purse and the civil list for such purposes. This was not at all what the *Oracle* had had in mind, for, as Fox represented the case, the wrongdoer was the King, not William Pitt. There was a small debate on the subject, Pitt defending the King; and, Fox having made no motion, the matter was dropped.

The *Oracle* said nothing about this development; the *World* of 10 March commented on it at length:

> Mr. Fox was on Wednesday evening . . . the able advocate for the Princes, and was forward in his wishes for the splendid support of the dignity of the throne. Mr. Fox . . . very properly maintained, that the Princes, when their establishments came to be formed, should [have been] furnished with a sum adequate to the occasion. Mr. Fox, however, certainly could not mean this to apply to the Duke of YORK. His Highness was possessed of a very large sum when he came of age, and the sale of the *Allerton Estate* since, brought him, if report err not, 120,000*l*. Mr. Fox could not surely mean to insinuate that this immense sum was already *spent* or *lost at play*?
>
> Mr. Fox . . . very artfully felt the pulse of the House with reference to a certain much-wished-for measure—*the payment of certain debts*—there was no encouragement, however, to bring on such a proposition.

Since, as everyone knew, the Prince would use the money to finance "*future dissipation*," the *World* felt that Parliament had acted wisely, and it could meanwhile "hope that the late remarks in the House of Commons will teach certain young *Gentlemen* a lesson of *prudence*, which will be more serviceable than the payment of debts twenty times over." Fox had not "felt the pulse of the House"; he had said emphatically that "*the payment of certain debts*" was the responsibility of the King. But, for the Prince of Wales, the effect was the same: the stud had to go.

On 10 March the *World* announced that the "PRINCE's Stud comes to the hammer on Monday." On Monday (12 Mar.) even the *Oracle* implored the

Prince not to change his mind: "The STUD./ —In the name of Heaven let it go. If it abridge the natural generosity of temper; if it curb the necessary shew of domestic establishments; if it (as pursuits may contaminate)—if it cast an insult upon a Character liberal in the extreme, let it go—and let it go—*for ever.*" On 13 March the *Oracle* reported, with every indication of relief, that the sale was underway: that on the previous day "7 COLTS, rising One Year Old," "9 FILLIES, rising one year old," and 32 other horses had gone under the hammer at Tattersall's and had brought 3,836 guineas. Since the Prince had paid many times this amount for them, the *Oracle* felt obliged to explain that the important item was not the sum realized from the auction, but the saving in upkeep. It stressed this point on 14 March, adding that the upkeep had been regularly estimated "at 30,000*l.* per annum." The opinions of other newspapers respecting the outcome of this first sale varied. It seemed to the *Public Advertiser* (13 Mar.) that the stud had sold very badly, and it attributed the cause to its numerous engagements: "The engagements of the . . . colts and fillies extend to the Lewes meeting of 1794, those most deeply matched being chiefly by Saltram. One colt by Saltram . . . is matched in sweepstakes to the amount of 1700 guineas; and a yearling filly by Saltram is engaged in a sweepstakes of a thousand guineas each for the next July meeting; for the October meeting in a sweepstakes of a thousand guineas, against five of the Duke of Bedford's, and five of Lord Grosvenor's; and in the oak stakes in 1793." The *Morning Chronicle* (13 Mar.) felt that the sale was mixed: "In general, the brood mares and aged horses, as it was expected, brought good prices, but the rising colts and fillies, being loaded with heavy engagements, had a very dull market." The *Star* agreed with the *Oracle* that the important thing was the saving in upkeep: "The number of racers and breeders sold on Monday . . . made *fifty-one*; which, with what are yet to come under the hammer, must have cost, on their keep alone, somewhat more than even the expences of a princely table./ The expences of race-horses are estimated, on an average, if a man keeps above three, at 100*l.* per annum each."

On 14 March the *World* stated that the "Stud sold well . . . except such horses as were saddled with engagements, and for them not a bidder could be found. One brood mare aged 23, was knocked down for 250 Guineas, and another by *High-flyer* for 270 Guineas." But by 15 March the *World* had changed its mind. Always alert to opportunities for extortion, it was now representing the outcome as calamitous, and it purported to be aghast at rumors that the Duke of York was re-entering the field:

> The Duke of YORK is reported to be going upon the TURF. We cannot believe the thing possible—nor would the PEOPLE grant SUPPLIES to be thus applied.
> The PRINCES of the BLOOD ROYAL of ENGLAND have a right to amuse themselves, if they do not call on the PUBLIC to furnish the means of their dissipation. If they do this, the Public in their turn will naturally and properly ask, "*Are they amusing themselves properly?*"
> The PRINCE of WALES's Stud sold very ill. Those who had once flattered the

judgment of his HIGHNESS in horses, seemed to have a different opinion—*at the sale.*

. . . . . .

NEWCASTLE.—STOCKS fell in the Stables 5 per cent. on the PRINCE's quitting the TURF: but rose *one half* on hearing the DUKE of YORK intended to enter at the Post.

On 16 March the *World* repeated that the stud had "sold very ill": "The sale of . . . brood mares and foals—are said, not to have paid the saddles and bridles in the time." On 22 March the *Oracle*, which yielded to no newspaper in matters of extortion, also reported that "the Duke of YORK means to purchase the Prince's [remaining] Horses.—Sir JOHN LADE is in future to have the management of the Royal Stables"; and on 23 March it expressed its utter disgust at the Duke's conduct. On the same day the *World* observed bitterly: "The DUKE of YORK is mentioned as likely to become the purchaser of the major part of the remainder of the PRINCE's Stud—if so, the public will be but little benefited by, or satisfied at the sale." There was no further reference to that subject.

On 5 April the Duke and Duchess of York's Establishment Bill, along with "An Act for Granting to His Majesty the sum of £400,000 . . . for the reduction of the National Debt," was presented to the King for signature, and on 7 April the *Oracle* reported that the Prince of Wales had gone "in State . . . to the House of Peers [to witness the ceremony], attended by Lords MELBOURNE, CLERMONT, and C[HARLES] SOMERSET. The DUKE of YORK was in the House in his Robes, and returned in the Carriage with the PRINCE." All three of the Prince's escort seem to have been members of his household, Lord Melbourne being a Gentleman of the Bedchamber. There was reason for celebration, for the Duke of York had got £18,000 a year from the consolidated fund, plus £7,000 from the Irish revenues, which, with the income from the Bishopric of Osnaburgh, gave him £70,000 a year, the whole to be computed from 5 July, 1791. The Duchess was to have £8,000 a year if she survived him. The £7,000 from the Irish revenues he owed to the Opposition, this not having been included in Pitt's original "proposition."

On 13 April the *Oracle* announced that the remainder of the Prince's horses had probably been sold:

> Yesterday was to come on at Newmarket, the Sale of His Royal Highness's remaining Horses, with their Engagements.
>
> There were thirty-three lots, of which seventeen were of horses and mares above three years old; eight of fillies rising three years old; three of colts rising two years old; and five of fillies rising two years old.
>
> These were to be sold with their engagements, which are, for the most part, very heavy; but *Escape* and *Traveller*, the favourite racers, are engaged only for fifty guineas each.
>
> The matches and sweepstakes engaged for are an hundred and seven; and the stakes depending upon them amount to twenty-four thousand three hundred and fifty-five guineas.

But this sale had not occurred. The Prince kept the horses until 1794. Since the newspapers said nothing more about them, the Duke of York had evidently bought off the entire press.

On 17 April the *Public Advertiser* reported the first conference respecting "THE PRINCE'S DEBTS": "The superior Officers of His Royal Highness's Household met, on Sunday [15 Apr.], at Lord Southampton's in Stanhope-street; and we understand, that, after some consideration, it was resolved to call in accounts from all his Royal Highness's tradesmen for the purpose of making a general statement to be laid before his Majesty./ About fourteen Noblemen and Gentlemen were present, among whom were Lord Southampton [Groom of the Stole], Lord Clermont, Lord Melbourne, Lord Charles Somerset, General Lake, and Colonel Hulse." It was apparently hoped that the King might be sufficiently impressed by the sale of the stud to reconsider payment of the debts. The money realized from the sale was meanwhile being spent on further renovations, for by 9 May, according to the *Morning Herald*, the "Prince of WALES [had] fitted up a room in Carlton-house, quite in the Chinese style, and it affords a very elegant specimen of Oriental taste. The cost of the chairs is estimated at about forty pounds each." Having "purchased General CONWAY's house and garden at the end of Warwick-street," he was now also planning to have the house "pulled down, and the premises immediately connected with the demesnes of Carlton-house, in order to form a return-way for carriages, &c."

On 7 March the *Oracle* published the first of a number of puffs of Lord Lauderdale. "Among the domestic felicities of the day," it said, "the most distinguished in private life are the Earl and Countess of LAUDERDALE, with whom the much-respected Mr. TODD of the Post Office, passes many agreeable hours." Since Lord Lauderdale did not puff himself in newspapers, this meant that he had been persuaded by Sheridan to subsidize the *Oracle*: for the first time, money for the support of the Opposition press was coming from the left wing of the party. What "*Game*" Sheridan had in mind this time was, however, still not evident, and, so long as the Prince of Wales continued to be financially interested in the paper, the Government, it was supposed, would in any event move with caution. In March, John Almon, quondam conductor of the *General Advertiser*, surrendered and was consigned without sentencing to King's Bench Prison, where he was to remain for almost fourteen months as an example to other critics of Pitt. But Bell and Stuart were in a different situation. No newspaper expected either of them to be brought to trial. The action against Bell for the libels on the Guards would, it was presumed, be quietly dropped and the various actions for the libels on Lord Lonsdale settled out of court. The presumption seemed to be warranted. Nothing further was said of the libels on the Guards, and by 27 April it was "understood that Mr. Stuart had made his peace with the Earl of LONSDALE; if so, nothing more would be said about [that action]" (*Star*, 28 Apr.). On 19 June the *Public Advertiser* reported that Lord Lonsdale had also settled with Dr. Wolcot, "on condition of his promising to prevent any more of the satiric poem in question being sold." Although the actions against Evans and Bell were still pending on 25 June, this "business," too, said the *Star* (26 June), would probably be "adjusted" shortly. It evidently was, since it was not mentioned again. Of the actual terms of the settlements, one can say only that it was a long time before Dr. Wolcot again wrote for the Opposition and, whether Lord Lonsdale had demanded money or not, the cost of defense had been quite an item in itself.

Had the Opposition press not been otherwise preoccupied, it might have made fine political capital of another situation, for, from early February on, the Ministerial newspapers were greatly alarmed about a quarrel between John Palmer and Charles Bonnor, officials in the Post Office. Palmer, a long-time proprietor of the Bath theater and currently also the lessee of the Brighton theater, had invented the device of substituting stage coaches for postboys on horses to expedite the delivery of mail and had been promised by Pitt in return the perpetual administration of the plan, plus 2½ per cent of the resulting increase in Post Office revenues for life. Since 1786 Palmer had therefore been Comptroller General of the Post Office. The following year Lord Walsingham had been appointed Postmaster General, and in March, 1790, Lord Chesterfield had been added to the staff as second Postmaster General. The affairs of the Post Office had always been notoriously corrupt, and these three appointments had not bettered the situation in that respect. Nor had they bettered it in any other, for, since Palmer did not readily submit to authority, the result had been a series of quarrels between him on the one hand and the Postmasters General on the other. Several of these quarrels had already flared up in the newspapers, the Postmasters General being invariably defended by the *World* and *The Times*, Palmer being defended by the *Morning Herald*, over which newspaper he was supposed[4] to have a controlling influence because of "particular favours" conferred. Palmer's ally in these struggles had been Charles Bonnor, originally an actor and dramatist with the Bath theater and later sporadically connected with Covent Garden. Bonnor had assisted Palmer with his enterprises from the start and in 1788 had been rewarded with the appointment of Deputy Comptroller General at a salary of £500 a year.

The trouble between Palmer and Bonnor began on 9 February, 1792, with the appearance of an advertisement in the *Public Advertiser*, announcing that there would be a meeting of "merchants" at the London Tavern on 15 February to discuss "the late delivery of Letters" and other "discrepancies" in the Post Office. Bonnor, who had heard nothing of such a meeting, made some inquiries and was advised that the advertisement had been inserted "by an Alderman," who had acted "with the blessing" of Palmer, and that it was part of a plot to get rid of "an authority which The Comptroller General could not combat," namely, the Postmasters General. Confronted with this information, Palmer admitted that it was correct and added that "a Magistrate" would deliver certain "papers" to Bonnor's home, which he would pick up on his way to the meeting.

Bonnor was momentarily reassured, but, after the "papers" were delivered, it occurred to him that he was going to be "made a cat's-paw" in the maneuver, and he therefore informed Palmer that he would retain the "papers" until he knew what was involved. Palmer responded (14 Feb.) by offering him and his wife a lifetime annuity in return for the papers and his immediately quitting the Post Office. Bonnor refused, and on 16–17 February he was subjected to threats and "other pressures." On 18 February he prepared a pamphlet, relating the above facts, exposing the machinations of Palmer, and extenuating his own conduct. The pamphlet was entitled *Facts Relating to the Meeting, Held on Wednesday last, the 15th of February, at the London Tavern, Respecting the Late Delivery of Letters; and an Explanation of Some Circumstances that have Led to a Difference between the Comptroller General and his Deputy. By Charles Bonnor, Resident Surveyer and Deputy Comptroller General of the Post Office.* A few days later, he published another extenuation in the *World*. He was immediately dismissed by Palmer, and, on 7 March, Palmer was in turn suspended by the Postmasters General.

On 9 March the *World* called the matter to the attention of the Minister: "Mr. PITT has now before him for his determination, the disputes at the POST OFFICE —Mr. BONNOR, who made his appeal in this Paper, has been dismissed by Mr. PALMER, who in return has been suspended by the POST MASTERS GENERAL. What will be the end of this is not known as yet." It was never adequately known, for Pitt was clearly not going to expose the affairs of the Post Office, always teetering on the verge of a national scandal anyway, to the public gaze. Everything which appeared in the newspapers subsequently was therefore either propaganda or rumor. On 12 March the *World*, heretofore a champion of Bonnor, suddenly joined the *Morning Herald* in eulogizing Palmer and denouncing the Postmasters General, who, it declared, had, in suspending him, not only "exceeded their authority," but also "sacrificed" every other "interest to their resentment." Bonnor, it now appeared, had been in league with them throughout in a counterplot against Palmer. On 23 March the *World* reported that "this day the POSTMASTERS GENERAL are to have an interview with the Minister, when we trust the unpleasant differences which . . . prevail in the Post-Office will be amiably terminated." But they were evidently not, for this interview was followed only by other interviews. In early May, Lord Walsingham turned over to Pitt a number of Palmer's letters, which Pitt returned without examination, and, by the end of May, the case was back in the hands of the Postmasters General. On 6 July the *Star* announced the results: "The long pending dispute in the post-office has at length been determined. The Post-masters General at the Board held on Wednesday [4 July], decided that Mr. PALMER should retire with a pension. Mr. BONNOR succeeds to the salary and official situation of the Comptroller." But it was the *Oracle*'s understanding (16 July) that Bonnor would merely perform the "duty" of Comptroller until a replacement could be found, and by 21 August it was the *World*'s understanding that the replacement would be Francis Freeling. Freeling did join the staff at approximately this time, per-haps as Deputy Comptroller, since Bonnor continued to function as Comptroller until 1795. Palmer was officially retired in 1793.

The Morning Post *and the* Westminster Election *of 1788*

The scandals in the Post Office were hardly mentioned by the Opposition news-papers, for Sheridan, who planned the stratagems of the Opposition press, was, to begin with, engrossed in the *Oracle*'s campaign against Pitt and later in the *Morning Post*'s campaign against Rose. The *Morning Post*, which had labored so hard to keep the issue of the 1788 election alive, had redoubled its efforts during February, and, at the end of February, everything which it had previously said was reissued as a pamphlet, entitled *The Trial of George Rose, Esq. Secretary to the Treasury, &c. for Employing Mr. Smith a Publican in Westminster, upon a Late Election, and Not Paying Him; on Which He was, on Thursday the 21st of July, 1791, Cast in the Court of King's Bench, by a Special Jury, in the Sum of One Hundred and Ten Pounds Five Shillings!* The pamphlet was dedicated to Lord John Russell, who was evidently subsidizing the maneuver, it was published by J. S. Jordan, and it was written by Charles Stuart, who had also been responsible for the material in the *Post*. All the Opposition newspapers purported to be horrified at the contents of this pamphlet, and so did Thomas Thompson, who on 1 March submitted a copy of it to the House of Commons, announcing at the same time his intention of moving for a thorough investigation of the Government's interference in the Westminster election of 1788. He was vigorously supported by Sheridan, who was in turn assailed by Rose. The result was a noisy exchange between Rose and Sheridan.

Since Rose was unprepared and angry and ineffectual as a speaker anyway, he was fighting at a disadvantage, but his newspaper, the *World*, nevertheless insisted that he had emerged victor. "Poor SHERRY has found to his cost, that a *Rose* has *thorns*, which will long stick in his side," it gloated on 3 March. "He has found, too, that *footing* in a *forest* is not quite so *smooth* as upon the *boards* of a *Play-house.*/ Sheridan cannot bear any allusion to his theatrical character. The reason of this we cannot divine, for he certainly cuts a better figure upon the boards of the Haymarket than of ST. STEPHEN'S. On the former too he is *Manager*—on the latter only a second-rate *Actor.*" On 5 March it added the observation: "The PARTY are attempting to raise an attack upon Mr. ROSE, because a number of their bad votes were detected at the *Westminster Election*. This is the manner in which they repay all *public benefits* to the country." This observation was elaborated on the following day:

> The best defence of Mr. ROSE, is allowing the PARTY all they would ask. Suppose then Mr. ROSE did employ a man to scrutinize into the *bad votes* of the *opposite Party*, and that there was a difference of opinion about *paying this person so employed*—What [difference] does all this make to the GREAT CONSTITUTIONAL QUESTION? Did not *these bad Votes* exist? YES. Did not *this very Trial* bring out the proof of them? YES. Did *these perjuries* and *assumptions of character* appear on the side of OPPOSITION? YES. Was not then the *guilt their own*, and the *detection* of it, only belonging to Mr. ROSE? YES! YES!

On the same day (6 Mar.), the *World* published a versification of its paragraph of 3 March, possibly supplied by James Boswell:[5]

> On the SPARRING-MATCH betwixt *Messrs.* SHERIDAN *and* ROSE.
> > Tho' SHERIDAN's sarcastic wit,
> > For tumults and confusion fit,
> > All order turns to scorn;
> > Yet when it plucks at TREASURY Sweets,
> > Prepar'd to sting in turn—it meets
> > The ROSE—*that has a* THORN!
>
> SWEET-BRIAR.

Sheridan had his own champion in the *Morning Post*.

Although Thompson had scheduled his motion for 9 March, he postponed it until 13 March, and, on the morning of 13 March, the Treasury papers announced a new pamphlet, entitled *A Refutation of Factious Calumnies on the Character of George Rose, Esq., Secretary to the Treasury*. But by this time there were additional "calumnies" to refute, for the Opposition had uncovered further evidence of irregularities, on the basis of which Thompson was able to accuse Rose of "making the revenue laws an engine for subverting the rights of free elections." Rose's refutation of this particular charge proved so inadequate that, as Ministerial candidate for Westminster in 1788, Lord Hood felt obliged to say something in his own defense, at the same time replying to the *Morning Post*'s charge that he had still not paid Frost. What he did say was that he had known nothing of Rose's activities on his behalf and that the payment to Frost had been "fully sufficient." Although Thompson's motion was defeated by a vote of 211 to 84, no newspaper could pretend that Rose had triumphed in this instance. The *World* chose to regard the outcome with a yawn. "BORE OF THE DAY.—Mr. ROSE's Trial," it observed typically on 17 March. "—While this can be kept going, [the Opposition's] own 600 detected votes, *perjured* and *suborned*, may be forgotten. This is truly being/ 'Under the ROSE.'"

The *Morning Post* of 14 March carried a full account of the debate and along with it an announcement that the evidence against Rose would be submitted to the electors. Rose, now fighting for the last shred of his prestige, responded in the only way he could by filing suit against the newspaper for libel, naming as defendants in the action the conductor, Richard Tattersall, and the printer, William Williams. The paragraph cited was Thompson's statement that he "[had made] the revenue laws an engine for subverting the rights of free elections." Although the action had no effect on the *Morning Post*, it at least heartened the *World*, which protested on 19 March: "If Mr. ROSE *be* guilty, he is the most imprudent man alive . . . to have the business of the *Excise Fine* sifted to the very bottom in a Court of Justice . . . ." The Westminster electors met on 20 March to prepare the petition for Rose's removal. The assembly was enthusiastic, and, except for the *Morning Chronicle*, the Opposition newspapers were equally so. The *Chronicle* expressed its opinion on 21 March in the verses:

ON A SHELTERED ROSE,
Inscribed to the Secretaries of the Treasury.
The lightning flies, the whirlwind blows,
But cannot hurt the SHELTER'D ROSE:
The full-blown flower no harm can hit,
Screen'd in a deep and hollow PITT.

The Ministerial newspapers said nothing of the charges against Rose, but on 22 March the *World* spoke up in defense of Lord Hood, who was only incidentally involved in the proceeding:

FROST *against* LORD HOOD.

The account between Lord Hood and Mr. FROST, for the Westminster Petition, having been very incorrectly stated, we are induced to give the following, which may be depended upon as the true state of the account settled by the Arbitrators:

	£	s.	d.
Amount of Bill delivered	12,168	6	0
Deductions made by the Arbitrators of sums, though charged, not paid, &c. &c.	2,929	6	0
	9,239	0	0
Received on account	7,634	10	7
Balance due by the Award	£1,604	9	5

Fox presented the petition to the Commons on 4 April, stating that he would make a motion on the subject later. Before he could make the motion, the *Morning Post* had been sued again, this time by the dowager Countess of Cavan on behalf of her daughter Lady Elizabeth Lambart.[6]

Of the six paragraphs cited by Lady Cavan as libelous, the first had appeared on 16 August, the last on 29 October, both 1791, and it would seem from the five later (13 July, 1792) reprinted by the *Diary* and the *Public Advertiser* that she was justified in regarding them as such. The second paragraph, published sometime in September, had read: "Lady Elizabeth L. has behaved with uncommon prudence since she satisfied her curiosity." The third, published on 4 October, had read: "SPORTING INTELLIGENCE./ Lady Elizabeth L-mb-rt, a very beautiful creature, and a very great favourite, was taken privately off the race ground, otherwise it is supposed she would have won several prizes." The fourth, published on 7 October, had read: "That beautiful young Lady of Quality, who made a Faux Pas with her Footman some time ago, has been restored to the embraces of her disconsolate friends." The fifth, published on 12 October, had read: "Lady Elizabeth—was induced to run away with her footman, because he used to *stand so often* behind her chair." And the sixth, published on 29 October, had read: "The beautiful young lady of quality, who eloped with her footman, but who has been since restored to her friends, is speedily to be led to the Hymeneal altar. Her lover knows of the transaction, but has settled an annuity on the gentleman of the shoulder-knot, on condition that he resides in another country." It seemed nevertheless odd that Lady Cavan should have waited so long to bring her suit, for the first of the paragraphs was at least eight months old, the last at least six, and, as the *Morning Herald* indicated on 30 April, she might have sued "several" other newspapers with equal justification and to better purpose, their libels being considerably more recent. It seemed quite as odd that she should have named Richard Tattersall as defendant, for, whereas Lord Lonsdale could have read Bell's name in the colophon of the *Oracle*, the colophon of the *Morning Post* identified only the printer, William Williams. Tattersall's connection with the paper was known to very few outside the *Post*'s office.

Although the presumption was that neither Lady Cavan's action nor Rose's action would come to trial, they may have had some influence on those "fourteen Noblemen and Gentlemen" who were pondering the debts of the Prince of Wales, for on 21 April the other newspaper in which he was interested, the *Oracle*, mentioned that the *Morning Post* could be bought at a bargain. Specifically, it said, "The *Morning Post* is now marketable at the rate of Seven Thousand Five Hundred Pounds, and there are bidders enough who would purchase the whole at Six Thousand Pounds which would certainly produce an Interest of nearly Ten per Cent. for the purchase-money." The Prince had bought into the newspaper at the rate of 12,000 guineas for the whole.

On 8 May Fox asked for a reading of the Westminster petition and moved that the petition "be referred to the consideration of a committee." The motion was rejected without debate by a vote of 81 to 34. Three weeks later the *Morning Post*, which had prepared the ground for the Opposition's attacks on Rose, lost its protagonist, Charles Stuart, who, it appeared, had not paid the entire debt of the spurious *Star* after all. On 8 May, 1789, he had borrowed £505 from the firm of Fraser and Hare, for which amount he had signed a promissory note, using in this instance the name, "Mathew Stuart." "Fraser" was John Fraser, "a maternal relation" of Mackintosh, in whose house Mackintosh had been "a boarder" from the time he arrived in London until his marriage in early 1789. In 1788 Fraser was, according to Mackintosh,[7] "carrying on the business of a wine merchant in Clipstone Street"; in 1789 he and Hare were in the nursery business and were certainly the most faithful advertisers the spurious *Star* had. But, after that newspaper expired, Hare had quit the firm, and Fraser, finding himself in financial difficulties, had borrowed £505 from Mackintosh, giving him Stuart's note for that amount as payment. The money did not save Fraser, for, included in the list of bankrupts for 24 December, 1793, was the name, "John Fraser, Nurseryman"; and Mackintosh, having tried in vain to recover from Stuart in any other way, was finally obliged to take the case to court.

Stuart was tried in Guildhall on 30 May, 1792, Lord Kenyon presiding, Mackintosh being represented by James Mingay, and Stuart being represented by the Prince of Wales's Attorney General, Thomas Erskine. The fact that the defendant and "Mathew Stuart" were the same person was established by samples of handwriting, but, since neither Mackintosh nor Stuart could afford to publicize his connection with the spurious *Star*, the reason for the original transaction was disguised, Erskine implying that it had had something to do with the exportation of fish. The transactions themselves turned out to be part of a snarl of transactions, and, since no one could have untangled it, the jury compromised by awarding Mackintosh £250 of his claim. The trial was attended by reporters from the spurious *Star*'s principal victims, the *World* and the original *Star*, long accounts of it being published by both newspapers on 31 May. The verdict was evidently Stuart's undoing, for he again disappeared from the scene, to reappear months later as writer for the Government. George Rose was already undone. Although Pitt could not dismiss him without admitting that the charges made by the Opposition were true, his usefulness in any of his former capacities was over.

That the Prince of Wales needed to rid himself of the *Morning Post* is clear from some documents later submitted to the "fourteen Noblemen and Gentlemen" as part of the "general statement" of his debts. The first[8] indicates that, during the six-month period ending 2 July, 1792, he and Tattersall lost over £522 on the lease:

Jan.	31.	By cash				£333	6	8
Feb.	3.	To a quarter's farm	£342	10	0			
		By cash				69	3	4
Mar.	6.	To duty for January	208	19	0			
	13.	By cash				99	5	6
May	3.	To a quarter's farm	342	10	0			
		To cash paid Mr. Bicknell	37	5	11			

| June | 2. | By cash | | 168 | 8 | 10 |
| | 18. | To duty for April | 261 12 0 | | | |

	£1192 16 11	£670 4 4
		£522 12 7

Balance due		
Mr. Tattersall,	½ £261	6 3½
Other [the Prince of Wales]	½ 261	6 3½

"Cash" would indicate the earnings of the paper, net except for advertisement duties, "duty" would indicate advertisement duties, and "farm" would indicate payments for the lease. As the Prince of Wales's solicitor, Charles Bicknell had acted as agent in Carlton House's purchase of the *Morning Post*,[9] and he was evidently still performing legal services in connection with it. Affixed to this audit was Tattersall's account with the Prince of Wales:

His Royal Highness the Prince of Wales to Mr. Tattersall.

Feb.	3	Quarter's farm		£29	15	8
May	3	ditto		29	15	8
July	2	To cash paid Benjafield	£175 0 0			
		To balance of other side	261 6 3½			

	436 6 3½	£59 11 4
	59 11 4	
	£376 14 11½	

The Prince was a lessor as well as a lessee, and, as owner of two twenty-fourth shares of the paper, he received £59 11s. 4d. each half year. This seems to account for the credits. On the debit side he owed Tattersall £175 for Benjafield's annuity, which Tattersall was paying on his behalf, in addition to half the newspaper's deficit.

There was a third document,[10] this one looking forward to the time when all the proprietors would have to be "[indemnified] against any depreciation of shares below £350, for each 24th."

Money to be paid, 3rd [July] 1793, for the *Morning Post*

	£	s.	d.
Mr. Skinner	1056	0	0
Hicks	867	11	4
Christie	505	0	4
Weltje	730	8	0
Furlonger	730	8	0
Weatherby	487	3	4
Mitchell	487	3	4
Hargrave	487	3	4

Davis   350   0   0
Tattersall   2596   13   4
                        _____
                        8297   11   0.

Affixed to this list of shareholders was the notation: "Suppose the twenty-four shares entire, it would at £350 per share amount to £8400—but Mr. Griffin has an annuity of £30 per annum for life which occasions fractions, and makes the above calculations nearly exact." "Mr. Griffin" was actually Mrs. William Griffin, who had been "tricked" out of printing the Morning Post in 1776, "under the assurance of . . . a stipulated annuity for life." [11] Also affixed to the list of proprietors was the notation: "If the sale is 2000 on an average six months before the expiration of the term, the proprietors are bound to take the paper," that is, without indemnification.

Having seen Rose through the worst of his tribulations, the World was itself leased in April. This information was provided by the Oracle of 21 April in connection with its advertisement for the Morning Post: [12]

> NEWSPAPER PROPERTY, with all its contingencies, produces an Interest superior to the best conditioned Freehold in Landed Estate; for instance, a Share in the Daily Advertiser was sold a few weeks ago, by public auction, at the rate of Twenty-five Thousand Pounds for the whole Property. The Property in the World sold a few years ago at the rate of Twelve Thousand Pounds for the whole Property; and even within these few days, that Paper has been lett on Farm by Captain TOPHAM, at little less than One Thousand Pounds per annum, well secured on long lease. The Morning Post is now marketable at the rate of Seven Thousand Five Hundred Pounds. . . .

The lessee of the World was the lawyer Isaac Swan, who, having been associated with the newspaper since at least October, 1790, [13] now had control of it for the next two years. There was no immediate change in the personnel. John Heriot, previously the paper's drama critic, continued at least to be a contributor, and, during the early months of the year, he also published a pamphlet, entitled An Historical Sketch of Gibraltar with an Account of the Siege which that Fortress Stood against the Combined Forces of France and Spain. Topham, too, was actively concerned in the newspaper as late as September, and he was alluding to the conductor's office as "my office" as late as October, [14] while the paper itself continued to support his interests, to puff his friends, and even during 1793 to publish information which only he could have provided. The character and policy also remained unchanged. For a few months the pages were occasionally adorned with the verses of "Amanda," "Fitz-Alan," "Ellen," "The Rural Bard," "Myra," and other convalescents from the Della Cruscan fever, but there was no actual improvement in the quality of the material, nor was there any alteration in the point of view. The Oracle's information that the World had been leased may in fact have been news to George Rose, for there is later evidence that he disapproved of the leasing and continued the Treasury subsidy only on condition that Topham would manage the political department as before. The leasing was not itself surprising. Topham had never been fond of responsibility of a confining nature, and he may have grown weary of being made a scapegoat in the Treasury's intrigues with Burke.[15] On 2 March the *World* had announced that "Simkin," whose epistolary verses ridiculing the trial of Hastings had appeared in that newspaper since 1789, would henceforth be replaced by his "friend," "Shonny Up Rees" (or, as he later signed his work, "Shonny Apreés"), "Simkin," it was "suspected," having been "forbid by the MANAGERS to record the SPEECHES of Mr. HASTING's Counsel." The verses of "Shonny Apreés" appeared in both the *Oracle* and the *World* until the end of April and in the *World* for the remainder of the year, along with the usual writings of Major Scott. In addition, Topham may have had some trouble with Rose, who could not or would not defend the newspaper against harassment from another quarter.

It was a long-recognized fact that the country had too many lawyers, and their practice of buying up notes at enhanced prices in order to sue for collection had been a national scandal for years. But, although the prisons were filled with victims of their machinations and a number of lawyers had already been disbarred for "improper practices," the newspapers indicated no concern until 9 February, 1792, when the *Diary* suddenly demanded that something be done to protect the press. The lawyers had, it appeared, discovered a new means of supporting themselves by threatening to sue printers and editors for publishing notices of fraudulent lottery schemes, in most cases innocently and in some cases many years earlier; according to the *Diary*, there were no less than 150 such *qui tam* actions pending at the moment. The *Diary*'s demands were immediately supported by other newspapers and on 13 February by the *World*, which stated categorically: "The PEOPLE of ENGLAND should find out, that while they are indulging the LAWYERS in what they laugh at, and which they term '*their Morning Breakfasts,*' namely—the continued prosecutions for what is termed LIBELS, they are themselves suffering to be borne down by expence, which is enormous, that VERY PRESS which makes ENGLAND superior to all other countries, and which awes, and will ever awe, a bad MINISTER into shame." Since the *World* was being paid £600 a year to refrain from "awing" Mr. Pitt, this was an odd statement, and it was followed by others, some of a threatening order, some evidently replies to arguments. On 27 February, for example, the *World* cautioned its readers with no apparent relevancy to anything: "NEWSPAPERS.— As a small lesson to such as are inclined to speculate upon this PROPERTY, it may not be amiss to know, that from the *short credit* given by the STAMP OFFICE, compared with what may be necessary to give to *trade in general*, a PAPER of established consequence is obliged perhaps to be from 1500*l.* to 2000*l.* in advance."

If the experience of the *Gazetteer*[16] is typical, then each action cost the newspaper £5 12s. 6d. for "Expences on Arrest," plus another £50 for settlement out of court; if the case went to court, the newspaper paid a fine of double that amount. Although most newspapers chose to settle, the *World* immediately declared that it would not give the lawyers one shilling and that it was holding the Government responsible for its fines. The declarations were repeated during March and April, and in April the paper was leased to Swan. Topham had made a good "bargain," for, in addition to the "little less than One Thousand Pounds per annum" on the "farm," he was reserving for himself the £600 subsidy from the Treasury and the £300 subsidy "for Theatricals." Swan, on the other hand, seems to have been assured that the ex officio actions pending against that newspaper would not be brought to trial, for by late April the *World* was warring with the lawyers rather than with the Government. A series of exposés of the profession generally was followed in early May by some blistering attacks on a "Mr. Crossley, attorney in the Adelphi," who, the *World* said angrily on 3 May, had already brought a dozen suits against newspapers "in hopes of getting *compromises*" and was now preparing another dozen. On 10 May it announced that, "[relying] on the evidence of a common *Informer*, [Crossley had] on Tuesday [8 May] brought another action against the PRINTER of THIS PAPER, for inserting some former *Lottery Office Advertisement*. This notice of the man will not be unnecessary [necessary?] to the COURT. With his views on the subject [of courts?], no man is unacquainted." On 13 May a bill was rushed through Parliament indemnifying newspapers inadvertently advertising illegal lottery schemes, but Mr. Crossley was undaunted. "[Mr. Crossley has] had the assurance to declare, '*He should [still] make a fortune by his Law Expences against the Public Prints*,'" the *World* exploded on 19 May. "What a JURY and a JUDGE will think of such Attornies, a little time will shew!"

By now the *World* was an out-and-out crusader for stringent legislation regulating the practices of lawyers, as well as for wholesale disbarments. "ATTORNIES," it observed bitterly on 21 June. "—It is said there are 500 in LONDON who have not one reputable cause, and who subsist by buying up *Notes*, and getting the *Law Expences* upon them. *Here*, indeed, the *Reforming Hand* of JUSTICE is much wanted." And on 2 July: "The most despicable Animal, as well as the most noxious in a country, is an ATTORNEY without reputable practice. As he is prepared to do every bad deed, so he is qualified. He should be publicly exposed whenever he is met with." By 3 July it seemed to the *World* that the problem was finally on its way to solution: "The race of *wicked* Attornies seems almost run. Three or four are struck off the Rolls continually, much to the honour of Lord KENYON [Chief Justice of the Court of King's Bench], who seems very properly resolved on the PURIFICATION *of the Practice*."

The Friends of the People

While the Pitt Government was taking steps to silence its own enemies, it was showing no concern about the enemies of the state. The *Oracle* and the *Morning Post* were under indictment, but the radical papers, the *Gazetteer* and the *Argus*, were not; nor had the Government indicated any awareness of the societies they represented. Even the *Diary* was puzzled. By the beginning of 1792, the Constitutional Society had become militant in its demands, and, six days before Parliament convened, Thomas Hardy had organized the London Corresponding Society. Like the Constitutional Society, the Corresponding Society was dedicated to universal male suffrage and annual parliaments, which goals it purportedly intended to achieve by legal means; but, unlike the Constitutional Society, which took its membership from the middle class, the Corresponding Society was made up of workingmen, who had real grievances and were not necessarily patient. The existence of this new organization was no secret, for the opening address, delivered by the Frenchman, Maurice Margarot, had been published in full by the *Argus*, and notices of the meeting had been carried by all Opposition newspapers and by the *Oracle*. Appeals to other malcontents to form similar societies elsewhere had resulted in an outcropping of such organizations, and these were also no secret, since every one of them advertised in two or three of the London papers. On 16 February the newspapers further announced the appearance of Part II of Paine's *Rights of Man*, and it was evident from both the *Gazetteer* and the *Argus* that this book was henceforth to be the Bible of all radical societies, although it was far to the left of the declared goals of any one of them. If the radicals needed any additional aid and comfort, the various scandals involving Rose and the 1788 elections provided it. But, instead of examining their petitions or even acknowledging their existence, the Government seemed determined to aggravate the offense. On 16 March the Commons was informed that, because of the fewness in number and the corruptness in character of the London justices of the peace, no man's pockets were safe against marauders and that the Government proposed to remedy the situation by augmenting the force, by substituting salaries for fees, and, if need be, by paying the salaries itself. The *Morning Chronicle* was exasperated. Pickpockets, it said, were not felons, and, although London probably had too many of them, the Treasury also had enough means of controlling elections without resorting to this ruse to add to the list. A number of individuals seem to have agreed, for, while the Middlesex Justices Bill was under consideration, a new society came into existence, called the Society of the Friends of the People. The prime movers were Lord Lauderdale, Charles Grey, and Philip Francis.

The Society of the Friends of the People, Associated for the Purpose of Obtaining a Parliamentary Reform was officially founded on 11 April. According to the "regulations" then adopted,[17] meetings were to be held on every first Saturday during the sittings of Parliament at the Freemasons Tavern, new members were to be admitted only if approved "by votes of nine-tenths of the Members present," and the "secretary" was to consist of a committee of "Twelve Persons, . . . one fourth of which shall be replaced by election at every General Meeting of the Society." The committee was to "conduct ordinary correspondence," "[prepare] all business and draw up all resolutions to be submitted to the society." The first committee consisted of William Baker, Charles Grey, Samuel Whitbread, John Wharton, Sheridan, Philip Francis, Thomas Maitland, William Henry Lambton, George Rous, John Godfrey, William Cunninghame, and James Mackintosh, all but the last four being members of Parliament. Lord Kinnaird and George Tierney shared the office of treasurer. It has frequently been said[18] that Mackintosh was also "appointed Honorary Secretary," with Daniel Stuart as "his deputy." The responsibility for this information is probably Mary Stuart's, since it was evidently she who furnished the obituaries of her father in which the information seems first to have appeared. It also seems to have no basis in fact. There is no mention of such "appointments" in the proceedings of the society or in the newspapers, and they would appear implausible in any event. The *Vindiciae* was now almost a year old, and thus far it had earned Mackintosh only an "honorary membership" in the Constitutional Society, which was disreputable indeed, compared with the Friends of the People. If Mackintosh was appointed "Honorary Secretary" at all, the appointment would have followed his *Letter to . . . Pitt*, which he published in July. But, since he went to some trouble to conceal his authorship of the pamphlet, it seems unlikely that the society would have avowed it by naming him "Honorary Secretary." Even if he received "the public thanks of the body" for the performance, as one of his biographers[19] insists that he did, "the public" itself was certainly not informed.

The "appointment" of a "Deputy" to an "Honorary Secretary" would meanwhile appear to be something new in the annals of societies, especially since the "Honorary Secretary" was represented as having numerous responsibilities, which the "Deputy" performed for him. To avoid this awkwardness, later historians and editors have suggested that Stuart was the actual secretary. But, in addition to the fact that he signed no letters as secretary and was not even a member of the organization, such an appointment would violate the regulations of the society. He himself later testified (*Oracle*, 3 Nov., 1794) that he was "not Secretary to the Society at large, but [had] acted as Secretary to the [Secretarial] Committee of the Society," although he had not been officially appointed to that position either. He was equally vague as to when he commenced his duties. On the one hand, he refused[20] to testify concerning the original members of the organization on the ground that that was "before I had any connection with it";

but he went on to admit that he had supervised the publication of the Declaration, which was authorized on 26 April, and that, by the beginning of May, he was having frequent conferences with Thomas Hardy of the Corresponding Society. The duties themselves seem to have consisted of delivering letters to and collecting information from other reformers and reform societies, the information being turned over to the Committee and on one occasion[21] to Fox. Also, according to his statement (*Morning Chronicle*, 4 Nov., 1794), he "inspected" the "printing" of "the proceedings of the Society." But this duty may have been added later, for his name does not appear on any of the publications until February, 1793, when the society may perhaps have taken over the Peterborough House Press, inactive since 1791, possibly moving at the same time into quarters at No. 52, Frith Street, Soho. The first publishers were James Ridgway, Henry D. Symonds, and G. Westley.

Since Stuart had no official connection with the Friends of the People and was not therefore on its payroll, one may well ask who was paying him. According to his daughter,[22] it was Lord Lauderdale: "Stuart . . . had the use of the Society's rooms . . . , where, having much leisure, he continued to write for The *Morning Post* and *Argus*, and also, under Lord Lauderdale's instructions, published some volumes of State Papers collected from newspapers. He was paid at the rate of £50 a volume, and was thus enabled to lay by a considerable sum, with which, when the Society broke up, he bought shares in *The Morning Post*. . . ." The "Society broke up" on 17 January, 1795, and, from 1786 to 1794, J. S. Jordan published ten volumes of state papers, entitled *Political State of Europe*. In 1794 John Debrett advertised another volume, entitled *A Collection of State Papers*, printed by himself, promising that a "Continuation of this work will be published on the eve of every Session of Parliament." The advertisement appeared in the *Morning Chronicle* of 24 and 31 March and 12 April, in the *Sun* of 25 March, and in the *Star* of 15 April. Although Daniel Stuart's name was not mentioned in connection with either series, he may have been the compiler of some of the volumes, and Lord Lauderdale may have provided helpful "instructions." But Lord Lauderdale would have had nothing directly to do with the publications, and Stuart would certainly have amassed no "considerable sum" from this £50-a-year enterprise. One is bound to suppose that Lauderdale was paying him a regular salary.

The founders of the Friends of the People, Daniel Stuart said later,[23] had been motivated by concern about the activities of the radical societies and the seeming indifference of the Government respecting them. Convinced on the one hand that the demands of the societies were extreme and on the other that they could not be ignored without danger to the state, they had hoped to ameliorate them and, by supplying firm and sane leadership, to "guide [the] popular commotion from errors and mischievous courses" into safe channels. This statement is generally supported by the Declaration to which members were asked to subscribe at the meeting of 11 April and which was said[24] to have been written, "either solely, or in a very principal degree," by Mackintosh:

> A number of Persons having seriously reviewed . . . the actual situation of public affairs, and state of the kingdom, and having communicated to each other their opinions on these subjects, have agreed and determined to institute a Society for the purpose of proposing to Parliament and to the Country, and of promoting, to the utmost of their power, the following Constitutional Objects, making the preservation of the Constitution, on its true principles, the foundation of all their proceedings.
> *First.*—To restore the Freedom of Election, and a more equal Representation of the People in Parliament.
> *Secondly.*—To secure to the People a more frequent exercise of their Right of electing their Representatives.
>
> . . . . . .

More important, said Stuart, the founders were determined to separate the society from The Party by excluding not only Fox, but his personal followers as well. This was a crucial consideration, for, since the society did represent the left wing of the Opposition and the right wing saw eye to eye with the Government on the matter of reform, there was otherwise the danger of a split. But, with Fox, who was "Mr. Party" himself, excluded, there was no such danger. The exclusion of Fox had a second effect, for, he being "The Man of the People," any movement with which he was identified was a popular movement, whereas Lord Lauderdale and his associates were determined that the people would have no share in this one. This was a Society of the *Friends* of the People, not a Society of the People; the dues were 2½ guineas a year, instead of a penny a week, as in the case of the Corresponding Society; and membership was not open to the public. Hence, although the society might fail to achieve its goals, it looked on 11 April as if it would at least do no mischief: either by creating a schism within The Party or by adding to the "commotion" outside. Everything went wrong.

The only reform which the Friends of the People had in mind was the elimination of election abuses, which would have the effect of "equalizing" the "representation" without actually extending the suffrage. This was the one reform which the Pitt Government could not tolerate, since it depended on these abuses to keep itself in power, but it had no reason, to begin with, for alarm. Without the support of Fox, the society was so weak, both inside and outside Parliament, that Pitt could justifiably regard its activities as only another "*cunning Game.*" In context they certainly seemed to be nothing else. On 13 March, Thompson had moved for an investigation of the Government's interference in the Westminster election of 1788; on 4 April, Fox had presented a petition from the Westminster electors to the same purpose; and, on 11 April,

167 "residents" (there were also a dozen "non-resident members") signed the Declaration of the Friends of the People, calling for an elimination by Parliamentary action of election corruptions in general. This was followed on 18 April by Sheridan's motion to abolish the self-electing power of magistrates in the Royal Burghs of Scotland, furiously opposed by an enraged Dundas, and on 26 April by a second meeting of the Friends of the People. This time the members approved an Address to the People of Great Britain, setting forth the objects of the society, and further resolved "that a motion be made in the House of Commons, at an early period in the next Session of Parliament, for introducing a Parliamentary Reform, . . . that Charles Grey, Esq. be requested to make, and the Hon. Thomas Erskine to second, the above motion," and that the Declaration of 11 April, the present Address, and the resolutions be published. Before these resolutions could be acted upon, the public learned that on 20 April France had declared war on the Emperor of Austria and on the King of Prussia in his capacity of King of Hungary and Bohemia. The Opposition press, which had represented Brissot as the man of peace and had expressed complete confidence in the Foreign Minister, the ex-Jacobin General Dumouriez, exonerated the French on the ground of extreme provocation, but the news was still an embarrassment to defenders of the French Revolution and advocates of British reform.

On 30 April the Declaration, the Address, and the resolutions were nevertheless published by all the Opposition newspapers, the *Oracle*, and the *Diary*, other newspapers declining on the ground that this was another harassment tactic; and that afternoon copies of the Declaration and the Address were submitted to the Commons. Although the texts of the documents were identical with the originals, the signatures were not. Instead of the 167 signatures to the Declaration, published in the *Proceedings*, there were now only 100, 76 having been omitted and 9 added. Added were such names as Dudley North, John Courtenay, John Curwen, Lord John Russell, and Lord Edward Fitzgerald; and among the omissions were the names of Alderman Coombe and a number of journalists: Robert Merry, James Perry, and D. E. MacDonnell, among others. On both lists were the names of John Cartwright (Chairman of the Constitutional Society), Alderman John Sawbridge, and the journalists, James Mackintosh, Thomas Christie, Samuel Rogers, Joseph Richardson, and Dennis O'Bryen. The names of the three Stuart brothers appeared on neither list. Grey's comments were brief. Having announced his intention of moving for "a reform in the representation of the people," Grey went on to indicate the purport of his motion. It was the consensus of the Friends of the People, he said, that certain "abuses had been permitted to creep into the Constitution through neglect, or had been introduced into it by corruption, and those abuses were of a nature so dangerous, that they threatened the very existence of the Constitution itself." The result had been a general unrest, for electors, misunderstanding the circumstances and knowing only that they were being deprived of their rights, supposed that there was something amiss in the Constitution. What the Friends of the People therefore proposed was the eradication of those abuses and hence a restoration of all the rights of free elections which the Constitution guaranteed. Such action, the members were sure, would "do away with every cause of complaint, and . . . preserve the peace of the public and the general tranquillity," whereas they were otherwise afraid that the present "agitation" might "produce all the miseries of civil commotion."

Except for a somewhat mysterious apprehension of Thomas Paine and the disruption of a dinner of the Constitutional Society,[25] the Government had heretofore indicated no awareness of a threat to the national "tranquillity," but it now appeared that Pitt at least had been very much aware of it indeed. As soon as Grey completed his remarks, he rose to say that, although he had once advocated reform, he had never advocated any changes in the Constitution, for he had then believed, and "he believed at this moment [that] we actually did enjoy as much happiness as we should, or that a rational man ought to hope for." He objected to everything Grey had said, and he objected in particular and "in the most decisive terms" to "the time and the mode in which this business was brought forward"; and he could assure his audience that "all the blessings we enjoy would be shaken to the foundation" if it were pursued. Since no changes in the Constitution were contemplated, Pitt's remarks were irrelevant, and, if only Fox had pointed out the irrelevancy or if, better yet, he had remained silent, disaster might have been averted. But there was a great deal of popular interest in this debate, and Fox took his responsibility as "Man of the People" seriously. The result was that he leapt into the trap by advocating what the Friends of the People had been intent on avoiding: changes in the Constitution itself. The Constitution ought to be changed occasionally, he declared: its "greatest beauty . . . is, that in its very principle it admits of perpetual improvement, which time and circumstances render necessary." He could not in fact believe that "any human institution is so very sacred as not to admit of being touched or looked at." With these words Fox not only made reform a party issue, he also made it a popular issue, and he transformed the type of reform from moderate to radical.

Even Burke, whose speeches were not noted for niceties of distinction, honored the difference between radical reformers and moderate reformers, and he saw eye to eye with the Friends of the People on the danger of "civil commotion." Hence, while the King and Pitt were talking of "tranquillity," he had stayed home; but, now that the subject was sedition, he had come down to the House, as he put it, "an old man" (he was sixty-three) and "unfit for business," now that he was "abandoned" by his "friends," to state his opinion. Most of it was a denunciation of Thomas Paine, Thomas Cooper, James Watt, Thomas Walker of Manchester, and other English radicals "who scruple not to enter into an alliance with a set in France of the worst traitors and regicides that have ever been heard of—the club of the Jacobins." There was also the usual denunciation of "theory" as responsible for the French Revolution and for the present clamor in England. But, unlike the Friends of the People, Burke wanted to deal with the problems by war and suppressions, and his only real objection to the "moderate or temperate reform" advocated by Grey was its essential "impossibility." The radicals, in his opinion, could not be converted to moderates; it seemed more likely to him that, under the present tumultuous circumstances, the moderates would instead become converted to radicals.

The Friends of the People never recovered from Fox's speech. Henceforth the people regarded the society as *their* society, and all of them thought that its goals were to extend suffrage by changing the Constitution. Although the members labored hard to correct these impressions, everything conspired to confirm them. Since the London society was originally intended to be only the first of many such organizations, one of its "regulations" had been the resolution "that all friends of reform be advised to organize themselves into similar societies." By early May societies had in fact sprung up everywhere, each calling itself "Friends of the People"; but not one of them purported to be anything but radical. Whatever influence the London Friends of the People might have had over the Corresponding and Constitutional societies was meanwhile destroyed. As Daniel Stuart put it,[26] the "Corresponding Society, while it accepted the countenance and protection of the Friends of the People, never intended to be guided by them. It was with them, as Horne Tooke said: 'I have no objection to travel in the same stage coach with one going only to Brentford, though I may be going to Windsor.'" All the Friends of the People had done was therefore to give aid, comfort, and support to the radicals. The Ministerial press made the most of it.

On 5 May the Friends of the People attempted to defend itself by resolving, "First, that ... occasion has ... been taken to throw out and propagate a variety of aspersions ... against the motives, objects and proceedings of this Association" and, "Second, that the aspersions and calumnies should be encountered and repelled by making the position of the association clear. ... If, after having done everything in our power, to obtain the Reform, which we think wanting, the country shall appear to be satisfied, with the present state of the Representation, we must and shall submit. ... [Whenever] its object is attained, our Association *is at an end*—WE GO NO FURTHER." The Declaration and Address were accordingly republished, these resolutions being added. On 8 May Fox's request for Parliamentary consideration of the Westminster petition was summarily rejected; and on 12 May the Friends of the People replied to a letter from John Cartwright, Chairman of the London Constitutional Society, dated 27 April, declining all "further intercourse with a Society whose views and objects" were so evidently at variance with its own, and ordered both letters to be published. On 14 May Samuel Ashton, Secretary of the Sheffield Constitutional Society, suggested that a "convention" of all reform societies be held in London. Although here was the opportunity to "guide [the] popular commotion from errors and mischievous courses" into safe channels, the Friends of the

People decided to do nothing while affairs were in the present state of ferment. A week later they took a drastic turn for the worse.

The Proclamation Against Seditious Writings

One has Lord Holland's word for it[27] that the Friends of the People resulted from the

> impetuosity of Mr. Grey, wrought upon by the restless activity of Lord Lauderdale, and the ambition of some of his younger friends, viz., Mr. Whitbread, Mr. Lambton, and Mr. Tierney. . . . It was originally founded . . . without the knowledge, certainly without the sanction, of Mr. Fox, who never was a member of it. It originated in a conversation, after dinner, at Lord Portchester's, who was very active in promoting it while under discussion, but who, when Mr. Francis brought pen, ink, and paper, to reduce the resolutions to writing, declined adding his signature, observing that they would not be *republican* enough for him.
>
> In a few months [Lord Portchester] publicly arraigned it as seditious, and obtained the Earldom of Carnarvon [as a reward]. . . . Many persons of weight and consideration in the Country, though connected with Opposition, loudly and vehemently condemned this Association; some who afterwards steadily adhered to Mr. Fox in his opposition to the war, such as the Duke of Bedford and Lord Derby, secretly lamented or openly disapproved of it. None of Mr. Fox's immediate and personal friends ([Richard] Fitzpatrick, [James] Hare, or Lord Robert Spencer) ever belonged to it.

Lord Holland was much too partisan. "[Persons] of weight and consideration in the Country" would of course have "disapproved" of the society, since they themselves probably controlled some elections, but the society would not have been mischievous without the "open," "impetuous," and thoroughly unenlighted support of Fox.

The Friends of the People had stated in the Declaration that its primary concern was to "preserve" the Constitution. In announcing his intention of moving for reform, Grey had again made it clear that the society opposed any changes in the Constitution, its only object being the eradication of those abuses which impeded its effectiveness. Pitt had wilfully misunderstood in a frantic attempt to confuse the issue, and Burke had tried to justify the confusion. He might have saved himself the trouble, for Fox said in effect that the Friends of the People did intend to alter the Constitution and that it ought to be altered. The die was cast. The people, the newspapers, and even some members of the society itself supported Fox's interpretation. The *Morning Chronicle* and the *Morning Post* joined the *Argus* and the *Gazetteer* as champions of the radicals, even of that ultraradical, Thomas Paine; and, had it not been for the exertions of Lord Lauderdale and a few others, the Friends of the People would have lost its equilibrium as well.

The situation was similarly altered so far as the Government was concerned. Although, by virtue of Fox's popularity throughout the country, it now had to regard Grey's motion with alarm, the propagandistic advantage had shifted to its side. The Ministerial newspapers made the most of it. The lines were now clearly drawn, they said, between the "Constitutionalists," who were fighting to preserve the Constitution, and the "reformers," who were bent on subverting it. Heading the "Constitutionalists" was Pitt; heading the "reformers" were the Friends of the People. Fox was not mentioned. The whole Ministerial press rallied behind the Constitutionalists. The newspapers published columns of denunciations of Tierney, Grey, and Lord Lauderdale, who were responsible, it appeared, for all the sins of Paine, Cooper, and Watt; and there were at least a dozen pamphlets on the subject—including the Rev. Robert Nares's *The Principles of Government Deduced from Reason* (London); *Remarks on the Proceedings of the Society, Who Style Themselves "The Friends of the People"*: and *Observations on the Principles of Government, as Applicable to the British Constitution. In Two Letters to a Friend* (London), sometimes attributed to Pitt's cousin, Lord Camelford; and *An Address to the Friends of the People* (Edinburgh), attributed by the *Telegraph* (21 Oct., 1796) to John Wilde, "professor of civil law in the University of Edinburgh." In the opinion of the *Telegraph*, the last pamphlet was "as extravagant in its manner, and as full of invective against the French revolution as any of Mr. BURKE's productions." Anyone reading the literature of the day would therefore have supposed that the Constitution was actually in peril. Added to this were fresh rumors of Pitt's dismissal, propagated by the Opposition newspapers, and rumors of French landings, propagated by the Ministerial press. The stock market went wild, and, in the midst of all this tumult, the King issued his Proclamation against Seditious Writings.

The Proclamation, which began, "Whereas divers wicked and seditious writings have been printed, published, and industriously dispersed, tending to invite tumult and disorder," went on to "charge and command" all magistrates to seek out "the authors and printers of such wicked and seditious writings," to charge everyone connected with law enforcement "to suppress and prevent all riots, tumults, and other disorders, which may be attempted to be raised or made by any person or persons, . . . on whatever pretext they may be grounded," and to "require and command all and every our magistrates . . . that they do, from time to time, transmit to one of our principal secretaries of state, due and full information of such persons as shall be found offending . . . , or in any degree aiding or abetting therein," so that they could be "vigorously" dealt with by law. The Proclamation was read on 21 May and printed by the newspapers the following day. Instead of clearing the atmosphere, it had the effect of another alarm, especially in light of the *Gazetteer*'s mention of 16 May that the "publisher of Mr. PAINE's work, on the Rights of Man, has received a notice of prosecution from the Attorney General" and the subsequent mention by several newspapers that Paine had received a similar notice. J. S. Jordan was indicted on 14 May; Paine's indictment was timed to coincide with the reading of the Proclamation, his trial being scheduled for 8 June. The passage of the Middlesex Justices Act on 23 May added further to the alarm, since the actual purpose of this legislation, it now seemed evident, was to enable Dundas to convert the London police into a Gestapo. On 25 May the Proclamation was debated in the Commons.

The Proclamation was the first in a long series of attempts to separate Fox from the Friends of the People. As the *Morning Chronicle* often enough pointed out, the Proclamation was unnecessary in every respect. Had the radicals "raised" any "riots, tumults, and other disorders," Pitt did not need a Royal Proclamation to "suppress" them; but they had not, nor did such "disorders" figure in their plans. The Proclamation was not in fact aimed at the radicals at all, but rather at the Friends of the People, which, it was already clear from the Ministerial papers, was to be charged with having fomented those supposed "disorders." It was equally clear that the Prince of Wales and the Duke of Portland would support the Government. This was hardly surprising, for the Prince of Wales, continually dogged by debts, was always susceptible to influence, and the Duke of Portland had a personal reason for preserving election abuses. But, as leader of the Opposition, Fox had to be deeply concerned. Whatever he thought of the Prince of Wales as a man, The Party had no hope of coming into office without him, and he was bound to the Duke of Portland by ties of friendship as well as expedience. The debate of 25 May promised, therefore, to be rather interesting.

As the Ministerial papers had anticipated, the issue throughout was the Friends of the People, and the Proclamation was supported, not only by Pitt and Dundas, but by Lord Guilford's friends, William Adam and Lord North, and by the Duke of Portland's friend, William Windham, the last expressing his "pain" at thus differing from those with whom he had been accustomed to agree. It was opposed by a dozen members of the society, who denounced it as a plot to intimidate and "defame" them by implying that they were "aiding" and "abetting" the radicals; and, in contradiction of such an aspersion, Grey again cited the resolutions, the Declaration, and the Address of the organization. It was also opposed by Fox, but without the vehemence of his former utterances. He even took care to point out that he was not a member of the society, that he had never subscribed to its principles, and that he did not intend to. Pitt must have been encouraged. On 31 May the Proclamation was submitted to the Lords, where the issue was the same. Here it was supported by the Prince of Wales in a maiden speech, subsequently much praised by the Ministerial newspapers, by his intimate, Lord Rawdon, by Lord Porchester, Earl Spencer, and the Duke of Portland. It was hotly opposed by the Earl of Lauderdale, who concluded some incidental remarks about the apostasy of the Duke of Richmond with the comment that he understood the Government was setting up a military camp at Bagshot "to overawe the people of the metropolis, and to destroy their endeavours to obtain a reform." He for one, he said, was "glad the Duke is to command that camp, for, if apostasy can justify promotion, he is the most fit person for the command, General [Benedict] Arnold alone excepted." The Duke of Richmond responded with equal heat, and an argument ensued, which Lord Lauderdale suggested, should be settled outside. Although the duel was averted by the judicious mediation of the seconds, Grey and Colonel Henry Phipps, the incident was widely publicized by the newspapers.

On 26 May the *World* announced that "[the DUKE of PORTLAND], *with all his interest*, has thrown himself into the scale of Administration." This announcement was repeated almost daily for the next several weeks, with no mention of Fox by any of the Ministerial papers. But the Government had obviously not forgotten him, for at approximately this time there was an odd twist of fortune respecting his Libel Bill. This bill, very dear to Fox's heart, had been slated for death in the Lords. Bowles had condemned it in several pamphlets, and the cause had been regarded as so hopeless that only Earl Stanhope had bothered to reply, his *The Rights of Juries Defended . . . And the Objections to Mr. Fox's Libel Bill Refuted* having appeared earlier in the year. The Opposition newspapers had not even printed excerpts from the pamphlet. Until mid-May everything moved along as expected. The bill was referred to the judges for an opinion, which would certainly be negative, since the judges would hardly recommend legislation calculated to deprive them of power, and Lord Grenville had said that he would act on that opinion, whatever it was. The opinion, negative, as anticipated, was submitted to the Lords on 11 May. But the Government indicated no eagerness to act on it until 21 May, when it suddenly reversed its position and "strenuously" urged that the bill be passed.

Lord Thurlow evidently refused to make the shift; and Pitt, who disliked him anyway, because of his support of the Prince of Wales's faction in 1788, apparently decided that this was a good time to get rid of him, for, on the morning of 21 May, the *World* informed its readers that Lord Thurlow was unworthy. He had, said the *World*, a "fractious overbearing temper," which interfered with the "successful exertion of ability," he was hostile to the Administration, and he was lamentably lacking in that "greatness of mind" required for the position of Lord Chancellor. On 22 May it said again that he really had "too much temper" for the post and that, although he would retire with "the TELLERSHIP of the EXCHEQUER only—which is about 3000*l.* a year," he had realized "a splendid fortune" during the period of his Chancellorship. On 24 May, the day before the Proclamation was debated in the Commons, the *World* abandoned generalities and accused him point-blank of having wilfully and in defiance of the expressed wishes of Government blocked the passage of the Libel Bill, which would otherwise, it implied, have become law months ago. It was especially bitter about his speech of 21 May. On 25 May it reported that he had just bought stock in the amount of £70,000, this sum supposedly representing only part of his ill-gotten gain; and, although no other changes in Government were contemplated, Lord Thurlow, said the *World* positively, must certainly go. Evidently encouraged by the mildness of Fox's remarks respecting the Proclamation, it repeated on 26 May and daily thereafter that *"the die is cast"* for Lord Thurlow and that the Libel Bill would become law despite him. But its patience with Fox was not inexhaustible, for on 2 June it turned on him with the mournful observation: *"Poor* CHARLES FOX finds himself in a very awkward situation. He now properly belongs to *no Party*—in wavering between the two, he is neither an *avowed Democrat*, nor yet a zealous supporter of the present establishment.—In short, he wants to get into *place*, and does not yet know the readiest way to it."

The Libel Bill passed the Lords on 11 June, Lord Thurlow's name heading the list of dissentients. The *World* was infuriated. "Lord THURLOW professes himself to be the *King's friend*," it sneered on 12 June. "It is an odd way of shewing his *friendship*, by opposing a measure which has the King's express approbation, and the object of which his *Majesty* has more than once recommended in his Speech from the Throne." On 15 June Lord Thurlow resigned, to be replaced temporarily by Sir James Eyre, but the *World* continued its harassments. On 23 June there were two full columns devoted to his bad temper, his unpredictable animosities, and his general pettiness. No newspaper rose to Lord Thurlow's defense, but some of his friends did. One of them, Sir John Scott, even tendered his resignation as Solicitor General, withdrawing it only at the request of Lord Thurlow himself. Lord Thurlow had not in fact been quite the scapegoat he appeared, for, not only did he leave office assured of the Tellership of the Exchequer for life and, the newspapers later suspected, a few sinecures besides, but on 11 June he had been quietly created Baron Thurlow of Thurlow, which title would pass to a nephew at his death. Since he had no children, this was for him an important consideration. Fox, for whom the Government had staged this farce, was meanwhile not influenced by it. On 15 June the Friends of the Liberty of the Press celebrated the passage of the Libel Bill at a public dinner. Fox, who was the guest of honor, accepted full credit for the legislation, and, if he acknowledged any debt to Pitt, he did not do so publicly. All the Government had gained thus far was, therefore, an empty seat on the woolsack, which looked most inviting to Lord Guilford's friend, the ambitious Lord Loughborough.

The Proclamation against Seditious Writings was a knell for the Friends of the People, but the dying was itself a slow process. On 24 May Grey had replied to Samuel Ashton's letter with the admonition that, if a "convention" of reform societies were held, the participating societies must "adopt clearly and state frequently their determination to support the Constitution": "It is only indeed with Societies who express the same moderation of principles, and adopt the same wariness of language, that this Society can entertain any correspondence, or promise any co-operation. . . . We have publicly disclaimed what we condemn . . . and . . . we have [already] been compelled to decline all intercourse with the Society for Constitutional Information in London." The question of whether the Friends of the People would even so participate in the "convention" had not, the letter concluded, been "decided," although, "[in] a more advanced stage of the business, it may become very fit matter for deliberation." The letter was approved on 2 June, and a few days later the Sheffield Constitutional Society joined forces with the London Constitutional Society. On 9 June the Friends of the People began to disintegrate. The occasion was a letter proposing Thomas Cooper as member. Cooper and Watt (the son of the inventor) were allied with the Manchester Constitutional Society, long headed by the cotton merchant Thomas Walker. They had gone to Paris early in the year, Cooper supposedly for reasons of curiosity, Watt for reasons of business, Cooper having returned in May. But, since Burke had charged in his speech of 30 April that they were in correspondence with the Jacobins, the Friends of the People felt obliged to question Cooper on the subject, and he admitted that they had in fact functioned as delegates from the Manchester organization and that he was still in communication with Robespierre. The proposal for his membership was accordingly withdrawn. Lord John Russell, William Baker, John Curwen, Dudley North, and John Courtenay protested that John Cartwright had frequently admitted that he, too, was in correspondence with the Jacobins as Chairman of the London Constitutional Society and demanded that he be ousted as well. This demand being rejected, all of them submitted letters of resignation.

The assumption that the Proclamation had nothing to do with the radicals was justified by subsequent events. The Ministerial newspapers continued to lambaste Tierney and Lord Lauderdale, without mention of Paine, Cartwright, and Cooper; and, despite the numerous "charges," "commands," "requirements," and "orders" set forth in the document, the Government made no attempt to interfere with the activities of the Constitutional and Corresponding Societies, although the Corresponding Society, with the shoemaker Thomas Hardy as perpetual secretary and John Horne Tooke as principal agitator, was supposedly growing apace. Tooke was by now also a frequent contributor to the *Argus*, still edited by John King. Not only were there no further arrests, but the Government even seemed reluctant to pursue the actions it had commenced. No date was set for Jordan's trial, and Paine's trial, scheduled for 8 June, was postponed for no apparent reason until December. The postponement puzzled the Opposition newspapers, since, once the Libel Act became effective, the decision as to guilt or innocence would be made by a jury, which the Government could not always control, rather than by a judge, whom it could. Paine of course used the reprieve to execute more "wicked and seditious writings" to be "industriously dispersed" among the populace.

On Dundas's motion, the Commons voted to abolish the slave trade "gradually," Dundas having in mind by 1800. The Opposition succeeded in altering the date to 1796, and the bill was referred to the Lords, where it would supposedly bog down. This over, Parliament concluded its business and on 15 June was thanked by a grateful King. The King said nothing about the Libel Act, although, according to the *World*, this legislation had had his "express approbation," but he again commended the Members for "the measures which you have adopted for the diminution of the public burthens . . . , for the reduction of the present national debt, and . . . for preventing the dangerous accumulation of debt in future." By this time Russia, with the connivance of Prussia and Austria, was invading Poland, Prussia and Austria were preparing to invade France, and there were rumors of new uprisings in Paris; but, although the King had "seen" these developments "with great concern," he still expected to "preserve to my people the uninterrupted blessings of peace." His only anxiety was the "sentiments in the minds of [these people]," but he was certain that the legislators would be "active and vigilant" in their "several counties" during the recess. Parliament was thereupon prorogued to 30 August.

For Lord Lauderdale there remained one mopping-up operation. Living in retirement and not himself being a Member of Parliament, General Benedict Arnold did not learn of the disparaging reference to him until after the prorogation. Since he had even better reason to complain than the Duke of Richmond, he also demanded a meeting, and, despite the inconvenience, the Earl of Lauderdale obliged. As the *Public Advertiser* put it on 3 July: "His Lordship had been at Brighton about ten days, and designed to have gone from thence to France, but the appearance of this affair detained him. He arrived in town on Friday [29 June], purportedly to give the meeting; and his Lordship having now settled all his disputes, we suppose he may proceed on his way in peace." According to the *Oracle* (2 July), the meeting occurred at seven o'clock on the morning of 1 July "near Kilburn-Wells," Lord Lauderdale's second being Fox, General Arnold's second being Lord Hawke: "Lord Lauderdale received the General's fire unhurt, and declined to fire in return."

The Theaters

The theaters had provided interest of another sort; nor was all of it connected with the stage. The first scandal involved Mrs. Billington. The affair of Mrs. Billington actually began in November, 1791, when she received a communication from the Opposition bookseller, James Ridgway, stating that he had purchased some letters which she might like to "suppress," inasmuch as they contained evidence of "indecent intercourse" with her brother and father. Mistresses of the Prince of Wales were likely to be preyed upon by blackmailers, since it was supposed that they had fared rather well financially; and Ridgway was an old hand at the blackmailing game. In early 1789 he had threatened to publish "500 libels" on Mrs. Fitzherbert, "declaring the P[rince] had forfeited his right to the Crown by marrying her," and had been deterred only by Sheridan's promptness in arranging payment; and in 1790 and 1791 he had been connected as publisher with two more extortionary ventures, Topham's *The Life of the Late John Elwes, Esq.* and Charles Stuart's *She Would be a Duchess*.[28] But he had not always been successful, and he was not successful in this instance, for Mrs. Billington turned out to be a woman of more spirit than prudence. On 18 November the legal firm of Neild and Bush informed Ridgway on her behalf that she would pay nothing for suppression and would certainly sue if the letters were published. Ridgway thereupon sent copies of two of the letters to her and, receiving the same reply from her lawyers, on 3 December advertised the work in the *World* and the *Morning Herald*. A few days later the *Morning Herald* published Mrs. Billington's account of the transactions, and on 8 December Ridgway was notified that "a suit was being commenced."[29]

Mrs. Billington actually brought two suits. On 7 January, 1792, the *Oracle* reported that "[a] Bill of Indictment was on Thursday [5 Jan.] presented to the Grand Jury at Westminster by Mrs. *Billington*, the celebrated Actress, against Mr. Ridgway, Bookseller; for writing what was termed 'Extortionary Letters on the subject of suppressing certain Memoirs of this Lady,' intended for publication. The Grand Jury threw out the Bill, and agreed unanimously, that Mr. Ridgway's conduct had been highly candid, manly, and spirited." The *Oracle* was of course delighted at this verdict, inasmuch as Peter Stuart had been a friend of Ridgway since 1782, when they had been associated on the *London Courant*,[30] and because the *Oracle* happened to be trading in blackmail itself. It was even more delighted at news that the *Memoirs* had gone to press. *Memoirs of Mrs. Billington, from Her Birth: Containing a Variety of Matter, Ludicrous, Theatrical, Musical, and——.... Written by Mrs. Billington, to Her Mother* emerged from the press in mid-January. According to the colophon, the pamphlet was published by "James Ridgway, York Street, St. James's Square"; and Ridgway had written most of it as well. There was a long "Advertisement," in which he referred darkly to the "uncommon pains [which had] been taken to prevent the publication" and went on to say that, in resolving to publish nevertheless, he had acted only in the interest of "decency," since, although Mrs. Billington had publicly "disavowed" the "authenticity" of the letters, she had not done so "by affidavit." The "Advertisement" was followed by a "Prefatory Address," mentioning that the letters had been purchased from someone who had surreptitiously got them from the executor of her mother's estate and again insisting that the publisher had never had anything further in mind than establishing their genuineness; and the "Prefatory Address" was itself followed by a biography of Mrs. Billington from 1783 to 1786. Since she was in Dublin during the greater part of this period, much of it had to do with Richard Daly, Manager of the Dublin theater and at the time her lover. The letters, dated 1783–1784, were few in number and far less sensational than they had been represented. On 1 February her lawyer, now the Prince of Wales's Attorney General, Thomas Erskine, nevertheless moved the Court of King's Bench for a prosecution of Ridgway as publisher of a malicious libel, entitled *Memoirs of Mrs. Billington.* The *Oracle*, which reported this development on 2 February, reserved judgment, being by this time in the pay of the Prince of Wales itself.

While Ridgway had been trying to blackmail Mrs. Billington, the *Morning Herald* had been trying to blackmail the Duke of Clarence's mistress, Mrs. Jordan. The Duke of Clarence had first threatened to sue and, thinking better of it, had appealed to John Palmer of the Post Office, whose influence over that newspaper, he had understood from Sheridan, was decisive.[31] Everything was peaceful for a short time. But, since Mrs. Jordan had not only preceded Mrs. Billington in Daly's affections, but was even beholden to him for one of her children, the *Memoirs* revived interest in her. By February she was the subject of considerable newspaper comment, and the Duke had also heard of "a book in defence of Mrs. Billington with anecdotes of Daly . . . , in which Mrs. Jordan is, and infamously scandalized." This time he wrote to William Adam, with instructions to "prosecute the editor." Having been assured by Adam that the book would not be published, he again instructed him to "attend to it if it is attempted to be published" and mentioned in addition that "there have been and there may be still in circulation handbills entitled, *Little Pickle* or the *Pretty Plotter* which book is to be published next Saturday. I believe it is merely a catch penny; but still it is worth looking after."[32] Mrs. Jordan had been called "Little Pickle" since 1790, when she had played a character by that name in *The Spoiled Child*, a trifle which she was thought to have written herself. *Little Pickle* was not published, but *An Answer to the Memoirs of Mrs. Billington. With the Life and Adventures of Richard Daly Esq. and An Account of the Present State of the Irish Theatre. Written by A Gentleman with Several Curious Anecdotes of All Parties* was, the colophon reading only "Printed for the Author. London, 1792." The Duke of Clarence evidently did not sue, and, since no one expected an actress to lead a celibate life, Mrs. Jordan was not damaged by the publicity. Nothing further was in fact said of her until 8 August, when the *World* announced that "Mrs. Jordan was, on Monday morning [6 Aug.], delivered of a child which died very soon after its birth. She had only gone for five months of her time." According to other newspapers, the birth had occurred in the Duke of Clarence's apartments. The suggestion of incest was, however, too much for Mrs. Billington. She seems to have had no engagements during 1792, and on 28 August the *Oracle* mentioned that, "in compassion to RIDGWAY's family," she had "generously consented to drop her prosecution." Sometime later she retired to the Continent with her husband and her brother, not to return until 1801.

The Billington scandal was succeeded by the Holman scandal. On 17 October "two morning papers," both certainly of an Opposition persuasion, published an "advertisement," stating that "Mr. [Joseph] HOLMAN of COVENT GARDEN THEATRE" had deserted "Mrs. HOLMAN, late Miss HUGHES" and "TWO INFANTS," leaving them in a state of destitution. Since the eighteenth century could not endure this kind of thing, "Mr. HOLMAN" leapt to his defense by publishing (19 Oct.) a one-column explanation of the affair in the Ministerial *Diary*, in which he maintained that the woman was not his wife and the children need not be destitute, having been nicely situated with his mother until "MISS HUGHES" removed them. Although this altered the situation somewhat, the public was not entirely satisfied, and letters poured into the office of the *Diary* until 10 November, when the conductor announced that he would publish no more of them, the case having been, so far as he was concerned, closed. Readers were also regaled with the various ordeals of Charles Dibdin.[33]

Dibdin was proprietor and manager of the Sans Souci, a theater in the Strand, where he sang songs which he himself had supposedly written. But the *Observer* was certain that the songs were stolen from Isaac Bickerstaffe, and, although Dibdin had defended himself by cramming the *Diary* and the *Public Advertiser* with puffs, he had finally lost his temper and on 18 March had filed an action for trespass against that newspaper, naming Isaac Swan as author and William Locke as printer of a paragraph which he had considered especially libelous. The *Observer* had since been silent, but, when, on 13 October, Dibdin opened his theater for the winter season, he was greeted with a barrage of abuse from the *World*. On 15 October the *World* reported that the songs were both "ill-written" and "wretchedly sung"; and yet, it added, "this man had the *modesty* to charge *five shillings* admittance." There was more of this kind of thing. On 16 October the *World* observed that "BICKERSTAFF's BAGATELLE was opened on Saturday night in the Strand, to a motley company, supplied with those *Paper Passports* called Orders [i.e., complimentary tickets]"; on 17 October it carried a derisive article, headed "BICKERSTAFF's BAGATELLE,/ SANS SOUCI, [*Or whatever it may be called.*]"; and on 18 October it added a mocking "ANECDOTE OF DIBDIN." On the same day Dibdin published a long letter in the *Diary*, dated "*Strand, Oct.* 17, 1792." He pointed out that some months earlier he had sued "the printer of a newspaper for a libel, whose prosecution will come up at the sittings after Michaelmas Term," and that he had then "sworn an affidavit" that he knew nothing of "Mr. Bickerstaff . . . since he absconded." He had supposed that that affidavit would end the matter, and yet he was not actually surprised at the resumption of the abuse, since "I do not give either the editors of newspapers, or their understrappers, general tickets"; and he had even decided to tolerate it, regarding it as "operating in the quality of so many advertisements, and begetting a saving in my expences of five or six shillings a piece." But he could not overlook the paragraph which had appeared that day in the *World*, and so he would "once more appeal to the laws of my country." To this the *Diary* appended some remarks of its own, strongly defensive of Dibdin.

On 17 October Dibdin did in fact file actions for libel against Isaac Swan as "sole Proprietor" of the *World* and Robert Bostock as printer. Since Swan was not a proprietor, he might have avoided the action on a technicality, but he did not; and it was an unlucky day for Dibdin on every account. The Sans Souci, it appeared, occupied premises adjacent to those of a Mr. Scott, "a man of some property and also a wine merchant"; and, as Mr. and Mrs. Dibdin were proceeding up the passage between the two buildings on the afternoon of 17 October, they were drenched with a tub of water from the wine shop. The drencher was called to account, but he was not repentant, saying only that he always dumped the water in the passage after cleaning the bottles and that it was up to the passer-by to watch out. The result of this argument was a free-for-all between Scott's employees and Dibdin's associates. Since Scott's crew was armed with bottles, there were numerous casualties, many of Dibdin's employees being badly cut in the face. On 18 October Dibdin delivered Scott to the Bow Street Station, where the presiding magistrate, Nicholas Bond, suggested that he apologize. Since Scott refused, he was charged with assault, but was released on bail, and the case was scheduled for a later hearing at Westminster. All of this was vividly narrated by the *Public Advertiser* of 21 October, which as usual was strongly in sympathy with Dibdin. The outcome of the hearing was not reported by the newspapers, and meanwhile the action against the *World* achieved nothing. On 20 October Dibdin was the subject of some sneering verses; on 22 October he was the subject of some sarcastic paragraphs; and on 24 October the *World* shifted its ground to politics: "DIBDIN, who is a very violent Jacobin, was greatly shocked when he heard the recent intelligence, that the French Troops had *evacuated Worms.*" Having exhausted its own ingenuity, the *World* of 25 October borrowed some verses from "Anthony Pasquin's" (John Williams's) *Children of Thespis.* At least part of this was unfair, since Dibdin seems actually to have had no interest in politics.

Mrs. Wells of Covent Garden was almost always in the news. She was certainly better known to readers of newspapers than any other performer, for there was hardly a day they were not called upon to weep over her latest misfortune. On 25 January she sprained her ankle and was unable to appear in *Notoriety* that evening (*World*, 26 Jan.). She had sufficiently recovered to appear in John O'Keeffe's *Wild Oats* the following night, but by 2 March she was so ill that, according to the *Oracle*, "the Public are likely to lose the professional talents of Mrs. WELLS, who is in such a precarious state of health as makes it very doubtful whether she will be able ever to appear again." On 25 April *Notoriety* was produced for her benefit, and she did her famous imitations between the acts (*World*, 26 Apr.), but she had not entirely regained her health, and on 28 April the *World* confided that more had been involved than illness. She had, it appeared, saddled herself with certain "incumbrances" in a valiant effort to "serve" her "family"; and, in order to "keep the secret," she had been living "in a foreign country amongst strangers: Her determination to let her own efforts only extricate her; Her resignation under a long and dangerous illness brought on by regret" could hardly fail, the *World* was sure, to melt the heart of every reader. She had in fact been arrested for debts incurred by her brother-in-law Emanuel Samuel, had been rescued by one lover, Major Topham, and had fled to the country and finally to Calais with another, the author of *Notoriety*, Frederick Reynolds.[34] There was a sentimental welcome-back in the *World* of 30 April, including the "Introductory Address" written for her benefit performance by Topham, and on 21 May the *World* congratulated her in another tribute: "GOOD ACTIONS never go without their reward. Such now attends the liberal conduct of Mrs. WELLS—who regardless of herself, has done so much to serve her family—From private letters received by the late ships, she learns that Mr. SAMUEL, who married her sister, has been called to the MADRAS station, with an additional appointment of 500*l.* per ann." Samuel had gone to Madras as auditor to the Nawab of Oudh, which position Topham had secured for him. In late May Mrs. Wells was back on the stage of Covent Garden with her imitations, and on 2 June Covent Garden was closed for repairs. The final performance was a benefit for the actors who were being dismissed, and, according to the *World* (2 June), she was as usual "regardless of herself": "Mrs. WELLS, the progress of whose whole life has been ACTS of KINDNESS to OTHERS—on this evening adds another act in giving for the relief of those who retire from the STAGE, the attraction of her Impersonations—to which some *new ones* are added." There was a lengthy account of this performance in the *World* of 4 June, including ecstatic references to her imitations. It was signed "Old Kent" and was supplied, as so were the earlier eulogies, by Mrs. Wells herself.

On 9 July the *Star* reported that Mrs. Wells was "down at Hastings, trying the benefit of the sea breezes upon a frame much impaired by ill health"; but the *Star* was in error, for on 10 July the *World* commended her for her fine work in O'Keeffe's *The Agreeable Surprise* at the Haymarket.[35] The *Diary*, which witnessed her performance in that play a few weeks later, was less enthusiastic: "[The] dainty dairy-maid of Saturday evening [28 July]," it observed on 30 July, "proved a *disagreeable surprise*, Mrs. W. being in a fair way to increase her family, and therefore by no means in a condition to undertake the part of *Cowslip*." But the *World* seemed to be unaware of her pregnancy, if in fact she was pregnant, for on 28 July it had announced that she would play in the Richmond theater, and on 30 July it added some eulogistic verses about her talents. Instead she went to Brighton, where on 1 August, according to the *Diary* (8 Aug.), "Mr. Palmer very kindly lent [her] the . . . Theatre . . .; she gave her Imitations, and cleared thirty pounds." Palmer's "kindness" may have owed something to the *World*'s defense of him during the Post Office quarrels. She was still writing theatrical commentary for the *World* as late as mid-September[36] and was evidently still living in Brighton at that time, for on 22 September the *Star* reported: "On Friday night [14 Sept.], Mrs. WELLS played Bridget in the *Chapter of Accidents* [a comedy by Sophia Lee], and *Cowslip* [in *The Agreeable Surprise*], to a large audience at Brighton, who were besides not a little amused by a squabble between her and some of the performers, from whom she appealed to the house; and such a scene of confusion ensued, that it was with the utmost difficulty the performance could proceed." This "squabble" may have ended her engagement there, for on 15 October she was back at Covent Garden to play Lady Anne in *Richard III*. She seems to have given her last performance on 28 November. Nothing further was said of her for several months.

There was one death. On 4 August died General John Burgoyne, "Colonel of the 4th Regiment of Foot, a Lieutenant-General in the Army, M. P. for Preston, in Lancashire, . . . Privy Councellor of the Kingdom of Ireland," and, most important, so far as the newspapers were concerned, playwright. Long obituaries appeared in the *Diary* and *Public Advertiser* of 7 August, the *Star* of 9 and 10 August, and the *Oracle* of 10 August; and accounts of the funeral, which occurred on 13 August, appeared in the *Oracle* and *Star* of 14 August and the *Public Advertiser* of 16 August. Most of his plays were thought to be unidentified. As the *Diary* put it on 7 August:

> Several pieces . . . were performed in America, of which we have no copies, and some even performed here, it is believed, attacked the town from the masked batteries of other names. This in an author may be modesty; it is however certainly prudence.
> The following is a list of such pieces as we can positively call his:
> The MAID of the OAKS, acted at Drury Lane, 1774
> The LORD of the MANOR, ditto 1781
> The HEIRESS, ditto 1783.[37]

In addition, General Burgoyne had left "five or six illegitimate children, with their mother, wholly unprovided for": surely, said the *Star* on 9 August, a mistress's "affection and fidelity deserve a better fate." "Out of respect to his memory," even the Ministerial *World* was "prompted to hope that the report is not true." Newspaper interest in Susan Caulfield and her four children, born between 1782 and 1788, continued until late August, when several newspapers reported that the Earl of Derby had provided for the group. According to the *World* of 1 September, "Lord DERBY's liberality is thus stated: To the creditors of General BURGOYNE 3000*l.* and a handsome provision for the surviving Lady and a large family." Lord Derby, who later took the family into his own home, bringing up the children himself, was a friend of Fox, but he was not politically prominent, and his exemplary character, added to the tragedy of his own situation, had won for him the respect of all newspapers. In 1778 his wife, Lady Hamilton, had become involved in an intrigue with that notorious wrecker of marriages, the Duke of Dorset, with whom she was apparently still living. Eight years later Lord Derby had fallen in love with the actress, Miss Farren, whom he was thought to have seen for the first time in a production of Burgoyne's *The Heiress*, and she had also fallen in love with him. They were still in love, but the affair was conducted on a very elevated plane and in an atmosphere of hopelessness, for, since he was opposed to divorce, there was no possibility of a consummation while Lady Hamilton was alive.

The theaters had their own problems, each of its own kind, the problems of Covent Garden relating mainly to personnel, those of Drury Lane mainly to housing, and those of the Haymarket mainly to the matter of Colman's salary. The problems were similar only in the sense that they were all grounded in politics. Having announced the renovation of Covent Garden, Harris had had considerable difficulty finding the money, and there were recurrent rumors that much of it was coming from Opposition leaders, who were thus surreptitiously acquiring a controlling interest in the theater. All such rumors had been vehemently denied by the Ministerial press. "The article in some of the daily papers, stating that the Duke of Bedford is to put 600*l*. on the rent of Covent Garden Theatre, for the sum he lays down to pay for its enlargement, is erroneous in the proportion of one third of the sum," declared the *Diary* for example on 9 January. But announced productions of works by Robert Merry, Thomas Holcroft, and the Rev. Henry Bate Dudley, all of them sympathetic with the Opposition's point of view, had tended to support the rumors. There was a strong feeling that Merry's work in particular should be withdrawn. Merry was not, however, a newcomer to Covent Garden, and his previous efforts, *The Picture of Paris*, a pantomime written by him and Charles Bonnor in 1790, and *Lorenzo*, a tragedy produced in 1791, had had nothing to do with politics. *The Magician No Conjuror* had a great deal to do with politics, for, although there was no "Jacobinism" in it, there was some stinging ridicule of Pitt, who, it was all too evident to the audience, was in fact "The Magician." The play was produced on 2 February, immediately withdrawn, and never printed, despite the acclaims of the Opposition papers. Holcroft's *Road to Ruin*, which made its debut on 18 February, turned out to be safe enough, since it poked fun only at the Prince of Wales. Like all of his comedies, it was also very popular, being many times reproduced and widely read, the printed version going through ten editions within a few months. Even so, Harris had second thoughts about Dudley's opera, for on 23 February the *Oracle* mentioned that *Witch of the Alps* would not be performed until the following season, supposedly because Shield had not returned from Italy in time to supply the music. It was not performed until 1794, by which time it had been retitled *The Travellers in Switzerland*.

On 11 April the *World* reported that "COVENT GARDEN THEATRE closes for the season the 2d of June, and then will be seen in its present state no more./ In the intended plan of COVENT GARDEN, Mr. HARRIS gives a *new room* to the *Old* BEEF-STEAK CLUB." This club,[38] now fifty years old and composed of all the personnel of the theater, its friends, and its publicists (actors, managerial staff, musicians, dramatists, Ministerial journalists, and politicians), took its name from the room in which it met, the room having previously been occupied by the original Beefsteak Club. Among those being dropped as members, were evidently the Merrys, for the *World*'s announcement was followed (17 Apr.) by one in the *Oracle*: "THEATRICAL.—We regret exceedingly to inform our readers, that with the close of the present Season, the talents of Mrs. MERRY [Miss Brunton] are lost to the stage." Mrs. Merry was dismissed on 2 June. On 4 June the *World* dropped a crocodile tear: "Mrs. MERRY we regret to hear, has, left the STAGE. These are not the days when valuable EXPORTATIONS should be permitted. . . ." With her went her husband, Robert Merry, "The Magician" having been more of a "Conjuror" than Merry realized.

The dismissal of Mrs. Merry seems to have been a blow to both the Merrys, who had not anticipated this means of retaliation. She immediately applied to the Haymarket, but, this theater being now completely Ministerial, the application was refused, and they spent the summer on the Continent. Although Merry was no longer connected with the Friends of the People, he was still writing for the *Morning Post*, which probably financed the trip. In any event, readers were not allowed to forget him. The *Oracle* of 15 June concluded a series of paragraphs with the information that "Mr. and Mrs. MERRY had taken the *Laurel* of *Liberty* with them to France.—The Poet presents his Ode to the NATIONAL ASSEMBLY, and no doubt will have the honour of a Seance." The *World* evidently added some paragraphs of its own, for on 4 July the *Oracle* snapped by way of comment: "Whoever 'makes the fortunes of Mr. MERRY,' Mr. MERRY in no narrow way helped on the fortunes of what *was* the World.—Nothing short of FOLLY could repay him with the most bare-faced ingratitude." By 11 July the *World* had returned to the subject with the comment: "Mr. MERRY is reported to have enlisted into a little Corps of JACOBINS at PARIS, to support the CONSTITUTION of FRANCE—'*As it was in the beginning*, but never *will be* again.'" The last mention of Merry for the moment was in the *Oracle* of 27 July, at which time he was supposedly in Calais.

It was a good summer for the Haymarket. On 30 June Mrs. Elizabeth Inchbald's *Young Men and Old Women* was presented to an appreciative audience, especially since the oblique reference in the title to the Prince of Wales's taste in mistresses was underscored by numerous asides; and on 25 July the Government finally acknowledged the loyalty of George Colman. Having employed the *World* to champion his cause, Colman had submitted a petition to Lincoln's Inn, asking £400 a year for supporting his father and an additional £600 for managing the Haymarket. The "Lunatic's" creditors had submitted a counterpetition, approving the £400, but vehemently protesting the £600, on the ground that £200 was more than adequate under the circumstances. At the hearing a spokesman for the group explained that, when the elder Colman was committed, his debts had totaled £7,000. Since then he had had an income of £3,446 a year, and in 1791 alone "a balance of £2870 was reported." Yet, not only had they as creditors not received a shilling, but the debts had now increased, they were informed, to more than £16,000. Surely, they felt, some economies were in order. The Chief Baron, Sir James Eyre, felt otherwise. Having ordered all "balances to be deposited in the bank" immediately and the "Lunatic's" house in Richmond advertised for rent, he went on to say that the creditors had been ill-advised, in his opinion, about the Haymarket. For, since it was more to their interest that the theater be efficiently managed than it was to Colman's, it seemed to him that they should have petitioned for even more than £600. The £600 was allowed. An account of the hearing appeared in the *World* of 26 July, and on 28 July the paper expressed its approval: "Young COLMAN will manage well this season for his Father's creditors. According to the present run, he will clear, at the end of this Season, 4000*l*. If the creditors were to act as they ought to do, they would *increase* rather than think of diminishing the Manager's Salary."

On 27 August Covent Garden, now completely redecorated, opened for the winter season. Although the Ministerial newspapers were delighted with the renovations, the opening itself was somewhat disappointing. The date had been set in the expectation that Parliament would convene on 30 August, but the prorogation had been extended, and so there was almost no one in town. Even Mrs. Wells was absent, being still in Brighton. Present, however, were evidently the Merrys, for on 28 August the *Star* noticed that "Mr. and Mrs. MERRY, with Mrs. FENNELL, arrived in London last night." Mrs. Fennell, previously Miss Porter, had married the actor, dramatist, and radical politician, James Fennell, earlier in the year. The Merrys remained in England until early November, although not always in London, since by 27 September, according to the *Oracle*, they were living in Bath; and it was the understanding of the Ministerial papers that they spent most of their time trying to get Mrs. Merry's engagement renewed. Taylor's recollection[39] that during this period Merry viciously attacked Harris "in the newspapers" may have been accurate, for the newspaper would have been the *Morning Post*, which is not available. Such attacks would also help to explain the *Public Advertiser*'s attacks on Mrs. Merry, typical of which was the slurring comment of 30 October: "Mrs. Merry does not grace the Stage this winter. What a loss to all lovers of nature and simplicity!" By this time the Merrys were back in London, and by 6 November, according to the *Public Advertiser*, they had finally realized that Covent Garden did not want Mrs. Merry and had returned to France, again probably at the expense of the *Morning Post*. As before, they were not forgotten. On 26 November the *World* mentioned that they had been seen in Paris and that Mrs. Merry was "reported to be in a thriving way," but this report seems to have been false. On 6 December the *Diary* remarked that Merry was trying to get a seat in the National Convention, and on 12 December the *World* stated with evident disgust: "When a *Gentleman* of the talent and manners of Mr. *Merry* is seen associating with the last dregs of human nature, such as are now assembled at Paris, no feeling Man can help sighing over—*a good man that is lost!*" To this the *Oracle* of 21 Decem-

ber added an amen: "The MERRY POET has now dwindled into a SAD POLITI-
CIAN."

The problems of Drury Lane had seemed meanwhile to be insoluble. During
the early part of the year, Sheridan was trying to sell 300 debentures at £500
each to finance the rebuilding, estimated by Holland, the architect, at £140,000,
and was having, the Ministerial newspapers understood, little success. Although
he had again contracted for the King's Haymarket for the 1792–1793 season, the
World insisted as before that the rent was exorbitant. "KEMBLE the *large*, has
made a tolerable season of it at Edinburgh," it remarked typically on 30 May.
"He ought to do so, for he has a *large* price to pay for the Theatre." On 29 June,
Sheridan's wife, Elizabeth Linley, died in Bristol, and Sheridan returned from
the funeral to face another problem. On 14 January the Pantheon, which housed
the opera company, had burned, and, although the King's Haymarket was not
yet officially licensed for operas, Taylor had succeeded in leasing it for Tuesdays
and Saturdays. The *Star*, which reported this development on 3 July, also
reported that Sheridan had dismissed all performers. The Treasury papers
concluded happily that this was the end of the Drury Lane company, but they
soon discovered that it was not. Sheridan, it appeared, had not dismissed the
performers, he had leased the Little Haymarket for those two nights, and he was
making commitments for the future. "Mr. SHERIDAN has kindly adopted a
bantling of Mrs. ROBINSON's," the *World* noticed grudgingly on 19 July. "It is
expected to make its appearance very shortly after the opening of the Haymarket
Winter Theatre." Mrs. Robinson had by this time gone to the Continent for her
health, not to return until December. The "bantling" was later (10 Jan., 1794)
identified by the *Morning Post* as an opera, entitled *Kate of Aberdeen*.

Drury Lane did not, however, open on 27 August, and there was again the
question of whether it would open at all or not, since Colman had suddenly
decided that he would not allow Kemble to manage a performance in his theater.
Kemble was therefore still in Edinburgh, where the Ministerial papers were
advising him to remain, since he was obviously not welcome in London. This
problem was seemingly resolved by the *Oracle*'s announcement of 29 August
that the Haymarket would not be necessary: that Sheridan had raised the
£140,000 for his own theater, that plans were being drawn for it, and that the
building would be ready for occupancy by Christmas. Construction was in fact
commenced in September, but, shortly after it began, Sheridan encountered a
new snag, and the date of completion was revised to September, 1793. Although
readers did not learn until the following year that Holland had increased his
price by £75,000, they were indignant, and so were the Opposition newspapers,
which refused to believe that all these impediments were coincidental. The
indignation was evidently effective, for on 3 October several newspapers
mentioned that Colman had reconsidered and was now willing to accept
Kemble as "acting manager," with the provision that he could discharge him if
he proved objectionable. This meant that the Government could oust the

company if it engaged in propagandistic activities, but, since Sheridan was lucky to get the Haymarket on any terms, the contract was signed, and arrangements were made for the opening. The Drury Haymarket did open without further incident.

The *Diary* of 9 November carried an interesting list of the arrangements made with performers at various theaters, the incidental puff of Miss Farren being inserted of course at her expense:

THEATRICALS.

MARA's engagement depends as it did last year, on her success.—In all events, she is to have a benefit.—And according to the event, from 10*l*. to 20*l*. up to a share of the profits.

The Storace has 10*l*. a night and a benefit.

Miss Farren, whose accomplishments lift her high above low life, whether of the great vulgar or the little, and whose private life is a model of unblemished purity, and improving elegance—continues in her gratifying employment, without demanding any augmentation of her establishment. She has 18 guineas the week.

Mr. Kemble has the same.

Mrs. Siddons is to perform this season. But the conditions of her engagement are not yet quite fixed. It will be probably by the night, leaving the number of nights to her determination. Perhaps it will be again 30*l*. a night.

. . . . . .

Mr. Lewis has 16*l*. a week and a stipulation for a benefit on the Saturday before Easter. Deemed the best night in the year.

Mr. Pope has 15*l*. a week—Mr. Holman 10*l*.—Mr. Farren 9*l*.—Mr. Palmer 14*l*.—Mr. Dodd 12*l*.

Some Aftermaths of the Prorogation

"The Opposition are now, poor Gentlemen, as much forgotten by their country, as if they did not exist in it—many of them, we fear, at any rate, have in it but a bare existence," the *World* declared on 23 July. But the Government knew better: however slight its strength in Parliament, the Opposition had the overwhelming support of the people. Hence, as soon as Parliament was prorogued, Pitt took steps to deal with his various enemies. The first of these was Sampson Perry, who on 9 July emerged from prison to resume the conduct of the *Argus*. Since, unlike the interim conductor, John King, Perry was an outspoken critic of Pitt, he was returned to court on 10 July to be indicted ex officio for having published a libel on the Commons. The libel, which had appeared on 8 May, while he was still incarcerated, had consisted of a quotation, printed without comment, from one of Pitt's early speeches favoring reform. No date was set for the trial, the hope evidently being that the indictment would be a sufficient deterrent. To the utter astonishment of all newspapers, the Government also moved against the *Oracle* and the *Morning Post*. On 9 July John Bell was tried in the Court of King's Bench for having published libels on the Guards in the *Oracle* of 5 and 7 January, Richard Tattersall was tried in the same court for having published libels on Lady Elizabeth Lambart in the *Morning Post* of August, September, and October, 1791, and Richard Tattersall and William Williams were tried for having published a libel on George Rose in the *Morning Post* of 14 March. Although Bell protested that the libels on the Guards were published "without his knowledge and to his embarrassment," he was convicted and ordered to remain available for sentencing. Lady Lambart and Rose were awarded damages. The trial of John Bell received little publicity; the trials of Tattersall received a great deal.

On 7 July the *World* had observed tauntingly: "A BARRISTER [Thomas Erskine], whose wit is proverbial, remarked on a [*certain*] TRIAL, that 'TATTERSALL *has certainly got in the wrong side of the* POST: and that the PRINCE had, *as many knew—an* ESCAPE!'" Actually it was Tattersall who had the "ESCAPE," for he could prove by documents that the Prince of Wales's agent, Louis Weltje, was legally responsible for everything printed by the *Morning Post*, his own responsibility being limited to the business management. Although he had said nothing about these documents before the trials, the Government was evidently uneasy that he might say something in court, for the action brought by Lady Cavan was tried first. But Tattersall continued to say nothing, pleading in his defense only that the libels on Lady Lambart were as shocking to him as they were to the plaintiff, that he himself "had very little to do" with the "arrangement" or "management" of the newspaper, and that he had "used every effort in his power" to identify the authors of the "calumnies." Lady Lambart was awarded £4,000 damages. Thus heartened, the Government tried the case of Rose versus Tattersall and Williams. Tattersall was again discreet, and Rose was awarded £100 from each of them. On 10 July Tattersall was returned to court to be indicted ex officio for having published a libel on the King. But, although he was willing to submit to damages, he was apparently not willing to go to prison, for the hearing turned out to be only an exchange of civilities. According to the *World* (11 July), Erskine entered a plea of guilty, but went on to say that "he did not believe the King had a more faithful and affectionate subject than the Defendant, and that all this misfortune had befallen him from his unfortunate connection with the *Morning Post.*/ Mr. ATTORNEY GENERAL [Sir Archibald Macdonald] thanked Mr. ERSKINE for the train in which he had put this cause./ The Noble and Learned Judge [Lord Kenyon] said he was sorry the Defendant had any connexion with a Newspaper, which had occasioned him so much trouble and expence." The action was thereupon quietly diverted to the printer,

William Williams, who spent twelve months in King's Bench Prison as a result. The date of his sentencing was not specified by the newspapers, and the *Morning Post* is lacking from 14 January to 6 December, by which time the printer was J. Norris.

The action brought by Rose was the subject of considerable newspaper comment, for, since the paragraph on which it was based was only a paraphrase of Thompson's speech respecting the Government's management of the 1788 election, the Opposition press thought that the plaintiff might more properly have been the Attorney General. The *World* thought not. "The manner in which Mr. ROSE brought action, was perfectly fair and constitutional," it snapped on 13 July. "By bringing it *civilly* for DAMAGES, he gave the Party an opportunity of JUSTIFICATION [of Thompson's charges], and *no Justification was attempted*. Of course, the JURY brought in the Defendant subject to DAMAGES, which all the PARTY-*wit* of Mr. ERSKINE could not do away.—Lord KENYON's charge amply testified this." Even more intriguing to the press was the action brought by Lady Cavan. Every newspaper carried a long account of the trial, the *Diary* and the *Public Advertiser* of 13 July added to their previous accounts another six columns, this time reprinting most of the libelous paragraphs, and references to the case persisted well into 1793.

Lady Cavan's action had always seemed suspicious to the Opposition newspapers, not only because it was filed so many months after the fact, but because the defendant was Tattersall, whose connection with the *Morning Post* was not then public knowledge. Although the reason for the delay was not explained at the trial, some attempt was made to account for Tattersall's involvement, one of the witnesses for the plaintiff, a Richard Barry, testifying that, as "Clerk of the Securities for the Stamp Office," he had on 20 April, 1791, "witnessed" a "bond," executed by Tattersall, making William Williams responsible for the content of the paper, and that the "bond" was still in existence. The fact that Lady Cavan had actually seen the "bond" was not established, and the testimony was irrelevant anyway, since Tattersall had already admitted that he was a proprietor of the newspaper. By implying that Lady Cavan might have read Tattersall's name from a document in the Stamp Office, the testimony did tend to allay the suspicion that she was acting for George Rose. Yet, without this suspicion, newspapers were at a loss to account for the fury of Lord Kenyon's instructions to the jury and the consequent amount of the damages, £4,000 being an unprecedented award for a grievance of this sort. While the *Diary* and the *Public Advertiser* were suggesting that perhaps the paragraphs had been especially abusive, the *Star* was wondering (12 July) if Lord Kenyon might have been influenced by a relationship: "Lady ELIZABETH LAMBERT, now rendered a topic of general conversation, is the relative by marriage of the venerable Judge GOULD, whose daughter is the Lady of her brother, Lord CAVAN." Lord Cavan had married a daughter of Sir Henry Gould, Justice of the Court of Common Pleas, in 1782.

As the *Morning Chronicle* had discovered by 1 March, 1796, the Prince of Wales was obligated to pay half the £4,000 damages, as well as half the £1,000 fee charged by Erskine for Tattersall's defense. But, since other newspapers had to pay all damages themselves, there was great dissatisfaction with the verdict. Whether the *Morning Post* was actually being punished for libeling Lady Lambart or whether it was being punished for libeling the Government, the verdict was interpreted as a threat to the press. No newspaper admired Lord Kenyon, and all newspapers agreed that the damages should be forgiven. The Ministerial *World* said so flatly on 17 July: "Lady ELIZABETH LAMBERT . . . should not take the damages awarded against Mr. TATTERSALL, who doubtless knew nothing of the CALUMNY." Such statements persisted in the *World* and other Ministerial papers throughout July and August with mounting hostility toward Lady Lambart, who, the *Oracle* observed bitterly on 23 August, was "[taking] the lead in all the country dances at *Margate*; and this she does with all the more glee, as TATTERSALL *pays the Piper*." On 9 September it repeated that "Lady ELIZABETH LAMBERT expects shortly to receive a considerable accession to her fortune. It comes by the falling in of a POST *obiit*." This statement was contradicted by the *Diary*, which announced triumphantly on 30 October: "Lady CAVAN has, with a spirit becoming her high birth, rejected the sordid proposal to take the sum awarded lately in damages to her accomplished daughter." But this statement was in turn contradicted by other newspapers, so that, until the end of the year, no newspaper knew what she would do. There was one additional development. On 18 July the *Oracle* mentioned that J. S. Jordan had on 16 July changed his plea from not guilty to guilty and was "awaiting the judgment of the Court." According to Paine,[40] he had made the revision after being "closeted" for a few hours "with the Solicitors of the Treasury." Although Jordan was under indictment for having published Part II of Paine's *Rights of Man*, he had also published *The Trial of George Rose*.

None of these actions seemed to have anything to do with the Friends of the People, and readers of newspapers during the summer of 1792 would hardly in fact have known that the Friends of the People was still in existence. Although on 4 July Mackintosh published his *Letter to . . . Pitt, on His Apostacy from the Cause of Parliamentary Reform*, it attracted no attention, since there was nothing courageous about it except the title. All Mackintosh said was that the reforms advocated by the Friends of the People were milder than those once advocated by Pitt, and he was evidently too frightened by the Proclamation against Seditious Writings to identify himself even with this statement, for the *Letter* was signed only "An Honest Man." This was his last service for the society. But Grey's motion for moderate reform was still on the Parliamentary calendar, and, included in an appendix to Mackintosh's pamphlet, was a notice that an investigation of the actual state of Parliamentary representation was in progress and would appear "later." In charge of this investigation was George Tierney, and the report would of course provide devastating justification for an elections reform bill. Everything the Government did subsequently seems to have been done with these considerations in mind.

The wooing of Fox, which had commenced with the passage of the Libel Act, was no longer conducted with subtlety. It was apparent to readers of all newspapers that, except for the office of Pitt himself, Fox could have anything he wanted, provided he repudiate the Friends of the People. The Ministerial press was plying him with compliments and urging him to join the Government as a matter of patriotic duty, and, by the end of July, it appeared, he was also being urged by the Prince of Wales. The *Oracle* was agitated. Having concluded its business transactions with Carlton House, the *Oracle* had been representing itself as the Prince of Wales's newspaper, but its principal concern had been to keep the Prince of Wales at a safe distance from Fox. Since a liaison between Fox and Pitt would remove Fox from the Opposition scene altogether, leaving Sheridan, it had thought, without a rival for the Prince's favors, the *Oracle* had approved of it; but it had had some very uneasy moments when the Prince had himself sanctioned the liaison by supporting the Proclamation against Seditious Writings. Having watched the situation closely throughout June, it had concluded that the scare was passed, and nothing it reported in July indicated any further involvement on the part of the Prince.

On 2 July the *Oracle* mentioned that the Prince had "recently purchased Stockbridge House, in Hants, the residence of the late Duke of CUMBERLAND": "His Royal Highness, by the above purchase, avoids again embrewing himself in brick and mortar to erect stabling . . . , Stockbridge House having convenient accommodation for at least sixty horses." On 12 July it suggested that he had been the victim of a plot at Newcastle and that the plotters were again active. "It is a little remarkable [at least]," it mused, "that since his Royal Highness . . . has declined the Turf, his horses have been singularly successful, and won most of their engagements. It has indeed been shrewdly hinted by some of the *knowing ones*, that this is only a decoy to bring him back again, but nothing can safely be asserted on such authority./ *Newcastle* suffers much this Meeting from the absence of the Princes. . . ." On 18 July it was again "sorry to learn, that the PRINCE's quondam *Horses* are now *successful*, for the honour of Society. With manners so amiable, who can bear to think that His Royal Highness has been deliberately and villainously plundered ?" The *Oracle* was also lavishing sarcasms on Mrs. Fitzherbert, who, it observed caustically on 14 July, "was last night at the Haymarket Theatre. *Young Men and Old Women* was *not* the entertainment." Mrs. Fitzherbert, it added on 30 July, "is very much indisposed at Brighton:— the cause is supposed to be occasioned by that *green-eyed Monster—*JEALOUSY."

But the Prince himself was evidently not at Brighton, for on 1 August several newspapers published rumors that he had been promised payment of his debts if he could bring Fox into the Government. One newspaper even suggested the personnel of the proposed administration and the plan for dealing with the Prince's embarrassments, the plan consisting of the usual economies, plus another appeal to Parliament. The *Diary* and the *Public Advertiser* of 2 August liked to think that the economies at least were a fact: "His Royal Highness . . . , we are informed has begun a diminution of his household, and intends to reduce it to the standard of a private Gentleman's, as shortly as can be consistent with the tenderness due to those who may have been withheld from other opportunities of promotion, by the hope of continuing in his service./ At Carleton house, therefore, the splendour and the honorary attendance, which are thought suitable to the condition of the Heir Apparent, cease for the present." The *Oracle* (also 2 Aug.) reacted with rage:

> A MORNING PRINT introduces the firm Administration which is to do every thing for the people, God alone knows when, with an intended first Message to Parliament for the liquidation of the Debts of an ILLUSTRIOUS PERSONAGE.
> The Party Prints preserve no sort of consistency in their reports touching an ILLUSTRIOUS PRINCE. They first told us his ROYAL HIGHNESS had forsaken the *Turf*. Then they made him purchase HOUSES he did not want, for which *they* gave 30,000*l*. *Now* they tell us his HOUSEHOLD is to be *discharged*, and then they make a MINISTER to obtain payment of DEBTS, which it is a libel upon the PRINCE to suppose he can owe.

To the great relief of the *Oracle*, nothing came of these negotiations, and a few weeks later the Prince of Wales was replaced as intermediary by the Duke of Portland.

The Government was also continuing its efforts to discredit the Friends of the People by subjecting to constant harassment Tierney and Lord Lauderdale. Almost every Ministerial newspaper had something to say about them, mainly of a generally abusive nature, since no specific charge could be made against either of them. Tierney was working on the report, and until 14 July, when the *Star* mentioned that he was leaving for Scotland, Lord Lauderdale remained in London "on business." Although on 4 August the *Star* reported that "yesterday morning the Earl of LAUDERDALE, Major MAITLAND, and Dr. [John] MOORE, set out from the Earl of LAUDERDALE's House, Hanover Square, for Paris," even the *World* could think of nothing more scathing than the comment (8 Aug.): "Lord LAUDERDALE is gone to the Continent for his health. His Lordship's *nerves* were much shook by the business of the last Session of Parliament." The radicals were not mentioned at all. Since the activities of the radicals provided the Government with its only argument against the Friends of the People, the Ministerial newspapers were evidently not going to discourage them at such a moment as this. Neither certainly was the Government itself.

The only plot against the state during the summer of 1792 was a plot to blow up King's Bench Prison, discovered on 7 July, when "50 lb. wt. of gunpowder" was removed shortly before it was to be exploded; and all newspapers agreed that the plotters were aggrieved inmates. Yet the radical societies were considerably more vigorous than they had been on 15 June, when the King called for "activity" and "vigilance." All of them protested the Proclamation against Seditious Writings and later the Duke of Brunswick's Manifesto, cheap copies of Paine's works were being even more "industriously" circulated, there was further talk of a British "convention," and Cooper, Walker, and Cartwright were still supposedly in correspondence with the Jacobins. On 18 August the newspapers were advertising *A Reply to Mr. Burke's Invective against Mr. Cooper, and Mr. Watt, in the House of Commons, on the 30th of April, 1792*, published by Joseph Johnson and written by Cooper, both in the full expectation that they would be indicted for a libel on the Constitution as a result. Tooke, who had nursed the Corresponding Society along to begin with, was now the moving spirit of the Constitutional Society and the acknowledged leader of metropolitan radicalism. Of the newspapers, the *Argus* was as democratic as ever, and it seemed to the *Oracle* that the *Gazetteer* was even worse than the *Argus*, owing to the activities of John Sotheby, one of the proprietors, and the editor, William Radcliffe. On 30 June the *Oracle* expressed its feelings on the subject:

HOW TO RAISE A LOW PRINT.

Get some ten-times broken AUCTIONEER accustomed to *Puffing*, to become an Honorary Proprietor, and some furious DEMAGOGUE to be the Editor.—Let the latter write *Treasons*, and the former *knock them down* to the best bidder.

The most effectual mode will be to *pass* the Puffer into all PUBLIC DINNERS; and there, when the liquor begets *valour*, and your REFORMERS are so ripe that they are ready—

"To smite the Air for giving *breath* to KINGS," let him pull out a *Cerberian* Print, and *put up* an article—leave the Paper upon the table, and do the same thing in other places. This is a received mode of tickling Trouts, and drawing forth the gaping gaze of the GUDGEON.

But the Government was not merely indulgent; it was actually helping the cause along. For on 17 July the *Oracle* reported that the Treasury writer, John Taylor had been arrested in Edinburgh on 6 June for "inciting" and "leading" some riots in that city against the Constitution, had been tried in the High Court of Justiciary on 12 July, and had been acquitted on evidence that he was acting on the instructions of the Government. Instead of there being too much "sedition," the Government evidently felt that there was not "sedition" enough.

The King's expectation of "[preserving] to my people the uninterrupted blessings of peace" was meanwhile completely disregarded by the Ministerial newspapers. The *World* was not even certain that one of these so-called "blessings," the reduction of taxes and the national debt, could be regarded as a "blessing" at all. While legislation for eradicating the debt was in progress, all newspapers had agreed that a national debt was an evil and, the sooner it was got rid of, the better off the economy would be. The King himself had been so pleased by the National Debt Act that he had thanked Parliament for it twice. Yet, once the act was passed, the Ministerial newspapers lost interest in it. The debt was not mentioned again until 5 July, when, instead of congratulating Pitt on having got rid of it, the *World* congratulated him in effect on having incurred it:

> Mr. PITT, not only by his general conduct, but by his excellent arrangement of the Taxes during the whole of his Administration, has solved the paradox, that the *National Debt* is a *National Benefit*; for having now redeemed us from the brink of bankruptcy, and a state of ruin and destruction, he has gradually improved our Finances, and replaced us at length on the rock of prosperity.—He has shown to Englishmen, and to all the world, that a *National Debt* is a *phantom*, formidable only in name, as there can be no real or permanent evil in the taxes necessary to pay the interest of it. This assertion is no longer general, for he has made [it] appear in *our* case, that where taxes are properly laid on, and also properly collected, then the *debt* is a *pretended burthen*, bearing equally upon the *whole*, and, consequently, bearing *in reality* upon *none*.

The reaction of the Opposition press to this piece of intelligence was typified by the *Morning Chronicle*'s comment of 6 July: "A Treasury Paper, as remarkable for the *sagacity* as for the novelty of its discoveries, has discovered that the *national debt* is a *national benefit*, and that the taxes imposed to pay the interest, bearing equally upon *all*, bear *in reality* upon *none*.—What may not a head of such acumen discover, if it but meet with proper treasury encouragement?" The *Oracle* was similarly disgusted. As it said on 9 July: "That the NATIONAL DEBT is a national benefit, is an assertion that insults the common sense of the country. . . . Surely the WRITER who makes the absurd assertion above alluded to, is mistaken in supposing himself Mr. PITT's *friend.*" The "monied men" evidently agreed, for the implication that taxes and the national debt would probably not be reduced after all did nothing to stabilize the economy, which had not completely recovered anyway from the Proclamation against Seditious Writings. There was a small increase in the number of bankruptcies, the stock market was erratic, and there were rumors that a leading stockbroker had absconded in panic with a large sum of money entrusted to him for investments. On 23 July the *Oracle* identified him as John Marplay, adding that he had taken only £10,000 and on 17 July had been apprehended and the money recovered.

While the Ministerial newspapers continued to talk of war, the Duke of Richmond, who on 30 July was elevated to the rank of Field Marshal for the purpose, moved to Bagshot to take charge of the great military camp. Lord Lauderdale's statement of 31 May that the purpose of this enterprise was "to overawe the people of the metropolis, and to destroy their endeavours to obtain a reform" turned out to be wrong. The purpose was more properly to glorify the Government, to popularize war, and hence to divert rather than "destroy" the clamor for election reforms. The games lasted a week and were managed singlehandedly by the Duke of Richmond, who conducted himself, the Ministerial papers agreed, brilliantly. Sham battles and other such entertainments were presented daily, and, since every Tory of consequence, not excluding the Royal Family, was in attendance, Bagshot was the social event of the year. The *World* was ecstatic. "The Duke of RICHMOND," it said typically on 1 August, "has long been allowed to be a good executive Officer. By the plans which he has laid down for the evolution of the troops in Camp, he has proved that he possesses the talents necessary for a General./ His Grace of RICHMOND, it seems forgotten by his enemies, served, the war before last, with great honour in Germany. At the celebrated battle of *Minden*, he was one of Prince Ferdinand's Aids du Camp, and distinguished himself much by his activity and spirit."

The climax of festivities was the Grand Review of 7 August, with the Duke the center of attractions which included, not only soldiers in quantity, but "The Large Ox," "The Learned Pig," and other such specimens, all brought together, said the *World* (8 Aug.), in a "great Tory show." Other newspapers reported that prices were ruinous, lodgings unobtainable, and the roads so jammed with traffic that only a fraction of the people who set out ever arrived. As the *Star* put it on 8 August: "Such has been the rage for visiting this military plaything, that six guineas were refused, and seven and a half absolutely demanded, for a pair of horses without a carriage, the night before the Grand Review./ The immense crowd that left town, for the purpose of seeing the Grand Review yesterday, is incredible. Upwards of ten thousand at least, have returned without seeing a single soldier." While the games were in progress, news arrived that on 24 July Prussia had declared war on France, and the Grand Review was itself climaxed by news that on 27 July the Duke of Brunswick, Commander of the Austro-Prussian forces, had issued a direful manifesto against the French revolutionists. To the Ministerial newspapers, these developments seemed quite in the Bagshot mood, giving the "show" a kind of fillip. Of Poland, which, now torn to shreds, was being parceled out among Russia, Prussia, and Austria, they said nothing.

Death of the Earl of Guilford

There were four deaths of political consequence during the year: John Stuart, third Earl of Bute, on 10 March; John Montagu, fourth Earl of Sandwich, on 30 April; Frederick North, second Earl of Guilford, on 5 August; and Constantine John Phipps, second Baron Mulgrave, on 10 October. Since all of them had been friends of the King during at least part of their lives, all of them had enjoyed honors and emoluments, which were listed by the newspapers as a matter of course. At his death, Lord Bute had been a Knight of the Garter, Chancellor of

Marischal College (Aberdeen), Ranger of Richmond Park, Trustee of the British Museum, and President of the Society of Antiquaries. Lord Sandwich had been a Fellow of the Royal Society, a Fellow of the Society of Antiquaries, a Doctor of Laws (Cambridge), a General in the Army, a Governor of Charter House, and Recorder of Huntingdon and Godmanchester. Lord Mulgrave had been a Fellow of the Royal Society, a Fellow of the Society of Antiquaries, and Elder Brother of Trinity House. But the death which most interested the newspapers was that of Lord Guilford, who had been, according to the *Star* (6 Aug.), "Lord Warden and Admiral of the Cinque Ports, Governor of Dover Castle, Lord Lieutenant and Custos Rotulorum of the County of Somerset, Recorder of Gloucester and Taunton, an Elder Brother of the Trinity House, President of the Foundling Hospital, and of the Asylum, and Governor of the Turkey Company." He had also been a Knight of the Garter and Chancellor of Oxford University. Obituaries of Lord Guilford appeared in the *Oracle* and *Star* of 6 August, the *Diary* of 6, 7, and 8 August, and the *Public Advertiser* of 7 and 10 August; accounts of the funeral, which occurred on 14 August, appeared in the *Star* of 15 August and the *Public Advertiser* of 16 August; and on 29 August the *Oracle* added an account of his financial situation.

For Pitt, who was certainly the darling of the gods, however he was regarded by his fellow mortals, these deaths could not have been more timely. Not only did one of them release Lord Loughborough, the Earl of Carlisle, Lord North (now third Earl of Guilford), Lord Stormont, Sir Gilbert Elliot, and Mr. Adam, all of whom were now free to defect if they wished, but together they returned to the coffer some choice patronage for redistribution. Only one of the prizes seems to have fallen through his fingers, the *Oracle* of 30 August reporting that the Duke of Norfolk had added the Recordership of Gloucester to the Lord Lieutenancy of West Riding, which he had held since 1782, and the High Stewardship of Hereford, which he had held since 1790. As to the redistribution of the remaining patronage, the respective heirs, it appeared, figured slightly in Pitt's thinking. The fourth Earl of Bute, who was still voting generally with the Whigs, got nothing and for that matter needed nothing, since he had been Lord Lieutenant of County Glamorgan since 1772 and had enjoyed a lifetime pension of £7,000 since 1782. The third Baron Mulgrave also got nothing, and the fifth Earl of Sandwich, Master of the Buckhounds since 1783, succeeded his father only as Recorder of Huntingdon and Godmanchester. Although the new Earl of Guilford had supported the Government in the debates on the Proclamation against Seditious Writings, Pitt evidently wanted him out of the country, for, shortly after he succeeded to the title, he was offered the post of Governor General of India, which, according to the newspapers, he indignantly refused.

To begin with, the newspapers showed only casual interest in the patronage, partly because the two plums, the Cinque Ports and the Chancellorship of Oxford, had long ago been promised to the Dukes of Dorset and Beaufort, respectively, partly because it would be used, they supposed, to reward the faithful. But it was soon evident that Pitt had something quite different in mind. Although, since August, 1791, when he had published his *Appeal from the Old to the New Whigs*, Burke had dreamed of a split in the Opposition, it could have made no difference to Pitt whether the Opposition was split or not, since he did not need additional support in Parliament and the split would not help him outside. The situation was now somewhat altered, for a series of defections, especially the defection of the Duke of Portland, might have a telling effect on Fox. Hence, while the Earl of Guilford was still in the act of dying, Pitt had taken steps to divert two of his followers. On 1 August Lord Mansfield, already Earl of Mansfield of the County of Nottingham, had been quietly created Earl of Mansfield of the County of Middlesex, with the provision that the title would pass at his death to Viscount Stormont, his nephew. Since Lord Mansfield was a very old man, this meant in effect that Lord Stormont had been elevated to the rank of an Earl. The newspapers also understood that Lord Loughborough had been offered the Lord Chancellorship vice Lord Thurlow. But, although both of them had supported the Proclamation against Seditious Writings, there was a vast difference, it turned out, between supporting the Government on a specific issue and identifying oneself with an administration which, the Opposition had always maintained, held office illegally. Even Lord Loughborough temporized. All the *World* could report on that score (31 July) was a certain comical development at Cambridge. Lord Loughborough had arrived there on 24 July, it appeared, "to open his Commission for Assizes," and, so certain was everyone that he would join the Government, that the whole faculty was on hand to greet him. But, while "the fellows of different colleges vied with each other to pay him their devoirs," they were pushed aside by the "vice-master of Trinity College," the Rev. W. W. Hodson, who rushed forward to be the first and "thus ensure a vacant See." Having forgotten to wear his spectacles and misjudging the distance required for an obeisance, he, however, struck Lord Loughborough such a sharp blow with his cap that "a torrent of blood streamed from his Lordship's nose." Stooping to recover the cap, he instead stumbled over it, so that he ended by falling flat "at his Lordship's feet," to "the universal ridicule of the surrounding crowd."

While Lord Loughborough was still considering his offer, the *World* was vehemently denying a rumor that the Duke of Portland had been offered the Chancellorship of Oxford. The report was preposterous, said the *World* scornfully on 8 August, for the Chancellorship had been promised to the Duke of Beaufort a long time ago. On 9 August the *World* repeated, although with less assurance: "The Duke of BEAUFORT, there is little doubt, will be elected Chancellor of the University of Oxford. His opponent is doubtless respectable: but the Duke of BEAUFORT has a superior claim, as a firm supporter of the present government. . . . The *Cinque Ports*," it added, "are likely to devolve by the patronage of the Minister, to the Duke of DORSET." But by this time no newspaper was certain of anything, for, although to begin with Lord Beaufort had been the unanimous choice of the Oxford colleges, all but two of them had since shifted to the Duke of Portland "as a recent convert." At this point there was an even more disturbing rumor: Pitt, it was said, had seized the Wardenship of the Cinque Ports for himself. The newspapers were stunned.

The *World* was the first to recover. "It is reported, that on Saturday [11 Aug.] the KING appointed . . . PITT to be Lord Warden and Admiral of the Cinque Ports," it said tentatively on 14 August. "We hope this is true—for every liberal man must think it is full time that the Minister, who has done so much for the Nation, should at last have something done for him." The *Oracle* was sure that the rumor was false, although, if it happened to be true, it said, it would "scotch" the suspicion (which the *Oracle* had itself originated) that Pitt was out of favor with the King. In any event the sinecure was, as the *Oracle* understood, a trifle, the "gifts" being "short of THREE THOUSAND a year." On 15 August the *Diary* added its own apology:

> Mr. Pitt has at last yielded to the wishes of his best friends (the foremost among whom may be mentioned the King and Queen) and accepted a provision. His Majesty, unsolicited, sent him the appointment of Warden of the Cinque Ports, &c. on Thursday [9 Aug.], by a Messenger, to Burton Pynsent.
> The income of the Lord Warden of the Cinque Ports has been variously stated. From the best reports we learn, that it netts the possessor near four thousand pounds a year, and is in every respect a complete sinecure.
> Mr. Pitt's seat in Parliament, as one of the Representatives of the University of Cambridge, will of course become vacant; to which, however, there cannot be a doubt of his being re-elected.
> Mr. Pitt's next excursion will be . . . to Hertfordshire; . . . and [he] will probably pursue his journey to Cambridge, to be elected Member for that University.

The *Star* (15 Aug.) reprinted the second paragraph of this account, omitting the remainder. Although there was now little question as to the truth of the report, the *Public Advertiser* of 16 August still preferred to deal with the subject hypothetically:

> If Mr. Pitt has really been appointed Admiral and Warden of the Cinq Ports, as stated in most of the newspapers, it may justly be said, that considering his numerous great services to his country, it was high time for him to obtain some matter of permanency. And all those who view the long list of places possessed until his death by the late Earl of Guilford, exclusive of many others procured for his family, and acquired during an Administration of far less importance in the national welfare than the present, will hardly begrudge the Minister, if true, this first and only appointment hitherto received for life.

On 18 August the *World* repeated, although this time with even less conviction, that the Chancellorship of Oxford would go to the Duke of Beaufort: "We understand that the Chancellorship . . . will be strongly contested; but have not any doubt of the Duke of Beaufort's success, as it is said to be supported by Administration." But this matter was settled by the *Morning Chronicle*, which announced on 22 August: "The Duke of BEAUFORT has withdrawn his unprofitable opposition at Oxford, and the Duke of PORTLAND has therefore no rival for the Chancellorship." By this time all newspapers were confused. The attempt to bribe the Duke of Portland indicated that Pitt was determined to remain in office; the seizure of the Cinque Ports indicated that he had decided to resign, the sinecure being provision for his retirement. Since he was also providing for friends and relatives, the *Morning Chronicle* clung to the supposition that a resignation was in the offing. But there was no announcement to that effect, and by 22 August the *Chronicle* had reached the end of its patience.

On 20 August the *Star* had mentioned: "The recent appointment of the Minister to the Wardenship of the Cinq Ports, is said to have given great dissatisfaction to the Duke of DORSET. His Grace was, it seems, amongst the candidates for this honourable office in the year 1778, when it was given to the ... Earl of GUILFORD." On 22 August the *Morning Chronicle* voiced some "dissatisfaction" of its own:

> The salary of the Cinque Ports is not more than 500*l.* a year; but when given in the present instance to a Prime Minister, it is made up out of the sinking fund to 4000*l.* a year, free of all deductions; and thus ingeniously, in spite of the Act of QUEEN ANNE, though they [the Government?] cannot create new places, they can so augment old offices as to make them temptations for *the most virtuous men* in the kingdom, as we find in the present instance; for how often and how loudly have we been told of the virtues of Mr. PITT? The Act of QUEEN ANNE was made for the purpose of preserving us against the extension of influence, and against the encrease of public burthen. This is avoided by this artifice, and the country has no other consolation than that there are good laws, if they were not defeated by Ministerial craft, and official corruption.
>
> The Prime Minister now feels the advantage of Lord THURLOW's absence from office. That Noble Lord, with his usual obstinacy, might have thought it fit to withhold the Great Seal from a grant which went to charge the Sinking Fund with 3,500*l.* a-year, in addition to a place of 500*l.* He would probably have said that the Minister, if he thought fit to become a pensioner, should take to himself a pension directly, and not smuggle it in under the name of a sinecure. It would not have been enough for him that the same juggle has been practised by former Ministers. An abuse is not less an abuse for having subsisted for a length of time.

There was more such "dissatisfaction" in the *Morning Chronicle* of 23 August:

WARDEN OF THE CINQUE PORTS.
In stating the addition made to the place of Warden of the Cinq Ports—it was said that the 4000*l.* a-year was made up out of the Sinking Fund—it should have been said out of the Civil List—but it comes exactly to the same end, if every

four or five years his MAJESTY comes to Parliament for 4 or 500,000*l.* more than the nation, in its magnificence, has allotted for his Household.

It remains yet to be announced to the public whether Mr. PITT is to receive the additional 3,500*l.* forth-with, or whether it is to commence only on his retiring from office—as a reward for past service. The Treasury writers have, unfortunately for his fame, been silent on this subject, which has greatly alarmed his friends in the City. They have been so much in the habit of extolling his disinterested virtue, that they were dumbfounded on hearing of his grant to himself—and said it could only be accounted for by the fact of his being about to quit office—"This really looks like retirement," said they, "for it is impossible that so noble a creature as he is should pocket the emoluments of a sinecure during the time that he is upon full pay as Prime Minister!"

We who do not give him credit for all the disinterestedness which they ascribe to him, yet do him the justice to believe, that he contents himself with the mere salary of the office, and that the pension does not take place until he shall be out of office.

As to the rumor of his having secured to himself also the reversion of the *greatest sinecure under the Crown*, the Auditorship of the Exchequer (for which also he is indebted to his own friends), we believe that it is not true, for a better reason than his virtuous forbearance—*because it is impossible.* The Auditorship of the Exchequer, though so enormous and so extravagant a place, is no other than a clerkship, and ranks under the Secretaries of the Treasury. It is conferred by a simple warrant from any three of the Lords of the Treasury—and it is ridiculous to say, that they can by any order, appoint a successor to the most noble and puissant Duke, who is the present clerk.

The present Auditor of the Exchequer was Henry Pelham-Clinton, second Duke of Newcastle, who had been awarded the sinecure in 1751. A close friend of the King, Newcastle was also, according to the *Star* (24 Feb., 1794), a Fellow of the Royal Society, a Knight of the Garter, "Lord Lieutenant and Custos Rotulorum of Nottinghamshire; Steward, Keeper, and Guardian of the Forest of Sherwood and Park of Tolwood, in the County of Nottingham; High Steward of East Retford . . .; Comptroller of the Customs in the Port of London; High Steward of Westminster, and President of the Westminster Hospital." Although Pitt had not in fact secured the reversion of the Auditorship for himself, he had secured it for his cousin Lord Grenville.

"The Writ is issued from the Office of the Clerk of the Crown, for a new election for the University of Cambridge, in the room of the Right Honourable WILLIAM PITT, appointed Lord Warden of the Cinque Ports, and who, it is imagined, will be re-elected without opposition," announced the *Star* on 22 August. But, as it turned out, the writ could not be issued until after Parliament convened. Since this meant that the country would have no Prime Minister in Parliament for the first several days, the Ministerial newspapers had some words of caution for the Opposition: "Mr. PITT will necessarily be out of Parliament for the first fortnight of the next Session," said the *Oracle* on 28 August, "—that is to say, he would be out as Member of *Cambridge*. But as he knows that OPPOSITION is ever ready to snatch at any little advantage, if any thing should concur of such peculiar delicacy or difficulty, as may require his presence in the House, he may in the interval between this and the meeting of Parliament, be elected for some other place, though he cannot immediately, be *re-elected for Cambridge*." Although Parliament was still scheduled to convene on 30 August, the prorogation was subsequently extended to 15 November.

A great deal had meanwhile been happening on the Continent. Goaded to fury by the Duke of Brunswick's Manifesto, the French had taken another violent step to the left. On 10 August the Tuileries had been stormed, the Swiss Guard murdered, the monarchy suspended, and the Royal Family confined under guard in The Temple. Lafayette had deserted his army and fled, to be captured and imprisoned by the Austrians. On 19 August the Revolutionary Tribunal had been established, and on 26 August the National Assembly had issued its decree against priests. More violence succeeded. On 2 September the French reacted to news of the Austro-Prussian successes with fresh riots, which spread from Paris into the provinces and resulted in the massacre of almost a thousand Royalists and priests; and on 21 September the monarchy was permanently abolished and France declared a republic. On 17 August the British Cabinet had met to discuss the events of 10 August and had resolved to recall Earl Gower, British ambassador to the Court of Paris since 1790, along with other members of the British Embassy. Gower had been instructed to say that the recall was motivated only by the King's concern "for the personal situation of their most christian majesties and their royal family" and was not to be interpreted as an act of belligerence, Britain still regarding herself as neutral. M. Chauvelin, French ambassador to the Court of St. James, was permitted to remain, so far as he knew, in his former capacity. To the astonishment of all newspapers, Ministerial as well as Opposition, the Government seemed otherwise unconcerned. The King went to Weymouth to remain through September, and Pitt visited his castles.

On 27 August, according to the *Star* (28 Aug.), "Mr. PITT, accompanied by Mr. Secretary DUNDAS, set off for Dover, for the form of taking possession of the Castle at that place, as being an appendix to the Wardenship of the Cinque Ports." On 31 August, again according to the *Star* (1 Sept.), Pitt "set off from his house in Downing-street for Mr. CASWALL's, Herts; from thence he will go to Deal-Castle, where he will reside about three weeks": "It is a pleasant prerequisite in his new office that it will give him half a dozen country houses, all on the sea coast." Timothy Caswall, occasionally mentioned by the papers as one of Pitt's drinking companions, was Commissioner of Excise from 1790 to his death in 1802. The *Oracle* had meanwhile been assuring its readers (e.g., 30 Aug.) that there would be no change of staff, "Mr. PITT having been induced" by his "liberality" to "[continue] under him as Warden of the Cinque Ports, all the friends, relatives, and *Eleves* of the late Earl of GUILFORD—all persons whom he knows to be his most inveterate enemies." This assurance was repeated by the *Diary* of 21 September with one qualification:

> Mr. Pitt sets off for Walmer Castle this day to take possession of his appointment as Warden of the Cinque Ports, &c. A party of friends go with him. His stay there will be about three weeks, in order to hold the different Courts, and swear in the officers under him. The Minister in this excursion puts on a General's uniform, as Constable of Dover Castle, we presume; and his servants wear military cockades.
>
> New Warrants are prepared, sealed with the Minister's family arms, for continuing in their several departments all the old Officers under the Lord Warden, the Secretary alone excepted, who is superseded by the appointment of Joseph Smith, Esq. the confidential secretary of Mr. Pitt, in his capacity of Prime Minister.

But this exception was followed by so many others that, by the end of the year, the newspapers could not think of a single "old Officer" who was still in place.

On 27 September the Duke of Portland was elected to the lifetime post of Chancellor of Oxford "without opposition." He was installed on 10 October in a very colorful ceremony. The *World* had cautioned throughout (e.g., 12 Sept.) that any "rumours . . . concerning the Duke of PORTLAND taking part in the Ministry are of *Blue* and *Buff* fabrication," and there was certainly no evidence to the contrary. The *Oracle* could not understand it. Behind all this, it told its readers on 24 October, was Edmund Burke, who, contrary to Pitt's wishes and in contempt of the Government's obligations to Lord Beaufort, had written a letter to the University, recommending the Duke of Portland "with much eloquence."

Will Pitt Resign?

The question of whether Pitt would or would not resign preoccupied the newspapers for many weeks. During September the consensus was that he would, and there was certainly an abundance of evidence to support it. He had now provided nicely for himself and his relatives; and, having failed to convert even the Duke of Portland, let alone Fox, he had indicated by the further prorogation of Parliament an inability to deal with the Friends of the People and Grey's scheduled motion for election reforms. Also he seemed completely indifferent, not only to affairs on the Continent, but to affairs at home. The *Oracle*, always fearful for Mackintosh, although his authorship of the *Letter to . . . Pitt* was still secret, took care to say on 16 August that he was "at *Boulogne*," not in Paris, and that he was not "vindicating the present MOBOCRACY of France." On 5 September it assured its readers that he had returned and was spending the month quietly at Margrave: he had categorically "rejected the proposal of being elected as a Member of the *French* NATIONAL CONVENTION," it added on 25 September. But Pitt evidently did not care what Mackintosh was doing; nor did he seem interested in the activities of Frost and Paine. Although no writings are presently attributed to him, "FROST, the Attorney," was furiously assailed by the *World* of 11 August for "blowing up the *Coals* of Sedition among his Fellow Citizens, by the publication of the most absurd and ill-written jumble of incoherences we have ever seen"; and on 14 September the *Diary* discovered that Paine had absconded. He had "fled" to the Continent four days earlier in order to avoid trial, said the *Diary*, and had taken with him "a large party of English." But on 22 September the *Public Advertiser* published a letter from Paine to Dundas, dated 15 September, in which Paine said that he had not left London until 13 September and that he had not "fled," but had simply been informed of his election to the National Convention and had gone to Paris to take his seat. The *Public Advertiser* still thought he had "fled," for his papers, which had been seized by the Customs House officers at Dover, were found to contain, it said, a notice of his trial. The *World* also thought he had "fled," although not on account of the trial, the date of which, it admitted, had not yet been fixed, but, as it had discovered by 23 October, on account of "various debts." All newspapers were at least agreed that Frost had gone with him and that Frost was also under indictment, but this information turned out to be equally mistaken: Frost had gone with him, but he was not under indictment. The Government said nothing, having evidently forgotten the reformers completely. In the case of John Almon, this forgetfulness was no boon. Having been imprisoned for over five months without even the courtesy of a sentence, he had finally persuaded William Woodfall to publish some excerpts from his *Anecdotes of the Life of the ... Earl of Chatham*, and excerpts had accordingly appeared in the *Diary* of 17 August, 27 August, and 10 September. The author was identified only as "one of the best informed men of the period," for Almon was reluctant to acknowledge his connection with the work until he collected the £900 owed him by the Opposition, and Pitt already knew that Almon had written it. Although the excerpts were complimentary to Pitt's father, they had no effect on Pitt.

More important, the Government seemed to have lost interest in the press. To most journalists of the day, the highhanded manner in which Pitt had appropriated the Wardenship of the Cinque Ports was even more shocking than the appropriation itself, since on all previous occasions Pitt had justified his actions in newspapers and pamphlets well in advance. Yet, in the case of the Cinque Ports and even the Chancellorship of Oxford, there was no preparation; nor was there any subsequent extenuation. The Ministerial newspapers were taken as much by surprise as the Opposition press, and, although most of them responded with apologies, the apologies lacked the impassioned quality of

Treasury propaganda. Throughout August and September the Ministerial papers did not in fact know what to say about anything. They did not know what the Government intended to do or even what it had done, and they did not know what position to take with respect to the little information they had. The Treasury writers seemed to be in a similar predicament. On 24 September William Augustus Miles informed Charles Long of the Treasury[41] that, although he doubted that "the fact . . . could be proved in Westminster Hall, and the purpose for which the money is paid," he had had "several hints . . . from Frenchmen in constant relation and intimacy with M. de Chauvelin and his family, that the editors of the 'Morning Chronicle' and of the 'Argus' have received considerable sums of money, and that they have each of them a large monthly allowance" from the French government. Miles himself had thought that the "hints" were worth some publicity and had therefore sent the story to several newspapers. *The Times* printed it on 24 September, withholding the names of the newspapers. On 25 September the *Morning Chronicle* demanded that the newspapers be identified: "A morning paper says, that there are two daily Journals of London actually bribed by the Jacobins of France, to spread sedition in England—and that one of them, in particular, has 10,000 livres per month for its treason. It would have been a faithful service to their country to have named the particular Journals, so infamously corrupted by foreign gold . . . that the Crown officers may bring the abandoned writers to legal punishment." *The Times* was silent, having apparently been advised by Long to forget the matter.

In only two possible instances did the Government concern itself with the newspapers, and both instances may belong to an earlier period. In the first case, it acted to protect Rose. In late May the Court of Chancery, still busy with Este's suit for collection of his £400 "pension," had ordered Topham to submit a complete account "within liberties or without" of the financial affairs of the *World*. Since this account was certain to embarrass a great number of people, the *Diary* had predicted on 1 June that the next hearing would make "more noise" than anything which had happened in the last twenty years. The most embarrassed man would, however, have been George Rose, whose reputation could ill afford another scandal. Hence, when the case again came up for consideration, as it did in August, the order was considerably modified. Este protested, but to no avail. In the second case, the Government acted to protect John Walter of *The Times*. In December, 1790, Walter had been sued for libel by John King of the *Argus*, and on 23 February, 1791, he had been tried and convicted. He had not been sentenced, and, when King protested, the Government moved against him instead. So at least said King; the newspapers did not interest themselves in his affairs until sometime later.

The story of King's persecution was later (London, 1798) detailed in three pamphlets: the first, written by King himself, being entitled *Mr. King's Apology: or Reply to His Calumniators*, the second, obviously written by Peter Stuart, although published anonymously, being entitled *The Real Calumniator Detected*; *Being Candid Remarks on Mr. King's Apology: or Reply to His Calumniators*, and the third, again written by King, being entitled *Oppression Deemed No Injustice toward Some Individuals. Illustrated in the Late Treatment of Mr. John King, under a Commission for Bankruptcy*. Although the first of these pamphlets is extremely rare, the gist of it with copious quotations is indicated in the second; and, even though the second and third cover a period of seven years in no distinguishable chronological sequence and are at times so garbled as to be incoherent, certain passages come into focus. Parts of the picture are also later supplied by the newspapers.

The original reason for the persecution, King charged, was that he had had the "audacity" to sue *The Times* and, having won a conviction from the jury, the further "audacity" to petition the Court for "judgment." Stuart, who was speaking for the Government, admitted the truth of this charge, but charged in return[42] that the jury did not know the facts, King having paid for the insertion of the paragraph on which the suit was based. The first part of the passage which follows refers to an incident which occurred in 1787, when Stuart was himself sued as printer of the *Morning Post* by a Mr. W. J'Anson.[43]

> The pages so carefully distinguished against the Times, bring to my mind, the case of a printer, who had rendered himself obnoxious to a numerous gang of *Swindlers*. An able, and an artful libel was written against them by Anonymous, and inserted in his paper—a prosecution was commenced, and he was convicted. After he had suffered punishment, the parties quarrelled, and the printer learnt, to his surprise and astonishment, that the gang of prosecutors had held a midnight council, formed a committee, actually designed, and carefully penned, the identical libel, for which they prosecuted the printer. If it were a general rule of courts of judicature never to dispense with the affidavits of the parties, the "stings of conscience," which are held by some as "very momentous," would preclude many a nefarious transaction from insulting the courts—There is at present nothing on record, upon the *oath* of Mr. King, that he never *saw*, or *heard*, of that paragraph, for which he prosecuted the TIMES, *previous* to its publication—When I see that, I shall know what to think, respecting that which I have learnt on the subject.

As to the nature of the "persecutions," Stuart was "surprized"[44] to hear "that about the year '92, 'a gang of marauders should *find out* Mr. King, and torment him for thirteen months.' .../ If these Marauders demanded money of Mr. King, it was, certainly, a very *audacious* offence; although, Mr. King *might* owe it them." He was nevertheless sure that King's own "offence . . . was worth at least, thirteen months torment, especially since "there was no law in existence that could [adequately] punish it." The "offence" to which Stuart was referring and the only "persecution" of which he was aware commenced, it appeared,[45] when two prostitutes visited the Bow Street Station to bring a "charge of a most scandalous sort" against King, "in which the *only weapon* 'charged in the indictment, was *whip-cord* and *wire, affectionately interwoven*, producing not' collision with the 'leper,' but only the 'pollution' which followed the 'contact' of the whip-cord and wire, with the *glowing* cushions of the two women before mentioned." Twelve hours later the prostitutes visited the Marlborough Street Station, where they "recanted" every word of the charge. But "Mr. [Nicholas] Bond in his official capacity as Sitting Magistrate" at the Bow Street Station tried the case nevertheless, and "numerous and respectable witnesses" appeared to testify to King's guilt, the prostitutes not being among them. King was convicted and fined £3,000. On the ground that the action had been contrived, King thereupon appealed to the Court of King's Bench, but to no avail. This "subsequent proceeding," said Stuart, "solemn and judicial, of men, in every shape, highly respectable—of men of fortune and character, . . . determined that Mr. Bond's proceedings on this occasion were RIGHT—*The Grand Jury of the City of Westminster found a True Bill for the Assault*:—a circumstance that stamps *legality* on the proceedings of Mr. Bond, proves them to be both *just* and *proper*." It seemed to King[46] that, had he submitted to this decision, the Government would have ceased its harassments, but he published a protest in a newspaper, obviously the *Argus*, with the result that, instead of £3,000, the verdict finally cost him £15,000. "The earnings of a whole life blow from me at a breath." The two trials and the protest probably belong to the late summer and autumn of 1792, and the "marauders" who "[tormented] him for thirteen months" thereafter were his clients, incited to such action by the Ministerial newspapers, especially, one supposes, by *The Times*.

The indications that Pitt would not resign were, so far as the newspapers knew, negligible and for that matter presumptive, since all of them related to Dundas rather than Pitt. On 1 August the *Diary* announced that "His Majesty has, in pursuance of the Act of Parliament, for the institution of a New Police for Westminster [the Middlesex Justices Act], caused to be established seven several Public Offices, and at each of them hath appointed three fit and able persons, being Justices of the Peace for the County of Middlesex and the County of Surrey respectively, to execute the Office of a Justice of the Peace in the said Offices, together with such other Offices for the said Counties . . . as may [seem] proper. . . ." But, since the creation of this "New Police" had been authorized in May, this was hardly a significant development. The changes in Dundas's staff seemed similarly insignificant. On 25 May the *World* had mentioned that Evan Nepean had resigned as Under Secretary for the Home Department and had gone to Jamaica, where on 5 May he had been sworn into office as Clerk of the Supreme Council, his successor in the Home Department being John (not "Jew") King. But on 8 August the *Oracle* reported that he was back. It now appeared that he had gone to Jamaica only "for reasons of health," that he had never intended to stay there, that he had not resigned, and that King had served on a pro tempore basis. So well had he served, however, that Bernard Scrope, the second Under Secretary, was resigning in his favor. Dundas was certainly, the *Oracle* added on 14 August, a model of "diligent application and deep penetration."

The *Oracle*'s enthusiasm about Dundas was probably owing to some negotiations between him and Peter Stuart's brother, Charles. Dundas finally referred the matter to Nepean, who seems to have acted as his paymaster throughout, with the result that Charles was promised an annual salary of £200, plus whatever "sums I might lay out for publishing, &c.,"[47] in return evidently for reporting any conversations he happened to overhear, defending the Government in street brawls, writing for newspapers, and turning out occasional pamphlets. Since Charles later mentioned[48] that his "quarter" ended on 9 December and since he was in the pay of the Home Department at least four days earlier, he probably commenced his labors on 9 September. In August Dundas also employed a Robert Watt to spy for the Government in Edinburgh. But of these activities the newspapers as yet knew nothing, and they would probably have regarded them lightly anyway, for the fiasco of John Taylor had revived the fiction that Dundas was a blundering fool, to be treated with banter rather than censure. Why, the *Morning Chronicle* asked its readers, would Dundas have paid Taylor to incite the Edinburgh riots unless he was at heart a reformer and meant to introduce a bill for major Scotch reforms as soon as Parliament convened? And how could the Scots be so ungrateful as to keep on burning his effigies? Such teasing continued throughout the summer and fall and even into November.

Now that his resignation was so evidently assured, criticism of Pitt was rampant, and, by the end of September, he was being assailed by a sixth newspaper, the *Courier*. The *Courier*, which joined the *Star* on 22 September as the second afternoon daily, was owned by a newcomer, John Parry, and, according to the colophon, it was printed by R. Harris at No. 38, Charing Cross. Although, according to C. H. Timperley,[49] the "printer of the *Courier* London newspaper [from] its commencement in 1792" until his death in December, 1819, was one Bryan M'Swyny, M'Swyny's name was not mentioned. The editor was the Rev. Charles Este, and among the personnel was Thomas George Street, heretofore known only as author of the pamphlet, *Aura; or, The Slave, a Poem* (London, 1788). Jerdan remembered Street[50] as a generous, gay companion and a "spirited" journalist, "with Shakespeare and Burke ever ready at his finger ends for quotation"; but there was little "spirit" in the newspaper at this point, for, since Este's forte was blackmail, its principal interests were scandal and politics. The *Anti-Jacobin Review*, which was not noted for accuracy, said later[51] that the *Courier* was thought to have been originally supported by Beaumarchais. Whether it was supported by Beaumarchais or Parry, it seemed to have no financial problems, for in early October Este told Robert Adair[52] that it was still politically uncommitted and offered to swing it to the side of Fox in return for Adair's verbal assurance that he would get a living when Fox came into office. For the newspaper he asked nothing. Adair communicated the offer to William

Adam, whose reply is not recorded, but Adam would hardly have refused. Since the *Courier* had always been hostile to Pitt, the only question was whether the paper would support Fox or Sheridan. Este evidently felt that Pitt's successor was more likely to be Fox; the *Oracle* was determined it would be Sheridan.

Throughout August the *Oracle* had been the usual mishmash: enthusiastic about Dundas, but equally enthusiastic about Sheridan and Lord Lauderdale. On 30 August it reported trouble with deliveries: "Complaints have been made against many of the Country Post-Masters, to the General Post-Office, in consequence of the irregular delivery and suppression of many of the London Newspapers. This matter has been taken up as it ought, and several dismissals will of course be the consequence." On 31 August it announced that the "Postmaster General [Lord Walsingham] has dispatched Messengers into Hampshire and Cambridgeshire, to discover, if possible, those worthy politicians who intercept the London Papers. If they can be detected, a dismissal from office, and a prosecution on behalf of the parties defrauded will instantly ensure." While this investigation was supposedly in progress, the *Oracle* turned to nonpolitical matters, such as (30 Aug.) the origin of the term "BEEF-EATERS.—When Yeomen of the Guards were first instituted to wait upon their MAJESTY, their station during all Entertainments was at the *Buffet*, from whence they were called *Buffetieres*. By an easy corruption of the vulgar, this name has been changed into *Beef-eaters*." Linguistic titbits of this kind simply fascinated Peter Stuart. By September the paper was pronouncing "Young [Thomas] SHERIDAN . . . one of the most intelligent youths in this or any other Country" and his father an out-and-out genius. It also had some kind words for Pitt, and as usual it adulated the Prince of Wales.

On 24 September, however, the *Oracle* underwent a transformation. Buchanan Millan was replaced as printer by James Bell, one of the original members of the Friends of the People and later a very active member of the Friends of the Liberty of the Press, the subtitle was dropped, the format much improved, and there were no further eulogies of Dundas and Pitt. Its idols were now the Prince of Wales, Lord Thurlow, Sheridan, and especially Lord Lauderdale, whose praises were sung in almost every number. Lord Lauderdale, said the *Oracle* again and again, was a "true friend to his country" and a steady "enemy" to everything represented by Pitt, as he was to everything represented by Paine. Lord Lauderdale was obviously financing the newspaper at this point, but he could not have known what the newspaper was doing, since he was still on the Continent. Although on 26 September the *Oracle* stated that he and Dr. Moore were returning, being even then in Calais en route, it noted on 11 October that they had changed their minds and had gone to Germany instead. Lord Lauderdale must have supposed that the *Oracle* was supporting the Friends of the People in preparation for the convening of Parliament, and to some extent it was. But its principal concern was the resignation of Pitt. What it had in mind was to restore Lord Thurlow to the Chancellorship and install Sheridan as Prime Minister. Since the other members of this proposed government were not stipulated, the choices were evidently to be made by the King. Sheridan, who was of course behind this maneuver, was counting heavily on the King's love for Lord Thurlow and his detestation of Fox to catapult himself into office. On 1 October there was another development.

There had always been an argument between Mr. Rose's "Gazette," the *World*, and Mr. Long's "Gazette," *The Times*, as to which of them was favored by the Government, and the blackout of news during August and September only made it more heated. On 8 September the *World* had, for example, observed with evident disgust that *The Times* "had recourse yesterday to its old expedient of circulating hand-bills as to the priority of French intelligence. The trick is too stale and notorious—it serves, however, to give publicity to *decline* and *dullness*." On 1 October both newspapers became subservient to the *Sun*. According to Heriot,[53] the *Sun* was commenced at the "repeated" suggestion of Burke, who, persuaded by Rose that the Treasury could not "direct" the newspapers already in its pay and exasperated with the treatment he was receiving from them, felt that the Government should have a newspaper of its own. Like the *Star* and the *Courier*, the *Sun* was an afternoon daily. It was printed by the *Oracle*'s ex-printer, Buchanan Millan, at No. 112, Strand, and it was edited by the *World*'s ex-drama critic, John Heriot. Since the proprietors went to some lengths to conceal their identity, even those people connected with the newspaper had to rely upon guesses. Miles, who was a frequent contributor, thought for example[54] that the proprietors were George Rose of the Treasury and Francis Freeling of the Post Office. William Jerdan, one of the later editors, thought[55] that the paper "had been established through the agency of George Rose, Charles Long, and other friends of Pitt." The *Morning Chronicle* sometimes thought that the paper was owned by Rose and James Bland Burges, Under Secretary of State for Foreign Affairs, sometimes by Long and Burges; and William Walter of *The Times* thought[56] that Rose and George Aust, another Under Secretary for Foreign Affairs, were at least interested. According to Daniel Stuart,[57] the *Sun* was "confidently said" to be the property of Long and Burges, except for one share, which was given to Heriot. A letter from Burges to Long[58] does seem at least to confirm their involvement, and, since it is likely that Heriot would have been offered a partnership, Stuart's understanding of the situation is probably correct. The money for the enterprise certainly came from the Treasury.

As editor of the *Sun* and its adjunct, begun three months later, the *True Briton*, Heriot received, said Daniel Stuart,[59] £600 a year; he also received allowances from the Treasury for printing pamphlets and writing "advertisements" for other newspapers. The material for the *Sun* was provided by Miles and other Treasury hirelings and by every member of Government who had a flair for journalism. In particular it was provided by Rose and Burges. So much of it was of their manufacture that anything which appeared was attributed to one or the other of them. The *Sun* immediately replaced *The Times* as the most detested paper in Britain. Because of Heriot's quarrel with Bell, the paper was resented by the *Oracle*; since Heriot had left Topham's employ without notice, it was resented by the *World*; and John Walter of *The Times* could not forget that it was Heriot's paragraphs which had sent him to prison for libel. But all the Ministerial newspapers were indignant, for whatever favors they had previously enjoyed were now lavished exclusively on the *Sun*. Although, as an afternoon daily, the *Sun* was strictly speaking in competition only with the *Star* and the *Courier*, both of them Opposition newspapers, it had announced in its first number that it would henceforth speak for the Government, that it would have "priority" of all "intelligence," and that every other Ministerial newspaper would be expected to copy. This was not idle talk. Not only was all news dispatched to No. 112, Strand, before it was released to other Treasury papers, but, if the news was of consequence, the Government bought up the edition for free distribution, with the result, said Heriot,[60] that the *Sun* "soon obtained an extensive, and, at that time, unparalleled circulation." To aggravate the offense, the *Sun* presented its information (and misinformation) belligerently, and most of the belligerence seemed to be directed at papers themselves in the pay of the Treasury. There were other reasons for alarm, one of them ethical, for, although the subsidizing or even leasing of papers for political purposes was considered right and proper, actual ownership of shares by members of a political faction was regarded as a violation of British freedom. But the ultimate outrage, so far as journalists were concerned, was the *Sun*'s "dullness." Abuse they could forgive, abuse being the prerogative of a newspaper, but abuse without "point" they could not. The *Sun* was a disgrace to the profession; or, in Dr. Wolcot's words, remembered by Redding many years later,[61] the *Sun* "was a Sun without a ray of light."

Because the *Sun* was brought out in the afternoon, it seems in retrospect to have been an experiment in concentration. If the experiment failed, the Government would still have its seven morning dailies; if it succeeded, it would not need them. But at the time no newspaper knew what was going on, and readers knew only that they were getting some news again, even though most of it was fiction.

Pitt Will Not Resign Willingly

Although the *Sun* was evidence enough that Pitt would stay in office if possible, the paper got off to an ignominious start. On 20 September the French had defeated the Prussians at Valmy. This defeat, which shifted the tide of events on the Continent, had not been reported by the newspapers prior to 1 October; nor was it reported by the *Sun* after that date. When the *Sun* burst on the horizon, readers were being regaled with accounts of Allied successes, and the *Sun* went on to proclaim the rout of the entire French army, backing the proclamation with a series of essays on the political state of Europe, signed "Alfred," "Alfred" being James Bland Burges. By 5 October the *Morning Chronicle* and the *Star*, which had recently combined their news-gathering facilities,[62] were skeptical, as so were the *Courier*, the *Diary*, and the *Morning Herald*. But skepticism, it appeared, would not be tolerated, for, whether it was rooted in "sophistry" or "Jacobinism," the *Sun* was bound to regard it as a libel on that government which had issued the reports. On 8 October the *Morning Chronicle* announced in somber terms that the skepticism had been justified:

> This day the public will have a convincing proof of the respect due to the Papers under the direction of Office. Our rivals must this day, with what grace we know not, submit to the task of retracting the assurance to which they have so vehemently pledged themselves; for yesterday Ministers received advices from Lord ELGIN [British envoy at Brussels], by which they learn, that his youth and inexperience had drawn him into the belief of Breteuil's fictions; and that he now finds the armies of the Combined Powers, enfeebled by famine and disease, after trying in vain to intimidate France by [the Duke of Brunswick's] manifesto, had been obliged to retreat to Verdun.

Breteuil was an ardent Royalist and a close friend of Marie Antoinette.

But there was no retraction in the *Sun* of 8 October, and on 9 October the *Star* also spoke out on the subject. Unlike the *Morning Chronicle*, which understood that the Government had itself been misled, the *Star* was convinced that the only dupe was the *Sun*, the Government having been aware of the situation all along. As yet no newspaper suspected that the *Sun* was actually owned by members of Government:

> ### THE THREAT.
> "We will set a mark on those audacious individuals, whether natives or foreigners, who dare to affront this generous nation by *imagining there are any in it sufficiently ignorant to be misled by their sophistry.*"
> So says a print which has only had an existence of six days, in every one of which, (as if it had credit to lose) it has pledged itself for the truth of General DUMOURIER's army having been defeated.—Its conductors have chalked out some work for themselves; for nine of every ten who have seen their rodomontade, not only *imagine*, but regardless of the mighty *threat*, even venture to *say*, that that paper itself has been *sufficiently ignorant to be misled*.
> They should throw out their future threats, not against those who *imagine them ignorant enough to be misled*, but *against those who have imposed upon their ignorance and credulity*—but this, we believe, they *dare not do*.
> The same paper makes a Correspondent ["Alfred"] *praise* it for DISCLAIMING NEUTRALITY, *in Politics*, and at the same time undertakes to *give a view of the*

present Political State of Europe, in which he will claim the favour of the public, by the *authenticity of his statements*, and the IMPARTIALITY *of his deductions—* How very consistent!

The retraction did appear on 9 October and was appropriately noticed by the *Star* of the following day:

THE CONFESSION.

The Public are not ignorant with what confidence some of our contemporaries denied the truth of the intelligence which we gave respecting the retreat of the Duke of BRUNSWICK's army. They will not be a little surprised when they hear those who had boasted of their ability to inform others, now confessing, that, notwithstanding of their confident assertions, they were, *at the time they made them, and even now are, "entirely ignorant"* and *"destitute of information"* respecting the events on which they *pledged their credit.*

That we may not, however, be accused of misrepresenting them, we shall give their confession in their own words:

. . . . "We are undoubtedly in a *state of* COMPLETE IGNORANCE. The whole period from the 28th of September [they should have said the 20th] to the 2d of October, *is at this moment a* BLANK *to us.* We have indeed been told, that, on the 30th of September, the Prussian army retired; but of the transactions of the two preceeding days . . . we are ENTIRELY IGNORANT. *Nor are we informed* with more precision of the events of the two following days: *still less* do we know what has happened since. . . . LABOURING UNDER THIS IGNORANCE OF EVERY THING *which can lead us to form a just opinion* on this important subject, we feel within us a repugnance," &c.

We shall not plague our Readers with a longer extract—the above is quite sufficient.

It was now three weeks since the Duke of Brunswick's defeat at Valmy.

There was still no overt activity. Pitt continued to visit his castles, Dundas was seemingly resting, and on 8 October the *Star* reported that Evan Nepean was on his way to Lisbon and would proceed to Spain, purportedly for purposes of relaxation. By 19 October it was understood that Parliament would again be prorogued, this time to 3 January, the reason being, said the *Sun*, that there was nothing to discuss. Even the *Public Advertiser* found this explanation ridiculous: the whole "state of foreign and domestic affairs" demanded "early action," it told its readers. The *Morning Chronicle* found it similarly ridiculous. The actual reason, in its opinion, was that Pitt was afraid of the popular reaction to Grey's motion for reform. This was evidently the case, for Fox was again being wooed by the Ministerial newspapers, every one of which was intent on a Fox-Pitt coalition. According to the *Sun*, Pitt was now willing to step down as Prime Minister, turning the office of First Lord of the Treasury over to the Duke of Portland and retaining only the office of Chancellor of the Exchequer. Fox would be Principal Secretary of State. All the Treasury newspapers entreated Fox to accept this "arrangement" for the sake of the country. As the *Public Advertiser* put it on 25 October: "Mr. Fox has been once termed the 'Man of the People'—that honourable title has long been disputed with him, and, we think, successfully: The times however are favourable to him, and by detaching himself from his *desperately situated*, and, of course, *seditiously inclined* partisans [the Friends of the People], he may again be hailed as 'the Man of the People,' and truly serve them by aiding Government in the maintenance of that constitution of which he has repeatedly professed himself, and we are inclined to hope truly, a zealous admirer." Two days later the *Public Advertiser* reported that the matter was settled: Fox would "recant . . . at the first convenient moment."

Pitt could also expect trouble in another area, for, once Parliament convened, he faced an election at Cambridge University. Since all the electors were staunch supporters of Church and King, there was no question as to the outcome, but it seemed even to some of the Ministerial papers that it would be wise for him to "stand" *in absentia*. Not only would there be the usual riots against him in the town, but there would probably be some demonstrations against him at the University. Religious radicalism among the student body was an old tradition at Cambridge.[63] Although it dated back to the early years of the century, Unitarianism had had nothing to show for its struggle there except a list of martyrs until 1772, when it had succeeded in limiting the rule that *all* candidates for degrees must subscribe to the Thirty-Nine Articles to candidates for advance degrees only, candidates for the A.B. being required merely to declare their membership in the Church. Heartened by this victory, the Unitarians had set out to attain their ultimate goal: the abolition of the subscription and the declaration altogether. The cause had enlisted some able leaders, dedicated to it and willing to sacrifice their careers to further it. One of them was Gilbert Wakefield of Jesus College, who took his A.B. in 1776, but refused to take his M.A. because of the subscription. Another was Robert Tyrwhitt, who resigned his fellowship in 1777 "for religious reasons." There were also Benjamin Flower, George Dyer, and William Frend. Of this group, the principal in late 1792 was Frend, a fellow of Jesus College. Upon his conversation to Unitarianism in 1787, he had relinquished his living, and in 1788 the University had canceled his tutorship; but he was still clinging to his fellowship and was extremely active in radical circles, where he was a glib talker and an ingenious arguer. Dyer was currently in London, writing for the newspapers. His first signed contribution appeared in the *Diary* of 13 October, 1792, and on 12 November the *Morning Chronicle* published his "Song for the French Revolution." He had also brought out (1792) a volume of verses, entitled *Poems, Consisting of Odes and Elegies*, and an enlarged edition of his *Inquiry into the Nature of Subscription to the Thirty-Nine Articles*, which had first appeared in 1789.

Cambridge radicalism was always fundamentally religious, and it might have remained entirely religious, had it not been for the political riots against its patron saint, Dr. Joseph Priestley, which had occurred in Birmingham in July,

1791. The Government's subsequent reluctance to prosecute the rioters had alarmed the Unitarians further, and after some deliberation the Unitarian Society had submitted a petition of protest, on the basis of which Fox had on 11 May, 1792, moved for the repeal of certain statutes discriminating against the dissenters. The motion had been strongly opposed by the Government, but the telling opposition came from Burke, who had denounced all Unitarians as *ipso facto* Jacobins. Although Burke had denounced them on the same terms in his *Reflections*, this time his words had more effect. His effigy was burned by Cambridge students, his works were publicly condemned, and he became overnight the antichrist of Cambridge Unitarianism. Pitt was almost as unpopular as Burke on this account, and Fox was of course a hero.

Students were also indignant about the treatment of the classicist, Richard Porson. Another radical, albeit active in different circles from Frend, Porson had held the Craven scholarship since 1781, had been a fellow since 1782, and had taken his M.A. in 1785. Here he had faced a problem, for the statutes of his college (Trinity) required that he take orders within seven years of receiving the M.A. or forfeit the fellowship, and, after much soul-searching, he had concluded that he could not conscientiously take orders. Had he done his soul-searching privately, the University might have felt different about him, but it was all presented to the public in a series of vituperative articles in the *Gentleman's Magazine* (1788–1789), signed "Cantabrigiensis," and in a book (1790), entitled *Letters to Mr. Archdeacon [George] Travis, in Answer to His Defence of the Three Heavenly Witnesses. 1. John, v. 7.* Since the University greatly disliked this kind of publicity, it had been more than eager to see the end of Porson. Porson also seemed willing to leave. The fellowship had expired in July, 1792, and, in anticipation of this event, he had removed himself to London early in the summer to take up residence at the Temple. But, having arrived, he had discovered that a lay fellowship, which did not necessitate his taking orders, had become vacant; and, since Dr. Thomas Postlethwaite, Master of Trinity College, had once promised it to him, he immediately called himself to Dr. Postlethwaite's attention. Dr. Postlethwaite had curtly advised him to take orders. Prior to this time, Porson's case had attracted no attention, but it now appeared that he had a champion in the *Morning Chronicle*, as well as a multitude of friends and admirers both in London and Cambridge. In a short time, £2,000 had been subscribed to provide him with a lifetime annuity of £100, in lieu of the £75 he had realized from the fellowship, and all readers of the *Morning Chronicle* were aware of the injustice. Under all these circumstances, Cambridge did not seem to be the place for William Pitt.

But, while the Ministerial newspapers were saying that there was no need for him to visit Cambridge, Pitt was himself making other plans. Porson's case, it appeared, was being reconsidered. The first fruit of the reconsideration was "a dividend" awarded to Porson for the year 1792–1793; the second was the Regius Professorship of Greek. The salary of the Regius Professor was £40 a year, and, since no Regius Professor had lectured at the University or even necessarily lived in the vicinity for over a century,[64] the position was an out-and-out sinecure. In 1780 it had been given to William Cooke, Jr., once a fellow of King's College and since 1785 Rector of Hempstead-with-Lessingham, Norfolk. Although Cooke had subsequently published an edition of Aristotle's *Poetics* (1785), *A Dissertation on the Revelation of St. John* (1789), and a number of sermons, he probably held the sinecure through the influence of his father, who had been Provost of King's College, Cambridge, since 1772, was Vice Chancellor of the University in 1773, and had been Dean of Ely since 1780. In any event, Cooke was somehow persuaded to relinquish it, and in late September Dr. Postlethwaite informed Porson that the place had been "unexpectedly" vacated, and, since it did not require subscription to the Thirty-Nine Articles, he strongly urged Porson to offer himself as candidate. On 6 October Porson accepted; but he accepted only on the condition that he could restore the sinecure to a professorship, return to Cambridge, and actually lecture.[65] The condition was enthusiastically agreed to.

By mid-October every reader of a Ministerial newspaper knew that Porson was joining the faculty of Cambridge, and, a few days later, he left London to resume his residence at the university. "Mr. Porson, the well-known scholar and writer, is gone to Cambridge, to be elected Greek professor there," the *Diary* announced on 20 October. "Some time since he lost his fellowship of Trinity, which could not be held after a certain term by a layman; now the University are giving him part of the recompence so much his due." On 24 October the *World* observed: "Yesterday Mr. PORSON was to be chosen Greek Professor at Cambridge. Is it Dr. *Young*, who says of singular merit, 'It makes a place stand candidate for him?'" Although the election was actually not held for another week, no newspaper questioned the outcome except the *Oracle*, which protested on 27 October: "A Morning Print [the *World*] is always announcing the intended appointment of Mr. PORSON to the Greek Professorship of Cambridge. As a profound Scholar, and a Gentleman of uncommon genius, Mr. PORSON may be unrivalled; but we have every reason to think, that there are insurmountable objections to the arrangement.—*Verbum sat.*/ Mr. PORSON has the strongest claim to the honourable pre-eminence; but the learned are not always liberal. There are certain peevish PROFESSORS who cannot forget old sores." The *Oracle* had greatly underestimated the influence of Mr. Pitt. Porson was unanimously elected on 1 November, and on 5 November the *Diary* reported that he had "begun [the month] in the Greek Professor's chair.... He read a delightful exercise upon Euripides the day before his Election. There was no one hardy enough to oppose him." That "delightful exercise upon Euripides" was the last lecture Porson ever delivered. Although he was never forbidden to lecture, it turned out that the University was cramped for space, and there were simply no rooms available.

Newspaper Reactions
to a Fox-Pitt Coalition

All Ministerial newspapers supported a coalition between Fox and Pitt, the *Sun* leading the pack. Yet the *Sun* was itself so detested that some of them tended to be more enthusiastic about the coalition than about the present government. *The Times* was especially resentful. Although it had been quite content to have no news so long as other newspapers were in the same situation, it was greatly alarmed by the obvious pampering of the *Sun*. On 15 October William Walter complained to Burges,[66] whom he regarded as "an impartial person," that Rose was said to be "patronizing" that newspaper and that there was evidence that the "early accounts of Foreign Transactions" were being provided by Aust. Walter was bitter about Aust, since Aust had once sent these "early accounts" to him. Burges found the complaint amusing. The *Diary* was also upset. William Woodfall had been ill, and the "agents" to whom he had entrusted the paper had such serious misgivings about the founding of the *Sun* and the appropriation of the Cinque Ports that he felt obliged to say on 10 October that there had been no change in the conductor: *"The Printer [it still] his own Editor."* But the usual avowal of confidence in the Administration was lacking, and there was even evidence of a shift toward the Friends of the People and moderate reform.

Of the Opposition papers, the *Courier* and the *Gazetteer* were now saying nothing about either the coalition or the *Sun*, and even the *Star* had been frightened into silence. Its victory over the *Sun* had turned out to be Pyrrhic indeed, for, having admitted that it had deliberately misrepresented the news, the *Sun* had returned to its former practices as if nothing had happened, propagating more misinformation and flailing away at other newspapers, Ministerial and Opposition alike. But on 11 October the *Star* reported that it was having trouble with the newsmen: "We have received many complaints that the Hawkers who vend the STAR in the evening charge sixpence and sometimes a shilling for the Paper. It is necessary to inform the Public, that these people are not our servants—they *buy* the Papers at the Office, and pay for them no more than other Newsmen who sell them at the price printed on the Paper [4*d*.].— We know of no remedy but the Purchasers *refusing to pay more than that price*." More important, since it was circulated largely in the country, the *Star* was having trouble with the Post Office, which was refusing to release the papers in the outlying towns. By 20 October these problems had evidently been solved, but by this time the *Star* had also withdrawn from the political arena and was engrossed in a battle as to who was legally entitled to compound and vend "Dr.

Waite's celebrated Worm Medicine in the form of gingerbread nuts." It was still so engrossed in early November.

The *Oracle* and the *Morning Chronicle* were at least agreed that Fox would never ally himself with Pitt, and both of them hoped that Pitt could not survive without him. But here the agreement ended, for the *Oracle* was fighting for the interests of Sheridan, the *Morning Chronicle* for the interests of Fox. The mode of fighting was also at variance, for the *Oracle* pretended that it was not fighting at all: in supporting the Prince of Wales's friends, it was simply supporting the Prince himself, without regard for politics. "Lord THURLOW's Character is too manly and honourable to incur the suspicion of connecting himself with the OPPOSITION," it said indignantly on 26 September. "No inference of that kind should be drawn from his intimacy with Lord RAWDON, whose friendship is coveted by everyone; nor from his attention to the PRINCE of WALES, for whom his Lordship always professed a great degree of attachment." It admired Lord Thurlow and Sheridan only because they were devoted to the Prince and, being gentlemen of excellent character, were bound to have an excellent influence. The *Oracle* was even convinced that the two would be able to cleanse the prodigal of his numerous sins and restore him to the bosom of his father as henceforth a dutiful son. Nothing had been said of the Prince's debts since the beginning of August, when the *Oracle* had vehemently denied that any debts existed. It now appeared that they did exist, for on 24 September the *Oracle* announced the formation of an *ad hoc* committee, apparently self-appointed, to advise the Prince on the subject. The committee consisted of Sheridan, Lord Thurlow, and Lord Rawdon, and, because of his great respect for the trio, the Prince had consented to listen to their advice and even to submit to drastic economies in order to speed payment. The *Oracle*'s announcement was disregarded by all newspapers except the *World*, which asked its readers on 26 September why, if he really meant to economize, was the Prince still paying "Mr. WELTJIE one thousand a year for the Marine Pavillion at Brighton"? And why was he still supporting Mrs. Fitzherbert?

On 16 October the *World* commented acidly: "A Morning Paper, remarkable for its Billingsgate abuse and infamous sedition, has got a *new Head* [i.e., masthead]—that of the Conductor too requires changing, for it is obviously *turn'd*." The comment was unfair, for the *Oracle* had no quarrel with Pitt or Fox, it had no opinion about the coalition, and it was seemingly unconcerned with politics generally. It was even indifferent to foreign affairs, for its only contribution in that field was the following item, which appeared on 20 October:

> ANTOINETTES FAMOUS THREE DROP DIAMOND EAR-RINGS.
> These precious Jewels, of matchless value, now prove honourable to the Commerce of this Country; and probably will remain in the wealthy bosom of *Britain* rather than be sent as a present by Government to the DEY of ALGIERS, as has been erroneously asserted.—Their price is set at *nine thousand Guineas*— a gift too rich for such a purpose—Besides, the fashion of the times requires

them to be re-set; having undergone no change since they first were purchased on the Marriage of their unfortunate late Royal Owner, at the price of *twenty-five thousand Louis d'Ors.*—They passed into this Country through the hands of Mr. [PETER] THELLUSSON [the merchant], and have been six months in the possession of Messrs. RUNDEL and BRIDGE, the purchasers and present owners.

But it should have been clear to everyone that Sheridan was playing another *"Game,"* this time on his own behalf. The immediate object was to reconcile the King and the Prince of Wales. The Prince would then plead Sheridan's cause, the King would appoint Sheridan as Pitt's successor, restoring Lord Thurlow to the Chancellorship, and they in turn would look after the interests of the Prince. Although the success of this plan depended entirely on the Prince, it looked, to begin with, as if he meant to co-operate.

On 12 October even the *Public Advertiser* mentioned that "Lord Thurlow and Mr. Sheridan, it is understood, are frequently in consultation with the Prince of Wales on the subject, as conjecture goes, of bringing forward a proposition for paying his Royal Highness's debts." The *Gazetteer* had heard some details of the "proposition," which it presented with equal evasiveness:

THE PRINCE's DEBTS.
We are desirous of being as delicate as possible upon this subject, and should, therefore, preface the following short statement by saying, that, though we believe it true, it does not come to us from any official authority.
A general account of the PRINCE's debts is intended to be made out for the examination of a Committee of Noblemen and Gentlemen, who will suggest to his ROYAL HIGHNESS by what annual deductions from his income they may be discharged within a certain term. The PRINCE is said to have determined upon retaining for himself a portion rather suitable to the comfort of a private gentleman, than to the dignity of an Heir Apparent, and is more likely to reduce than increase the allotment, which may be proposed for him by his friends.
When the dividends, and the periods of payment have been ascertained, the creditors will be invited to transfer their debts into loans, of which the interest will be paid half yearly, and the principal by certain instalments. The property of the Prince of WALES and the Duke of YORK, will be the security for this loan, the shares in which, as in others, will be transferable. . . .
The late Chancellor [Lord THURLOW], Lord RAWDON, and Mr. SHERIDAN, are the confidential friends of the PRINCE upon this subject, and the former nobleman is now a frequent visitor at Carleton-house, where he has a room allotted solely to his use on mornings.

Except for the *Oracle*, no newspaper gave Sheridan credit for the transformation. The Ministerial newspapers were inclined, to begin with, to give the whole credit to the Prince himself, for, as the *Diary* pointed out on 13 October, his quitting the turf having been "his own idea" and not the result of "coercion," there was no reason to suppose that the plan for retrenchment was otherwise.

The *Morning Chronicle* credited by innuendo the Friends of the People: "The PRINCE of WALES, in curtailing his household, pays a handsome compliment to the spirit of reform, which is so generally raised in the kingdom," it commented on 25 October. "He devotes five-sixths of his income to the liquidation of his debts, and with the remaining 12,000*l.* a year, he will, with a small house, served by half a dozen domestics in brown frocks, enjoy all the comforts of a private gentleman—and gratify at the same time his most prevailing passion—benevolence to the wretched." By this time the Ministerial newspapers were crediting Lord Thurlow, whose "preaching" of "oeconomies" had in their opinion effected the change, if there was one. But on this point several newspapers were now frankly skeptical, and even the *Public Advertiser* felt that a little more "preaching" would not be amiss. "At this critical moment all Princes ought to act with circumspection," it stated on 27 October. "The money intended to uphold them with the proper splendor of Royalty, is taken from the hard earnings of the industrious; and though cheerfully bestowed, it ought to be oeconomically disbursed. The donors never intended their gifts to be either squandered at an hazard table, or lavished at a horse-race. It is given to support dignity, and not to feed dissipation." The *Oracle* hastened to assure the *Public Advertiser* that "dissipation" did not enter into the Prince's plans. "The PRINCE intends, by the advice of Lord THURLOW, to relinquish the Establishment of Carlton-House, and to retire to General CONWAY's adjacent, on 12,000*l.* per annum until his debts are paid, and his noble mansion completed," it said on 29 October. This information was revised by the *Diary*, which noted on 30 October that "CARL-TON-HOUSE is to be evacuated in form, in the course of ten days;—*Kemshot* will then be the PRINCE's place of general residence."

The trouble was that no one could remake the Prince of Wales into anything resembling his father's image, and so much of the *Oracle*'s effort had been expended in denials. "By the appearance of the PRINCE of WALES at Egham, it is not to be inferred that he means to return to the Turf," the *Oracle* had said for example on 8 September. "He was merely a spectator, and totally unconcerned in the Race." He was "a spectator" at every race which followed, and his brother was evidently something more, for on 2 November the *World* mentioned that the Duke of York was "again a considerable loser at the Newmarket Races." The Prince was also a regular attendant at the faro tables, and there was the constant embarrassment of his continued association with Mrs. Fitzherbert and Louis Weltje. On 31 October readers of the *Public Advertiser*, who had previously been acquainted with Weltje only in his relations with the Prince, were regaled with an account of his domestic life. The account was a report of a case tried on 29 October, the plaintiff, Amelia Louisa Weltje, who described herself as the wife of "Mr. Weltjie, a person who some time since held a lucrative situation under … the Prince of Wales," accusing Betty Callaway, "Mr. Weltjie's servant," of assault. William Garrow, who represented Mrs. Weltje, charged that for years she had been "ill treated by her husband," frequently "turned out of doors by him and otherwise been treated with brutality"; but the situation had worsened during the summer, he said, when, although she was very ill, her husband would not permit the servants to care for her or even to change her bed linen. On 2 July she had risen and, waiting until the kitchen was clear, had stolen some clean sheets from the laundry; but, as she was returning to her room, she was viciously attacked by Miss Callaway. When she complained to her husband, he defended the servant, stated that she had acted on his instructions, and refused to dismiss her. Mrs. Weltje thereupon took her to a magistrate, but Weltje followed, provided bail, and escorted the servant back home. "Happily," said Garrow in conclusion, Weltje was not "an Englishman," but only "an arrogant purse-proud foreigner, who had got rich in the service of the most illustrious subject of this country." The jury found Miss Callaway guilty, and she was sentenced to two months' imprisonment. There was no fine because, said the magistrate, Weltje was so "gallant" that he would have paid it for her.

On 1 November the *Diary* protested: "The affair relative to Mr. and Mrs. WELTJIE, lately agitated at Hick's Hall, was the result of those matrimonial disagreements which are unhappily too common in life, and which are wholly unfit to be a subject for the aggravating misrepresentation of public prints. The idea of any *gallantry* in the matter was the mere *sportive* license of the bar, as the servant, who is confined for the alledged assault, is an old woman." At the same time, the *Diary* had another word of preachment for the Prince:

> With every applause for the virtuous determination of the P—ce to live, comparatively speaking, retired, until his creditors demands shall be liquidated, the Nation must cordially wish, that the voice of dissipation will not be suffered by him to intrude, from any quarter, to weaken his highly commendable resolutions.
> The plan at present agreed upon for the arrangement of a certain Personage's affairs, is as follows, viz—for his Highness to live in future on the 10,000*l.* per annum, which he derives from the civil list—and to appropriate the annual sums arising from the late grant of Parliament, and the revenues of the Duchy of Cornwall, towards the payment of his debts by instalments.

On 2 November the *Diary* added: "A Great Personage seems now in good earnest to be entering on a plan of retrenchment. C—House, with establishment, is obviously quitted, *pro tempore*, for retirement to a private seat; and where we doubt not, but the Great Personage will participate infinitely greater happiness, than while living in sumptuous Palaces, at an expence incompatible with the present state of his affairs." A few months earlier the *Diary* had thought it was improper for the Heir Apparent to be living the life of a simple country gentleman; it now thought it was quite proper, the only question being whether he would actually do it or not.

This question lingered until 27 November, when the *Diary* announced that on "Friday [23 Nov.) the Plate of . . . the Prince of Wales was removed from Brighton, in order to be conveyed to Kempshot, Hants, where his Royal

Highness will chiefly reside during the winter./ The Prince will, in a few days, also remove his stud from Bagshot, not intending to reside at the place in future./ The Prince, it is now determined, will not use General Conway's late house, during his short visits to town in the winter, but will retain a suite of apartments in Carlton-House." This announcement was followed on 1 December by the announcement:

CARLTON HOUSE.

The sacrifice at the shrine of true honour, on the part of the Prince of Wales, by a retrenchment of his expences to be enabled to discharge the just demands of his numerous creditors, was on Thursday [29 Nov.] announced in form to the Pages and Servants of every description who were ordered to attend at one o'clock.

They were informed by Colonel Hulse that . . . their services would be dispensed with, after the expiration of the present quarter—that all arrears would be paid up to the day of their discharge, and that a final pension to each would be allowed as a compensation for their loss of employment.

But the *Oracle*, which had labored so hard to bring these "retrenchments" about, had long since lost interest in them. By early November it was involved in a variety of personal quarrels, including a dispute with the *Diary* over the relative merits of editions of Shakespeare. This dispute, which began on 10 November with the *Diary*'s comment that George Steevens was "giving forth a new edition of SHAKESPEARE, although it seems unnecessary after [Edmund] Malone's work," raged until 21 November, when the *Oracle* announced that it would say nothing further on the subject for the moment: "STEEVENS and his prodigious labours are to appear immediately after Christmas. And then the great question between MALONE and him will be decided, as to the authenticity of certain Copies of the great Bard, and a world of other matters." Two things seem to have happened. Lord Lauderdale, who had been paying the newspaper to support the Friends of the People, discovered that it was playing another "*Game*" altogether. On 1 November the *Oracle* had declared that "Lord LAUDERDALE is a firm and independent young NOBLEMAN, to whom the Country does and ought to look up.—He is no respecter of *persons* or of *situations*. The most advantageous *heights*, occupied by the most *practiced* GENERALS, and fortified by the most terrible ordnance of *venality* [a sarcastic reference to the Duke of Richmond and the camp at Bagshot], cannot dismay him./ 'I tell you what you yourselves do know:/ Shew you your sinecures, poor, poor dumb mouths!/ And bid them speak for me.'" This was the last mention of him, and although by 21 November Lord Lauderdale had returned from France and was, said the *World*, expected in London "hourly," there were no cheers from the *Oracle*, which was now entirely in the Ministerial camp. More important, the Prince had again been negotiating with Pitt, and so Sheridan had had to revise his own plans. His present hope was to join the Pitt Government in lieu of Fox.

Rumors of Pitt's resignation were still rampant during October and November, but no newspaper took them seriously. "It was yesterday reported that Mr. Pitt had resigned, but nobody believed it to be other than a stock-jobbing fabrication," the *Oracle* remarked typically on 20 November. Rumors of Fox's defection were equally rampant, and these were taken seriously. "Yesterday," said the *Diary* of 28 November, for example,

> a variety of rumours relative to a change in Administration were extremely prevalent. Different arrangements were stated as possible, but the most credited was the following:
> Earl Fitzwilliam, *First Lord of the Treasury.*
> Lord Loughborough, *Lord Chancellor.*
> Mr. Fox, *Principal Secretary of State.*
> Mr. Wyndham, *Secretary of the State.*
> Mr. Pitt, *Chancellor of the Exchequer.*
> The Duke of Portland, *Lord Lieutenant of Ireland.*
> Mr. Secretary, *Secretary for Ireland.*

But Fox had not defected, and, since it was now clear that Pitt meant to stay in office anyway, the question was whether he could be ousted. By early November Sheridan and therefore the *Oracle* had evidently decided that he could not. The *Morning Chronicle* thought he could, but it did not think the task would be easy. Hence, in addition to the campaign being readied by the Friends of the People, the *Chronicle* commenced a campaign of its own, expanding the issue of the Cinque Ports into the general issue of official corruption through patronage. Since many of the positions the Government was giving away, such as Recorderships and Chancellorships, were actually elective, the two campaigns were not entirely separate.

Patronage per se was not originally the issue, for oppositions had always respected a government's right to reward the faithful, while newspapers had regarded the practice as so proper that they had not been particularly curious as to who was being rewarded or how. This was still the case in September, 1792, for the *Diary*'s mention of 6 September that "Mr. Dundas's son [Robert] is appointed Joint Keeper of the Signet with his father, and [is] to have the reversion of that office" was not intended as an aspersion on any one, even though the young Dundas was only nineteen years old. Pitt's crime was to use the patronage for purposes other than rewards, attempting to bribe the Duke of Portland with the Chancellorship of Oxford and using the Wardenship of the Cinque Ports to augment his own present income, not to provide for his retirement. It was this improper use of patronage with which the *Morning Chronicle* was originally concerned. But, since most of Pitt's followers had once been his opponents, it was so difficult to separate the rewards from the bribes that by 1 November all patronage was being represented as corruptive and Pitt as the archcorrupter.

The contents of the book of patronage, commonly called "The Red Book," had never been publicized. Whatever the Opposition newspapers could learn about them now was. Even the *Star* joined the sport by announcing on 23 October that the Treasury writer, John Bowles, had been appointed Receiver General of the South District of Wiltshire. Other papers provided a great deal of such information. Pitt's secretary, Joseph Smith, had, it appeared, been appointed Receiver of Stamp Duties as well as Secretary of the Cinque Ports, having since 1786 also been Comptroller of Coinage and the Mint; and £300 of the £500 salary enjoyed by William Augustus Miles had been converted into a lifetime pension. The Duke of Beaufort, who had failed to get the Chancellorship of Oxford, was already Lord Lieutenant of Monmouth, of Brecknock, and of Leicester, as well as Knight of the Garter, whereas Lord Dorset, to whom the Cinque Ports had been promised, had had to console himself with the Lord Stewardship of the King's Household. The Duke of Richmond was not only Master General of Ordnance and Field Marshal, but Lord Lieutenant of Sussex, his private secretary being his nephew Charles Lennox, who had been a Colonel in the Coldstream Guards until his duel with the Duke of York in 1789, when he was transferred as Lieutenant Colonel to the 35th Regiment of Foot. The Lord Chancellor of Ireland, Lord Fitzgibbon, was also Vice-Chancellor of the University of Dublin; Lord Onslow was High Steward of Kingston-on-Thames, Lord Lieutenant of Surrey, High Steward of Guilford, and Lord of the King's Bedchamber.

Charles Jenkinson, Lord Hawkesbury, was President of the Board of Trade, Clerk of the Pells, Chancellor of the Duchy of Lancaster, and Collector of the Island Customs, enjoying altogether £14,000 from "absolute sinecures" alone, as well as control of a large amount of subordinate patronage. Pitt's cousin, Lord Grenville, was Foreign Secretary, President of the Board of Control, Ranger and Keeper of St. James's and Hyde Parks, and possessor of "a lucrative place in Ireland." Although the second Secretary of the Treasury, Charles Long, had thus far nothing to show for his services but a Fellowship of the Royal Society, awarded him on 2 February, 1792, the first Secretary, George Rose, was Master of the Pleas in the Court of Exchequer for life, Verderer of the New Forest, and Clerk of the Parliament, his wife having in addition a lifetime pension of £300. Dundas was Home Secretary, Treasurer of the Navy, Commissioner of the Board for Indian Affairs, Keeper of the Signet, and possessor, it was supposed, of a half-dozen other sinecures, all marked for reversion to his son Robert. "EQUALITY," groaned the *Morning Chronicle* on 1 December. "— The appointments of Mr. ROSE are as much as the revenue of the Duke of CLARENCE;—and Mr. DUNDAS, in salary, &c. has more!" The person most wounded by these revelations seems to have been Lord Mountmorres, who, having no sinecure whatever, reminded the Government in a preface to his *The Principal Transactions of the Irish Parliament* (London, 1792) that he had always been a friend to Pitt and had defended him in particular during the Regency crisis of 1788–1789, when he had published numerous letters in the *Public Advertiser*, over the signature, "Themistocles."

The Opposition press had got much of its information from Thomas Paine and Charles Pigott. When Paine departed, he left behind him a manuscript, entitled *Letter Addressed to the Addressers on the Late Proclamation* [*against Seditious Writings*]. The work was intended for publication, and it was published with Paine's signature, but with no publisher's name, the colophon reading simply, "London. Printed for the Booksellers 1792." Paine had written his *Address to the Addressers*, as it was popularly called, in June or July and had dedicated it, not to the Government, but to those who "addressed" the Government, especially to "the numerous rotten Boroughs and Corporations" whose testimonies of loyalty to King and Constitution were then filling the pages of the newspapers.[67] Unlike his earlier publications, this one called for immediate revolution on the ground that "abuses" were too deeply entrenched to be eradicated quietly and that the Friends of the People had no actual interest in eradicating them. Everything Paine said was underscored by *The Jockey Club: or A Sketch of the Manners of the Age*, Parts II and III of which were now also in print, although Pigott's name was not attached to them.

Much of Paine's work and almost all of Pigott's consisted of exposés, and, since Paine and Pigott were hostile to the whole political system, the Opposition fared almost as badly as the Government. Grey was depicted as a monster, posing as a reformer in order to preserve corruption, and Fox was represented in much the same terms. The angelic Lord Derby, it was pointed out, had been Lord Lieutenant of Lancaster since 1776 and the independent Earl Spencer, High Steward of St. Albans since 1783. Lord Clermont, who had been Governor and Custos Rotulorum of County Monaghin since 1775, had in 1784 also been appointed Customer and Collector of the Port of Dublin. One of the most notorious cases of corruption was, according to Paine,[68] the next Earl of Mansfield, Lord Stormont, who "draws from the public . . . not less than six thousand pounds a year" as "Justice General of Scotland and Keeper of the Scoon." But all of this was more than offset by two items respecting the "incorruptible" Burke. In the first instance, Paine, who was charging that Burke was as greedy as the other defectors and was prevented from accepting a reward only by public opinion, went on to say that in 1782 the Rockingham Whigs had given a £1,500 pension to a certain person, who, when the pension was put up for sale or mortgage, turned out to be Edmund Burke.[69] Pigott was more specific. When the pension was offered, he said,[70] that "Pseudo Patriot . . . betrayed all possible avidity to get hold of [it]; but a PENSIONED PATRIOT appeared a Paradox irreconcilable, and he conceived that a knowledge of the transaction might injure him. . . . He longed after the pension, but he had not made up his mind to the disgrace and obloquy generally annexed to it. It was therefore agreed, that the pension should be issued out under a *fictitious* name, in order to satisfy the Gentleman's scruples. . . ."

In the second instance, Burke was accused of negotiating with Pitt at least six months before he published his *Reflections*. Paine presented the evidence as a reminiscence:[71]

> I was in England at the time the bubble broke about Nootka Sound; and the day after the King's Message . . . was sent to Parliament, I wrote a note to Mr. Burke, that upon the condition the French Revolution should not be a subject (for he was then writing the book I have since answered), I would call on him the next day, and mention some matters I was acquainted with respecting that affair. . . .
>
> When I saw Mr. Burke, and mentioned the circumstances to him, he particularly spoke of Mr. Grey as the fittest Member to bring such matters forward; for, said Mr. *Burke, "I am not the proper person to do it, as I am in a treaty with Mr. Pitt about Mr. Hastings's trial.*

The King's message regarding the vessels captured by Spain in Nootka Sound was sent to Parliament on 5 May, 1790, and on 12 May Grey moved for the introduction of all papers relating to the affair. Burke's *Reflections on the Revolution in France*, to which Paine's *Rights of Man*, Part I, was an "answer," appeared on 1 November of that year.

The Insurrection Which Wasn't

So far as readers of newspapers knew, the situation remained basically unchanged until late November. They learned from the *Sun* that the war was still going badly for the Allies. They knew that on 6 November the Austrians suffered a stunning defeat at Jemappes and that on 14 November General Dumouriez captured Brussels. They knew in particular that on 16 November the French Executive Council declared the Scheldt and the Meuse open to and from the sea and that on 19 November it dedicated itself to the support of liberation movements everywhere. But, since the Government indicated no concern, they did not regard these developments as ominous. As to domestic affairs, they read a great deal about a new organization, called The Association for Protecting Liberty and Property against Republicans and Levellers, commonly known as The Crown and Anchor Association or merely The Association. According to the prospectus, which was published on 6 November, the purposes of the society were to suppress seditious publications, to discredit French philosophy, and to encourage the formation of similar societies in other parts of the country; and heading it was John Reeves, classical scholar, lawyer, and strong supporter of William Pitt, who had last figured in the news on 4 July, 1791, when the *Star* mentioned that he had just been appointed "Chief Justice in the Court of Civil Jurisdiction" in Newfoundland, where he would "[determine] causes during the fishing season only." The first meeting was to be held at the Crown and Anchor on 20 November. But, despite Reeves's intimacy with Pitt, The Association was supposedly not sponsored by the Government; nor would it be connected with it in any way, all activities to be planned and financed by individual members.

The Government itself was seemingly still unaware of the reformers. In late October, John Frost returned from France and on 6 November visited the Percy Coffee House, where he was heard by a Mr. Yatman, a Mr. Savignac, and a Mr. Bullock, to utter the words: "I am for equality; I see no reason why one man should be greater than another; I would have no king; and the Constitution of this country is a bad one." He thereupon returned to France, with no objection on the part of the Attorney General. It even looked as if the Government might finally release John Almon, who on 19 November was at least permitted "to assign errors to his outlawry." Henry D. Symonds and Thomas C. Rickman had affixed their names as publishers to a new edition of Paine's *Letter Addressed to the Addressers*, and Maurice Margarot and Joseph Gerrald were now prominent in the Corresponding Society. In Dublin the Society of United Irishmen, founded by Wolfe Tone in 1791, was causing a little trouble, principally because of the activities of the secretary, Archibald Hamilton Rowan; and on 21 November the delegates of the Associated Friends of the People in Edinburgh (totally unrelated to the London Friends of the People) resolved to hold a convention on 11 December. But, insofar as these events were reported, they were reported only by the Opposition papers, which could report in addition that, on 7 November, James Mingay had been elected to the Whig Club. Since Mingay had once been attorney for the Ministerial *World* and only recently had represented Lord Lonsdale in his actions against Bell, Wolcot, Evans, and Peter Stuart, the election was reason for rejoicing.

Even the *Sun* had apparently mellowed. Emboldened by the change, the *Star* mentioned on 7 November that moderate reform was no longer in its opinion a party issue, for certain "*abuses* . . . are admitted [by *all parties*] to have crept into our happy Constitution," and these "abuses" ought to be "eradicated." On 15 November the *Star* angrily denied that it was controlled by the Friends of the People. It was owned, it told its readers, by the "same Persons by whom it has been conducted for more than three years," the "rumour" to the contrary was "malicious," and it would pay 100 guineas for the name of the "perpetrator." It simply believed in the cause of moderate reform. Although the *Sun* was still preoccupied with affairs on the Continent and with the Fox-Pitt coalition, it seemed to William S. Bourne, writing to William Adam on 13 November,[72] that the "real purposes [of that newspaper] are to garble the debates of Parliament and to send them into the world in such a state as to bias the minds of the unwary in favour of whatever measure the ministry may think proper to adopt, and against whatever may derive from real independence." What Bourne proposed was "to change my weekly publication [the *Observer*] to an every day one" and thereby provide "a decided opposition . . . —detecting misrepresentation and correcting error." Because of "a situation I hold in the Post Office," he thought he could also "counteract in a great degree the exertions which are making to extend the circulation of [the *Sun*] throughout this kingdom." Adam was evidently discouraging.

But there was a great deal going on of which the newspapers knew nothing. They did not know, for example, that Lord Auckland had been sent to The Hague to promise Holland British protection in the event of an invasion and that M. Chauvelin's attempts to preserve Anglo-British relations were being coldly regarded by Lord Grenville. They had heard nothing of a possible war with France since the beginning of August. They were also unaware of Dundas's activities. Dundas later told Farington[73] that "during the French Revolution . . . He & Mr. Pitt had [had] spies amongst [all disaffected persons] who regularly reported to them all the proceedings. In one of these Societies . . . , they had bribed the *Secretary* of the Society, who after each night of their meeting . . . regularly brought their books with all the minutes of their proceedings." Most of these spies and informers were engaged during November, for, by the end of the month, every reform organization, as well as every debating society, coffeehouse, and tavern, was riddled with them. Like John Taylor and Robert Watt, most of them were also agitators, posing as enemies of the state and often themselves inciting the acts of sedition which they subsequently reported.

The Association was formally organized on 20 November, Reeves being elected "Permanent Chairman" and Edward Topham secretary. It was not what the prospectus had indicated. Readers of Ministerial newspapers had been given to understand that the principal subsidizer would be Sir Joseph Banks. His patriotic virtues and "princely fortune" had been much extolled by the *Sun* and the *Oracle*, and on 19 November the *Diary* reported that he had just acquired another "7000*l*. per an." through the death of an uncle. But, although Banks was now a thoroughgoing alarmist and a firm believer in home inspections and regular signings of loyalty oaths, he seems not to have contributed a shilling. Nor did anyone else. According to Daniel Stuart,[74] The Association was always financed in one way or another by the Government. Reeves himself, said Stuart, "besides enjoying about half a dozen places under government," was to his knowledge "paid between three and four thousand pounds" a year for his services. It worked in close co-operation with the offices of the Attorney General, the Solicitor General, and the Home Secretary, it used the Government's newspapers, the *Sun* and (after 1 January, 1793) the *True Briton*, as if they were Reeves's personal "tools," and it had only one original purpose: to persuade the people that the Constitution was in imminent jeopardy. Reeves's *modus operandi* seemed in fact to be identical with that of Dundas. The *Gazetteer* later (16 Aug., 1793) maintained that the actual "projector" of the society had been John Bowles. Whether this was the case or not, Bowles's next pamphlet, *A Protest against T. Paine's "Rights of Man" : Addressed to the Members of a Book Society*, was "*Printed by Order of the Crown and Anchor Society.*" But The Association was also publishing cheap editions of Paine's *Rights of Man* without the imprint. Like Dundas, too, it relied heavily on spies and agitators, who were quite as likely to be inciting riots against the Constitution as they were to be inciting riots for it.

With the founding of The Association, the political climate changed completely. On the evening of 20 November, there was a near-riot at the Drury Haymarket, for, while the audience was calling for "God Save the King," someone in the gallery called for "Ça Ira." There were hisses and groans, followed by a frenzied search for the offender, who was not found. The Opposition newspapers took a very sober view of this incident, which, none of them doubted, had been arranged by the Government. The *Morning Chronicle* felt that an inquiry into the Government's long harassment of Drury Lane might now be legitimately demanded; it also felt that a protest might be submitted to the King, who was stooping to "party prejudice" by regularly patronizing Covent Garden and conspicuously avoiding Drury Lane. The *Morning Chronicle* had much to say on this subject during late November and even early December. On 22 November there was a more disturbing development. Although Parliament had voted to cut the Army budget, the *Star* reported that the Army was being augmented. The *Sun* scoffed at the report until 24 November, when it admitted that the Admiralty had sent "word" to the "Marine Barracks at Plymouth" to add to the forces there. The *Star* repeated its statement on 27 November, this time with some vehemence:

> In the STAR of Thursday last [22 Nov.], we announced that different regiments and the Marine corps had received orders to fill up their companies to their full complement.
>
> On Thursday one of our contemporaries [the *Sun*] manifested its *want of information* by asserting from *high authority*, that there is no truth in the statement, and its *malignity*, by insinuating that we had fabricated the report for *stock-jobbing* purposes.
>
> We offer no proof of a fact now so notorious, that the very walls are covered with bills offering encouragement to such volunteers as may present themselves.

On 27 November, too, the *Star* announced that, having devoted a lifetime to ridiculing George III and his friends, Dr. Wolcot was now on George's payroll. "PETER PINDAR," said the *Star*, "clears 300*l.* a year by the KING. 'Produce me a *subject* [i.e., any one of the King's subjects],' he says, 'that will bring me this sum, and I will write a *farewell Ode to his* MAJESTY.'" Wolcot had not written for the Opposition since he was sued by Lord Lonsdale. The *Morning Post* was also in the news. On 13 November the *Diary* had mentioned regretfully that "Lady Cavan has demanded the four thousand pounds damages obtained the last term from Mr. Tattersall"; and on 24 November it noticed even more regretfully that the money had been paid: "The Solicitor of Lady Cavan yesterday received Four Thousand and Fifty-two Pounds of Mr. Tattersall, in the presence of his Attorney, Mr. Hodson, Chancery-lane, being the amount of damages and taxed costs, obtained by Lady Lambert against him, as proprietor of the Morning Post. Thus, after all the papers has [*sic*] urged *pro* and *con* [i.e., whether she would or would not demand payment], her Ladyship has received the money." As it turned out, Tattersall had paid the full amount himself, the Prince of Wales having failed to provide even his moiety. He also paid the full amount to Rose. But, when it came to collecting from William Williams, now in prison for the libel on the King, Rose was magnanimous. The *World* was proud of him. "Mr. ROSE, much to his honour, has forgiven the hundred pounds recovered against the late Printer of a Morning Paper," it told its readers happily on 1 December. "He took the damages awarded against the Proprietor— properly distinguishing between him who was capable, and the one who was not."

By this time the Ministerial press was in a state of frenzy, and the frenzy was obviously effective, for, according to the *World* of 28 November:

> The representation of [Reynolds's] *Dramatist* [at Covent Garden] was last night delayed near a quarter of an hour beyond the usual time of the perfor- mances commencing, by the perseverance of the audience in their call for "God save the King;" and it was not until they had repeatedly been assured that it should be given in full chorus at the conclusion of the entertainment, that the performers were suffered to proceed. . . .
>
> "God Save the King" was the finale, it was twice sung, and each time followed by shouts of loyalty, bordering on enthusiasm.—We heard two Jacobins hiss. . . .

On 29 November *The Times* exhorted its readers to report any suspicious activi- ties to The Association, especially activities on the part of those purporting to be only moderate reformers, they being the most dangerous kind. It continued its exhortations on 30 November, and on 1 December the *Diary* announced that the Attorney General, Sir Archibald Macdonald, had on 28 November "pre- ferred seven bills of indictment for libel against publishers and printers, all of which were found true bills by the Grand Jury." That afternoon the *Star* identified one of the seven as James Ridgway, a publisher for the Friends of the People and a long-time foe of William Pitt. Ridgway had provided bail on 31 November and was awaiting trial. But, by the time this item appeared, every- thing was in a state of pandemonium.

The excitement began, according to the newspapers, early on the morning of 1 December, when all mail coaches and other vehicles were stopped to be searched for "traitors," who, it was understood, were removed and delivered to the Tower by the thousands. An hour later it was understood that the "traitors" had escaped and were storming the Tower. By mid-morning it was understood that they were not yet storming the Tower, but were on their way, marching on London as an army. By noon they had supposedly arrived. The Thames was now said to have been poisoned, the Lord Mayor of London, Sir James Saunderson, was said to be seizing large quantities of firearms, and the Duke of Richmond was standing guard at the Tower. At this point the King called out the militia, which, it was thought, battled the rebels throughout the day and well into the night. The people had long since barricaded themselves in their houses, expecting to be murdered any second.

By the following day the violence seemed to have subsided, but more violence was evidently expected, for extraordinary measures were being taken to defend the country against its citizens. On 4 December the *Diary* reported that the Bank was now under heavy guard, since "the Bank would no doubt, be the first thing to be levelled," if "any circumstance kindle the present popular discontent into more serious commotion." In addition, it said:

> The Duke of Richmond is intent upon restoring the fortifications of the Tower, where there is a spirit of vigilance and preparation which the present generation have never yet witnessed. Several hundreds of men are employed about the walls; . . . the Tower gates are shut at nine o'clock, two hours sooner than usual; a stranger is with difficulty admitted in the day time, and no persons but officers and sentinels are suffered to appear upon the ramparts. . . .
>
> We have the pleasure to inform our country readers, that Government are taking the most active and vigorous measures to preserve the activity and property of the people. . . . It is generally believed that Government had discovered an infernal plot, planned by some foreigners, and certain unnatural incendiaries of native growth, to seize the Tower and the Bank, and, after diverting the Stream of the New River, to set the city in flames.

Similar accounts appeared in all the newspapers. The *World*, for example, reported that barracks were being hastily constructed around the Tower, under the supervision of the Duke of Richmond, to defend the capital against "the disaffected at home," while the Army was being dispersed to all parts of the kingdom to deal with "the disaffected" there. The *World* seemed to feel that the situation was much worse than anyone supposed and that insurrections were probably bursting forth everywhere. So evidently did the Duke of York, who, according to the *Morning Chronicle* of 5 December, had "entirely relinquished Newmarket, and sold his few running horses" in order to devote his attention to national defense. So, too, it appeared, did Lord Loughborough, for on 7 December the *World* announced that he "certainly leaves the Duke of PORT-LAND's friends—by which the Ministry will have an accession of great legal experience and political knowledge." The Duke of Portland was himself evidently still adhering to Fox.

Although there had been no fresh outbreaks in London, the state of tension there was indicated by numerous street fights. One of them inevitably involved Charles Stuart, who was always cursed with an excess of zeal and a consequent penchant for violence. According to the *World* (6 Dec.), which never neglected an opportunity to embarrass the personnel of the old spurious *Star*, Stuart had been "brought before [Alderman Brass Crosby, evidently on 5 Dec.], charged with assaulting and beating a Watchman in Castle-yard, Holborne./ He was committed to the New Compter to answer for the assault." By 4 December, according to the *Diary*, the King had proclaimed a bounty of £3 for able seamen, £2 for ordinary seamen, and 20s. for able landsmen in order to encourage enlistments in the Navy; and by 7 December the *World* had discovered that the Duke of Richmond was strengthening the fortifications of the parks, the guns being inspected, serviced, and, if need be, replaced. But the immediate danger, it now felt, lay outside London, and the Army would need to be greatly augmented to deal with the numerous "seditious Clubs." The *Morning Chronicle* did not protest the augmentation, but it strongly protested the billeting of soldiers in barracks. As it repeatedly urged, the billeting of soldiers in their own homes or in private homes in their own general neighborhoods was not only an honored British tradition, but a guarantee that the Army would remain a thing of the people. Moving soldiers to alien neighborhoods and billeting them apart from the people besides, transformed the Army from a friendly force to a potentially hostile one: a powerful weapon in the hands of an unscrupulous and desperate minister. The protests were unavailing; the Duke of Richmond constructed barracks in every city.

The Opposition papers were similarly uneasy about the purges. On 30 November, it appeared, Lord Sempill, who had joined the Army in 1771 and had been commissioned Lieutenant in 1781, had been cashiered for "[corresponding] with the Friends of Freedom in France." On the same day Lord Edward Fitzgerald, an original member of the London Friends of the People, had been cashiered for attending a dinner in Paris and there participating in a toast to the abolition of hereditary titles. On 4 December the *Diary* reported that the King had on 3 December "struck" another two colonels and a major "off the army list." The major was never identified, but, according to the *Star* of that afternoon, the colonels were William Dalrymple and Norman Macleod. This time there was no specific charge, and the trio was apparently guilty of nothing except a connection with the Friends of the People and an interest in the reform movement in Scotland. The *Star* was distressed. "Colonel DALRYMPLE and Colonel M'CLEOD have left the army, his MAJESTY having signified his royal pleasure to this effect," it observed sadly. "Colonel M'CLEOD raised a regiment at his own expence while serving in India, where he received no less than six wounds. Colonel DALRYMPLE has for a series of years [he had been Colonel of the 2nd Footguards since 1782] served with eclat, but is now President of the Glasgow Association." The *World* (7 Dec.) responded with the sneer that Colonel

Macleod's "late conduct at heading a party of Jacobins [evidently at the meeting of the Associated Friends of the People on 21 Nov.], is not the first instance he has given of his *fixed* principles." The Edinburgh convention was evidently to be discredited before it could begin. Commissions were meanwhile being handed out to the faithful, one of whom, Lord Lonsdale, was now Colonel of the Cumberland militia.

The Crown and Anchor Association had meanwhile flourished. Every city and town now had its own cell, each supposedly independent of the rest and yet all working in the same manner toward the same end. As Daniel Stuart put it:[75]

> The affiliated Jacobin Clubs of the French Provinces have been made the model of the Reevesian Associations and Committees, against Republicans and Levellers at home; and in the English Parochial, as well as in the French Popular Meetings, the Constitution, as declared by Reeves, Pitt, and Co. has been formally approved. Every President or Chairman of these *"Conventions"* becomes a *"Municipal Inquisitor:"* Sir Joseph Banks makes his *visites domiciliares* in the parish of St. Anne, and keeps a register of the complexion, age, employment, &c. of lodgers and strangers. The *"section"* of St. James's *denounce* for *incivism* every house-keeper who does not oblige his servants, workmen, and apprentices, to sign their acceptance of the Constitution. . . . Every man is called upon, more palpably than in France, to declare our Constitution glorious and unreformable; and if any one is more consistent than [those apostates] Mr. Pitt and the Duke of Richmond, and signifies a wish for the removal of abuses in the construction of the House of Commons, he is branded as a Jacobin, and, if possible, utterly ruined.

The newspapers were of course crammed with loyalty addresses, individuals vying with boroughs and corporations to attest their devotion to Church, King, and in particular Constitution. The principal threats to the Constitution, readers of Ministerial newspapers would now have supposed, were Lord Lauderdale and Thomas Erskine, Lord Lauderdale because he was fighting for election reforms, Erskine because he was fighting for freedom of the press. The attacks on Erskine had actually begun on 29 October, when the *Diary* accused him of trading "principles" for "fees," which, in 1791 alone, it said, "produced above 8,500*l.*—The late Chancellor THURLOW's business at the Bar was about 1,200*l.*" By 20 November Erskine was being assailed by all the Treasury newspapers in the evident anticipation that he would represent the new batch of indictees. It now appeared that anyone indicted by the state was *ipso facto* guilty and that any lawyer who appeared against the state was just as guilty as his client.

The Convocation of Parliament

The fiction that on 1 December the Government had "discovered an infernal plot, planned by some foreigners, and certain unnatural incendiaries of native growth," and had acted just in the nick of time to prevent a full-scale revolution persisted for almost a week. But, as to what had happened on that memorable day, the newspapers knew nothing, and by 7 December it had occurred to the *Morning Chronicle* that no one had seen anything either. The Government needed such a "plot," for months it had been encouraging the radicals to devise one, and, having failed in this endeavor, it had simply invented one out of its own "fiendish imagination." The *Chronicle* made its point in a long editorial, which was epitomized in the verses:

NATIONAL ALARM.
There can be no harm in giving alarm,
And scaring the People with strange apprehensions;
By brewing this storm, we avoid a Reform,
And securely enjoy all our places and pensions.

The editorial had an immediately sobering effect on the Opposition newspapers and the *Diary*, but not on the public, which continued to be "scared." Although the people had no confidence in Pitt, they had too much respect for the King to believe that he would have called out the militia to put down a phantom or that he would sanction the fortification of buildings and parks, the construction of barracks, the stationing of troops throughout the country, the augmentation of the Army, along with the seemingly irrelevant augmentation of the Navy, the purgings, and the inquisitions unless he had good reason to expect trouble. There was probably also the element of excitement, and this was no spectator sport. Everyone was called upon to participate, and a man could therefore visit taverns in search of Jacobins, he could help burn an effigy of Paine, or, if he had nothing else to do, he could drop by the local Association to sign another loyalty oath, always with the self-satisfying assurance that he was fighting the enemies of his country.

The newspapers alone were probably worth the price of a little delusion, filled, as they were, with rumors of traitors being brought to justice and other heroic achievements of an alert citizenry. In fact, there seem to have been no arrests, although the Government did take action in two cases. By 6 December it had issued an order for the arrest of John Terrence Frost, whom it charged with using seditious language in the Percy Coffee House on 6 November. Since everyone knew that Frost was in Paris, no time was wasted searching for him.

He was outlawed on 8 December and a £100 reward offered by the Treasury for his apprehension. On the same day, the Government tried Sampson Perry, under indictment since 10 July for a libel published in the *Argus* on 8 May. According to the *Gazetteer* (10 Dec.), the trial was brief, Perry being convicted on evidence that he was a proprietor of the paper at the time the libel appeared. The facts that he was then in prison and that the libel was shown to be a direct quotation from one of Pitt's earlier speeches were dismissed as irrelevant. Perry was himself not present, the lawyers for the Crown having persuaded him to flee to France a few weeks earlier; hence he was also outlawed and another £100 offered for his apprehension. By 7 December the Government had got rid of the *Argus*. This achievement was reported by the *World*, which stated simply: "A Paper, obscurely known for its seditious and libellous character, was put to death this week by an irresistible attack of a *Stamp Office Fever.*" According to Sampson Perry,[76] the maneuver was planned and executed by James Bland Burges, who was assisted possibly by James Mackintosh, certainly by Sheridan, "with the view, no doubt, of making his way to ministerial favour and preferment, by an *amende deshonorable* for his former refractory conduct." Since Sheridan had promised Perry that "I might fully rely on *his* attention, as *one* of my friends, for . . . preserving . . . the *Argus*" and had himself strongly urged Perry to flee, this was an act of unmitigated perfidy. Sheridan's newspaper, the *Oracle*, added to the offense by reporting gleefully on 11 December: "The ARGUS last week suffered the fate of the DAMNED,—but with a ceremony that would have graced a better cause. A numerous party of Gentlemen, attended by a Band of Musicians, at the Crown Inn, PECKHAM, caused the Constable to make a fire, into which was thrown a bundle of the deceased [*Argus*] that contained the treasonable articles against the KING and the Constitution." Since the *Oracle* was now as dedicated to witch-hunting as the *Sun* and *The Times*, it concluded this account by calling on its readers to join the search for "Mr. ST. FOY, . . . late a Proprietor of the *Courier de l'Europe.*" The *Argus* reappeared on 1 January, 1793, as the Ministerial *True Briton*, the morning edition of the *Sun*.

There was still much talk of the various fortifications, and on 10 December the Ministerial newspapers announced the biggest social event since the Grand Review at Bagshot: an inspection of the work which was underway to prepare the Tower "for the defence of this country." Among the inspectors were the Prince of Wales, the Duke of York, dignitaries from the Army, the Navy, the *Corps Diplomatique*, and the Government. The arsenals were displayed, soldiers lined the streets, bands played, the Duke of Richmond was everywhere at once, and the ceremony was pronounced a huge success. The *World* added to its account a note of personal rapture: "ENGLAND, at this crisis, proudly boasting of a popular Administration, an unbounded Commerce, a judicious extent of Civil and Religious Liberty, comprehends every thing that a generous heart can conceive, or an honest ambition desire; and Britons accordingly think themselves fortunate in living under the auspicious reign of GEORGE THE THIRD." The

World was so gratified to see the Prince of Wales in attendance that by 12 December it was apologizing and even lying for him: "The Prince of WALES has undoubtedly run beyond his income—but when he has relinquished the disgusting and degrading scenes of the TURF, it should be recollected he has had many to impose on him, and that in no other species of gaming has he ever indulged."

Since 20 November *The Times* had been assuring its readers that all was well financially: that, thanks to the activities of The Association, "the monied men" again felt secure. But there was no indication of such a feeling, for the number of bankrupts was alarming, and the stock market was more convulsive than ever. Since nobody knew what the country was being fortified against, rumors of a war between Britain and France and rumors of insurrections were almost equally rampant. The propagation of rumors for the purpose of manipulating the stock market was an old practice. The Russian ambassador, Ivan Simolin, was accused of doing so in 1781, Pitt was accused of doing so in 1785,[77] and other members of Government had been accused of doing so since. A conspiracy between a broker and a newspaper for stockjobbing purposes was something new, the only instance of it occuring in early 1783, when the Stuart brothers had engaged in such an enterprise, even forging a document to assure the suppression of certain information until it served their interests to release it.[78] But, by late November, 1792, such conspiracies were evidently a commonplace, for almost every newspaper felt obliged to state from time to time that it was not stockjobbing. At least half of them were.

The most notorious of the stockjobbing newspapers was the *Oracle*, which, having lost the financial assistance of Lord Lauderdale and for the present, it appeared, even of the Prince of Wales, was now purporting to be an authority on finance. But its financial reports were largely collections of rumors, and the fact that the rumors were always presented incidentally, as if they were common knowledge, and, more often than not, with apparent skepticism, made them none the less effective. The financial column of 8 December read, for example:

THE FUNDS,

By the alarming Rumours propagated yesterday at the 'Change, sustained a Depression of 3 per cent.

What we mentioned the preceeding day concerning apprehended Commotions in *Scotland* [as a result of the Edinburgh convention, still scheduled for 11 December], appeared to have some shadow of foundation—although we then disbelieved the Report, and have still every reason to think, that the whole is calculated for the purposes of Deception in the *Alley*.

Be that as it may, this assertion formed the chief cause of the Fall of the Funds; and the despondency of the MONIED MEN was not a little aggravated on account of the Distractions in *Ireland*, by which lately the Funds of the Sister Kingdom fell about 20 per cent.

The STOCK-BROKERS also experienced a considerable Panic from the declaration, that a War against *France* is now inevitable; that a *Tender* had some hours before been towed up to the *Tower* against the tide; and that Press Warrants were expected immediately to be issued.

We give these conjectures merely as they occurred, without pretending to vouch for the truth of the various Reports, although their calamitous effect is beyond contradiction; but we hope this day's transactions will produce a favourable change.

That day's "transactions" were of course worse, since several of these reports were news to "the MONIED MEN." The financial column of 11 December was similarly gloomy, but this time the gloom was justified:

THE FUNDS,

Continued to decline. Yesterday they closed at about 76½, being one half per cent. lower than on the preceding day.

The belief of a WAR—the Resolution of DUMOURIER to make an immediate Invasion of *Holland*—the Revival of the Trade of *Antwerp* by the opening of the Scheldt—the apparent determination of the NATIONAL CONVENTION to dispatch the FRENCH KING and ROYAL FAMILY, by which Annihilation of ROYALTY, the whole Government of *Europe* may perhaps be seriously affected—all are circumstances which concur to convulse the PUBLIC CREDIT. . . .

A "war against *France*," it was now generally felt, was in fact inevitable. The *Star* of 8 December had reminded the Ministerial newspapers that, for every effigy of Paine which was being burned in England, at least one effigy of Dundas was being burned in Scotland; but, since the Scots had been burning effigies of Dundas ever since they became acquainted with him, the burnings would have had nothing to do with the convention of the Associated Friends of the People. Contrary to the statement of the *Oracle*, no "commotions" were "apprehended" in connection with the convention, and no "commotions" occurred. It was held in Edinburgh on 11 December, as planned, and lasted three days, being attended by 180 delegates, representing eighty reform societies. The chairman was the ex-Colonel William Dalrymple, the vice-president Thomas Muir, the secretary William Skirving. The minutes indicated no radical agitation on anyone's part, and the resolutions, a copy of which was subsequently sent to the London Friends of the People,[79] were mild. The Government was evidently well represented, for on 26 December Dundas, "transmitting" for the King's "perusal" a letter he had received "under cover of the Lord Advocate [Robert Dundas]," went on to explain that "Mr. [Alexander] Scott is the confidential person employed by [the] Lord Advocate, and J. B. is the spy who attends the meeting of *The Friends of the People* now calling themselves in Scotland *the British Convention.* . . ."[80] "J. B." was probably James Boswell.

But the Ministerial papers indicated little interest in the convention, the *World* remarking only (12 Dec.) that the Government had "very properly, [taken] away the Commission of two officers [Col. Macleod and Col. Dalrymple] —who seem, by their conduct, better disposed to fight *against their* KING, *than for him.*" They were greatly interested, however, in the sudden and violent defection of the life-long radical and onetime editor of the *Argus*, John King. King had not only defected: he had mounted the rostrum in Egham to proclaim his admiration for William Pitt, to defend the Constitution, to denounce all reformers, and to declare his utter detestation of the French Revolution. The Egham speech was printed in full by the *Morning Herald* of 12 December, reprinted in part by other newspapers, and later reissued as a pamphlet.[81] The Opposition newspapers were much more concerned about the riots in Manchester, which began on 11 December and lasted two days, thus coinciding with the convention in Edinburgh. The point of departure in this instance was a meeting of the townspeople for the purpose of preserving the Constitution against "incendiaries"; and, so enthusiastic was the audience, that, on the way home, it attacked all the dissenters in the area, finally burning to the ground the homes of Thomas Cooper and Thomas Walker. James Watt was still on the Continent. The Association could compliment itself in every respect. "If, as Shakspeare says, 'The Players are the brief abstract and Chronicle of the Times,' then Loyalty never was more truly conspicuous than at this moment," observed the *World* on 18 December. "At every Provincial Theatre in the Kingdom the tune of 'God Save the King' is continually called for."

Having called out the militia, the King was bound by law to convoke Parliament within fourteen days. Much of what had happened was preparation for this event, and the *World* further prepared for it by announcing on 12 December that the Army was being augmented "by adding ten men to every company" and that the "seceders from Opposition are, the Duke of PORTLAND, Lord LOUGH-BOROUGH, Mr. WYNDHAM, and Mr. ANSTRUTHER." Parliament did convene on 13 December, but anyone who expected finally to learn why the King had employed the militia was doomed to disappointment. In his opening address, the King referred vaguely to certain "seditious practices," which, having "in some measure" been "checked" as a result of the Proclamation against Seditious Writings, had lately been "more openly renewed, and with increased activity": "A spirit of tumult and disorder . . . has shown itself in acts of riot and insurrection, which required the interposition of a military force in support of the civil magistrate.—The industry employed to excite discontent on various pretexts, and in different parts of the kingdom, has appeared to proceed from a design to attempt the destruction of our happy constitution, . . . and this design has evidently been pursued in connexion and concert with persons in foreign countries." Without specifying the nature of this "evidence," he went on to say that, although he had tried to "[observe] a strict neutrality in the present war on the continent," he could not overlook "the strong and increasing indications which have appeared there of an intention to excite disturbances in other countries"; nor could he overlook France's apparent designs on The Netherlands, "who have observed the same neutrality with myself." Hence, in order "both to maintain internal tranquillity, and to . . . [preserve] the blessings of peace," he had not merely called out the militia, but had "thought it right to take steps for making some augmentation of my naval and military force." He had "no doubt" that the Commons would "make a due provision" for these "extra-ordinary expences, which may, for a time, prevent the application of additional sums . . . to the reduction of the national debt, [and] retard . . . a further diminu-tion of taxes"; and he was sure that the Lords would continue "on their firm determination to defend and maintain that constitution, which has so long protected the liberties, and promoted the happiness of every class of my subjects." The war in India, it gave him "great pleasure" to add, had been concluded, owing to "the brilliant successes of the British arms, . . . under the able conduct of the Marquis [so created on 8 Oct.] Cornwallis." Having said this much, the King took his departure, and on the following night the Royal Family attended the Drury Haymarket for the first time.

The speech led to lively debates in both houses, the debates following the same general pattern. Those opposing the Address of Thanks demanded evidence that an insurrection had occurred, as well as evidence that a wholesale preparation for war was the best way to preserve peace. Those supporting the Address replied with attacks on those supposedly responsible for the insurrection and fulminations respecting the conduct of France, so that the "debates" were in effect only so much angry oratory. In the Lords the opponents to the Address included the Duke of Norfolk and Lord Lansdowne, the latter objecting at length to the "darkness and mysterious silence" which had characterized "this business." He also took occasion to express his disapproval of the activities of The Crown and Anchor Association and to add his opinion that there had been no uprising, that Parliament had been "illegally assembled," and that "the real motive" behind all this was "war." It had always been the case, he said, that "men who enjoyed sinecure places" would do anything to keep them, but to plunge the country into war was going somewhat too far. What he therefore proposed was a reform bill which would deprive Pitt and his friends of their patronage before they could do further damage. To these pronouncements Lord Grenville responded with the sneer that it was Grey's notice respecting similar reforms which had brought about the present situation. Thanks to the Friends of the People, he said, subversive societies were now rampant, and seditious literature was available to all at twopence a copy.

Lord Stormont was glad to "range" himself "under the broad banner of the Constitution" on this occasion and to "add one to the great phalanx that is to shield it from the poisoned arrows directed against it," as so were Lord Por-chester and the Duke of Clarence. The Duke of Clarence added that he had already "made an offer of his professional services to his country" in the event of war, and he was personally convinced that war was unavoidable: "It is plain the French are directed by objects of ambition and aggrandizement; they have already annexed the Duchy of Savoy to their dominions as the eighty-fourth department, and, if they conquer Holland, I suppose they will make it the eighty-fifth." The Duke of York and the Prince of Wales were not present, but the Prince of Wales's friend, Lord Rawdon, sided with Lord Lansdowne. He had "come down to the House" to support the Government, he said, expecting that the Government would certainly present evidence of an insurrection before it called on Parliament to "sanction" such "precipitous measures"; but, "inferring" from Lord Grenville's silence that "no tumults existed," he was taking his stand with the Opposition instead.

The debates in the Commons were more heated. In the absence of Pitt, who, since his election was still pending, was not at this point a member, the Address of Thanks was moved by the Lord Mayor, Sir James Saunderson. Saunderson talked mostly of the present situation, which he represented as even more alarming than it had been earlier, inasmuch as the societies were now working "less openly and more cautiously" and hence were "the more dangerous." Foremost among the respondents was Fox, who stated as his "firm opinion, that there is not one fact asserted in His Majesty's speech which is not false." The whole speech and everything which preceded it he regarded as "an intolerable calumny on the people of Great Britain; an insinuation of so gross and black a nature, that it demands . . . the most severe punishment. . . . An insurrection!" he exclaimed. "Where is it? Where has it reared its head? Good God! an insurrection in Great Britain! No wonder that the militia were called out, and Parliament assembled in [this] extraordinary way. . . . But where is it? . . . I will take upon me to say . . . that it is not the notoriety of the insurrection which prevents [the Government] from communicating to us the particulars, but its non-existence." Certainly, he admitted, the societies had published pamphlets "containing doctrines tending . . . to subvert our establishments," but there was no law prohibiting such publications; the law stated only that, if the publication had mischievous effects, the Government could "take cognizance of the fact in a court of law." But the Government had chosen to waive the law, to decide for itself whether publications were mischievous or not, and to suppress them on its own authority. To achieve its ends, it had established a system of spies and informers, set up an inquisition, and introduced all the other paraphernalia of a despotism. To counteract the doctrine of the rights of the people, it had even revived the "exploded" doctrine of the rights of kings, as evidenced by a recent handbill issued by Reeves's Association, entitled *One Pennyworth of Truth from Thomas Bull to his Brother John*. The result of all this, and this result was the one he particularly "dreaded," would be to drive everyone to extremes, for it was an unhappy truth that "one extreme naturally leads to another." Although he would himself continue to "stand in the gap, and oppose myself to all the wild projects of a new-fangled theory, as much as against the monstrous iniquity of exploded doctrines," he foresaw the time when he would be standing there alone. As to developments on the Continent, Fox was utterly opposed to interference on behalf of Holland or any other country; he was particularly opposed to supporting Austria and Prussia. He could even sympathize with those Englishmen who had celebrated their defeats, for he would confess that he himself had heard of them with some gratification, as so, he was sure, had every lover of liberty who had read the Duke of Brunswick's Manifesto. Having appealed to his "valued friends" not to fall victim to the Government's "snares" and having again taken his place with the moderate reformers, Fox concluded by moving an amendment to the Address, stating in effect that the Commons would require some definite information about the insurrection before it proceeded. The amendment was supported by Grey, Erskine, and Sheridan; it was opposed by Fox's "valued friends," William Windham and John Anstruther, as well as by Dundas, Sir Archibald Macdonald, and Burke. As evidence that he at least had not been "remiss" in his duties, Macdonald mentioned that he now had "on my file two hundred informations" awaiting prosecution.

It was the opinion of the *Morning Chronicle* that "the real motive" behind the "present business" was less "war" than politics, the principal object being, as it had been in the case of the Proclamation against Seditious Writings, to separate Fox from the Friends of the People. Burke seems to have felt that it was a little of both. Having defended despotism as sometimes necessary and at all times better than the kind of "liberty" enjoyed by the French, he went on to say that war was not only inevitable, but long overdue. As he put it: "What renders the factious in this country particularly dangerous is their connexion with the French robbers and assassins. The French have declared war against all Kings, and of consequence against this country. . . . Their power has already become formidable to the whole of Europe, and, if we would not have Europe torn from us, it is necessary that we interpose by the most effectual means to stop their farther career." The "factious" singled out for special invective were now Joel Barlow, John Frost, Lord Sempill, and that "complete model of depravity" from "the deepest recesses of Hell," the Duke of Orleans, who had returned to France to support the republican cause. Barlow was actually an American, although he had lived in England since 1790. However, Burke also expressed his profound regret that a man so talented as Fox had not seen fit to accept a position in the Government or even to support the Government in this moment of crisis; and, so far as he was concerned, this seemed to settle the matter. Fox's motion was defeated by a vote of 290 to 50.

On 14 December Fox moved a second amendment, praying that the King would "employ every means of negociation, consistent with the honour and safety of this country, to avert the calamities of war." It was supported by Adam and Sheridan and opposed by Dundas and Burke, the latter contending that it was too late for such negotiations, France having already declared war on England. The amendment was defeated and the Address approved by the same vote of 290 to 50. On 15 December, Fox moved a third amendment, this time praying that the King would send a minister to Paris "to treat with those persons who exercise provisionally the functions of executive government in France." The ensuing debate was even more heated than those which had preceded. The principal supporter of the motion was Erskine, who backed his own statements with numerous quotations from Dr. Johnson; the principal opponent was Burke. This was in one sense a rather solemn occasion, for, by taking his seat for the first time on the Treasury bench, Burke had indicated that he saw no hope of an understanding between himself and Fox. But the effect was somewhat obscured by the recent exposés of Pigott and Paine; and, in order to guard against a possible misinterpretation, he felt obliged to state that he had not been bribed by William Pitt. "I have made no provision for myself or family," he said. "We are not in the possession of any office; neither cajoled by the reversion of place, nor by the promise of pension." Having clarified this matter, he then dismissed the quotations from Dr. Johnson as "a good common-place against war," sneered at Erskine for setting himself up as an "instructor," and embarked on the usual denunciation of the French Revolution. But this time his fury was completely out of bounds. "Will you," he demanded, "tamely surrender yourselves to Citizens Frost and Paine? Forbid it, heaven! forbid it, justice! forbid it, humanity! Yield to traitors to their King? To a nation of murderers? Stain the illustrious pages of our history with such profanation and impiety? May God, in his infinite mercy, add vigour to our arms, and enable us to check the encroachments of those monsters of society!" The reason for his rage, it finally became apparent, was Erskine, who, he had just heard, would represent Thomas Paine, whose trial was now scheduled for 18 December. Although the motion was negatived by the usual majority, this debate aroused so much interest that the *Oracle* of 17 December devoted six pages to it, distributing the extra half sheet gratis. By 18 December it had recollected with panic that the half sheet had been unstamped, but it assured its readers that it had made amends by filing an affidavit at the Stamp Office. The affidavit, a copy of which was included, stated that 2,825 copies of the paper had been printed. It was signed by John Beswicke, "Publisher and Superintendant of the Printing Press of THE ORACLE." *The Times*, now printed by Thomas Thirlwind, had sold approximately 2,900 copies.

It was evident from the debates of 13, 14, and 15 December that Parliament would support a war, but, since Parliament always supported the Government, this fact was hardly noteworthy. The question which remained unanswered was what effect Fox's three motions had had on the people, who would have to fight the war if there was one and who would be disinclined to do so unless they believed that the Constitution was actually imperiled. It was generally admitted that Burke, who was not loved by the populace and whose reputation had already been impaired by Paine's *Letter Addressed to the Addressers* and Pigott's *Jockey Club*, had not helped the Government's cause. His speeches were applauded by no newspaper, and they greatly alarmed the Opposition press, the *Courier* even wondering if he was entirely sane. They also alarmed the *Diary*, which, being quite as afraid of Burke as it was of Paine and uneasy about Pitt besides, was tending to support Fox. Other Ministerial newspapers ignored Fox, but redoubled their attacks on the radical reformers, all of whom were represented as agents of the French. There was considerable gloating over the flights of Frost, Paine, and Sampson Perry and over the demise of the *Argus*, the *World* announcing on 15 December: "We are exceedingly sorry to inform the Public, that Mr. HORNE TOOKE has lost the use of one of his limbs.—A few days ago died a Paper, called The ARGUS." This was the first serious mention of Horne Tooke, who had previously been dismissed as nothing but a publicity hound.

Although nothing was said for the moment of the moderate reformers, the Friends of the People could not feel that it had gained any advantage. Meeting on 15 December to reconsider their situation, the members resolved after lengthy deliberation to "persevere in their endeavours to accomplish . . . the object of their Association . . . until the object is obtained, or shall be found to be . . . unattainable." But they also resolved to republish their "motives and intentions" in order to demonstrate that they were not "Republicans and Levellers," and they respectfully declined an invitation from the United Irishmen of Dublin, dated 26 October, to support Catholic emancipation. On the following day (16 Dec.), several members of the United Irishmen, among them Archibald Hamilton Rowan, the Secretary, were arrested for trying to overawe the Irish Parliament, but all of them were subsequently released. The *Morning Post*, which by 6 December was being printed by J. Norris and on 17 December dropped its subtitle, calling itself henceforth only the *Morning Post*, was now carrying the most complete accounts of radical activities and was also the principal champion of the Friends of the People.

The Alien Act

On the day Parliament convened (13 Dec.), riots erupted in Cambridge, the result of the same "manipulated panic"[82] which had caused the riots in Manchester two days earlier and following much the same pattern. As before, the point of departure was a meeting of the townspeople for the purpose of suppressing seditious publications, the rioters were the people who attended the meeting, although they were led, according to the *World* (17 Dec.), by the chimney sweeps, and the victims were the dissenters. The riots continued through 14 December, upon which day the Commons moved a writ for a special election at the University, and 15 December, when the townspeople met again, this time to declare a state of emergency. Instead of blaming the rioters for the trouble, they, however, blamed the victims for having distributed seditious literature and otherwise propagated "treason" in the first place, and they resolved to persist in their efforts until they had hunted out and punished every one of the "traitors." By the time Pitt arrived, the Town of Cambridge was therefore under martial law, and the dissenters were in hiding. Everything was also quiet at the University, since students were still under the impression that Porson was an active member of the faculty. Hence, at ten o'clock on the morning of 18 December, Pitt was unanimously re-elected Member of Parliament for Cambridge University, and that afternoon he returned to London, his "popularity" being, according to the *Oracle* (19 Dec.), "rather increased than diminished."

On 13 December Sir Archibald Macdonald, the Attorney General, had greatly deplored "the length of time necessary to be employed in taking the previous steps before a prosecution could be commenced," but he was supposedly making some progress on his "two hundred informations," for on 18 December the *World* reported the arrest (17 Dec.) of James Ridgway of York Street and William Holland of Oxford Street, both of whom had been indicted by a Grand Jury, Ridgway for selling Paine's *Rights of Man*, Part II, Holland for selling his *Letter Addressed to the Addressers*. They were being imprisoned until they found bail, for which they had been ordered to give forty-eight hours notice. This was the second indictment of Ridgway. The Opposition had maintained throughout that these prosecutions were illegal. As Fox had reminded the Commons on 13 December, the law permitted any and all publications, the Attorney General had no ground for complaint unless he could prove that a publication had resulted in overt acts, and thus far the Government had traced no overt acts to the writings of Thomas Paine. Nor had it presented evidence of such acts. On the other hand, said Grey on 17 December, he was prepared to show that *A Pennyworth of Truth from Thomas Bull to his Brother John* had helped to incite the riots in both Manchester and Cambridge, and, since he had traced the handbill to The Crown and Anchor Association, he could very properly move for the prosecution of John Reeves as publisher of a "mischievous libel." The motion was negatived, and, on the following day, Paine was himself tried as author of the *Rights of Man*, Part II.

The trial was held in Guildhall before Lord Kenyon and a special jury, Paine, who was still in France, being represented by Thomas Erskine. Paine in fact figured only slightly in the proceedings, for, as the trial progressed, Erskine became the prosecutor, and the Government, as defendant, stood charged with subverting the law by trickery. Without in any sense condoning Paine's writings, Erskine concluded with an impassioned defense of the existing law of libel as the basis for freedom of the press and of freedom of the press as the basis for rational liberty. But, although the address is still regarded as a masterpiece and long excerpts were subsequently printed by the *Morning Post*, it failed to influence the jury, which convicted Paine and as a result exonerated the Government without even waiting for the concluding remarks of the Attorney General. Since this verdict enabled the Government to proceed against Ridgway, Holland, and the numerous other publishers of Paine's works, the Ministerial newspapers should have been happy. They were not. Because Erskine had interrupted his discourse on two or three occasions to say that he was exhausted and on one occasion to say that he felt faint, he was jeered at constantly by *The Times*, the *Sun*, and the *World* as "The Swooning Philosopher" or "Tom Ego"; and the fiction that he was just as guilty as Paine was revived with venom. At the end of the year, the *Sun* reprinted one of its attacks in a collection, entitled *A Speech at the Whig Club [4 Dec., 1792] ; or a Great Statesman's [Mr. Fox's] own Exposition of His Political Principles. . . . An Answer to Two Letters . . . published in the Morning Chronicle. . . . A Consoling Epistle to Mr. F[rost], on his late Accident. An Admonitory Epistle to . . . Thomas Erskine. . . . The Bishop's Wig, a Tale. All published originally in The Sun.* It was apparent that Erskine was going to be punished, for the burden of much of the material (see, for example, *World*, 19, 20, 21, 24, 25, and 28 Dec.) was that, whereas the unhappy King of France had no one to defend him, Thomas Paine had "the PRINCE of WALES's ATTORNEY GENERAL." The Ministerial papers had been kind to the Prince since 12 December, and on 21 December the *Public Advertiser* announced that "His Majesty allows 20,000*l.* per annum for five years, towards the complete liquidation of the Prince's debts; at the end of that period, the whole 400,000*l.* will be paid off. The small debts, amounting to 60,000*l.* have been all discharged within the last fortnight." Since this announcement and others like it seem to have had no basis in fact, they were no doubt intended to quiet some of the Prince's creditors; but the Prince was not as yet so grateful as to dismiss Erskine.

Whatever object the Government had in view, the discrediting of the Friends of the People, the winning over of Fox, the preservation of its patronage, or the commencement of a war, depended for its realization on a succession of alarms. The worse the radicals looked, the better off, in short, was William Pitt. On 19 December there was another alarm, this one consisting of a bill, introduced by Lord Grenville, "for establishing regulations respecting Aliens arriving in this kingdom, or residing therein in certain cases." The Alien Bill, which, along with the Army and Navy budgets, preoccupied Parliament for the remainder of the year, provided for strict surveillance of immigrants, including periodic examinations, frequent registrations, confinement to certain "safe" areas, and a system of "passports." It was supposedly necessitated by the fact that there were now over eight thousand immigrants from France, including "persons disaffected to the government of this country." The Opposition newspapers objected to it on the ground that it was intended only to frighten the populace, that it was hastily contrived in order to confuse the public further as to that phantom insurrection of 1 December, and that it amounted to a declaration of war against France. It passed the Lords on 26 December and the Commons on 4 January. Although the debates during this period had as usual little to do with the issues under consideration, they were certainly not lacking in drama. The first bit of such drama ended Sheridan's dream of joining the Government.

While his newspaper, the *Oracle*, had been faithfully supporting Pitt, Sheridan had been faithfully supporting Fox, but on 20 December he began to waver. The occasion was a debate on the Navy budget. Sheridan had risen to say that, considering the present state of Continental affairs, he realized that the country must prepare for the possibility of war and he would "heartily" have approved the budget if it had called for an additional 40,000 seamen instead of a mere 9,000. If war came, he would "heartily" support it also; nor had he ever actually opposed it. He had simply said, as the King had himself said, that it should be averted if possible. He said the same thing today. His principal concern at present was the situation of the French Royal Family and especially the King. Since he was personally convinced that there still "existed" in France "a sincere disposition to listen to and respect the opinion of the British nation," he did feel that the French might spare Louis's life if they were acquainted with "the temper" of the British. Burke was enraged. Purporting to interpret Sheridan's remarks as an "unfounded, indecent, and impertinent" slur on his own conduct, he went on to accuse him, not only of being "in the secrets of the French ministers," but of speaking as their agent. Fox defended Sheridan, Pitt supposedly attempted a reconciliation, but the damage was done.

Since there was nothing offensive in Sheridan's speech except the perfidy behind it, Burke could have reacted only to that, although not necessarily on his own initiative, for it is highly unlikely that Pitt ever intended to take Sheridan into the Government. Although he was no doubt grateful for his assistance in stifling the *Argus* and for the support of the *Oracle* during the 1 December alarms, he had nothing to gain by his defection, which would have had no influence on Fox or on the people. If this was in fact an act of guile on Pitt's part, it at least succeeded, for the *Oracle* held Burke singly reponsible for quashing whatever arrangement Sheridan and Pitt had agreed on. On 22 December the *Oracle* expressed its opinion of that gentleman:

> We have yet a doubt upon our minds, whether the aggravated peril of LOUIS be not derivable from the CRUSADE so fatally preached by Mr. BURKE to the *Sovereigns* of *Europe*.
>
> It is astonishing, that when every other Member in the House sees the necessity of conciliating all PARTIES, Mr. BURKE, regardless how they may affect his cause, scatters his brands of division, and hurls his menaces of arrogant defiance; together with imputations, which a temper as ungovernable as his own might resent in a way we deprecate exceedingly.—We have need of the collective talents of this Country.—All unworthy Spleen should be expelled, as disgraceful to the temper and feelings of British Senators.
>
>> "Are we turn'd Turks, and to ourselves do that,
>> Which Heaven has forbid the Ottomites?"

We are concerned to see so great a man as BURKE flying out in starts of mis-becoming invective.—By his strange attack upon Mr. SHERIDAN, it should seem he is disinclined even to bear the commiseration of another for the SUFFERERS, whose cause he has wished to make his own.

There was more on 24 December:

> How ridiculous does the irritable Temper of BURKE make his praise or censure! He one day throws his Contempt as liberally as the Husbandman *dung* upon the soil—the tilth rears up prematurely, the Day following a full crop of flowering Praise.
>
> "Why look you, I am whipt and stung with Adders,
> When I think of those French Politicians."

And on 25 December: "If the unhappy LOUIS stood in the parallel state of Trial with Mr. HASTINGS, he might yet attain the latest longevity without decision; and come at last by his *death* without a *sentence.*" It looked as if this would not happen to Louis, however, since on 20 December the French had declared all Bourbons, except those presently confined in The Temple, forever banished from the empire. While the *Oracle* continued its diatribes, Sheridan, who was nothing if not resilient, assisted Mackintosh, O'Bryen, Erskine, Tierney, and others in reviving the Friends of the Liberty of the Press as an antidote to The Association. He had no difficulty explaining matters to Fox, since Fox had evidently been unaware of the intrigue.

Although Burke now regarded Fox as lost and was quite as exasperated by his loyalty as he was by Sheridan's perfidy, the Government still had one trick left. Pitt's supposition that, if the Duke of Portland defected, Fox would defect with him had at least not been disproved, since the Duke of Portland had not defected. Except for William Adam and Lord Guilford, most of the right wing of the Opposition had been voting with the Government, several of them, notably William Windham, Lord Stormont, and Lord Loughborough, having spoken in defense of the Government as well. But the differences with Fox had always been represented as extraordinary and not indicative of any actual break; and so for the moment they continued. On 21 December the Duke of Portland rose to say that he would support the Alien Bill, now in its second reading, and added as usual that he was not motivated by "any personal attachment to the present administration," for "I cannot forget the manner in which they came into power; I cannot forget the many circumstances in their conduct by which they have forfeited all title to the confidence of the nation. I cannot forget that to their misconduct many of our present difficulties are owing." He was followed by Lord Stormont, who added his support on the same terms; and on 22 December Lord Stormont was followed in turn by Earl Spencer. On 24 December Fox restated his position, protesting in passing the dismissals of various Army officers, especially of Lord Sempill and Lord Edward Fitzgerald, without even the courtesy of a court-martial. They had done nothing illegal, it seemed to him, unless soldiers were understood to have no civil rights. Burke accused him of "impertinence." The Government, he snapped, "judges the conduct of its military officers" in exactly the same way as "a jury judges of the tendency of a seditious libel," and it was the King's "prerogative to dismiss any of his officers" at any time "without assigning a reason" for the action. This time Burke had nothing complimentary to say about Fox's "talents." The newspapers were still in the main complimentary.

On 26 December there was the first actual defection. By this time readers were being told of further setbacks for the Austrians, now commanded by the Prince of Saxe-Coburg, and further victories for the French, who already occupied much of the Austrian Netherlands. The Alien Bill having been read in the Lords for the third time, the Earl of Carlisle, a follower of the late Lord Guilford, reacted to this news by stating that, not only would he support the Government in this instance, but he would henceforth support it in all instances as a matter of policy. Although he still believed that "a change of administration is the only thing that can be of essential service to the country," he believed that a change at this particular time would be "of very dangerous consequence," inasmuch as Fox clearly favored negotiations. The bill was thereupon passed by the Lords and on 28 December was delivered to the Commons.

On the morning of 28 December, all newspapers reported that the Duke of Portland had accepted a second sinecure, the Presidency of the Foundling Hospital. Even the *Morning Chronicle* was bewildered. Without actually commenting on this development, it affixed to its announcement the observation: "We must apply to Placemen and Pensioners for the causes of Lord GRENVILLE's Bill, and the intended suspension of the Habeas Corpus. . . ." The purpose of this announcement, it became apparent later in the day, was to add a touch of plausibility to a story which was being readied for Fox, the teller of the story to be another follower of the late Lord Guilford, Sir Gilbert Elliot. Elliot performed very well. Shortly after the debate began, he rose to inform the Commons "with extreme reluctance" that there was now an irreconcilable difference of "sentiment" between the Duke of Portland and Fox. Although he personally hoped that "private friendships" would continue, he was speaking for the Duke when he said that "Fox's conduct" during the last several weeks had effected a "whole turn of thinking." Like himself, the Duke considered it "the duty of every man to stand forward in support of His Majesty's government, and thus to maintain the Constitution, and to save the country" at this critical moment in its history, and he could no longer, therefore, continue his political association with Fox.

Fox was aghast. At first he refused to believe it. He and the Duke of Portland, he said, had "lived seventeen years on terms of friendship, and for ten of those seventeen have been in habits of the greatest intimacy and affection." If the Duke of Portland felt that there was a permanent schism, he would not have informed him in this manner, especially since he had expressed his personal contempt for the Pitt Government only a few days earlier. A schism was impossible. There was of course disagreement respecting the Alien Bill, but they "agreed on every thing else"; or there was at least no "difference" which could not be resolved by "a fair discussion." If the Duke of Portland somehow felt otherwise, all he could say was so be it. He had so long acted with "characters whom I esteem and love" that the prospect of acting without them was almost too painful to endure. Still, if he "should be driven, which God forbid! to the situation of acting without, or even against those characters, I hope and trust I shall have sense enough to discern my duty, and fortitude enough to perform it." This was a great moment in the life of Charles James Fox, but it failed to impress Burke, who, having referred sneeringly to "the phalanx," which now constituted the Opposition, went on to express his "astonishment" that Fox should have called the disaster at Jemappes "a glorious victory." The newspapers were similarly astonished, for, although Fox had indicated on 13 December that he was not sympathetic with the Allies, no newspaper could remember that he had called Jemappes "a glorious victory." But, since the Ministerial press was happy to take Burke's word for it, the statement was credited to Fox from this moment on, and the Opposition was henceforth referred to as "the phalanx."

But Burke's speech of 28 December at least gave tit for tat, so far as the newspapers were concerned, for, in the course of it, Burke snatched a dagger from his pocket, hurled it to the floor in a fine frenzy of rage, and, pointing a trembling finger in its direction, thundered: "This is what you are to gain by an alliance with France." Waving the dagger above his head, he then dedicated himself anew to "[keeping] the French infection from this country, their principles from our minds, and their daggers from our hearts. I vote for [the Alien Bill], because I consider it the means of saving my life and all our lives, from the hands of assassins. . . . When [the French] smile, I see blood trickling down their faces; I see their insidious purposes; I see that the object of all their cajoling is— blood!" This performance the Opposition press remembered for many months.

On 31 December Sir Gilbert Elliot amended his remarks, which, it appeared, had not been "authorized" by the Duke of Portland after all: they had merely represented the tenor of his own thinking and the thinking of some of his friends. The Marquess of Titchfield thereupon pledged his own support to the Alien Bill and to all future legislation necessary for national security, but, like his father, the Duke of Portland, he could not "too explicitly declare that in no other respect can I give [Pitt] any share of my confidence." William Adam voted with Fox. There was certainly a difference of opinion, and it seemed to Fox, commenting on Elliot's apology, that it was perhaps greater than he had previously supposed. Essentially, he thought, it was a difference "on the state of the country": the Duke of Portland "thinks the country is in danger, and therefore very properly thinks that the executive power should be strengthened. I, on the contrary, am not aware of such danger, and [therefore] see no necessity for the [Alien Bill]." Although Fox did not say so, there was also a considerable difference of opinion respecting the matter of free elections.

Notes for Part II

1. For a fuller account of these developments, see Lucyle Werkmeister, *The London Daily Press 1772–1792* (Lincoln: University of Nebraska Press, 1963), pp. 346–349, and elsewhere.

2. For other such enterprises see *London Daily Press*, pp. 98, 163–164, 268–315.

3. For newspaper reactions to these suits, see *London Daily Press*, pp. 351–352.

4. *Mrs. Jordan and Her Family*, ed. Arthur Aspinall (London: Arthur Barker, 1951), pp. 12–13.

5. This suggestion is based on the several facts that Boswell was writing for Ministerial newspapers at this time, that the *World* was rising to his defense in 1792, and that the name signed to the verses is similar to a pseudonym he had previously used, "Old Salusbury Briar." See Lucyle Werkmeister, *Jemmie Boswell and the London Daily Press, 1785–1795* (New York: New York Public Library, 1963), pp. 11, 47, 48.

6. Although the newspapers spell the name *Lambert*, the newspapers seem to be in error. The precise date of Lady Cavan's action is not given by the press.

7. See *Memoirs of the Life of the Right Honourable Sir James Mackintosh*, ed. Robert James Mackintosh (Boston, 1853), I, 41. For the machinations of the spurious *Star*, see *London Daily Press*, pp. 219–316.

8. Published by Aspinall. See Arthur Aspinall, *Politics and the Press c. 1780–1850* (London: Ernest Benn Ltd., 1949), p. 279.

9. See *London Daily Press*, p. 103.

10. Copied from Aspinall. See *Politics and the Press*, pp. 278–279, 280.

11. See *London Daily Press*, p. 24.

12. The paragraph which follows effectively repudiates my previous suggestion (*London Daily Press*, pp. 215–216) that the *World* was probably not leased prior to its sale in 1794.

13. See *London Daily Press*, p. 207.

14. See *London Daily Press*, p. 208.

15. See *London Daily Press*, pp. 199–200, 205, 327, 329.

16. Robert L. Haig, *The Gazetteer 1735–1797* (Carbondale: Southern Illinois University Press, 1960), pp. 224, 226.

17. All references to the proceedings during the year 1792 are taken from *Proceedings of the Society of Friends of the People; Associated for the Purpose of Obtaining a Parliamentary Reform, in the Year 1792* (London, 1793).

18. See for example the obituaries of Daniel Stuart, *Gentleman's Magazine*, n.s., XXVII (1847), 90 and XXVIII (1847), 322; *Letters from the Lake Poets . . . to Daniel Stuart*, ed. Mary Stuart (London, 1889), p. x; Mackintosh's *Memoirs*, I, 79.

19. Mackintosh's *Memoirs*, I, 80.

20. *State Trials for High Treason. Reported by a Student in the Temple* (London, 1794), I, 203.

21. Daniel Stuart, "The Newspaper Writings of the Poet Coleridge," *Gentleman's Magazine*, n.s., IX (1838), 579.

22. *Letters from the Lake Poets*, p. x.

23. "The Late Mr. Coleridge, the Poet," *Gentleman's Magazine*, n.s., X (1838), 125.

24. Mackintosh's *Memoirs*, I, 79.

25. See *London Daily Press*, p. 356.

26. *Gentleman's Magazine*, n.s., X, 125.

27. *Memoirs of the Whig Party during My Time. By Henry Richard Lord Holland*, ed. Henry Edward Lord Holland (London, 1852), I, 13–15.

28. *London Daily Press*, pp. 175, 347.

29. This account is taken from Ridgway's "Prefatory Address" affixed to Mrs. Billington's *Memoirs*.

30. *London Daily Press*, p. 129.

31. *Mrs. Jordan and Her Family*, pp. 12–13.

32. *Mrs. Jordan and Her Family*, pp. 18–19.

33. This account supplements my previous one in numerous particulars. See *London Daily Press*, pp. 216–217.

34. For an account of her wanderings, see *Life and Times of Frederick Reynolds. Written by Himself* (London, 1827), II, 134–160. But Reynolds's dates are not always correct.

35. *The Agreeable Surprise*, first performed on 3 September, 1781, was many times revived.

36. [Mary Wells], *Memoirs of the Life of Mrs. Sumbel, Late Wells* (London, 1811), I, 74.

37. The only plays now attributed to General Burgoyne are *The Maid of the Oaks* (Drury Lane, 5 Nov., 1774), *The Lord of the Manor* (Drury Lane, 27 Dec., 1780), *The Heiress* (Drury Lane, 14 Jan., 1786), and *Richard Coeur de Lion. An Historical Romance from the French of Sedaine* (Drury Lane, 24 Oct., 1786).

38. For a list of some of the members, see *London Daily Press*, pp. 98, 156–157, 158.

39. John Taylor, *Records of My Life* (London, 1832), II, 271–272.

40. *Letter Addressed to the Addressers on the Late Proclamation. By Thomas Paine* (London, 1792), p. 25.

41. For a fuller account of these events, see *London Daily Press*, pp. 366–367.

42. *The Real Calumniator Detected*, pp. 24–25.

43. See *London Daily Press*, pp. 91, 298.

44. *The Real Calumniator Detected*, pp. 27–28.

45. *The Real Calumniator Detected*, pp. 2–6, 8–9, 28–29.

46. *Oppression Deemed No Injustice*, p. 24.

47. *Politics and the Press*, p. 421.

48. *Politics and the Press*, p. 421.

49. C. H. Timperley, *Dictionary of Printers and Printing* (London, 1839), p. 875. But Timperley himself contradicts this statement on page 801 by stating that in 1799 the printer was John Vint.

50. William Jerdan, *Autobiography* (London, 1852–1853), I, 92.

51. See *Politics and the Press*, p. 103.

52. See *London Daily Press*, p. 379.

53. This account supplements the account previously presented. See *London Daily Press*, pp. 368–371.

54. *The Correspondence of William Augustus Miles on the French Revolution 1789–1817*, ed. Rev. Charles Popham Miles (London, 1850), II, 344, note.

55. Jerdan, I, 93.

56. See *London Daily Press*, p. 370.

57. Daniel Stuart, *Peace and Reform, against War and Corruption* (London, 1794), p. 20, note.

58. See *London Daily Press*, p. 370.

59. *Peace and Reform*, p. 20, note.

60. See *London Daily Press*, p. 368.

61. Cyrus Redding, *Fifty Years' Recollections, Literary and Personal, with Observations on Men and Things* (London, 1858), I, 96.

62. See *London Daily Press*, p. 379.

63. Arthur Gray and Frederick Britain, *A History of Jesus College, Cambridge* (London: Heinemann, 1960), pp. 121–122. The discussion which follows is based on Gray and Britain,

pp. 122–124, and Martin Ray Adams, *Studies in the Literary Backgrounds of English Radicalism* (Lancaster, Pa.: n.p., 1947), pp. 234–235.

64. Martin Lowther Clarke, *Richard Porson. A Biographical Essay* (Cambridge: Cambridge University Press, 1937), p. 34.

65. Except for the contextual material, the above account is taken from Clarke's *Porson*, pp. 31–34, and *Recollections of the Table Talk of Samuel Rogers. To Which is Added Porsoniana*, ed. Rev. Alexander Dyce (London, 1856), pp. 313–316.

66. See *London Daily Press*, p. 370.

67. *Letter Addressed to the Addressers*, p. 2.

68. *Letter Addressed to the Addressers*, p. 6.

69. *Letter Addressed to the Addressers*, p. 43.

70. [Charles Pigott,] *The Jockey Club: or A Sketch of the Manners of the Age*, Part III (London, 1792), p. 199.

71. *Letter Addressed to the Addressers*, p. 48.

72. *Politics and the Press*, p. 450.

73. *The Farington Diary by Joseph Farington, R. A.*, ed. James Greig (London: Hutchinson and Co., 1922–1928), V, 163.

74. *Peace and Reform*, pp. 9, 20–22.

75. *Peace and Reform*, pp. 18–19.

76. For a fuller account of the demise of the *Argus*, see *London Daily Press*, pp. 363–365, 376, although the account mistakenly supposes that the *Argus* survived until the end of December. The account also exonerates Sheridan, who, it now appears, should not have been exonerated.

77. See *London Daily Press*, pp. 121, 138.

78. See *London Daily Press*, pp. 67–68.

79. For copies of minutes and resolutions, see *The Parliamentary History of England* (London, 1817), XXXI, 870–879.

80. Quoted from *The Later Correspondence of George III*, ed. Arthur Aspinall (Cambridge: Cambridge University Press, 1963), II, 138.

81. *Mr. King's Speech at Egham with Thomas Paine's Letter to Him on it, and Mr. King's Reply, as They All Appeared in the Morning Herald* . . . (Egham, [1793]).

82. Walter Sichel, *Sheridan* (London: Houghton, 1909), II, 245.

III

THE FIRST YEAR OF THE WAR: 1793

Character of the Newspapers:
The Opposition Press

There were fifteen dailies at the beginning of 1793, two of the fourteen in existence at the beginning of 1792 having been discontinued and three new ones having been commenced. The sale of newspapers had also increased, and it further increased during 1793, as the "following . . . comparative state of the duties paid for Newspaper Stamps," which appeared in the *Star* of 2 September, indicates:

		£	s.	d.
From Aug. 1791 to Aug. 1792,	14,219,760	118,498	0	6
Aug. 1792 to Aug. 1793,	17,073,621	142,280	3	0
	2,853,861	23,782	2	6

The character of newspapers was considerably altered. For one thing, poetry was no longer regarded as essential. Several newspapers, notably the *Diary*, the *Public Advertiser*, the *Public Ledger*, and *The Times*, were abandoning it altogether in favor of librettos of popular songs, taken from the "operas" or more properly the operettas being performed at Drury Lane and Covent Garden; and other newspapers, such as the *Gazetteer* and the *Morning Herald*, were printing poems only occasionally. But, although interest in poetry was limited to certain newspapers, there was still a great deal of it, and there tended to be more as the year progressed. The sonnet with a somewhat nostalgic theme was especially prominent. The *Morning Chronicle* and the *Morning Herald* each published a half-dozen such sonnets by William Lisle Bowles, and the *Morning Post* even had a sonneteer on its staff. Della Cruscan verse was still being offered by the *Oracle*, and Mrs. Robinson, although an infrequent contributor, attracted considerable notice. There was much political verse, usually satirical and often on the level of doggerel, and there was much poetry of a rather high order, owing principally to the *Morning Chronicle*, which, during the last six months of the year, was most specifically "The Paper of Poetry."

Sports were generally neglected. The newspapers had always disapproved of horse racing, and, now that the Prince of Wales and the Duke of York were engrossed in military games, they were inclined to forget it altogether. They had disapproved of boxing even more, and in this instance there was little to report, since, before the year was over, most of the "bruisers" were employed by the Government as "crimps." The sole remaining patron of boxing seemed to be the Duke of Hamilton, an amateur boxer himself. Gambling was another matter. For several years ladies of quality had been conducting gambling "entertainments" in their homes, usually for the purpose of recouping the family fortunes. These had been patronized by the Prince of Wales, the Duke of York, Mrs. Fitzherbert, and everyone else, it appeared, who was even loosely attached to the Carlton-House coterie. But, although such "entertainments" had been the center of London social activity, they were ignored by the press until early 1793, when the blackmailing newspapers became interested in rumors of financial ruin on the part of the guests and pandering activities on the part of the hostesses. By the end of the year, the "Pharo tables" were themselves news. As the name implied, the principal game had been faro, and the ladies continued to prefer it to anything else, but the gentlemen were experimenting with a new game, called "casino," and by midyear rouge et noir had been imported from France. Rouge et noir evidently proved to be a real money-maker, for by 8 August, according to the *Morning Post*, the "managers of the table at Charing Cross" were realizing £10,000 a year from it. Every newspaper carried a daily column on the subject of the Court. Readers knew what the King and Queen had done almost every hour of the previous day, and they were as well informed about state functions as anyone present. This *was* the society column, whereas paragraphs about the gambling tables were regarded only as scandal. Yet, since this was the first time newspapers had noticed any extra-Court social activity, the paragraphs were at least harbingers of the society column of today.

The year 1793 also marked the beginning of the fashion column. There had been no fashion column before because there had been no fashions. The King, the Queen, and the Princesses dressed as they had always dressed, and, since the Queen frowned on innovations on the part of her guests, styles had remained unchanged for over thirty years. The Prince of Wales, although supposedly a rebel against the inelegance of the Court, had rebelled only to the extent of dressing more elaborately than his father: he had never been so recalcitrant as to alter the mode. Whatever news there was on the subject of clothes had therefore been woven into accounts of state functions, it had consisted only of descriptions of individual dress, and it had concerned nothing except material, color, and ornamentation. But a full-scale rebellion was in the making, and, by the beginning of 1793, it was everywhere in evidence in the form of a feminine undergarment, called "the pad," the effect of which was to make the wearer look many months pregnant. No one knew who had introduced the pad. It may have been Mrs. Wells, since the *Diary* of 30 July, 1792, seems to have been quite mistaken in supposing that she was "in a fair way to increase her family." For similar reasons it may have been Mrs. Merry. The pad in any event was not admired by the newspapers. Having ignored it as long as possible, they tried hard to censure or ridicule it out of existence, but to no avail. The horror of the Queen was also ineffectual. Her announcement before every state function that wearers of pads would not be admitted seemed rather to strengthen the rebellion; for, whereas pads were worn, to begin with, only by ladies with husbands in the offing, they were soon worn by women of every condition, social and marital. The pad also introduced other vogues, dress and coiffure being adjusted to conform with the *enceinte* appearance and additional eccentricities being adopted whenever occasion suggested. The Ministerial newspapers felt sorry for the Queen, who, several of them pointed out, was not altogether opposed to change, since she and the Princesses had adopted the bathing machine. Yet, since the pad did persist and since it was accompanied by so many other innovations, no newspaper could ignore the fact that there had been a genuine rebellion against the Court in matters of dress and that fashion had henceforth to be part of the journalistic fare. The first fashion column may have appeared in the *Morning Herald* of 5 July. By 1794 even the Queen seems to have been reading fashion columns, for, although she and the Princesses never succumbed to the pad, they did succumb to later vogues.

Continental news was of course much in demand, and, having learned from their experience with the *Sun* how little they could trust the Government's accounts, newspapers were scrambling to establish independent sources; but the results were not very happy. The *Oracle*, for example, had had an independent source for years in the person of the Rev. William Jackson, who was still living in France to avoid his creditors, but, if Jackson knew what was going on, it was certainly not evident from the *Oracle*. Foreign newspapers were very expensive, and, even when arrangements had been made to ship them, their deliveries were so impeded by the Post Office that the news was stale indeed by the time it arrived. Hence, although all newspapers prided themselves on their "foreign intelligence," much of it was hearsay and guessing. If the guess turned out to be lucky, the newspaper never allowed its readers to forget it; if it turned out to be unlucky, it ridiculed the "intelligence" offered by other newspapers. Much of the news, too, was pure fiction, manufactured by the editor or conductor for stockjobbing purposes. Stories of Allied victories were published one day and retracted the next, and, since the original publication was often a second edition, second editions were in ill repute. The year 1793 was, however, distinguished for its maps. Maps were themselves no innovation. As early as 12 November, 1781, the *Morning Herald* had offered its readers a map "*of the late Naval* ACTION *of the* CHESAPEAK," which had been followed during 1782 by another half-dozen such diagrams. But the diagrams were evidently too crude to interest anyone, for by 1783 the project had been discontinued. The map was revived by John Bell, whose copper engravings were certainly the newspaper achievement of the decade.

The *Daily Advertiser*, still printed by Joshua Jenour at No. 33, Fleet Street, and still selling at only 3*d*., was generally unchanged in character. On 12

October, 1793, it experimented with a new format, putting the news on the first page and pushing the advertisements toward the back. This was the first time such an arrangement had been attempted by any newspaper, and readers evidently did not like it, for it was discontinued after a few days. As before, the paper was politically neutral, presenting facts, not opinions. The *Star, and Evening Advertiser*, still printed and edited, under the close supervision of the proprietors, by John Mayne in Temple Bar, was also regarding itself as neutral or at least "impartial." The shift was justified (1 Jan.) on the ground that subscribers expected it. As the *Star* put it: "Our task is more arduous than that of any of our contemporaries; for, all of them are the avowed supporters of some party; and from them impartiality is not expected—from us it is. . . ." This would certainly have been news to the subscribers, who had been told on 7 November that they "expected" the paper to support the Friends of the People. But, because of its large country circulation and its consequent dependence on the Post Office, the *Star* had had to consider the Government's "expectations" as well, so that in effect the shift represented a compromise of "expectations." In addition, there was a strong Ministerial faction among the proprietors, which also had to be placated, one of the leaders being John Mac Murray. Mac Murray died on 6 November, "after a long and painful illness," probably leaving his shares to his son, John Murray, a minor; but his death had no effect on the policy of the newspaper. In general, the *Star*'s "impartiality" turned out to be largely expedience. Although the paper could never bring itself to support the war or to applaud the Government's corruptive practices, it supported such a large part of its legislation that, for much of the year, it seemed to be more Ministerial than Opposition. Its editorial sins were, however, offset by certain virtues, for the paper did not wilfully misrepresent the news, and, because of its continuing link with the *Morning Chronicle*, its foreign and legal "intelligence" was the best of any available.

The *Courier*, the *Gazetteer*, the *Morning Chronicle*, and the *Morning Post* continued to support the Opposition. The *Courier* was now representing the radical reformers, the *Gazetteer* was moving toward moderate reform, the *Morning Chronicle* was championing Fox, and the *Morning Post* was defending the Friends of the People. Except for the *Morning Chronicle*, which was still collecting its £300 annuity from admirers of Fox, the Opposition press was shifting for itself. Lord Lauderdale had lost interest in newspapers for the moment, and the right wing of The Party had withdrawn its support altogether. On 2 August, 1793, Earl Fitzwilliam indicated that he had made no contributions for "a year and a half," and on 28 September he told Adam that, although the Duke of Portland would contribute "£200 towards payment of debts," he would contribute "not one shilling . . . [for] any other purpose, . . . particularly not to any newspaper writer whatever." The Duke of Devonshire was to be approached instead.[1] Lord John Russeil had persevered long enough to finance the *Morning Post*'s attacks on George Rose, but by now he had also abandoned the cause, as so had Lord Robert Spencer. In addition to having financial problems, the Opposition press was constantly harassed by both Reeves's Association and the Post Office, The Association doing everything in its power to persuade the country that the papers were opposed to the Constitution and hence treasonable, and the Post Office doing everything it could to impede delivery. Neither tactic was very successful, for, treasonable or not, these four papers do seem to have reflected public sentiment on the basic issues of peace and reform, and, except for the *Courier*, they were not sufficiently dependent on the Post Office to be injured by Freeling's machinations. Since they continued to function as a unit, they were more powerful than one might have supposed: more powerful certainly than the Ministerial papers and considerably more powerful than the Opposition itself. The two most effective newspapers of the Opposition group were now the *Morning Chronicle* and the *Morning Post*, the *Courier* tending to dissipate its energy in generalized abuse and the *Gazetteer* sinking slowly into the quagmire of vapidity.

On 24 December, 1792, the printing office of the *Morning Chronicle* had been moved from No. 1, Great Shire Lane, Temple Bar, to No. 5, Exeter Street. There was otherwise no change in the colophon, and the paper was still conducted by James Perry and James Gray. As usual, it had little interest in the theater, less interest in sports, and a downright contempt for fashions and fashionable people. But it was becoming increasingly interested in poetry. During the early part of the year, it published several sonnets by Bowles, along with occasional verses by Rutt, and, from June on, it published poetry in quantity. Among its poets were Richard Porson, Samuel Taylor Coleridge, and Robert Burns,[2] in addition to George Dyer and numerous unidentified correspondents, such as "Brogue," "L.," and "Tom Fool," "L." being possibly Hannah More. As a reporter of the debates, the *Chronicle* still had no rival, and its foreign and legal "intelligence" was matched only by the *Star*, which shared it. The *Chronicle*'s major achievement was, however, the editorial. The spurious *Star* had consolidated "paragraphs" into a coherent whole as early as 1789.[3] Not only did the *Chronicle* duplicate this feat, but it altered the character of the whole from ranting propaganda to critical analysis. Supplementing the editorials were epistolary contributions of a particularly astute sort, and supplementing the epistolary contributions were the brilliant satires of Richard Porson, that Regius Professor of Greek, for whose lectures there were still no rooms available at the University of Cambridge. In all such respects this was a golden year for the paper. Since Perry and Gray were not given to boasting, one knows only that on 16 October they were desperately in need of compositors, for whom they were offering a weekly wage of £1 10s. But, according to Farington,[4] they were doing well financially, clearing, it was "computed," about £6,000 a year and paying "about £25,000 . . . to Government for stamps." In other respects the year was less golden, for, as representative of Fox, it shared the fate of Fox. Hence, from 29 December, 1792, on, it was daily denounced by the Ministerial press as "that

Jacobin print," and, shortly after the new year began, it was indicted for a libel on the Constitution.

The colophon of the *Courier* remained unchanged during 1793, but there were some changes in the masthead. On 1 January it was carrying the motto, "NEC CORRUMPERE, NEC CORRUMPI," which had been dropped by 27 July; and on 27 November the paper had a subtitle, being now the *Courier, and Evening Gazette*. The subtitle, added sometime after 21 March, had disappeared by 12 December. Although only scattered copies of the *Courier* have survived, all of them support the radical reformers, and, since the paper was, to begin with, still edited by the Rev. Charles Este, all of them are intent on blackmail, a paragraph in the issue of 2 January being typical: "Not a little *gossip* is passing, with respect to a late *confinement* before marriage. The anxiety is to know, whether the Lady liked her lover so little as to be likely to run *from* him; or so much as to be in danger of flying to him *too soon!*"

There was also no change in the colophon of the *Gazetteer, and New Daily Advertiser*, although there was a change of editor. According to Haig,[5] the proprietors had been so pleased with the accomplishments of William Radcliffe that in October, 1792, they had increased his weekly salary from four to five guineas, and, during the last three months of that year, the sale of the newspaper had increased as well, rising from a daily 1,507 in October to a daily 1,904 in December. But on 31 December Radcliffe resigned, having "entered into a connection with another Paper," and on 16 January, 1793, he was replaced by "Mr. Bourne," probably Frederick Bourne. In February, Bourne was replaced by D. E. MacDonnell, who remained with the *Gazetteer* until 1794. MacDonnell had last been mentioned (*Morning Post, World*, 23 Apr., 1791; *Morning Chronicle*, 25 Apr., 1791) as editor of the *Morning Post*, and his availability at this particular time would indicate that he had just quit that newspaper. He was not a great editor. He had had little success with the *Morning Post*, and he had as little success with the *Gazetteer*. Since he was connected with the Friends of the People, the *Gazetteer*, which had previously supported the radical reformers, was now supporting the moderates, but the support tended to be perfunctory, and by September, 1793, the *Gazetteer*'s sale had dropped to 1,396 copies.

Although the *Morning Post* is lacking for the first half of 1793, it was still being printed by J. Norris in Blake Court, Catherine Street, Strand, from 1 July on. Readers were also still being advised to leave advertisements "at Mr. Hargrave's Rainbow Coffee-House, Cornhill," but, according to the *St. James's Chronicle* (31 Jan.) and the *London Packet* (1 Feb.), Jeremiah Hargrave, the proprietor of that coffee house and one of the proprietors of the *Morning Post*, had died on 28 January. Neither newspaper mentioned who had inherited the properties. It may have been the "J. Hargrave" who, said the *Morning Chronicle* and *Oracle* on 25 April, had appeared in the Court of King's Bench the previous day regarding custody of "four infant children." Hargrave had been "insane," it appeared, "the paroxysms of insanity" having been "produced by excessive and habitual intemperance," but he was again normal and was promising the court never to drink again. The children were restored to their mother pending "negotiations." The editor during at least the early part of the year was no doubt William Radcliffe, since the *Morning Post* was the only London newspaper with which he could have "entered into a connection" on 31 December, 1792, there being no change in the editorship of the other two Opposition dailies, the *Courier* and the *Morning Chronicle*. A change in the editorship of the *Post* at this time was even to be expected, since, if the sale of the paper averaged two thousand copies a day from 3 January on, the lessees would not have to buy the paper when the lease expired on 3 July. Radcliffe, it was evidently hoped, might effect this miracle; MacDonnell very evidently could not. Among the contributors were evidently still Daniel Stuart, Robert Merry, and Dennis O'Bryen; and there was also a sonneteer in the person of Joseph Haslewood, the antiquarian, who signed his verses, "J. H., Conduit Street."

As before, the Opposition was also supported by the *English Chronicle, and Universal Evening Post*, by the *General Evening Post*, and by the *London Chronicle*. The colophons of the three were unchanged. In addition, there were the weekly papers: the *Craftsman, or Say's Weekly Journal*; *E. Johnson's British Gazette, and Sunday Monitor*; the *London Recorder, or Sunday Gazette*; *Ayre's Sunday London Gazette, and Weekly Monitor*; the *Westminster Journal, and London Political Miscellany. By Simon Gentletouch of Pall Mall, Esq.*, and the *Observer*, which had by now dropped its subtitle and by 21 July, 1793, was being printed by J. Desmond, No. 6, Newcastle Street, Strand. Colophons and titles were otherwise unchanged. On 14 April a new weekly was commenced, the *Sunday Reformer, and Universal Register*, this one being published by George Riley, No. 33, Ludgate Street; and on 25 April the *Morning Chronicle* was advertising Volume II of the *Patriot, or, Political, Moral, and Philosophical Repository*. This journal, published fortnightly by G. G. J. and J. Robinson, seems to have expired after the tenth number of the third volume. Since the Opposition had little support among the country newspapers, the advent of the Cambridge *Intelligencer* on 20 July at least deserves mention. The founder of the *Intelligencer* was the Unitarian, Benjamin Flower.

The Ministerial Press

Since the elections of 1784, it had been the Government's policy to subsidize as many newspapers as possible; but, on 1 October, 1792, the Treasury had founded the *Sun* as an experiment in concentration. As an experiment, the *Sun* could hardly be regarded as a success; yet the Government seemed to feel that it was not altogether a failure either, for, by the end of that year, it was arranging for what appeared to be a compromise. Plans were being made for a morning companion of the *Sun*, to be called the *True Briton*; subsidies of a number of newspapers were being canceled; salaries were being translated into pensions, places, and sinecures; and certain other financial encouragements were being shifted from the Treasury to the Home Department and the Post Office. One effect of these changes was to remove "honest George Rose" from the scene as paymaster and thus spare Pitt further embarrassments on that account. Henceforth Rose was only a journalist, and, although on 4 December, 1793, George Canning remarked[6] that no one could continue long in politics without making his acquaintance, he had by this time no influence over any journal except the *Sun* and the *True Briton*. Any transaction involving money was handled by the second Secretary of the Treasury, Charles Long, whose reputation was as yet comparatively unsullied.

Of the numerous writers once carried on the Treasury's payroll, only two remained: William Augustus Miles, who on 9 April, 1793, collected £250 in settlement of his account "to Lady Day," and L. Wolfe, who on 9 July collected £159 2s. in settlement of his account for 1792 and on 25 July an additional £457 16s. for "Parliamentary business" during 1793.[7] So far as one can ascertain, all the others were now "pensioned," some of them receiving sinecures as well; and handsome provisions were later made for Miles. John Taylor, who in March, 1793, collected £120 as his "Allowance 3/4th Year to [Christmas, 1792],"[8] was probably being paid by Dundas, as so were Charles Stuart and a regiment of informers. Of the London newspapers, the only dailies still subsidized at the beginning of 1793 were the *Diary*, the *Morning Herald*, *The Times*, and the *World*; the only nondaily was the *Evening Mail*. Even these newspapers seem to have been on probation, the continuation of the subsidies depending on the conduct of the papers during the next several months. The remaining newspapers, it was evidently hoped, would continue to support the Government anyway, with a little piecemeal encouragement from time to time. Since the afternoon papers and the nondailies were at the mercy of Francis Freeling of the Post Office, who had turned out to be extremely co-operative, very little trouble was expected from them; and the dailies had nothing to gain by defecting, since the Opposition was not subsidizing newspapers either. It looked, therefore, as if the Government could still count on nine of the fifteen dailies: the *Diary*, the *Morning Herald*, the *Oracle*, the *Public Advertiser*, the *Public Ledger*, the *Sun*, *The Times*, the *True Briton*, and the *World*. The principals of the group were, of course, the *Sun* and the *True Briton*.

The *Sun* was still printed by Buchanan Millan at No. 112, Strand, and John Heriot edited the newspaper until 1806. The last Treasury payments recorded for him are £100 on 13 December, 1792, "Fifty Eight Pounds, & Ten Shillings & Sixpence for Advertisements in different Papers" on 28 December, "One

Hundred & Seventy Two Pounds Sixteen Shillings & three pence for Printing Pamphlets and advertising in different Papers &c." on 16 March, 1793, and another £100 for an unmentioned reason on 22 June.[9] The payments of £100 seem to represent an allowance, the odd sums expenses. The *True Briton*, which made its appearance on 1 January, 1793, was also edited by Heriot, but it was located at No. 5, Catherine Street, Strand, and it had its own printer, A. Wilson. According to Amphlett,[10] the "principal supporter" of the publication was Lord Kenyon, but Amphlett seems to have referred to a much later period, for the only names mentioned in connection with it at the beginning were Rose, Burges, and Heriot, and Burges was thought to be only a contributor. The *Morning Chronicle* always (e.g., 7 July, 1793) regarded the *True Briton* as "*honest* GEORGE ROSE's paper," and it seemed to the *Morning Post* of 19 July that the whole "*gasping* Journal" was sustained by Rose's "paragraphical pursuits." As to its financing, the *Morning Post* stated flatly on 1 June, 1796, that "the very materials for the printing, the fitting-up of the house, and every other expence attending its introduction, was paid by money issued from the Treasury"; and its later (12 Nov., 1796) statement that Rose had "furnished the money necessary to give [the paper] existence" was evidently not meant to imply that the money had come out of Rose's pocket. But the Treasury at least had some assistance from another Government agency, since the premises, the press, the type, and many of the materials had belonged to the *Argus* before that newspaper ran into "trouble with the Stamp Office."

Figuring prominently in the masthead of the *True Briton* was the motto, "NOLUMUS LEGES ANGLIAE MUTARI," so that there was no doubt that the primary object of the newspaper was to defend the Constitution against the reformers. But the newspaper did not itself say so until 28 January, when it presented the following address:

TO THE PUBLIC.

If ever there was a period when we were all invited to exert ourselves in the defence of those Public Principles which we have adopted as the foundation of our actions, to counteract the effect of false Theories, and to establish those which have stood the test of time and experience, that period is now arrived. It shall be our task to perform this useful, and, at the present moment, peculiarly necessary duty.—No person who feels as a BRITON *ought to feel, can be indifferent to the public Acts of the Nation, or to those events in other Countries with which the state of our own is necessarily so intimately connected.*

These sentiments induced us to undertake the publication of a New Paper—We appeal to our Readers for the accuracy with which we have stated facts, and the promptitude with which we have conveyed interesting intelligence. It is probable that the ensuing Session will afford as much important business as any that has preceded it—In pursuance of our Plan, we pledge ourselves to detail correctly the PROCEEDINGS OF PARLIAMENT; *and our Readers may depend upon seeing the* DEBATES *fully, accurately, and impartially given.*

It is impossible for us to address the Public, without expressing our Gratitude for the distinguished favours which have been conferred upon us—We trust, that by our perseverance in defence of the Constitution, we shall be best entitled to a continuation of such support.

The reports of the debates were being supplied by "Mr. Wolfe," and one of the writers for the paper was John Taylor. Although the *True Briton* never acknowledged the contributions of Rose and Burges, it did encourage the suggestion that it was intimately associated with the Administration, as, for example on 15 February, when it noted approvingly that "Mr. SHERIDAN, Mr. B. DUDLEY, &c. are kind enough to publish every where, that we have the determined support of Government." It also made no secret of its connection with the *Sun*, Heriot's editing of the two papers being often enough mentioned. To begin with, the *True Briton* was in fact little more than a reprint of the *Sun* of the previous afternoon. But, as an afternoon paper and a notoriously inaccurate one at that, the *Sun* soon yielded both its priorities and its functions, so that by March it was almost as innocuous as the *Daily Advertiser*, while the *True Briton* was setting a new record for scurrility and misinformation. James Bland Burges was nevertheless very proud of these newspapers. "Have you heard," he asked Lord Auckland excitedly on 2 February,[11] "that we have got two papers perfectly attached to us and considered as the authentic vehicles of such matters as Government choose to make them? Their titles are *The Sun* and the *True Briton* and I really think they are much superior to any we have seen." The Government evidently thought so too, for Francis Freeling said later[12] that copies of these two papers, along with "a three day paper, occasional Gazettes, etc etc.," were regularly delivered to "many of the respectable country papers . . . at the expence of Government. . . ./ This originated in the year 1792 with Mr. Chas Long & was placed under my management. The condition with the proprietors was that they should from time to time insert any articles having for their object a refutation of the dangerous principles disseminated by Paine & others for the subversion of every established principle & order."

One of the functions of the *True Briton* was to whip into line the four newspapers still in the pay of the Treasury. The only newspaper of this group to be ignored was the *Diary, or Woodfall's Register*, still printed by William Woodfall in Salisbury Square, since the principal concern here was evidently to keep the paper in existence. The *Diary*'s admiration for William Pitt had been flagging for months, owing to Woodfall's illness. But, on 1 January, Woodfall resumed the management, and the New Year's address not only rededicated the paper to Administrative policies, but absolved "The PRINTER" from responsibility for its aberrations. Having reminded his readers that he had "now been five and twenty years in [the public] service," during "the whole [of which] time, . . . he [had] uniformly adhered to one object: the support of the existing Government," Woodfall explained that he had unfortunately "been precluded from the execution of his public duty, for some weeks past, by a severe illness." Although he had been "aided" during "this exigency . . . by most able assistants," the "assistants" had not been quite so devoted to the Government as he. But he had now recovered, and the *Diary* would not only resume its support of Pitt, but, "on Monday next, . . . will be printed on an entirely new type." The *Diary* was in fact printed on "new type," but the type may not have been purchased with the *Diary* exclusively in mind, for, from late January on, Woodfall and Andrew Strahan were publishing legal works as "Law Printers to the King's Most Excellent Majesty, for Whieldon and Butterworth, Fleet Street." On 17 April the *Diary* mentioned that "Mr. Whieldon, for many years a bookseller in Fleet Street," had died in Brompton four days earlier, but his death did not affect the Woodfall-Strahan publications, which continued to appear under the same imprint. This appointment would have meant a great deal to Woodfall, inasmuch as his son, William Woodfall, Jr., was being trained in the law, and it was probably intended as a bonus. In addition, the *Diary* was subsidized until midsummer. In March, 1793, Woodfall collected £200, which the Treasury had owed him since the previous Christmas, and on 20 July he collected another £200, due evidently since 25 June.[13] One month later the *Diary* ceased to exist. Woodfall had tried to sell it earlier, "had several offers, and was for some time in treaty, but could not effectuate a bargain before the end of the . . . Session of Parliament." The *Diary* did support the Government during the last eight months of its life, but, since it was unenthusiastic about the war and somewhat suspicious of the alarmists, its support was not zealous. As before, the paper shared its information with the *Public Advertiser*, and, as before, it was a champion of Charles Dibdin.

The Times, still printed in Printing House Square, was by 5 January again being printed by A. Anderson, who remained with the newspaper through at least 8 June, but by 11 November had been replaced by C. Bell. The editor was still William Finey and the conductor the elder John Walter, with William Walter evidently functioning as his assistant. The *True Briton* detested this newspaper. "The *Morning Weather-Cock* is veering again," it shrieked on 8 February; and on 13 May: "The *political weathercock* has veered within the last week to every point in the compass. It is supposed that it will fix at *Bis-Aspostacy* at last." On 31 July it again compared *The Times* with a "weather-cock," which, it added, "[verifies] the adage, '*Tempora mutantur et nos mutamur in illis!*'" Rose had never liked *The Times*, which had been Pitt's and Long's "Gazette" rather than his; and he particularly disliked it now, since it was eclipsing his own *True Briton* in every respect. But Rose's opinions were no longer of consequence. Hence, on 23 January, Walter collected £200 from Charles Long for *The Times* and the *Evening Mail* to Christmas, 1792, and on 25 July he collected another £200 "to Midsummer," 1793.[14] At this point the subsidy was translated into a £300 "pension," supposedly as a "Reward for Fidelity, & as compensation for actual Sufferings" while Walter was in prison.[15] The pension was paid until

1799, and until 1805 Walter was also Printer to the Customs. In December, 1792, *The Times* was selling less than three thousand copies a day; in November, 1793, it boasted that its sale was averaging "near 4000 daily,"[16] and it was Farington's understanding[17] that, for the next three years, the paper "cleared to the Proprietors £24,000." A considerable part of this income probably came from stockjobbing, for which *The Times* was notorious; but it also had as much Continental "intelligence" as the Government. For this it was indebted to the Foreign Undersecretary, George Aust; and, although Aust may have charged for his informations and the informations were not necessarily reliable, still he continued to provide them until his retirement in 1796.

The *Morning Herald* continued to be printed by H. Roaf at No. 18, Catherine Street, Strand, through 2 March, 1793; and, although the address remained unchanged, Roaf was on 4 March replaced as printer by H. Brown. The *World* was still printed by Robert Bostock at No. 335, Strand, and leased to Isaac Swan. Neither paper was doing at all well. By the end of 1793, the *Herald* was "said not . . . to sell more than 800 a day. Two or three years ago between 4 and 5,000 were sold."[18] The *World* was probably worse off, and, in addition, it was involved in several litigations. The three actions being brought by Charles Dibdin, two against Swan, one against Bostock, were still pending, as so was the action brought by the Rev. Charles Este against Major Topham. The last one was a continuing embarrassment, for on 16 January Este charged that Topham's refusal to submit an account of the financial affairs of the *World* had been "scandalous and impertinent" and petitioned the Court to cite him for contempt. The hearing, to which the *Oracle* (18 Jan.) devoted over a column, was extremely dramatic, but the Court responded with evasions, and so nothing was settled.

The *Morning Herald* and the *World* had been subsidized by the Treasury in the amount of £600 each, the subsidies having been arranged by Rose. But, when Rose contracted for the support of these papers, they were conducted by their respective proprietors, Rev. Henry Bate Dudley and Edward Topham, who happened to have a special talent for conducting newspapers; and it was Rose's understanding that they would continue to be so conducted. They were not. Dudley, already rector of North Fambridge, had in 1780 also bought the advowson of the rectory of Bradwell Juxta Mare, Essex, leasing the glebe and tithes as well, and, as soon as he had settled with Rose, he quit the *Herald* altogether and moved to Essex, installing himself as curate.[19] Although Topham had continued his connection with the *World*, his interest in that paper had been desultory at best, and he was now spending most of his time in Yorkshire, living the life of a country gentleman and directing The Association's activities in that area. Rose was annoyed, and the *World*'s announcement of 15 January that the King had been "pleased" to appoint Topham a Deputy Lieutenant of the East Riding of the County of York annoyed him further. This man, the *True Briton* informed its readers day after day, was being paid by the Treasury to manage a newspaper, but the newspaper was going to wrack and ruin while he luxuriated in the country.

Since the *Morning Herald* and the *World* had been his newspapers and had been supporting him under the most desperate circumstances, it is hard to believe that Rose wanted to ruin them. One is rather inclined to suspect that he was battling to save them, having perhaps been promised that the subsidies would be continued or converted into pensions, provided Dudley and Topham resumed the management. The result in any event was the same. On 28 January the *True Briton* reflected bitterly that "[it] seems to have been the general practice with the Proprietors and Conductors of Newspapers, after taking some pains to establish the credit of their Prints, to neglect them entirely—in many instances to sell the property of them to persons under them, and to retire into the Country to enjoy the Pension they derive from their Paper. . . ." This reflection was followed by a series of lectures, addressed specifically to Dudley and Topham, and on 7 February by the triumphant announcement that the *True Briton* had finally "taught the Proprietors of other Prints, that a Newspaper is not a *sinecure*—One person has quitted his Farm, and another his Sport, in the country, to endeavour to repair the effects of long *neglect* and *inattention.*" But the *True Briton* was mistaken on both accounts. In Dudley's case, it understood (16 Feb.) that "discontent [had] arisen from his not thinking himself sufficiently consulted in the disposal of *Church Preferment*—Some, indeed, say that he expressed his disappointment at not being the last-created *Bishop.*" In Topham's case, it did not know what was the matter, but on 6 March it concluded a diatribe on the subject of newspapers generally with the announcement that the demise of the *World* was imminent: "*The World*, which is nothing new, is becoming ungrateful; for it is customary for *The World* to be illuminated by THE SUN, without feeling those obligations for the blessing, which it ought. Truth to say, it is a *vile World*; and we should almost suppose it made for *Frenchmen*; for it seems desirous to have it forgot that THE TRUE BRITON flourishes, and will soon put down all its Enemies—for *The Herald* speaks falsely, *The Times* are changeable, *The Oracle* is dumb, *The Chronicle* is partial, *The Post* is stupid, and *The World* is approaching to *its end.*" On 18 March the *World* was again assailed, this time on the ground of loyalty: "The Proprietor, as we suppose, of a Morning Paper, which, in spite of its name, the *World* seems to give little credit to, has adopted a very poor artifice to bring that Paper again into favour. A Card is sent to various parts of the Country, stating the Newspapers favouring the Constitution, and those adverse to it; and at the top of the former is the Paper alluded to—Sure we are, that if that Print can be said to be favourable to the Constitution, it ought to be at the *bottom* of such a list." Similar statements appeared throughout April, May, and June. On 26 April, the Rev. Henry Bate Dudley had meanwhile collected £300 from the Treasury as settlement for the *Morning Herald* "in full," [20] thus ending the Government's connection with that newspaper; and on 25 July Edward Topham collected £150 for the quarter ending 20 June,[21] this payment being terminal for the *World*. Although the *World* had indeed been "a *vile World*," it could not justly be accused of political apathy, for most of the material in it was propaganda for the Government and The Association, the remainder being puffs, extortionary paragraphs, exposés of the legal profession, and news of Topham's activities in Yorkshire.

The *Oracle* was still located at the *Oracle* office, British Library, Strand, and the colophon still carried the name of James Bell, albeit sometimes as printer, sometimes as publisher, sometimes with a "Jun." affixed, sometimes not. As before, the "literary department" was being managed by Peter Stuart and James Boaden, with Sheridan standing at their elbows, and John Bell was still the proprietor and publisher. Although Bell had been convicted on 9 July, 1792, of having published two libels on the Guards, he had not been sentenced, and it looked as if the Government had forgotten the matter. The *Oracle* had accepted the cancellation of its subsidy with good grace, and it was evident from the thanksgiving statement with which it greeted the new year that the cancellation would have no effect on its politics. "As BRITONS, the year 1792 has given us abundant cause of thankfulness," it said. "—We have seen the attacks of treasonable Reform defeated by the collective energy of a great People—The understandings of Englishmen have been too strong for the infusion of French Spirits to intoxicate. Our masculine sense has kept us from the newly distilled dregs of *our* old ingredients, which experience has laid by as destructive and faithless [a reference to the Revolution of 1688]—giving a gay delirium to the brain, and banishing comfort from the heart." It repeated this declaration on 2 January, at which time it dedicated itself absolutely to "CONSTITUTIONAL DOCTRINES" and "*elegant Literature.*" The numbers which followed were filled with vituperations of Fox and eulogies of Pitt, Dundas, and Reeves; and, in defending the war and damning the reformers, the *Oracle* outdid the *Sun* and the *True Briton* at every turn. Far-fetched conclusions and wildly imaginative arguments were its forte. But the incessant attacks on Burke and the constant praise of Sheridan offset the effect of all this. Sheridan, it appeared, was still holding Burke responsible for the disruption of his plans, and he had been encouraged to hope that a liaison with Pitt might yet be possible despite him.

Although Bell seems to have profited little from the *Oracle*'s stockjobbing, Stuart and Boaden were evidently doing very well, for during 1793 the paper was much less interested in gossip than it was in the market. "Monied Men and Persons interested in the Funds may look with perfect confidence to the Oracle for faithful reports of the Daily State and Fluctuation of the stocks," it announced on 4 January. As usual, most of these "faithful reports" were based on "intelligences" respecting the state of the war, and, except for the proceedings of the French Convention, which the Rev. William Jackson was probably able to report first-hand, all of them were rumors. But, with the elimination of much of the extortionary material, the *Oracle* was able to devote more space to "*elegant Literature*" than before, to the delight, no doubt, of Stuart, who thought of himself as primarily a man of letters. To show that it at least recognized "*inelegant Literature*" when it saw it, the *Oracle* was the severest critic of the Poet

Laureate, Henry James Pye. On 4 January it devoted a half-column to his "Ode for the New Year, 1793," in which it demonstrated that the poem was "lacking in boldness," that "the thoughts are not just—the expression is bald— . . . it wants often common sense," and the "epithets are all common place." There was more of this on 6 June, when the paper commented on Pye's "Ode for His Majesty's Birthday," which it had published two days earlier: "Whatever may be pretended about the *ingredients* of the present Laureate *Pye*, it is certain that this Poetical Pastry cook is not out in his *season.*/ [Thomas] WARTON bestowed upon the Annual Ode much topographic splendour and bold impersonation. He was a man of Genius. [William] WHITEHEAD was before PYE every way; but neither of them are Ode Writers. A cold creeping cluster of baby rhymes does not constitute an Ode." This comment was followed on 7 June by "INSTRUC-TIONS TO THE LAUREATE" on how to write odes so that they would have some "*Sense* as well as *Numbers.*" The author of such material is supposed to have been George Steevens, whose edition of Shakespeare had already been defended by the *Oracle* against that of Malone.

Since the *Oracle* was similarly alert to "*inelegance*" in prose, it was a steady sneerer at the kind of writing which was appearing in other newspapers. "LANGUAGE," it observed bitterly on 7 June, "—A literary Print informs us yesterday from *Sligo*, that seven wild Irish Defenders were by the Volunteers *killed* DEAD upon the spot. Another literary Vehicle has conveyed a *gratuitous gift* from the States of *Brabant* to the EMPEROR of 800,000 florins." "When SWIFT wrote his plan for refining English, he complained of our fashionable *abbreviations*, and the natural dissonance of unrelieved consonants," it remarked again on 6 July. "We have to struggle with other evils; for instance now, of OBSCURITY, that may be called *easy*, take the following polite specimen: 'No apology can be offered for laying any uncorrect publication before you, except that you should judge it one.' So says a Modern to the PUBLIC." The *Oracle's* notion of "*elegance*" in prose was evidently the writing of Peter Stuart, who was responsible for these critiques. Its notion of "*elegance*" in verse was the poetry of "Laura Maria" (Mrs. Robinson), whose contributions were always presented with rhapsodic headnotes. But, since her contributions were few, the *Oracle* also published the work of other Della Cruscans. The principal, to begin with, was a new poet, "Themira," "Themira" being succeeded by the lovesick team of "Julia" and "Arno."

The *Public Ledger* was printed as before by John Crowder at No. 12, Warwick Court, and, on 23 October, 1793, the editor was still Alexander Chalmers. On 4 March the Treasury transmitted to it the sum of £100, which settled the account for "One Year to Christmas [1792]."[22] This is the last recorded payment. Although very few copies of the paper for the year 1793 have survived, Chalmer's continued association with it indicates that it remained generally Ministerial. The newspaper which suffered most from the cancellation was the *Public Advertiser*, still printed and conducted by Henry Sampson Woodfall at

No. 1, Paternoster Row. Although no Treasury payments to Woodfall are recorded, there can be no doubt that the paper had been as regularly subsidized as other Ministerial papers and that the subsidy was discontinued at approximately the same time. Woodfall seems to have been greatly disturbed, for, having begun the year as a crude propagandist for war, the *Public Advertiser* was soon printing anything without regard even for coherence. An article which appeared on 5 February began, for example, with the declaration: "Nothing can be more obvious than the necessity of declaring war against the French at this critical juncture." But, having repudiated Fox's arguments against the war and impugned the motives of the peacemongers, the article concluded with a plea for negotiations: "Our Court sycophants run about the town, saying the dear English surely cannot treat with France; what, a Monarchy treat with a Republic? These learned personages seem to forget, that Cardinal Mazarin, nearly as good a politician as Mr. Pitt, treated with the Commonwealth of England after the decapitation of Charles the First." Similarly, an article which appeared on 9 February, again strongly urging the necessity for war, concluded with the admonition: "Let but France alone, and it most probably in six months time will have a civil war within itself." But by March the paper was back in the Ministerial fold, and there it remained until it expired. The *Public Advertiser*, still selling for $3\frac{1}{2}d$., instead of the usual $4d$., was not a disreputable newspaper, despite its ranting approach to politics. Its information, identical with that of the *Diary* until the *Diary* ceased publication and thereafter identical with that of the *World*, was adequate, and its interest in material relating to historical and literary figures of the past was unique. Its principal contributor continued to be James Boswell.

The colophons of the various triweekly newspapers—the *Evening Mail*, the *London Packet*, *Lloyd's Evening Post*, the *London Evening Post*, the *St. James's Chronicle*, and the *Whitehall Evening Post*—were unchanged, as so were the titles. The papers also continued to support the Government, despite the cancellation of subsidies. In the case of the *Evening Mail*, the subsidy was paid until mid-1793; in the case of the *London Evening Post*, the *St. James's Chronicle*, and the *Whitehall Evening Post*, the subsidies were canceled at Christmas, 1792, the accounts not being settled, however, until March, 1793.[23] Another Ministerial journal was commenced by Dr. John Trusler on 1 January, 1793, under the title, *Monthly Communications*. According to the numerous advertisements, this one, although modeled on a newspaper and selling at the same price as a newspaper ($4d$.), was offering readers somewhat broader coverage. *Monthly Communications* seems to have expired, however, after the first number.

Much of the material appearing in the Ministerial newspapers was provided by the corps of "pensioned" writers and published at the Government's expense. But, with the cancellation of regular subsidies, the Ministerial papers were no longer obliged to support the Government on every issue. The result was that, for the first time, they enjoyed some degree of independence, and, before the year was over, they were combining with the Opposition papers on matters of interest to themselves. One such matter was the lawyers, by whom they continued to be harassed. Another was laws respecting debtors, and yet another was the state of the prisons, with both of which newspapermen were all too well acquainted. There was also a common resentment of ex officio prosecutions, for one newspaper almost always sided with another against the Attorney General, however much it disagreed with it politically. On the other hand, the cancellations did create financial problems. Two newspapers, the *Diary* and the *Public Advertiser*, ceased publication, others became obsessively concerned with "hush money," and there was a growing reliance on stockjobbing. Fortunately, Pitt never disapproved of stockjobbing.

Passage of the Alien Act

The debates on the Alien Bill had seemed to be widely digressive, but in fact they were not, for the real question at issue, it was now evident, was the question of war or peace; and, since it was never clear whether the war was intended to defend the Constitution by keeping French principles out of Britain or to protect commerce by maintaining the balance of power on the Continent, almost anything was relevant. The final clash was due on 4 January, 1793, when, having already passed the Lords, the bill was scheduled for its final reading in the Commons. There was considerable activity by way of preparation.

The newspapers were filled with reports of arrests in Scotland and Ireland, and in England the Government seemed to be fighting a last-ditch stand against alien aggressions. The Plymouth dockyards, now heavily guarded and "closed to strangers of any rank," "wear," said the *Morning Chronicle* sadly on 1 January, "the appearance of war." The search for traitors had reached a point of frenzy and, as far as the *Morning Post* was concerned, ludicrousness. "Government are teized by the representation of the Treasury SPIES, who, to shew themselves deserving their guinea a-week, are eternally obtruding lists on their employers, of rebels, traitors, and Sans Culottes, who disturb the peace of the country," said the *Post* on 1 January. "The fact is, that some of these infamous villains have given in the names of men, whom Government know to be as attached to the King and Constitution as the most loyal subjects in the realm; but, still, for what reasons we know not, these fellows are still retained in the respectable occupations of *spies* and *informers*." But the search continued. "His Majesty's Ministers are still indefatigable in their researches after French Assassins and Domestic Traitors; convinced from daily evidence, that their exertions hitherto have only/ '—Scotch'd the SNAKE—not killed it!'" observed the *Public Advertiser* on 3 January. The public at large seemed to be equally "indefatigable," for Addresses of Loyalty from cities, boroughs, parishes, and clubs continued to flood the newspapers, the one circulated "in the neighbourhood of Holborn" having, according to the *Morning Chronicle* of 4 January, a column to the left for the signatures of those who refused to sign, with an adjacent column for their reasons. Along with these addresses were announcements of additional bounties for enlistments being offered by spirited individuals or societies, formations of new clubs to defend the Constitution, and fresh burnings of Paine's effigy.

But, as the *Morning Chronicle* pointed out on 3 January, there were also multiple burnings of Dundas's effigy, and these were not inspired by The Crown and Anchor Association: "Mr. DUNDAS, when he last gave notice of a motion for repealing the coal-tax in Scotland, found it necessary to state his reasons, lest it should be thought a catch at popularity. He did not state all his reasons: we understand that the Scotch having consumed almost all their fuel in burning the Right Hon. Gentleman's effigy; the price of coals must be reduced, before they can afford to pay the same tribute of respect to *Thomas Paine*; and the more so, because burning the first was voluntary—the other is to be by *command*." Since respect for the law had somehow got lost in all the concern about the Constitution, it is perhaps not surprising that a number of people were doing more than burning effigies. This was particularly true in London, where there was a sharp increase in the number of major crimes. When the Middlesex Justices Act became effective on 1 August, 1792, Londoners were harassed by nothing more formidable than pickpockets; they were now harassed by robbers, rapists, murderers, and arsonists. Crime, all newspapers agreed, was now a genuine problem.

The newspapers which supported the Alien Bill and hence the war were directing most of their abuse at "Citizen" Lauderdale, at "Chicken" Taylor, at Grey, and, for the first time, at Fox and the "Jacobin *Chronicle*," *The Times* concentrating on Lord Lauderdale, the *Sun* on Fox and the *Chronicle*. There was also much ridicule of the Opposition generally because of the defections, the *Public Advertiser* again announcing on 3 January that the Earl of Carlisle had "seceded from the miserable ranks of Opposition with his friend Lord Lough-borough." The newspapers which opposed the Alien Bill were eulogizing "Fox in ENGLAND, the Duke of LEINSTER in IRELAND, and Lord LAUDERDALE in SCOTLAND": these three, along with William Lambton, were certainly, declared the *Courier* on 3 January, "the tutelary geniuses of their respective nations!" The Duke of Leinster was a brother of Lord Edward Fitzgerald, a cousin of Fox, and had for many years been a leader of the Opposition in the Irish Parliament. The principal targets of these newspapers were Dundas, of whom the Opposition press had formed a quite different opinion during the last several weeks, and Burke.

Burke was attacked on every possible ground. Although most of the Ministerial newspapers were momentarily ignoring him, their very silence seemed suspicious to the *Oracle* in light of Paine's statement that Burke had once been *"in a treaty with Mr. Pitt about Mr. Hastings's trial."* On 4 January for example the *Oracle* noticed with evident relief that the *"Trial* has withdrawn its annual pomp.— Bows no longer bend the scarlet Peer—The bustle of the Major [John Scott]— the *allbum* of the Captain [Edward Topham], and the impersonation of BECKY [Mary Wells]—all are passed away. These we have *lost."* But it also noticed in a following paragraph that "[the] *slavish* PRINTS have completely forgotten the *madness* they once imputed to BURKE. The *Old* WOMAN [*The Times*] also rests from her labours—'Tis strange!" The *Morning Post* was addressing letters to him from "The Swinish Multitude," a phrase he had unfortunately used in his *Reflections* and which Cooper had subsequently employed to good advantage in his *Reply to Burke's Invective*; and the *Morning Chronicle* was ridiculing him as an alarmist. Some of the ridicule was general, a paragraph in the *Chronicle* of 4 January being typical: "Mr. BURKE, and the associators for suppressing insurrections, that the most quick-sighted *natural eye* has not been able to discover, have adopted from SHAKSPEARE the following apt motto—

> Get thee glass eyes,
> And, like a scurvy Politician, seem
> To see the things thou dost not."

Much of it had to do with the dagger incident of 28 December, already hilariously caricatured by James Gillray. The following items appeared for example in the *Morning Chronicle* of 1 January:

EPIGRAM.
On Mr. BURKE producing the Dagger in the House of Commons.

> BURKE from his coat the dagger drew,
> And mark what follow'd after;
> With rage quite frantic—thro' and thro',
> He *struck* them all—*with laughter*!

TOBY.

Mr. BURKE's *Dagger*, though the object of so much laughter at the time, was certainly not to be laughed at by the gentleman who was next him. For it was not a mock dagger that he brandished about, such as is used by players for stage effect; but as much a real dagger, as that with which the Jesuit put an end to the Fourth Henry of France!

Lord BEAUCHAMP was the gentleman who was on the right-hand of Mr. BURKE, and with becoming prudence he shifted his place.

According to the *Courier*, also 1 January, Burke's performance impressed even the players: "We have the satisfaction to hear, that the favourite low Comedian, Mr. PARSONS, . . . was in the gallery when Mr. BURKE raised much laughter with the *dagger.*/ Mr. BUNBURY has made a delightful sketch of a late dagger-scene.

—Mr. KEMBLE has furnished the motto, a new reading from SHAKESPEARE, viz.
—/ 'I will use daggers to her, but speak none.'" Henry William Bunbury, an
amateur artist and caricaturist, was celebrated for his lampooning of the Prince
of Wales's turf transactions, especially the one involving Escape. The *Oracle* of 4
January supported the cause with some verses:

EPIGRAM

UPON BURKE'S DAGGER.

I see thee still in form as palpable as this. MACBETH.

    "The Days of Chivalry are past!"
    I must deny it to the last.
    Though BURKE, in haste to prove his love,
    Forgot to throw them down his *glove*,—
    No doubt a TRAITOR's *mind* to stagger,
    He thought it best, to *draw his Dagger*.

PUNCTILIO.

"We hear," said the *Morning Chronicle* on the same day, "that it has been suggested to Mr. BURKE to try what effect a pistol, *properly levelled* is likely to
produce." The *Chronicle* was punning, Reeves's Association being designed
to protect "Liberty and Property against Republicans and Levellers."

As it turned out, the squibs were wasted, for Burke did not participate in the
debates of 4 January. Neither did Sheridan, who was evidently biding his time,
hoping for a resumption of negotiations with Pitt. The bill was opposed by
Taylor and Maitland on the ground that it amounted to a suspension of the
Habeas Corpus Act, endowing a government which already held office "unconstitutionally" with power to suppress whatever "freedom" remained. Jenkinson
replied with a denunciation of the Constitutional Society, the activities of which
would alone, he felt, justify a suspension of the Habeas Corpus Act; and, in any
event, he declared, surrendering one's "freedom" was itself a kind of "freedom."
The fact that Pitt had got into office "unconstitutionally" had, in his opinion,
nothing to do with the present crisis, which was caused by the French Revolution, not by the British Government. Grey objected to Pitt's demanding "extraordinary powers" without telling Parliament any of the facts, "the whole to be
done upon a footing of confidence in his judgment." He admitted frankly that
for some time he had not known what he was voting for. Had the country armed
to go to war or to negotiate? Was the Alien Bill intended to prevent a war or to
foment one? Was it supposedly necessitated by danger threatening the country
from within or danger threatening it from without? The Government's statement that an answer to these questions would defeat the purpose of the bill he
regarded as an insult to the Commons. Lord Mulgrave, who had quit the
Opposition in 1784, along with the Duke of Richmond, supported the bill, not
because of the Constitutional Society, which he considered too "contemptible"

for notice, but because of the Friends of the Liberty of the Press; and his objection to that organization, it developed, was that it had censured the jury for convicting Thomas Paine and that it had admitted Erskine to membership. He felt very strongly on the subject of Erskine, and he could only thank God that Erskine's "eloquence and labour . . . were not a match for the plain common sense of twelve honest men."

The bill was also supported by Lord Titchfield, by William Windham, who mentioned parenthetically that, although he could "imagine" a better government than the present one, he would continue to vote for it so long as it continued to do its "duty," and by Thomas Grenville, who, since he was shifting sides, tendered the usual apologies to Fox. Fox had a good deal to say in reply. To begin with, he refused to believe that any danger threatened the country from within, for it was unthinkable that French theories could take root in a land of "rational freedom"; nor would such danger explain the augmentation of the forces. The Government did not need a large army and navy to try Thomas Paine. He supposed, therefore, that the Government must apprehend danger from without. But the only danger from without resulted from the lack of any "public means of communication," for Britain certainly had no grievance which could not be settled by negotiation. The opening of the Scheldt, it was true, was a *fait accompli*, and it was a violation of the treaty of 1788, which had virtually guaranteed the navigation of that river to the Dutch. Still, the terms of treaties were not to be insisted upon if the consequences were disastrous; and in this case Holland seemed to have thought that they were, for she had chosen to overlook the violation rather than go to "the danger and expence of a war." Why then should Britain go to war for her? But perhaps negotiations were impossible because Britain was warring against French "opinions" rather than against France. If this was what the Government had in mind, then Fox would like to remind it that "opinions" were not crushed by armies, but by fortifying the people against them and especially by respecting their complaints. The glorification of the British Constitution was all very well, and Fox was quite as zealous in his defense of it as any of the alarmists. But he would not believe that a good constitution was a static one: a constitution had to change, to improve, or it was in a state of decay. He would also not believe that a constitution was subject only to subversion by the populace: it was also subject to the abuses and encroachments of the executive power, and at this point, he thought, it was in far greater danger from above than from below. Finally, Fox would like to ask the Government when a war waged against "opinions" could be regarded as won. Would the Government demand the restoration of the old French regime, or would it fight on until every Frenchman was exterminated? Having expressed his personal gratitude to Erskine for his fine defense of Thomas Paine, Fox thereupon concluded by moving that further consideration of the bill be postponed three weeks in order to permit an inquiry into its necessity. Pitt objected that such a delay might be a national catastrophe, although as usual he declined to say why.

The motion was accordingly negatived, and the bill passed without a division. It was to become effective on 22 January.

The *Sun* of 5 January surveyed the scene with mixed feelings. On the one hand, it thought that "Mr. PITT was too liberal in the Debate of Friday [4 Jan.], when he rated OPPOSITION at *ten* or *fifteen*"; on the other hand, it was disappointed that there had been no defections among the Duke of Portland's faction, and it was particularly annoyed that every member of that faction had prefaced his support of the Alien Bill with the reminder that Pitt held office "dishonestly." "We appeal to the Duke of PORTLAND himself, how far it answers its own purposes, or is consistent with his intentions, at the time that he declares His MAJESTY's Ministers ought to have the confidence of the People, to accompany that Declaration with a charge, which, if it were founded, would necessarily lead the People to distrust them," it said. But the Duke of Portland was evidently not to be dealt with in this manner, for the *Sun*'s remonstrance was not repeated, and other Ministerial newspapers seemed determined to re-establish good relations. As usual, the *Oracle* outdid them all, although not necessarily on its own initiative, since the Duke was a notorious purchaser of puffs. "The DUKE of PORTLAND, now acting diametrically opposed to some of his former Friends, cannot fail of bringing a valuable accession of talents and virtues to the Party which he embraces," it declared on 18 January. "Munificent and generous in his expence; polite and elegant in taste; benevolent and humane to his fellow-creatures; he possesses, in an eminent degree, those endearments which command esteem, affection, and popularity."

Pitt's estimate that all but ten or fifteen Members were supporting the Alien Bill was not for the moment disputed by the Opposition newspapers, for, not only had Fox been deserted by most of his old friends, but the Whigs' attempts to import some new ones had failed in every instance, the numerous by-elections which followed the convening of Parliament having resulted only in more victories for the Government. Since there was ample evidence of irregularities, the Opposition had challenged the outcomes as a matter of course; and, during the remainder of January and most of February, the contests were being reviewed by the Commons. No newspaper expected any reversals, and the expectation was in the main justified. The election which had attracted the most attention was the one in Thetford, where the Whigs had entered as candidate their recent convert, James Mingay. Mingay had campaigned as a member of the Friends of the People, and, according to the *Morning Chronicle* of 3 January, had got "a hero's welcome" from the electors. But, when the votes were counted, he had lost overwhelmingly. The *World* interpreted these events as a major defeat for the cause of moderate reform. As it said on 11 January, "'*The Friends of the People*,' are now called by the people '*The Society of Agitators*'—only fit to fraternize with French Republicans and Levellers."

Since the consensus of the Parliament was no index to the consensus of the people, the Ministerial newspapers labored hard to persuade them that the Alien

Act was necessary. The principal laborers in this particular vineyard were the *Public Advertiser* and *The Times*. Having heartily congratulated the country on its new law, the *Public Advertiser* of 5 January argued at some length that the law was not only necessary, but long overdue:

> The good effects of the Alien Bill are fully demonstrated by the swarms of suspicious Frenchmen with which the Dover coaches have been loaded *downwards*, ever since this salutary measure received the sanction of the Legislature. Though so many doubts have arisen in the breast of those who *cannot believe* the necessity of the *Alien Bill*, if they would give themselves time to make enquiries in their several neighborhoods; if they would observe on the mysterious conduct of several Foreigners, or listen to their conversations in Coffee-houses and public places, they would soon see the necessity of it, and give due credit to Administration for taking so timely and necessary a step.
>
> Amongst the many instances which may be given of the necessity of the above Bill, the following fact is sent to us by a Correspondent of veracity:
>
> About a fortnight before Christmas, a woman who keeps a kind of Ordinary for Foreigners in the neighbourhood of Soho-square, was informed by a little boy who supplied them with porter at table, that the Gentlemen were talking all manner of treasonable conversation—This induced the woman to listen at the door of the parlour where they dined, when she heard such Toasts given against the King and British Constitution, as shocked her. The woman, . . . instead of reporting what she had heard before a magistrate, rushed into the room, upbraided them with their conduct, and desired them to march out of her house directly.
>
> Messieurs took her at her word, and decamped to the number of *fourteen*, without paying their reckoning.
>
> These men, with many others of the same complexion, are still hanging about town.

The Times could report even more ominous incidents.

It had always seemed to the *Morning Chronicle* that William Pitt was bent on war, but, by the time the Alien Act was passed, it had concluded that war did not figure in his plans after all: that the advocates of moderate reform were to be overawed by nothing more than a succession of alarms. Since the archwarmonger was therefore Burke, the *Chronicle* continued its ridicule of him with another series of verses relating to the dagger incident. The last in the series appeared on 11 January:

A DANGEROUS BORE.

The dagger that the Thane with terror fill'd,
  Was but a shadow to the moonstruck mind;
But Burke,—in daggers more than Shakspeare skill'd
  Throws fancied shadows to the wind.
The murderous weapon waves in air before us,
And if he can't convince us,—swears he'll bore us!

The *Chronicle*'s assessment of the situation seemed to be supported by the abuse of Burke which was again appearing in the Ministerial papers, even though most of it had to do with the trial of Hastings. On 9 January, for example, the *Public Advertiser* had reprinted Paine's statement about the *"treaty with Mr. Pitt,"* under the heading, "Anecdote respecting Mr. Hasting's Trial, from Mr. Thomas Paine's Letter to the Addressers"; and it seemed unlikely that the paper would have thus discredited this enthusiast for war unless there was to be no war. No newspaper, however, agreed with the *Chronicle*. *The Times* and *Evening Mail* spoke for the Ministerial press when they announced on 6 January: "FRANCE no doubt sees with terror the preparations making in this country to arrest the progress of her plundering system, and every nerve is at work to prevail on us to desist. But our Ministry are not to be wheedled or threatened out of that duty which Great Britain owes to her own safety, and that of her allies. The general welfare of Europe demands our interference, and as it is with the universal approbation of the public we take up arms, our success cannot be doubted." Although the other Opposition papers were skeptical about the "success," they had no doubt that a war was in the making.

It was at least evident that the British Government was not going to be "wheedled" by M. Chauvelin, for, on 31 December, 1792, Chauvelin had been notified by Lord Grenville that, since he had been accredited to the Court of St. James only as representative of Louis XVI, he had had no "public character" since Louis's imprisonment on 10 August. Whether the Court of St. James would receive him as representative of the Executive Council of the French Republic or not was a "new question," which Britain was not called upon to decide at the moment, no credentials having been submitted. On 7 January Chauvelin, acting on instructions of the Executive Council, informed Lord Grenville that the application of the Alien Act to the French immigrants would be regarded as a violation of the treaty of commerce of 1786 and demanded to know whether such application was intended. The note was returned, and on 8 January the *Sun* advised its readers that Chauvelin was a dangerous subversive: that there was no valid reason for his being in England, inasmuch as the British had had no ambassador in France since the recall of Earl Gower on 17 August, and that he had taken advantage of British hospitality since to direct the activities of all the French agents in the country and to propagate his "vile" doctrines through the medium of the *"seditious Chronicle."* Chauvelin had also protested that vessels carrying foreign grain destined for France were being unlawfully detained in English ports by order of Government; and, although Lord Grenville stated that he did not receive this note until 9 January, it and all previous correspondence[24] were turned over to the Ministerial papers on 8 January. Since the correspondence was published piecemeal with much insulting commentary, Chauvelin was subjected to daily indignities at the hands of the Ministerial writers, in addition to the arrogance of Lord Grenville.

A Time for Conjectures

While the Ministerial newspapers were reporting the flights of other enemy aliens and urging that M. Chauvelin be sent packing as well, the Government was calling for the augmentation of the Army by one hundred independent regiments, and the *Sun* was trying to augment the Navy by persuading cities to offer additional bounties for enlistments. London came through magnificently. On 18 January *Lloyd's Evening Post* reported: "Every good seaman can now receive eleven pounds bounty, five from Government, two from the City of London, two from the Trinity-House, and two from the Jockey Club." The *Sun* expected the rest of the country to do as well. "*Bristol, Liverpool,* and other large Trading Towns, we have no doubt, will follow the example of London, in offering a Bounty to Seamen," it said on 14 January. Fortifications of buildings and parks were also progressing, although the Duke of Richmond was no longer mentioned in connection with the work, since on 10 January, according to the *Morning Chronicle* (15 Jan.), he had "unfortunately" broken both his legs.

But the *Morning Chronicle* was still unconvinced that Pitt actually intended to fight. "It is determined to raise one hundred Independent Companies; so that the career of rank is open to all aspiring young men who have interest with Ministers," it observed on 10 January; and on 12 January it repeated that the sole purpose of the "skeleton regiments" was to provide Mr. Pitt with more commissions to give away. "It is the boast of Mr. PITT," it went on to protest,

> that the party of his rival is reduced to ten or fifteen, (a fact, however, about which he is grossly mistaken) but surely if so, and if the sense of Parliament is so entirely with him as he pretends, the country have a right to see him conduct the affairs of Government without jobs and corruption. If it be true, he has no need to court favour by improvident and lavish means. It would seem either that he loves the most extravagant way of doing business by habit or by choice; or that his sounding boast of a demolished Opposition is untrue, and that he dreads a speedy end to the delusion he has spread over the country, and is willing to secure the time-servers by the only argument which is effective with them.

On 16 January, having reported a sharp rise in the stock market, owing to "rumours of peace," the *Chronicle* added: "That the British Ministers never had an idea of a serious rupture with France, however well calculated to provoke one their conduct has been, and daily is, the measures of the War-Office fairly prove; for our readers will have seen that instead of vigorous means having been taken to recruit the old corps, the usual job of independent companies has been instantly adopted, as if from a consciousness that the war-hoop would not last long enough to enable them to give away five hundred commissions." The *Chronicle*'s conviction that no one wanted a war except Burke was evidently shared by John Courtenay, whose *A Poetical and Philosophical Essay on the French Revolution. Addressed to Mr. Edmund Burke* was published by Ridgway on 17 January.

But by this time even the Ministerial newspapers were talking of peace, and all reports from Government offices indicated that war had been averted, at least for the moment. The *Morning Chronicle* was confused. As it said on 18 January:

> It is certain that Ministers appear solicitous of giving to the public mind an assurance of peace. The City of London, in answer to their offer of a bounty, of forty shillings to seamen, were told by Lord CHATHAM [Pitt's brother, who since 1788 had been First Lord of the Admiralty], that his Majesty thanked them for their zealous and patriotic offer, but at present the proposed bounty was not considered as necessary.
>
> And during the present week the answer at the War-Office to the offers of raising Independent Companies, has been that all which it was intended to raise at this time were engaged for, and that they could not accept of any more offers.
>
> To these symptoms of pacification may be added another, that some officers who were ordered to join their regiments with all possible speed, have received intimation that they need not put themselves to any inconvenience in obeying that order.
>
> These are signs of peace; but they may be fallacious; for at the same time we see the most scandalous means taken to provoke and insult the French people, as if it were a fixed design to irritate them to hostilities. In the very Journal in which they publish their own State Paper [the *London Gazette*], *pending a negotiation* . . . , they have suffered calumnies on the person whom they acknowledge to be "the accredited Minister of the King of France" [M. Chauvelin]— of so gross and personal a kind, that he cannot as a gentleman *live* under the imputation; and which the French, as a people of honour and delicacy cannot *overlook*. When we see this done in a Journal set up for the purpose of publishing State Papers, and of being a kind of record of their actions, not once or twice, but in a regular series; and making it evidently their object to vilify and slander the French Minister by the most horrid falsehoods, it can scarcely be believed, that they mean seriously to negotiate, though they have begun a negotiation.

But the newspapers had been misinformed on almost every point. On 19 January the *Chronicle* mentioned that, "[in] common with many other persons we were taught to believe that Ministers had said to the city of London, that their proposed bounty was not immediately necessary. The fact we understand is not so; they have accepted the offer, and therefore this is not to be held as one of the symptoms of peace." The War Office had also not refused the offers of independent regiments; and, if there had been any negotiations, M. Chauvelin was unaware of them.

On 13 January Chauvelin had transmitted to Lord Grenville a long explanatory letter from the French Foreign Minister, M. Le Brun; and on 17 January he had requested an interview for the purpose of submitting his new credentials. On 18 January he had been informed by Lord Grenville that Le Brun's explanation was unsatisfactory, and on 20 January he had been advised that the King had not "[thought] fit, under the present circumstances," to "receive" the credentials and that Chauvelin was therefore being "[returned, as a private person,] to the general mass of foreigners resident in England." Hence, if there had been any deliberations, they would have been concluded on 18 January; but until 22 January all newspapers were under the impression that negotiations were in progress. To strengthen this impression, the Government released on 20 January the letter from M. Le Brun, which was therefore published by all newspapers the following day. Since the conduct of Britain's prospective allies was always an embarrassment to the advocates of war, the *Courier* reacted with pleas for interference on behalf of Lafayette, still a hero to the English and now imprisoned by the Austrians, directing its appeals to Pitt, to Dundas, to Lord Grenville, and even to the Prince of Wales. The *Gazetteer* and the *Morning Post* reacted with similar pleas for interference on behalf of Poland, now on the eve of a second partition among Russia, Prussia, and Austria, after a last desperate struggle for independence, under the leadership of General Kosciusko. There was no such propaganda in the *Morning Chronicle*, which could only repeat what it had said earlier. "We are unable for this day to make the observations that occur to us on the reply of Le BRUN to the Answer of Lord GRENVILLE," it told its readers on 21 January. "It is obviously put into the power of the British Cabinet . . . now to acknowledge M. CHAUVELIN, as letters of credence are given to him from the Republic; and on every other of the topics at issue between the two countries, the British Ministers on a fair, open negotiation, may yet extricate themselves from the unprovoked danger in which they have so rashly brought the nation, by meddling with what they had no business, and irritating the people whom they described to be insane." But, as to "the intentions of our Ministers," the *Chronicle* could "form, as yet, no precise idea. We see a great deal of that sort of bustle, which gives countenance to jobbing, and none of the alacrity and vigour which indicate war. We find that Ministers have, by this alarm, found means to give commissions, &c. to their expectants, but we see no grand preparations to avert from the commerce and manufactures of the kingdom, the storm which they have collected around us, and which threatens to burst on our heads." On 22 January readers were informed that M. Chauvelin's credentials had not been accepted.

On 22 January, too, the Alien Bill became effective. Henceforth passports would be required from all Frenchmen entering or presently residing in the country and fresh passports for those changing places of residence, each one being issued only after an examination of the applicant and a search of his possessions. Henceforth also Frenchmen could not settle within ten miles of the coast or more than fifty miles from London. The *Public Advertiser* of 21

January was so pleased with the prospect that it even expressed its gratitude to Burke: "The country is infinitely indebted for its present safety to Mr. *Burke*— for it was Mr. *Burke* who sounded the alarm of danger; he exposed the *Secrets* of the Prison House, and held up to public view, and to public abhorrence, a party of men eager to render themselves indebted for their fortune and elevation, to the ruin of the Empire." Commendations of Burke were extremely unusual, and the *Courier*'s reaction to this particular outburst (22 Jan.) was at least succinct: "*Independence!* — 1. THE NEW RAISED COMPANIES! — 2. MR. EDMUND BURKE." The question of what would happen to M. Chauvelin was still unanswered. On 22 January the *Oracle* mentioned that he was "extremely uneasy in remaining here, as from this day he becomes subject to the Alien Bill, and is liable to have his Papers examined. He has applied to Lord GRENVILLE on the subject, but has been given to understand that he would be considered in no other light than that of any other Alien." By 23 January the *Oracle* understood that he had "set off for Dover, on his way to *France*." He did in fact leave two days later.

The execution of Louis XVI was announced by all newspapers on 24 January. Although the particulars were lacking, readers learned that he had been condemned to death on 20 January and sent to the guillotine the following day, the Committee of Public Safety being established at the same time. They also learned that on 28 January Dundas would present to Parliament a message from the King, asking for an immediate augmentation of the forces. The newspapers purported to be stunned, but they were not so stunned as to overlook the political advantages. The *Sun* and the *True Briton* at once blamed "Citizen Fox" for the "murder," *The Times* blamed that "Jacobin," Lord Lauderdale, and the *Oracle*, the *Courier*, and the *Gazetteer* attributed the whole thing to Edmund Burke. The Duke of Orleans, who had at least voted for the execution, was not mentioned. As usual, only the *Morning Chronicle* surveyed the situation calmly. "Mr. SECRETARY DUNDAS's notice of a message from His MAJESTY to the House of Commons on Monday next, to call for a considerable increase of our Armaments, may be considered as a certain indication of war," it told its readers on 24 January. "The murder of the late FRENCH KING, an act of such complicated injustice, cowardice, cruelty and impolicy, as is scarcely to be paralleled, has this aggravation of its inherent atrocity, that it will serve to make a war with France popular, which certainly neither diligence nor wisdom on the part of the administration has been exerted to prevent." On 25 January it spoke up in defense of Fox and Lord Lauderdale:

> The friends of liberty in England are not to be libelled by any imputation of their approving of the diabolical conduct of the National Convention of France. They have uniformly exerted themselves, by all the means which private men had in their power, to save the unhappy monarch. If our Ministers had used the same diligence, candour, and zeal, there is no doubt but Louis might have been saved; but then, perhaps, there would have been no popular argument for war. A war is now indubitable. The popular argument drawn from the KING's

murder—for death, contrary to the established forms of the law of a kingdom, is murder—will be successfully used; and the blood and treasure of England will be lavished, under the pretext of bringing a nation of madmen and ferocious beasts, back to reason and humanity.

. . . . . .

Yet, in the present fever of the multitude, we see ourselves devoted to this chevalresque pursuit; and the few men who have virtue and bravery to demand simply, that Englishmen will deliberate before they sally out, are doomed to every invective that a heated imagination, with a malignant heart, can suggest.

On 26 January the *Chronicle* presented with evident sarcasm the "one argument for this war" which "it is impossible to deny." For, since, said the *Chronicle*, "we have in truth no foreign enemy to fight with, the money that it will cost us, whatever it may be, will not go out of the kingdom. The people may be taxed indeed, but that is of no consequence, for the money will only be taken out of the pockets of the industrious poor, to be put into those of placemen, pensioners, and contractors, with a certainty that through the canals of luxury, dissipation and vice, it will return again into the common stock, and perpetuate to the poor the industry from which it was originally drawn."

On the morning of 28 January, readers were advised that M. Chauvelin had gone home. On 24 January the King had, it appeared, been "pleased . . . to direct that Monsieur Chauvelin, late Minister Plenipotentiary from the Most Christian King, should depart this realm, on or before the 1st day of February next," and he had actually departed early the following day. The insults had evidently continued right up to the end, for, according to the *London Packet*, Chauvelin had been "arrested in Oxford-street, on the day of his departure, upon a writ for forty-five pounds, but was liberated in an hour or two." The *Packet* suspected that there were other debts, for it was very certain that "this *ci-devant* Ambassador" was not what he had pretended to be. He "has an estate of three or four thousand a year in France," said the *Packet*; "but had never, as has been said, the rank of Marquis." Readers were also advised that Lord Loughborough had accepted the post of Lord High Chancellor. "Upon what personal conditions the Noble . . . Lord takes this high situation, we do not know," said the *Morning Chronicle*. "Report says that he is to have the reversion of Lord MARCHMONT's place of Keeper of the Great Seal of Scotland; and, by another rumour, it is said that he would not consent to accept of them without a pension of 6000*l.* a year on his retirement." Finally, readers learned of the publication "this day" of *A Letter from the Right Honourable Charles James Fox, to the Worthy and Independent Electors of the City and Liberty of Westminster.*

Advertisements for Fox's *Letter* appeared in almost all the newspapers, excerpts were printed by the *Public Advertiser* without comment, and a few newspapers called attention to the work editorially. One was the *Morning Chronicle*, which represented it as a work of vital importance to all Britons; another was the *Oracle*, which took advantage of the occasion to attach a vindication of Sheridan. Since Burke had already (20 Dec.) accused him of speaking for the National Convention rather than the King, the *Oracle* was evidently afraid that he would make more serious accusations in the heat of that afternoon's debates. "Mr. Fox, severely wounded by implications, which annoy the Patriotism he aspires to," said the *Oracle*, "this day addresses to the Public and his Friends a vindicatory Pamphlet, which, as it is the first in his life, has, perhaps, the commission to elucidate the most critical period of it./ It is a fact, that one of the strongest papers in favour of the unfortunate KING of FRANCE was written by Mr. SHERIDAN: it is said to have been translated by the elegant pen of Madame SILLERY, and very much circulated by the *Brissotins*. Monsieur SILLERY's speech on the subject, did him the *greatest honour*." The "paper" has not been identified, but, since the Marquise de Sillery lived in England from October, 1791, to November, 1792, during which period she was in frequent communication with Sheridan, a collaboration is possible. The Marquis de Sillery defended Louis against his accusers.

The *Letter* was dated 26 January. Hence it had been written after the country learned of the execution of Louis XVI and rushed through the press in order to appear on this particular day. As the title indicated, it was addressed to the Westminster electors, and its purpose, said Fox himself, was to explain the motions of 13, 14, and 15 December. Approximately half of the pamphlet was devoted to this explanation. Fox began by repeating that the King's action in summoning the militia was "illegal." The King could, it was true, summon the militia in case of an emergency, but he must advise Parliament as to the nature of that emergency, and he had not done so; nor had there been any evidence of an emergency. On 13 December Fox had therefore moved for an investigation. Of those who opposed the motion, many admitted that in their opinion no emergency existed, but they had opposed it anyway, because, as they said, they were uneasy about the propagation of "French opinions" and wanted to prevent an emergency in the future. To this group Fox would say that the militia could be lawfully summoned only to deal with a present "evil," not to deal with an "evil" which might or might not occur at some later date; and, as to the expedience of the measure, he could think of no surer way to transform "opinions" into "overt acts" than to fight them with "force." Others who opposed the motion did so because they felt that ignorance under the circumstances was an advantage: that the "obscurity" would arouse a "terror" which in turn would put the country on guard against "French opinions," whether they had as yet made any inroads or not. To this group Fox would point out that the "terror" had thus far fostered only "systems of crooked policy and pious fraud." "Is it nothing," he asked, "to destroy peace, harmony, and confidence, among all ranks of citizens? Is it nothing to give a general credit and countenance to suspicions, which every man may point as his worst passions incline him? In such a state, all political animosities are inflamed. We confound the mistaken speculist with the desperate incendiary."

On 14 December Fox had moved that Britain should attempt to "avert the calamities of war," so long as its doing so was "consistent with the honour and safety of this country"; and here, it seemed to him, the reason was obvious. For, "if it be true that there are seeds of discontent, War is the hot-bed in which these seeds will soonest vegetate; and of all wars, . . . that war is most to be dreaded, in the cause of which Kings may be supposed to be more concerned than their subjects." The same reason explained in part the motion of 15 December to send a minister to Paris to confer with "those persons who exercise provisionally the functions of executive Government in France." Of the opponents to these motions, almost all had felt that Britain could not honorably communicate with a government from which it had suffered "injury" and "insult." This argument, Fox admitted, he could not understand, for, if it was true that the present French government had "injured" and "insulted" the British nation, then it was precisely that government to which the British must complain and from which they must demand satisfaction. The remainder of the pamphlet was an impassioned plea for peace, which concluded with a plea to his friends in the Commons not to support the King's request for an augmentation of the forces. "To declare war, is, by the Constitution, the prerogative of the King," Fox reminded them; "but to grant or with-hold the means of carrying it on, is (by the same Constitution) the privilege of the People, through their Representatives; and upon the People at large, by a law paramount to all Constitutions—the Law of Nature and Necessity, must fall the burdens and sufferings, which are the too sure attendants upon that calamity. It seems therefore reasonable that they, who are to pay, and to suffer, should be distinctly informed of the object for which that war is made. . . ."

It is easy to suppose, as most of the Ministerial newspapers did, that the first part of this pamphlet had little to do with the second, that Fox had been goaded into writing it by fear, and that it was actually an appeal to the Duke of Portland not to desert him; but the supposition would be wrong. When Fox made the motions of 13–15 December, the only argument for war which was likely to impress anyone was that the British Constitution was imperiled by French "notions." Fox had contended that this was not the case, and he had done so, it appears, on good authority. Although there were many reform societies, all of them were known to be small except the Corresponding Society, which "boasted of . . . scores of thousands all over the kingdom," probably on the "advice" of Horne Tooke that, "if you wish to be powerful, pretend to be powerful." Since this society was extremely radical and its members consisted of "mechanics, labourers, porters, coal-heavers, and persons of that class," it would have constituted the peril, if there was any; and hence it was important to Fox to know exactly how large the membership was. Fox seems to have consulted Sheridan, who in turn consulted Daniel Stuart. As a nonofficial subsecretary of the Friends of the People, Stuart was acquainted with the Secretary of the Corresponding Society, Thomas Hardy, who told him the "truth about the numbers": that in fact they consisted of only a few thousand. Sheridan, said Stuart,[25] thereupon "called [Fox] out of the House that I might personally communicate to him [this] agreeable information." This was the only time Stuart ever met him. Fox could not divulge this information, since it was confidential, but he could say with certainty that the Constitution was not in peril. He could also know that he was expressing the consensus of the people when he said so.

Since, if the British Constitution was not in peril, the British King was also not in peril, the murder of the French King did not, in Fox's opinion, alter the logic of the situation. But, as the *Morning Chronicle* had been saying, it would prove difficult under the present emotional circumstances to explain this fact to the people, especially since anyone who had the "virtue and bravery" to try would be "doomed to every invective that a heated imagination . . . can suggest." As "The Man of the People," Fox nevertheless felt bound to make the attempt, and all he was asking of his "friends" in Parliament was that they did not take advantage of "the present fever of the multitude": that they withhold financial support of the war until the situation could be viewed calmly and the people, who were "to pay, and to suffer," had been "distinctly informed" as to what they were "to pay, and to suffer" for. But the Duke of Portland, to whom this appeal was principally addressed, was by this time subjected to other influences.

The Government and the
Friends of the Liberty of the Press

The Government's only argument in favor of war was, as Fox said, a supposed threat to the Constitution, which was also its only argument against reform. But its attempts to "popularize" the argument had not succeeded. The reason was that, since Pitt enjoyed no public confidence, he was obliged to work deviously; and, although he was ingenious, ingenuity was sometimes not enough.

In Ireland the Government had blundered badly in arresting several members of the United Irishmen the previous December. The *Courier* of 1 January was greatly upset about the arrest of Archibald Hamilton Rowan in particular, protesting at length that Rowan was "a Gentleman most deservedly popular" in Ireland and certainly undeserving this kind of treatment. But, by the time the protest was published, Rowan was released, having been charged only, as the newspapers understood, with using "seditious words." Ireland presented a problem of its own, for, since Catholic sympathies were with France rather than England, there was no possibility that the Irish would rally to the defense of the

Constitution; and there was a possibility, as the Opposition had argued, that, in the event of a war, they might even assist the French. Since any tumult in Ireland tended to strengthen this argument, what the Government needed in that area was a semblance of calm. Hence Dundas sent no agitators to Ireland, and, owing to a bit of strategy on the part of the King, the country was in fact lulled into a state of comparative quiet until the war was underway. The strategy was much deplored by the *Morning Chronicle*, not because the *Chronicle* was opposed to Catholic demands or because it suspected, as it should have, the King's sincerity, but because it was uneasy about his interfering in such instances. As it said on 19 January in a summation of the situation: "When the Irish Catholics applied to [the Irish] Parliament last Session, their petition was not even suffered to lie on the table, but contemptuously kicked over the bar. The Irish Catholics have now applied to the King, and his Majesty has commanded the Lord Lieutenant [the Earl of Westmorland], in his Speech from the Throne, to recommend their complaints to the consideration of Parliament. What is this but a branch of the system so often and so justly reprobated—for withdrawing the affection and confidence of the people from their Representatives, and directing all their hopes to the Crown . . . ?"

Dundas managed affairs in Scotland, where, as in England, it was to the Government's advantage to incite as much sedition as possible and to advertise that it existed by a succession of prosecutions. Since Lord Braxfield, often called "The Hanging Judge," was presiding over the High Court of Justiciary in Edinburgh, everything should have gone very well; but there had been blunders here, too. On 3 January, according to the *Star* (10 Jan.), "Mr. MUIR, Advocate, was apprehended at Glasgow, and brought from thence to Edinburgh gaol. He has found bail for his appearance before the Circuit Court of Justiciary." This turned out to be only part of the story. Although Thomas Muir had officiated at the convention of the Associated Friends of the People the previous December, the Scots had seen nothing objectionable in his conduct, and, regarding him, as the Irish regarded Rowan, as "a Gentleman most deservedly popular," they had protested, and the Government had supposedly revised its plans. According to the *Gazetteer*, it had apologized to Muir, informed him that the charge, which consisted only of "lending the works of Thomas Paine to a friend," would be dropped, and released him. By 10 January Muir was on his way to Paris. Since then the Government had concentrated on "Gentlemen" who were not so "deservedly popular." The London newspapers reported six trials for sedition during the month of January. James Tytler, tried on 7 January, was charged with writing or publishing a seditious libel, addressed "To the People and their Friends"; John Elder and William Stewart, tried on 10 January, were charged with publishing another "seditious libel"; and John Morton, James Anderson, and Malcolm Craig, tried on 8, 9, and 11 January, were charged with urging soldiers at the Castle to drink seditious toasts. Tytler was outlawed, having been persuaded to flee the country rather than face trial; the others seem to have been sentenced to nine months in prison, plus heavy securities for good behavior for an additional three years. But the effect was impaired by a protest from the last three that they had acted on instructions from Dundas.

In England the Government had fared worse, although for different reasons. At the beginning of 1793, its principal achievements had been to drive Sampson Perry and Thomas Paine out of the country, to outlaw John Frost, and to frighten into an apparent apostacy the moneylender, John King. Since then it had lost ground rather than gained it, but King at least continued to be helpful. His speech at Egham, published by the *Morning Herald* on 12 December, had finally been read by Paine, who, having regarded King as his protégé and knowing nothing of his predicament, responded with some remonstrance and advice. The letter, headed "Paris, 3 Jan. 1793," read in part:

> DEAR KING,
>
> I don't know any thing these many years, that surprised, and hurt me more, than the sentiments you published in the Courtly HERALD. . . . You have gone back from all you ever said.
>
> When I first knew you in Ailiffe-street, . . . a child, without fortune or friends, I noticed you; because I thought I saw in you, young as you was, a bluntness of temper, a boldness of opinion, and an originality of thought, that portended some future good.
>
> I was pleased to discuss, with you, under our friend *Oliver*'s lime-tree, those political notions, which I have since given the world in my "Rights of Man."
>
> You used to complain of abuses, as well as he, and wrote your opinion of them in free terms—what then means this sudden attachment to *Kings*? this fondness of the English Government and hatred of the French?—If you mean to curry favour, by aiding your Government, you are mistaken; they never recompence those who serve it; they buy off those who can annoy it, and let the good that is rendered it, be its own reward. . . .

King did his duty. He replied from "New Burlington-street" on 11 January with a second recantation. He was no longer, he said, "a friend of the French," having "renounced" that "friendship" and the "prejudice I had too hastily adopted" as soon as they revealed themselves as "oppressors." This statement was followed by a long diatribe on French theories and British reformers and finally by a bit of counteradvice: "Mr. PAINE—such men as *Frost, Barlow*, and others, your associates, shew the forlornness of your cause. Our respectable citizens do not go to you, they remain at home, attached to their country—the whole nation, as one man, is roused against you. . . ." King thereupon turned both letters over to the *Morning Herald*, with which he was probably now associated. The *Herald* published them on 22 January.

The implication in King's letter that "citizens" could choose between supporting William Pitt and getting out of the country, if not intentional, at least reflected the Government's thinking. Of the major reformers, only two, Sampson Perry and Thomas Paine, had been brought to trial, and both of them had been tried *in absentia* and, as it happened, at a time when the populace was in a state of panic, owing to a supposed insurrection. Not only was the Government averse to trying such cases with the defendants present and under normal circumstances, but it was averse to trying them at all. Its usual policy was to frighten the offenders into flight or, if they were already out of the country, to discourage their return by threatening to prosecute. Flight was always celebrated by the Ministerial newspapers as a great victory for Pitt. In the case of Perry, *The Times* was still shouting its good riddance on 5 January: "The *Argus* news-paper was intended to be reprinted in Paris on the 1st of January. The Conductor may there give unlimited scope to his treasonable abuse of our Government." As an example to outlaws who might think of returning, there was still John Almon, in prison since March, 1792, and as yet unsentenced. But by now the policy seemed to be creating more problems than it was solving.

Except for the *Sun* and the *True Briton*, no newspaper approved of the treatment of Almon, and, appeals to Pitt having failed, several of the papers appealed to John Wilkes, who had been closely associated with Almon during his own radical days.[26] As Chamberlain for the City of London, Wilkes had ripened into a complacent Tory with enough influence, it seemed to the newspapers, to do something about the situation. It finally appeared that Wilkes was looking into the matter, for on 9 January the *Diary* reported: "Last week, Mr. WILKES paid a visit to his old friend, Mr. ALMON, in the King's Bench, who has been there a long time for a Libel, published near five years ago, no ways relating to the present times." The paragraph reappeared in the *Star* and *Oracle* of 10 January, with the addendum in the *Oracle*: "Mr. ALMON's patient Sufferings claim some Relief from the Hand of Power. We forbear any opinion on the Merits or Demerits of his Case: suffice it to say, that he has already amply atoned for the Trespass alluded to; and that his Enlargement would reflect honour on the Feelings of those whom his Imprisonment may have concerned." With the Almon case already an issue, the Government must have been saddened indeed to learn that John Frost was also returning.

Although the *Public Advertiser* had reported the arrest of Frost as early as 31 December, 1792, the report was premature, for, unlike Almon, Frost did not merely reappear. Instead, he wrote a letter to William Pitt, dated "PARIS, DECEMBER 19th, 1792," sending a copy to the *Morning Chronicle* for publication. The *Chronicle* published it on 1 January, 1793. Frost had just heard of his indictment and of the reward offered for his apprehension, and he did not like any part of what he had heard. He did not like the assertion that he had left England to avoid prosecution, "as no prosecution to my knowledge was com-menced while I was in England, and my departure was no secret": in stating otherwise, "the Proclamation states a falsehood." Nor did he like Pitt's deciding who would and who would not live in the country. He would "return to my trial," he assured Pitt, not only to "afford an opportunity to some fellow citizen to profit by the proposed bounty of the Treasury," but to "adjust an account with you," who, in May, 1782, had promised to labor to "obtain redress of the abuses in government," then represented as "essentially necessary to the *independence of Parliament, and the liberty of the People,*" and had since labored so hard to prevent it. The only comment on Frost's letter came from the *Oracle,* which remarked on 2 January: "When a Paper will stain itself with the disculpation of a being like the Delegate of a *treasonable* Association, its Constitutional *Spirit* may be presumed above *Proof.*" Other Ministerial newspapers were dealing with the problem differently. Frost had not fled to avoid the Attorney General, they agreed, but only to avoid his creditors, since he was very heavily in debt and had no hope of extricating himself. This tactic succeeded nicely. On 8 January the *London Gazette* included in its list of bankrupts the name, "John Frost, late of Spring Gardens, scrivener, to surrender Jan. 12, 23, and Feb. 19, at twelve, at Guildhall." On 9 January the *Morning Chronicle* published an anguished letter from Mrs. Eliza Frost, entreating her husband's creditors, whoever they were, to "suspend judgment," for his debts, she knew, were trivial and his property substantial. Every debt, she promised, would be liquidated immediately upon his return and would have been liquidated earlier had liquidation been requested. Although she was not surprised, in light of the "repeated suggestions" in the newspapers, that "a commission of bankruptcy against him" should have been applied for, she was dumbfounded that the application should have been granted, since the most superficial investigation would have established his solvency.

The Government's most serious problem was, however, Erskine and the Friends of the Liberty of the Press. As it turned out, the Government had made a tragic mistake in trying Paine, for, although it had won its case in court, it had lost it everywhere else. Erskine had emerged as the champion of the law, the Government as corruptor, and, to emphasize the fact, the recently activated Friends of the Liberty of the Press had honored him with a public dinner, censuring in passing the jury, the judge, and the Government. For Pitt, the situation was extremely awkward. The passage of the Alien Act should have been followed by a flood of indictments, especially since the Attorney General, Sir Archibald Macdonald, had boasted on 13 December that he was then processing two hundred of them, but so sensitive was public opinion by this time that only two trials were reported by the newspapers for the month of January and only one arrest. Thomas Townley Macan was convicted of attempting to blow up King's Bench Prison on 7 July, 1792, and was sent to Newgate for three years; and on 7 January, according to *Lloyd's Evening Post* (9 Jan.), a Mr. Carter was tried at Clerkenwell for publishing a libel, called "An Address from the London Corresponding Society to the Other Societies in Great-Britain, United for the Purpose of Obtaining a Reform in Parliament." Publication had consisted of his posting the "Address" on the corner of Crown Street, St. Giles's, on 5 December. Although Macdonald admitted that it might seem "odd" to prosecute "a poor miserable Bill-sticker," still the libel was so "alarming" that he felt that no one connected with it should be ignored. The Court agreed. Carter was convicted and sentenced to six months in prison. On 13 January, again according to *Lloyd's Evening Post* (16 Jan.), Thomas Spence, a bookseller in Chancery Lane, already under indictment for selling Part II of Paine's *Rights of Man*, was arrested on a second charge and confined in New Prison in Clerkenwell. In this instance, the Government had acted out of desperation, for, not only was Spence a publisher for the Friends of the People, but, at the end of 1792, he had assailed the Administration in a pamphlet, entitled *The Case of Thomas Spence, Bookseller, who was Committed for Selling the Second Part of Paine's "Rights of Man."* On 14 January the *Morning Chronicle* reminded its readers that these cases were supposedly only the beginning:

> There are no fewer than two hundred indictments prepared by the Crown Officers, to be presented to the Grand Juries throughout the kingdom for libels and seditious words. They are of all kinds, some against newspapers, some against pamphlets, hand-bills, &c. and of the seditious words some were uttered from the pulpit, and some in the ale-houses, in moments of jollity and inebriation. On the slightest computation, the trial of these indictments in law costs, and the value of the time of the imprisonments that may follow conviction, cannot be less [for the indictees] than 50,000*l.* to say nothing of the utter extinction of free opinion.

The public, in other words, was to continue its vigilance.

Since it was unable to act on its own, the Government had relied heavily on its newspapers and The Association, although here, too, the results had not been altogether gratifying. The regular burning of Paine's effigy had been urged by the *World* as a matter of patriotic duty, and The Association evidently saw to it that effigies were burned, for, as late as 14 January, *Lloyd's Evening Post* reported that the burnings were "[continuing] in every part of the Kingdom." There were incessant denunciations of "the *Jacobin Chronicle*" in the *Sun* and incessant demands in the *World* that readers burn "the seditious print" wherever they found it. On 10 January the *World* reported happily: "Several PUBLIC PRINTS, inimical to the Constitution, have lately been burnt by public spirited Gentlemen, in the *principal* Coffee-houses in this Metropolis. This example should be followed generally throughout the kingdom." To enable "public spirited Gentlemen" in the provinces to know what newspapers to burn, lists were provided, indicating which newspapers were "for the Constitution" and which were against it. This was not a good idea. Since *The Times* and the *Sun* regarded themselves as considerably more "for the Constitution" than the *World*, neither newspaper was pleased to see the *World* heading that list; nor was either of them willing to yield priority to the other. The quarrel as to which newspaper was most "for the Constitution" was still going on in March. There was also a question as to whether being "for the Constitution" was an advantage. The *Morning Chronicle* of 14 January maintained that it was not: "We are favoured with a copy of a printed Letter sent from London by post to various parts of the country, dividing the London papers into two classes, with the titles of *For the Constitution—Against the Constitution*. The severest punishment to the authors of this calumny, is to inform them that the Papers they attempt to slander, as against the Constitution, sell [as a result] more than three times the number of those they recommend, as for the Constitution." On 15 January, having traced the letter to Topham, the *Chronicle* added the sarcastic notice that "persons holding places of profit and large sinecures under Government, are— deeply impressed with a sense of our excellent Constitution; and truly sensible of the blessings they enjoy." Topham, along with Thomas Vavasour, had just been appointed "Deputy Lieutenant of the EAST RIDING of the County of YORK" and had prepared for his new duties, according to the *World* (17 Jan.), by moving the gallows from the area in front of the County Jail to the yard in front of the Castle. The reputation of The Association had by now so deteriora- ted that Banks invested in another series of puffs, reassuring the people that he was a very fine man despite his connection with Reeves. "The name of Sir JOSEPH BANKS should never be omitted in the enumeration of those who are friends to the exertions of Genius in the cause of Knowledge," proclaimed the *Oracle* on 18 January. "His ample fortune is cheerfully dedicated to this purpose; and there are at this time individuals in the various quarters of the globe enabled by his bounty to prosecute their pursuits, whose object is the public good."

It had seemed to Lord Mulgrave on 4 January that the activities of the Friends of the Liberty of the Press were reason enough to support the Alien Act. The Ministerial newspapers had agreed. There was no group in their opinion as "Jacobinical" as this one and no individual as contemptible as Erskine. The advertisement for another public dinner, to be held on 19 January, upset them altogether, and, as it turned out, with good reason, for the dinner was a great success. It was attended by over eight hundred people, and, in charge of the arrangements, were Charles Grey, John Courtenay, George Byng, George Rous, James Mackintosh, Captain Charles Morris, who provided the song for the occasion, and Sheridan and Erskine, who made speeches. Sheridan's speech was later sent to the newspapers to be printed as an advertisement; Erskine's speech, too lengthy for the newspapers, was separately printed for free distribution, in an edition, according to the *Star* (24 Jan.), of 100,000 copies. The speech was mainly an indictment of The Crown and Anchor Association, whose members, said Erskine, were not only the accusers and witnesses in the Government's prosecutions of the press, but also the judges, inasmuch as they were regularly used to pack juries. Also a speaker at the dinner was Horne Tooke, although he seems not to have been invited and was not allowed to conclude. According to some of the newspapers, he was interrupted by a flying bottle, which narrowly missed his head; according to others, he was simply asked to desist; according to the *Public Advertiser* (23 Jan.): "Mr. Horne Tooke was not only pulled down from a table, on Saturday, for having *freely* spoken his opinion to the friends of the *freedom* of the press, but himself and his supporters were thrust from the room.—It was thought, however, shortly afterwards, that such a transaction might disgrace the meeting, and Mr. Rous was one of a Deputation sent to negociate a peace with Mr. Tooke. His interference was successful; Mr. Tooke returned; and the series then took place of commendatory speeches between him and Mr. Sheridan." Except for the *Sun* and the *True Briton*, the Ministerial newspapers allotted this dinner a great deal of space: the *Oracle* (21 Jan.) gave it almost two pages, the *World* nearly as much, whereas the *Morning Chronicle* gave it only four and one-half columns. Although a few of them represented it as a brawl, not one of them suggested that it was seditious, and most of them were sympathetic with Erskine's remarks. Freedom of the press was, after all, a matter of consequence to them.

Inspired perhaps by what Erskine had said, Thomas Law delivered to the *Morning Chronicle* a letter he had written to Reeves on 17 December, 1792, announcing his resignation from The Association. He had told Reeves that, when he joined The Crown and Anchor Association, he was given to understand that its purpose was to counteract the spread of "republicanism" by the distribution of "anti-republican" tracts; he had since discovered that its purpose was to agitate for war by "inflaming the popular passions against the French" and to collect informations for the Government. He had been appalled, he said, to find that The Association was "encouraging anonymous letters," that the letters were being regularly scrutinized by a five-member committee, and that whatever information could be gleaned from them was being turned over to the Solicitor General, Sir John Scott. Law's letter was published by the *Morning Chronicle* on 24 January and was immediately reissued as a pamphlet. Only the *Public Advertiser* commented. "The very dregs of Opposition can only assemble, halloo, and hoop against the conduct of Administration, and cry aloud the Liberty of the Press is in danger," it snorted on 25 January. "But the good people of England know that it is false; for the whole matter in issue must be submitted to a Jury." In light of Erskine's remarks about "packed" juries, this was hardly an effective rebuttal. The Government obviously had to do something about Erskine; this meant that the Prince of Wales would again be figuring in the news.

A Message and a Postponement

Although nothing further had been said about the King's allowing "20,000*l.* per annum for five years, towards the complete liquidation of the Prince's debts," the story had not been denied, and an advertisement, published by all newspapers on 7 January, had even seemed to confirm it: "CARLTON HOUSE./ *5th January,* 1793./ THE CREDITORS *at large of His Royal Highness the Prince of Wales, are requested to send in their respective Bills,* (*made up to the above date*) *to the office of His Royal Highness's Treasurer* [*Colonel Hulse*], *in Pall-Mall, in order that the said Bills may as speedily as possible be arranged and put into a state of liquidation.*" On 22 January, according to the *Oracle* and *Lloyd's Evening Post* (23 Jan.), there was another "Treasury Board," followed by a further reduction of the Prince's household, "two Pages of the Presence, three of the Back Stairs, Cook, &c." being "paid up to the last quarter" and "retired on a pension of half their salary." But the Prince was still living in Carlton House, still giving small parties, and, as *Lloyd's Evening Post* noted (9 Jan.), still dining at times with Mrs. Fitzherbert "at her house in Pall-Mall."

The Prince was politically inactive during the early part of the month, but by mid-January he had renewed his intimacy with Sheridan, and, since it seemed to Sheridan that the only obstacle to his joining the Government was Burke, it should have surprised no one to learn that the Prince had "expressed a desire" to talk to him. On 24 January the *Oracle*, which was again greatly interested in the Prince's affairs, reported that the two had met: "Mr. BURKE yesterday at noon had a long audience of the PRINCE of WALES. His Royal Highness had last week expressed a desire to see Mr. BURKE and that Gentleman had appointed Saturday [19 Jan.].—The PRINCE could not then conveniently receive him, and mentioned the beginning of the week. Mr. BURKE accordingly visited the PRINCE yesterday. The nature of the conversation cannot be known, of course./ His Royal Highness, however, ... more than ever seems inclined to afford his countenance to His MAJESTY's Ministers; satisfied, that the melancholy lesson of a neighbouring Nation should not be neglected by a Prince who feels for the dignity of his Family and his own Interests." The implication that the Prince had expressed a willingness to support the Government under certain conditions seemed to be justified, for on 25 January, according to *Lloyd's Evening Post* (28 Jan.), he had an even longer "conversation" with "Mr. Pitt and Mr. Dundas."

It was clearly Sheridan's understanding that Burke had agreed to support his interests, for the *Oracle*, which had previously detested him, was devoted to him from this point on. It was also devoted to Mrs. Fitzherbert, who was evidently assisting Sheridan in this intrigue, as she had assisted him in earlier ones. Having on 26 January mentioned that "the PRINCE of WALES passes much of his time, *en famille*, with Mrs. FITZHERBERT, at her House in Pall Mall, in all the laudable pursuits of a private Gentleman and Man of Honour," the *Oracle* went on in subsequent numbers to praise her virtues and her fine influence over the Prince. The news of the Prince's defection on 30 January was almost too much for the already enraptured *Oracle* to endure:

THE PRINCE OF WALES.

At a period as critical to all *Europe*, and so interesting to the hearts of Englishmen, we are happy when the Pen of TRUTH can witness actions beneficial to Society, and honourable to individuals.

The PRINCE of WALES, whose conduct upon all occasions bespeaks the most honourable mind, has withdrawn himself from the Political Discord, and attached his name where the laws of NATURE suggested the Propriety of Alliance! The KING, as a FATHER, looked for that affection which a feeling mind could not shake off, in a Son who is an honour to Human Nature, and the Country that gave him birth! Upon all critical subjects, at every moment where the heart dictated, the PRINCE has manifested a Dignity of Character, so finely blended with exquisite feeling, that it is difficult to decide which is most to be admired, his head or his heart.

No longer swayed by Prejudice, or shackled by Party, throwing himself into the bosom of a LOYAL and FREE PEOPLE, we congratulate his Royal Highness on the laudable step he has taken, and anticipate the joyful gratulations of every HONEST ENGLISHMAN.

The PRINCE, who never loses sight of the most gentlemanly manners, previous to his withdrawing himself from the PORTLAND PARTY, wrote a well-judged and handsome Letter to the Duke, thanking his Grace and his Friends for their attachment to him, and assigning the best reason for his change of political sentiments—THE SACRED TIES OF FILIAL AFFECTION! The PRINCE of WALES has now an opportunity of distinguishing who are his REAL DISINTERESTED FRIENDS; and it is to be hoped a Character so ILLUSTRIOUS and so AMIABLE will scarcely find a single enemy in the BRITISH DOMINIONS.

The *Oracle* said again that the letter to the Duke of Portland was an act of simple courtesy and was interpreted as such by the Duke himself: "His Grace of PORTLAND saw without the smallest surprise, the polite renunciation of the PRINCE—He has been an hundred times upon the point of desertion himself; and now if the word *Constitution* were swept away from the banner of the Phalanx, he would fly it with horror. His confidence is certainly unbounded in Mr. Fox./ 'Better to fear too far, than trust too late.'" All credit for the Prince's conversion was given to Burke. "The PRINCE has reposed full confidence in Mr. BURKE," said the *Oracle*. "—After the conference we stated to have been held [on 23 Jan.], His Royal Highness was fully convinced, and the measures which followed have proceeded from the undeniable claims of his own honour and dignity." The *Oracle* understood that Burke was being "mentioned as the Secretary for the Home Department" vice Dundas as a result of this coup, and it for one thought that this would be an excellent arrangement: "It is an Office, wherein every lover of good Government would see him with pleasure. Such a Man it is impossible to reward, and hardly possible to honour by any appointment."

Sheridan's "confidence" in the Prince of Wales was also "certainly un-, bounded," for, if ever "trust" was misplaced, it was misplaced in this instance. The Prince may have commenced negotiations in good faith, but Burke, who had not liked Sheridan to begin with and would have liked him even less after his speech to the Friends of the Liberty of the Press on 19 January, would have seen in this overture only a means of dealing with Erskine. Since Burke was not adroit in such maneuvers, he had turned the matter over to Pitt and Dundas, who talked to the Prince on 25 January. But by this time the situation had changed. The papers had announced the execution of Louis, the King was to ask for an augmentation of the forces, and Pitt's immediate concern was what Fox would say on that occasion. Since there was no possibility that Fox would support the request, Pitt's only hope was to minimize the effect his speech would have on the people. Hence, in addition to the dismissal of Erskine, Pitt now wanted something tantamount to a public censure of Fox, namely, a letter to the Duke of Portland, in which the Prince announced his own defection and urged the Duke to defect as well. In return, he promised the Prince two things he very much wanted: a colonelcy and assistance with payment of his debts. Although, if Sheridan's affairs figured at all in these arrangements, they figured only incidentally, the *Oracle* was under the impression that they were the very core of the discussions, and it was certainly not prepared for the Prince's letter to the Duke of Portland. But, having persuaded itself or having been persuaded by the Prince that it was all a matter of "manners," the *Oracle* continued to sing the praises of the Prince and his "REAL DISINTERESTED FRIENDS."

On 28 January, Parliament was to hear the message from the King. That morning the Ministerial newspapers reported Chauvelin's departure, Lord Loughborough's acceptance of the Chancellorship, the dismissal of Erskine, and the Prince's letter to the Duke of Portland. The last two announcements were made by the *True Briton*. "It was yesterday *whispered* in some fashionable Circles, that *Counsellor Ego* has received intimation from a certain great Personage, that his services as Attorney General will in future be dispensed with," said the *True Briton*. The letter, in which the Prince had stated why he was pledging his full allegiance to William Pitt and why he thought "at this critical time every person ought to concur in supporting his Majesty's Government," was reviewed at some length with high praise for its "manliness." The effect of this announcement was somewhat damaged, however, by a notice in the *Morning Chronicle* that, as soon as the Prince had signed the communication, he had been awarded "the commission of Colonel of the 10th Regiment of Light Dragoons"; and the effect of all announcements was more than offset by Fox's *Letter . . . to the . . . [Westminster] Electors*. That afternoon Dundas laid before the Commons copies of all official correspondence with M. Chauvelin, most of which had already appeared in the newspapers. He also presented the message from the King, who, it appeared, "[relied] on the known affection and zeal of the House of Commons to enable [him] to take the most effectual measures . . . for maintaining the security and rights of his own dominions; for supporting his allies; and for opposing views of aggrandizement and ambition on the part of France, which would be at all times dangerous . . . , but are peculiarly so, when connected with the propagation of principles which lead to the violation of the most sacred duties, and are utterly subversive of the peace and order of all civil society." Although the debates had been scheduled to follow immediately, the Government suddenly decided to postpone them until 1 February. Behind this decision was no doubt Fox's *Letter*.

Fox's *Letter* was published on 28 January and was sympathetically noticed by several newspapers of that date. On 29 January the *Morning Chronicle* remarked that it demonstrated "the candour, manliness, and consistency, of a heart that speaks only to be clearly understood, and that refrains from all reproach of the desertion, calumny, and insult that it has suffered"; on 30 January the *Diary* printed some additional excerpts without headnote; and on 31 January the *Morning Chronicle* reported that the demand for the pamphlet was far exceeding the supply: "Ten thousand copies of Mr. Fox's Letter to his Constituents are already sold, and the Publisher has never yet been able to get them from the press so fast as they are called for." The work was now in its fourth edition. The Government was obviously uneasy about the effect of the *Letter* on the people, for the Ministerial newspapers were publishing epistolary replies, usually signed "A WESTMINSTER ELECTOR," in addition to their own comments; and on 1 February they advertized the first pamphlet: *A Letter to the Right Hon. Charles James Fox, upon the Dangerous and Inflammatory Tendency of His Late Conduct in Parliament*. The author, although not identified in the advertisements, was Richard Bentley. But the real concern was the effect on the Duke of Portland, for, if the Duke yielded to Fox's appeal, opposing an augmentation of the forces until the people made its will known, the Government would be in an embarrassing situation. Until the Government knew what he intended to do, there would clearly be no debates.

On 30 January the *Morning Chronicle* reacted to the King's message with the declaration:

> War is now resolved on; the British Nation is committed. Is it not strange that even now the question is to be asked, *For what are we going to war?* Is it to reinstate the French King? alas! That is impossible! He has been murdered by a despicable faction! Is it to preserve the dynasty of France? Neither in the Speech nor in the message from the Throne, have we a syllable in support of the Family of Bourbon; and indeed it would have been curious to have had any such pretext

set up by his Britannic Majesty, who in his own Royal titles, disputes with the family of Bourbon, their pretensions to the Throne of France.

The pretext first stated in His Majesty's Speech, and repeated in the message is, that we are to oppose "The propagation of principles which lead to the violation of the most sacred duties."—In other words, we are to oppose the metaphysics of Frenchmen! If we are to judge of their pertinacity from our own, there never was so quixotic a crusade.

The "murder" of Louis, which the *Chronicle* had once predicted would be used by the Government as the "popular argument" for war, had in fact been almost forgotten. Although the Ministerial newspapers had previously talked of little else and had already announced the Rev. Robert Nares's pamphlet on the subject, *A Short Account of the Character and Reign of Louis XVI*, only the *Oracle* now referred to it and it only incidentally. "The sufferings of LA FAYETTE are unquestionably great," it agreed on 31 January; "but if the report be true, that he encouraged the flight of the ROYAL FAMILY, and afterwards betrayed them, they are not unmerited. The deplorable effect of this treachery must give him severer pangs than any he has hitherto felt." This, at least, it seemed to the *Chronicle*, was all to the good, since, as it pointed out on 29 January, the fate of Louis was actually only another argument for reform:

> The melancholy catastrophe of Louis may . . . afford many salutary lessons to Despots and Autocrats. It may admonish them, that if they withhold, in a season of (what may be called) orderly ferment, moderate concessions of usurped power, and either reject with proud contempt or stifle with oppressive violence the voice of a people supplicating for rights, a painful period may come, when they will review their former arrogance with all the bitterness of unavailing repentance, and when their fate will be in the hands of those whom they had irritated by insult, and rendered desperate by encreasing accumulated grievances.

The war, if, as the *True Briton* was now saying, "we are unhappily forced into it," was clearly to be fought in defense of the Constitution. Nor was the Constitution to be defended against the French. Although on 30 January the *World* told its readers that "*Citizen* LAUDERDALE, previous to his departure from France, dined with DUMOURIER, who assured him that he should return the visit in England, and bring with him more company than Citizen LAUDERDALE could entertain," there was no serious suggestion of an invasion, and rumors of raids were credited by no newspaper. "A Report prevailed yesterday, which was spread for Stock Jobbing views, with great avidity, that the French had taken two Vessels laden with Corn and Cheese [en route] from London to Liverpool," the *World* mentioned casually on 31 January. The Constitution was obviously to be defended against British reformers, who had somehow become imbued with "the metaphysics of Frenchmen." As a "pretext," the defense of the Constitution had numerous advantages. It was more vague and hence more comprehensive than the execution of Louis, and it was much more likely to appeal to the people. For the Government, confronted, as it was, with demands for election reforms, no other justification would have served at all, and the Duke of Portland would never have supported the war on any other terms.

The Government had already indicated that it meant to defend the Constitution willy-nilly by announcing on 28 January a strengthening of the King's legal counsel. Being added to it were John Anstruther, Robert Graham, Thomas Plumer, Sylvester Douglas, William Garrow, and a "Mr. Leycester." These six, described by the *True Briton* as "the best talents of the age," had earned their reward. Anstruther, once a close friend of Fox, had been supporting the Government since 12 December; Plumer was performing brilliantly as counsel for Warren Hastings. Douglas, a son-in-law of the second Earl of Guilford, had been active on Pitt's behalf since his father-in-law's death; and Hugh Leycester had always been loyal to Pitt, as he was always loyal to any government which happened to be in power. Although Leycester was already the King's Attorney in Cheshire and Flint, some trouble evidently developed respecting the present appointment, for, when the "silk gowns" were finally conferred on 7 February, he had been replaced by William Grant. Grant was also deserving. Having been brought into Parliament by the Government in 1790 as Member for Shaftesbury, he had conducted himself properly since, and it was not his fault if he was tedious. The announcement of these appointments in the *Morning Chronicle* (28 Jan.) was succinct: "Six silk gowns are to be given away in the Court this day; Mr. GARROW is to be honoured with one of them." The *Chronicle* was bitter because Garrow had once been a protégé of Fox and had always posed as a friend to the Opposition. But, since the Government never lost a case to him, there had been suspicions. John Almon's complaint[27] that, when Garrow represented him in 1789, he had "deceived" him at every step of the "proceedings" was neither the first nor the last such accusation.

The dismissals of Thomas Erskine and Arthur Peary Pigott as Attorney General and Solicitor General respectively to the Prince of Wales were formally announced on 29 January, as so were their replacements: "His Royal Highness . . . has been pleased to appoint Robert Graham, of the Society of the Inner Temple, Esq. to the Office of His Royal Highness's Attorney General, and John Anstruther of the Society of Lincoln's Inn, Esq. to be Solicitor General to His Royal Highness." The *True Briton* was very happy. "*Counsellor Ego* now stands by himself—divested of that honourable office of which he used to boast so much . . . ," it exulted on 30 January. It was even happier to have "heard" on 1 February "that the *resignation* of Messrs. ERSKINE and PIGOTT, as Attorney and Solicitor General to the PRINCE of WALES, has been followed up by a message to Mr. SH[ERIDA]N, intimating 'that his future visits to Carlton-House would be dispensed with.'" The reaction of Erskine added to the merriment. According to the *Oracle* (23 Jan.), "Lord RAWDON and Mr. ERSKINE had [had] Audiences of the PRINCE of WALES" on 22 January. Erskine had apparently not seen him since; nor had he had any warning that a dismissal was contemplated. As soon as he recovered from the shock, he applied for an audience, and the application was curtly refused. But he continued to apply. According to the newspapers, he was still petitioning the Prince on 1 February "to have an opportunity, either personally, or by letter, of making some representations to [him] on the subject of the late removal."

Erskine certainly interpreted the "removal" as an act of censure, the Prince having disapproved (although he had not indicated so on 22 January) both of him and of the Friends of the Liberty of the Press. Since the Friends of the Liberty of the Press had impeded the activities of the Attorney General and of The Association, the Ministerial papers regarded the dismissal as a great victory for the Government. The Government seemed also to regard it as such, for at approximately this time it indicted the *Morning Chronicle* for a libel on the Constitution. The libel consisted of a political advertisement for a reform society in Derby, printed by the *Chronicle* on 25 December, 1792. The Association itself had, however, suffered another setback, for on 30 January the *Oracle* replied to Law's letter to Reeves, which the *Chronicle* had published on 24 January. Although the reply purported to be a defense of Reeves, it was actually only a confirmation of Law's charges:

MR. LAW.

The Fact concerning this Gentleman's Secession from the Association at the Crown and Anchor has never been clearly understood.—We beg leave to state it. . . .

When the circumstance of Anonymous Letters was the subject of discussion, Mr. LAW proposed that they should be burnt without examination—The Gentlemen acting in the Committee with Mr. LAW were of opinion, that, although Anonymous Letters were *prima facie* to be reprobated—and although they, as much as he, detested the idea of holding up any individual as an object of suspicion and prosecution from such evidence—yet it was possible that Letters without Signatures might contain what would warrant the attention of the Committee. They would not therefore consent to have such Letters hastily and without examination destroyed.

"The Prince of Wales is now pursuing a line of conduct, which will ensure him the esteem and admiration of all ranks of society," said the *Diary* on 30 January. The statement was subject to dispute. The dismissal of Erskine was an act of sheer perfidy, and, although the Prince had thereby struck a blow for the "Constitution" and against the reformers, he had also struck a blow against freedom of the press. Except for the *Sun*, the *True Briton*, and the *Public Advertiser*, the newspapers were unenthusiastic. The colonelcy was an embarrassment. Although the *Morning Chronicle* had announced it on 28 January, the Ministerial papers insisted that it was not actually granted until 29 January, so that there was some time lapse between the letter to the Duke of Portland and the reward. They also insisted that the reward was a trifle. The Duke of York would "command the brigade of Foot Guards," *Lloyd's Evening Post* reminded its readers on 30 January, but the Prince would "command" nothing: he would hold the rank of Colonel in the Army and Colonel Commandant of the 10th Regiment of Light Dragoons and might even "encamp with his regiment," but Sir William Pitt would still be the actual commander. Although other newspapers were under the impression that the Prince would be the actual commander, they understood that he had declined to accept the emoluments and would therefore derive no financial benefit from the appointment; and, with the last part of this statement, at least, every newspaper could agree. As the *Star* subsequently (4 Feb.) put it: "It has given the PRINCE of WALES great pleasure, being appointed Colonel of the 10th Regiment of Cavalry, as he has long ardently wished for it. The emoluments of a Regiment of Horse are about 1400*l.* a year; but we are confident, from the PRINCE's known generosity, that it will prove no addition to his income."

The Prince's new "line of conduct" certainly had no effect on the Duke of Portland, but something did, for, by 1 February, Pitt was ready for the debates, having at least been assured of the Duke's silence. The first announcement appeared in the *Oracle*, which stated on 31 January: "Mr. FOX was never so deplorably deserted as at present. His PARTY in the House of Commons consists exactly of SIX, to which when the friends of the Marquis of LANSDOWNE are added, the amount will be FOURTEEN! Such is the formidable Opposition Mr. PITT has to encounter." On the following day, the *London Packet* announced another defection, the Prince of Wales's friend, Lord Rawdon, having, it understood, "completely withdrawn himself from the ranks of Opposition." At the same time, readers were informed that Lord Howe would assume command of the Grand Fleet with the temporary title of Admiral. They were not informed that France had sent a new ambassador to England with instructions to make almost any concessions to avoid war. M. Maret had arrived on 30 January, had presented his credentials to Lord Grenville, and was now in conference with Miles.

Debate on the King's Message and the Declaration of War

On 1 February, Pitt addressed the Commons on the matter of France. He began by denouncing the "murder" of the King as a necessary consequence of those "French principles" which were now invading every country and went on to eulogize the British Constitution as "never before equalled in the annals of mankind" and secure against everything except "imported opinions," "studiously and industriously brought into this country." He then reviewed the correspondence between M. Chauvelin and Lord Grenville in order to demonstrate that Britain had remained neutral until France's evident determination to conquer the Netherlands, to murder all kings, and to "propagate her principles all over the world" forced her to take a stand in her own defense. It must also be remembered, he added, that Britain was bound by treaty to "support" and "assist" Holland in this crisis, and Holland's failure to "call upon us" was not necessarily chargeable to "indifference": it might "perhaps" be owing to "motives of policy." The speech concluded with a motion for augmentation of the forces. The motion was supported by Lord Beauchamp, who, with obvious reference to Fox, stated to begin with that he was not sympathetic with the French and had never "gloried" in the defeat at Jemappes. The most "suspicious" thing France had done, in Lord Beauchamp's opinion, was to "leave an ambassador here after ours had been recalled," and he was frankly relieved to hear that the "spy," M. Chauvelin, was gone. As to Holland's attitude toward the opening of the Scheldt, he would say only that Holland had to be "saved" whether she wanted to be "saved" or not, for the country had been "raised up" by Queen Elizabeth as a barrier to England against France and Spain, and, despite their many frictions since, England and Holland remained "natural allies." A war so obviously necessary as this one ought, he thought, to be declared at once, and he was sure that "we may expect a speedy and happy termination," since every major power would support Britain. Austria would support her because she wanted The Netherlands back, Prussia because she needed to recover prestige, Holland because her existence depended on it, Italy because she was interested in returning Savoy to the King of Sardinia, and Spain and Portugal because they recognized the threat to themselves of French arms and French "opinions." The motion was also supported by the Prince of Wales's new Solicitor General, John Anstruther, and by Burke's disciple, William Windham. Windham, it was clear, wanted to continue the fight until the Bourbons were back on the French throne. The motion was opposed by Samuel Whitbread, by Lord John Russell, and by Fox, Sheridan remaining silent.

Fox began, as had Pitt, by expressing his detestation of the "murder," but, in his opinion, this "catastrophe" had no bearing on the relationship between Britain and France, for no nation had a right to punish another nation for acts not affecting itself. Unlawful interference in French affairs had, he was sure, caused all the trouble to begin with, for France had had a right to alter her constitution if she wished, and Austria and Prussia had had no right to form an alliance for the purpose of "[invading] the kingdom," of "[moulding] its government according to their own caprice," and of "[restoring] the despotism, which the French have overthrown." To this alliance and to the subsequent and numerous crimes of the Duke of Brunswick, Fox attributed everything which had happened in France since, including the "murder" of Louis. The "murder" should not, therefore, be permitted "to blind the judgment, by rousing the passions": the only possible grounds for war were, as they had been before, the danger to Holland, resulting from the opening of the Scheldt, the French decree of 19 November, and "the general danger to Europe from the progress of French arms." As to the first, Britain was bound by treaty to assist Holland if assistance was called for, but not otherwise. As to the second, the correspondence between M. Chauvelin and Lord Grenville was proof that the French were willing to retract and that their overtures were rebuffed "with haughtiness un-exampled." And, as to the third, it would be awkward indeed for Britain to show concern about a few French victories when she had watched with "scandalous indifference" the invasion of France by Austria and Prussia and "the entire conquest of Poland." Hence these were not legitimate grounds for war, but mere "pretexts." The actual ground, although the Government was "ashamed" to admit it, was the same as it had been for Austria and Prussia: the "destruction" of the French republic and the "restoration" of French "despotism." Fox entreated his friends not to involve Britain in such an affair; for, even though the war was at present "thought to be popular," the time would soon come, he predicted, when it would be "generally execrated" as a war of kings, not of nations or of peoples. Nor would it be short-lived, for, having no stated "object," it would have no discernible end, but would drag on and on while Britain sacrificed the last remnant of her prestige "fighting the battles for despotism!"

Having thus argued his case, Fox concluded with the plea that, whether his friends supported him or not, they would at least respect his motives. He was, he said, "no stranger" to the fact that "calumnies" were being circulated by the newspapers and by handbills: he could no longer "walk the streets without hearing whispers that I and some of my friends have been engaged in improper correspondence with persons in France." He did not blame the people, for, having "been told by their representatives in Parliament that they are surrounded by dangers, and . . . shown none," they were of course "full of suspicion and prompt of belief." But he had, he admitted, been distressed to hear Burke, Lord Beauchamp, and William Windham imply that he was a "partizan of France." If they had any evidence to support such charges, he begged them to present it rather than to attack him by innuendo; meanwhile he fervently hoped that "the House will give me the credit of being innocent till an open charge is made; and, if any man hear improper correspondence imputed to me in private, he will believe that he heard a falsehood, which he who circulated it in secret durst not utter in public." Pitt's motion passed without a division.

On the same day (1 Feb.), the same motion was debated in the Lords, having been introduced by Lord Grenville. Here it was supported by the Earl of Carlisle, by the Earl of Kinnoull, by Lord Porchester, by Lord Stormont, and by the new Lord Chancellor, Lord Loughborough. The Duke of Portland said nothing. It was opposed by Lord Derby, by Lord Stanhope, by Lord Lansdowne, and by Lord Lauderdale. Lord Stormont agreed with Lord Beauchamp that the war would be short: he expected France to collapse economically before it could even get started. He pointed out that she had reported a deficit of "seven millions sterling, in one month [alone]; and what country on earth can sustain such a deficiency long? If the report be true, the Convention has issued eighty millions in assignats, but where is the fund to render them of any value, or to give security to those who take them?" He was answered by Lord Lansdowne, who insisted that Britain could not afford the war either, the last two wars having left the nation 150 millions in debt. He also ridiculed the notion that the war would be brief, on the ground that the French were "enthusiasts," and "one enthusiast can beat ten mercenaries." The French had already shown themselves to be too "formidable" for Austria and Prussia, he said: why should Britain share their "predicament"? But the major clash was one between Lord Lauderdale and Lord Loughborough. In rising to oppose the motion, Lord Lauderdale had referred to "the low and pitiful invectives that daily issue from the press" in order to discourage his "prosecution of those reforms that I think essential to the public happiness"; and he had later interrupted his remarks to say a word in defense of Brissot, whom, he declared, he was "proud to rank . . . in the list of my friends. His virtues and talents merit the acknowledgment." Lord Loughborough commented acidly that "friendship and attachment" were, in his opinion, "matters of taste," and he was happy to say that he personally had no "taste" for "revolutions, massacres, war, confusion, and the murder of kings" and that he did not "envy" this "taste" in others. The motion was again approved without a division.

The *Oracle* later (4 Feb.) boasted that, although the "Houses of Parliament [had] not [broken] up till Friday Midnight," it had had its newspaper on the street on "Saturday Morning at Eleven o'Clock, . . . containing Sixteen Columns, which had been written and printed from Memory within Eleven Hours," whereas newspapers carrying "only half that amount of Debate" had not appeared until later. Since the silence of the Duke of Portland and his friends was a victory for the Government, the Ministerial press could be pleased indeed with the way things had gone. "To the grief of the Party, but not of all parties, old Lady Blue and Buff died last week, after having long been in a declining state," the *Public Advertiser* announced on 5 February; "she was attended to her grave by the citizens Fox, Sheridan, and Erskine. . . ." There was special rejoicing over the rebuke administered by Lord Loughborough. "The LORD CHANCELLOR gave Lord LAUDERDALE a most complete dressing in the House of Peers on Friday evening," gloated the *True Briton* on 4 February. "—The friend of the Incendiary BRISSOT was glad to hide his little head behind the *brazen Marquis* [Lord Lansdowne]./ The *miserable remnant of Opposition* seems to be now employed in attempting to make the War (if we are unhappily forced into it) unpopular. . . ." According to Holland,[28] Lansdowne "was too suspicious to feel, and too restless in his dealings with public men to inspire, implicit confidence"; and, although "he had some imagination, some wit, great

William Pitt addressing a session in the House of Commons.
Painting by Henckel.

Bettmann Archive

Charlotte Sophia

George III

William Pitt. Painting by Thomas Gainsborough.

Charles James Fox

Edmund Burke. Painting by Romney (?).

Richard Brinsley Sheridan. Painting by Gainsborough, 1786.

Mrs. Fitzherbert

The Prince of Wales, later George IV. Engraving
after a painting by Sir Thomas Lawrence.

Thomas Erskine. Engraving after a painting by R. Cosway

animation, and both in sarcasm and invective not infrequently rose to eloquence," his "publick speeches . . . wanted method and perspicuity, . . . justness of reasoning, . . . judgment, and . . . taste." Because of their experience with him in the past, the Whigs, whom he supported, had had in addition, "not only a distrust, but an unwarranted hatred, of his very name." For all these reasons perhaps, Lord Lansdowne had been ignored by the newspapers, but his new intimacy with Lord Lauderdale altered that situation, so far as the Ministerial papers were concerned. Lansdowne was now also a reprobate. The Opposition papers were still unwilling to say anything on his behalf, but the new attacks on Lord Lauderdale were at least parried by the *Morning Chronicle*, which on 7 February even honored "his efforts for the public weal" with a sonnet. Fox, however, fared the worst. Here, said the *True Briton* on 5 February in a sputter of rage, was "a man debased by early Profligacy, and the desperate extravagance of Play—first ruined by the folly of the Box [dice], and then restored, yet more dishonourably, by the peculation of the Pharo-Bank—growing old in open Debauchery, despising Decency, and lost to all Religion—In Politics, the most abandoned of Prostitutes—In Place, the foremost to attack all Rights, grasp at all advantages, and brave all clamours—Out of Place, an everlasting Sycophant to popular opinion, yet always losing popularity by wanting even the appearance of Principle. . . ." By this time his *Letter* was in its seventh edition and, according to Coleridge,[29] was "quite the *political Go* at Cambridge," where it was "[converting] many souls to the Foxite Faith." By 8 February it was in its ninth edition.

The Prince of Wales had meanwhile "converted" no one. He had not "converted" the Duke of Portland, the announcement of Lord Rawdon's defection had turned out to be unfounded, and there was even some question as to the extent of his own defection. He had not broken with Sheridan, and he had evidently hinted to someone that Erskine's "removal" had had nothing to do with politics, for on 2 February the *Public Advertiser* expressed its "[surprise] indeed at the impudence and folly of writers in saying that Mr. Erskine was not *turned off* on account of his *political principles* and *professional conduct*. What must be the political principles and professional conduct of that man who was advocate for a wretch [Thomas Paine] whose doctrines attempt to explode hereditary Monarchy, and to overturn the Government of this Country ?" But the Prince had performed his part of the agreement, and the Government was bound to reciprocate. Hence on 4 February the *True Briton* notified his creditors that all debts would positively be paid: "A certain Personage is said to have made a present of a very large sum of money to his eldest son.—60,000*l*. is stated to be the sum./ We applaud the conduct of his Royal Highness the Prince of Wales, in giving his firm and decided support to the present Administration. We know how to excuse the wanderings of youth, and we always trusted that observation and experience would induce His Royal Highness to do that which is right." The eulogy was continued the following day: "His Royal

Highness the PRINCE of WALES, by his noble conduct at the present crisis, has endeared himself to the whole Nation, the Jacobins alone excepted. . . ." The *Morning Chronicle* was disgusted. "The PRINCE of WALES has, through the whole of Mr. PITT's Ministry, had the honour of daily abuse from the Treasury Papers: he is now doomed to endure the more bitter calumny of their friendship," it said on 5 February. "They announced to the public yesterday, that in consequence of his Highness's change of principles, the King had made him a present of sixty thousand pounds! In this gross and indecent way, do these hired writers insult, by impossible rumours, the highest personages." But, except for the *Oracle*'s mention of 6 February that "Mr. PECK was last week engaged in discharging the Debts of his Royal Highness . . . at Brighthelmstone," the Prince was spared further "calumny" of this sort, and by 8 February he had "pensioned" all servants except those to whose "attendance" a "private Englishman is accustomed." On 6 February and again on 11 February, according to *Lloyd's Evening Post* (8 and 13 Feb.), "Mr. Dundas and Sir William Fawcitt had an interview with . . . the Prince of Wales, at Carlton House." There were no further such interviews, the Government's interest in him having apparently ceased. One other person profited from the transactions between the Government and the Prince of Wales. On 8 February Sir William Pitt, who had been succeeded by the Prince as Colonel of the 10th Regiment of Light Dragoons, was advanced to the rank of General. Also rewarded was Lord Mulgrave, who, on the same day, was commissioned Colonel of the 31st Foot Regiment. Mulgrave had furiously assailed Erskine and the Friends of the Liberty of the Press in the debates on the Alien Bill.

Since Holland had not asked for British aid, the Opposition newspapers had not expected Pitt to refer to Holland at all. Otherwise they found nothing surprising in his speech. As they had anticipated, the "pretext" for war was to be the defense of the Constitution, the situation in France being deliberately confused with the demands for reform, especially moderate reform, at home. The speech was immediately preceded and followed by another show of legalistic strength, although certainly an unimpressive one. On 4 February *Lloyd's Evening Post* announced that "[a] great number of informations for libels have within a few days been filed by the Irish Attorney-General [Arthur Wolfe], particularly against printers of newspapers." But the "printers" were not identified, and the only "action" of any kind reported by the London newspapers involved a "Thomas M'Donnell," who on 1 February, according to the *Morning Post* (7 Feb.), was "put to the bar of the House of Commons, and discharged after a reprimand from the Speaker [John Foster], for publishing the Resolutions of the Freeholders of the County of Dublin, assembled by the High Sheriff agreeable to their requisition." In Scotland, Walter Berry and James Robertson were brought to trial on 28 January for publishing *The Political Progress of Great Britain*. The author, James Thomson Callender, failed to appear and was outlawed. The trial of Berry and Robertson dragged on with long interruptions until 18 March, when, although the verdict was ambiguous, Berry was sentenced to six months in Tolbooth Prison, Robertson to three. James Smith and John Mennons were tried for sedition on 4 February, but the newspapers did not know the outcome. On 1 February the *Star* also reported that "[an] indictment was served on Saturday last [26 Jan.] against THOMAS MUIR, Esq. Advocate, younger of Huntershill, for trial . . . upon the 11th of February next, for the charge of sedition." The *Gazetteer* was infuriated, pointing out in a series of paragraphs that, since everyone knew Muir was in France and could not possibly return by that date, the real object of this maneuver was to declare him an outlaw. The *Gazetteer* was still under the impression that Muir was being charged only with "[*lending*] PAYNE's Works to a Friend!"

In England the Government was employing a similar tactic. Except for Perry, Gray, and Lambert of the *Morning Chronicle*, there were no new indictees, but readers would have inferred from the Ministerial papers that John Horne Tooke, Thomas Walker, and Thomas Cooper, if not already indicted, would be indicted shortly and that the charge in these instances would be high treason. Although not one of them was frightened into flight, the *Diary* liked to think (9 Feb.) that Horne Tooke was at least frightened into retirement: "HORNE TOOKE, little inviting as the country is at this season, lives now almost entirely at WIMBLE-TON. Perhaps he begins to think that the speculations of such men as TOM PAINE are no longer worthy of his notice, and that the calm decline of life [he was fifty-seven] is better employed in philosophical reflection than political experiment." Cooper, according to the *Oracle* of 6 February, was not frightened at all: "Mr. COOPER, the adversary of BURKE, who is under prosecution for a Libel, has avowed his intentions of pleading his own Cause, and of going, as he terms it, at large into the Question." The Ministerial newspapers said nothing further of Cooper. Nothing was ever said of John Bell, whom the Government dealt with in another manner and with more success. Bell's indictment for the libels on the Guards was now thirteen months old, his trial seven months old, and he was suddenly ordered to appear in the Court of King's Bench on 5 February for sentencing. But the order was followed by a visit from the Crown lawyer, Edward Bearcroft, who somehow persuaded him to ignore it. Bell did. Bearcroft thereupon informed the Court of Bell's refusal to appear and asked that its judgment be taken out against him. His name was called three times, and, since there was no response, an order was issued for his arrest. A report of these proceedings appeared in the *Public Advertiser* of 7 February. There was no mention of them in the *Oracle*.

Bell's hearing was also not mentioned by the *True Briton*, but, in case there was any doubt as to the reason for the action, the *True Briton* of 7 February notified its readers that John Bell's paper, the *Oracle*, was "an insidious Print, which aims at sapping the Government under the mask of attachment to the Administration." The "sapping" had begun on 30 January, when, purporting to defend The Association against Law's accusations, the *Oracle* had admitted that the accusations were true. There was another such paragraph on 31 January, when the *Oracle*, reviewing the correspondence between M. Chauvelin and Lord Grenville, interrupted its praise of Lord Grenville to say that, as Grey and Sheridan, "with their accustomed acuteness," had noticed, there was "a *chasm* in these Letters from July 8 to November 19, 1792." With a war at stake, the Government could not afford this sort of thing. The Prince of Wales's letter to the Duke of Portland did not jar Sheridan's confidence in the Prince, but it seems somehow to have jarred his confidence in Pitt, for the "sapping" began when the *Oracle* first learned of it. Pitt responded by ending the negotiations. On 1 February Sheridan was given to understand by the *True Briton* that his attentions to the Prince were unwelcome to the Government, and on 5 February he was notified by the *Public Advertiser* that his attentions to Pitt were equally unwelcome. The Government, in short, did not want him.

Having strengthened its staff of lawyers, the Government commenced a shuffling of superior personnel. On 9 February Sir James Eyre, previously Lord Chief Baron of the Exchequer and always a loyal supporter of Pitt, replaced Lord Loughborough as Lord Chief Justice of the Court of Common Pleas; and on 12 February Sir Archibald Macdonald, previously the Attorney General, took his seat on the bench as Lord Chief Baron of the Exchequer. On 15 February he was made a member of the Privy Council. On 13 February Sir John Scott, who, as Solicitor General, had collaborated so beautifully with The Association, re-placed Sir Archibald Macdonald as Attorney General. Scott was already loaded with honors. In 1787 he was elected Chancellor of Durham; in 1788 he was knighted; on 13 December, 1792, he was elected Fellow of the Society of Anti-quaries; and on 14 February, 1793, he was elected a Fellow of the Royal Society. His replacement as Solicitor General was John Mitford, described by the *St. James's Chronicle* (12 Feb.) as "one of the King's Counsel, a Welsh judge and Member for Beeralston in Devonshire." Mitford, recently a vehement spokes-man for the Government, had been knighted on 15 January. But, before the shuffling was complete, Pitt had accomplished his object: the country was at war.

Except for what it could learn from the correspondence between M. Chauvelin and Lord Grenville, readers of newspapers had known very little about the progress of affairs until 4 February, when they were suddenly presented with three documents: Lord Auckland's Declaration of 16 November, the King of Prussia's Declaration of 6 January, and Lord Auckland's Memorial of 25 January. Since none of these documents was likely to "popularize" the war, the Government's object in releasing them was a mystery to the *Morning Chronicle*. The King of Prussia's Declaration was addressed to the Poles and was one of several such edicts preceding the second Treaty of Partition, news of which had not yet arrived. Lord Auckland's Declaration and Memorial were addressed to the Dutch and were acts of out-and-out incitement. As Ambassador Extra-ordinary and Minister Plenipotentiary to The Hague, Lord Auckland had assured the Dutch, in the Declaration of 16 November, that Britain would "execute . . . , with the utmost good faith, all the different stipulations of the treaty of alliance so happily concluded in 1788" and had entreated them to join her in resisting "any attempts . . . to disturb the internal tranquillity of the provinces." As a token of that "good faith," Britain had thereupon dispatched "a small squadron, destined to protect the coasts of [Holland] until their own maritime force should be assembled." The second communication, a very emotional piece of writing, denounced the French for numerous crimes against religion, morals, and decency and censured the Dutch for permitting its "solemn treaties" to be "infringed" and its "rights and territories . . . violated." The British would not stand by, said Lord Auckland, while the whole social order was subverted, and he could assure the Dutch that every word he said had the "unanimous approbation of a people, who abhor anarchy and irreligion, and who love their king, and will maintain their constitution." The Memorial concluded with a plea for "conformity of principles and conduct," which "can alone give to the united efforts of the two countries, energy necessary for their common defense."

The *True Briton*, which had previously talked as if war might be averted, was now certain that it was imminent, because, as it told its readers, the French did not want to negotiate. M. Chauvelin had absconded without so much as a word to Lord Grenville, and his successor, M. Maret, although representing himself as Chargé d'Affaires, had not even been provided with credentials. The "author" of this "false statement," Miles thought,[30] was Burges, but at least it was news to the readers that M. Chauvelin had had a successor. On 6 February the newspapers reported an increase in bounties for seamen enlisting in London: they now totaled £13, an additional £2 having been offered by independent "associations"; and on 9 February they announced that Britain was at war. The declaration had come from the French. Already fighting Austria, Prussia, and, as a result of the occupation of Savoy and Nice, Sardinia, the French had reacted to M. Chauvelin's report by adding to the list Holland and Britain. The declaration was dated 1 February, and the text of the document was printed by all newspapers on 11 February.

None of this mitigated the rage of the *True Briton*. It continued to rail at M. Chauvelin for supposedly refusing to talk to Lord Grenville and at M. Maret for supposedly neglecting to bring along credentials, and it was especially incensed with General Dumouriez, who, it now appeared, had approached Lord Auckland with a view to reopening negotiations, even offering to come to England for the purpose. This, it seemed to the *True Briton*, was the ultimate insult, for the French had issued their "infamous" declaration before Lord Auckland had received instructions from Lord Grenville.

Early Reactions to the War

Copies of Lord Auckland's Declaration and Memorial and of the French declaration of war were presented to Parliament on 11 February, along with the inevitable message from the King. Like the *True Briton*, the King seemed to feel that the declaration of war was, to say the least, uncalled-for, and he seemed also to regard it as of little moment. The "powers of France" having, "on the most groundless pretences, actually declared war against his majesty and the United Provinces," the message read, the King was certain that he could rely "with confidence on the firm and effectual support" of Parliament and on "the zealous exertions of a brave and loyal people" to "[prevent] the extension of anarchy and confusion." Dundas responded at once. Although the Address was not moved until the following day, so strong were his feelings that he concluded the reading with some remarks about Lord Lauderdale. Since Thomas Maitland rose to the defense of his brother, there was a fine preliminary skirmish, which resulted, it seemed to the *True Briton* of 12 February, in an ignominious defeat for Maitland: "Mr. DUNDAS made last night a happy hit at BRISSOT's Noble Friend—It was so home, that Major MAITLAND could mumble out but a very awkward justification of his brother's *friendships*."

The message was debated on 12 February. In the Commons the Address was moved by Pitt, who urged that, since war "now is not only declared, but carried on at our very doors," the Members would forget "whatever differences of opinion might formerly have existed" and "unanimously" proclaim their "fixed resolution" to defend "with ardour and firmness" the King, the Constitution, and "those inestimable blessings they have so long enjoyed under its influence." Why the French should have taken this action, Pitt purported, as had the *True Briton*, not to know, for, despite repeated provocations, the British Government had "pursued to the last a conciliatory system, and left every opening for accommodation, had the French been disposed to embrace it." But the French were evidently bent on war. The grievances listed in their declaration, it seemed to Pitt, were preposterous, since they were essentially reducible to three: "first, . . . we loved our constitution; secondly, . . . we detested their proceedings; and lastly, . . . we presumed to grieve at the death of their murdered king. Thus would they even destroy . . . sentiments of compassion. . . . Thus would they deprive us of that last resource of humanity—to mourn over the misfortunes and sufferings of the victims of their injustice." The motion pledged "firm and effectual support" in prosecuting this "just and necessary war" and looked forward to "cordial co-operation" between Britain and other European powers "in preventing the extension of anarchy and confusion, and in contributing to the security and tranquillity of Europe."

The motion was seconded by Thomas Powys, who, like the other renegades, felt bound to "lay [his] jealousies and distrust of the present Ministers aside" for the good of his country. In Powys's opinion, France was a "monster" which had to be destroyed, not because she constituted a military threat, but because she encouraged "the combinations of bad men at home"; and he for one "less [feared] the arrows that fly by day, than the pestilence that walketh by night." Powys had defected on 14 December, 1792, as a result of the phantom insurrection two weeks earlier. The motion was opposed by Fox. Fox prefaced his remarks with the hope that what he was going to say would be properly understood; for it seemed to him that, whenever the people were asked to support a war "with their property and their lives," they had a "right" to know its "true ground" and that he had a "right" to inform them without being accused by his one-time friends of "sowing disaffection." He then proceeded to evaluate the situation, showing that the Government had discouraged negotiations at every stage, that it had consistently insulted the French, that it had "alarmed the people that their own constitution was in danger," and that it had "made use of [the execution of Louis XVI], which, however it might affect us as men, does not concern us as a nation, to inflame our passions and impel us to war.... And, now that we are at war," he said, "they durst not avow the causes of it, nor tell us on what terms peace might have been preserved." In short, he was convinced that the war could and should have been averted, he was not "sanguine" of its success, and he would not indulge in any "crooked reasonings" with respect to that man whose "misconduct" had brought it about. Although he had no choice but to support the war, now that it was a fact, he would not support an address which misrepresented the situation, which implied that Britain was fighting, as were Austria and Prussia, for the restoration of despotism, and which said nothing about peace. He would therefore move to strike out almost the whole of it and to call instead for "exertions ... to induce France to consent to such terms of pacification as may be consistent with the honor of His Majesty's crown, the security of his allies, and the interest of his people."

Fox was answered by Dundas. He was also answered by Burke, who, in a long and often savagely personal speech, accused him of everything from "repetitiousness" and demagoguery to treason. In support of the last accusation, Burke read from the *Moniteur* an account of a dinner, held by the English Friends of the People in Paris, at which toasts were supposedly drunk to "Citizens Fox, Mackintosh, Sheridan, Paine, Barlow, and other friends of liberty who have enlightened the people of England." Sheridan had said nothing since 21 December, awaiting the outcome of his negotiations with Pitt, but, those negotiations having collapsed, he leapt into the fray as defender of Fox and incidentally of course of himself. Whatever his shortcomings as a person, Sheridan was brilliant as a debater and never quite so brilliant as when he was dealing with Burke. For some time Burke had been calling the Opposition a "phalanx" in sarcastic reference to its size, and he had made the mistake on this occasion of saying that the few remaining members of the "phalanx" were not even in agreement with each other. Sheridan demurred. He was astonished, he said, that Burke should have such an "odd" conception of a "phalanx"; for certainly a "'phalanx,' whatever its extent, must consist of a united band, acting in a body, animated by one soul, and pursuing its object with identity of spirit, and unity of effort." The Opposition was a "phalanx" in precisely this sense. Sheridan went on to examine Burke's other statements, answering sarcasm with sarcasm and insinuation with insinuation, coming finally to the matter of that dinner in Paris. "This anecdote," he told the Commons, "wants only one little ingredient to produce possibly some effect, namely, fact. The truth is, that neither my health nor Mr. Fox's health were drank at that meeting; and it is a little unlucky that [Mr. Burke], who ransacks every corner of every French paper for anything that will make for his purpose, should have overlooked a formal contradiction of such toasts having been given, inserted by authority in the *Patriote François*. . . ." But then Mr. Burke twisted everything to suit his purpose, for this was not a meeting of the Society of the Friends of the People, as he had implied, but only "an idle dinner of English and others." Sheridan having concluded, Fox's amendment was rejected and the original address agreed to without a division.

In the Lords the Address was moved by Lord Grenville, who said much the same thing as Pitt; and, evidently to everyone's surprise, it was warmly seconded by the Duke of Portland, who "pledged" his "firm support to a war, the object of which is, to resist doctrines that . . . go to the overthrow, not merely of all legitimate government, . . . but even of religion itself, and of every thing for which society is instituted." It was opposed by Lord Stanhope, who moved an amendment, stating in effect that Britain was entirely at fault and demanding to know what "objects" the King "proposes to obtain" by the war. At this point Lord Stormont congratulated the Duke of Portland on "the manly avowal of those sentiments which have just now taken place" and added his personal "prayer" that, if Britain failed to "suppress that pestilential contagion of opinions, . . . an earthquake . . . will bury these islands in the bosom of the deep, while the morals of the country remain pure." Lord Stormont was succeeded by Lord Lauderdale, who, very much shaken by Portland's speech, stated, to begin with, that he was distressed to find himself differing from "the majority of this House, and what is of infinitely greater consequence, . . . [from] the majority of the people of England," for he regarded the judgment of the popular majority as more trustworthy than the judgment of any individual, whatever his position. If in this instance, he went on,

the public opinion was under no improper influence; if the minds of men had not been agitated by groundless fears; if the most designing arts had not been employed to warp their judgment; if the most interested and despicable characters had not too well succeeded in their impostures, I should feel myself perfectly safe in appealing to this or the most public tribunal, upon the necessity or policy of the war. . . . But is there a man in Great Britain ignorant that the most wicked arts have been practised, to irritate and mislead the multitude? Have not hand-bills, wretched songs, infamous pamphlets, false and defamatory paragraphs in news-papers, been circulated to rouse the indignation of this country against France, with whom it has been long determined . . . to go to war?

Lord Lauderdale concluded his remarks by moving the same amendment Fox had moved in the Commons. The original Address was thereupon supported by Lord Hawkesbury and the Duke of Leeds. The Duke of Leeds, always an enthusiast for war, had resigned as Foreign Secretary in April, 1791, because of the Government's failure to fight the Russians. The Address was opposed by Lord Lansdowne, who especially objected to Parliament's being "called up" to "approve" this war "upon some twenty-four hours notice"; and, both amend-ments being negatived, it was agreed to.

The *St. James's Chronicle*, which always wanted to get rid of Lord Lauderdale, had complained on 12 February: "The present Parliament was chosen in the year 1790. In the year 1793, the election of the Scotch Peerage is not determined. The impeachment [of Hastings] is not the only thing that goes on slowly." Although the Government certainly shared this point of view, it was evidently unwilling to deal with that situation at present, but it did act to strengthen its hand in others. During February and March, the Commons tried fifteen more contested elections, and all of them were resolved in favor of Pitt's candidates. The *World* was especially pleased to hear that James Mingay would not be sitting for Thetford. "Counsellor MINGAY wants to get into Parliament, to support his 'learned Friend,' Counsellor EGO [Thomas Erskine]," it remarked on 18 February: "the good people of Thetford, however, *bar* this *Coalition.*" There were also more by-elections, owing to the recent appointments, and here again victory was on the side of the Government. There was particular rejoicing over the re-election on 6 March of the new Attorney General, Sir John Scott, as Member for Weobley.

The declaration of war had meanwhile activated many of the King's friends, who, for one reason or another, had lost interest in politics; and, although William Adam and the new Earl of Guilford were still supporting the Opposi-tion, all other followers of the late Earl of Guilford were not only supporting Pitt, but would obviously accept office if they had an opportunity. This was not the case with the Duke of Portland, and he was apparently still able to control his followers, for a rumor that William Windham would succeed Dundas as Home Secretary turned out to be false. The Duke's strong endorsement of the war was nevertheless interpreted by everyone as a defection. It was obviously so inter-preted by Lord Lauderdale, for, as the *True Briton* noted with malicious satisfaction on 14 February: "Lord LAUDERDALE actually shed tears the other night in the House of Peers, when he deplored the conduct which the Duke of PORTLAND seemed inclined in future to pursue. They seemed, however to have but little effect upon any one in the House. His LORDSHIP's feelings were not much calculated to excite *sympathy.*" The *Evening Mail* made much the same comment on 15 February: "Lord LANSDOWNE whined out his grief at the loss of such a support to Opposition [as the Duke of Portland], and Lord LAUDERDALE cried, or as *Sir John Suckling* says, 'if there were no tears, he seemed to wipe away that none.'" While the *True Briton* was estimating the opposition to the war in the Lords as three, the *World* was estimating the opposition in the Commons as eleven. The Opposition, it announced derisively on 15 February:

> talk of seceding from Parliament, and in solemn form; for we understand they are all to be conveyed from the House of Commons in a *Mourning Coach*.
> The Mourning Coach will not hold all the Minority within side, so *Chicken* TAYLOR will be perched on the roof, and *Jackall* JEKYLL is to ride in the Boot.
> Strange things may come to pass—for the *Stage* of Politics, perhaps, the two great Minority Leaders, FOX and SHERRY [Sheridan], may take to the *Stage* as Mountebanks—Doctor CARLO the *Quack*, and SHERRY, the *Merry Andrew*.
> Mr. FOX says, "all his Friends have forsaken him, and he cannot tell why." An ATTORNEY, once very much afflicted with the gout, in a very violent paroxysm, cried out—"O Heavens! What have I done to deserve this?" A Friend, who sat by him, replied—*"Look into your Office!"*—The ATTORNEY was satisfied.
> Mr. FOX's Letter precisely ascertains the *number* of his friends: each of them took an *edition*.

The *Letter* was now in its eleventh edition.

Despite such jeers the Ministerial newspapers were agitated to hear that Fox would move resolutions against the war. The *Public Advertiser* expressed its opinion on 13 February in a long editorial, which read in part:

> If the miserable fragment of OPPOSITION wish to gain any credit by an appearance of *patriotism*, they should not at this period attempt to embarrass Administration by vexing and frivolous motions, but co-operate in supporting those vigorous measures which are now become absolutely necessary for the honour of Great Britain. The question of the propriety or impropriety of WAR is determined, and even such advocates of the French as are not lost in sedition, and dead to humanity, must confess that they have been the aggressors in the present hostilities; for though this country was putting itself into a position of defence, it was only to enforce the faith of treaties, and no positive breach of peace had appeared on the part of the British nation when the French usurpers thought proper to declare war against us.
> It has been confidently affirmed by the Party Writers, that HOLLAND was by no means disposed to enter into a war on the question of the SCHELDT, but that THE DUTCH have been actually forced into impending hostilities by the Ministers of this country. This affirmation on the part of the Opposition Writers, is obviously a wretched invention of factious malignity. . . .

There was more of this in other Ministerial newspapers, and on 16 February the newspapers were advertising a pamphlet, entitled *Mr. King's Speech at Egham with Thomas Paine's Letter to Him on it, and Mr. King's Reply, as They All*

Appeared in the Morning Herald [*of 22 January*] (Egham and London). On 18 February there was a second pamphlet: Arthur Young's *The Example of France a Warning to Great Britain*. Both of them were sponsored by The Association. On the same day (18 Feb.), there were advertisements for a third pamphlet: *An Inquiry Concerning Political Justice and its Influence on General Virtue and Happiness. By the Rev.* [*William*] *Godwin*, 2 vols. quarto, published by G. G. J. and J. Robinson, price £1 16s. But, unlike King's *Speech* and Young's *Example*, this one was not published for propagandistic reasons, and, although it had much in common with Mackintosh's *Vindiciae Gallicae*, it was too expensive to attract purchasers and much too philosophical to appear relevant to the present situation. So little in fact did it impress the Ministerial newspapers that it was many months before they were even aware of its existence.

Fox moved his resolutions on 18 February in a speech which was mild to the point of being conciliatory. He made it very clear that he would support the war, even though he thought it was unnecessary, and that, in proposing the resolutions, he meant only to suggest to the Government a possible "guide" for its conduct and a "landmark on which to fix their attention for the attainment of peace." He even suggested that the Ministers might have been "imposed upon" and "misled" by persons who, inordinately concerned about France's internal affairs, had wilfully misrepresented her attitude toward Britain. Having been accused of "repetitiveness," he would not, he said, review the grounds of the war, but would confine himself to Poland, the recent dismemberment of which was, he felt, relevant to the present situation. The body of the speech was therefore an account of that kingdom, concluding with the second Treaty of Partition. This treaty, signed on 23 January, had given Prussia Danzig, Thorn, and the district of Posen, Russia at least four times as much, and Austria almost nothing. The result had been a new quarrel between Austria on the one hand and Prussia and Russia on the other. Having stressed the fact that these were Britain's prospective allies, Fox ended the account with a fervent hope that England would not ally herself with "that detested league" or enter into any "engagements" which would "prevent us at any time from making a separate peace." This was the burden of the fifth resolution. The fourth deplored the recent indifference of the Government to the invasion of Poland, and the first three stipulated that interference in French affairs was not the object of the war, that all differences between France and Britain might have been adjusted by negotiations, and that negotiations were not attempted. Burke replied with the usual sneers that Fox was an agent of Brissot and with the usual tirade against the French. He, it was evident, meant to continue the war until a Bourbon was back on the throne. Burke was supported by Jenkinson and others, Fox by Grey, Jekyll, Lambton, Major Maitland, Sheridan, and Adam, the latter stating that in his opinion the resolutions would at least "define the object of the war" to the satisfaction of the people and, unless it was so defined, he feared that they would be "adverse to the burthen of fresh taxes, and that discontents will arise." Fox, speaking in reply to Burke, stated that, since he was "not acquainted with M. Brissot," he could not comment on his point of view; but, as for himself, he had "finished [his] task" and could "with confidence say *liberavi animam meam*! . . . If the part which a regard to the interests of the country obliges me to take is not popular, it is not my duty to be influenced by that consideration." The resolutions were defeated 270 to 44, and on 21 February the *True Briton* published some supposed correspondence between "Citizen Fox" and "J. S. S./ Inspecteur du Pantheon, Paris," the purport of which was that Fox wanted his bust placed in the Pantheon and was competing for that "honour" with such "candidates" as Robespierre and Danton.

Despite the overwhelming defeat of Fox's resolutions, Grey moved on 21 February to "embrace the earliest occasion . . . of restoring . . . the blessings of peace," and on 22 February Taylor moved to reaffirm the principle "that in time of domestic peace the soldiers should live intermixed with the people, that no separate camp, no barracks, no inland fortresses, should be allowed; and that a circulation should be thus kept up between the Army and the people, and the citizen and the soldier be intimately connected together." The first motion was not even dignified by a debate; the second was defended by Fox, who maintained that the erection of barracks was only one instance of "a design on the part of Ministers to teach the Army to look solely to the Crown, without regard to the House of Commons." As other instances he cited the creation of independent regiments, the dismissal of officers for political reasons, and the "increase of the soldiers' pay last year . . . , an increase which the King had no authority to give till voted by the House of Commons." It was also defended by Grey, who concluded by censuring "the erection of barracks, as a measure new in its principle and dangerous in its consequences." Pitt argued, on the other hand, that a state of civil war did exist in some of the manufacturing towns because of the seditious activities in those areas and that barracks were desirable elsewhere because of the prevalence of "revolutionary ideas," which might otherwise prove too seductive for the soldiers. Neither motion came to a vote; and, as to the second, said the *Sun* on 23 February: "It is well known throughout every corner of England, that the erection of Barracks for the Military is a measure which has long been desired—it frees the Publicans from a burden which has long borne heavily upon them, and the Soldier enjoys infinitely greater comfort. In every point of view therefore, this is a measure which ought to be applauded." In preparation for this debate, the *Morning Herald* had published on 22 February a second letter from John King to Thomas Paine. This one, dated 12 February, was as furiously anti-French as any of Burke's speeches.

Daniel Stuart said later[31] that, to begin with, the war enjoyed a "courtly popularity" in the sense that it was "a popularity, originating in the Cabinet" and subsequently "re-echoed" through the kingdom by "Proclamations, camps, and addresses." Most readers of newspapers would have agreed with Stuart, for the war seemed at this point to be as enthusiastically endorsed by the country at large as it was by Parliament. The papers were again crammed with loyalty addresses, one of which was signed by 465 inmates of King's Bench Prison, who only seven months earlier had almost succeeded in blowing up the building. "The Ladies" had set up a "patriotic subscription for the relief of the widows and children of such sailors or soldiers who may fall in the present war" and had already collected several hundred pounds; and the Duke of York, who was to command the British forces, was so eager to get into the fray that, according to the *Morning Chronicle* of 18 February, he "expected to embark for Holland" ahead of his troops, serving in the Prussian army until they arrived. But this plan was evidently altered, for on 23 February the *Oracle* announced that he would "[set] off with his Troops for *Holland* on Monday morning, and His MAJESTY goes to the Tower to see them embark./ The *ardour* of the GUARDS to serve under their spirited Leader, cannot be too warmly commended. . . ." The "first three battalions of Guards" did in fact sail on 25 February, the Duke of York leaving a few days later. Although no one knew how the war was going, there were rumors of French victories, "circulated," *Lloyd's Evening Post* thought (22 Feb.), "for the purpose, probably of depressing the Funds," the last of which indicated "that Dumourier [*sic*] had been successful in his attempt upon Breda." But, since no one doubted that the British would speedily set everything to rights, the reports only added zest to the collection of subscriptions and to the scramble for commissions. Even those gentlemen who were not engaged in the scramble planned to visit the Army during the course of the summer, provided the war lasted that long. This, it appeared, was to be the really "great Tory show," topping even the Bagshot Grand Review.

Lord Chatham, still First Lord of the Admiralty and a member of the Privy Council, was now also a colonel in the Army; and two of the Prince of Wales's friends, Colonel Hulse and Major General Gerard Lake, were preparing to embark with the Duke of York. The Prince, although necessarily remaining behind, was setting a fine example for the rest by devoting himself to his regiment. "The PRINCE daily visits his Regiment, and finds in military parade and exercise an employment that fills his active mind," said the *Oracle* proudly on 6 March. "—His Royal Highness rides down unattended by even a single domestic." Also remaining behind was Sir John Lade, who, having threatened to sue for what Charles Pigott had said about him in *The Jockey Club*, was now threatening to sue for what Pigott had said about him in another pamphlet, this one entitled *Persecution. The Case of C. Pigott; Contained in the Defence he had Prepared [in Case Sir J. Lade Sued]*. Another nonparticipant was the Prince's boon companion, Richard Barry, Earl of Barrymore, familiarly known as "Hellgate." Barrymore had died, said the *Oracle* (8 Mar.), on 6 March "as a result of an accident"; succeeding to the title was his brother, "the Right Hon. Henry Barry, of Olethan and Ibawne in Ireland." Because of a club foot, the new Lord Barrymore was known as "The Lame Lord" or "Cripplegate."

The Duke of Clarence, who, on 13 December, 1792, had delivered a rousing oration in favor of the war and had then already volunteered his services, was proving to be the only laggard. The *True Briton* had apologized for him until 30

January, when it informed its readers that he had been ill, but it "hoped" that he would "soon be sufficiently recovered to embark on the element [*sic*] of British Glory." By 6 February it "understood" that he intended to "serve under Lord HOWE in the Grand Fleet" as soon as he put his affairs in order, and it still "understood" so on 12 February. By 18 February all the Ministerial newspapers were desperate, and, evidently determined that no one would miss the adventure, they appealed to him to join "the Grand Fleet" now. The Duke of Clarence did not respond. Another laggard seemed to be Lord Lonsdale, but he was only the butt of some malicious byplay. According to the *Morning Post* of 9 February, 1798, Lonsdale "gave [PITT] a seat in Parliament in 1780, and in return [PITT] exalted the Knight into Lord LONSDALE." But *The Times* of 21 February, 1793, had a different story. "If we recollect," it mused, "Lord LONSDALE got his title by very handsomely promising to build a 74 gun ship at the end of the American war, for the service of Government—As that war ended before the ships timbers were laid, and he has been enabled by the interest of the money unexpended to save a sum equal to the principal, which would have been sunk at that time, it is supposed his Lordship will now carry his patriotic *intention* into immediate *execution*." Lord Lonsdale, who never gave anything away if he could help it, certainly had no such intention, but, since he was disliked by all the newspapers, the sarcasm was echoed by most of them. On 23 February the *Gazetteer* reported with mock seriousness that "Lord LONSDALE has given orders to set immediately on the stocks, the *seventy-four* gun ship, which he so *munificently* promised during the late war. She is to be called the '*Better late than never.*'"

The enthusiasm which characterized the fashionable classes supposedly characterized the lower classes as well. On 6 January *The Times* had declared that the war had "the universal approbation of the public," and every newspaper had subsequently agreed, as so had every member of Parliament. Fox said repeatedly that the war was "thought to be popular," and, although Lord Lauderdale maintained that the public had been duped by Pitt and Reeves, he admitted that, in opposing the war, he was opposing "the majority of the people of England." But, to the fashionable classes, the war was primarily, as the *Morning Chronicle* had put it, a "chevalresque" pursuit, a kind of knight errantry, designed to "[bring] a nation of madmen and ferocious beasts, back to reason and humanity"; and, since the lower classes had no time for romantic ventures, they would not have supported it simply as an act of gallantry. They had to be convinced that the war was necessary to the defense of the Constitution. Although the Government had insisted throughout that they were so convinced, it had hesitated to declare the war itself, it was clearly apprehensive about the effect of Fox's *Letter . . . to the . . . [Westminster] Electors* and speeches, and readers of its newspapers were now given to understand that the British were fighting only because the French would have it so.

There was good reason for uneasiness, for, while "The Ladies" were setting up charities for prospective widows and orphans, the populace, which was expected to provide those widows and orphans, had shown from the outset a marked reluctance to do so. Even the Ministerial newspapers admitted that the bounties had not proved enticing, and, once war was actually declared, enlistments seem to have dropped off almost altogether. In the case of the Army, the Government had tried to solve the problem by turning the task of recruiting over to one hundred individuals, commissioning each of them a colonel and holding him responsible for filling his own regiment. But, since this had proved to be a difficult and costly assignment, most of these "independent regiments" remained "skeletal." The Navy, for which no such expedient was possible, was even worse off. On 12 February the *Morning Chronicle* accused the Government of bungling: "It has struck the commercial part of the public with astonishment, that Ministers who have for four months past, been *goading* and *provoking* the French to war, by every species of insult, and who therefore ought to have foreseen the calamity, have at the same time taken no adequate precautions to guard our trade against capture." The accusation was not quite fair, for the Ministerial newspapers had done everything possible to encourage enlistments, as so had organizations the country over. By 15 February the *Public Advertiser* could report that the "praise-worthy example of the Corporation of London, in giving bounties to Seamen, in addition to that of 5*l.* from Government, has been followed by most of the principal sea-ports in the kingdom"; but instead of enlistments the newspapers could report only desertions. Hence on 18 February *Lloyd's Evening Post* announced the first presses: "A press took place on the River yesterday morning. All the seamen were taken from the colliers, and the gangs were very successful./ Thursday night [14 Feb.] a hot press took place in Hamoaze, Catwater, and Plymouth. Near 200 seamen were picked up, and distributed among the men of war."

The obvious solution would seem to have been a conscription, but Pitt could never have enforced it. There had already been a few small demonstrations against the construction of barracks, the independent regiments were much resented, a press was likely to set off a riot, and, in the case of desertions, public feeling was always on the side of the deserter, as the following item, taken from the *True Briton* of 19 March, indicates:

> Last week Sergeant Sagar, of the King's Dragoon Guards, now upon the recruiting service at Leicester, being in search of some Deserters, in the neighbourhood of Loughboro', he accidentally detected a deserter from the 59th regiment of Foot, at Woodhouse Eves. After much altercation, some of the inhabitants so far favoured the man as to enable him to make his escape, when the Sergeant fired after him with a pistol, and the contents unfortunately lodged in his groin; in consequence of which the man is since dead, and the Coroner's Inquest have returned a verdict of Wilful Murder against Sagar, who has been committed to gaol to take his trial for the same.

On 2 March the newspapers announced that the King would pardon all deserters surrendering by 30 April, but no surrenders were reported.

The Government and the Reformers

Despite the activities of all the spies, informers, agitators, and street hecklers, employed by Dundas and Reeves, the lower and middle classes obviously did not regard the war as "necessary." Although they did not demonstrate against it, they did not feel that it represented anything worth dying for, principally because they were not convinced that the Constitution was jeopardized by the French. Under these circumstances the war created a number of new problems for the Government without solving any of the old ones. It had no evident effect on the clamors for reform, and it provided Pitt with no pat method of dealing with them, so that he was compelled to rely as before on ingenuity and luck. The abolitionists were still managed by Parliament. Since almost none of the newspapers was interested in their cause, Pitt could afford to be personally sympathetic without adding fuel to that flame. Parliament was so adroit that, although William Wilberforce introduced or tried to introduce a number of additional motions for ending the slave trade and the Quakers presented petition after petition, the abolitionists actually lost ground during 1793; for, whereas the Commons had previously resolved that the trade should be abolished by 1 January, 1796, it now thought otherwise, and the Lords seemed disinclined to think about the slave trade at all. In the case of legal reform, which was much more important to Pitt than abolition, no such evasive tactic was possible.

The demands for legal reform originated with the newspapers, as essentially a consequence of their battles with the lawyers. Although the *World* had once (3 July, 1792) hoped that the "race of *wicked* Attornies [was] almost run," the profession, as it turned out, had been able to spawn them faster than Lord Kenyon could disbar them. Nor was there any actual ground for disbarment, since what they were doing was not illegal. The real culprit was the law, which compelled the public to meet their demands or go to prison for debt. But the obvious solution to the problem, namely, a revision of the laws respecting debtors, was not seriously suggested by the newspapers until the case of Lord George Gordon called it to their attention. In this instance the laws were being exploited, not by the attorneys, but by the Government, and, although such exploitation was an accepted part of the legalistic procedure, this happened to be a notorious and particularly glaring example of it. Lord George Gordon, a brother of the wealthy Duke of Gordon, was a long-time trouble-maker. Having led the anti-Catholic riots of 1780, he had been tried for treason in 1781; and, acquitted of that offense, he had gone on to become a tireless fighter for peace and various reforms and a close friend of anyone of comparable complexion, especially of Thomas Hardy. On 6 June, 1787, he had been tried for libeling the judges in a pamphlet (*The Prisoner's Petition*) advocating prison reforms, and on 13 June he had been tried for libeling Marie Antoinette in the *Public Advertiser* of the previous year. Convicted in both instances, he had been sentenced on 28 January, 1788, to serve five years in Newgate Prison, to pay a fine of £5,000, and to find two securities for good behavior for another fourteen years in the amount of £2,500 each. But he had not been forgotten. He had frequently been mentioned by Burke, who had slated him in his *Reflections* and in various speeches, and he had also been mentioned by the newspapers, chiefly because of his conversion to Judaism. Hence, when he completed his sentence on 28 January, 1793, all newspapers had had reporters on hand.

The hearing was both comical and pathetic. Lord George had brought to court with him his two securities, both of them common laborers, the first being "a numberer of carts in the City of London, at the salary of 12s. a week," the second being similarly employed but earning somewhat less. Neither of them had saved any money, and Lord George himself had only £500, which sum, he explained, he had borrowed from his brother. Although he had hoped to turn over to the Court his own income of £500 a year, his brother, who provided it, had refused his permission. Before the Court replied to these explanations, it instructed him to remove the "uncommonly large round slouched hat" which he was wearing, and, when Lord George ignored the instruction, the hat was removed by one of the officers. Lord George thereupon "desired the Court to observe, that his hat had been pulled off his head by force and violence. He pulled a white night-cap out of his pocket, and put it on, and a red and white pocket handkerchief over it. He then, with great composure, stroked down his beard, which is at least ten inches or a foot long. This unusual appearance excited . . . a mixture of risibility and astonishment." But the performance was not over, for, having explained to Lord Kenyon that he wore the covering, not "from contempt or disrespect to the Court, but solely from a religious motive," he took from his pocket a petition, respectfully addressed to the Court by Israel Abraham George Gordon. The "petition" cited "the 18th chapter of Leviticus and various Jewish writers" as authorities for the covering and was evidently a very scholarly document; but the reporters did not hear all of it, for the Treasury solicitor, Joseph White, interrupted the reading to say that there was no point in continuing, since the securities were in any event unsatisfactory. Gordon was accordingly removed, and, still wearing his nightcap and handkerchief, returned to Newgate, where he would evidently spend another fourteen years, this time for debt.

Although the hearing was reported by all newspapers on 29 January, not one of them found it altogether "risible." The Opposition papers were outraged by the failure of the Duke of Gordon to pay the fine and provide the securities, especially since, in light of his rewards, it looked as if he was actually conniving with Pitt to keep his brother in prison. It seemed to most newspapers, too, that the Government could have released Lord George Gordon without jeopardizing its own interests. The more fundamental question of whether the Government should be empowered to make such decisions was not raised, but by early February a number of newspapers were suggesting that a revision of the laws respecting debtors might be in order. Since the Government wanted no agitation of this sort, Lord Kenyon hastened to announce that the lawyers were the real offenders, that the situation could be remedied by disbarments, and (*Lloyd's Evening Post*, 6 Feb.) that, not only would the disbarments be accelerated, but henceforth attorneys who advised their clients "to prosecute groundless or frivolous actions, for the sake of the costs, . . . would be compelled to pay the expences themselves." The *World* was not satisfied. On 15 February it called for remedial legislation:

> ATTORNIES.—Every hour the LEGISLATURE is more and more forcibly called upon to check the Progress of these Harpies. In LONDON they have half filled the Prisons with unfortunate Beings, the Victims of their Charges alone; where a *trifling Debt* has been swelled by their Costs on it to *four times the original Sum*. Lord KENYON, who has been justly stiled the *moral Judge*, should, perhaps, institute an inquiry into these enormities, for such wretches scarcely ever appear in the COURT of JUSTICE. They sit in their own Chambers, getting into their hands *Bills* and small *Debts*—on which they institute a practice as abhorrent from honesty as it is from Justice. Here it is that HUMANITY calls for a REFORM!

Lord Kenyon was called "the *moral Judge*" because of his feeling about adultery. Adulterers appearing in the Court of King's Bench could count on heavy damages and an impassioned lecture besides.

The *World* seemingly admired William Garrow and Francis Const. "Mr. GARROW, by his professional abilities, having obtained a silk gown, Mr. CONST stands foremost to succeed to much of his business," it said on 19 February; and on 10 July: "Mr. CONST seems succeeding as fast as possible to the business of Mr. GARROW, now moved upwards within the bar." Garrow had been elected a Bencher of Lincoln's Inn. Since Const had once been[32] and probably still was the legal counsel for the newspaper, he had probably inserted the puffs himself in the hope of obtaining through Garrow's influence "a silk gown" of his own; for otherwise the *World* hated everyone in the profession. It was also becoming increasingly sensitive to the plight of debtors generally, as so were other newspapers. What they needed was a Parliamentary spokesman, and by late February it looked as if they had found one in the person of the Prince of Wales's friend, Lord Rawdon, who had announced his intention of moving for a modification of the laws respecting debtors. The newspapers were ecstatic. Lord Rawdon became overnight the toast of all except the *Sun*, the *True Briton*, and the *Oracle*. He was not the toast of the *Sun* and the *True Briton*, because any tampering with these laws would hamper the Government, and the result would inevitably be the repeal of the laws altogether. He was not the toast of the *Oracle*, for, since John Bell was trying to adjust his own affairs with the Government, having failed to appear for sentencing, that newspaper had to proceed with extreme caution. "It is with infinite pleasure we see the confidence of the PRINCE reposed in a Nobleman of such distinguished merit as Lord RAWDON; whose courage and conduct in the field are not more conspicuous than his strict integrity and rigid rectitude in all the transactions of private life," it observed on 22 February. "His Lordship's sentiments of honour are, indeed, so refined, as sometimes, in the opinion of his friends, to be carried to extremes. Certain it is, they frequently prove detrimental to his *interest.* . . ." Since the Insolvent Debtors Bill or, as the newspapers called it, the Debtor and Creditor Bill was to be justified on "the great principles of justice and humanity," it promised to cause Pitt a great deal of trouble.

One of the first effects of the war was an increase in the number of bankrupts, most of whom, as the *Gazetteer* noticed on 23 February, were builders. Many of them, too, were solvent, but, because of the enormous costs involved in the proceedings, very few were able to extricate themselves. Since the incomes of the Commissioners of Bankrupts depended on the number of bankrupts, there was a growing suspicion that many of these actions were suborned, but the suspicions had not yet crystallized into an issue, to the great good fortune of the Government, which relied on bankruptcies to solve some of its own problems. The only trouble with this tactic was that it did not always succeed. It did not succeed in the case of John Frost, who, despite the indictment and the "commission of bankruptcy," returned to England on 9 February and, having adjusted matters with his creditors and engaged Erskine as his counsel, had by 14 February, according to the *Morning Post*, "voluntarily surrendered himself" and been "admitted to bail." The bail was actually furnished on 15 February, at which time Frost pleaded not guilty to the charge of using seditious words. On 20 February *Lloyd's Evening Post* reported that he had again sued Lord Hood, this time to recover £242, which, he said, he had been forced to pay on his behalf for services performed during the 1788 election. Sir James Eyre, now Lord Chief Justice of the Court of Common Pleas, had exonerated Lord Hood on the ground that Frost had contracted for the services and was therefore obliged to pay for them himself.

The Government had underestimated the resources of John Frost; it had overestimated the resources of John Bell. On 5 February the Court of King's Bench had issued a warrant for Bell's arrest; and, although Bell did not leave the country, as Bearcroft had no doubt suggested, the heavy expenses of defending himself against two long-drawn-out actions, the one brought by Lord Lonsdale, as well as the one brought by the Government, had taken their toll. Bell was having financial difficulties. From 14 February on, the *Oracle* devoted almost a full page to advertisements for his British Library, his rental library, his prints and engravings, and his enterprises generally:

PRINTING BUSINESS
in general.
Mr. Bell, of the BRITISH LIBRARY, *Strand*, respectfully informs the *Public* that his

PRINTING ARRANGEMENTS

Are now completed. His PRESSES are of a peculiar Construction, which enables him to execute the *Printing Business* in the most perfect manner:—He assumes to himself the merit of having revived the Taste for *Fine Printing* in ENGLAND; and he is still emulous to raise that Art to the highest degree of Perfection: but his *Future Productions* will best prove his Pretensions to a preference in this Line of his multifarious Concerns.

Should any Persons be desirous of having their Works,—Applications to Parliament or Proceedings therein, or any Communications printed in a *correct* and *beautiful* manner, they may be assured of their being executed by Mr. BELL with the utmost accuracy and dispatch, and if desired, with as much privacy as if the Presses were under their own immediate Management. . . .

Since the Government was quite happy to settle the matter with a proceeding of bankruptcy, it had no objection to negotiating its own grievances. Negotiations seem to have been underway by 23 February, for the *Oracle* of that date went out of its way to puff the Guards; and they seem to have been completed before the Duke of York left for Holland. On 6 March the *Star* reported that Bell had fulfilled his part of the bargain:

THE GUARDS.

The following Apology which had been previously approved by . . . the Duke of YORK, was read yesterday on the Parade, to a Circle of the three regiments of Foot Guards.

APOLOGY FROM MR. JOHN BELL.

Two most scandalous Libels on his MAJESTY's Regiments having appeared in The ORACLE, in January, 1792, for which I have been prosecuted by indictment, and convicted by a Jury in his MAJESTY's Court of King's Bench; but having represented to the Officers and Soldiers of the Guards, that I was not the Author of those Libels; but on the contrary, I have ever reprobated them from principle, although by being Proprietor of the Newspaper, I have been considered as being responsible for those Publications therein; they have been pleased to drop all further proceedings in the said prosecution, on condition of my paying the costs, and of my making a public apology.—I therefore feel a pleasure in making the best atonement in my power to the Officers and Soldiers of the three Regiments of Foot Guards, by declaring now, as I ever have done, that the Libels in question have always had my sincere and hearty reprobation; and further, I think it necessary to thank them for their handsome conduct towards me, and for granting their pardon.

The payment of those "costs" proved Bell's undoing altogether.

There were still remarkably few trials. The Government wanted no trouble in Ireland, and neither at this point did the Irish, who, convinced that the King was looking after their interests, were confidently awaiting the passage of the Roman Catholic Bill. But Lord Mountmorres was attacking the bill in newspapers and on 27 February John Foster strongly opposed it in Parliament, so that Pitt could expect uprisings in that area shortly. In Scotland Lord Braxfield tried Walter Berry and James Robertson on 28 January, 18, 19, and 22 February, and 18 March and concluded, he hoped, his business with Muir. The handling of Muir's case was a work of art. The *Gazetteer*, which seemed to be well acquainted with his plans, had stated daily that Muir would positively return for his trial, but that he could not possibly return by 11 February. Since the trial was thereupon postponed indefinitely, the *Gazetteer* was under the impression that it would probably not be held at all. As it put it on 22 February: "Several prosecutions for Libel, &c. were commenced by the agents of Government in the first effervescence of their zeal, which in the present cooler moment, we imagine, they may not be disinclined to withdraw. Such, for instance, was the indictment against Mr. MUIR, an Advocate of Edinburgh, where the crime alledged was, that he had actually *lent* PAYNE's Works to a Friend! Beyond this charge, if it be sustained, there is but one step remaining, and that is, to indict men for *reading* the works which Ministers, or their agents, shall regard as exceptionable." Muir had meanwhile written to the Associated Friends of the People in Scotland, stating that the notice of his trial had reached him on 8 February and that he had notified the Court at once that he could not be in Edinburgh by 11 February, but would be there as soon as he could arrange transportation. Transportation had now, he thought, been arranged, he was leaving Paris at once, and he hoped to arrive in Edinburgh almost as soon as the letter. The letter was dated 13 February, and a copy was sent to the *Morning Chronicle*, which printed it on 26 February. Muir arrived too late. On 2 March the *Gazetteer* reported that, having failed to appear before the High Court of Justiciary on 25 February, he had been outlawed, and a reward was being advertised for his arrest. The charge had been expanded to cover all his activities during the previous six months, including reading to the Edinburgh convention in December an address from the United Irishmen, sent to him by Rowan.

Pitt liked to punish his own enemies as inconspicuously as possible, always preferring devious devices to open trials. He liked to deal with enemies of the state in the full glare of sunlight, but, with The Association in disrepute, because of the letter of Thomas Law, and the Friends of the Liberty of the Press seemingly undaunted by the dismissal of Erskine, he had had to move cautiously, especially in England. On 1 February Fox had mentioned parenthetically that he could not be "much surprised at any aspersion on my character" in light of Law's statement that the Crown and Anchor Association "not only receives anonymous letters reflecting on individuals, but corresponds with the writers of such letters, and even sometimes transmits their slanders to [Mr. Dundas]." Burke had struck back on 12 February by denouncing Fox, Mackintosh, Sheridan, Paine, and Barlow as alike enemies to the Constitution, but The Association had derived no benefit, since his authority was subsequently demolished by Sheridan. On 14 February the *True Briton*, evidently feeling that something had to be said, stated that the actual "ground upon which Mr. LAW chiefly disagreed [with The

Association at the Crown and Anchor] was *French*—That Gentleman had money in the French Funds, and was *tender* of any measure that reflected upon the conduct of that humane, amiable, just and moderate people." But the Friends of the Liberty of the Press was meanwhile advertising another public dinner, to be held at the Crown and Anchor at the end of February, and by 21 February there were so many reservations that the dinner had to be deferred until 9 March, when the entire tavern would be available. On the same date (21 Feb.), 2,500 residents of Nottingham petitioned the Commons for "a general plan of reform," including universal male suffrage. The petitioners did not mince words. They stated flatly that, since the Constitution no longer recognized "the right of free election," the people were "amused" by the fiction that the Commons was a representative body and that, unless something was done, their "confidence" in Parliament, already "weakened," would be "destroyed."

The notion that, in its pristine state, the Constitution had guaranteed every freeman the right to vote was an invention of Major John Cartwright, and it had no basis whatever in fact. But this was not the issue, for the Constitution did guarantee the people a right to petition, and this right at least Pitt had not previously questioned. On this occasion he did. He seemed now to think that, although the people had "a fair right to petition, for the redress of any supposed wrong," Parliament's "reception" of the petition was largely a matter of courtesy; and, when the language showed such lack of "respect" for the Commons and "reverence" for the Constitution as the Nottingham petition did, then it was "impossible" for the House, "consistently with dignity or propriety," to accept it. Fox objected that it had accepted other petitions in which "the disrespect was more glaring than in the present one" and that, for reasons of simple expedience, the Commons could not afford to be "over nice in examining petitions presented from its constituents." But the objection fell on deaf ears: the petition was refused by a vote of 109 to 21.

Although Pitt's speech on the Nottingham petition was a *cause célèbre* with the Opposition newspapers for years, the overwhelming rejection of the petition by the Commons seemed to restore some of his self-confidence. On 15 February John Frost, who was an enemy of the state, as well as one of his personal enemies, had been released, with no date set for his trial. But on 23 February, according to *Lloyd's Evening Post* (25 Feb.), the Government dealt with three other culprits. Thomas Spence, tried at the Middlesex Sessions for selling Paine's *Rights of Man*, Part II, was acquitted, owing to a flaw in the indictment. William Holland, tried in the same court for selling Paine's *Letter Addressed to the Addressers*, was convicted, sentenced to one year in prison, and fined £100. Henry D. Symonds, tried at the Old Bailey for selling the *Rights of Man*, Part II, was convicted, but sentence was postponed, "pending an investigation of his financial state." Symonds was also under indictment for selling Paine's *Letter Addressed to the Addressers* and Pigott's *Jockey Club*. On 27 February the *True Briton* spoke out against reformers generally in a long address, beginning "BRITONS! behold the herd of hapless, forlorn and friendless French Emigrants, who infest your streets," and ending "In a word, read in the sad destiny of these miserable Fugitives your future fate, should you, like them, be seized with the contagion of Reform; and in beholding their ruthless condition, tremble at the consequences of destroying that harmony and that strength by which the wonderful Fabric of Society is at once supported and adorned." The address was probably intended as a harbinger of the Traitorous Correspondence Bill, for the press was seemingly unprepared for the news (28 Feb.) that Sheridan would introduce a motion respecting seditious practices.

On 4 March there was a flurry of activity. In anticipation of the dinner of the Friends of the Liberty of the Press, the Ministerial newspapers announced publication of John Bowles's pamphlet, *A Short Answer to the Declaration of the Persons Calling Themselves the Friends of the Liberty of the Press*, and the Government showed its contempt for that society by harassing the press further. Richard Phillips, printer and editor of the Leicester *Herald*, was sentenced to eighteen months in the Leicester jail for selling the *Rights of Man*, Part II, and it was understood that the Manchester *Herald* had been suppressed altogether. In Cambridge Dr. Isaac Milner, the Vice Chancellor of the University, met with twenty-seven members of the faculty and resolved to prosecute William Frend for publishing (16 Feb.) a pamphlet, entitled *Peace and Union Recommended to the Associated Bodies of Republicans and Anti-Republicans*. Although this resolution seems to have originated with certain resident Fellows, not with Pitt and not even with Milner, it was the kind of resolution Pitt would supposedly approve, and Milner was ambitious. His militant support of the Government had already earned for him the Presidency of Queen's College (1788) and the Deanery of Carlisle (1791); he was currently working for the Mastership of Trinity College as successor to Dr. Postlethwaite. On 4 March, too, Sheridan rose to introduce his motion.

Except for the *True Briton*'s sneer of 2 March that "Mr. SHERIDAN's *Seditious Motion* comes on on Monday," the newspapers had said nothing about the motion, but it had evidently caused some concern, since everyone was on hand for the debate. What Sheridan proposed was "that this House will, upon this day sevennight, resolve itself into a committee of the whole House, to consider of the Seditious Practices and Insurrections, referred to in His Majesty's most gracious Speech at the opening of the present session of Parliament." In short, he proposed an inquiry into the supposed uprising of 1 December, 1792, to determine if "the danger in this country was real" or "not real" and, if "the whole was a false alarm," to determine whether the Government was the victim of "a delusion" or whether "the whole was founded on a systematic plan, laid by Government for deluding the sense, and finally subduing the spirit, of the people." He felt that the inquiry was important, he said, because that alarm had led to further alarms, to the strengthening of the executive power, to the "weakening" of "the rights of the people," and to war. Everyone had been affected by the "panic." Sheridan referred in particular to William Windham, who "has been panic-struck, and now strengthens the hand of Government,—he who, last session, to use a vulgar adage, 'rolled His Majesty's Ministers in the dirt,'" and to Burke, who "has been so affected, that he sees nothing but a black and clouded sky" and "takes refuge in the Ministerial gabardine, where he hopes for security from the approaching storm." Although it seemed to Sheridan that, if the Ministers were innocent, they would welcome the opportunity to defend themselves, he did not think that any defense was possible, so overwhelming was the evidence against them: the "connivance" of the Government in circulating the works of Paine and Pigott, the founding of The Association to suppress works which the Government and The Association were themselves circulating, the lack of any indication of an insurrection, Pitt's silence on the subject, the constant propagation of rumors, the incitement of riots against the Protestant dissenters, the search of mail by the Post Office, and terrorizing of the press. Sheridan had a great deal to say on the last subject.

Sheridan pointed out that the Government had bought the support of newspapers, whenever possible, "one paper in particular," the *Sun*, even being "the property of members of this House," and that it had stopped at nothing to destroy the others. He knew positively that publicans were being asked, "Do you take in the *Morning Chronicle* or *Morning Post* ?" And, if the answer was yes, they were warned to "take care there is no sedition in it; for, if there is, you are liable to punishment for distributing it to your customers." He knew, too, that the solicitors to the Treasury, William Chamberlayne and Joseph White, had sent letters to attorneys in various parts of the country, suggesting that they search out booksellers who were distributing the works of Paine and Pigott and commence actions against them, although it was common knowledge that attorneys were "not distinguished for superior morality" and that it was precisely this practice of suing in their own interests, not in the interests of clients, which the Courts had supposedly been trying to check. The Government was obtaining its own names, Thomas Law had revealed, from The Association, and on 13 December Sir Archibald Macdonald had informed the House that he then had two hundred of them on file, awaiting prosecution. But what had happened to those prosecutions ? If the country was in a state of insurrection, why, Sheridan wanted to know, had the Government "brought forward" only a few of the two hundred ? And why had it given priority to "miserable bill-stickers" and to booksellers who had merely "sold in the way of trade, the *Rights of Man*, omitting all the parts objected to . . . in the trial of Mr. Paine, the *Address to the Addressers*, and the *Jockey Club*" ? Sheridan frankly wondered if the Government even intended to try John Frost. What Sheridan had said was amplified by Lambton, Fox, Colonel Macleod, and Thomas Maitland. It was assailed by Windham, who defended his apostacy and The Association, with which he was now identified; by the Lord Mayor, Sir James Saunderson, who defended his conduct during the phantom insurrection and since; and by Burke, who defended the Government, interrupting the defense to denounce Priestley, Cooper, Watt, and the *Morning Chronicle*, the latter for extenuating the September massacres. The assault on Cooper was not quite fair, since Cooper was no longer sympathetic with the French Revolution. The motion did not come to a vote.

On 7 March the *Morning Chronicle* announced that William Frend, Fellow of Jesus College, Cambridge, would be tried in the Vice Chancellor's Court shortly for publishing his *Peace and Union*. The *Chronicle* was strongly on the side of Frend. On 8 March it announced that the stewards for the public dinner of the Friends of the Liberty of the Press would be Alderman John Sawbridge, M.P., J. G. Lemaitre, David Godfrey, Charles Sturt, M.P., James Bell, Captain Charles Morris, John Bonham, John Wharton, M.P., Edmund Calamy, William Breton, Henry Howard, M.P., Thomas Rogers, Charles Goring, Robert Knight, Nicolls Raynsford, Joseph Richardson, Harry House, Alderman Nathaniel Newnham, Richard Weld, John Courtenay, and James Losh. There had evidently been some resignations, for, attached to this announcement, was the notice: "Some of the greatest characters in this country have been proud of their names being recorded as *defenders* of the liberty of the press, but gentlemen who are sometimes *professionally* obliged to be advocates against it, and have long been in the habit of trying to prove that *wrong* is *right*, are apt in process of time to think it so, and therefore become ashamed of that in which men of any other description would glory."

The dinner was held on 9 March, as scheduled. Although the *Morning Chronicle* of that date did not mention the dinner, it celebrated the occasion by striking another blow at The Association:

> *Wanted*, for immediate employment . . ., one hundred affidavit men; as they are to mix in good company, it is expected that they appear in tolerable coats, with a change of linen. They are to insinuate themselves into families and societies, to mark carefully, and, as soon as opportunity offers, to commit to paper all discourses, and even words casually dropped, that have any the most distant tendency to matters of Government, taking for their general rule with respect to seditious words or writings, Judge ALIBONE's definition, viz. "All discourses or writings, on political matters, without the express permission of Government." No half measure, squeamish men need apply, as it may sometimes be necessary for them to swear to the truth of documents already prepared. Persons who have attended the Old Bailey as principles will have a preference. —Apply to the Society for anonymous defamation.

The dinner was in fact a disappointment. Among those present were John Thelwall, Horne Tooke, and James Mackintosh, but not Erskine. The speeches were made by Grey and Sheridan, and these were followed by toasts to Lord Lauderdale, Thomas Maitland, and Colonel Macleod. Although Horne Tooke proposed a toast to Joseph Gerrald as well, it was apparently not drunk. Only five hundred attended, as opposed to the eight hundred who had attended the dinner of 19 January, no arrangements were made for publication of speeches, and, except for a subscription to defend freedom of the press, there was nothing noteworthy about the resolutions. The Opposition papers were unenthusiastic; the Ministerial papers ignored the event until 15 March, when the *Public Advertiser* remarked: *"The Liberty of the Press*, that sacred right without which freedom cannot exist, and which, in the hands of good men, has been the promoter of every blessing this country enjoys, can never be hurt more dangerously, than by a set of vain-glorious pseudo-patriots, who meet together to make it a mere stalking horse for the abuse of the Ministry. This semblance of virtue is more detestable than the most open vice. . . ." But eulogies of The Association were now rampant. "To the merits of the Crown and Anchor Association there is no praise adequate," declared the *Public Advertiser* on 14 March; "the present general spirit of patriotism in the kingdom rose from their most laudable example. . . ."

Elections, the War, and Mr. Fox

On 9 February the members of the Friends of the People assembled to hear the Report on the State of the Representation of England and Wales, finally completed by Tierney and his committee. The report was approved, publication authorized, and it was further resolved that Tierney would draft a petition for election reforms on the basis of it. No reform group frightened the Government as much as this one, and this one could not be dealt with in any of the usual ways. The members could not be driven into bankruptcies, imprisoned for debt, goaded into flight, or even brought to trial; nor could the Government procrastinate, as it could in the case of the abolitionists. All it could do was to insinuate in and out of Parliament that Lord Lauderdale, Grey, and the society's patron, Fox, were agents of the French; and this it had been doing right along with no particular success. But as usual events seemed to play into Pitt's hands, for the reading of the report coincided with the announcement of the war, and the trio could therefore be represented as traitors. The Ministerial newspapers made the most of the advantage. The *True Briton* and the *Public Advertiser* devoted whole issues to exposés of supposed correspondence between Fox and the French or between Lord Lauderdale and the French, and the Ministerial pamphleteers seemed to feel that Fox's opposition to the war was proof enough that such a correspondence existed. Young's *Example of France*, advertised on 18 February as an answer to Fox's *Letter . . . to the . . .* [*Westminster*] *Electors*, included a diatribe on the Friends of the People, as so did *Modern Patriotism;* *in Answer to the Letter of . . . Fox*, advertised on 26 February. Another pamphlet, entitled *Address to the Friends of the People [in Verse]*, included a diatribe on Fox. This one, signed only "A Friend of the People," may have been written by Major Waller, who, according to the *Diary* (6 Mar.), was contributing satirical verse to many of the Treasury papers during this period, under the name "Jonathan Slow." On 21 February Pitt redefined the right to petition, most certainly with the Friends of the People in mind, while Burke expressed a stern hope that, in view of the war, the organization had revised its plans and had sunk back into a state of coma. Sheridan assured him that it had not: that, despite rumors to the contrary, the Friends of the People was "neither dead nor sleeping," but was "in the full vigour of activity"; and on 23 February the *Gazetteer* announced publication of *The State of the Representation of England and Wales.* According to the advertisement, the pamphlet was printed, "by order of the Society [of the Friends of the People] for D. Stuart, No. 52, Frith-Street, Soho," and was "sold by all the Booksellers in Town and Country." On 25 February advertisements appeared in all Opposition newspapers and in some of the Ministerial nondailies, and on 1 March pirated editions were announced by Ridgway, Symonds, and R. H. Westley, respectively. A report on the representation in Scotland, much less detailed, appeared somewhat later and was ultimately incorporated with the earlier report.

 The State of the Representation of England and Wales, prepared almost entirely by Tierney, noted, to begin with, that "a majority of what are called the representatives of the Commons are returned by the 170th part of the male subjects of England paying taxes, even supposing these only to amount to two millions," and that, of this "170th part," only a fraction could possibly be regarded as "independent electors":

> Your Committee report, that the gross defects and abuses . . . have established A SYSTEM OF PRIVATE PATRONAGE, which renders the condition of the House of Commons *practically* as follows.

71 Peers and the Treasury nominate—	90	
Procure the return of—	77	
Patronage of 71 Peers and the Treasury—	—	167
91 Commoners nominate—	82	
Procure the return of—	57	
Patronage of 91 Commoners—	—	139
		306 *out of*
	513 *Members.*	

Of the 306 Members, the Treasury returned seven, five by influence, two by nomination; Lord Lonsdale also returned seven, five by nomination. Several peers returned six: Lord Edgcumbe, Lord Eliot, the Duke of Newcastle, and the Marquess of Buckingham. Earl Fitzwilliam and the Duke of Marlborough returned five each; Lord Lansdowne, the Duke of Bedford, Lord Ailesbury, the Duke of Northumberland, the Duke of Devonshire, the Marquess of Stafford, and the Duke of Rutland returned four; Lord Sydney, Lord Radnor, the Earl of Sandwich, and the Duke of Beaufort returned three; the Duke of Dorset, the Duke of Richmond, the Marquess of Bath, Lord Egremont, Lord Westmorland, and Lord Cornwallis returned two; and, included in the long list of those returning one, were the Duke of Norfolk and the Duke of Portland.

The "gross defects and abuses" which made such "PRIVATE PATRONAGE" possible were detailed at considerable length. The principal item was the cost of running for office. Since all electors assembled at one voting place, it was "customary" for the candidate to provide transportation for the "non-residents," to support them during "three to seven days' residence" in the voting place, and to add compensation for "loss of time and trouble." Thus a voter living fifty miles away cost the candidate at least £5 4s., a voter living 250 miles away at least £18 16s. In many areas almost all the voters were "non-resident," and, even in a metropolitan area like Bristol, the nonresident voters represented an expense of £9,793. In addition, the "act passed *to prevent giving meat and liquor at elections*" had "customarily" been ignored with respect to "voters from the country," being deemed applicable only to local voters; but, since it was "impossible . . . , during the tumult of an election, to distinguish one description of electors from another," every voter "was permitted to participate in the distribution of liquor," so that "the whole town is a scene of drunkenness and confusion, to . . . the intolerable expence of the candidates." Added to this were heavy poll taxes, which every voter should have paid for himself, but which were so "generally" paid by the candidates "that from custom it is never considered as an act of bribery"; and there was also the "indispensable and heavy cost" of "counsel, and solicitors" to make sure that the election conformed with the "numerous points of law." The longer an election lasted, the greater was the cost; and elections might last fifteen days. If no vote was cast within a "reasonable time after the officer has made three proclamations," the officer might declare the election over earlier; but, if one of the candidates was having financial difficulties, the other was certain to prevent the curtailment by "feeding" votes, that is, by sending one voter in just before the polls were declared closed, or by insisting upon "the six oaths," which he could legally require from the voters at any time.

Since only a man who was himself very wealthy or had a very wealthy patron could afford candidacy, there were few actual contests. In some instances the patron simply "named" two candidates, who, running unopposed, were *ipso facto* elected; in other instances the elections were "*compromised*," for patrons with a conflict of influences preferred to enter only one candidate apiece rather than submit to the "*intolerable expence attending contests*." In both instances the voting was "meaningless." Even when an election was free from single influence, when it was not "compromised," and when the candidates were reasonably circumspect, the voters often had less to do with the outcome than did the "returning officer," who decided when the election would begin and when it would end and who was qualified to vote and who was not. Being in "sole command" of the election, he could twist the results to suit himself, and, in cases of disputed elections, his word was final. Since he was "*notoriously illiterate and needy*," was "*appointed by intrigue and cabal*," and hence was an "*avowed partizan of one of the candidates*," no election could, strictly speaking, be regarded as "free" nor any Member of the Commons as an actual representative of the people.

Although the report was not mentioned by the newspapers, the numerous editions would indicate that it was widely read, and there was an abundance of corroborative evidence in the accounts of the various contested elections. Because of its connection with the trial of Warren Hastings, the most scandalous of these was the Stockbridge election. Since Hastings's trial was now much more embarrassing to the Government than it was to the Opposition, the Opposition had no desire to end it, and the Government could not end it without alienating Burke. The Government was therefore in a very awkward situation, and, to make it even more awkward, the Opposition saw to it that the trial remained an issue by moving from time to time for its curtailment. One such motion had been made on 11 February, when Thomas Maitland asked for the appointment of a committee to consider means of expediting the proceedings, which, as he pointed out, had now gone on "nearly six years," Hastings having been "under accusation" for nine. The facts that Hastings had returned from India already broken in health and that the hearings were always "thinly attended" were additional arguments, he said, for concluding them as speedily as possible. Dundas supported the motion, this time on grounds which Burke himself might respect, namely, that the trial was getting bad publicity on the Continent and that the French newspapers were making capital of it by calling it "The Farce." Although Dundas made it very clear that he did not blame Burke or the other managers for the prolongation, it did seem to him that, if the accusers and the accused compared their evidence privately, some of the speeches could be abbreviated. Motions of this sort were always strongly supported by the newspapers, since those which were not in the pay of the Government were likely to be in the pay of Hastings's agent, Major John Scott. "*One Hundred and Twenty one* changes have taken place in the House of Lords, during Mr. HASTINGS's Tryal," said the *St. James's Chronicle* on 16 February: how can such a "jury" weigh the evidence? This time there was even a pamphlet: John Williams's *Authentic Memoirs of Warren Hastings, Esq. . . . By Anthony Pasquin, Esq.*, published by John Bew.

Scott had, however, been working at a disadvantage, for he had lost his seat as Member for West Looe in 1790, and the Government had evidently been unwilling to incur Burke's wrath by giving him another one. In early 1793 he had taken matters into his own hands and got himself and a John Cator elected as Members for Stockbridge. The election was followed by charges of wholesale misconduct. "No less than eighty-four actions of bribery are brought on the business of the Stockbridge election," *Lloyd's Evening Post* reported on 1 March; "the penalties sued for amount to 42,000*l*." The case was reviewed by the Commons on 22 February with all Members on hand and the Government clearly on the side of Scott. But, in light of the overwhelming evidence against him and Burke's vehement feelings on the subject, it yielded to the extent of supporting the contestants, and Joseph Barham and George Porter were therefore seated instead. The Government would not, however, countenance the prosecution of Scott, and, since there was no doubt that briberies had occurred, it contrived to shift the guilt to the bribees. A committee was accordingly appointed to look into the conduct of the Stockbridge electors, and Scott was returned to the world, his reputation unsullied. The *Morning Post*, which saw eye to eye with the Government on the matter of Hastings and hence Scott, said so on 25 February. "We are happy to find," it observed, "that the Major is not involved in the Bribery transactions; for however much we differ from him in Politics, there is no man who has had the happiness of being acquainted with him that does not cordially esteem him."

Burke's reaction to this turn of events was not indicated, but his reaction to another one was. On 28 February Burke complained that the Lords had convened for the trial so early that, had he not gone directly to Westminster Hall without waiting for the preliminary "proceedings," the hearings would again have been postponed. His conduct was approved by the Commons, and that afternoon Maitland's committee for suggesting means of expediting the trial reported in effect that it could not think of any. Dundas's proposal that the evidence be presented in private had not been considered. The *Oracle* purported to be exasperated. "Mr. HASTINGS suffers certainly more than ever was endured by any Man, before any *Tribunal* in the known world," it exploded on 9 March. "And his inhuman Persecutor is filled with spleen against any one who shall dare to propose a mode of shortening his pain.—The voice of the People should be listened to—That of the great assemblage of Citizens in these realms is loud in its complaint of the *tedium* and *expence* of the trial."

The Government's tactic of denouncing all advocates of election reforms as Jacobins, with Fox as the arch-Jacobin, had the disadvantage of consolidating the forces of peace and reform and of reaffirming Fox's position as representative of the interests of the people against a prowar, antireform Government. There can be little doubt that, had Fox appealed to the people, there would have been a rebellion against both the corruptions and the war; and it is therefore greatly to his credit that he did nothing of the sort. On the contrary, he was scrupulously cautious. Although he supported all petitions for reform, he did not solicit them, and he strongly denounced attempts to influence the Commons by extra-petitionary means; as to the war, he said at all times that, although he did not regard it as either "just" or "necessary" and would do everything in his power to negotiate an early peace, he would support it while it lasted. The Government was not grateful, and it became less grateful as the war progressed.

The French had seemed to begin the war at a disadvantage, for the execution of Louis had resulted in a struggle for power in the Convention, and the Prussians, moving more rapidly than anyone expected, had undertaken the defense of Holland. But on 16 February General Dumouriez crossed the border, on 26 February he captured Breda, and on 1 March he went on to capture Gertruydenberg. The Government handled the situation badly. On the evident assumption that an unpopular war was not likely to be made popular by a succession of defeats, it suppressed the news, and, since newspapers were therefore dependent on rumors, everything seemed to be worse than it actually was. The fall of Breda, positively announced by the *Oracle* on 6 March, had been announced by other newspapers as early as 22 February, and the fall of Gertruydenberg had been regularly reported since 25 February. In addition, the argument that Britain was fighting to protect Holland, still insisted upon by the *True Briton*, looked rather silly in view of the fact that Holland was making no effort to defend herself. "One is tempted to wonder, how, after the declared intention of *France* to invade *Holland*, the preparations for repelling any Enemy so powerful should have been so tardy," the *Oracle* reflected on 9 March. "The phlegm of the Dutch Character has never been successfully raised into exertion but upon the Ocean. . . ." None of this spurred enlistments. Neither did the complaints, reported by Opposition newspapers, that the bounties promised by the Government were not being paid. On 2 March the King acted to proclaim 19 April a general fast day, and on 6 March he acted again to request that 12,000 Hanoverian troops be employed to assist the Dutch. The purpose of the fast day was to drive the masses to churches, where they would be subjected to furious diatribes against the French, thinly disguised as sermons. This was by now a very old trick and one all too familiar.[33] The Government could think of nothing except getting rid of Fox. By 27 February the Ministerial newspapers were suggesting that he and his friends ought to be indicted for high treason, and on 15 March the Government introduced the Traitorous Correspondence Bill.

The Traitorous Correspondence Bill, in part a reaction to *The State of the Representation of England and Wales*, in part to the increasing unpopularity of the war, was a desperate expedient, prepared for well in advance. The Government did not rely entirely on the dissemination of rumors, for on 4 March Sheridan mentioned that his letters were being "stopped at the post-office," and he was evidently afraid that the "paper" he had sent to the Marquise de Sillery "in favour of the unfortunate KING of FRANCE" had been seized, since he went to some trouble to defend it. Fox referred to persistent reports that the Ministers also possessed incriminating correspondence of his, which they had got from the Post Office and thus far withheld for reasons of "lenity," and that they had the word of numerous informers that he had talked with French agents. Fox was not frightened. Of course he had talked to Frenchmen, he said, and, as for treasonable correspondence, he would rather suppose that the Government, provided it had any, might find it "an awkward thing to produce letters opened at the post-office." It certainly had none of his, for, except for a letter to Lord Lauderdale, he had sent no communication to France in more than two years. "Is it not a situation of the country horrible to relate," he asked, "that men's correspondence and conversation are to be pried into with such inquisitorial jealousy, as to make it dangerous for them to commit their thoughts to paper, or to converse with a stranger, but in the presence of a third person?"

The Government had also been active in another area. On 1 March the *Gazetteer* had announced a meeting of the Whig Club, to be held on 5 March at the London Tavern, with George Byng as chairman and the Earl of Albemarle, Alderman Skinner, and Alderman Coombe as stewards. The purpose of such meetings had always been to honor Fox, but on 4 March Sheridan announced that the purpose of this one was to embarrass him: that Windham had been soliciting resignations, at the behest of the Government, to be presented to him on the occasion. Fox very much regretted that Sheridan had mentioned Windham's conduct, for he was personally certain that Windham had nothing more in mind than to establish "a sort of independent corps," without realizing that many would join it as a graceful means of deserting an old friend. Windham positively denied that he had been "canvassing for Government," and Burke purported to know nothing about it, although he felt strongly that Fox ought to be deserted. Fox was. On 6 March the *Gazetteer* reported that the chairman had opened the meeting by reading a letter of "secession," signed by Burke and forty-four others, including Lord Sheffield, William Windham, and Alderman Newnham, but not including the Duke of Portland, who in fact had sat on the Chairman's right while the letter was read. On 7 March the *Gazetteer* printed the letter and the signatures. No newspaper was quite as happy as the *True Briton*, which added to its account of the meeting (6 Mar.) the observation:

MODERN WHIGS.

A few years ago, when the Whig Club was in a flourishing condition, several of its Members were displeased at the admission into their *august* Body, of the two Conductors, *par nobile fratrum*, of a certain Jacobin Print [James Perry and James Gray of the *Morning Chronicle*]. The Club, in consequence, came to a resolution, not to admit in future any persons of that description, who might lessen the dignity of the Collective Body.

At this time, when such an havoc has been made among the *rank and file* of the Whig Forces, Volunteers, it is rumoured, will be accepted on any condition. . . . A few well-known Newspaper Reporters, the outrageous license of whose tongues has so often appalled the loyal frequenters of the Gallery of St. Stephen's Chapel, will shortly have their coat-buttons decorated with the Insignia of the Order.

. . . . . .

The only surprising name on the list of "seceders" had been that of Alderman Newnham, a member of the Friends of the Liberty of the Press, long a supporter of the Whigs, and until 1790, when Pitt had got rid of him, a Member of

Parliament for London. Newnham had signed his name at the last minute, having just learned that on 2 March Brook Watson had been appointed Commissary General to the Duke of York's army, that he had resigned as Member for London, and that an election would be held on the following day. Since the Government wanted to replace Watson with another of its friends, Alderman John William Anderson, announcement of the appointment and hence of the election had been deferred until it was supposedly too late for anyone else to enter himself as candidate. Newnham, however, did; and, to improve his chances of election, he resigned from the Whig Club and on 6 March inserted advertisements in the newspapers, stating that he was politically "independent." All newspapers were disgusted. The Opposition newspapers supported neither candidate; the Ministerial newspapers supported Anderson. The *Diary* supported Anderson on the ground that his "father and mother were *both British born* subjects" and he had never associated with "traitors." "If ever there was a time which called upon all ranks of Englishmen to exert themselves in the defence and preservation of their rights and liberties, it is at the present moment, when we are not only actually engaged in a war with our old enemies the French, now rendered barbarians and savages by impracticable theories and mob principles, but those very principles . . . endeavoured to be defended and inculcated in this country, by a set of men and their *followers*, who call themselves *Englishmen*," it declaimed on 6 March. "It is therefore peculiarly incumbent on the Livery of London, . . . to be wary in selecting either Magistrates or Representatives in Parliament, who are, or *have been any way connected with men of the above description. . . .*" The *World* supported Anderson on the ground that the "independents" were themselves a party: "Mr. NEWNHAM, in his public advertisement, tells the Livery of London, that he has disengaged himself from every connection of *Party*, when it is notorious that he has only left the Whig Club to act in conjunction with those Gentlemen who have withdrawn their names from that Society, and who have constituted themselves a distinct and separate Party. Let us, therefore, hear no more about Alderman WEATHERCOCK's *independence*." The *World* even had a word of commendation for Thomas Skinner, who had protested the shift by resigning from "Mr. NEWNHAM's Committee": "Let Mr. Alderman SKINNER's political Principles be what they may, he is certainly consistent. . . ." Skinner's "political Principles" had been considerably in doubt. On 6 March Anderson was elected as Member for London, and, later in the year, the Government brought Newnham into Parliament as Member for Ludgershall.

From 6 March on, every Ministerial paper was crammed with ridicule of Fox and his friends, especially Grey, Sheridan, and "General Jackoo" (Jekyll), but on 11 March Fox was suddenly advised that the die was not cast after all: that he would have one final opportunity to recant. That afternoon Pitt presented his budget. The *Oracle* said nothing about the recantation or the budget, but it made some seemingly random remarks about the Government's appointments:

Among other Gentlemen who will derive official advantage from the present War, are two, whose respectability of character may challenge the Tongue of Calumny—The first, . . . THOMAS STEELE: and the second, . . . DUDLEY RYDER, joint Pay-masters General.

The late Mr. RIGBY, when Pay-master General [1768–1782], is said to have cleared 50,000*l.* in one year by his perquisites, &c. But Mr. BURKE's Bill of Oeconomy has reduced the profits more than three-fifths. . . .

BROOK WATSON, Esq. whose experience justly entitles him to the appointment of Commissary General for the Forces abroad, will certainly be no loser by the calamities of War, notwithstanding his uncommon efforts of Patriotism. One of his predecessors in *Germany*, the late Sir LAURENCE DUNDAS, cleared nearly half a million; and the late Mr. TAYLOR, who died miserably in the Fleet Prison some few years ago, is reported to have had claims against Government to the amount of 700,000*l.* sterling. But the last Gentleman had not influence to obtain a final settlement, and perished in jail almost unnoticed.

These paragraphs were a typically Sheridanesque performance: blistering criticism and scathing exposés masquerading as commendation. Steele and Ryder had been appointed Paymasters General in February, 1791, after careers which "[challenged] the tongue of calumny" indeed. Steele had been Joint Secretary of the Treasury with Rose from 1783 to 1791, when he was removed because of scandals connected with the 1788 elections. Ryder had been Under-secretary for the Foreign Office during 1789 and 1790, a member of the Privy Council in 1790, Comptroller of the Household from 1790 to 1791, and he was still Vice-President of the Board of Trade, to which post he had also been appointed in 1790. Ryder had been much in the news during the King's illness of 1788–1789 because of his services for the Queen and William Pitt. The reference to Burke's "Bill of Oeconomy" was another sarcasm, since this legislation had been ignored for years. The only "experience" which qualified Watson for his new assignment was the chairmanship of the Commons' committee on the Regency Bill, and for this he had been rewarded well in advance. His wife had been getting a pension of £500 a year since 1783, and he himself had been a director of the Bank of England since 1784.

Although seemingly unaware of the jibes in the *Oracle*, Pitt was not unaware of the popular reaction toward the war, for much of his speech of 11 March was another attempt to show that the war was "just and necessary." This time he dealt in generalities. The nation was fighting, he said, to defend "a beloved monarch," a "constitution which is the source of our pride and the cause of our happiness," a "religion which our ancestors professed, and on which we rest our hopes of felicity," and "our liberties and privileges as an independent state." He apologized profusely for any "inconvenience" the war might cost the people and sincerely hoped it would be slight. He expected to continue his "funding" of the national debt, he said, he did not expect to increase taxes, although he could not reduce them either, and he saw no reason that "commerce" should not continue to "flourish." The budget amounted to something over £11,000,000, some £3,000,000 of which he intended to raise by loans, partly from the "Commissioners" in charge of the fund "for paying the national debt," partly from private individuals. He stressed the fact that he had represented the situation at its worst. Because of possible unforeseen expenses, he had estimated each item "at a very high average," and, because of possible unforeseen "misfortunes," he had supposed that the war might last four years. He felt, for example, that perhaps 45,000 seamen would not be enough and that the present "allowance of 4l. a month per man" might prove inadequate. But the outcome of the war was certainly in no doubt: 12,000 Hanoverians were now "being taken into British pay," with the expectation that "other foreign forces" would be added to them, and, without going into the matter "much at length," he might mention that there was a vast difference between France and Britain in "internal government and sources of revenue." The last half of the speech was addressed to Fox, who, Pitt remembered, had once said that "the only, or almost the only ground on which war ought to be undertaken was, to vindicate national honour." This war, Pitt told him, was unique in that it had been undertaken for just that reason. The lecture covered much the same ground as Pitt had covered earlier in the speech, but the tone was mild and even respectful.

Sheridan, the first to respond, supported the budget, but was uneasy about Pitt's intention of employing other "foreign mercenaries," and he regretted that Pitt should have deluded the people with optimism respecting "trade and manufactures," which would of course suffer, he said, both in Britain and elsewhere. He concluded his speech with some advice, namely, that, before the Commons "lay a new burthen of a single shilling on the people," the Members "[scrutinize] . . . all useless places, and reversionary sinecures," for the people might like to know, he said, that "all unnecessary expences and unmerited stipends" have been abolished before the Commons "applies to their pockets." In light of the *Oracle*'s exposés of that morning, the advice amounted to a threat. Fox also supported the budget. He was in fact relieved, he said, to discover that Pitt meant to finance the war "on a large scale," for, since the country was engaged in it, it should certainly "provide for [its] vigorous prosecution." Fox's objections were essentially those already voiced by Sheridan. He disliked the mention of other "foreign forces" and possible alliances, he felt that the inevitable damage to "trade and commerce" should have been admitted, and he pointed out that failure to reduce taxes when a reduction had been promised amounted to increasing them. He also had a great deal to say on the inclusion of revenues from the East India Company, the charter of which had not yet been renewed. As to the "justice" and "necessity" of the war, he knew only that whatever Britain was fighting for could more quickly, more certainly, and more humanely have been gained by negotiations.

There was no immediate comment on Fox's speech, but the *Public Advertiser* of 12 March commented obliquely on Sheridan's: "The good sense and virtue of this country must look with honest indignation upon all those persons, who, in the present state of it, propose Reforms of Parliament, or impede the operations of Government, by impotent, yet spiteful attacks upon its powers.—They must look upon them in the same light, both as to sense and to honesty, as upon a surgeon, who, employed to cut a patient for the stone, should bestow his time and attention upon a small pimple that happened to have made its appearance upon the sufferer's body." There was more of this on 14 March: "Sunk and degraded as a certain faction are, in the opinion of all rational and honest men, it is astonishing that they can persevere in proposing measures that only tend to render them still more odious and insignificant in the eyes of their country. . . ." *The Times* agreed. "Messrs. Fox and Sheridan made but a lame business of their remarks on the Budget," it observed. "They *limped* when they came to the *test*, and *halted* through inability to proceed in their charges against the maladministration of the present Cabinet." The *Oracle* was silent, but the *Morning Chronicle* compensated with some really telling sarcasms. "To ease as much as possible the public burthens in carrying on the war, Mr. Secretary Dundas is to contribute the whole of his emoluments as Treasurer of the Navy," it announced. "Lord Grenville [will contribute] the annual produce of all his sinecure places. Mr. Rose, his fees, as Clerk of the Parliaments. The Duke of Richmond the accumulated produce at compound interest of his salary, since he was first appointed Master General of the Ordnance; and Lord Loughborough, the difference between his income as Chancellor, and Chief Justice of the Common Pleas." The Traitorous Correspondence Bill was introduced on the following day.

The Traitorous Correspondence Bill

On 1 December, 1792, the King had "proved" that a state of insurrection existed by calling out the militia; on 19 December the Government had "proved" that the Constitution was threatened by French *émigrés* by introducing the Alien Bill. On 12 March, 1793, the Attorney General, Sir John Scott, announced that he would shortly move "that leave be given to bring in a bill more effectually to prevent during the war, all Traitorous Correspondence with, or Aid or Assistance being given to, His Majesty's Enemies"; and it was clear enough from the *Public Advertiser* that the same old trick was to be employed again. If there was to be a Traitorous Correspondence Bill, that paper said in effect on 14 March, then there must be traitorous correspondence:

> The proposed Bill of the Attorney General for preventing any treasonable correspondences between disaffected individuals in this country, and our detestable enemies abroad, is likely to prove an admirable supplement to that act

[the Alien Act] which drove a tribe of incendiaries out of the kingdom. This measure is a proof that Ministers are vigilant at their posts; and we doubt not that they have good reasons for what they are about, as there are wretches in this country who would seize all opportunities in order to furnish our foes with intelligence that might . . . be turned to the prejudice of their country, though these wretches dare assume the sacred name of *patriots*.

Inasmuch as Fox had been accused of corresponding with the French since the beginning of the year, he was obviously one of the "wretches," and anyone who read the *True Briton* during this period knew that the Friends of the People were the others. "Mr. GREY and Mr. SHERIDAN seemed *alarmed* at the notice of the ATTORNEY-GENERAL on Tuesday evening, of his intention to bring in a Bill to prevent *treasonable Correspondence*," it sneered typically on 14 March. "*Why* should those Gentlemen be alarmed? SURE they are *honourable* men./ It cannot be supposed, that the Bill to be brought in . . . can have any reference to the conduct of certain persons calling themselves the *Friends of the People*, or the *Friends of the French*, or by some such name—Unless those Gentlemen *betray* themselves, by putting themselves forward as the objects of the Bill, we shall certainly not accuse them." Bowles, who always readied pamphlets for such occasions, was in this instance a day late, *The Real Grounds of the Present War with France. By John Bowles* being advertised on 16 March. But this lack was more than compensated by a notice in *Lloyd's Evening Post* and other newspapers of 15 March: "Yesterday stocks rose upwards of Three per cent. The principal reason for this great rise, was the account of the Declaration of War by France against Spain." The declaration was dated 7 March.

As it turned out, the Traitorous Correspondence Bill was a trick within a trick, for, although all Ministerial newspapers had repeatedly and positively stated that the bill would have to do with letters, Sir John Scott opened his speech of 15 March by announcing that this was not the case: that he was using the term "correspondence" only in the "legal sense." The bill would not interfere with the exchange of letters, he said, since such interference would disrupt "commercial communication," and it would certainly introduce no innovation in "principle." It would merely clarify the "statute of the 25th Edw. 3rd," which was the basis for the present law of treason, by bringing it into line with subsequent statutes or by specifying what was already implicit in its "spirit," as defined by Sir Matthew Hale. In brief, the bill would prohibit the sale or delivery of any articles, military or otherwise, which could be used by the French army; it would prohibit the purchase of French lands or French funds; it would prohibit travel from Britain to France unless the travel was licensed by the King and travel from France to Britain unless the traveler possessed a "passport" or a "license"; and it would prohibit the insuring of any vessels passing to and from France. The motion was supported by Frederick North; it was opposed by Fox, Erskine, and Curwen.

Erskine protested that Hale was a very questionable authority, since, by ignoring the element of "intention," he had completely misunderstood the "spirit" of the law. He also protested that Scott had presented no evidence to justify the bill: "Has the Attorney General a single indictment against any one person now depending?" he asked. "Has he even any well-founded suspicion that treason anywhere exists?" But in fact the bill seemed to have only three objectionable features. It enabled Pitt to banish for the duration of the war all British subjects who were currently in France; it supposedly complicated the financial affairs of Lord Lauderdale, who, it was thought, owned considerable property in that country; and it was misnamed. As Fox said, there was no reason to call it a "Traitorous Correspondence Bill" except for the effect of the term "correspondence" on the people; and he would therefore charge that the bill was introduced "with no other view than to disseminate through the country false and injurious ideas of the existence of a correspondence between some persons and France." To this Scott replied that, whenever "the Constitution" was involved, Fox seemed to be upset, as if he had "a consciousness of something." The bill was thereupon read. It was again read on 21 March, and the House was in committee on 22, 26, and 28 March and on 4 April. After some debate on 8 April, it passed the Commons on 9 April. The most tumultuous sessions were those of 21 and 22 March.

The debates of 21 March began with another speech by Curwen, who opposed the bill on the ground that it jeopardized British commercial interests, another speech by Frederick North, who liked to misrepresent himself as a sudden convert to the Government's point of view, a speech by Maitland, who was obviously intent on protecting Lord Lauderdale's investments, and a speech by Fox. It seemed to Fox that this was a bill which "every good Whig, as a Whig, must heartily reprobate," and, as far as he could ascertain, "every good Whig" did, for "no bill has ever been brought into Parliament which is more unpopular." On behalf of the people, he objected to every part of it as either "ineffectual, impolitic, or tyrannical," and he especially objected to its being "hurried through the House" before the people could object for themselves. Fox was answered by Pitt and Sir John Scott, who were in turn answered by Sheridan: although the *True Briton* of that morning had addressed a long letter to him, signed "MILES," the purport of which was that he should keep quiet, and the *Public Advertiser* had backed this advice with some threats. Sheridan agreed with Fox that the bill was "a foul calumny" on "the people of this country," and, like Erskine, he challenged the Attorney General to "name one man he suspects." But no, said Sheridan, the Attorney General will say only that there must be an "evil," since he has a "remedy." It seemed to Sheridan that "hypocrisy" and "deception" had been the stock in trade of the present Government, but the people were becoming weary of the "stale attempts" to "delude" them: "Ministers begin to feel that the story of seditions, and all the trade of the alarmists, begin to flag, and therefore this bill is brought in to revive the delusion. . . ."

On 22 March Grey voiced his personal objections to the title and preamble of the bill, both of which "[imply] that there are among His Majesty's subjects some dangerous mal-contents, who aim at the . . . complete overthrow of our constitution." Fox concurred. In addition, he said, he was tired of hearing that the Government was defending the Constitution, when it was in fact subverting it at every opportunity; and, "if the Constitution . . . is to be destroyed," he concluded, "I do not care whether its overthrow comes from France, or origin-ates at home. I will support Ministers in carrying on the war, but I will not agree to undermine the Constitution [by supporting their legislation]." It was almost a convention that Burke would attack Fox and be flailed in return by Sheridan. Hence Burke's rising to reply to Fox's last several speeches could have surprised no one. Burke began by applauding the bill and the "wisdom" of the Ministers for having thought of it, and he proceeded to disagree with the statement that "every good Whig" ought to "reprobate" it. A "Whig," said Burke, was a man who, "on any public misunderstanding," would support "the aristocracy and democracy of the country. . . . A Tory was a person who [favored] on all occasions the prerogative of the Crown." Whether one should be a Whig or a Tory depended on the circumstances, and, when the Constitution was threatened by mobs, every man, it seemed to Burke, should want to be a Tory. Fox had suggested that the Government had been "remiss" in dealing with enemies of the state. Burke agreed. But "a little rest from the fatigues of business," he said, "is as necessary to the body politic as to the body natural": "Sleep [the sister of death] is a cessation of all our faculties. It is a relaxation which infuses into the vital stamina a new portion of health and vigour, and enables all the members to exert their various functions with a greater impulse and effect." Fox had further suggested that the present bill "implies and requires that a man should surrender part of his natural rights to obtain those that belong to society." Here, too, Burke agreed; but surrenders of this kind were sometimes necessary. He agreed that the bill gave the Ministers "unusual powers," and he even agreed that the Ministers might misuse them. But misuse of powers was, he thought, "infinitely preferable to the situation we must be in if Dumourier and his barbarians are to come amongst us," to usurp the Government, to murder the King, to destroy the Constitution, and to introduce their "*Visite Domiciliare,*" their "*Tribunal Revolutionnaire,*" and their "*Douce Fraternité.*" Burke concluded on a personal note. Although he had no objection to an Opposition, he said, there was "a considerable difference between a well-tempered vigilance and watchfulness, which calmly point out to an administration the error of their plans . . . and a frivolous, cavilling, vexatious, petulant faction, which thwart every thing from obstinacy, peevishness, and envy. Whether the conduct of certain gentlemen bear a greater resemblance to the one or the other of these, I will leave it to the country to judge." It was now Sheridan's turn.

Sheridan thanked Burke heartily for his speech, congratulated him on his "eloquence," and expressed great admiration for "his wit, his mirth, and humour," even though Burke had "applied" them to "subjects which do not perhaps call for either," such as "wars, treasons, murders, and massacres." These sarcasms over, Sheridan reviewed the speech word by word. To begin with, said Sheridan, the speech supposed that there was a conspiracy against the Constitution; if there was no conspiracy, the whole thing was a network of "deceptions." "And how actually stand facts with respect to sedition in this country?" he asked. "Why, I believe there is one editor of a newspaper [Sampson Perry] who has been frightened by Ministers, and has run away; an attorney [John Frost] is under prosecution on a charge for which he has given bail, and a bill-sticker [Mr. Carter] is in gaol. These are the mighty proofs of the whole country being in a state of insurrection!" As to Burke's "observations . . . on the necessity of rights remaining in a state of inaction for a long time, that they may require new vigour, and the simile of sleep to the body natural being the same as inactivity for a time to the body politic," no one can doubt, said Sheridan, that the simile "is beautiful enough, and applicable too, for the Minister has often sung a sort of lullaby to the Constitution." But "sleep" is still "the sister of death, and, . . . although a human being may sleep to recover his health," rights, once suspended, are likely to remain suspended.

Sheridan hoped indeed that "French principles can be avoided; but if in resisting the new, we incline to imitate the old system of government in France, we shall have no reason to congratulate each other upon our prudence. If we hate anarchy, it is not necessary that we fly from it into the arms of despotism." At present, it seemed to Sheridan, the Government was adopting the worst of both systems. The "*visite domiciliare*," which so horrified Burke, was already standard procedure with The Association. Burke might see, without leaving London, "the *visites domiciliares* thriving wonderfully under the auspices of Mr. Reeves, and the society of which he is so worthy a president: as also under Mr. Luke Ideson, and Sir Joseph Banks. These gentlemen, by themselves and agents, particularly the latter, have entered into a great number of houses, and have called upon the occupiers of them to give in a particular description of their inmates, the sex, the age, the stature, the colour, the complexion. Sir Joseph particularly has examined into these circumstances, with all the curiosity of a naturalist." Why, finally, Burke should be so "peevish" about the Opposition, Sheridan did not know, for "gentlemen have . . . gone over to the Minister in such numbers, that there is not room for them all." Sheridan was succeeded by George Hardinge, Member for Old Sarum, who declared, in the course of a very tiresome speech: "With respect to commerce, I will cut the knot and say, 'Let it perish,' if to keep it alive the war must be fed by the expenditure of more blood." But, by some quirk or other, the declaration was subsequently credited to Windham, who was supposed more specifically to have said, "Perish commerce! Let the Constitution live!"

It was Fox's understanding (21 Mar.) that the Traitorous Correspondence Bill was to be rushed through Parliament as speedily as possible, but this was not the case. After 22 March the debates were spaced, jumping from 22 March to 26 March, from 26 March to 28 March, and from 28 March to 4 April. Since, except for Burke and members of Government, no one of any prominence had spoken up for the bill, it seemed to be as "unpopular" as Fox had said it was, and the delays gave Pitt an opportunity to rally his forces and to revise his campaign. On 26 March the Ministerial newspapers announced publication of a pamphlet by Alexander Dalrymple, Hydrographer to the Admiralty, entitled *Mr. Fox's Letter to his Worthy and Independent Electors of Westminster, fully Considered in a Letter to a Friend*; and on 28 March the *St. James's Chronicle* reported that "Messrs. ERSKINE and MINGAY, it is said, are about to relinquish the sweets of the English bar for the tranquil liberty of the American States." But Dalrymple's pamphlet was primarily a defense of the war, and Erskine and Mingay were identified with the Friends of the Liberty of the Press rather than the Friends of the People. Fox and the Friends of the People, who had once been represented as the only reason for the bill, were now ignored, and the legislation was justified on strictly legal grounds. The Ministerial papers had nothing to say about Fox's speeches or even Sheridan's. The Opposition papers had something to say about Burke's.

"Mr. BURKE's idea of passing the Traitorous Correspondence Bill, in order to give an *opiate to the Constitution*, must be very consoling to the people, and particularly to the Associators," the *Morning Chronicle* remarked on 25 March. "It is probable too, that by repeating the dose, the Constitution may soon sleep the sleep of death." And on 27 March: "The Ministerial Papers learn of Mr. BURKE to talk of plots and conspiracies, and correspondence with the enemy, as fluently as if they knew of any such practices. They forget that their great leader, after all his denouncings, and the repeated calls upon him for proofs, has never been able to produce any./ Even Mr. Chairman REEVES, with all the secret powers of his inquisition, has never been able to detect a single traitor; and the whole effect of his researches, except the encouragement given to anonymous slander, has hitherto been to frighten poor publicans and ignorant bill stickers." Burke was also assailed by the *Oracle*, which on 1 April printed a letter from Dr. Priestley, denying that he had sanctioned any correspondence between the English Revolution Society and the Jacobin clubs. The letter was dated 7 March and was a reply to Burke's charges of 4 March. Although the *Oracle* was purporting to defend both the Alien Act and the Traitorous Correspondence Bill, the defense as usual left something to be desired. On 3 April, for example, the paper concluded some remarks on the wisdom of the Alien Act with an attack on an "*affected* and *malignant* writer, himself a CLERGYMAN, [who] is labouring to incite hatred against the unhappy EMIGRANTS, who, bred to the sacred function, have among us no manual occupations, and are therefore blamelessly poor." The "CLERGYMAN" was probably the Rev. Robert Nares.

On 22 March, according to the newspapers (on 2 April, according to later accounts), Dundas married Jean Hope, sixth daughter of John Hope, second Earl of Hopetoun; and on 26 March, according to the *Star*, he was "chosen Governor of the Bank of Scotland." These were less happy days for William Pitt. On 5 April he settled the year-old problem at the Post Office by retiring John Palmer, as the *Oracle* had discovered by 16 April, "upon a pension of 3000*l.* per annum"; but he had not settled the problem of Lord Rawdon's Debtor and Creditor Bill. The introduction of the bill in late February had been followed by another rash of disbarments, and on 6 March the *True Briton* announced that the legal profession was purged and the bill was unnecessary: "The *Wig* Club having lost, at one cut, eighteen of its most ornamental Curls, is now degraded to a mere Scratch, with a Tyburn Top." Pitt was working from another angle. The person most likely to influence Lord Rawdon was the Prince of Wales, and, from early March on, the newspapers reported that Pitt was frequently at Carlton House. The visits achieved nothing, for on 27 March the Lords listened to a second reading of the bill and another speech by Lord Rawdon.

The purpose of the bill, said Lord Rawdon, was to distinguish between the "fraudulent agent" and the innocent debtor: between what should be regarded as a "crime" and what should be regarded as a "misfortune." The bill was also an attempt to standardize practices. As the law now stood, "the creditor is enabled to deprive the debtor of his liberty, upon a simple swearing to the debt." If the affidavit was submitted to the Court of Common Pleas, the debtor might "enlarge" himself without bail by submitting a counteraffidavit; if it was submitted to the Court of King's Bench, bail was required, and the bail was always fixed at "double the debt sworn to." Once arrested, a man could not adjust his affairs by paying the debt, for he was now subject to "fees of office," which might well be considerably more than the original debt. It had already been discovered, said Lord Rawdon, that most of the persons arrested were arrested for debts under £20 and that approximately 150 were imprisoned annually, "not because they have not paid their creditors the debts which were due to them, and for which they were originally arrested, but because they have not money sufficient to pay the [costs]." His bill would "prevent all arrests for less than 20*l.*," it would "prevent excessive bail from being required," it would prevent a prisoner's being "hurried to gaol when in a state of sickness and insanity," and it would compel the Government to publish monthly lists of "persons convicted of fraudulent transactions," so that the public would know who they were. The bill passed its second reading with great applause from the newspapers, especially from the *World*, which reminded its readers daily that no debtor was presently safe from the practices of "*Pettifogging* ATTORNIES." Pitt continued to confer with the Prince throughout March and April, but as usual the Prince seemed to be faring better than he. By late March the newspapers understood that Pitt was effecting a reconciliation between the Prince and his father, and on 6 April the *St. James's Chronicle* mentioned that the Prince would "reside at Windsor Castle during the time that his regiment does duty at the Royal Regiment." By mid-April he was back in the bosom of his family, and newspapers were expecting some announcement about his debts.

Having failed to quash the Debtor and Creditor Bill and having overplayed his hand with respect to the Traitorous Correspondence Bill, Pitt ran into further trouble with his economic program. It had seemed to the *Morning Chronicle* that he had decided to finance the war by loans because he was afraid the people would refuse to finance it by taxes. The *Morning Chronicle* disapproved of this plan, and so evidently did the speculators, for the economy, which was already in a bad state, took a turn for the worse as a result of the debate on the budget. The market fell sharply, the number of bankruptcies soared to several times their pre-war average, and unemployment rose. On 21 March the *Morning Chronicle* introduced a long editorial on the subject of Pitt's economics with the announcement: "Another Banking-house in this city yesterday stopt payment. The dreadful consequence of the war, for which the Jesuitical authors of the delusion that has involved us in it care nothing, is swelling to such a sum of calamity as never was known in the memory of man. The first question now asked is, What houses have stopt to-day? And we are sorry to say, that for three weeks past, no one day has the question been answered with a negative./ Already by these bankruptcies two millions of people, artisans, manufacturers, and labourers, are thrown out of all employment." The *Oracle* of 27 March denied that the bankruptcies resulted from the war, although it admitted that the market had taken a dive and that the country bankers, who had invested with "the property of the Consumers," had been forced "to sell out at the loss of 15 or 20 per cent." The *Public Advertiser* also denied it, the denials being furnished by Lord Mountmorres.

But the loan troubled even the *Public Advertiser*. "There will be a meeting, by appointment, of the monied men, this day, at the house of the Chancellor of the Exchequer, in Downing-street, to settle the terms of the new Loan," it announced on 18 March. "The ensuing Loan will be a circumstance entirely *nouvelle* in the annals of financiering. . . . [Millions] to be borrowed for public service, and no new taxes to be laid on the subject to defray the interest thereof! It has the appearance of something paradoxical to those who do not know, or will not acknowledge, the eminent talents of the present Chancellor of the Exchequer as a Financier." On 20 March the *Public Advertiser* reported that the meeting had occurred: "On Monday there was a meeting of the monied men at the house of the Chancellor of the Exchequer . . . , for the purpose of agreeing about the terms of the new Loan. The only gentlemen who attended this meeting, besides the Governor and Deputy Governor of the Bank, were Mess. Johnston, Angerstien, and Devaynes. We before stated it as our opinion, that the Bank would advance the money, which we are informed is the real fact. The terms . . . are not yet made public." The terms were evidently still unsettled, for on 26 March the *Morning Chronicle* published the following paragraphs:

THE LOAN.

Yesterday Mr. PITT agreed for the loan of 6,000,000*l.* of three per cents at 72, the price of that fund in the market being 77, which is a bonus to the Money-lenders of 300,000*l.* The Contractors are Messrs. ANGERSTIEN and JOHNSON, but they have lists in which a great number of the Minister's friends are included.

The Commissioners for liquidating the National Debt have no part of the loan, so that while the nation by this most improvident bargain is borrowing money at 72, they will be daily employed in buying at 77! If it should be asked why Mr. PITT has made this bargain so obviously against the true interests of the country, the answer is plain—*the loan is a good thing*, and is to be parcelled out among so many expectants that a million and a half could not be conveniently spared to the Commissioners!

If it were possible to procure a true list of the men who have the loan, (every thousand of which they might yesterday have sold for fifty pounds without advancing a shilling) we should see that those who had profited from the American war had not been so eager to break their honourable connections, and to involve the country in a new contest *without substantial reasons.*

The *Oracle* (28 Mar.) protested:

THE LOAN.

The Minister must naturally expect to have all the floodgates of abuse opened upon him, for the obvious disadvantage he laboured under in effecting the late Loan.—But all that could be done was done.—He left the supply open to com-petition, and naturally, the state of the market considered, expected more liberal offers. But the true fact is, that MONEY has been excessively rare, and the perilous state of paper currency makes our Houses of stability slow to part with the *Specie* which, when *discounts* can be had, must be their only resource.—Add to this, that the firmest Merchants cannot be without alarm, lest the circle of their own connection should be impaired, and unlooked-for demands be made for the support of their intimate friends.

If to the above obvious, and to us apologetic, reasons, we add the super-risk of Commerce in a time of war; the heavy *onus* of insurance and freight, so increasing always; the *paucity* of OFFERS will be no longer surprising, and the MINISTERS no longer *blamed.*

The *Oracle* pursued this curious argument on 29 March, and on 30 March the *Morning Chronicle* spoke out again:

THE LOAN.

We find a set of ready writers disposed to do that for Mr. PITT, which he could not do for himself—to find that his bargain was remarkably oeconomical. There are some simple facts in this transaction which we recommend to these ingenious gentlemen to explain.

1. There were originally three parties of bidders for the loan; here there was a competition, but instead of pursuing this advantage, and giving it to the lowest, by some means or other a *coalition was formed*, and they shared it among them. How did the auctioneer bring this about?

2. These parties had previously made application to their monied friends, and desired them to put down their names for such sums as they would agree to lend on the terms that might be agreed upon, trusting to them for good terms. After the bargain was made, and the coalition formed, these confiding men were cut down to a half or one third of their original sum, in consequence of the coalition and the reserve.

[3.] The Minister reserved one million seven hundred thousand of the loan *for the public companies*, as it was called. We will thank their advocates for a correct account of the distribution of this part of the loan.

4. Mr. PITT says it would have been highly injurious to the public if he had made a present saving of 160,000*l*. by giving 1,600,000*l*. of the loan to the Commissioners for Liquidating the National Debt—and yet he gave to the money-lenders the option of taking the whole loan, or of leaving this part of it to the Commissioners. We will thank these ready reasoners to conciliate Mr. PITT's practice with his argument.

5. Mr. PITT urges as the great reason for not making a better bargain, the difficulty of getting so large a sum at a time when money is so *scarce*. Will the same worthy friends of the Minister inform us why Mr. PITT, in such scarcity, preferred making the bargain for this *large* sum, when an Act of Parliament directed him *how to find more than a third of it*, without giving a single shilling out of the pockets of the public for premium?

These facts are of some consequence to the character of Mr. PITT as a Minister and a man. The public have not forgot the jobs of 1784 and 1785, when his only other operations in finance (except in the two hundred and odd new taxes that he has laid on the people) were done upon terms that cost the nation seven hundred thousand pounds more than they ought to have paid: we mean, the terms on which he funded the outstanding debt.

The loan was debated on 3 April. The debate reached its climax in a clash between Pitt and Fox, from which, it seemed to the *Oracle*, Pitt emerged victor. "Mr. Fox and his puny Party have not been very parsimonious of their invectives against Mr. PITT for the terms of the Loan. They, forsooth, insinuated, that, had they been in power, the public money would not have been lavished away with such criminal prodigality.—'*Eight* per cent. for a Loan, when money might have been obtained at five or six!...' This was the impudent language of OPPOSITION. But ... Mr. PITT completely silenced the clamour, by calling to their recollection, that, when Mr. Fox was last in power, a Loan was made at the extravagant terms of ELEVEN *per cent!*" Other newspapers ignored the clash, the *Public Advertiser* (also 4 April) stating only that Pitt was "not to blame in that business of the loan, because he could not effect the bargain upon better terms in these critical times."

It looked for a while as if Pitt's luck had deserted him altogether, for, in addition to everything else, the papers continued to be filled with accounts of French triumphs. On 18 March the *Oracle* reported that within ten days General Dumouriez had captured Breda, Klundert, and Gertruydenberg, and it now seemed likely that Williamstadt had also capitulated. On 25 March it reported that Dumouriez had made himself Commander-in-Chief, that he now had eighty thousand men, and that on 13 March he had defeated the Austrians, commanded by the Prince of Saxe-Coburg. There were also persistent rumors of the execution of Marie Antoinette. The Ministerial newspapers repeated that the war was unavoidable, and, to support this statement, they announced on 23 March the "speedy" publication of a pamphlet, entitled *Alfred's [Burges's] Letters; or, A Review of the Political State of Europe, to the End of the Summer 1792. As Originally Published in The Sun*. They could report, too, that the press of seamen was going along nicely, the press gangs, according to *Lloyd's Evening Post* (25 Mar.), having been especially successful at Newcastle, Shields, and Sunderland. By 28 March the picture had changed. The picture had actually changed much earlier. The victories in Holland had been costly, and on 8 March General Dumouriez had been recalled to explain the losses. On 14 March there had been the first revolt in La Vendée, there was disaffection in Lyons, Marseille, and Normandy, and General Dumouriez, returning to find his forces demoralized, had been defeated by the Prince of Saxe-Coburg at Neerwinden on 18 March. Already at odds with the Convention and fearing that all was lost, Dumouriez had commenced negotiations with the Prince on 22 March, had denounced the Convention and threatened to block supplies to Paris on 23 March, and on 24 March had pulled his troops out of Brussels. On 25 March he had concluded a secret treaty with the Austrians, agreeing to evacuate The Netherlands altogether. While the evacuation, which was completed by 31 March, was in progress, he was making further threats against the French, but he had lost the support of the soldiers, and, when he finally defected to the Austrians on 4 April, only a few of them joined him.

Readers of newspapers learned of these developments slowly and, to say the least, imperfectly. On 28 March the *Morning Chronicle* reported that the French had been driven out of Holland and that Breda and Gertruydenberg had already surrendered to the Austrians. On 29 March the *Oracle* announced that the Austrians were expected to capture Ostend that day and that Dumouriez had been seriously wounded and was now a prisoner of the Austrians in Brussels. On 30 March it stated that he was not a prisoner, that he had got heavy reinforcements from Brussels and Antwerp, was occupying a strong position, but seemed nevertheless to be evacuating Holland and the Belgic provinces. It did not know why. It had also heard that on 18 March he had been defeated by the Austrians "near Tirlemont, at Neer-Landen," the French having lost "6000–10,000 men, killed; Austrians 4000–5000," and that civil war was expected hourly in Paris. On 4 April the *Morning Chronicle* and the *Oracle*, the latter supposedly a specialist in foreign news, reported that "The Netherlands may now be considered as entirely evacuated by the French." In addition, said the *Oracle*, Lord Elgin had reached Vienna, and "a Treaty between *England* and *Germany* may soon be expected." The Government had already (25 Mar.) signed a treaty with Russia, but of this the newspapers knew nothing. On 5 April there was a spate of news. According to the *Oracle*, Dumouriez had again been defeated, and the Royalists had risen, had subdued the whole province of Brittany, and had taken Orleans. According to the *Morning Chronicle*, Paris was in a state of utmost confusion and might even be under siege. It had in fact been under siege, said the *Morning Chronicle* on 8 April, General Dumouriez having marched on the capital with all his troops. The *Oracle* elaborated:

COUNTER REVOLUTION IN FRANCE.

The Lords of the Admiralty received an express on Saturday morning [6 April] from Admiral McBride, with the important intelligence that General DU-MOURIER had stated to the NATIONAL CONVENTION that the Combined Powers were an irresistible force; that they had refused to treat with any but a Crowned Head, and that it therefore became absolutely necessary to proclaim Louis XVII. The NATIONAL CONVENTION immediately sent six Commissioners to arrest DUMOURIER, who having had notice of their intention, assembled and harangued his Army, submitting to them what he had done, and calling upon them for their support.—The troops unanimously declared that they would stand by him— tore the three-coloured Cockade from their hats, and mounted the white. DU-MOURIER then seized the six Commissioners, and after sending them as hostages to CLAIRFAIT, instantly marched towards *Paris*.

This story was absolutely confirmed by the *Oracle* of 9 April and even 10 April, although by 10 April the *Oracle* understood that Dumouriez had only two French regiments with him, the remainder being Austrian. The *Morning Chronicle* knew only that "DUMOURIER is said to have been persuaded to change sides by the *ambi-dexter* [*sic*] negotiations of Lord Auckland."

Passage of the
Traitorous Correspondence Act

When the Traitorous Correspondence Bill was introduced, the war seemed to be going badly for the Allies; by 28 March it seemed to be going well. The faster the war was over, the more popular it was likely to be; yet, with victory apparently on the threshold, there was no justification for the Traitorous Correspondence Bill. This fact seems to explain the Government's continuing silence about developments on the Continent, for Pitt must certainly have known more about them than the newspapers indicated. The Traitorous Correspondence Bill had proved to be a blunder in any event, for, although the Commons could be counted on to support the war and oppose reformers, it had demonstrated a reluctance to support legislation so obviously intended as a censure of the Friends of the People and, much more importantly, Fox. The reluctance persisted, for the speakers during the last days of the debates were essentially the same as those during the earlier ones. There was one exception. Sheridan, who had been Fox's right-hand man during the earlier sessions, was silent from 4 April on; and, from 4 through 9 April, the *Oracle* was enthusiastically on the side of Pitt and bitterly censorious of Fox. That the Prince of Wales had something to do with these changes was suggested by the *Oracle* itself, which declared on 5 April, for example:

> Mr. PITT is a frequent visitor at Carlton-House.—This *looks* like business; and of the *right* tendency!
> The PRINCE, whose *constant* devotion to Mrs. FITZHERBERT has been the *routine* of many years, now passes *all his time* in the society of that Lady, to whom he appears *more attached* than ever.
> Brighton and Kempshot will feel the loss of the PRINCE the ensuing Summer!
> —His Royal Highness's new residence [Sir Horace Mann's house in Bourne] will, no doubt, among the Kentish Belles, produce many a "Canterbury Tale."—But his Royal Highness's *motto* is—"Constancy and Honour."

If the negotiations did turn out to be "business," Sheridan and Mrs. Fitzherbert meant to be part of it.

Despite Sheridan's silence, the Government had to yield on several points in order to get the bill passed at all. Although Scott had stated that it was to be applicable to Ireland as well as Great Britain, the Commons had on 28 March limited it to Great Britain; and on 4 April the clause preventing the return of British subjects from France without the King's license was deleted altogether. Scott consented to the deletion on the ground that the same effect could be achieved by Royal proclamation and that the King had already turned back by such proclamation "certain persons lately arrived from France at Dover." Whitbread and Fox immediately protested that the King had no power to "hinder the return of a man to his native country," and Fox demanded a "canvas" of the Dover incident: "I am justly alarmed for the liberties of this country," he said, "when such exploded doctrines upon the King's prerogatives are attempted to be revived." This debate was cut short by Pitt, who, having said a few words about the "principle" of "proclamations," dismissed further comment on the subject as irrelevant. On 8 April the Opposition moved to insert a clause entitling offenders to regular trials. Although the motion was defeated by a vote of 110 to 32, too many Members were abstaining to make the vote meaningful.

On 9 April the Traitorous Correspondence Bill was read for the last time. The event was celebrated with no new pamphlets, but the *Morning Herald* did publish a third letter from John King to Thomas Paine. This one began, "SIR./

You told Mr. ——, that you would not continue a correspondence with a man, who had changed principles. . . . Though you may be for ever silent, I shall persist in writing, that you may see I condemn anarchy as much as I love freedom"; and most of it was a condemnation of reformers, all of it justified on patriotic grounds: "I am of no party, Mr. PAINE; I am only for my country. . . ." The letter was dated 9 April and, like the others, was reissued as a pamphlet, being entitled *Third Letter from Mr. King to Mr. Thomas Paine, at Paris* (Egham and London). According to the colophon, the second letter was now in its thirteenth edition. Fox, who led the opposition, hoped that the various amendments would not induce the House to accept the bill, for he objected personally to almost every clause in it. In particular, he objected to indicting on evidence of intention and to the elimination of regular trials. As the text now stood, he said, a man who merely agreed to deliver certain articles to France or who merely agreed to purchase an estate in that country was guilty of treason and could return "to his native land" only on penalty of death. He concluded his speech by deploring the absence of Erskine, who had been called away on business; but he "consoled" himself "with reflecting, that I have discharged my duty to my country in giving the present bill every opposition in my power." Burke also regretted Erskine's absence, but he "consoled" himself with the "reflection" that Erskine was doing his duty as he saw it: defending the enemies of his country and filling his pockets with money. As to Fox's speech, he said, it "resembled more a prize declamation at a university than the substantial arguments of a statesman," but he would nevertheless reply to it. The reply consisted of a long lecture on the nature of the Constitution, the function of law, and the history of the law of treason. The bill passed the Commons by a single vote: 154 to 153. It still had to be approved by the Lords.

King's letter to Paine was a reminder that the Traitorous Correspondence Bill was necessitated by the activities of certain reformers. There was another reminder in the *True Briton* of 10 April. "Mr. BURKE last night clearly proved, that the objects of the Opposition to the *Traitorous Correspondence Bill* were frivolous and ill-founded," said that newspaper. "—The anxiety of the Faction to prevent the passing of this Bill, proves, indeed, that they have *particular* reasons for the opposition which they give to it." Since no member of the "faction" had been accused of selling supplies to the French and, except for Lord Lauderdale, not one of them had been accused of owning property in France, the *True Briton* was referring to actual "*Correspondence*," hoping that its readers would infer the content of the bill from its title. The *True Briton*'s admiration of Burke was by no means shared by the *Morning Chronicle*. "Mr. BURKE, who has given no assistance in amending the Traitorous Correspondence Bill in the committee, came down yesterday to make a speech in its defence on the third reading; and with his usual candour, he avowed his motive," the *Chronicle* remarked on 10 April. "He approved of the Bill because it tended to cut off all fellow feeling that might arise from intercourse or common interest, and to leave no sentiment but enmity between Great Britain and France." On 15 April the Opposition newspapers advertised *The Gallic Lion, or Modern Pandemonium: a Political Fable, dedicated by Permission to The Right Hon. Edmund Burke, M.P.* Although the author and printer were unnamed, this pamphlet was followed by a quick succession of similar pamphlets, written and published by the surgeon and paleontologist, James Parkinson: *Pearls Cast before Swine . . . Scraped together by Old Hubert; The Soldier's Tale . . . with . . . Words of Advice. By Old Hubert; The Budget of the People. Collected by Old Hubert;* and *An Address to the Honourable Edmund Burke. From the Swinish Multitude. By Old Hubert, Secretary.*

The fate of the Traitorous Correspondence Bill in the Lords was still in question. No newspaper suggested that either the Prince of Wales or the Duke of Clarence would support the legislation, but the Prince was at least behaving himself, and the Duke was finally, it appeared, going to "embark on the element of British Glory" as well. According to *Lloyd's Evening Post* of 12 April, "the Prince, it is now planned, is not to serve in the Kentish encampment, this year; with a view to which, his Royal Highness had taken Sir Horace Mann's house, at Bourn. As an establishment there would be very expensive, from the necessity of keeping a table that should be accessible to all the superior Company, his Majesty has been intreated to order the Prince's Regiment upon duty at Windsor, where his Royal Highness can have apartments in the Castle, and avoid all extraordinary expenditure." By 17 April *Lloyd's Evening Post* could report that "Apartments are now fitting up in the North West Wing of the Quadrangle of Windsor Castle, for the occasional summer residence of . . . the Prince of Wales." Similarly gratifying was an announcement in the *Star* of 11 April: "His Royal Highness the Duke of CLARENCE kissed the KING's hand, on receiving the command of the LONDON, of 98 guns, which is put into commission at Plymouth; his Royal Highness the Duke of CLARENCE is to hoist his flag on board her, as Rear-Admiral of the Channel fleet. Captain KEATS is appointed to the command of her." The Duke of Portland and his friends were now expected to oppose the bill, although their position had been doubtful. As the *Morning Chronicle* put it on 11 April: "The Ministerial papers have renewed their abuse of the Duke of PORTLAND—as it is part of their instructions to abuse every man who is not ready to support Ministers in every measure, they must have been very ill informed when they remitted their daily labours with respect to his Grace." But the Government could now count on two votes from Lord Stormont.

On 15 or 16 March, depending on which newspaper one read (actually, it appears, on 20 Mar.), the Earl of Mansfield died; there being "no issue," said *Lloyd's Evening Post* (20 Mar.), "Lord Stormont, his nephew, succeeds to the title and much of the property." The death was of little interest to the newspapers, partly because the Earl had been in retirement for years, partly because he had amassed almost nothing by way of honors and emoluments. But it was of great interest to Lord Stormont, for the title of Earl of Mansfield, County

Nottingham, passed to Lord Stormont's wife, Louisa, and her heirs, and the title of Earl of Mansfield, County Middlesex, was now his. Pitt, who was rarely mistaken in judgments of character, had prepared the elevation on 1 August, 1792, by arranging a second Earldom for the aged Earl of Mansfield "with sp. rem. to [his] nephew, Lord Stormont." Although Lord Stormont had been a follower of the late Earl of Guilford and was at that time still voting with the Opposition, he reversed his position on 13 December and had since labored hard in the Government's interests. The Earldom had evidently been only bait, for, sometime during this period, the new Earl was "elected" Chancellor of Marischal College, Aberdeen, which position had been vacated by the death of the third Earl of Bute in 1792, and appointed Joint Chief Clerk of the Pleas in the Court of King's Bench, the emoluments of the latter office being, according to the *Star* (9 Sept., 1796), £6,000 a year. He held both sinecures until his death. In addition, he was still Lord Justice General of Scotland and Keeper of the Scoon, from which "*places*," for they "are not," said the *Star*, "employments," he derived an additional £4,000 a year. If he was not worth all this to "the public," he was apparently worth it to Pitt, for, although he was now a peer in his own right and therefore no longer a Representative Peer, he voted as both. *Lloyd's Evening Post* was somewhat uneasy about this double voting. Now that the new Earl of Mansfield "has been seated, a vacancy of course happens for one of the sixteen Peers of Scotland," it mentioned on 12 April. The Government seemed to be unaware of a vacancy.

The Traitorous Correspondence Bill had its second reading in the Lords on 15 April, at which time it was supported by Lord Grenville, Lord Hawkesbury, and Lord Darnley and opposed by the Earl of Guilford, the Earl of Lauderdale, the Marquess of Lansdowne, the Duke of Norfolk, and the Earl of Kinnoull, the latter only because of the insurance clause. The Duke of Portland, who had heretofore said nothing, rose finally to state that he would "not oppose" the commitment of the bill, even though he found "several parts of it highly objectionable," especially "making the agreeing to do certain acts equally criminal with the acts themselves." As to legislation in general, he wanted to repeat that he would "give a fair and honourable support to the war, because I think it both just and necessary." What he seemed to be saying was that he would vote for the bill, provided it was altered to suit him, but it seemed to *The Times* of 17 April that he had given it "stout support," thus "[proving] to the world his strong opposition to the political principles of Mr. Fox."

While the bill was being tailored to the Duke of Portland's taste, the newspapers were adding their usual commentaries. "INFORMERS," observed the *Morning Chronicle* of 17 April with obvious reference to the speech of Lord Lansdowne. "Notwithstanding the great encouragement held out by Government, no plots against the State have yet been discovered. Are we from hence to suppose that informers are not as numerous as they were wont to be, or that they are ashamed of their employment?" "We are authorised to say, that Lord

LAUDERDALE was last Tuesday [16 April] in the House of Lords," the *True Briton* announced on 20 April. "The report, therefore, of his Lordship being gone on a visit of condolence to PHILLIPE EGALITÉ, is void of foundation." The French had established the first Committee of Public Safety on 6 April, and all the Ministerial newspapers hoped that the Duke of Orleans would be an early victim. There were other concerns. On 17 April the *Public Advertiser* attempted to demonstrate that bankruptcies, properly interpreted, were a sign of affluence. The *Morning Chronicle* was disgusted. "A Ministerial paper most facetiously undertakes to prove 'that the late failures, in almost every instance, are indicative of the prosperity and flourishing state of the country,'" it noticed on 18 April. "Such pleasantries are somewhat too refined for the comprehension of merchants and manufacturers." On 18 April the Society of Antiquaries met to award Fellowships to the deserving. Although the Duke of Norfolk was now (lifetime) president of that organization, the deserving turned out as usual to be friends of the Government or persons whose friendship the Government was hopeful of acquiring. Among the group on this occasion were Baron Mulgrave, who, since his succession to the title, had specialized in attacks on Erskine, and Lord Rawdon, who was obstinately sponsoring the Debtor and Creditor Bill.

On 18 April, too, the newspapers published Lord Auckland's Declaration and Memorial to the States General, executed on 5 April. The *Oracle* wanted Lord Auckland removed at once, and a motion to that effect, it told its readers, was already in the making. That afternoon Sheridan moved for a copy of the Memorial. The effect of this document, the Government seems to have hoped, would be offset by all the propagandistic sermons, since 19 April was the day appointed by the King for a general fast. The fast was not altogether a success. Except for the *Morning Chronicle*, which on 18 April published some sarcastic verses, "Hymn on the Fast: a Poem by G[eorge] Dyer, B.A.," the Opposition papers ignored the event, and the enthusiasm of the Ministerial newspapers was evidently effective only with members of The Association. "Yesterday being the day appointed for a *General Fast*, it was properly observed by all those who are friends to their country, and admirers of the *best Constitution in the world!*" reported the *Public Advertiser* on 20 April. Those who missed the sermons could have read long excerpts from them in any of the Ministerial newspapers of the next several days. Although the pious might have found something lacking, the sermons did prove that, in his feelings about the French, Lord Auckland was a piker compared with the Church of England. Daniel Stuart later collected some of the excerpts for his *Peace and Reform*[34] as examples of "the sentiments of our high church pastors: Such is the religion, the benevolence, the humanity, they teach! To exterminate for opinion. . . . To erase a whole nation from the earth!"

On the day following the fast (20 April), the Friends of the Liberty of the Press held another dinner. The attendance was estimated at between four and five hundred, Grey was in the chair, and Horne Tooke was very much in evidence. The question under debate was whether the £400 collected to defend freedom of the press should or should not be used "to resist the laws of libel." Tooke insisted that it should, but the company resolved to consider the matter at a later meeting. The *Oracle* gave the dinner two and one-half columns. The *True Briton* had some words of advice for Tooke. "Before Parson TOOKE attempts to break the LAW, because he may deem it a bad one, he had better ask a little good advice: he may have something round his neck not quite as heavy as a mill-stone, but at the same time very troublesome to the wearer," it cautioned on 23 April; and on 25 April it told its readers that "HORN [*sic*] TOOKE has quietly betaken himself to the country, for the purpose of studying more peaceably new plans of riot."

The Traitorous Correspondence Bill passed the Lords on 22 April. It had been altered somewhat. The "agreement to sell to the French a pair of old boots," as Lord Lansdowne had put it, was still treason, as so was the purchase of property in France, but the mere "agreement" to purchase property was not, and neither was the purchase of funds. In addition, as the *Star* mentioned on 19 April, "the Lords . . . have restored to the subject the ancient right of trial in cases of treason, which, as the bill was brought from the Commons, it completely took away." The passage of the bill in its amended state was evidently regarded as no triumph for anyone, since the newspapers hardly referred to it. By this time the issue was Lord Auckland's Memorial and Sheridan's forthcoming motion on that subject. The Memorial, dated 5 April, informed the Dutch that "Divine vengeance" was at hand: that the "detestable regicides" who remained in France would soon be destroyed by "famine, anarchy, and civil war" and that those who had fled could now be hunted down and exterminated. Auckland entreated the Dutch to do their duty. He reminded them that they had already promised to deny "asylum" to anyone who "directly or indirectly participated in the . . . crime"; he now exhorted them, in the name of "religion, morality, and humanity," to "deliver [the wretches] up to justice." The *True Briton* passionately supported every word Auckland had said, and it was infuriated with Sheridan.

On 25 April, nevertheless, Sheridan called for a reading of the document and went on to say that, although he had no "respect or esteem" for Lord Auckland as a person and regarded "the haughty, arrogant style" of his pronouncements as "inexcusable," he would confine himself to the content of the note by asking Ministers for "an explanation of the real intent, nature, purpose, and object of the war in which we are engaged." By the "treachery" of General Dumouriez, certain Commissioners of the National Convention had been turned over to the Austrians, and the British Government was now asking the Dutch to "murder" them. There had been divided notions as to the "necessity" and "justice" of the war, and various "objects" had been suggested by Pitt, but Pitt had not previously suggested that there was to be "a general massacre" of all French citizens or even of "all prisoners of war." If Pitt now believed that "about eight or nine millions of people, must be put to death, before we can negociate for peace,"

Sheridan begged him to be honest enough to say so. If this was to be strictly a "war of vengeance," Pitt might also be good enough to explain why Russia, Prussia, and Austria were not also being punished for their crimes against Poland. Sheridan concluded with a long motion, expressing the "displeasure of the House" at every sentiment enunciated in the Memorial.

Pitt purported to be astonished at the mildness of the motion, it having been his understanding that Sheridan would ask for Lord Auckland's "removal" and subsequent "impeachment." The war had not of course been "entered into" for reasons of "vengeance," he said, and yet a few examples of "vindictive justice" were not amiss, considering the "horror" of the crime of regicide. This country had gone to war because "France had declared war against this country": "our objects" then were "to repel her unjust attacks, and, if possible, to chastise and to punish her, and to obtain indemnification for the past, and security for the future." Pitt could not feel that the Memorial "affected" these objects; nor, for that matter, could he feel that the Memorial was very important, since the five Commissioners were not at present "in the custody of the Dutch" and were not likely to be so. If, however, any of the regicides tried to find refuge in the British Isles, Pitt did believe that "we ought to deliver them up to justice," that is, "to a competent tribunal." The thing which puzzled him most was that Sheridan, once a friend of Lord Auckland, should have thus maligned him, and he sincerely hoped that the motive was not personal animosity. Fox reassured him that Sheridan's motive was "his sense of public duty"; he further protested that Pitt had defended the Memorial only on the ground of "its meaning nothing at all." The motion was ultimately defeated by a vote of 211 to 36, but it was not ineffectual, for Lord Auckland was subsequently recalled. The comments in the Opposition newspapers relied heavily on Fox. "Lord AUCKLAND has not obtained a very creditable victory from the late decision in his favour," said the *Gazetteer*, for example, on 5 May. "The charge against him was that he *meant* mischief.— The defence set up in his favour was, that he meant—*nothing!*"

The Battle for Election Reforms

The original purpose of the Traitorous Correspondence Bill had been to discredit by innuendo Fox and the Friends of the People just before Grey moved for election reforms. But legislation for the purpose of innuendo apparently did not appeal to the Commons and appealed even less to the Lords, for allusions to the "traitorous correspondence of certain Gentlemen" became sparse and disappeared from the Ministerial newspapers altogether before the bill was even passed. The bill was a blunder, and Pitt blundered again with respect to the Stockbridge affair. Major Scott's attempt to get back into Parliament had resulted in his being charged with "eighty-four actions of bribery" and being sued for "penalties" totaling £42,000; and, in order to spare the Major the cost and embarrassment of all this litigation, the Government had shifted the guilt to the electors and approved an investigation of their conduct. Pitt could not have anticipated the consequences, for, while the newspapers were announcing new editions of *The State of the Representation of England and Wales*, the Commons was being informed (18 Mar.) that the Stockbridge electors were unionized: that they had formed "a club . . . for the purpose of proceeding regularly upon the business of bribery and corruption," that the members "debated upon their own corruption, and settled the sum that each elector should take for his vote, as well as the security he should require for the payment of it," and that they had appointed "a common agent to transact the business." A motion for "the preventing of bribery and corruption [in future Stockbridge elections]" was inevitable, and the Stockbridge Election Bribery Bill was accordingly introduced on 20 March. Its second reading was scheduled for 11 April, but on 10 April another bill was introduced, incapacitating "those Electors who have been found to be guilty of . . . bribery and corruption [in the recent Stockbridge election]." The Government protested that the bill was too severe; Francis protested, on behalf of the Friends of the People, that it was too "partial." It seemed to him that, since the "rich man" who offered the bribe was more guilty than the "poor man" who took it, "pains and penalties" in such instances ought to be inflicted on the candidates. He was particularly opposed to penalizing the Stockbridge electors, "who are in no way distinguished from their neighbours." A "system of bribery and corruption prevails almost universally," he told the Commons: "votes" are a "commodity . . . every day bought and sold by wholesale." What was actually needed was therefore a general reform program. The Stockbridge electors agreed in part, for on 11 April they petitioned the rejection of the first bill on the ground that their "property" would "sustain [injury] if the bill . . . should pass into law." Since the House was lacking a quorum, further consideration of the Stockbridge Election Bribery Bill was postponed indefinitely. The second reading of the Stockbridge Electors Incapacitating Bill had been scheduled for 6 May, but on 3 May this reading was postponed for three months, on the motion of George Rose. It now looked as if there might be a general reform bill after all.

Grey had given notice of a motion for election reforms on 30 April, 1792. On 23 February, 1793, the Friends of the People had brought out *The State of the Representation of England and Wales*; on 18 March Ridgway had published an anonymous pamphlet, entitled *Letters to the People of North Briton on the Universally Allowed Corruption of the Commons House of Parliament*; and on 29 April members of the Constitutional Society, meeting for their anniversary dinner, with John Frost, Thomas Walker, Maurice Margarot, Thomas Hardy, Hamilton Rowan, and Lord Edward Fitzgerald as stewards, had voted to support any action adopted by the Friends of the People with respect to election reforms. But, although the Government had been afraid of Grey's motion right along and had tried to block it in numerous ways, it seems finally to have been taken by surprise. The Traitorous Correspondence Act having failed in its purpose, the Ministerial papers were currently silent on the subject of Fox and his friends, and, at the urging perhaps of Wilkes, the Government was even preparing the release of John Almon. On 26 April, according to the *Oracle*, on 27 April, according to the *Morning Chronicle* (both 29 April),[35] the Court of King's Bench had ordered "the outlawry against the Defendant to be reversed" because of "an error in the proceedings"; and it was understood that Almon would be sentenced for the libel on 1 May. Almon was represented by Alan Chambre. By 1 May the situation had changed. The Ministerial papers were charging the Friends of the People with trying to "incorporate the same political innovations which have already led to the wreck of France," and, instead of dealing with Almon, the Court of King's Bench was dealing with Henry Symonds and James Ridgway, both of them publishers of *The State of Representation* and other reform pamphlets. Symonds, already serving a two-year sentence in Newgate Prison for selling Paine's *Rights of Man*, Part II, had pleaded guilty to selling his *Letter Addressed to the Addressers* and Pigott's *Jockey Club* as well; and Ridgway, under indictment for selling the same three works, had by now also pleaded guilty. Thomas Erskine and Arthur Pigott, who represented the pair, hoped that the sentences would be light. Lord Kenyon having promised to consider the matter, Symonds and Ridgway were "committed to Newgate," said the *Evening Mail* (3 May), to await the results.

Although the Commons was overwhelmingly opposed to the eradication of election abuses, the Friends of the People expected to overcome the opposition by petitions, and it seems to have been singly responsible for the flood of petitions which deluged the House from the end of April on. Daniel Stuart, still secretary to the Secretarial Committee of that organization, mentioned later[36] that he had given "[several] books with a printed declaration in favour of Parliamentary Reform, and with many blank leaves annexed, . . . to Thomas Hardy, the Secretary to the London Corresponding Society, then keeping a shoemaker's shop at the east end of Piccadilly, that he might circulate them through his divisions to obtain signatures in favour of Parliamentary Reform. He did so; but very few signatures were secured." The reason, Stuart thought, was that the Corresponding Society had very few members, but the probability is that that particular petition was too cautious. Stuart was also in touch with Joseph Gerrald, who was currently "haranguing" the Constitutional Society, and with all the reform groups in Scotland. The response was impressive. Petitions poured in from all over England and Scotland, and, although many of them "prayed" for universal suffrage and annual Parliaments rather than the mere eradication of abuses, they at least agreed that there was something the matter with the present system of electing Members of Parliament.

There had been considerable question as to whether the people had a "right" to actual representation or not, but the "right" to petition, like the "right" to a free press and the "right" to trial by jury, was supposedly guaranteed by the Constitution as the very "bulwark of British freedom": when the people spoke out loud and clear, the Commons was bound to listen. The people had last spoken out two years earlier to protest the war with Russia, and there was no doubt in the minds of the Opposition that their petitions had decided the matter. But Pitt's interpretation of the "right" to petition had since undergone some revision. In the case of the Nottingham petition (21 Feb.), Pitt had stated in effect that, although the people had a "right" to complain, they had no "right" to be heard; and this dictum was enthusiastically applied in the present instance, numerous petitions being refused on one pretext or another. A petition presented by the Constitutional Society, carrying 1,300 signatures and "praying" for universal male suffrage, was accepted after a long debate, but a petition from "the inhabitants of the town and neighbourhood of Sheffield" was refused (2 May) by a vote of 108 to 29 because of "evident disrespect to the House," and a petition "signed by upwards of 3700 inhabitants of the city of Norwich" was refused (6 May) without a division because it was printed. In addition to the dozen petitions which were refused, there were at least a dozen which were never presented, for, not only had the people lost the right to be heard, but the Government had taken advantage of the economic situation to stifle their complaints.

The commercial state of the country had gone from bad to worse. On 25 April the *Morning Chronicle* had reported: "Alarming as is the *catalogue of ruin* in every Gazette, it does not exhibit a tenth part of the distresses of the day; every man in an extensive trade receives hourly information of unpaid bills, and houses on which he has claims, praying for time." And on 27 April it had carried a long letter, signed "MANSFIELD'S GHOST," which began: "SIR,/ One hundred and thirty Attorneys admitted this Term!!!—Thriving happy times for Old England! four prisoners in one room in the King's Bench, and Fleet prisons— forty-six bankrupts in one week, and the body of Merchants soliciting the Prime Minister to turn *pawnbroker*. Strong proofs that we are all very happy!" There were further such lamentations in the *Chronicle* of 29 April:

> One of the Treasury papers again assures its readers, that the *prosperity* and manufacturers of the country were the immediate causes of the late failures.— It must be highly flattering to the writer of such an article [most likely Lord Mountmorres in the *Public Advertiser*] to find his theory confirmed by the long list of Bankrupts in each succeeding Gazette.
> *One hundred and eighteen bankrupts* in *five* succeeding Gazettes! Amidst this horrid scene of ruin, it is some consolation to every virtuous heart, that the

enormous fees arising therefrom flow into the purse of a Noble Chancellor [Lord Loughborough], who changed his friends and his office only because the Constitution was in danger, and without any view of bettering his situation in life.

But the appeal to Pitt by "the body of Merchants" had been effective. On 25 April a select committee had been appointed to look into the situation, and on 29 April it had submitted its report and recommendations. What it proposed was that the Treasury lend money to merchants, provided they showed evidence of need and could furnish adequate securities. It proposed more specifically the issuance of "exchequer bills not to exceed five millions" "in sums of 100*l.*, 50*l.*, and 20*l.*," bearing "an interest of two pence half-penny per cent. per day" and repayable in four installments over a period of one year. The proposals were debated on 30 April, the Commercial Credit Bill was introduced on 1 May, and it was passed on 8 May.

The list of bankrupts continued to be long. On 1 May the *Oracle* mentioned that "the Gazette of last night contains Twenty-seven bankruptcies," and on 6 May the *Morning Chronicle* reported: "Thirty-three more bankrupts on Saturday [4 May], making 178 in seven succeeding Gazettes! The fees to the Chancery purse on the seven batches are upwards of *five thousand pounds*! Ruin is profitable." The Commercial Credit Bill was nevertheless an innovation, and everyone was uneasy about it. "Mr. Pitt is adopting the most effectual measures in his power for the restoration of public credit; and should he fail in succeeding to the extent of his wishes, he will, at least deserve well for these his best endeavours," the *Public Advertiser* apologized on 26 April. Dundas, in the debates of 30 April, "protested," to begin with, "against any declaration that the present embarrassment of the merchants and manufacturers, is the effect of the poverty of the country. I consider it as precisely the reverse, and will maintain, however odd it may sound, that it is occasioned by the uncommon prosperity of the nation." How effective the bill would be, Dundas did not know, but Fox's suggestion that the Government might abuse its powers he regarded as too preposterous to answer. The *Morning Chronicle*'s comment on the first part of this speech appeared on 6 May: "It does not yet appear that the prosperity of our manufactures and commerce, of which Mr. DUNDAS says the Bankrupt lists are proofs, is much greater than before those lists were so long!" The *True Briton* and the *Sun* had already commented very effectively on the second.

The *Morning Chronicle* of 4 May carried two statements about the petitions. The first was brief: "The number of Petitions for a Parliamentary Reform, is already very considerable; and nothing, we are convinced, could have prevented it from being greater an hundred fold, but the gross fraud of representing the Constitution as in danger; and men's minds having been too severely occupied by their private distresses, to leave them at leisure to attend to public grievances." The second supplemented the first:

COMMERCIAL CREDIT.

In two papers, perfectly well known in the narrow circle to which they are confined to be under the immediate direction of the Treasury [the *True Briton* and the *Sun*], an address has been inserted, the pretended object of which was to dissuade the inhabitants of Birmingham from signing a petition for Parliamentary Reform; but the real object of which seems to be to warn all commercial men, that if they hope to participate in the public aid, intended to be given by Parliament, they must be careful to do nothing, that may be disagreeable to Ministers.

In the papers alluded to, it was introduced with a preface—

"The following Address to the Inhabitants of Birmingham, has been circulated in that town. It contains so much good sense and sound reasoning, that we wish to promote its circulation all over the kingdom, and with that view, give it a place."—

And it contains the following remarkable passage—

"Independent of the war, the public calamity of the failures among the commercial part of the nation, too much occupies the attention of a very respectable part of the Community, to permit them to lend their assistance in discussing or promoting such a measure (were it otherwise adviseable), and their help should not be despised, for their opinions would have very great influence in getting it carried into effect:—but while *they are obliged to solicit Ministry for assistance to support their general Credit, and to enable them to continue to employ the industrious workmen dependent upon them, how can they propose to countenance any measure which may be disagreeable to Administration?*"

Here we see the objection urged, in the House of Commons, against the proposed mode of granting relief, viz. that it would be made a mere instrument of ministerial influence; and repelled by Mr. DUNDAS as too absurd and incredible to deserve a moment's attention, openly avowed and inculcated by the understrappers of Ministers.

On the day Grey introduced his motion (6 May), petitions were nevertheless submitted from Westminster, Suffolk, Poole, Aldgate, Warwick, Huddersfield, Dundee, Paisley, Montrose, Kilmarnock, Kirkcaldy, Newmilns, Perth, Edinburgh, Dunfermline, Irvine, Strathaven, Galston, Roxburgh, Linlithgow, Anstruther, Nottingham, and Norwich; and the Ministerial papers had little to offset them. In addition to the aspersions in the other newspapers, the *Diary* had on 4 May introduced a column, entitled "S'YERG [GREY'S] BEGGAR'S OPERA,/ BEING A COMPLEAT PARODY/ of GAY's BEGGAR's OPERA." The column was introduced by the headnote: "One of our fashionable Wits had so far back as last October *dreamt* a compleat Parody of Gay's Beggar's Opera, but it was thought proper to reserve its publication till after the Reform Motion. In the mean time accept of the Airs, and if agreeable you shall have the prose also." The "fashionable Wit" was Charles Stuart, and, although it was never "agreeable" to present "the prose," the "Airs," which were somewhat crude lampoons on Fox and members of the Friends of the People, were continued through 15 May, usually reappearing in the *Public Advertiser* a day later. Grey began by submitting a petition from the Friends of the People. It had been written by Tierney and was probably familiar to most of the Members, since it had been published that morning under the title: *Authentic Copy of a Petition Praying for a Reform in Parliament, Presented to the House of Commons by C. Grey . . . and signed only by the Members of the Friends of the People.* The language was meticulously respectful, the avowed purpose was "to preserve in its purity a constitution [the petitioners] love and admire," and the gist was that the Commons did not "adequately represent" the people. The "mischiefs . . . which arise from the present state of the representation" were detailed at great length, and the petitioners offered in every instance to "prove" that the "mischief" in fact existed. As soon as the reading was concluded, Burke demanded to know the addresses of the petitioners. Grey protested that addresses were not usually added in such cases, but he assured Burke that "all the subscribers reside either in London or near it" and proceeded with his speech.

Most of the speech was a diatribe on Pitt, whom, Grey admitted, he did not "trust" and certainly would not "bargain with." The speech was long and by no means brilliant, but it concluded appropriately with a motion "that the said petition be referred to the consideration of a committee." The motion was opposed by Jenkinson, Powys, and Windham, who agreed that suffrage was not a question of "right," but of "expedience," and that it was extremely "inexpedient" at the moment to extend it. Under any circumstances, it seemed to Windham, nothing could be quite so "calamitous" as legislators who were "agents of the people"; and, as to the Constitution, he said, "its faults cannot be corrected, without removing all its valuable parts." This led him into a discussion of "metaphysics," to the great amusement of the House and subsequently the Opposition newspapers, since Windham had no idea what the term meant. After a speech by Erskine, who of course supported Grey, the debates were adjourned until the following day.

Although everyone was eager to "deliver" his "sentiments," the debates of 7 May yielded little that was new. Francis, who undertook to reply to Windham, lamented that the "French Revolution is [Windham's] answer to every thing; the French Revolution is his everlasting theme, the universal remedy, the grand specific, the never-failing panacea, the perpetual burthen of his song": whatever the issue, Windham "[serves up to us] a cold, flat, insipid hash of the same dish, . . . till at last . . . the taste revolts, the palate sickens at it." Francis could not see what bearing the French Revolution had on the present issue except that the world might learn from it the consequences of ignoring the voice of the people. Burke having implied that signers of the petition had no settled addresses, Francis assured him that he knew the majority of them personally and that "all of them . . . are gentlemen who, in point of rank and fortune, are on a level with the generality of this House." Francis was followed by the Earl of Mornington, who was very happy that Grey had proposed no specific plan of reform, for the basic question, it seemed to him, was whether an alteration of "the very genius and spirit of the British government" was "necessary for the public good." Lord Mornington thought it was not, and he said so at great length: learnedly, but not without prejudice. He then considered the "tenor" of the petitions on the table, and, although it appeared to be generally "moderate," he could not help noticing that it pointed in the direction of universal suffrage and that some of the petitions demanded it. He noticed in particular a petition "from sundry inhabitants of London, Westminster, and their vicinity," which called for annual Parliaments as well as universal suffrage, and he was struck by the fact that, heading the list of signers, was Thomas Hardy, Secretary of the Corresponding Society and a notorious sympathizer with the French Revolution. He also seemed to remember that the Corresponding Society had been advertising for signers of the petition. The Corresponding Society, he was quite sure, would not be content with moderate reform, and he could see no evidence that the Friends of the People had had a moderating influence on other organizations. On the contrary, the Friends of the People had "actually coalesced with many leading characters in the Constitutional Society" to form the Society of the Friends of the Liberty of the Press. The more he thought about it, the more Lord Mornington was convinced that the reformers would not even be content with universal suffrage: they would insist upon governing the country themselves, in accordance with that "curious theory" set forth "in a treatise, intituled 'The Social Contract,' written by J. J. Rousseau."

Whitbread protested that, if Hardy had violated the laws, he should have been prosecuted and that, having not been prosecuted, he had a right to express an opinion. He also protested that "preserving" the Constitution was a different thing from "subverting" it, he denied that the Friends of the Liberty of the Press had anything to do with the Friends of the People, and he regarded it as a very "bad omen" that "the appellation by which the society to which I belong is distinguished, 'The Friends of the People,'" should "be always received with a sneer." He would not say that the House of Commons ought to represent the people, but he would say that there ought to be "an identity of interest between the two" and that, "whenever the people speak, their voice [ought to be] heard and attended to." As to the present motion, Whitbread had had too much "experience" with "the influence possessed by [Mr. Pitt] on all the deliberations of this House" to anticipate its success; but the people will persevere, he promised, and "the things will be done." Anstruther and Pitt opposed the motion on the usual ground of expedience. Pitt added that, although he had no objection to petitions, he found these petitions unimpressive, since the similarity "in substance and expression" indicated that they were the "fabrication of a few individuals" and did not express "the sentiment of the people. . . . If I am asked, then, what weight they ought to have, the answer is easy. None. . . . The fraud is too gross and palpable. . . ." For over a year now, he went on, the Friends of the

People had been doing everything in its power to propagandize the cause of moderate reform, and, since all the petitions except its own "carry a suspicious and dangerous appearance," it had clearly not made one convert. The members had once resolved to disband if their object proved unattainable, and he now called upon them to do so and "to join with us in opposing a reform which is not even desired and which cannot be granted with any propriety." Pitt concluded with a lecture on the nature of "rights," which he represented as deriving only from governments, and on the nature of the Constitution, which he represented as a triumph of expedience.

Sheridan charged in reply that Pitt was afraid to refer the people's "complaints" to an investigative committee, since he knew what the investigation would reveal. It would reveal, said Sheridan:

> that Peers of the other House send members to the House of Commons by nomination; that the Crown sends members into that House by nomination too; that some members of that House send in members by their own nomination also—all these things make a farce of an election . . .; that men are created peers without having been of the least service to the public in any action of their lives, but merely on account of their Parliamentary influence—the present Minister has been the means of creating a hundred of them . . .; that corruption is the pivot on which the whole of our public government affairs turns; that the collection of taxes is under the management of wealthy men in Parliamentary interest . . .; that neither in the Church, the Army, the Navy, or any public office, is an appointment given, but in consequence of Parliamentary influence, that in consequence corrupt majorities are at the will of the Minister. In short, whether the eye is directed to the Church, the Law, the Army, or to Parliament [or, Sheridan might have added, the Royal Societies or the Universities], it can only serve the seeds of inevitable decay and ruin in the British Constitution.

Like Whitbread, Sheridan however promised that the Friends of the People would not give up: it would persevere in its object, he said, until that object was "effectually accomplished." William Adam, who had heretofore supported "the phalanx," declined to support it on this occasion, but Fox remained loyal. The motion was defeated by a vote of 282 to 41.

Immediate Aftermaths of Grey's Motion

Most of the battles between the reformers and the "Constitutionalists" were battles between the people and Pitt. Only the radicals suggested that the Commons ought to "represent" the people in any arithmetical sense or even that it ought to comply with popular demands; but even the reactionaries conceded that it was bound to listen to their complaints and to defend their interests against the interests of property, as represented by the Lords, and against the interests of the Crown. The people could advertise their complaints either directly through petitions or indirectly through the press. The newspapers estimated that one out of every hundred male adults had signed a petition for election reforms during late April and early May, and, even if this meant that 99 per cent of the population was content with the present state of elections, as spokesmen for the Government had contended, the number of malcontents was not negligible. The Commons should have listened, but the voice of the people could no longer be heard above the voice of William Pitt.

The radical reformers, convinced by the vote of 7 May that nothing was to be gained by petitions, prepared for a revision of plans. On 17 May, Thomas Hardy and Maurice Margarot reopened correspondence with William Skirving, Secretary of the Associated Friends of the People in Scotland, and a convention was arranged to discuss the situation. By late May there was fresh trouble in Ireland, and by early June that country seemed almost to be in a state of civil war. Radicals were returning from the Continent in droves. On 2 May the *Oracle* reported that "MERRY, the Poet, is at *Calais*, waiting that channel of communication to be opened that will give us back a delightful Writer." Merry, probably still employed by the *Morning Post*, subsequently settled near Norwich and was soon an intimate of Tooke, Godwin, and other reformers. By 1 June, William Beckford was also back from France, "completely democratized," said the *World*. Radical publications continued to pour from the press, the one which attracted most attention being John Lovett's *The Citizen of the World*, which appeared on 18 June. The Government showed its customary lack of concern.

On Thursday, 9 May, the *Oracle* reported the release of John Almon, in prison since March, 1792, for a libel published on 18 November, 1788:

Court of King's Bench.
Wednesday.
The King, v. Almon.
The Defendant was brought up by his own order for Judgment . . . : the ATTORNEY-GENERAL, however, opened the case in the most polite and gentleman-like manner; and after admitting many circumstances in Mr. ALMON's favour,

which he acknowledged to have been acquainted with, Mr. Justice BULLER interrupted him, by asking, *Why Mr.* ALMON *had not been pardoned?*—The ATTORNEY GENERAL replied, that he thought it was the most honourable, as well as the most respectable for Mr. ALMON's character, that he should have a public acquittal by the most public testimony of his innocence. The Court immediately ordered Mr. ALMON to be discharged upon his own recognizance of 100*l. sine die.*

The Times reported (9 May) that, Almon having already been imprisoned for fourteen months, Sir John Scott hoped the Court would be lenient, that Lord Kenyon promised to take the matter under advisement, and that Almon was meanwhile released on a bail of £100. Instead of being acquitted "by the most public testimony of his innocence," Almon was therefore subject to recall at any time. The result was that he immediately became a pamphleteer for the Government. On 9 May Joseph Johnson was advertising *Thoughts on the Causes of the Present [Commercial] Failures*, a work by William Roscoe. At the end of the month, Almon replied to it with *The Causes of the Present Complaints Fairly Stated and Fully Refuted.* "Mary Bryant, otherwise Broad," who had escaped from Botany Bay, "[crossing] over 3000 miles of sea in an open boat, along with several male convicts," fared better. According to the *Public Advertiser* (13 May) and the *World* (15 May), the King granted her a full pardon.

Although the Ministerial newspapers hinted at possible actions against Thomas Cooper, Thomas Walker, and James Watt, none of the Manchester group was molested, and neither were Hardy, Tooke, Margarot, Gerrald, and other radical leaders in London, although the Government was well aware of what they were doing. But on 27 May the Government finally tried Frost, under indictment since December, 1792, for "seditious words" uttered on 6 November. Frost was defended by Erskine, and appearing against him were four informers, Yatman, Savignac, Bullock, and John Taitt, Taitt's name having recently been added to the list. Frost was convicted largely on the evidence of Bullock, who had taken down every word he said in shorthand, and, bail having been refused, he was committed to Newgate to await sentence. According to the *Oracle* (15 June), he was returned to the Court of King's Bench for the purpose on 14 June, but judgment was postponed. He was again returned on 19 June, when, said the *Oracle* (20 June), he was sentenced to six months in Newgate, one hour in the pillory at Charing Cross between the hours of noon and two o'clock in the afternoon, and ordered to furnish securities for good behaviour for five years thereafter, he for £500, two others for £100 each. His name was meanwhile being struck from the list of attorneys. Frost's real crime was embarrassing the Government by repeatedly suing Lord Hood and of course his outspoken criticism of Pitt. On 8 June the Irish Government also formally indicted Archibald Hamilton Rowan for distributing on 16 December, 1792, a "seditious paper," beginning "Citizen Soldiers, to arms!" The paper urged the Irish "Volunteers" to resist a Government proclamation tending to dissolve them.

Since the "Volunteers" were currently at war with the "Defenders," the indictment seemed to be justified, even though it was six months late. But Rowan was freed on bail, and that seemed to be the end of the matter.

The trial which attracted most attention was that of the Cambridge radical, William Frend, but Frend was not being tried by the Government, and the prosecution had not been initiated by Pitt, even though he was expected to approve of it. The first announcement of the trial appeared in the *Morning Chronicle* of 7 March. In April there were reports of hearings and appeals, but the results were indecisive, and on 3 May the trial began. It was held in the Vice-Chancellor's Court, with Dr. Milner presiding, and it lasted most of the month. Frend, who was charged with publishing *Peace and Union* and thereby violating statutes and laws of the University by impugning the established religion, chose to defend himself. His defense consisted of defiance, derision, and ridicule, to the delight of the undergraduates and the Opposition papers, most of which carried running accounts of the trial. The Court was remarkably lenient. On 26 May, according to the *Morning Chronicle* (1 June), "the Vice-Chancellor acquainted Mr. FREND that he had been found guilty of the charges exhibited against him, and ordered him to recant his errors in words to the following effect;—'I, WILLIAM FREND, M.A. Fellow of Jesus College, &c. &c. by order of the Vice-Chancellor, do acknowledge, that I have offended against the latter part of the *Statute de Concionibus*, by having published a pamphlet, entitled PEACE AND UNION, &c. and I do hereby recant my error.' He was allowed till Thursday next [30 May] to consider of complying with this order." Frend refused. Protesting that the statement did not specify what "opinions" he was recanting, he insisted that the Court read a long paper he had prepared on the subject. The paper was read "in adjournment," and, the Court having reconvened, he "[stretched] out his right hand [and] replied—Recant! I would sooner cut this right hand off." According to the *Oracle* (4 June), Frend argued his case on this occasion with "ingeniousness" and "erudition," and, although he "too frequently descended to quibbles, and low wit," the "Under Graduates testified by frequent plaudits their disapprobation of such a prosecution." The *World* observed only (1 June): "CAMBRIDGE—Mr. FREND made a defence in the SENATE HOUSE [on 30 May], of three hours and an half. Some of the young Men were forbidden to applaud by *clapping their hands*, so they *stamped their feet*. Mr. FREND defended with some ingenuity, a very stupid publication of his own." The hearing concluded with a long speech by Dr. Milner, who, having defended the prosecution, denounced "our 'atheistic enemies,' the French, and expatiated on the respect and attachment due to the best of Governments, and the most perfect of Constitutions, . . . solemnly pronounced the sentence of banishment from the University against Mr. FREND."

It is notable that Dr. Milner and "The Committee of The Twenty-Seven" did not reap the rewards they expected, but Pitt did not like to be embarrassed, and the trial of Frend was a major embarrassment. To aggravate the situation, it was heavily publicized, not only by the newspapers, but by the "Proctor in the Vice-Chancellor's Court," John Beverley, whose *The Trial of William Frend* was announced on 16 July. In addition, the "sentence of banishment," so "solemnly" pronounced by Dr. Milner, failed to end the matter, for the *Morning Chronicle* ridiculed the proceedings throughout June, while Frend provided fresh copy by appealing the case. On 10 June the *Morning Post* reported that on 31 May he had "appealed to the University against the sentence pronounced by the Vice Chancellor on the preceding day" and that on 1 June "the Proctor, in the name of the University, [had] inhibited the Vice Chancellor from putting his sentence, during the appeal, into execution." By 24 June, according to the *Oracle*, a new Board of Delegates had been appointed to "[consider] the appeal," and on 4 July the *Morning Chronicle* announced the results:

CAMBRIDGE.

Last Friday and Saturday [27–28 June], the Delegates sat on Mr. FREND's cause, and after due deliberation, affirmed the sentence of expulsion. Sir WILLIAM WYNNE, who acted as the mouth of the Council, went through the whole process, as managed by the Promoter and Co. and not only adjudged them to be right in the gross, but clearly decided them to be perfectly correct and legal in the particular steps of the accusation. What steps Mr. FREND may take in consequence of this *equitable* decision, we are perfectly ignorant. We believe, we hope at least, that he will appeal to the Court of King's Bench. We shall then see whether there be left any remnant—[*sic*]

The University had also divorced itself from Wakefield. On 19 June the *Morning Chronicle* mentioned that, although the "university of Cambridge had published, at their press, the three first parts of Mr. GILBERT WAKEFIELD's *Silva Critica*, . . . the times growing very ticklish, they have refused to extend their patronage to the fourth. . . . The purity of an orthodox university shrinks even from the possibility of heretical infection. Mr. WAKEFIELD, however, submits to this mortifying refusal with a very good grace, and even pays a brace of handsome compliments to his orthodox refusers, Mrs. MILNER and KIPLING, . . . in his preface."

The only radical reformer actually prosecuted by the Government had therefore been John Frost, whose perpetual suits against Lord Hood constantly reminded the public of the disgraceful elections of 1788. The moderate reformers, who asked only for the eradication of election abuses, the Government could not prosecute; and, now that Pitt had altered the Commons's thinking about petitions, prosecutions would seem to have been unnecessary. But Whitbread and Sheridan, who had promised that the Friends of the People would fight on until its object was attained, obviously did not think the battle was over; and neither certainly did William Pitt. William Grant, who had been appointed King's Counsel in February and Joint Justice of the Carmarthen Great Sessions in April, failed to be re-elected as Member for Shaftesbury, and, although the Government would ordinarily have smuggled him back into Parliament as Member for some other borough, it chose to get along without him. Further hearings on the Stockbridge Election Bribery Bill were delayed until 27 May, when the bill was quietly voted out of existence. In addition to preventing new election scandals and quashing the old ones, the Government struck out at the Friends of the People and the friends of the Friends of the People by every means in its power.

On 8 May, the day following the defeat of Grey's motion, Ridgway and Symonds were returned to the Court of King's Bench, where Ridgway was sentenced to two years in Newgate for publishing *The Jockey Club*, a third year for publishing the *Letter Addressed to the Addressers*, and a fourth year for publishing *Rights of Man*, Part II. He was fined £100 for each of the last two offenses and ordered to furnish securities for good behavior for another five years, himself in the amount of £500 and two others in the amount of £250 each. Symonds, already serving two years in Newgate for publishing the *Rights of Man*, was sentenced to two additional years and fined £200 for publishing *The Jockey Club* and the *Letter Addressed to the Addressers*. Securities for subsequent good behavior were the same as those imposed on Ridgway. The two immediately combined their businesses. On 22 May they advertised John Williams's *Life of the Late Earl of Barrymore. By A. Pasquin. Published by Ridgway and Symonds: First Year of Our Imprisonment in Newgate, May 15*; and on 1 June they advertised Parkinson's *An Address to the Hon. E. Burke from the Swinish Multitude. By Old Hubert, Secretary. Published by Ridgway and Symonds: Newgate, May 28, First Year of Our Imprisonment*. Other such publications followed, but so long as the pair published nothing for the Friends of the People, the Government was evidently content.

Another publisher for the Friends of the People, the bookseller William Holland, who was already serving one year in prison for selling Paine's *Letter Addressed to the Addressers*, was brought back to King's Bench on 10 May, where, according to the *Public Advertiser* (13 May), Bearcroft moved that a second criminal action be filed against him for having published in 1792 *Gloucester Bastile!!! Pathetic Particulars of a Poor Boy Sentenced to Suffer Seven Years Solitary Confinement in Gloucester Gaol*. Still another, the bookseller Thomas Spence had hardly advertised an edition of the *Authentic Copy of a Petition Praying for a Reform in Parliament, Presented . . . by Charles Grey*, when he was arrested and imprisoned. The bookseller Daniel Isaac Eaton, who had also brought out an edition of the *Authentic Petition*, was tried in the Old Bailey on 3 June for publishing the *Rights of Man*, Part II, having been indicted for the offense on 20 February. He was defended by Felix Vaughan and John Guerney, both of them newcomers, Guerney having just been admitted to the bar, and representing the Crown were the Treasury solicitors, William Chamberlayne and Joseph White. "The Jury, after some deliberation," said the newspapers, "brought in a verdict, *Guilty of publishing, but not with a criminal intention.*" On 7 June the lawyers debated the meaning of this verdict. According to *Lloyd's Evening Post* (10 June), Vaughan and Guerney argued that the verdict meant not guilty; Chamberlayne and White thought otherwise, but they consented to release Eaton on the same bail as before until the matter was settled. The *Morning Chronicle* was strongly on the side of Vaughan. "The KING *v.* EATON, is in some respects similar to a trial [1–5 Sept., 1760] in the reign of our 2d CHARLES, the KING *v.* WILLIAM PENN, and WILLIAM MEAD; where these two honest Quakers were indicted for having spoken seditious words in Gracechurch-street. The Jury's verdict was, '*Guilty of* SPEAKING *in Gracechurch street,*'—and as *speaking* was no crime, and the Jury would not see the sedition, to the great mortification of the Court and gratification of the country, the record was amended to *Not Guilty,*" it said on 8 June. The question was further debated on 27 June, when it was decided "that the case should be laid before the Judges, in order that they might enter the proper verdict, and settle the law upon this matter." The outcome of their deliberations, if there were any deliberations, was not noted. The truth was that, since "intention" was the determining factor in cases of libel and the jury could now judge the law as well as the fact, Eaton was technically innocent. But, instead of acquitting him, the Government chose to try him on another charge.

Since on 1 May advertisements for the British Library appeared in the *Morning Chronicle* rather than the *Oracle*, readers would have supposed that John Bell had quit the *Oracle* and was not therefore responsible for its support of Sheridan and the Friends of the People during the days which followed. But nothing, it appeared, could save Bell, for on 11 May he announced his bankruptcy. The announcement appeared in both the *Oracle* and the *Sun*, and it was accompanied by no advertisements for the British Library:

JOHN BELL,
OF THE
BRITISH LIBRARY, STRAND, LONDON,
TO HIS CREDITORS IN GENERAL.

THE GAZETTE of this Night will proclaim me a Bankrupt.

Many years have I ambitiously laboured in hopes of avoiding the present Calamity. The Destinies seem to have decreed otherwise; and to this complexion am I come at last.

A retrospective view of my various efforts and Productions would prove that I have deserved a better Fate—but wherefore should I murmur.—Although I am the Source from which Government has actually received nearly Half a Million of Money, by different Duties—although Hundreds have been nourished daily and solely for years in my Employment—although the Arts have received some lustre from my enterprise—yet I see many names much more respectable than my own, in the gloomy Catalogue of temporary Misfortunes.—I have, however, yet one Consolation, which I will boldly assert,—that in the innumerable and unprecedented Difficulties and Embarrassments which have assailed me, I have not forfeited the Character of an Honest Man. I speak thus boldly in the Face of the World; and challenge the World to prove otherwise. Severities have frequently pressed hard upon Propriety;—but place the Complainers in my Situation, and I am convinced that Approbation would supersede Reflection.

Speaking perhaps more materially to your satisfaction, I will declare what can be proved, that my present Property, with a fair, free, and deliberate operation, would be adequate to all your demands; and, according to my opinion, leave also a handsome surplus to myself. That Property is now in your hands, but must be subject to inevitable defalcations.

In all Situations, and under all circumstances, I hope I shall feel a proper Thankfulness and Gratitude for every Favour and Indulgence that I have experienced from you,

JOHN BELL.

The *London Gazette* of 11 May did "proclaim" as bankrupt: "John Bell, of the Strand, Bookseller, to surrender May 14, 25, June 22, at twelve, at Guildhall, London. Attornies Mess. Hearne and Pearce, Paternoster-row." On 14 May the *Star* further advertised the immediate sale of an "old and well-established . . . COUNTRY NEWSPAPER." Anyone interested was asked to address "P. Q. at Anderson's Coffee-house, Fleet Street, London." This newspaper may have been an adjunct of the *Oracle*.

Throughout June the *Oracle* was vehemently opposed to both peace and reform, and, from mid-May on, the paper carried many advertisements for Cadell and a sprinkling of advertisements for other booksellers. Bell's enterprises were not again mentioned until 3 June, when the *Oracle* announced John Hughes's *The Siege of Damascus*, now available as No. 90 in Bell's British Theatre. On 7 June there was a puff of Lady Manners's poetry, a volume of which would be brought out by the British Library within a week, spare copies being sold at a guinea apiece; and on 10 June there was a column of advertisements for the British Theatre, followed by an address "TO THE PUBLIC IN GENERAL." This address, a quotation from the previous address to the creditors, was followed in turn by a second address:

JOHN BELL,
TO THE SUBSCRIBERS TO THE BRITISH THEATRE.

The preceding Declaration renders it unnecessary for me to make any further Apology for a temporary Suspension of the Publication of THE BRITISH THEATRE; but I will not deny myself the Gratification of returning my most sincere and respectful Thanks for the honourable Patronage which THAT WORK in particular has experienced from you. It has ever been my Endeavour and my Pride to fulfil to the utmost of my Power all my Engagements, and all my Professions: Whenever I have failed in either, the Disappointment has entirely proceeded from inevitable necessity, and not from Neglect or Disposition. Under such Consciousness, although my Purposes have been occasionally defeated, I trust I shall feel Spirit, Resolution, and Power enough to rally again.

THEREFORE permit me to entreat and hope for your kind Indulgence, until I shall be enabled to resume the Publication of THE BRITISH THEATRE; as I have no doubt of still completing that VALUABLE WORK, not only agreeably to my original Plan, but also with very enriched Additions and Improvements. The Continuation, I may be bold to say, will not be delayed very many Weeks—for as that WORK and my beautiful Edition of THE FUGITIVE POETRY are the only Public Undertakings of mine which remain unfinished, they shall be the first Objects of my renovated Exertions and Attention.

SUCH are my Resolutions; and I would gladly hope that they will be countenanced and supported by your kind Indulgence and Approbation.

JOHN BELL.

June 10, 1793.

On 13 June there was a column of advertisements for Bell's British Library. Although Bell's "Character" as "an Honest Man" was in considerable dispute, no one could deny that he was diligent.

Those advocates of moderate reform who could not be prosecuted were being assailed in newspapers and pamphlets. Excerpts from Charles Stuart's "S'YERG'S BEGGAR'S OPERA" appeared in the *Diary* through 15 May and in the *Public Advertiser* through 16 May. On 11 May the *Public Advertiser* supplemented Stuart's verses with some abusive verses by "Mr. JERNINGHAM." There was also an abundance of prose. Rumors that residents of Sheffield and Birmingham were signing new petitions, this time asking only the eradication of election abuses, moved the *Public Advertiser* to demand (13 May):

Ye sons of Sheffield and of Birmingham, famed for ingenuity, industry, and integrity, what are your projects? Are you turned Reformers? Do you want Representatives for your towns? Alas! "Ye know not what ye ask:" you have a good trade, you are respectable people, you live under the best Constitution in the world,—enjoy your happiness. Seek not for troubles; for in what every city or town there is an election, that city or town for the time being is in a state of slavery. . . . Do you want more Representatives? you wish for more plagues. Do you want them to be chosen more frequent [*sic*]? You want sorrow and misery to fill your towns? Elections are diseases, which in many cities and towns are not cured at the end of a septennial Parliament: the blood is inflamed, and the fever rages more or less from election to election.—O! consider what ye are! great and flourishing towns, valued and esteemed by all the world: and would you sink yourselves into slavery, by pinning your faith on the sleeve of a disappointed man, or men: rest assured, not one of the leaders for Reform, want any sort of Reform: that will not place them in a situation to partake of the loaves and fishes. . . . "Shoemaker, stick to your last," is a good old proverb: while the towns of Birmingham and Sheffield support their great characters, as the first manufacturers in the world, let them leave politics to Statesmen: wonderful are the works of thy hands, O Birmingham and Sheffield!—Yet thou art not fit to guide the helm.—Great was the father of the present Minister, acknowledged the

Saviour of our country:—if possible, the son excels him. No Minister ever had to combat with such an enemy as France now is: but, give him your confidence, and he will shew you the father yet lives in the son.

While the *Sun*, the *True Briton*, *The Times*, and the *Public Advertiser* were publishing lectures and diatribes, the *World* was addressing crude letters to Fox, Sheridan, Francis, and other supporters of Grey's motion. The author was most certainly Charles Stuart, who was therefore writing for the *World* in early June. There were also the inevitable pamphlets. Bentley, it was understood, was readying a second *Letter to Fox*, and Joseph Cawthorne was finishing *The Celebrated Speech of Sir Robert Walpole against Short Parliaments. With a Preface on the Times*. On 10 May *The Times* announced publication ("price 1s.") of another answer to Fox's *Letter*, entitled:

> A SHORT REVIEW: addressed to the Right Honourable CHARLES JAMES FOX. Wherein is displayed his glaring inconsistency from his Speeches, respecting the French Faction; the consistency, wisdom, and patriotism of the present Ministry, proved in their Treaty with France; and Mr. Burke's Speech about the French, more than three years ago, demonstrated to have been prophetic; the Counter-Associations vindicated, and the Object of the Liberty of the Press Society, and Mr. Erskine's Declaration developed. BY A WESTMINSTER ELECTOR. Dedicated to JOHN REEVES, Esq. Promoter of the Associations for the Protection of Liberty and Property against Republicans and Levellers. Sold by J. Parsons, No. 21, Paternoster Row.

An abbreviated form of this advertisement appeared in the *Star*. The "WESTMINSTER ELECTOR" was Charles Stuart, who, having "circulated some hundred copies," was applying to Nepean for payment. Although the "application was rejected,"[37] the *Diary* did print (6 June) a two-column excerpt. *The Works of C. Tacitus* by Arthur Murphy appeared on 31 May, and on 1 June the *True Briton* noticed that "Mr. MURPHY has dedicated his Translation of TACITUS to Mr. BURKE. His Dedication is distinguishable for classic chasteness and for obvious truth.—Every man must allow, that no praise can be too high for the patriot part which Mr. BURKE has acted in the defence of the Constitution of his Country." The dedication had already (31 May) been reprinted by the *Diary*. The last item in the series was a monthly journal, *British Critic*, advertised by all Ministerial newspapers on 1 June. The *British Critic*, established, according to Redding,[38] "principally by the activity of . . . Nares," was an organ of the Church and hence a strong advocate of war and the "Constitution."

Although Burke had said almost nothing during the debates of 6–7 May, he was the principal target of the Opposition papers. Possibly because he could be libeled with impunity, the *Gazetteer* and the *Morning Chronicle* were filled with quotations from his early speeches on reform. The charges and insinuations in the Ministerial papers were ignored by the Opposition press except in the case of Maitland, who was defended on 21 May by the *Gazetteer*: "It has been asked in a

Treasury paper, what is become of Major MAITLAND? With one of the usual treasury insinuations, that his absence from Parliament is improper.—The answer is short.—Major MAITLAND is on his voyage to join his regiment in Jamaica." New editions of the *Authentic Copy of a Petition Praying for a Reform in Parliament, Presented . . . by Charles Grey* continued, however, to appear; John Wharton gave notice of another motion regarding "corruptions"; and on 25 May the Friends of the People resolved that it would continue the fight. It was still convinced that its object could be attained by petitions, provided they were submitted by "a great majority of the kingdom"; it attributed the vote of 7 May to "the silence of the principal cities and counties"; and it attributed their silence to the constant "alarms, . . . which we have no doubt were excited and inflamed for the special purpose of checking the disposition of the country in favour of a Reform, and of calumniating the characters of those who promoted it." If it turned out that "the Nation" was either "adverse or indifferent . . . , then indeed it will become us to abandon all thoughts of a useless vexatious perseverance in so deserted a cause"; but thus far, it seemed to the Friends of the People, the results had been "encouraging." The resolutions were subsequently published, under the title, *Address to the People of Great Britain*. The author was again Tierney.

On 31 May John Wharton moved for an inquiry as to "whether any, and which of the provisions" resulting from the Glorious Revolution of 1688 "had been invalidated or taken away." The motion was negatived by a vote of 71 to 11. Lambton thereupon gave notice that on 10 June he would move against the interference of peers in elections. This motion was not made. According to the *Oracle* (10 June): "Mr. DUNDAS, on Friday last [7 June], during the exclusion of the strangers from the Gallery, intimated to Mr. LAMBTON, that Mr. PITT had that day given notice by a Messenger, that on account of his continued indisposition, it would be impossible for him to attend on Monday next, [this day.]/ Mr. LAMBTON, in consequence of this information, withdrew his Motion concerning the Interference of Peers at Elections, pledging himself to bring it forward at an early period next Session of Parliament." The only purpose of such motions anyway was to keep the issue alive. The Government had meanwhile extended the influence of peers in elections to include the elections of peers themselves. As the *Star* put it on 1 June:

> The late decision of the House of Lords respecting the right of Scots Peers created British Peers since the Union to vote at the Election of the Sixteen Representatives of the Peerage of Scotland, is so far extraordinary, that it is made to operate as an *ex post facto* law. It sustains the votes of the Duke of QUEENS-BERRY and the Marquis of ABERCORNE, although tendered at the last Election in direct opposition to precedent, and to two former decisions of the House of Lords.
>
> It also creates a new and distinct order of men in the Constitution, viz. men who are Lords of Parliament in their own right, and have also votes in the election of sixteen other Lords of Parliament.

And on 13 June: "By the late decision of the House of Lords, the Marquis of TWEEDALE, who is the brother-in-law of the Earl of LAUDERDALE, is deprived of the seat to which he would have been entitled, if the votes of the Duke of QUEENSBERRY and the Marquis of ABERCORN had not been confirmed./ The contest for the representation in the British Peerage, declared vacant by the Committee of Privileges, will be between Lord HOPETOWN, Lord GALLOWAY, and Lord KINNAIRD. Had Lord KINNOUL's vote been tendered, Lord KINNAIRD would have been the sitting Peer." On 25 June the *Gazetteer* reported that "the Earl of LAUDERDALE has entered a very spirited and argumentative Protest against . . . sustaining the Votes of the Duke of QUEENSBERRY and the Marquis of ABERCORN, at the last General Election of the Peers of Scotland." Although Lord Lauderdale had himself survived the new ruling, he would not, it was now very clear, survive another Scots election.

The Government and Lord Rawdon; the Government and Mr. Burke

While Pitt was battling the advocates of election reforms, he was also battling the advocates of other reforms, and in every instance victory was on his side. Except for the *Sun*, the *True Briton*, and the *Public Advertiser*, the newspapers were unanimous in demanding reforms of the legal profession, reforms of the bankruptcy proceedings, reforms of the prisons, reforms of the penal codes, and reforms of the laws respecting debtors. On 30 May the *Star* calculated that the "Commissions of Bankruptcy recorded . . . in the month of February last, amount to 512—and the sum for which they have stopped payment is computed far to exceed the total amount of all the coined money in Great Britain!!" The worst of it was that a sizable amount of every estate was swallowed up in "fees" before the claims of the creditors were even considered. The "fees to the Chancery Purse [in the last three and one-half weeks] are upwards of *five thousand pounds!*" the *Morning Chronicle* proclaimed on 6 May; and this was only one item. For, in addition to Lord Loughborough's "fees," there were "fees" due to the Commissioners of Bankrupts, of whom Arthur Murphy was now one, and "fees" due to the lawyers. The legal profession was growing apace, adding to its ranks at the rate of 520 members a year, although there was no reputable employment for half of the previous ones and the prisons were already crowded with their victims: four in every cell in the Fleet and the King's Bench, said the *Morning Chronicle* on 27 April, and Newgate was even worse off. Lord Loughborough, who had maintained throughout that the prisoners, however crowded their quarters, would be healthy enough if only they were kept at work, revised his opinion somewhat after an investigation of the situation. His *Observations on the State of the English Prisons, and the Means of Improving them ; Communicated to the Rev. Henry Zouch*, published as a pamphlet on 29 May and reprinted by the *World* on 29 and 30 May, admitted that some alterations were desirable and even "imperative"; but he was disinclined to take the initiative himself, and so evidently was everyone else.

What the newspapers lacked in most areas was a Parliamentary spokesman. On 1 May Lord Lauderdale submitted a petition from James Robertson and Walter Berry, who were protesting the sentences imposed by Lord Braxfield. As in the case of Eaton, the jury had found them guilty only of printing and publishing the pamphlet in question without finding them guilty of intentional libel, but Braxfield had waived their motions for acquittal, and Berry was now serving six months, Robertson three months, in Tolbooth Prison, Edinburgh. The committee, to which the petition was referred for "solemn deliberation," voted to reject it. On 31 May Sir Thomas Charles Bunbury, with the object of "[lessening] the sum of human misery" and "[preventing] an unnecessary expenditure of the public treasure," moved somewhat tentatively for revisions in the treatment of convicts under sentence of transportation. Although these sentences were also imposed by Lord Braxfield, Dundas purported to approve of the revisions and, in order "to consider the resolutions more maturely," moved that the debate be adjourned three months. But, since the injustices of Lord Braxfield were still somewhat peripheral to their own interests, the London newspapers had been pinning their hopes on Lord Rawdon, who was fighting to amend the laws respecting imprisonment for debt.

The Debtor and Creditor Bill had passed its second reading on 27 March, and on 6 May the Lords went into committee on it. At this point it encountered unexpected opposition from the Prince of Wales's friend, the ex-Chancellor, Lord Thurlow, who found almost every clause legalistically objectionable. Despite indignant protests on the part of Lord Rawdon, further consideration of the bill was thereupon postponed until 31 May. On 13 May the *True Briton* informed its readers that the bill had been a mistake: "Lord RAWDON certainly means well and acts from an honourable impulse, in his attempts to meliorate the condition of the unfortunate Debtor; but we have to regret that his Bill should be liable to so many legal objections as to make it likely that it will be lost." The *World* took no such view. As it put it (also on 13 May): "LORD RAWDON'S BILL.—The encreasing Calamity of every week makes all possible attention to this Bill a PUBLIC DUTY in every MEMBER of PARLIAMENT: for, from unforeseen circumstances, the honest, but unfortunate DEBTOR, may daily fall into the hands of the lowest class of wretches, the *Pettifogging* ATTORNIES. On every ground of policy and humanity, the DEBTOR, be he who he may, on fairly and unequivocally surrendering up *his all*, should have free liberty of Person. The monstruous Barbarity of shutting up a set of Beings for no purpose but to gratify the malice and the extortions of ATTORNIES and BAILIFFS, grows too crying an Infliction on the justice of the Country!" It seemed to the *Gazetteer* that something might also be said for the creditors. "Lord RAWDON acts with the true spirit of a British Senator, by endeavouring to reform that pest of society, the pettifogging part of the law," it remarked on 25 May: "It is an evil of magnitude, that, to recover above 40*s*. a creditor is put to 50*l*. expence, should he not gain his cause; and, if he does, the taxed costs leave him four times as much as the debt *minus*."

An item in the *Diary* of 31 May provided a classic example of what could happen to "the honest, but unfortunate DEBTOR": "DIED./ Monday [27 May], in the King's Bench Prison, in an advanced age, and broken down by misfortune T[homas] Attwood, Esq. formerly Chief Judge of the Island of Dominica, and afterwards of the Bahamas." But the item had no effect on the debates of that afternoon. By this time Lord Thurlow not only objected to the Debtor and Creditor Bill, but also objected to the practice of "enlargement within rules," that is, of allowing prisoners who had "acted fairly with respect to one or two debts" to live just outside the prison until they paid the remainder. Even so, he thought the bill might be "so modelled as to become a beneficial measure," and he was therefore willing to recommit it. So was Lord Loughborough, who thought it ought to be turned over to the judges "to frame upon their ideas." Lord Rawdon was furious. He would rather have the bill killed at once, he said; and he wanted also to "complain loudly" about the manner in which he had been treated. Lord Loughborough's assurance that he would be given full credit for the bill, whatever it turned out to be, failed to placate him. By a vote of 10 to 5, the bill was held over to be reconsidered in modified form two months hence. According to the *Star* (1 June), very few Lords were in attendance.

The newspapers accepted the defeat in silence, but by mid-June several of them had again become interested in the case of Lord George Gordon, still imprisoned for debts owed the Government. Visitors reported that his spirit was broken and that he was in a state of such deep despondency that he hardly recognized his friends. On 26 June the *Morning Herald* protested: "Lord GEORGE GORDON has already remained five months in Newgate for want of bail, since the expiration of his sentence of five years imprisonment; so that his punishment, though ending apparently after the term of five years, amounts, in fact, to confinement for life; it not being in his power to procure two persons in bail for so large a sum as two thousand five hundred pounds each." The protest reappeared in the *Gazetteer* of 29 June and in other papers thereafter. Lord Rawdon, who on 20 June succeeded to the Irish title of second Earl of Moira, was not forgotten. The newspapers were certain that he would continue the fight during the next session of Parliament with a variety of other bills. But Pitt also remembered. Before Parliament reconvened, the new Earl of Moira had been elevated to the rank of Major General, and the expectation was that he would be shipped to the Continent.

Burke fared quite as badly as Lord Rawdon. Burke had already suffered considerable humiliation at Pitt's hands, since none of his reform legislation was presently being enforced, and the humiliation had only begun. On 11 March

Pitt had included in his four-year budget the income from the East India
Company, although its charter was due to expire in April, 1794, and Burke had
said repeatedly that he would never consent to its renewal. Fox had protested,
and so had the Opposition newspapers, but Burke had not. On 23 April Dundas
moved that the charter be renewed, since it seemed to him that it had functioned
to everyone's advantage. The only major change which he proposed was that
members of the Board of Control, who had previously served without salary, be
henceforth salaried by the Company. He had rejected, he said, a proposal that
"the appointment in the governments and supreme councils in India . . . be
vested in the Crown," and he would like to explain that he had done so for two
reasons. One was that the King already had "the power of recalling these
officers, if their administration appears to be directed by any but public
measures"; the other was "that a minister might be prevailed upon, from private
motives, or by solicitations from those whom it might be difficult to resist, to
appoint persons whom he himself might not entirely approve of. The case,
however, is widely different when a minister can only recommend a character to
the judgment of [the] twenty-four [members of the Court of Directors]."
Francis, who was as well acquainted with the workings of the East India
Company as Dundas, exploded. Having demonstrated that the Company was
"unfit to manage and govern either for the benefit of the people or for [its] own
advantage," he considered Dundas's argument that the government ought not to
be directly vested in the crown, because the patronage would become "a
formidable source of corruption, if left to the disposal of the King's ministers,"
and it would become an "occasion" of constant "jealousy," if left to the disposal
of Parliament. "I ask the right hon. gentleman, where this dangerous patronage
is vested at present," he said:

> Will he descend from that character of frankness which his friends attribute
> to him, and which he professes himself—will he submit to say that it is *bonâ fide*
> left to the Court of Directors to dispose of the powerful and lucrative offices of
> India; that governors and councillors, that the judges and their train, that the
> commanders of armies, general and field officers, the chiefs of provinces, and the
> collectors of revenue, are really and unequivocally subject to the unbiassed
> nomination of the Court of Directors? We all know that directly the reverse is
> the fact, and that, in all the great and lucrative departments of government, the
> Directors have no more real power than I have. Like other individuals, if they
> want a service or a favour, they must carry their solicitations to the fountain head,
> that is, to the right hon. gentleman himself, who pretends to be so much shocked
> at the thoughts of patronage, and at the suspicion of possessing it.

"NEWSPAPERS," the *Star* remarked on 27 April. "—The India Company pay *one
million* a year to the revenue. It is generally known that the newspapers of
England pay *two hundred thousand pounds* a year to the revenue—that is one-fifth
part as much as a Company who are the Sovereigns of 30,000,000 of souls, who

keep a large standing army, and who have patronage to the amount of several millions a year."

On 13 May Dundas's bill for renewal of the charter was debated clause by clause. Fox objected strongly that the bill not only preserved all the former evils, but introduced some new ones, and he could not help contrasting it with the one which Burke, to his "immortal honour," had introduced in 1780. He repeated these statements on 17 May, and on 24 May he protested passionately that the bill was "nothing but a continuation of that system of deception, fraud, and rapacity, which has marked the conduct of Ministers in the management of the affairs of India" throughout, and that its only purpose was to make the East India Company "the tool of Ministers" by vesting all of its patronage in the Crown. He begged the Commons at least to support an amendment, altering the expiration date of the charter from 1811 to 1797. The Commons refused. Fox's amendment was defeated 132 to 26, and the original bill was passed.

Burke attended the debates on the institution of a Board of Agriculture on 15 May, for on 17 May *Lloyd's Evening Post* reported that he had "introduced two French Clergymen into the House of Commons, and applied to the Speaker to let them sit under the Gallery. The application . . . not being complied with, Mr. Burke showed strong marks of displeasure, applying, as it is said, the appellation of '*Barbare*' to a certain High Character, and that rather loudly." He was not in the House on 24 May. He had been "attending all the day the trial of Mr. Hastings," said Lord Inchiquin; "and the fatigue of that attendance may well be admitted as an excuse for his absence [here]." Where, then, asked the *Morning Chronicle* on 27 May, had he been on 11 March, on 23 April, on 13 May, and on 17 May:

THE INCONSISTENCY OF MR. BURKE.

No person went *such lengths* in reprobation of Mr. DUNDAS's system for the Government of India as Mr. BURKE has done, not only by his speeches in the last Parliament, but by publications to which his name is affixed. One of these publications was a speech made by Mr. BURKE, on the 28th of February, 1785, in which he directly accuses Mr. DUNDAS "of having adopted a system, by which *his faithful band* of Indian sepoys were to be gratified, at the expence of millions of sufferers in India"—of "*perpetuating*" every abuse by his system which Mr. Fox's bill was intended to remedy;" of having "outdone in his *imitation* the crimes that he had reprobated in volumes of Reports, and in sheets of bills of Pains and Penalties;" and after accusing both Mr. PITT and Mr. DUNDAS, of doing "acts of corruption, unequalled in the heroic times of Roman iniquity," he concludes by giving the *following solemn pledge to the world*: "Whoever therefore shall, *at any time*, bring before you *any thing* towards the relief of our distressed fellow-citizens in India, and *toward a subversion of the present most corrupt and oppressive system for its Government*, in *me* shall find a *weak*, I am afraid, but a *steady, earnest*, and *faithful assistant*."

Subsequent to the date of this publication, Mr. DUNDAS brought forth a plan to give the Governor General additional powers. This plan Mr. BURKE *also* most vehemently opposed on the ground of its being the most *arbitrary* and *unconstitutional system* that ever entered into the imagination of man.

In this year Mr. DUNDAS brings into the House of Commons a bill, by which his *system*, that system *so abused by* Mr. BURKE, is to be continued *in all its parts* for twenty years, giving to the Public 500,000*l*. a year from *the plunder of India*, as Mr. BURKE has so often called it, and a dividend of ten per cent. to the Proprietors.

Forgetting *his solemn pledge and engagement*, not chusing to *recollect*, that by this bill the *distressed Princes of India*, whose cause he is pleading in Westminster Hall, are cut off *from every hope of redress for ever*, Mr. BURKE *absents himself* from the House of Commons, in every stage of the discussion of this bill. We do indeed commend his *prudence*, though we can say nothing for his *justice*; for it must have been *extremely awkward* for Mr. BURKE *silently* to hear the assertions of *his new* friend, Mr. DUNDAS, that Bengal had *flourished*, and that the people were happier under our Government, than under their former Sovereigns—that the Bengal resources exceeded five millions—that *his system*, the *system so reprobated by* Mr. BURKE, had *answered*. To be sure all this must have been *poison* to Mr. BURKE, who day by day affirms [in his prosecution of Hastings], that Bengal is *ruined*, and that the resources of the Government were produced by fraud, rapine, murder, and breach of treaty. It was wise therefore in him, rather to subject himself to the *gentle correction* of Mr. FOX and Mr. SHERIDAN, than to be present at a discussion in which he could not remain NEUTER without disgrace, nor speak without differing from his ministerial friends.

"Mr. BURKE was the author of the India Bill in 1780," the *Gazetteer* remembered on 28 May: "A bill is now brought forward in direct hostility to every principle of that produced by Mr. BURKE, yet this he suffers to pass without a syllable of remark. It would be a curious question to decide, whether Mr. BURKE has changed his principles, or whether his consistency is overborne by his fears of offending Mr. DUNDAS."

The Government had made a mockery of the prosecution of Hastings. It had ridiculed it in most of its newspapers; it had rewarded at least two of Hastings's lawyers, Thomas Plumer having been appointed King's Counsel and Edward Law having been appointed King's Attorney and Sergeant for the County of Palantine in Lancaster; and it had contemned the whole of Burke's argument by renewing the charter of the East India Company. The worst was not over. On 21 May the *Oracle* reported that Hastings would testify in his own defense: "Six days are talked of as appertaining to an ORATOR of no little impeachment, and then he rests from his labours *for ever*." The newspapers were generally enthusiastic about Hastings's address, and so evidently was the Archbishop of York, for on 25 May he lost his temper at one of Burke's interruptions. It was "impossible," he said, "to sit silent, to listen to the illiberal conduct of the Managers [of this trial]: they examine a witness as if he was not a witness, but a pickpocket. If Marat or Robespierre were here, they could not conduct the impeachment in a more scandalous manner." The statement was quoted by every newspaper except the *Sun* and the *True Briton*, and most of them commended the Archbishop of York. Even the *True Briton* insinuated into its defense of Burke (28 May) the suggestion that he was a fanatic: "Mr. BURKE, with a becoming attention to a cause in which he so zealously embarked, and from a due respect to public opinion, has never been absent from the Trial of Mr. HASTINGS.—We are sorry to remark, however, that he has sometimes been almost the only Manager in the Box for a whole day together." According to *Lloyd's Evening Post* (29 May), the Archbishop's statement was first called to the attention of the Commons on 28 May, when William Baker produced a copy of the *World*, read the quotation, and denounced it as a libel on the Managers and the House. But, Burke having protested that a motion on the subject would only "stir up more Party attacks," Baker consented to "desist."

Hastings's counsel had concluded its defense much earlier than anyone anticipated, and, having waived the "right to make a general opening," the prosecution was not prepared to present a rebuttal. On 28 May Burke therefore moved for the appointment of a committee to consider the matter, and on 30 May the committee recommended that further hearings be postponed until 12 June and that the Lords be so notified. Prior to this time, Burke had been supported by the *Sun* and the *True Briton* and Hastings by all other newspapers except the *Public Advertiser*, which had been noncommittal. On 29 May the *Public Advertiser* spoke up in defense of Hastings. "There is so much of rebound and of resource in Mr. Hastings's great mind, that many years ago, before his last expedition to India, he had thoughts of setting up an academy for the Oriental languages," it said. "If his trial should last much longer, the expences incurred by it to him may perhaps oblige him to have recourse to his old design." Reacting perhaps to this pronouncement, Burke moved that the Managers prepare a detailed history of this trial in order to demonstrate that they had not been responsible for the previous "delays." The constant insinuations made by newspapers and by members of both Houses to that effect impugned, he thought, the "dignity" of the Commons, "the character of the Managers," and the very "honour of the British nation." The motion was supported by the Opposition and opposed by the Government. Pitt insisted that, no specific charge having been made, the report was "needless," and he strongly recommended that Burke withdraw the motion, as so did Dundas. Burke refused. Everything, he said, depended on the outcome of this trial. If the Commons refused to defend the Managers, its "delegates," against the insolence of the Lords, if the Lords were permitted to "decide this cause on feeling, not on justice, depend upon it, we are gone. It is the last case of the kind that will ever come before that tribunal, on which rests the main security of our Constitution." The motion was defeated. "The Trial of Mr. HASTINGS begins every where to have the appearance of a *last Will* and *Testament*," the *World* commented wearily on 1 June. "The *Defendant*, the *Counsel*, the *Lords*, and the *Managers*, all talk of dying under it."

Burke was obviously approaching a point of exasperation, and, with the intention, one suspects, of precipitating the crisis, Grey moved on 6 June that the hearings be delayed until the next session of Parliament. As one of the Managers, he could attest, he said, that an earlier hearing would seriously jeopardize the cause of the prosecution and greatly assist the cause of Mr. Hastings. Dundas, now genuinely concerned, supported the motion and, even more unexpectedly, admitted that the Lords had been responsible for all the previous delays, but the House nevertheless voted to continue the hearings on 12 June. Burke immediately announced that, in view of these "extraordinary proceedings," he would, on the following day, "bring forward a motion, . . . necessary for the justice and honour of this House." Burke was anticipated by Grey, for, before he could get to his feet, Grey rose (7 June) to state that he interpreted the rejection of his previous motion as an act of censure and that he would therefore demand that the House either "dismiss" him as Manager or give him the opportunity to "discharge" his "task" competently. Burke repeated the demand. More importantly, he said, he would like to know what the "sentiment" of the House was respecting the trial. He knew only that every time it was mentioned, "gentlemen" reacted with "mirth" or with words of "compassion" for Hastings, although Hastings had lived in India "fourteen years, enjoying in salaries and emoluments the sum of 40,000l. a year" and had "caused two unfortunate women to be robbed of one million of money" in addition. At this point he was called to order, and, the Speaker (Henry Addington) having "begged" him "to abstain from further observations on the general question at the present moment," Dundas hastily moved that the hearings be postponed until the next session. The Lords subsequently consented.

Feeling as he did about the French Revolution, Burke would never have rejoined the Opposition, but he might have retired in a rage or, worse, have joined the Duke of Portland's faction, supporting the Government's measures while constantly damning the Government itself. Pitt could afford neither alternative, and, in order to widen the breach, which the Opposition supposed still existed, Whitbread again called the House's attention to the *World* of 27 May with the quoted comment of the Archbishop of York and on 12 June moved for prosecution of the printer. The House might also, he thought, consider the conduct of the Archbishop of York. Francis supported the motion with a stirring eulogy of Burke, who, he implied, had been betrayed by his new friends and would be "a fool indeed" to trust them again. Dundas protested that the insult did not appear in the "records" of the Commons, that the motion should have been made at once, that the Lords was in recess for several months, and that it would be very embarrassing if the printer was acquitted. He therefore moved that the House adjourn and forget the matter.

The proceeding was a farce, for everyone knew that the *World* was Burke's severest critic, that it had been abusing him daily for years, and that two prosecutions of the printer, Robert Bostock, had already been ordered for similar reasons with no results, the first on 16 June, 1789, the second on 21 May, 1790. No action whatever had been taken in the first case; in the second, Bostock had been tried on 7 June, 1790, convicted, and forgotten.[39] But Burke seemed oblivious to these facts. Although he did recommend that, in all such instances, the House handle matters itself rather than "delegate" its powers to "any court whatever," he seemed to have little resentment toward the *World*, he was inclined to forgive the Archbishop of York, in view of his "age and . . . the impatience generally attendant upon it," and he "assured" Francis that he "trusted" no one except God: neither "princes" nor "people." The House voted to adjourn, to the disappointment of Sheridan and the *Oracle*, the latter protesting on 14 June: "The reproach of the ARCHBISHOP of YORK to the Managers is so far the more grating, as he has been for many years one of the most intimate friends of Mr. BURKE." But nothing had seemed "grating" to Burke, for, between 7 and 12 June, Dundas and Pitt had closed the breach by somehow persuading him that they were on his side. On 20 June the Treasury did discontinue its subsidy of the *World*. This cancellation and the postponement of the impeachment hearings were Burke's compensations.

It is notable that the prosecution of Bostock was to be based on the quotation. Although the newspapers had been reporting the debates without particular incident since 1771,[40] only Sheridan suggested that they had a "right" to do so and that the prosecution should therefore be based on supplementary material. The *Oracle* still preferred to regard the reporting of debates as a privilege, which needed to be exercised cautiously. As it put it on 17 June: "Nothing can be more *liberal* than the remark of Mr. SHERIDAN, that it is not criminal in a Newspaper to *report* expressions used in a Court of Justice, or in a House of Parliament even though they be offensive. Yet without assuming it as a *right*, for it is not one, there should be no comment on the part of the Reporter, introductory approbation, or other favouring adjunct: for by this means the Paper adopts the sentiment of the libellous paragraph, and by its circulation, in two ways presses it upon the minds of men—as an assertion made by one of note, and farther strengthened by the Writer's *own* opinion."

Patronage, Politics, and the War

On 27 May the *Morning Chronicle* accused Pitt of "[sacrificing] private friends, to make room for his new associates," but the charge was not entirely fair. On 1 May, according to the *Star* (2 May), John Thomas Townshend was "sworn in as one of the Lords in Commission of the Treasury." Townshend was an old friend of the Government, having been Undersecretary in the Home Department from 1783 to 1789 and Lord of the Admiralty from 1789 to 1793. Another old friend, Robert Hobart, was being added to the Privy Council, and Dundas, it was always understood, could have anything he wanted. When one of the Government spokesmen suggested (17 May) that the new Board of Agriculture would provide places for promising young men, Sheridan replied that there were places enough already, but everything of importance had been appropriated by Dundas or Pitt "If . . . it is asked why one of [the young men] should not be appointed Clerk of the Signet in Scotland, the answer is, that that position is already held by the Treasurer of the Navy; or why one of them should not be appointed to the office of the Treasurer of the Navy, the answer is that that position is already held by the Secretary of State; or why one of them should not be appointed Warden of the Cinque Ports, the answer is, that that position is already held by the Chancellor of the Exchequer." No one ever understood Pitt's attachment to Dundas. The *Gazetteer*'s suggestion (17 May) that Dundas played the political game as Pitt liked to see it played was probably as good an explanation as any: "Mr. DUNDAS, who mixes more good humour as well as more enjoyment with his politics than any of his colleagues, was the agent of Lord LOUGHBOROUGH's conversion," the *Gazetteer* added. "His report on succeeding was—that his Lordship was now '*done to a turn!*'"

Everything the Opposition papers could learn about Dundas had been reported, the *Star* of 12 April mentioning, for example: "A warrant has just passed the Treasury Board, for issuing the sum of 200*l.* secret service money, to . . . HENRY DUNDAS, his Majesty's Secretary of State for the Home Department." None of these items helped his reputation, and, after the debates on the East India Company Bill, his reputation needed some help. Although the *Oracle* did what it could, its ministrations were evidently not enough, for by mid-May all newspapers understood that Dundas would retire as Home Secretary. On 17 May the *Morning Chronicle* announced that his successor would probably be Lord Auckland: "Lord AUCKLAND, it is reported, is to be recalled, created a British Peer, and made Secretary of State; while Mr. DUNDAS, with a snug salary under the India Bill, is to continue President of the Board of Controul, Treasurer of the Navy, and a Member of the Cabinet." The *Star* had heard only (17 May) that Lord Auckland would quit The Hague and be appointed "to an ostensible situation in this country" instead. On 18 May the *London Gazette* announced that "the Right Honourable William Lord Auckland of the Kingdom of Ireland" had been created a British peer, with the title, "Baron Auckland of West Auckland in the County of Durham"; but the newspapers were still certain that he would succeed Dundas as well. The *Gazetteer* said so on 18 May, the *Oracle* on 20 May, the *Oracle* having heard in addition that "Lord MALMSBURY is to be appointed Ambassador at the *Hague vice* Lord AUCKLAND." Dundas was now strongly defended by the *Diary*, and, to help the cause along, he himself announced that he would relinquish his salary as Home Secretary. The *Diary* responded with more eulogies. "Mr. Dundas, as Secretary for the Home Department, has had, perhaps, the most arduous task of any one in that Office since the Rebellion of 1745," it remarked on 24 May. "How well he has executed it, a loyal and grateful nation can bear witness. He has shewed capacity and firmness tempered with coolness, vigilance, and humanity; and he has so ably conducted himself, not to mention his *unparallelled refusal of salary*, that he merits the thanks of Parliament, being one great means of stifling commotion without bloodshed, fully as much as an Admiral or General, who performs a great exploit tending to the glory and welfare of his country!" On 28 May the *Diary* introduced a column, headed "Dialogues of the Dead and Living," the first "Dialogue" being entitled "On *Dundas*'s Secretaryship" and the point of all "Dialogues" being that Dundas was a great man. But Auckland was not, it appeared, acceptable to Pitt, and, according to the *Morning Chronicle* of 31 May, "Mr. PITT has carried his point, so strongly contested against the King's party, that Lord AUCKLAND shall not come into the Cabinet as Secretary of State—It is imagined, however, that his triumph has gone no further than a compromise. Another friend of the new Chancellor is likely to succeed to the situation." Auckland had been retired on a pension of £2,300 a year.

On 6 June the *Morning Chronicle* repeated: "Some difficulties have occurred in the Cabinet about the appointment of LORD AUCKLAND to the Office of Secretary of State; and according to the latest determination, the Earl of CARLISLE is to relieve the over-loaded shoulders of Mr. DUNDAS." The *Gazetteer* agreed. "The Earl of CARLISLE is certainly the candidate, who looks to the Secretaryship of State . . . with the prospect of success," it told its readers on 7 June. "His Lordship's friends . . . say, that his nomination is already made out, and only waits the Royal signature." "Mr. DUNDAS is very naturally anxious to get rid of the office of Secretary of State," it added on 8 June. "When he professed to give up the *pay*, it was not to be expected that he should retain the *trouble*." On 12 June the Earl of Carlisle succeeded the late Earl of Guilford as Knight of the Garter, having resigned the Order of the Thistle for the purpose, but he did not succeed Dundas as Home Secretary. By 14 June the *Oracle* was sure that "Mr. DUNDAS is shortly to have a peerage"; and on 19 June the *Public Advertiser* mentioned that Pitt might quit: "It was yesterday strongly rumoured in the City that Mr. Pitt will be out of office before the end of next month. If such an event should take place, it will remain to be seen, whether it is a remove [*sic*] of policy to afford an opening for peace, or whether he is disgusted with the Hawkesbury influence in the Cabinet." Dundas did not get a peerage, and Pitt did not quit.

According to the *Star* (2 May), Townshend had replaced Eliot as Lord of the Treasury on 1 May, and the *Star* was usually reliable, but the *True Briton* of 19 June was still speaking of this change only as a possibility: "Mr. J. T. TOWNS-HEND, it is said, is to be a Lord of the Treasury in the room of Mr. ELIOT." It did mention, however, that Edward George Eliot and Robert Banks Jenkinson had been appointed to the Board of Control, and on 21 June the Opposition newspapers reported that so had Dundas, the King having appointed him "President of the East-Indian Board, with a yearly salary of 5000*l.*" By this time the *True Briton* was implying that Dundas would be succeeded as Home

Secretary by Windham, he being "now quite in the habits of intimacy with Mr. PITT, and his immediate appointment to some reputable situation [being] no longer a matter of doubt." There was less criticism of Dundas's appointment than one might have anticipated, partly because it was no surprise, partly because it was expected to be followed by his resignation as Home Secretary, and partly because it was overshadowed by the appointment of Jenkinson, who had no qualifications for the post whatever. The *True Briton* argued stoutly that the very purpose of the appointment was to train him, but this explanation failed to satisfy the *Gazetteer*, which stated on 21 June: "Mr. JENKINSON has obtained an admission into the INDIA School of Politics, with a salary for his labours. The confidential aid [and heir] of Lord HAWKESBURY is thus properly repaid. But it is rather whimsical to find HARRY DUNDAS accepting of a similar salary, and entering into the same school for the purpose of *finishing his Education!*"

The newspapers of 24 June were still predicting that Dundas would be replaced by Windham, but on 25 June the *Gazetteer* announced that he would be replaced by Cornwallis and that he had been persuaded to continue as Home Secretary until Cornwallis could "perform the *duty* and receive the *salary* of that important office: Lord AUCKLAND's political principles in the opinion of the Minister, are not yet sufficiently *decided*, it seems, to entitle him to a seat in the Cabinet." This announcement was followed by another defense of Dundas, the *Oracle* of 26 June railing at that "*Party Print*, [which] with bitter invective reprobates Mr. DUNDAS and the other COMMISSIONERS of INDIA AFFAIRS, for accepting of *salaries* to enable them to discharge their duty more faithfully to the Public"; and the defense was followed in turn by another appointment. According to the *Star* of 28 June, the King had appointed Dundas "to be Custos Rotulorum for the County of Middlesex." "Mr. DUNDAS, by his appointment to the Lord Lieutenancy of Middlesex, will have the regulation of all the Police Officers in London and Westminster," the *Star* added on 29 June. The *Oracle* put this somewhat differently. "Mr. DUNDAS's appointment to the Lord Lieutenancy and Custos Rotulorum of Middlesex must afford the greatest satisfaction," it said on 29 June, since the "new Police-officers will be more under his immediate controul." The posts had been "vacant since the death of the late Duke of NORTHUMBERLAND."

Other friends of Pitt fared less well. On 6 June the Duke of Richmond was elected a Fellow of the Society of Antiquaries; on 12 June the Earl of Westmorland, presently Lord Lieutenant of Ireland, was elected Knight of the Garter, although the election was not announced until 12 July and he was not invested until 1795; and by late June George Rose, Jr., had been appointed secretary of the Legation at the Court of Berlin. "Honest George" himself got nothing except possibly some more pensions for his relations. "Mr. ROSE is too *disinterested* to put the *gain* of his newspaper into his private purse," said the *Gazetteer* on 26 June. "He intends to give them—*when any arise*—to his mother and sister, who are at present supported by a *Government pension*, in Edinburgh!" The *Morning Post* felt very sorry for him, since, as it pointed out on 7 June, all he got for his literary labors was flattery: "The place of Paragraph Writer to the Treasury, has been performed gratuitously by the FLOWER of Politics for several years; at present a stipend is allowed to the persons who fill such employments, and nothing is required but to LIBEL all the worth in the Country, and to compliment the *odoriferous* Secretary for his *manliness*, and the possession of all the *virtues* under Heaven."

Of Pitt's recent friends, Jenkinson had been appointed to the Board of Control, and on 21 June the *Evening Mail* announced that "ARTHUR YOUNG Esq. is to be Secretary to the New Agricultural Board." Although Young was being rewarded for his *The Example of France a Warning to Great Britain*, still he had had considerable experience with agriculture and had even published on the subject. The Duke of Portland and his followers got nothing, although this was their fault, not Pitt's. On 14 June the *Star* reported that "yesterday the Duke of PORTLAND and Mr. DUNDAS had audience of Mr. PITT, at his house in Downing-street"; but the report had evidently been fabricated by the *Sun* and the *True Briton*, for on 15 June the *Morning Chronicle* declared: "It is *not true*, as stated by two Treasury Papers yesterday, that Mr. PITT had an interview with the Duke of PORTLAND, nor is it true that he will have the honour of dining with his Grace on Sunday." The *Morning Chronicle* was apparently right. By 3 July, according to *Lloyd's Evening Post*, Earl Spencer had been offered and had declined the Lord Lieutenancy of Ireland. Not content with distributing pensions, places, and sinecures, the Government was also padding expenses. The first reference to this practice, of which there were subsequently many, appeared in the *Star* of 19 June: "A warrant has passed the Treasury, for an allowance of 1,000*l*. to Lord HENRY SPENCER, Secretary to the Embassy at the Hague, to defray the expences of a journey from the Hague to Vienna, and back again."

While Parliament was concerning itself with domestic problems, Lord Grenville had been trying to organize the various enemies and potential enemies of France into a grand coalition, and, since he was offering subsidies, he was making good progress. On 25 March a treaty was signed with Russia, on 10 April with Hesse-Cassel, on 25 April with Sardinia, and on 25 May with Spain. It looked as if the war could not last very long, for the defection of Dumouriez and the outbreak of a counterrevolution in La Vendée had been followed by fresh violence in Paris, culminating in the overthrow of the Girondists on 2 June. The Reign of Terror had begun on 31 May and would last for well over a year. With the French army and navy totally disorganized and France itself almost in a state of civil war, every advantage was, to say the least, on the side of the Allies, and for a while victory seemed to be on their side as well. The plan was to attack the French on three fronts, through the Low Countries, in La Vendée, and in the French West Indies, the "Grand Fleet," under the command of Lord Howe, having meanwhile sought out and destroyed the French navy, so that there would be no interference with shipping. The "Grand Fleet" did set sail in late May, on 14 April the Prussians had commenced a siege of Mainz, which the French had added to their territories on 14 February, and by late April the British had moved five thousand troops into Holland. These troops, plus the Hanoverians and some Hessians, constituted the Duke of York's army, which was to be added to the Austrian army in an attack on Dunkirk. On 8 May the Duke of York captured St. Amand and on 23 May commenced a siege of Valenciennes.

Except for daily rumors of the execution of Marie Antoinette, the London newspapers were rather well acquainted with political developments in France, but they seemed to know little about the state of the war. One reason was their persistent interest in stockjobbing. Reports of victories, defeats, invasions of Ireland, and negotiations for peace were part of the daily fare, all of them having been manufactured for a purpose. On 30 April the *Oracle* stated, for example: "The Funds yesterday, experienced a considerable rise; the Scrip, for instance, got up as high as 79¼. The reasons assigned were various as to particulars, though they all pointed to one great end, viz. PEACE." "The Stocks were very heavy on Saturday morning, from a rumour in circulation, that the Combined Army could not proceed from a total want of provision and forage," said the *Gazetteer* on 13 May. And on 20 May the *Oracle* announced: "Orders were given, that no Papers should be delivered to the public on Saturday [18 May]; and that letters should not be given out till this day: The Particulars of our Letters from *Brussells*, and from *our Correspondent with the British Army*, cannot therefore be communicated until *to-morrow*." No other newspaper had heard of such "orders," and the implication that a peace was in the making was denied by the *True Briton*, which mentioned on 21 May: "A week and ill-informed Print, apparently in the pay of some desperate jobbers still persists most obstinately in asserting, that the French Executive Council has transmitted Commissioners to treat for Peace with this Country. . . ."

Another reason for the paucity of war news was willful misrepresentation on the part of the *True Briton*, which not only pretended to be, but actually was, the spokesman for the Government. So far as that newspaper was concerned, the news was an uninterrupted succession of Allied victories. Since none of the stories was ever retracted, a map, published on 29 June, with the caption, "A Sketch of the Position of the Combined Armies before Valenciennes and Conde," proved quite a shock to the readers, who had been given to understand that both cities had been captured weeks earlier. It was no shock to other newspapers, which had been suspicious of the stories right along. The *Gazetteer* had charged on 13 May that Heriot and Miles were manufacturing the stories in order to "please their employers"; and on 15 May *The Times*, always more interested in priority than accuracy, charged that the stories were not even decently manufactured:

> One of the morning papers of yesterday, because it belongs to a few Clerks in some of the Public Offices, has the impudence to assume to itself the *exclusive*

monopoly of all the NEWS that comes to this country. This observation is the more arrogant and presuming, as the fact is directly the reverse, as the columns of that paper can testify, many of them being daily filled with extracts from the TIMES of the preceding day.

We wish not to trouble our readers with observations on our own, or on those newspapers belonging to other proprietors. The Public will always, and very properly, judge for themselves. As the paper in question has however chosen to give an opinion of this, we shall for once condescend to notice it, by observing— that it is a compilation of *absurd bombast, fulsome panegyric, libellous calumny*, and is conducted under the most *abject servility* that ever disgraced a newspaper.

The *True Briton* was meanwhile (15 May) accusing *The Times* of "sporting" with the "feelings" of the Duchess of Gordon. This was a grave accusation, for newspapers were expected to extort money only from members of the opposite party, and the Duchess of Gordon was the social leader of the Tories.

Despite all the supposed victories, the war continued to be unpopular, and by mid-May the Government had resolved to devote the summer to military entertainments, which, it hoped, would stimulate enlistments. The Ministerial newspapers were enthusiastic; the *Morning Chronicle* was not. "The Duke of RICHMOND is bravely resolved not to be an inactive spectator of the war," it said on 21 May. "His Grace will put himself at the head of one of the holiday camps that are going to be formed; and woe to the enemy that shall dare to approach his wooden redoubts, manned with pasteboard grenadiers." Heading the war party, so far as the newspapers were concerned, was now Edmund Burke rather than Pitt, for the same papers which were denouncing his prosecution of Hastings were quoting with admiration his own denunciations of the French Revolution. Heading the peace party was Fox, whose principal crime, in the eyes of the *True Briton* (e.g., 1 June), was "his intemperate and unjust eulogium of the Battle of *Jemappe*." The Princes seemed to be divided. Every report indicated that the Prince of Wales shared all the views of his parents, with whom he was now on very comfortable terms; and, according to *Lloyd's Evening Post* (27 May), he was even moving in Tory circles, having recently attended "a grand public dinner," given by the Duchess of Gordon at her house in St. James's Square. He was devoted to his regiment, or, as the *Oracle* put it on 25 April: "The PRINCE seems partially attached to the *uniform* of his Regiment— A wise provision makes it impossible for his military ardour to be farther gratified." There was also no doubt about the "military ardour" of another Prince. "PRINCE ERNEST," said the *Oracle* on 21 May, "is with the advanced Guard of the Army.—The conduct of the young Nobility in the War against *Democracy*, is well calculated to erase all low prejudices against RANK 'often useful, always beautiful.'" A third Prince had been swept away by "ardour" of another sort. The first announcement of the marriage of Prince Augustus appeared in the *Oracle* of 23 April: "An ILLUSTRIOUS young English Personage, now on his travels in Italy, is said to be lately married to Lady AUGUSTA MURRAY, the eldest daughter of Lord DUNMORE. They were united at *Rome*. His R[oyal] H[ighness] is just twenty years of age, the Lady turned of thirty. This event will cause much investigation in the political circles, on the score of precedence." Prince Augustus was not in any event interested in the war, and neither, it had appeared, was the Duke of Clarence. On 21 May the *Oracle* had declared that the "reason why his Royal Highness of CLARENCE is treated in so scurrilous a way in the Party Papers, appears to be his *aversion* to REFORM and attention to his DUTY." Readers must have wondered what "DUTY" the *Oracle* had in mind, for there had been no indication that he was "attending" to anything except Mrs. Jordan. But on 1 June the *True Briton* again announced that he would assist "the War against *Democracy*": "The DUKE of CLARENCE has reduced his Household, and is preparing for his departure to sea." The same announcement in modified form appeared in the *World*: "The Duke of CLARENCE previous to his departure for sea, will sell off all his household furniture, the *Jordan* excepted—which is to be preserved as a *keep-sake*." It also appeared in the *Star*, which reprinted the item from the *World*, substituting "pickling-dish" for "keep-sake," Mrs. Jordan being known as "Little Pickle."

On 5 June the Ministerial newspapers were stunned to learn that a group of "NOBLEMEN AND GENTLEMEN" were meeting at the Crown and Anchor to set up a fund for payment of Fox's debts. Presiding at the meeting was James Adair, the motion for establishment of the fund was made by Francis, the committee in charge of planning consisted of Lord John Russell, Lord George Henry Cavendish, Philip Francis, John Crewe, a Mr. Cyner, William Wrightson, Alderman Skinner, Alderman Coombe, and Adair, and the trustees were Mr. Coke of Norfolk, Thomas Pelham, and George Byng. The *Morning Chronicle* immediately supported the fund on the ground that Fox might be enjoying the patronage of Dundas, Rose, and Lord Grenville, had he been willing to eat Pitt's "toads," and that he certainly deserved some reward as a man of principle, who had sacrificed everything to the interests of the people. The Ministerial newspapers, well aware of the propagandistic effect of such arguments on the people, retaliated generally with ridicule and protests, but the *Public Advertiser* of 7 June was compelled to admit that the collections were mounting apace: "Mr. Fox's Subscription Fund, under the direction of Mr. Serjeant Adair and Mr. Francis, is said already to exceed forty thousand pounds, deposited in the hands of Mr. Coke, of Norfolk; and the exertions of the Party will no doubt encrease that sum to the amount of one hundred thousand pounds at the ensuing meeting of the Whig Club, under the auspices of Lord Petre." The *World* and *True Briton* (8 June) protested that Fox had not been neglected: "Mr. Fox's friends, in their zeal to serve him, had advanced what is not strictly true, viz. that Mr. Fox has never received any emolument or benefit from his Country. Mr. Fox was once in possession of a place in Ireland *for life*, which produces about 1800*l*. a year, but which, from his extravagance, Mr. Fox found it necessary *to sell*." This was the Clerkship of the Pells, which Fox inherited in

1774. But such protests were outweighed by the *Oracle*'s announcement of 11 June, "The Subscription for Mr. Fox increases rapidly. *Ten Thousand Pounds* are expected from his Grace of BEDFORD," and the *Public Advertiser*'s announcement of 14 June: "Seventy Thousand Pounds are the present amount of the Fund raised by the Friends of Mr. Fox. The Dukes of Portland and Bedford very handsomely grant an annuity of two thousand pounds for Mr. Fox's life, at the price of 22,000*l.* taken from this Fund." However, the *Public Advertiser* continued:

> [when] Mr. Fox talks of "receiving from the *Public* a disinterested proof of their affection," he is much mistaken—it is to his Party—his particular friends—and NOT the Public, to whom he is beholden for whatever subscriptions may be raised in his favour—To prove this, let a general subscription be open at the bars of several coffee-houses about town, and then see what sums the general mass of the People would subscribe for this man, who "never had any object in view but the good of the PUBLIC!" Perhaps they would remember the Middlesex Election [of 1788]—the Coalition [with Lord North]—the Regency Bill—the *glorious fabric* of the French Revolution—the *joy* for the Victory of Jemappe, &c. &c.

On 15 June the *Public Advertiser* suggested that the fund was not what it purported to be:

> Many people have presumed to suspect that the *charitable subscriptions* for the support of Mr. Fox, is not so much intended for the relief of the *indigent Patriot* him*self,* as to raise a large sum in order to supply the wants of a *bankrupt Party.* Indeed there seems to be some reason for this suspicion, if a report may be trusted which says, that two Noblemen have agreed to allow Mr. Fox an annuity of two thousand pounds, for the sum of *twenty-two thousand pounds*, which they have each taken from the *charitable fund.* One of the noblemen [the Duke of Bedford] is too rich to stand in need of the sum he is said to have taken for the annuity, but the other [the Duke of Portland] is not supposed to roll in affluence, and therefore if the first of the report is well-founded, may be thought to have assented to the measure by way of a blind, to cover the necessities of the other.

The case was argued for an additional column. To the annoyance of the *Morning Chronicle*, the *True Briton* was indulging in similar argumentation.

Fox, the War, and the
"Ingratitude" of Mr. Burges

The Times had approved of Fox's fund, not, as it said, because it agreed with his opinions, but because it respected his principles. The *Morning Chronicle* expected similar approval from the *True Briton*, for the evident reason that James Bland Burges had once been befriended by Fox. But the *True Briton* did not approve, and on 15 June the *Morning Chronicle*, having accused it of perfidy and railed at length about its prostitute status, went on to assail its principal contributors:

> A correspondent remarks that in perusing the newspapers of the Treasury underlings, the paragraphs of the two *Secretary-Editors* are easily known by a curious species of analogy between the style in which they are written, and those avocations by which it was the pride of their early days to be distinguished. Each of these ornaments to the quill coming late into literature, it is not to be wondered that each should have transfused into his compositions some of the spirit and peculiarities of his former condition. Thus the ribaldry of *Rose* puts us continually in mind of the damaged stores of a Purser; while the balderdash of *Burgess*, like the refuse of an oil-shop, resembles an *amalgama* of mouldy mushrooms, and corrupted cabbage, dealt out by a retailer of *putrefying pickles*.

Rose had once been in the Navy, although not necessarily as a purser; Burges was being deliberately confused with one of the *True Briton*'s advertisers, "J. Burgess," the "pickle-man." Further comment was delayed by a notice that on 17 June Fox would move for peace. The *Morning Chronicle* always supported such motions wholeheartedly.

As it happened, General Dumouriez was in London when the motion was made, but, after his defection, only the *Oracle* had indicated any interest in him, and its information had been slight. On 19 April it had reported that "Du-MOURIER, since his flight to the Austrians, has issued a second Proclamation, in which he calls all the Generals who refused to join him traitors; and talks as confidently of the frank and noble Proclamation by the Prince of COBOURG, as if he did not know that Proclamation to be a mere delusion.—Treachery defeated often leads to fatuity." It had been upset to hear on 20 April that he was to fight on the side of the Austrians. Lafayette, it remembered, was thrown into a dungeon, although he "fought only to preserve *freedom* for *France*, [but] the *darling* HERO of *Republicans*, whose ambition ravaged *Brabant*, and was rapidly running over *Holland*, is trusted for apostacy with command, and confided in as the faithful ABDIEL of an infernal Host!" By 6 May it had discovered that he had not been trusted: "General DUMOURIER is said by some accounts to have gone to *Vienna*, and by others to have retired to *Switzerland*; but it is agreed on all hands, that the PRINCE de COBURG did not choose to entrust him with any military command whatever." On 15 June Dumouriez appeared in England, but so little notice was taken of his visit that readers would hardly have been aware of it. On 19 June the *Star* mentioned that he had arrived in London on Saturday and "received an order from the Secretary of State for the Home Department to quit the kingdom in 48 hours"; on 20 June the *Public Advertiser* remarked that, on "Monday night [17 June]," he had "got one of the notices authorised by the Alien Bill, to quit the country on Tuesday morning" and had accordingly departed; and on 21 June the *Morning Chronicle*, which was now rather fond of him, thanked the Government for protecting the people against this desperate alien. "The Duke of RICHMOND is said to have been awake and *personally* on watch in the *Tower*, during the three nights that M. DUMOURIER passed in London," it added. On 1 July, the newspapers understood, Dumouriez was arrested in Ostend.

There was almost as little interest in Fox's motion as there was in the visit of Dumouriez. On the morning of 17 June, the *Gazetteer* mentioned parenthetically: "The old fiction that Mr. Fox 'glories in the battle of *Jemmappe*,' is revived with additions by the Treasury Clerks in their paper. The obvious malignity of the lye at the present moment is all that entitles it to notice. The public sufficiently remember, that the phrase in question fell from Mr. COURTENAY, and the name of *Jemmappe* was never mentioned by Mr. Fox, but to blame Ministers for a waste of blood, which, by their efforts, properly directed, might have been averted." The *World* struck a blow at Burke, although Burke was certain to support the Government: "POLITICAL FRIENDSHIP.—BURKE subscribes nothing to CHARLES FOX." And the *Diary* at least provided Fox with some ammunition by observing: "A warrant has passed the Treasury Board for 100,000*l*. to Baron Alvensleben, being part of the grant of Parliament for the corps of Hanoverian troops, in British pay, now serving under the command of . . . the Duke of York." The national debt had again been an issue, principally because of the appearance on 11 June of Edward King's *Considerations on the Utility of the National Debt ; and on the Present Alarming Crisis : with a Short Plan of a Mode of Relief, and an Explanation of the Solid Inherent Grounds of Great National Prosperity, that Exist in this Country*. King felt that a large national debt was the very ground of a nation's prosperity.

Although only the *Morning Chronicle* had indicated any concern, Fox made a good speech. He would not, he said, indulge in recriminations: he would even suppose, for the sake of argument, that the war had originally been justified. The question with which he would concern himself was whether there was any justification in continuing it. Having concluded that there was not, Fox went on to mention that an "immediate termination of [hostilities] is almost the universal desire of the people in this country." This was perhaps the most important statement in the address, since, on all previous occasions, he had said that the war was "thought to be popular." Although Windham opposed the resolutions, even he admitted in effect that public sentiment was on the side of peace, but he could not think that "simple illiterate persons" ought to be deciding "questions of state . . . —particularly with regard to war." The resolutions were also opposed by Burke, who added a word of praise for Dumouriez: "no mean man," he said, and one whom he himself was "rather glad to see as a guest here in London." The resolutions were defeated by a vote of 187 to 47. Pitt was so sure of the outcome that he took the opportunity to announce that there would probably be "fresh taxes" within the next year, and Dundas laid before the House copies of the treaties with Russia, Hesse-Cassel, and Sardinia. The treaty with Spain, although signed on 25 May, was withheld.

While the debates in the Commons were progressing according to expectation, there was a real surprise in the Lords, where the issue was Lord Auckland's Memorial of 5 April. Earl Stanhope had concluded a denunciation of that document with a motion that it be "publicly disavowed by His Majesty," and, the motion having been vigorously opposed by Lord Grenville, the Duke of Clarence suddenly announced that he would like to "say a few words, and they shall be but few." Readers had last heard of him on 7 June, when the *World* had reported that he would be joining the fleet momentarily: he "certainly sells off all his moveables at Petersham—the *fixtures* are to remain; the *Jordan*, of course, is reckoned amongst the latter." Without specifying his intentions, the Duke made it clear that he had previously been sympathetic with the Government, but Lord Grenville's speech had convinced him, he said, not only of the injustice of the Memorial, but of the stupidity of the war, both as to purpose and present conduct; and he, for one, would play no part in it. The motion was negatived, and on 21 June the King prorogued Parliament to 13 August.

The Duke of Clarence's announcement was a bombshell to the press and evidently to the Government, since, from 19 June on, there were reports of frequent conferences between Dundas and the Prince of Wales and between the Prince of Wales and the Duke of Clarence. Reactions to it varied. The *Public Advertiser* confined itself (19 June) to the facts: "The Duke of Clarence's speech may be said to have made more impression on the House, than that of any Noble Lord who delivered his sentiments on the subject of Lord Auckland's memorial, for it not only turned the Ambassador's conduct into ridicule, but opposed the sentiments of the Ministry in both houses." The *True Briton* (19 June) sneered: "The DUKE of CLARENCE said, in the House of Peers, that he believed HIS MAJESTY's Ministers would be at a loss to declare *where* we were carrying on the War. This is a proof that the Royal Sailor holds no correspondence with his Brother of YORK, who certainly could inform him pretty accurately *where* the War was carrying on with vigour, honour, and success." The *Morning Chronicle* (19 June) predicted trouble for the Duke: "The Duke of CLARENCE having declared his disapprobation of perishing in a war, in which the people of this country can gain nothing, but increase of death and taxes, will find the disgusting praise of the Treasury papers converted into abuse." *The Times* was convinced (21 June) that something sinister was going on: "That *the Duke of* CLARENCE should vote for making PEACE with the French Regicides, when the British Army, in conjunction with the Combined Forces, were triumphantly erecting the Standard of Loyalty over the Tree of Rebellion and Democracy, is *strange— very strange*, indeed!" The *Oracle* (26 June) was seemingly determined to think the best: "Some People attempt to account for the Duke of CLARENCE's extra-ordinary opposition to the War, in various ways. We are inclined to ascribe to him those motives which redound most to his *credit*." But the *Oracle* was in fact thinking the worst, since it was alluding again to that Dutch loan. A later hint that the Duke was miffed because he was not commanding the Grand Fleet instead of Lord Howe probably came closest to the truth.

With the focus of interest on the Duke of Clarence's pronouncement, other events of 17 June tended to be forgotten, but on 21 June the *Gazetteer* at least remembered the treaties. "Three treaties, made in the month of March and April last, are just now laid on the tables of the two Houses of Parliament," it reported. "The first of these treaties, with the EMPRESS [of Russia], binds us to continue the war at her pleasure. The second is for a quantity of that *live stock*, commonly called soldiers, from the Landgrave of HESSE CASSEL. The third obliges us to contribute 200,000*l.* per ann. to enable the King of SARDINIA to defend his own dominions." Other papers were remembering Fox and the fund for payment of his debts. He was now subjected to the daily ridicule of the *True Briton*, with the assistance from time to time of the *World* and the *Public Advertiser*. "I have lost my money at the Gaming-table and at Newmarket," the *True Briton* whined on 18 June. "—I have sold a Place for life which produced 1800*l.* per annum—I have been an Advocate for the Rights of Man, and triumphed in the glorious Victory of *Jemappe*! Do, good Christian! subscribe something to my support!" "It is a very singular circumstance," the *Public Advertiser* expostulated on 19 June,

> that Mr. Fox has been often accused of having exulted in "the *glorious victory* of JEMAPPE," according to the very words which Mr. Fox was said to have used soon after that victory was made known, and yet that no friend of Mr. Fox, and no literary tool devoted to his party, ventured to deny that he had expressed any such exultation till after the *eleemosinary* fund was set on foot, for the purpose of *securing* Mr. Fox in the *interest* of the Party. If Mr. Fox did not utter such an expression, why was not the contradiction published before, since it has so often been charged upon him? Does the *arch Patriot* begin to fear, that a supposed zeal in the cause of France, may lessen the *charitable fund* in the opinion of English-men?

But the *True Briton* was now (19 June) attacking from another angle, replying in effect to the *Chronicle*'s charge of 15 June that Burges was "ungrateful":

The *Jacobin Chronicle* accuses us of deriving all our information upon Public Subjects from the Public Offices. This is an accusation which we deem an honour, and which is certainly very much calculated to advance our interest— but we think we could point out a *good-natured man* in Office, who, by stealth, sometimes conveys the same intelligence even to the *Jacobin Chronicle*.

Is it a *very safe topic* for the Conductors of the *Jacobin Chronicle* to touch upon the *manner* in which intelligence is obtained? Perhaps they would not be pleased if we were to point out, by name, an *inferior Clerk* in one of the Public Offices, who is in habits of intimacy with Mr. Fox, and who has been *strongly suspected* of a *trifling breach of confidence*, in communicating to him, as well as to certain Jacobin Papers, the little official information [his position] gives him an opportunity of knowing.

Burges, the *Gazetteer* remarked on 19 June, was a bore: "Mr. Deputy Secretary BURGESS is not only a *Poet*, but a *Musician*: he has lately written and set to music, an Ode to *Sleep* of such exquisite *characteristic* merit, that it is impossible to read, or to hear it, without *yawning!*" By this time the *Morning Chronicle* had resolved to silence the *True Briton*, if possible, once and for all. Except for the *World*, no newspaper had thus far survived a siege of unremitting ridicule, and, despite the Treasury's ministrations, financial and supervisory, even the *World* had failed to recover the circulation, dignity, and influence it lost in 1789. Since the *True Briton* was actually owned by the Treasury and whole editions were circulated throughout the country at the Treasury's expense, it could not be damaged financially, but a newspaper at which every one was laughing was no credit to the Government. The siege began on 16 June and continued until 1 August.

On 16 June the *Morning Chronicle* stated flatly that Fox had not "gloried or exulted in the victory of Jemappe" and that, when Captain Berkeley had accused him of doing so in one of the debates, he had been called to order and compelled to admit that he was mistaken. As to the *True Briton*, the *Chronicle* went on, it would be very glad to trade exposés with Burges and Rose any day in the week. This statement seems to have had some effect, for the *True Briton* discontinued its abuse of Fox, and the *Morning Chronicle* of 21 June indicated that Burges was making a peace offering, which, it also indicated, it would not accept: "Terms of accommodation have been proposed to us by BURGESS, who feeling himself somewhat embarrassed how to express his pacific dispositions in the most satisfactory manner, has packed up a *set* of his finest *olives*, which we understand are now on the way to the Printer of this Paper./ If BURGESS's paper scorns to *receive* a bribe, this anecdote will shew that he is not above offering one. But we scorn his insidious *delicacies*! '*Timeo Danaos*, &c. *dona ferentes*.' We translate for the Under Secretary's benefit—'*We could not eat his olives though they were as plenty* [*sic*] *as blackberries*.'" On 22 June Burges was assailed as a dullard and an ingrate:

> That Secretary *Placid* [a pun on the name *Bland*] is a dull man, is no fault of his, it may be said. Genius and abilities are given but to few; and surely it is

rather in his favour, at least on the score of spirit, that he should still persevere in a struggle to be thought a wit, after the many defeats to which he is daily subject, and to the continual admonitions of his best friends, to abandon so desperate an undertaking. We are far from combating such pretensions to praise as these on the part of Secretary *Placid*; but when dullness is associated with ingratitude to benefactors—when stupidity allies itself with envy—when eternal efforts to be comical, instead of ending in a joke, possibly bad enough, but excuseable from having some coarse good nature in it, produce nothing but an heterogeneous mixture of buffoonery and malice, we must confess, that a character possessed of these qualities, so far from having a claim to the common, compassionate toleration usually extended towards men of shallow understandings, excites in us a feeling which can only not be denominated contempt from its being necessarily accompanied with aversion and disgust.

On 25 June the *Morning Chronicle* was joined by the *Gazetteer*, which contributed several paragraphs to the cause: "The LORD CHANCELLOR [Lord Loughborough] has certainly not subscribed any part or period of the profitable commissions of bankruptcy to the subscription now pending at the Crown and Anchor Tavern." "It is useless to ask for lists of casualties in this war, for it is asserted in the morning paper of GEORGE ROSE [the *True Briton*], that the infantry can turn aside the balls with their hands; and in his evening of Saturday [the *Sun*], it is asserted that the cavalry avoid the balls by the *fleetness* of their horses." "We are authorized to assure the publick and the *curious* in *fish sauce*, that a respectable tradesman in the Strand, whose *name* has of late been frequently alluded to in a Morning Paper, has no connection in *politics* or *pickles*, with a certain Under Secretary of State." The name of the "respectable tradesman" was J. Burgess, and the *Morning Chronicle* had suggested the "connection" by misspelling Burges's name. Still silent on the subject of Fox, the *True Briton* of 26 June ventured the comment that the *"Jacobin Chronicle* has been dealing largely in *pickles* lately—it probably will become well peppered," which the *Chronicle* of 27 June dismissed with some verses:

> BURGESS, I frankly must confess,
>   No *Attic* salt, dear Sir, is thine!
> If any salt thou dost possess,
>   'Tis salt of *Pickle*, *Sauce*, and *Brine*.

A VERY SERIOUS REFLECTION.
How chang'd for the worse Nature every day grows,
  To exclaim with the ancient Poet of Rome!
Who'd believe, from that beautiful thing call'd a ROSE,
  Such loathsomeness, foulness, such stenches could come!

On 29 June there was a long letter, signed "A FRIEND TO THE HONEST BURGESSES," which protested that the oil and pickle business was an honourable business and that "J. Burgess, the oil and pickle-man, in the Strand," objected to being confused with James Bland Burges, since "Mr. B. the oil-man is a worthy man, and does no dirty work, except in his shop and his cellar . . .: he is *grateful for favours*, and civil to his customers."

The *Chronicle* of 1 July was crammed with letters from "correspondents" respecting the origin of Burges's name. The *Chronicle* itself thought it was Italian:

> We are happy to announce a delicious repast for our tasteful readers. In a small box in which the *jar of olives*, sent as a peace-maker to our Printer, was carefully packed, he found a parcel, entitled,—"*An assortment of Sprigs and Scraps of Poetry*," which we find to be the genuine composition of Mr. Under-Secretary Placid himself. He seems to have known how to tempt all our palates. The Printer praises the olives, as being high-flavoured, and we can assure our readers, that the poetry has the true Italian gusto;—a circumstance which seems strongly to confirm the assertion of the Under-Secretary (notwithstanding the contradiction of our correspondent Blandoso) that he is sprung from the illustrious house of *Borghese*, and to reconcile it with his degradation into an oilman; for on a scrap hardly legible, . . . we have made out the two following lines:
> "Ah me! what changes in this life we view;
> "I sells the olives, as my fathers grew."

There were more letters on 2 July, the "correspondents" agreeing that Burges had once been a "pickle-man," but disagreeing as to whether he was originally Spanish, Swiss, or Italian. The *Chronicle* could state positively that he had been a "pickle-man," even though he was admittedly not the J. Burgess who was "in the Oil and Pickle trade" at present. As the *Oracle* remarked on 8 July, the publicity was at least "[operating] very beneficially for our friend BURGESS [the pickle-man]. He ought really to pay for the Paragraphs as *Advertisements*."

In addition to ridiculing Burges and Rose, the *Morning Chronicle* had been running a serialized eulogy of Fox, who was now being daily belabored by the *World*. The gist of the *World*'s squibs was that the fund had failed, and on 6 July the *True Briton* ventured a similar comment: "Mr. Fox resides in seclusion at St. Anne's Hill, watching with anxious eye, and, we fear, an aching heart, the slow progress of his Subscription./ Mr. SHERIDAN, in subscribing a thousand pounds to the relief of Mr. Fox, was not so much a *pigeon* as has been supposed, but more of a *decoy-duck*." This comment was ignored, but almost every other statement made by the *True Briton* was greeted with jeers by the *Morning Chronicle*. A puff of the Duke of Richmond moved the *Chronicle* to remark on 11 July, for example:

> Nothing can be a stronger instance of the large cargoes of *perishable* panegyric now in the treasury *stores*, than that *rations* of it are served out even to the DUKE of RICHMOND. As for GEORGE ROSE and Secretary PLACID, they are store-keepers general of this mouldy commodity, and may always order for their own use whatever quantity they please.

The *Wit* of Under-Secretary *Placid* is like the *appetite* of his customers—"*keen—devilish keen!*" How pleasant it must be for him to carry in his mind all the resources of his warehouse! We are at a loss to compare his excellence with any thing but what DRYDEN has described of ZIMRI—

> "His trade so various, that it seem'd to be
> "Not one, but every trade's epitome;
> "'Twas, in the space of one revolving moon,
> "Pimp—fiddler—scribbler—oilman—and buffoon."

On 13 July the *True Briton* ventured another comment on Fox: "Mr. Fox has completely failed in the object of his Subscription, by the indiscretion of his friends. If they had let it rest upon the footing of charity *merely*, he might by this time have raised a very comfortable sum./ We have not heard that the Trustees of a certain Mendicant have yet *touched* SHERIDAN's Thousand." This comment was also ignored, but on 16 July the *Chronicle* replied to the *True Briton*'s condemnation of "pharo parlours":

> Under-Secretary *Placid*, in his paper of yesterday, has shewn us how wonderfully a *good conscience* sets a man at his ease, and with what happy effect it enables him to inculcate the lessons of honour and morality. Gaming, that horrible sin—that crying, extraordinary vice—that unheard-of offence against God and man—that wicked practice, by which so much good money is *lost*, is still the burthen of his song, still animates him to those sublime exertions which proclaim so incontestably to the world, that gratitude to benefactors is not the only virtue contained within his precious bosom. Like the great teachers of old, *Placid* Under-Secretary perceives the necessity of seasoning instruction by example; and we are happy to know, in confirmation of the good opinion we have ever expressed of him, that he *never touches a card*, or is addicted to any *such* methods of getting money. The Under-Secretary knows that there are other means, far less hazardous, by which little and low men *descend from their garrets*, and are enabled to vie in their purchases with the most *opulent pursers* [a reference to Rose], and to raise themselves in society to a level with the most *eminent under-strappers* of the age!

On 19 July the *Morning Chronicle* replied to a slur on Lord Lansdowne:

> Mr. *Secretary Placid* is very liberal of abuse on the MARQUIS of LANSDOWNE, and with a very good cause. The noble Marquis was the political foster father of Mr. PITT; and with respect to favours received, Mr. *Placid* judges of Mr. PITT's *feelings* by his *own*.
>
> Under-Secretary *Placid*, it is known, is an avowed enemy to *gaming*. In his paper of yesterday he declares himself as strongly against *private calumny*.
>
> On this last subject the Under-Secretary is tolerably safe. Not being given to panegyrick, he is exempt from the charge of calumniating others, while his own character is such as to make it impossible that any thing in the resemblance of calumny can be said against himself!

On 20 July the usual prose denunciations were supplemented by verse:

SECRETARY PLACID'S FAC-TOTUM ROOM.
There vapid paragraphs in bundles lay,
Here rang'd around the olives take the shelf,
Poetry and music, stop the passing way,
Whilst in the middle, stands—his mighty Self.

For the last ten days of the month, the *Morning Chronicle* talked of nothing except the stupidity, crudity, and hypocrisy of the *True Briton*, and, since the Opposition newspapers were likely to co-operate in such enterprises, it was probably supported by the *Gazetteer*, the *Morning Post*, and the *Courier*. The *Gazetteer* was in fact still scoffing at Rose on 14 August: "Mr. GEORGE ROSE, ever 'tremblingly alive' to fame, is so much gratified by the approbation of his fellow-citizens, that he has been at the expence of an advertisement in his own Journal, to announce a vote of thanks to himself from a county *smoking club!*" The *True Briton* was not destroyed; nor was it silenced on the subject of Fox. On 25 July it even expanded its tactic by announcing that, since the public had been reluctant to trust Fox with a flat sum, the fund was being converted to an annuity, to which all readers were urged to subscribe. The announcement appeared in the form of a letter, which was followed on 31 July by the statement: "There is nothing surely so honourable in Mr. Fox's friends, as raising for him an annuity of 3000*l.*; and nothing can prove so much their *reliance* upon his *prudence* and *honour*, as their settling it upon him in such a way as that he cannot alienate it, or, in other words, *gamble it away.*" Since even the *Oracle* was admitting (31 July) that on paper, at least, the fund was growing apace ("The *Subscription* for Mr. Fox exceeded 100,000*l.* a week ago. How the *Cash* comes in we are not informed."), this tactic was temporarily abandoned, and, for the next few weeks, the abuse was leveled more directly at Fox. "Bravo!" exclaimed the *True Briton*, for example, on 3 August, "at it again! Mr. Fox *did not* support the doctrine of *General Warrants* upon his first coming into Parliament! Mr. Fox *did not* rejoice in the Victory of *Jemappe!* Mr. Fox *did not* applaud the glorious Fabric of the French Revolution! Oh, no! Mr. Fox *never did any thing!/* Truth, Honour, and Consistency, what are ye to a Jacobin!" But by mid-August the *True Briton* had returned to its old theme. "CRUEL ROBBERY!" it shrieked typically on 17 August; "—There is a report in circulation, that, as CHARLES FOX was going a few days ago to ST. ANNE'S HILL, he was robbed of *his whole Subscription*, which he was carrying home in his breeches pocket." The attacks continued throughout September. Although the *World* contributed a few items, noting, for example, on 26 September, "NEUTRALITY.—SHERIDAN has not contributed to CHARLES Fox's Fund; he has, however, positively declared, that he will not take any thing from it," the principal assailant was the *True Briton*. Yet the *Morning Chronicle* had not labored in vain, for Fox emerged with a gift of £70,000, and Rose and Burgess with a badly battered newspaper. J. Burgess, the "pickle-man," was not heard of again until November, when advertisements for "cases of pickles, cases of rich sauces, potable soups, dried tongues, Hams, &c." were again appearing in the *True Briton*. Readers interested in these commodities were invited to visit his warehouse at No. 107, Strand.

The Finer Arts and Artists

On 31 January the *Morning Chronicle* advertised "*Descriptive Sketches in Verse* . . . by W. WORDSWORTH, B.A. of St. John's, Cambridge./ Printed for J[oseph] Johnson, No. 72, St. Paul's Church-yard," and on 5 February the *World* announced that "The Shakespeare, by Mr. STEEVENS and Mr. Isaac READ, is completed. It is in octavo." Neither work attracted any attention. There was a belated interest in *Poems by G. Dyer. Late of Emanuel College, Cambridge,* "lately published by J. Johnson" and on 29 May advertised by the *Gazetteer*, and poems by Burns were always greatly in demand. But, if readers trusted the newspapers, no living poet could hold a candle to Lady Catherine Rebecca Manners, and Mrs. Mary Robinson was probably the greatest poet of all time. Lady Manners, whose husband, William Manners, had only recently (12 Jan., 1793) been created a baronet, had selected John Bell as her publisher, with the result that her poetry was widely publicized by the *Oracle*. The *Poems*, first mentioned on 7 June, appeared on 17 June, and, from 13 June on, the *Oracle* talked of little else. On 5 October it announced with rapture that it would soon be offering its readers original poems by this literary giant, and the first of the poems did appear on 25 October. Mrs. Robinson was eulogized by all news-papers, as so for different reasons was the Duchess of York, now estranged from her husband. Almost every day readers were told by one paper or another that the Duchess was a saint and Mrs. Robinson a genius; and the appearance of Mrs. Robinson's *Three Poems* on 16 July was heralded as the literary event of the century. The *True Briton*, not usually interested in books, was ecstatic about this one, and the *Morning Post*, which did not even carry book advertisements, not only advertised the *Three Poems*, but on 17 July printed excerpts with an extrav-agantly laudatory headnote. On 2 August the *Oracle* announced that another poem, *Modern Manners*, which was so delighting the public and which had been variously attributed to Richard Tickell, Joseph Richardson, and Edward Jerningham, was also the work of Mrs. Robinson, and on 6 August it printed excerpts from this pamphlet. The *Morning Post* repeated the announcement on 3 August, adding its own opinion that the poem was another "striking proof of the versatile talents of this elegant and intelligent Author." The *Oracle* and the *Morning Post* became more enthusiastic as the year progressed, and both news-papers were greatly upset when, on 27 November, the *True Briton* referred to

Mrs. Robinson as "the *first Poet* now living." She was simply, they protested, "the *first Poet.*" The *Oracle* had an equally high regard for her talents as a librettist, but its evaluation in this respect was not shared by Kemble.

Covent Garden completed its 1792–1793 season to the satisfaction of the Ministerial newspapers. Of the new plays, Mrs. Inchbald's comedy, *Every Man Has His Fault*, first performed on 29 January, was very popular, as so was Reynolds's comedy, *How to Grow Rich*, performed on 18 April. The latter play, which had something to say about "low Attornies," was, however, obscured by an epilogue, written by Miles Peter Andrews and recited by William Thomas Lewis with the aid of a pad, which he suddenly displayed to the hilarity of the audience. Cumberland's comic opera, *The Armourer*, was performed on 4 April with less acclaim, and Hurlstone's musical interlude, *To Arms; or, The British Recruit*, performed on 3 May, was passed over in comparative silence. There had been some scandals. On 15 January the *Morning Chronicle* had carried a long advertisement in which "Mrs. Holman" (Miss Hughes) maintained that, in addition to deserting her and his two "infants," Joseph Holman was using his influence to prevent her appearing at Covent Garden. She was now determined to vindicate herself by publishing an account of the affair, and, since she had no money, she was appealing for subscribers. But the Opposition newspapers were evidently weary of her, for not one of them supported the cause, and the account did not appear.

A more important scandal involved Madame Mara, who, having concluded a series of concerts at Oxford University, had been singing oratorios at Covent Garden. This scandal began on 13 March, when the *World* published a letter, signed "COMMON SENSE," which accused her of disappointing audiences and showing other signs of contempt for the Royal Family and the British people. On 22 March the *Oracle* published a reply to this letter, submitted by Madame Mara's husband, John Mara, the cellist; and on 25 March it published a reply to the reply, submitted by James Harrison, who, it appeared, was author of the letter signed "COMMON SENSE." On the same date, the *Diary* and the *Morning Chronicle* published the whole of the correspondence between Mara and Harrison, and on 27 March the *Diary* reprinted Harrison's reply. Nothing further was heard of this matter until 6 December, when, according to *Lloyd's Evening Post* (9 Dec.), it was the subject of two suits. Both cases were tried in King's Bench, and in both instances Erskine represented the plaintiff, Mingay the defendant. In the first instance, Harrison was being sued by a Mr. Ashley, who stated that he had employed Madame Mara to sing the oratorios at Covent Garden, that Harrison's letter in the *World* of 13 March had so aroused the public that she had been afraid to sing, and that he had consequently lost all his profits on the enterprise. Ashley was nonsuited by Lord Kenyon on the ground that the "civil power would have been well able to handle riots had any occurred." In the second instance, Harrison was being sued by Madame Mara, who accused him of vilifying her character. She was awarded 1*s*. damages. "Two rather remarkable facts appeared on this trial," *Lloyd's Evening Post* added, "viz. that Mr. Ashley, in a few nights, got upwards of 3000*l.* and that Madame Mara had 50*l.* every night she sang."

"COVENT-GARDEN THEATRE is expected to close about the 10th instant, with the greatest receipts ever known there. DRURY-LANE has, unfortunately, had just the reverse," said the *World* on 3 June. The Drury Lane Company had in fact had a very troubled time. According to the *World* of 5 February, Colman was charging a rent of "somewhat less than 20*l.* a night," but the theater was so small that, having an opportunity to return to the King's Haymarket, the company quit that theater very early in the spring to spend the remainder of the season there. Its performances were constantly assailed by the *True Briton*, which on 28 January denounced them generally as a national disgrace, and, during much of the time, Sheridan was having difficulties with Holland, who had increased the cost of the new building by £75,000, and with the courts, which were suddenly disinclined to honor his patent. For weeks no newspaper expected the company to survive, and even the *Oracle* mentioned on 30 March that, according to "report," "Mr. SHERIDAN means to dispose of his Theatrical dominions at the end of next Season." But on 13 April the *Morning Chronicle* announced that the patent at least was assured:

DRURY-LANE THEATRE.

We learn with pleasure that the legal difficulties which have so long retarded the conveyance of the titles and interest in the *dormant patent* to the Trustees for DRURY LANE THEATRE, are entirely got over to the satisfaction of all the parties. It is an extraordinary fact, that the circumstance of the Patent in question having been separated from Covent Garden Theatre, and played under in another house for the space of eleven years, was not known even to Mr. HARRIS, till proved by the acute remarks of Mr. HARGRAVE. The question in discussion was, what length of *dormancy* might be supposed to *merge* a right, and produce invalidity? This doubt, though in fact of little importance to the interest of Drury Lane, where the assent of the Crown and of all parties had admitted the perpetual right of renewal in their other patents, was by Mr. HARRIS's Council deemed necessary to be completely done away under a legal arbitration, as otherwise a doubt might appear to be thrown on the other patent of Covent Garden, no person being in fact able to say which has been the dormant and which the active patent. The investigation has produced the most perfect proof of the validity of both.

The untangling of this legal snarl, which had cost Sheridan another £31,500, was followed by more newspaper attacks. "Mr. SHERIDAN has lately been more particularly the object of attack by the understrappers of the Treasury; and as the consistency and openness of his political conduct renders that somewhat dangerous, for the advocates of Apostates of all descriptions to assail, they, with their accustomed liberality, endeavour to injure him in his property," the *Morning Chronicle* remarked on 25 April. "—Hence all the paragraphs about stale plays and empty benches at the Haymarket Theatre." The *Chronicle* and the *Oracle* struck at least one blow in return by publicizing (25 April) the private life of that ex-alcoholic, Harris's lawyer, "J. Hargrave."

On 3 June the *Gazetteer* reported: "The quibbles of the gentry of the Long-robe, so long hostile to 'Poor old Drury,' are at length done away, and the public will be gratified with the immediate sight of that structure rising into new splendors." And on 19 June: "The disputes, which have so long retarded the erection of the *Drury-Lane* Theatre, were yesterday finally adjusted at a Meeting of the Proprietors and Trustees held at the *St. Alban's Tavern*. The work is, in consequence, to proceed immediately, and with the utmost expedition." According to the *Morning Chronicle* (26 June), the building was "going on with as much dispatch as the greatest number of men that can be employed without being in the way of one another can give," and it was expected to be completed by January. On 13 July the *Oracle* explained that "Mr. SHERIDAN, obtaining possession of the Haymarket House, for the accommodation of the Drury-lane Company, [had] agreed with the Proprietors of the Opera, to furnish that [the opera] of [1792–1793]. This has been done with great credit to the Managers, and next season Mr. TAYLOR resumes his rights." But on 3 July the *Oracle* denied that the opera had "netted 7000*l*. this last season . . . : it may be 700*l*. after the expences are paid. The proprietors of Drury gave in the first place 5000*l*. for the House. But for the ability of the MANAGERS, [the opera] must have been a loss." No newspaper denied that the "Proprietors of Drury" had lost.

The program had not been brilliant. On 7 March the Drury Lane Company presented Boaden's musical melodrama, *Ozmyn and Daraxa*, and on 18 March Arthur Murphy's tragedy, *The Rival Sisters*, written many years earlier, but not previously performed. The first play was hardly mentioned by the newspapers; the second received more publicity, partly because it starred Mrs. Siddons, partly because the *Oracle* charged (27 Mar.) that the epilogue, which Murphy insisted was his, had been stolen, "every idea of it," from Vaughan. Of the plays which received most publicity, one was not performed at all, and the other was performed only once. From the beginning of January on, the *Oracle* was greatly concerned about Mrs. Robinson's opera, *Kate of Aberdeen*, which Kemble had still not produced, and both it and the *Diary* were concerned about Mrs. Jordan, who had been absent for some time. On 19 January the *Diary* told its readers that the opera would be performed and that Mrs. Jordan's absence was tem-porary: "Mrs. JORDAN certainly returns to her theatrical duty this season, and two causes are stated; one, that she wishes to have the pleasure of appearing in Mrs. ROBINSON's coming Opera, and the other, that she has a new comedy to bring forward written by a particular friend. . . . [The] public will be glad to recover so sprightly a votary of the laughing muse." But the *Diary* was mistaken. On 29 January Mrs. Jordan wrote a letter to Sheridan, asking to be released from her contract on the ground that she was "in the receipt of a very large Salary, without being permitted to perform" and that her numerous complaints to Sheridan and Kemble had been ignored. The letter was published by the

Oracle of 30 January and the *World* of 31 January, and on 31 January the *Oracle* explained the nature of the difficulty:

> Mrs. JORDAN has been engaged at a very liberal Salary—The conditions of the obligation were these:—To make her First Appearance in a NEW CHARACTER: that Character to be in a Play, the production of her Female Friend—and which Play was agreed to be accepted for the purpose.—Delay increased impatience, and occasioned remonstrance. Ever ready on her part to fulfil the duties of her Professional Engagement, she demanded a stipulated time for the commencement of her salary—Acquiescence on the part of the MANAGER produced only mortification by the silence with which the Play has been treated—and hence an appeal to Mr. SHERIDAN, through the medium of THE ORACLE.—We think—an experiment would gratify the Public—ascertain the judgment of the Patroness—and *benefit* the *Proprietors*—if confined even to one Night's Representation.

The play in dispute was *Anna*, which Kemble had accepted, but was refusing to produce; and, although the contract stipulated that Mrs. Jordan would make her seasonable debut only in *Anna*, it did not compel Kemble to produce it. On 4 February the *World* announced the capitulation of Kemble:

> *The* JORDAN *and the* KEMBLE.
> This dispute between *Sock* and *Buskin* is likely to terminate without a Duel, the statement of which is simply as follows:—*Sock* is heartily tired of her old *parts*, and is extremely anxious, for the gratification of herself, to have *new ones*. *Buskin*, however, objects to, and will not allow her to please herself, but wants to *force* upon her such *parts* as in his opinion she can best *manage*. Thus the matter at present stands—*Sock* will not give up a point—*Buskin* remained stiff in his sentiments till last Friday [1 Feb.], when he was obliged to yield to the ability and persuasion of this charming daughter of THALIA.

The *World* was fond of *double entendre*, and it was not fond of Drury Lane. On 6 February the *True Briton* however repeated that "Mrs. JORDAN, it is said, is again reconciled to the Haymarket Theatre, which she was so anxious to quit. The Deputy Manager and she had long been jarring." And on 25 February *Anna* was produced.

On 23 February the *Gazetteer* announced that the "new Comedy, *Anna*, in which Mrs. JORDAN is to appear next week, we have authority to say, is not written by the Duke of CLARENCE." The announcement came just in time, for the play evidently had nothing to recommend it. The *Oracle*, which had been puffing Mrs. Jordan in every issue, said only (26 Feb.) that "Mrs. JORDAN last night made her first appearance this season, in a Comedy then also performed for the first time. The Actress was welcomed with the most eager approbation. Of the Play it is not our wish to speak, seeing that it suffered some displeasure of the Audience." Other Ministerial newspapers found it almost plotless, and the audience, although seeing it through, would not allow it to be repeated. Yet there were extenuating factors. According to the *Star* (1 Mar.), Kemble had resented Mrs. Jordan's employment of the newspapers on her behalf, had accepted defeat with bad grace, and had deliberately encouraged the audience's "displeasure": "Mr. KEMBLE and *Dora* JORDAN were restored to tolerable amity through the three first acts of *Anna*, but in the fourth, Mr. KEMBLE, pulling out his snuff-box, began to take the *pinch of contempt*; and before the fifth was half through, with an air of triumph he exclaimed, 'So much for an appeal from the judgment of the MANAGER to that of an audience.'" There was also some trickery respecting the epilogue, which turned out to be a castigation of the Opposition and its newspapers. According to the *Morning Chronicle* (26 Feb.), Mrs. Jordan, who was supposed to recite it, refused when she discovered the hoax, and the epilogue was omitted. On 9 March the *Oracle* published an advertisement respecting authorship of the play: "A CARD./ SIR,/ Being informed that Paragraphs have appeared in many of the Public Prints, asserting or insinuating that Mrs. JORDAN is the Author of the Comedy of *Anna*—I think it incumbent upon me to declare, that those assertions and insinuations are totally without foundation—and that I am the Author of that Comedy. . . ./ I am, Sir,/ Your most obedient Servant, C. Cuthbertson./ *St. Alban's Street, March* 8, 1793." *The Times* did not believe it. "Mrs. JORDAN's muse has died of grief for the loss of her bantling, so that there are no hopes of her ever *obliging* the public with another dramatic production," it remarked on 14 March. But Mrs. Jordan was at least back on the boards.

Having settled the matter of *Anna*, the *Oracle* redoubled its efforts to get Mrs. Robinson's opera produced as well. On 23 March it suggested that perhaps Kemble found the opera too patriotic: "Mrs. ROBINSON's Opera is said to breathe that spirit of Loyalty, which would at this period render it highly popular. Why is it not produced? It would have been in a better channel, had she presented it to Covent Garden Theatre, for a variety of reasons." On 30 March it announced that "Mrs. ROBINSON has wholly WITHDRAWN her promising Opera from the Haymarket Theatre. We hope, however, to see it *elsewhere*, and most likely with flattering success." On 5 April it again blamed Kemble: "Mrs. ROBINSON's Opera had the approbation of the *best Authors living*, before she presented it to the Theatre, who were unanimous in their opinion of its claim to Public Patronage; indeed, there has been but ONE person, among the wide phalanx of Critics, who has not pronounced it a most promising production. Mrs. ROBINSON's LITERARY FAME is built upon the *invulnerable* basis of universal *public opinion*. She has nothing to fear from the shafts of ENVY and MALEVOLENCE." The *Oracle* was still talking about this opera on 30 October. By this time it planned to print the opera itself as soon as Mrs. Robinson returned to London, along with "a full explanation of her reasons for withdrawing it from DRURY-LANE THEATRE." There was one final harassment during the 1792–1793 season. On 22 June the *Oracle* printed a letter from Eliza Charlotte Bateman, who was accusing Sheridan of bad faith. More than a year earlier, she said, she had had a series of interviews with Kemble, respecting an acting career at Drury Lane.

The interviews had terminated after five months because, as she understood it, Kemble had heard that she was intimate with the proprietor of a newspaper, which had lambasted his performance in *School for Scandal*. She had thereupon appealed to Sheridan, who had promised her "a contract, a benefit, &c.," but she had got nothing. She had subsequently talked to several of his friends, who had interceded on her behalf, and she had just talked to Mr. Windham, who had also interceded to no purpose. All she wanted to say was that Sheridan seemed to be blind to merit and deaf to the "voice of friendship," even when it came "from such men as Mr. GREY, Mr. LAMBTON, and Mr. WYNDHAM." The letter, dated "Soho Square, 19 June, 1793," was, however, answered only by the *Oracle*, which mentioned on 4 July: "Mr. BATEMAN stands well for a *title*—one better than the *Theatre* at least can give her. Her husband succeeds to Lord BATEMAN." Her husband did not succeed. The title became extinct at the death of the second Viscount.

Charles Dibdin was also in the news. On 18 March, 1792, he had filed actions for trespass against William Locke and Isaac Swan, then connected with the *Observer*, and on 17 October, 1792, he had filed actions for libel against Robert Bostock and Isaac Swan, then connected with the *World*. On 26 February, 1793, the first of these cases was finally tried. Locke was brought into the Court of Common Pleas, where he was found guilty of printing a paragraph stating that Dibdin had stolen his songs from Bickerstaffe, but the assessment of damages was postponed, and the case attracted little attention. Although it was mentioned by the *Oracle* of 28 February and by the *Star* of 13 March, it was not mentioned by either the *Diary* or the *Public Advertiser*, which were always violently partisan when Dibdin was involved. On 18 May Swan was tried in the same court on supposedly the same charge, but in fact the charge had been altered, for the libel now consisted of several paragraphs, allegedly implying that Isaac Bickerstaffe was hiding behind the curtain of the Sans Souci, engaging in "disgusting relations" with Dibdin. This case did attract attention. *Lloyd's Evening Post* (22 May) gave it almost a column, the *Diary* and the *Public Advertiser* (20 May) gave it almost four columns, and, by the end of the month, the *Diary* was advertising *The Trial of Isaac Swan* as a pamphlet. Representing Dibdin on this occasion were Sergeant Adair and Mr. Reader; representing Swan were Sergeant Bond and Mr. Const. It was established that, when the libels were published, the *Observer* was being edited by Frederick Bourne and printed by William Locke, Swan being a contributor and a "Mr. Logan" a compositor; and William Woodfall and "several performers" attested that the implication was unfounded inasmuch as Bickerstaffe had left the country several years earlier "on a violent suspicion of having attempted some unnatural practices" and had not returned. Since Swan's attorneys maintained that the paragraphs had implied nothing obscene, they presented no witnesses. Dibdin was awarded £100 damages from Swan and another £100 damages from Locke. On 25 June Swan and Bostock were tried in the Court of King's Bench for the libels in the *World*, they being represented by Erskine, Dibdin by Mingay. But the libels consisted only of statements respecting Dibdin's "dullness" and dishonesty, and the damages were fixed at 1*s*. Brief accounts appeared in all newspapers, Swan being described by the *Morning Herald* as editor of the *World*, by all other papers as "Proprietor" or "sole Proprietor." Since damages in such instances were customarily paid out of newspaper budgets, it may be of some consequence that the *Observer* was an outspoken critic of the Government, the *World* an impassioned defender.

State of the Theaters During the Parliamentary Recess

The summer of 1793 was quiet. Although the *Oracle* and the *World* could not say enough in praise of Colman, the only news of consequence was reported by the *Oracle*, which announced on 10 July that "Mr. KEMBLE, the Drury-Lane Manager, is visiting some country friends for a few weeks; at the end of which he . . . *performs* in the MOUNTAINEERS of the younger COLMAN at the Summer House." The play was produced on 3 August, and on 5 August the *Oracle* and the *World* pronounced Colman a genius. Each paper gave the play a column and one-half. There was little news even from the Provinces, the *World* mentioning only (16 Sept.) that "Anthony Pasquin" was now connected with the theater in Glasgow. On 16 September Covent Garden was reopened for the winter season, and on 20 September the *Public Advertiser* reported that Colman, "having made the necessary arrangements with the Proprietors of Drury-lane Patent (who could not finish their new House in time for the customary commencement of the season) yesterday opened the Hay-market Theatre, under the sanction of their authority. . . ."

As the *Public Advertiser* and the *World* had told their readers on 14 September, Covent Garden was renovated:

> A great part of this summer has been passed in effecting [further improvements in Covent Garden.].
> The most material has been the raising of the roof, by which, in point of air and coolness, every part of the house is benefited.—What was not so certainly to be expected, is also produced by the alteration, a *Coup d'Oeil*, the most complete that any theatre in this country can shew. The view from the side-boxes and pit, over the three stages of boxes and the two galleries, to the stained ventilator of the upper one, which completes the whole, is so happily managed by the proportion and relativeness of the ornaments, placed in parts, before untouched, that it might be doubted whether it was a good policy to invite so much attention

from the stage, if it was not to be supposed, that such objects are observed, while there are no performances upon it.

In part of the space, thus gained, a new gallery has been erected, which, though it is forwarder, and therefore, better for its company, than the old one, leaves the under gallery much more open than in the former Theatre, and does not interrupt the view from any part of it. To the latter gallery there are now four entrances, which will divide the company, so as to prevent any obstruction, or inconvenience by a crowd.

In the fronts of the three stages of boxes, the compartments of the decorations are stained with a new colour, which is expected to be more grateful to the eye by candlelight than the former. Last season, the divisions between the boxes, which were of a plain red, were unsuitable to the adjoining decorations, and broke the line of splendour intended to be preserved in that part of the house. These are now gilt, in front, and have a well-fancied scroll ornament on the sides. The backs of the first division of front boxes have also a gilt cornice; and a considerable improvement in this part of the House is the substitution of an arched, instead of a solid border below the second and third rows of Boxes.

The Theatre has been lighted, before a small party, that the effect of these improvements might be tried. Mr. Sheridan, who is now busily engaged in the choice of decorations for his own Theatre, was one of the number, and was not the least warm in praise of them.

The presentations, the Ministerial newspapers thought, were worthy of the renovations. A modernized production of *Hamlet*, evidently assailed by one of the Opposition papers, which did not like *Hamlet* anyway, was stoutly defended by the *Oracle* and supposedly by one of its correspondents, since on 9 October the *Oracle* published a long letter on the subject:

REVIVAL OF HAMLET.
Mr. Conductor.

I observe your Paper particularly attentive to the Drama of our country. In consequence, I trouble you with a few remarks called forth by a Writer, who, in another print, mentions the *revival* of Hamlet properly dressed.

When any attack is made upon the fame of Shakespere, it should always be met; because herein controversy can produce no particle of *acrimony*, and may be ultimately beneficial to the cause of literature. With what gentlemanly temper the Commentators upon the great Bard have treated each other, the whole world can bear them witness.

. . . I will now come immediately to the points in question.

The Writer thinks the Poet out of his *latitude*, when he mentions the "daily cast of brazen CANNON;" it is an anachronism, I freely confess; but he should be told that Shakespere invariably bestows the manners of *his age* upon characters of all times—He does not like an Antiquarian scrupulously preserve the costume of periods long past, but uses their personages as vehicles rather for informing his own —

> To shew the very age and body of the time,
> His *form* and *pressure*.

By thus palliating the first charge, we go on to the *second*; and a very serious one it is; viz. That "he has much exceeded the *longitude* of COMMON SENSE, when he makes HAMLET observe, upon the UNDISCOVERED COUNTRY, from whose bourne *no traveler returns* just after he has *seen* the SPIRIT of his FATHER."

Now, Sir, the expression cavilled at, means not more than this—A COUNTRY, whose modes of being no travellor or voyager could ever *disclose* for the benefit of MAN, in this life at his return. The GHOST expressly says, that he is *forbid* to TELL the secrets of his prison-house—but by some dolorous hints, dropt at *hazard*, he does leave no room to doubt, that at present he is but in PURGATORY—

> "Condemned to walk the night,
> And for the day confined to fast in fires."

You will see that this was not, even by the SPIRIT himself, thought a *peep* into *that* COUNTRY, from whose bourne he could not HIMSELF have returned.—He was then merely upon his purgation, fasting in *fires* during the DAY, and walking upon the earth in the *night-time*, like a *Will o' The* WHISP.

DANTE.

"The Manager of [the Covent Garden Theater] is now prosecuting an object, that must be dear to the lovers of SHAKSPEARE," the *Oracle* added on 10 October: "it is to give to his immortal productions the advantages of the most picturesque scenery and appropriate dresses."

On 13 November Covent Garden presented Jerningham's tragedy, *The Siege of Berwick* and on 23 November O'Keeffe's comedy, *The World in a Village*. The authors in both instances were finally identified, although, as late as 21 November, the *Morning Post* thought that *The World in a Village* had been written by Lord Courtenay. The *True Briton* particularly admired the prologue, since it had been supplied by its own drama critic, John Taylor, and was, in its opinion, just what the country needed. "Mr. TAYLOR's Prologue to *The World in a Village*, has travelled through all the Villages as well as Towns of Great Britain, exciting every where that general admiration and applause which an elegant eulogium on our Constitution, so justly and at the same time so poetically expressed, cannot fail to excite in the bosoms of Englishmen," it said typically on 20 December. Dudley's opera, *Witch of the Alps*, was not performed, and by 20 December the *Morning Post* understood that it had been shelved: "The Rev. BATE DUDLEY is busily employed on a New Opera; if it does not possess more merit than the Woodman [performed on 26 Feb., 1791], we trust the good sense of the Manager will prevent its appearance."

On 30 October the *Oracle* announced that "Mrs. WELLS has a daughter of twelve years of age about to make her appearance at Covent-Garden Theatre— Of her Musical Powers the promise is very pleasing." Mrs. Wells herself was lacking, having spent most of the year in Fleet Prison. On 14 December the *Morning Post* entered a protest: "We are of opinion that the creditors of Mrs. WELLS should not provoke her, but come into terms with her immediately, and suffer her to follow her profession. As a married woman, we are of opinion, that if she put in that plea, she could not be detained; and the humanity, or at least self-interest, should urge those to whom she is indebted to enlarge her immediately." By 23 December she was thought to have been "enlarged," and the *Morning Post* "understood" that she "intends very shortly to perform French and English Theatrical Imitations between the Acts of the Grand Concert at Hanover-square Rooms." Still lacking, too, was Mrs. Merry. On 15 July, according to the *Morning Post*, Mrs. Merry was performing with her father's company in Norwich and intended to remain with the company during the summer. "It is probable that Covent-garden will have this pleasing Actress next Winter," the *Post* added. On 29 August both the *Oracle* and the *World* announced that "Mr. and Mrs. MERRY have retired to *Switzerland*." The announcement was repeated by the *Gazetteer* of 30 August, but on 2 September the *World* mentioned that they had been visiting friends in Norwich, and on 4 September the *Morning Post* stated that "Mrs. MERRY is engaged at Covent-Garden Theatre—Mr. MERRY of course remains in England." Although all newspapers understood that Mrs. Merry had in fact been engaged, her name appeared on none of the bills, and on 2 October the *Public Advertiser* again announced Merry's departure: "Mr. Merry . . . passes the winter in Switzerland. We are glad to hear that this gentleman is by no means so enthusiastically devoted to French politics as he was before. The report that Mrs. Merry is engaged at Covent Garden theatre is probably premature." The *Public Advertiser* had apparently got its information from the *Morning Post*, and, since Merry was traveling with Charles Pigott, the possibility that he was undergoing a political change of heart should have seemed slight. The travelers got only as far as Harwich, but why they turned back, no reader knew, for nothing further was said of Merry until 12 October, when the *Oracle* noticed that "MERRY, the Poet, is in town. His benevolent wishes for *peace* are more likely to find gratification *here* than elsewhere." There was one final report on the Merrys. On 22 November the *Morning Post* and the *Oracle* mentioned that they were leaving London and "are going to reside in a private way, at Scarborough, in Yorkshire." Merry was still a close friend of Edward Topham.

For one reason or another, Harris seems to have encouraged Mrs. Merry to believe that her contract would be renewed, and he would have been far better off with her than he was, as it turned out, with Mrs. Esten. Harriet Esten, who had married James Esten in 1784, had been a performer at Covent Garden for years, and, like the other performers, she usually played in one of the Provincial theaters during the summer. During the summer of 1793, she was attached to the Edinburgh theater, and there she met the Duke of Hamilton. The Duke of Hamilton had been married since 1778. Although he was a Knight of the Thistle and a good Tory, he was fonder of boxing, women, and low company than he was of honors and politics. His dinner guests were usually bruisers, hackney coachmen, and such, and in 1787 he had seduced and deserted the Countess of

Eglinton, whose husband had divorced her the following year. The Duchess of Hamilton had endured all this, but Mrs. Esten was evidently too much, for on 2 September the *World* announced: "Mrs. ESTEN is on a *visit* to the Duke of HAMILTON, at Hamilton House, in Scotland. His amiable Dutchess, of course, is not there." "The Scotch Peer, who has discarded his Lady, to give place to an Actress, has *lost* no reputation by this act of modern gallantry; and the Performer, it is well known, had none to lose," the *World* added on 13 September, and on 14 September: "The Pension given by a certain Ducal Scotsman to Mrs. ESTEN, is 1000*l.* per ann. secured upon landed property. This fact we state as an extraordinary instance of *Caledonian Economy.*" But Mrs. Esten did not forget her professional obligations, for on 30 September the *World* reported: "Mrs. ESTEN on Thursday [26 Sept.] had an *audience* of the Manager of Covent-Garden Theatre, and for that purpose came to town in the Duke of HAMILTON's carriage, drawn by four horses, and attended by his Grace's servants." By December she was again a regular performer; nor was there any evidence of public displeasure, to the astonishment of the *Morning Post.* "Since the affected Actress insults the audience every night, by the display of the jewels of an amiable and ill-used Duchess, she goes by the name of *Queen of Diamonds!*" it exclaimed on 16 December. On 18 December it called on audiences to protest: "Mrs. WRIGHT is appointed Milliner to Mrs. ESTEN. This Lady now appoints her trades people with as much form as though instead of being a *Birmingham* Duchess, she was a Princess of the Blood." On 19 December it shed a tear for the rightful Duchess: "The benefit of the *Queen of Diamonds*, must be attended by all the modest women in town. She, who feeling for the cruel treatment of an amiable Duchess, wears her picture on the public stage, set round with brilliants, next her *heart!*" But for the present, at least, Mrs. Esten remained.

The competitive theater during the last months of 1793 was not Drury Lane, but the Haymarket. The housing of the Drury Lane Company had been a major item of news from July on, for Sheridan's relations with Colman were not satisfactory, and, although Sheridan had got along with Taylor, the Opera House was not available for the coming winter. "Mr. TAYLOR is to resume his Opera next season," the *Oracle* repeated on 10 July, "and under the patronage of the Duke of BEDFORD, he is disposed to try the effect of an auxiliary amusement— This is a GRAND CONCERT." On 23 July the *Oracle* seemed to think that the new building might be completed in time:

DRURY-LANE THEATRE

Is proceeding rapidly—there are above 300 men at work now, and that number will be doubled by the end of the week.

Mr. SHERIDAN was there himself on Saturday [20 July], and suggested various improvements, such as his superior knowledge of the Stage supplied. KEMBLE too was there all day.

Mr. HOLLAND the Architect, exhibited the whole of his plan; and, not being crippled in the means, when executed it will form the finest Theatre in Europe.

The principal changes in the construction will be *upon* and *below* the Stage— There is so vast a depth, that in machinery things may be done which have hitherto been impracticable.

In addition to the Theatre, it is the design of Mr. SHERIDAN to have a very elegant Tavern and Coffee-house, from which passages will communicate with the Lobbies: and the ENTERTAINMENT, which is so properly termed the *most rational*, will therefore be attended with every comfort and accommodation.

The *firm* liberality of the Duke of BEDFORD is mentioned in the warmest terms. He determines to see the NEW DRURY flourish, in despite of all difficulties. A munificence worthy his princely fortune.

Colman obviously did not think the building would be completed by September, for on 3 August the *Morning Post* mentioned that he had obtained permission to keep the Haymarket open until Christmas. The *Oracle*, still engrossed in the construction, seemed unaware of this development. "Saturday night [3 Aug.] Mr. SHERIDAN gave a supper to the Workmen employed in building Drury-lane Theatre," it announced on 5 August; "they were divided into parties of forty, and each party were allowed a sheep and a fillet of veal, and a gallon of beer each man." But on 31 August the *Oracle* concluded another progress report by admitting that Sheridan had in fact come to terms with Colman:

DRURY-LANE THEATRE.

The Strut, or Brace, as it is variously called, being a large beam or rafter of *one hundred and ninety feet* in length, with bevil joints, was yesterday carried on a couple of jacks to the new Theatre, to be placed beneath the roof, and keep the walls from swerving.

The ceiling will be eighty-five feet in width, which is about fifteen feet wider than that of the Theatre at Oxford built by Sir CHRISTOPHER WREN, or the Tuscan roof of St. Paul, Covent Garden, one of the boldest constructions of INIGO JONES.

From Drury Lane, totally distinct from all other entrance, the Stage Door will communicate, and the front of the Theatre, which is in Russel-street, will be faced with Portland stone.

It is intended to be opened on the first of January. In the mean time Mr. COLMAN and the Proprietors of the Summer Theatre have again consented to let the Drury-Lane Company perform there till the new building is completed.

The *Oracle*'s announcement was a signal for the Ministerial newspapers, which at once opened fire on the Drury Lane personnel. "*Wonders* will never cease," said the *World* on 9 September, "—Mrs. SIDDONS is about to perform *gratis*!! and for *three nights*. So let us hear no more of her *parsimony*. She is going to Dublin, and is to have *only* 1000*l.* for twenty five nights. This is as much as it is said another celebrated Actress [Mrs. Esten] is to have for two years *playing*; but then there is a wide difference in the nature of their engagements; as the latter Lady's *performances* are to be all *in private* and *behind the curtain*, for the sole *amusement* of a *certain Duke*; while the former is to appear in public, and play for the entertainment of the whole City." The discovery that Colman would be managing the Haymarket, not Kemble or Sheridan, necessitated a shift of ground, but the Ministerial newspapers were agile. Colman, they now said, had rescued the Drury Lane Company, which Sheridan had deserted, and he had done so at an enormous expense, no part of which was to be paid by Sheridan. The stables alone, said the *True Briton* on 16 September, would cost Colman £2,000. On 17 September the *Oracle* protested that Sheridan had already paid "*four thousand* pounds" for those stables, and on 23 September "A FRIEND TO TRUTH AND JUSTICE" set the record straight altogether. His letter, which was published by the *Morning Post*, read in part:

> There never was an idea of not providing an Asylum for such of the Company as had not other engagements, or were likely to feel a temporary suspension of their employment.
> The question was simply, whether the Proprietors of Drury-lane should rent the Hay-market of Mr. COLEMAN, which they proposed to do; or Mr. COLEMAN rent the Drury-lane Patent from them? The latter was preferred; because, as it was probable that the late period in which the New Theatre would open, would occasion a necessary encroachment on the ensuing summer season, it was but just to give Mr. COLEMAN's Theatre an opportunity of advantage in the winter. It is a mistake that Mr. COLEMAN is *burthened* with the Renters. The Proprietors of Drury-lane are to pay a proportion, at all events; and unless the undertaking is profitable to Mr. COLEMAN, they receive no rent or advantage whatever. . . .

The odd thing is that the Drury Lane Company might apparently have had the Opera House, which, instead of being devoted to opera, was handed over to architects for renovation. According to the *Public Advertiser*, the renovations were still underway on 13 December:

> OPERA HOUSE.—The interior of this building is now nearly ready for the upholsterer. The covering of the seats is to be crimson sattin. The figures,which appear to support the several tiers of boxes, are grotesque; sphynxes below,— then griffins—and after these, rams heads; all richly gilded. With these figures, gilt brackets alternately occur; and the paper lining of the boxes, which is of white ground, with coloured flowers, has a gold border. The pit, though somewhat reduced by the useful extention of the stage, is rendered more accessible than ever, a passage having been sunk between the orchestra and the lower seats, so that there are now six entrances to this part of the Theatre.

Since the Haymarket was as Ministerial as Covent Garden, most of its plays had already been produced at Harris's theater, and all that was demanded of the Ministerial newspapers was occasional puffs of the authors. "REYNOLDS, the *Dramatist*, is gone to YORK," observed the *Oracle* and the *World*, for example, on 28 and 30 October, respectively. "A pleasanter fellow no county can well contain. TOPHAM is there, and MORTON to give him welcome." A musical trifle by Morton, *The Children in the Wood*, was performed at the Haymarket on 1 November, but, since it was performed anonymously, the puffs of Morton were not very helpful. The only other new piece was Prince Hoare's operatic farce, *My Grandmother*, performed on 16 December.

The *Oracle*, always enthusiastic about Sheridan's projects, was keeping its readers up-to-date on the latest one. On 10 September it issued another progress report:

NEW DRURY.

An Interruption to the process of the Building took place yesterday, occasioned by accident. A piece of timber fell from the upper scaffolding, amongst the Gentlemen of the *Hod*, but hurt none of them. *Paddy* however felt himself affronted, and conceived it at the moment intentional. A remonstrance ensued between them and the Carpenters; the latter, conscious it was an accident, but unable to convince, menaced them. A battle royal ensued, in which HENDY, Foreman to Mr. SAUNDERS, employer of the Carpenters, received a dangerous wound with a saw in his left leg.

The Officers of the Police being upon the spot interfered, and fortunately quelled the disturbance; the consequence was, all the hands, upwards of 500, struck.

Mr. HOLLAND, Architect and employer of the whole, being fortunately in town, arrived amongst them, and recommended a hearing before Mr. Justice BOND, at the Public Office in the evening, as necessary to satisfy all parties; which proved truly so. The Magistrate . . . delivered to them a lecture, in which he pointed out the consequence of maiming a man (as it was proved they had HENDY), that immediately affected their feeling faculties. They cheerfully asked pardon in a manly manner of him that was suffering, and departed friends, to drink the health of the Magistrate and their employers, in a Butt of Porter, with every man a Loaf, the gift of Mr. Sheridan.

The letter from "A FRIEND TO TRUTH AND JUSTICE" in the *Morning Post* of 23 September concluded the discussion of Sheridan's arrangements with Colman, and throughout October the Ministerial newspapers were maintaining instead that the theater would not be ready for occupancy by 1 January. The *Oracle* replied with more progress reports, and by Saturday, 26 October, the roof was on. "The new DRURY THEATRE will stand the test, in point of elevation, with any of our public buildings," declared the *Oracle* on 28 October. "On Saturday last it was completely covered in; after which the different workmen drank success to the undertaking with the loudest acclamations. A speedy completion of the whole may therefore be anticipated." The event was also noted by the *Morning Chronicle*: "On Saturday the workmen finished laying the slates on the roof of the New-Drury Theatre Royal; and, as usual on such occasions, the men drank its success; and on Wednesday [30 Oct.] the raising dinner will be given; at which time the Theatre will be decorated with a variety of Flaggs; the workmen will man the scaffold, and be again regaled by the several builders who have contracted to raise the same."

The "dinner," of which there were at least three accounts (all 31 Oct.), was evidently a huge success. The *Morning Chronicle* reported:

NEW DRURY-LANE THEATRE.

This stupendous edifice being completely covered in, yesterday was a day of general gala for the workmen employed in its structure. On various parts of the building a variety of flags, with appropriate inscriptions, were displayed. The scaffolds were manned by the different artificers, amounting to eleven hundred men, and beer, &c. distributed to them. The toasts were repeated to the various scaffolds by persons stationed for that purpose. The King, the Proprietors of the Theatre, &c. &c. were drank with repeated huzzas. A supper was to have succeeded in the building, but for fear of any tumult arising in consequence of the previous liquor, it was deferred to Saturday night, when 100*l.* given by Mr. Sheridan, is to be divided among them. Mr. Sheridan, and a number of the admirers of the Drama, were present.

The *Morning Post* reported:

DRURY-LANE THEATRE.

This noble structure having been roofed in yesterday, a number of elegant flags were displayed on the ends of the scaffolding poles, with the King's Arms and other devices, worked in gold and silver on silk.

At three o'clock, the workmen manned the scaffolding, and upwards of five hundred of them attracted the notice of the Public, by loudly huzzaying and manifesting their joy in atchieving this important object before the setting in of the rainy weather. In the evening, the workmen marched in procession through the streets, and were afterward regaled by the Proprietors. The principal Gentleman concerned in the undertaking dined at the Shakespeare, and the Public will feel gratified to be assured, that there is not a doubt but this costly and grand edifice will be fit for their reception in the time originally stated by Mr. HOLLAND.

At night the Cupola was brilliantly illuminated, and exhibited a splendid spectacle for many miles round the metropolis.

Even the *World* was enthusiastic:

DRURY LANE THEATRE

Was yesterday completely covered in. The ventilator, and other parts of the building, were ornamented with flags and other trophies, with the proper arms of the two cities, Westminster and London, and the names of the two Parishes, St. Paul, Covent Garden, and St. Martin in the Fields, to both of which the new property conjunctively belongs.

At five, the Proprietors partook of an elegant dinner at the Shakspeare Tavern, after which a number of toasts, suited to the occasion, were drank; the musical performers of each Theatre attended; and the evening was spent with the utmost hilarity. That all ranks of people engaged in this structure might share the pleasure attending their success, sixteen butts of porter were exhausted among the workmen with a plentiful supply of provisions.

Within also, the building proceeds as rapidly as without. The arches are already turned, upon which the Pit will be raised, and all the timbers are coppered to prevent any accident from fire. GREENWOOD, and the other Painters, are busied, in the mean time, in painting the Scenery at Ranelagh Rotunda.

That the Theatre will open in January next, is the common opinion of all. *Macbeth* will be the first performance, with a grand *spectacle* from the French.

Where the Royal Standard was yesterday hoisted upon the Cupola of the Ventilator, a Statue of SHAKESPEARE is to be raised, which will be seen not only in the most open parts of the town, but all round the vicinity of London.

Last night the Cupola was illuminated.

There was evidently a fourth report, for on 2 November the *Morning Post* stated: "A very malicious attack has been made on the new undertaking in Drury-Lane, which, in *spite* of every *jealous* suggestion, will . . . be not only a very distinguished national ornament, but amply reward the Proprietors for their liberality and popular labours."

Readers heard little of the new theater during November. On 12 November there was a short item in the *Morning Chronicle*: "DRURY-LANE BUILDING./ Yesterday two men were severely hurt by the falling of a scaffold, on which there was a considerable weight of stone, preparing for the cornice of the new houses in Little Russel-street.—They were taken to the Middlesex Hospital.—This is said to have been the first accident that has happened, which . . . is a circumstance both fortunate and extraordinary." The incident was also reported by the *Oracle*. There was another item in the *Oracle* of 16 November: "NEW DRURY./ An extraordinary precaution is to be taken here against the communication of fire from one part of the Theatre to the other./ An *iron curtain*, the ruler of which will be sufficiently heavy to bring it down, is to be ready for use at the front of the stage, so that, if the scenery should, at any time, take fire, the flames will be prevented from reaching the audience part of the Theatre./ The precaution must be somewhat superfluous, for, as the Theatre will be lined, like that of Covent Garden, with iron plates, no accident among the scenes, and even of that there has not been an instance for several years, would take effect upon it." And on 22 November the *World* reported: "At Drury Lane Theatre such is the expedition with which the new building proceeds, that workmen are employed all night to finish it. They work by moon-light." There was no mention of the theater in December.

Fads and Fashions of 1793

The pad, or, as the *Morning Post* called it (22 Nov.), the "six-month pad," was first mentioned by the newspapers on 19 April, Lewis having displayed a sample of the article on the stage of Covent Garden the previous night. For the remainder of the month and throughout May, the *Star* was deluged by letters from indignant readers, and on 23 May the *Star* assured them that their protests had been effective: "The *Pad*-system at length gives way to the just ridicule that every where attends it; *green girls* begin to be ashamed of *assuming* a shape, which modesty forbids to be natural to them—and the *dowagers* will soon be *hooted* out of it in the streets, for affecting that which is *impossible!*" Although the *Star* was indulging in some wishful thinking, the "just ridicule" at least continued. Comedians at the theaters inserted references to the pad at every opportunity, and on 27 May Covent Garden even produced a play on the subject, Robert Woodbridge's one-act farce, *The Pad*. *The Pad* was evidently very popular, for it was published on 6 June and was still delighting audiences at the Haymarket on 2 August. There were also several pamphlets, and, from mid-May on, the newspapers were filled with quips, the following, taken from the *Morning Chronicle* of 30 May, being typical:

ON THE PAD
The Pad performs a generous part indeed;
For whilst it makes the barren Matron breed,
Fond Miss might love (still innocent, and chaste),
Blest Maid! might love, nor fear a swelling waist.

On 1 June the *Diary* repeated that the ridicule had been effective:

THE PAD.
The ridicule which this indelicate ornament has excited, has been the means of greatly lessening its sale. The PAD Venders have had a meeting, who, perceiving the impossibility of the continuation of the flattering patronage already bestowed on their taste of invention, have agreed unanimously to part with their stock under prime cost; which resolution, unfortunately for those gentry, came to the ears of our frail fair, who have determined (imagining their intentions, as soon as they had rid themselves of the false protuberances, were to plan some new appendage to the female attire, more expensive to the purchasers, and more troublesome to bear) to continue the *Pads* no longer than those they have in wear shall keep their shape, during which time they will fix on some more *decent* sign which will equally signify—*this House soon to be let*!!!

Those ladies who have given their support to the Pad, are more to be pitied than censured. Modesty will ever stand unshaken against the attacks of frailty, and though virtue may be insulted, it will seldom turn to vice, unless the mind is so weak to yield to the temptations of *Fashion*, which often stamp infamy on the credulous, whose understandings, had they been properly cultivated, would spurn the idea of adding to Nature, where she has not been kind. *Barton*, in the Battle of Hexham, may be here quoted; his speech, in the third act, to *La Varenne*, at once justifies the assertion, that Beauty is seldom encreased by Ornament—it stands thus:

"I' faith if we would but leave nature to herself, her works are pretty equal, but we will be garnishing with worldly nonsense, till we so besmear the face of it, that we can scarcely trace sweet natures out-lines."

It would be a difficult task to convince the majority of the female sex, of the justness of *Barton*'s remarks; it is therefore hoped that time will take effect where reasoning has power, and that decency will stand unmoved against the arts of *Fashion* and the *encouragement* of Men-milliners.

Colman's play, *The Battle of Hexham*, was first performed in 1789. William Woodfall's advice about "the temptations of *Fashion*" fell on deaf ears. By June even the Post Office was affected by the new interest in dress, for a decision to put its employees in uniform stirred up an animated discussion among the ladies and hence the newspapers as to color and type. The ladies themselves, as the *Star* noticed with anguish on 29 June, had topped the pad with another grotesquerie: "FASHION.—The Nemplish bonnet, which first nodded over the *forehead*, and then withdrew towards the *left temple*, has now reached the back part of the head, and is gradually assuming a larger form. Its *position* there, which is very unbecoming, must be not a little painful to the wearer, held, as it is, from falling over the *shoulders*, only by a strong *grappling* of steel pins!" "FASHION" was still an object of contempt. But on 5 July the *Morning Herald* came to terms with the situation by offering its feminine readers serious information on the subject, presented in a sympathetic manner:

The *fashionable* female dress is now thus arranged:—

The hair is still dressed flat upon the forehead and temples, but the ringlet begins to yield in charms to the *queue renversé*. On one side a *turban cap* is brought very low down upon the temple;—on the other, the hair is drawn through an opening in this cap, and is so suspended till it falls gracefully on the shoulder. Two or three long feathers, chiefly white, or straw-coloured, are placed in front.

The *handkerchief* is pinned low, and the tucker raised high; but not so high as entirely to hide the neck.

Pads continue to be worn; and on account of these the dress is still a loose gown of white muslin flounced in front, appearing to be put on with the negligence permitted to the supposed situation of the wearers. A narrow sash ties it at the waist.

Silk stockings with coloured clocks are the *supreme rage*.

Other newspapers continued to be disgusted. "The *Pad* is universally banished from all well regulated families; its place is supplied with the cooler ornament of a small hoop or a straw petticoat," the *Gazetteer* remarked hopefully on 12 July; but on 26 July it bewailed the obstinacy of this garment in a poem, entitled "On the Present Fashionable Phenomenon,/ The Pad." The poem was signed "A Friend to the Sex."

The pad remained, but the bonnet evidently did not, for on 14 August the *World* mentioned: "The Cap *en Militaire*, now sported by our fashionable *Belles*, is called the *Valenciennes* Helmet." And on 8 September it added that "Helmets are become the reigning mode for the decoration of the Ladies' heads [at Margate]. In this warlike dress, Lady WALLACE far exceeds her female competitors; for she has, instead of the feather, which others modestly substitute, actually put the flowing tail of a horse, which in/ 'Graceful ringlets down her manly shoulders flows.'" If it was inevitable that fashions should be influenced by the war, it was equally inevitable that Lady Wallace, who looked like an Amazon and was as militaristic as any lady in the country, should be in the vanguard of that influence. A sister of the Duchess of Gordon, Lady Wallace had gone to France shortly after the Revolution and in 1789 had been arrested by the French as a British agent. When the newspapers next heard of her, she was an intimate of General Dumouriez, and it was suspected that she had had something to do with his defection. Once the defection was complete, she had returned to England, entertained him during his brief visit there, and subsequently published *The Conduct of the King of Prussia and General Dumouriez Investigated*. On 17 December she was back in the news, the *Oracle* having published an exposé of her amorous adventures with one Thomas Wright: possibly, although improbably, Thomas Wright, the bookseller and one-time (1785–1786) mayor.

The gentlemen were not totally neglected. Although they got no fashion advice from the newspapers, they came in for a share of the ridicule, the *Courier* of 27 November remarking, for example: "The fashionable morning dress—a grey mixture frock, with a scarlet *envelope* close round the neck—gives our modern beaux the appearance of a groupe of *turkies*, with their throats cut." Their conduct was also subject for comment. On 5 September the *World* reported that the ladies of Brighton were complaining "of the indelicacy of the Gentlemen, who collect in considerable numbers on the Beach, near their Machines." They were not "collecting" on the beaches of Margate because the bathing machines there were equipped with canvas awnings, which shielded the users from their gaze. But the gentlemen figured most prominently in stories about the faro entertainments, since these were an issue, and almost all issues during this period were basically political. The frequenters of the entertainments were overwhelmingly Whigs. These included the Carlton House coterie, all Whiggish except the Prince of Wales himself, and leaders of the left wing of the Opposition, who had long been represented by the Government press as having impoverished themselves at the tables. Since all of them were natural prey for the *Oracle*, *The Times*, and other Ministerial newspapers with a taste for extortion, the marvel is that oblique references to scandalous incidents connected with faro parties had not appeared in those newspapers before. They did appear at the beginning of 1793. According to the Ministerial newspapers, one of the heaviest gamblers was Charles James Fox, and the institution of a fund for payment of his debts encouraged the *True Briton* to take a moralistic stand on the subject. Gambling, it said in mid-July, was wrong. The *World* went one step further. Gambling, it told its readers on 29 July, was Jacobinistic: "When certain of OUR NOBLES are losing their time, their health, their estates, at FARO, does it never occur to them, that they are laying the FOUNDATIONS OF DEMOCRACY ?" The *Morning Chronicle* had replied to such statements with derision. The *Morning Post* adopted another tactic. Not only did it agree that gambling was wrong, but, from August on, it indicated just how wrong it was by publishing accounts of the earnings and practices of the owners of the tables. Since, unlike the patrons, the owners were almost entirely friends of the Government, the Ministerial papers were willing to forget the matter; but not so the *Morning Post*, which on 24 December announced without comment that the new season had begun: "Lady HORTON has commenced her winter's entertainments; Pharo, Sunday and Friday." Readers were obviously going to hear more on the subject.

There were weddings, but, since weddings were not regarded as social events, they interested newspapers only if they seemed to have some political importance or if one of the parties to the match was personally known to the editor. The marriage of Louise of Mecklenburg-Strelitz to Prince Frederick William of Prussia on 24 September received more publicity by far than the marriage of Dundas, since the Princess had been mentioned as a possible bride for the Prince of Wales. The "late" marriage in Wales of Thomas Chambre, solicitor in Chancery, to Miss Fitzroy Crofties was mentioned only by *Lloyd's Evening Post* (23 Jan.) and the *Morning Chronicle* (24 Jan.), and the marriage of the bookseller, Charles Rivington, was mentioned only by the *Diary* (20 May), but the marriage of Lady Elizabeth Lambart, on whose behalf Lady Cavan had collected £4,000 damages from the *Morning Post*, was overlooked by no newspaper. The *Morning Post* had been a poor loser and Lady Cavan a spiteful winner, for, when, on 3 August, the *Post* had referred disparagingly to both her and her daughter, Lady Cavan had threatened to sue again. The *Post* hastily (7 Aug.) apologized, the apology being signed by the printer:

LADY CAVAN.

The following letter we received yesterday, from Lady CAVAN, *which we freely insert, considering that the contradiction of the paragraph complained of, cannot proceed from better or more satisfactory authority, than her Ladyship. On our own part, we profess, that we conceive the Letter from* Lady CAVAN *superfluous, as we were well convinced that neither her Ladyship, nor* LADY LAMBART *would have appeared in public until they were persuaded that no danger could arise to his Lordship, as the paragraph certainly explains.*

Upper Seymour-street, Tuesday,
the 6th of August, 1793.

SIR,
    Understanding that the following Paragraph has Appeared in Your Paper, of the MORNING POST, on the 3d instant, which Attacks my Character, as A *Mother* and Lady ELIZABETH LAMBARTS, as A *Sister*, I must *insist* on your Contradicting of it directly in the said Paper, to prevent *very* unpleasant Consequences, as neither my Daughter or myself *were ever at any* Place of Public Entertainment *whatever*, until long after We *knew*, from private letters, that Lord CAVAN was *perfectly Recovered of his wound*, and *on Duty* before Valencienne,
        "Lord CAVAN is quite well of his wound, which must be a matter of great satisfaction to his mother and sister, who, since they heard he was shot, have visited ALL places of public amusement, to alleviate their GRIEF, and CONSOLE them for the misfortune."
    I am your humble servant,
                J. NORRIS, *Blake-court,*
                Catherine-street, Strand.

On 14 November all newspapers reported the marriage: "On Saturday morning [10 Nov.], at St. George's Hanover-square, [of] Capt. Ricketts, of the Royal Navy, to the Right Hon. Lady Elizabeth Lambert, sister to the Earl of Cavan"; and, in almost every instance, the announcement was followed by a squib, sometimes referring to the damages, sometimes not, the *Oracle*, for example, adding only that the "beautiful and accomplished Lady ELIZABETH LAMBERT, has been confined since Saturday with the RICKETTS!" The newspapers did not wish Lady Lambart well.

Expiration of the
Tattersall-Weltje Lease

On 21 June Parliament was prorogued to 13 August, on 13 August it was prorogued to 29 October, and on 29 October it was prorogued to 21 January. The reason for these additional prorogations, the Opposition press thought, was that Pitt needed a string of military victories to back up a request for increased taxes. On 17 June he was sure he would have them by 13 August, but he did not have them then or on 29 October. The sequential manner of dealing with the prorogation had in any event an effect on the newspapers. Very few newspapers made money during the Parliamentary recess. Although production costs were lower, sales dwindled, advertisements fell off, and, most important, political propaganda was in little demand. A newspaper which was regularly subsidized could survive a long recess with no great difficulty, but a newspaper which was paid for its propaganda piecemeal, as most of the Treasury newspapers now were, would have given a seven-month prorogation some serious thought. The division of the prorogation into stages helps to explain why the *Diary* was not discontinued and the *Public Advertiser* sold on 21 June. It helps to explain why the *Morning Herald*, which lost its subsidy on 26 April, remained loyal until mid-July and why the *World*, which lost its subsidy on 20 June, remained loyal until October. It also probably accounts for the survival of the *Morning Post*.

The expiration of the Tattersall-Weltje lease was a crisis for the Opposition press. Radcliffe had not succeeded in raising the sale to 2,000 copies a day, and the "farmers" were therefore obliged to buy out the other proprietors at the rate of £350 a twenty-fourth share. The last document on the subject[41] specifies what it would "probably" cost the Prince of Wales to pay his half of the indemnification and settle his debt with Tattersall:

An Estimate of the Probable Sum to be paid for the *Morning Post*, 3ʳᵈ July 1793.

Balance of account including the ½ year delivered and Mr. Benjafield's annuity to Christmas [i.e., the amount presently owed to Tattersall, obviously including half of the £5,000 damages paid to Lady Cavan]	£3192
Loss on the farm, ½ year from Christmas to July 1793	600
12 shares, ½ the property to be purchased, July 1793 at £350 per share	4200
Amount of money to be paid	£7992
From which deduct two shares in possession at £350	700
Balance to be paid	£7292

Exclusive of the annuity of £350 granted to Mr. Benjafield.

Tattersall was better off, for, since he already owned almost seven and a half shares, he needed to purchase only an additional four and a half to make up his dozen, whereas the Prince needed to purchase ten. The "improbable" alternative was evidently to persuade some or all of the other proprietors to retain possession of their shares, paying them the difference between the actual value and the £350 guaranteed by the lease. The possibility that any of them would consent to such an arrangement seemed slight. It looked as if Tattersall and the Prince of Wales, finding themselves on 3 July the sole owners, would recover whatever money they could by selling the press and materials, and the *Morning Post* would cease to exist. But in fact it did not.

By 12 February, 1796, the *Morning Post* was owned by Daniel Stuart and John Fuller; on 1 January of that year, the *Post* mentioned that "the present Proprietors" had "[undertaken] the Conduct of this Paper" on 27 July, 1795; and on 6 July, 1795, the *Post* announced that it had been sold. What happened to the proprietary between 3 July, 1793, and 6 July, 1795, is to a large degree a matter of conjecture, although certainly not entirely. Of the proprietors, one, Jeremiah Hargrave, had died; another, Mr. Davis, was, according to the *True Briton* (4 July, 1796), still a proprietor in 1794; and a third, Louis Weltje, seems to have quit the paper in 1793. On 9 December, 1793, the *Morning Post* reported that "*A Change . . . has taken place in the Property of this Paper*" and that "*it is only necessary to add, that the Proprietor who during the last Winter interfered in the conduct of this Paper has no longer any Connection with [it].*" The only proprietor who could and did "interfere" was Tattersall, but, since the *Morning Post* of 10 July, 1794, spoke of "the secession of Mr. TATTERSALL from the property" of the *English Chronicle* as if it were a very recent occurrence, one must suppose that the earlier "seceder" from the *Morning Post* was Weltje. Although Weltje had not "interfered," *The Times* had been afraid that he would,[42] and his connection with the paper had been common knowledge. It is true that the *Post* was indifferent to the affairs of the Prince of Wales from July, 1793, on, but, since it had been indifferent right along, this fact is inconsequential.

Other clues are provided by the character of the newspaper or by incidental references. The proprietors, for example, still owned the *English Chronicle*, for on 24 August readers who missed the *Morning Post* were referred to that newspaper, and on 28 November the *Post* announced a contribution of "10 shillings" from the "Compositors of the English Chronicle" to its fund for "Indigent Manufacturers." Among the contributors listed on 23 November were "C. D. H." and "Mr. Legge," who, since they gave as much as the *Post*'s editor, were probably somehow concerned. The principal advertisers during the last half of the year were Tattersall, Skinner, Dyke, and Christie, all auctioneers, although, from 21 October on, Christie was also advertising in the *True Briton*. Book advertisements were almost entirely lacking. The personnel was in some respects unchanged. Joseph Haslewood was supplying most of the poetry, with occasional help from "Peter Pindar," who was again publishing in many of the newspapers; and Robert Merry was at least an occasional correspondent. Certainly chargeable to him is a letter, signed "PHILO-PITTI," which the *Post* published on 22 July. The letter complimented the Government upon its multiple achievements, especially the "great patronage bestowed on several newspapers, which propagate such intelligence, and such opinions as it is necessary from time to time to issue from the Treasury. Among these a Morning Paper, and an Evening Paper lately set on foot, claim and deserve the pre-eminence: being the property of certain Clerks in office, they are entirely, and with propriety, at the disposal of the Minister, to retail whatever he thinks proper." There were, however, alterations, indicating that the "*Change*," reported by the *Morning Post* on 9 December, had actually occurred by 9 July.

The principal alteration in personnel was the introduction of "NOVICE JOHN," who henceforth furnished the editorials. Although his essays tended to be treatises on political philosophy, they did supply an element of dignity. On 9 July, too, the *Morning Post* published the first of a series of boasts, indicating that it had recently extended its news-gathering facilities: *"Our Readers will perceive, by the Yesterday's Evening Papers, if they have read them, and the Morning Papers of This Day, that they have availed themselves of our* PRIORITY *in French Intelligence. We hope, in future, to gratify them in this particular—without having recourse to the stale trick of adopting* SUBSEQUENT DATES, *or hazarding a mention of that, as fact, which, with respect to the Treasury Prints, never has, nor never can occur."* There was a second boast on 12 July: *"Our Patrons, the Public, will perceive, that our exertions in procuring for them a* PRIORITY *in Continental Intelligence, has succeeded even beyond our most sanguine expectation.—With respect to Foreign Information, all the Papers in London this week have been* totally *indebted to the* MORNING POST." On 13 July the *Post "again [challenged]* ALL *the Papers, printed this Day in London, to a Competition"*: and on 20 July it proclaimed: *"The Public are alone our Patrons.—We seek no favours from the* Treasury, *and as long as the* PEOPLE *flatter us with their encouragement, we shall feel no reluctance in courting a comparison with our Competitors. Our own honest and independent exertions we consider as the best claims to public favour."* The proclamation was repeated on 22 July, with the addendum: *"We despise the idea of soliciting* that *favour, under the barren praise of being the* unworthy *instruments of* unworthy *men, however exalted; for Power is seldom the reward of Virtue."* The *Morning Post* was probably counting on Merry's returning to the Continent as correspondent, but Merry refused to go so long as there was a possibility that Mrs. Merry would be engaged by Covent Garden. When he finally did leave, in late September or early October, he got only as far as Harwich, and by 29 November "Novice John" had gone instead. From 29 November through 27 December, his essays were headed "Brussels," although, since he was still writing political philosophy, the essay of 29 November dealing, for example, with the politics of the Italian poet, Ariosto, he might as well have stayed in London.

Foreign news was not in fact the *raison d'être* of the *Morning Post*, which was clearly in business to support the interests of Lord Lauderdale. Like Lord Lauderdale, it wanted peace and reform. It hated the *Sun* and the *True Briton*, which were still attacking him despite his appeals to the Attorney General, to the Secretaries of the Treasury, and even to Pitt.[43] It hated the Duke of Richmond, with whom he had almost fought a duel, and it hated those other archapostates, Burke and Pitt. On 19 September it printed the Glasgow petition for peace, which was Lord Lauderdale's special project, the petition being otherwise printed only by the *Morning Chronicle* (18 Sept.) and the *Oracle* (19 Sept.), both of which explained that the petition was printed at his request and therefore at his expence. Always an apologist for radical reformers, the *Post* was obsessed with developments in Scotland from September on. It was the only newspaper to publish minutes of the Convention, it carried the most complete accounts of the trials, especially the trial of Muir, and on 30–31 December it published the whole indictment of William Skirving. Lord Lauderdale seems to have attended the October meetings of the Convention, and he was greatly agitated about the trials. The *World*'s observation of 19 April, 1794, that Lord Lauderdale had "a Paper of his own" was very evidently overdue: he had had the *Morning Post* since 9 July, 1793. Two facts, however, seem obvious. Since he knew nothing about newspapers and had no literary ability, he was not managing the *Post* himself; and, since any legal connection with the paper would have been discovered and publicized, he was acting even in his business negotiations through someone else. The evidence that his agent in both instances was Daniel Stuart is, to say the least, substantial.

There is every indication that Daniel Stuart managed the *Morning Post* from 9 July, 1793, on. The previous editor, William Radcliffe, had been engaged by the lessees of the paper; his contract therefore expired with the expiration of the lease, and there is no evidence that he was re-engaged. Nothing further is heard of him until September, 1794, when the proprietors of the *Gazetteer*, having decided to recall him as their editor, had considerable difficulty finding him. It turned out that he was living in the country, having been in retirement for some time.[44] Daniel Stuart would in any event have been a likely choice as Radcliffe's successor, since he was writing for the *Morning Post* at the time and knew the paper intimately, having been connected with it since 1782. He had even edited it from 1787 to 1789. For Lord Lauderdale, there would have been no other possibility, since Stuart was already on his payroll as Secretary to the Secretarial Committee of the Friends of the People. Indications that Stuart was in fact the new editor appeared very early. Because of his work for the Friends of the People, Stuart had become acquainted with Thomas Hardy, Horne Tooke, Joseph Gerrald, and other radical reformers, and the *Post* always knew more about their activities than the *Gazetteer* or even the *Courier*. From May on, he was also in correspondence with William Skirving respecting the Edinburgh convention and the trials, and on 2 September Skirving wrote to him, as "Secretary to the Society of the Friends of the People," explaining his testimony at the trial of Muir. The letter was published by the *Morning Post* and the *Morning Chronicle* on 6 September, the *Morning Post* stating that "a copy" had been sent to its editor, the *Morning Chronicle* stating that its editor had been "requested to insert [it]," the implication being that the "insertion" had been paid for. In a letter, submitted to the Commons on 6 June, 1794, Stuart mentioned incidentally that "Skirving sent me the printed minutes of the [Edinburgh] convention." The *Post* was the only newspaper to publish these minutes, and, when the pamphlet version of Skirving's trial appeared (1794), it included an introduction by Daniel Stuart. At the end of 1793, Stuart published, on behalf of the Friends of the People, another pamphlet, entitled *Peace and Reform, against War and Corruption. In Answer to a Pamphlet, Written by Arthur Young, Esq., entitled "The Example of France, a Warning to Britain."* Although the pamphlet was not announced until 21 December, excerpts disguised as editorials appeared in the

Morning Post from 16 August on, the first being an attack on Young. The first excerpt, identified as such, appeared in the *Morning Chronicle* on 20 December, and, on 21 and 24 December, the pamphlet was advertised by the *Oracle*, still managed by Daniel's brother Peter. On 23 December the work was finally announced by the *Morning Post*, and on 27 December the *Post* published the same excerpt, a defense of Fox, which had already appeared in the *Chronicle*. The name of the author of *Peace and Reform* was withheld until later, although the publishers were identified from the outset as Ridgway and Symonds.

The extrapolitical activities of the paper are also revelatory. Many newspapers printed stories with a view to influencing the market; the Stuart brothers had long since refined that practice. Their *modus operandi* was to forge a document substantiating the story and send it along to another newspaper for publication, diverting suspicion from themselves by loudly deploring the evils of stock-jobbing. The three of them had collaborated on such a project in 1783,[45] and Peter Stuart had forged several documents since in connection with his editing of the *Oracle*. But his forte was Government bulletins, written in English and supposedly issued by a member of the Administration; Daniel Stuart's specialty, as it became all too evident later, was foreign material, written in French and supposedly transmitted from the Continent. On 25 October, 1793, the first of such manufactures was delivered to the office of the *Sun*. The *Sun* published the story that day, retracted it on 28 October, and on 29 October was accused by the *Morning Post* of having perpetrated the hoax itself:

> The Public should be on its guard against the tricks of the Stock-Exchange against the Settling Day [of the war]. We have had already one *Forged Official Bulletin*, published in a *Government Print*; and this, we have no doubt, will be practised in similar Papers, which, from their conduct, care not how far they deceive the Public.
>
> OFFICIAL BULLETINS.
>
> A Government Print of yesterday evening has the following article, for which it asks the *forgiveness* of their few readers. We publish the apology, in the hope that it will obtain that pardon which it so earnestly solicits.
>
> "The *Official Bulletin* transmitted to us from Flanders, and which we gave in our Paper of Friday, proves to have been a Forgery. It could not have been published by any authority, and must have been fabricated for some private and interested purpose. We may express a hope, however, that it is only anticipative of some near event."
>
> Of the prognostics of this gentleman we shall make no comment. They have so often failed, that until we have more dependance on their prophecies, we shall not attempt to support ministerial predictions.

"A political poulterer [Michael Angelo Taylor] observes, that in consequence of the lunatic excesses to which Stock Jobbing is carried on at present, that we shall have a greater plenty of *Lame Ducks* this Winter, than was ever before remembered," the *Post* added on 21 November. Taylor's prediction was accurate, and a good part of the money lost by those *"Lame Ducks"* turned up in the office of the *Morning Post*.

In addition to everything else, the *Morning Post* of late 1793 conformed generally with what Daniel Stuart said a newspaper ought to be or at least with what every newspaper which he is known to have managed was. From July, 1793, on, there is no difference in the essential character of the *Morning Post*. None of his contemporaries regarded Stuart as a stylist,[46] and, except for *Peace and Reform*, which was probably polished somewhat by Mackintosh, his writings were so awkward that readers were sometimes left to guess what he was talking about. The boasts, which appeared in the *Morning Post* from 9 July on and which characterized all his newspapers, are good examples. Fortunately, he did little of the writing himself, and he was as canny in selecting his staff as he was in planning his various enterprises. In effect, the Stuart newspapers were a combination of the *Morning Chronicle*, as it was currently conducted by James Perry, and the *Morning Post* and the *Morning Herald*, as they had once been conducted by the Rev. Henry Bate Dudley. As in the case of the *Chronicle*, the principal feature of his papers was a very dignified political editorial, backed by hard-hitting paragraphs with "point." The editorial writer in late 1793 was "Novice John," Stuart himself supplying the paragraphs. But, unlike Perry, Stuart thought[47] that a newspaper ought to be "cheerfully entertaining" as well, "not filled entirely with ferocious politics"; and, by "cheerful entertainment," he meant "poetry and light paragraphs," that is, fashionable gossip with an emphasis on "personalities." As he saw it, the paragraphs ought not to be "tame," but neither ought they to be "low, scurrilous, or violent." To modern readers, these paragraphs seem quite as "ferocious" as the paragraphs on politics, and in fact Stuart always printed anything, provided it was coherent with the politics of the paper and provided it was paid for. In 1793, as later, the *Post* had to remind its readers occasionally that certain paragraphs *"would, if inserted, be charged at the Stamp-Office."* The paragraphs paid for in 1793 evidently included the attack on Lady Cavan and her daughter and an item, published on 7 August, which read: "A boarding-school Miss of THIRTEEN has eloped with papa's footman, a fellow about six feet high. The circumstance is doubly mortifying to the mother, as he was also the favourite of mama!" Paragraphs of this kind, of which there were many after 1795, gave a newspaper, in Stuart's opinion, spirit. Stuart's notion of "poetry" was the effusions of Mrs. Robinson, and in late 1793 the *Post* was publishing the sonnets of Haslewood and the satires of Dr. Wolcot instead. But this was obviously not the fault of the editor, for no one was more enthusiastic about her poetry than he.

A final bit of evidence that Stuart was managing the *Morning Post* from at least 9 July, 1793, on is supplied by one of his own statements. "[The *British Press* and the *Globe*] took from me my chief assistant, George Lane . . . ," he said in 1838.[48] "Mr. Lane, as he owned, was indebted to me for all he knew of newspapers. At first he was slow and feeble, but his language was always that of a scholar and a gentleman, rather tame, but free from anything low, scurrilous, or violent. After several years of instruction by me—I may say, education—he had become a valuable parliamentary reporter, a judicious theatrical critic, a ready translator, and the best writer of *jeux d'esprit* . . . I ever had. . . . Lane had little knowledge of politics and little turn for political writing; but he was a valuable assistant. He resided near the office, was ready and willing . . . to go any where, , and report any thing, and he would do every thing." "It is sometimes difficult," Stuart said again,[49] "to say what it is that occasions the success of particular enterprises, and it is common for every one who has assisted to claim pre-eminent merit. . . . Sir James Mackintosh never did; but my brother Peter and others did for him. . . ." The description of George Lane as political writer exactly describes "Novice John"; and Lane's competence as "a ready translator" explains the appearance of the forgeries in French, for Stuart himself knew only English. Although letters signed "Novice John" were still published by the *Morning Post* in late 1795, Lane had been replaced as principal editorial writer by Mackintosh. In mid-1793 Mackintosh, along with O'Bryen, Erskine, and Sheridan, were active in the Friends of the Liberty of the Press, but, if he was then writing for any newspaper, it would have been the *Oracle.*

The Tattersall-Weltje lease expired on 3 July, 1793, and, on 6 July, 1795, the *Morning Post* announced that there had been a change in the property. Since the interval was almost exactly two years, Lord Lauderdale had evidently taken a two-year lease on the newspaper, similar perhaps to the previous lease and inevitably including another indemnification clause. This would have been a mutually happy arrangement, for Lord Lauderdale, who expected Parliament to convene on 13 August, had need of a newspaper, and the *Morning Post,* which would otherwise have succumbed, had need of Lord Lauderdale. The actual lessee, one can be certain, was Daniel Stuart, but to what extent Stuart bought into the paper during this two-year period remains a question, and his own statements on the subject are not very helpful. Since he was known as a man of "inviolable secrecy"[50] and was always especially secretive about his radical activities, one cannot expect him to say more than need be, and in the main he said less. Although it was public knowledge, for example, that he and Fuller had owned the *Post* since at least 6 July, 1795, and that he had conducted the "literary department" thereafter, he was inclined to set the date forward. The first statement reasonably attributable to him appeared in the *Courier* of 11 January, 1811, which asserted that he had "purchased [the *Morning Post*] for the paltry sum of Five Hundred Pounds" and that, "a very few years" after the purchase, namely, in 1802, he had "*sold* [it] for *Sixteen Thousand Pounds.*" In 1835 he mentioned in a letter:[51] "In August, 1795, I began to conduct *The Morning Post,* the sale of which was so low, only 350 per day, that a gentleman at that time made a bet with me that the Paper was actually extinct. . . . *The Morning Post* [in 1799] was selling 2,000 daily." In 1838 he made several such statements: "In 1795, my brother Peter purchased the copyright of the Oracle newspaper, then selling 800 daily, for 80*l.* There were no house or materials; and I joined in purchasing the Morning Post, with house and materials, the circulation being only 350 per day, for 600*l.* What it was that occasioned such a depreciation of newspaper property at that time, I cannot tell."[52] "Soon after I joined the Morning Post in the autumn of 1795, Christie, the auctioneer, left it on account of its low sale, and left a blank. . . . But in 1802, he came to me again, praying for re-admission."[53] Stuart's daughter, however, understood[54] that he had paid "a considerable sum" for the *Morning Post* and that he had bought it in early 1795.

The reference to Christie has always been interpreted to mean that Christie quit the newspaper in 1795 as proprietor, but it is clear from the context that Stuart is talking about Christie as advertiser. Christie began to retire as advertiser on 21 October, 1793. More baffling is the statement that Stuart bought the *Morning Post* in order to provide a home for the *Oracle*, just purchased by his brother Peter. Peter bought the copyright of the *Oracle* on 26 August, 1795, and there is no indication in the colophon or elsewhere that it was ever printed, published, or edited at the address of the *Morning Post*, although perhaps it was. Especially baffling are the statements respecting circulation and price. On the one hand, Stuart insisted that he paid only £500 or £600 for the paper and that, at the time he bought it, the circulation was only 350 a day; his daughter, on the other hand, said that he paid "a considerable sum" for the property, and her statement is supported by the newspaper itself, which announced on 6 July, 1795, that the new proprietors (Stuart and Fuller) had had to pay "more POUNDS" for the property "than it originally cost PENCE!/ This [is an] indisputable fact. . . ." But in context Stuart appears to have been talking about the copyright, house, and materials, and it seems evident from the announcement that, prior to 6 July, 1795, the *Morning Post* had been essentially defunct, having perhaps even ceased publication. His daughter may have been talking about the cost of shares. Here lies the real puzzle: what shares, if any, did Stuart and Fuller own prior to July, 1795? The simplest answer is that they owned all of them, but this answer is far from adequate.

Fuller's involvement is easily explained, for in early 1794 Topham sold the *World* to "a Gentleman," and, since John Fuller had been connected with the paper since at least 1791,[55] he was very probably the purchaser. On 30 June, 1794, the *World* was consolidated with the *Morning Post*, and Fuller would therefore have become half-owner of the *Post*. But the *Post* was leased to Lord Lauderdale, and Lord Lauderdale could have arranged no such consolidation unless he was also the sole proprietor, and it appears quite possible that he was. Davis, it was later (2 July, 1796) established, was still a proprietor on 14 April, 1794, but there is no further mention of him, and the other proprietors may have quit earlier. Lord Lauderdale would have acquired the newspaper through the offices of Daniel Stuart. For Stuart was certainly realizing enough from his forgeries to buy out all the shareholders, and yet, as agent of the lessee, he could probably not buy the shares for himself. Until there is evidence to the contrary, one may therefore suppose that Daniel Stuart was the manager and nominal lessee of the *Morning Post* from July, 1793, to July, 1795, that he was obliged to conduct the paper during this period in the interests of Lord Lauderdale, and that he finally purchased his half of the newspaper from Lord Lauderdale himself.

The First Prorogation: Punishments

The first prorogation of Parliament (21 June) was followed by a flood of prosecutions, but as usual the Government was giving the impression of vigilance without actually disturbing any of the radical reformers. The victims were either talkers or booksellers. The names of the talkers had been provided by Dundas's agents and by Reeves's committee for the encouragement of anonymous defamation, recently denounced by Thomas Law. The Association was evidently still active in this respect, for on 5 August the *Morning Chronicle* protested:

> INCENDIARY POSTING BILL.
> Again we think it our duty to announce the diabolical attempt which some ruffians are now daily making to stir up the people to fury by means of horrid and perfidious hand-bills; The paper that we noticed some days ago, replete with the most scandalous abuse of the King and Royal Family, under the attractive shape of a theatrical bill, was posted up on Saturday night in various places in the city, to meet the eye of the crowds that Sunday draws abroad, and this was done without any interruption from the vigilance of magistrates. It is impossible to conceive any thing more horrible than the tendency of this paper, which has been so copiously distributed in the streets, thrown into shops, and pasted upon the walls, as to make it impossible to be regarded as the act of a single ruffian. Its malice is also so obvious as to betray the source from which it comes, and this in truth may account for the criminal supineness with which certain sycophant magistrates have acted on the occasion. If it had been an affair in which traps were to be laid for peaceable citizens—spies to be placed on tavern conversations—or the meetings of boys to be disturbed, we should have had numerous panegyrics on the zeal and activity of the independent and loyal guardians of the peace.

On 16 August the *Chronicle* protested again: "One of the brown-paper publications, distributed gratis by the Crown and Anchor Society is admirably calculated to set old friends and neighbours at variance—it is a description of such *words*,

&c. as the law deems seditious, either before or after the third bottle; and for which any loyal butcher ought immediately to convey any disloyal baker or other neighbour, to the nearest jail." The trials, all of which were held in the provinces, began in July and continued throughout the year. With one exception, the defendants were laborers or petty shopkeepers, the "seditious words" had been uttered in taverns, and convictions were immediately followed by prison sentences. The exception was the Baptist preacher, William Winterbotham, who was accused of preaching two "seditious and atrocious sermons," the first on 5 November, 1792, the second on 27 November following. He was tried for the offenses on 25 and 26 July at Exeter, but, although he was convicted in both instances, sentences were postponed indefinitely.

The *Morning Chronicle* was similarly indignant about the booksellers. "The prosecutions in the country go on with unabated rigour," it announced on 8 August, "and at every Assize, at every Quarter Session, there are indictments presented for words spoken in liquor—for selling or for lending pamphlets—and they are chiefly against men whose independent spirit, arising from successful industry, makes them scorn to consult their ease by ignominious submissions to the tools of office. In most instances they [the Government] have failed. And the case of Mr. PHILIPS, of Leicester, still stands unimitated, as well as unprecedented, in severity. It was his misfortune not to be tried by any of the Judges of England." The year 1793 was in fact a calamitous one for booksellers. There were several deaths. In 1790 the trade lost only "Honest George Kearsley," who was eulogized by the *Diary* on 10 December; in 1791 it lost only Lockyer Davis, who died on 23 April; in 1792 it lost no one; and in 1793 its numbers were reduced by four. On 12 April the elder John Bew of Paternoster Row died; on 13 April Mr. Whieldon of Fleet Street died; on 6 November John Mac Murray (or Murray) of Fleet Street died; and on 1 December William Owen of Fleet Street died. Mac Murray had been a proprietor of the *Star*; Owen had been a proprietor of the *Gazetteer*. On 12 August the *Gazetteer* also reported the death two days earlier of "Mrs. Holland, wife of the bookseller in Oxford-street, presently in Newgate for selling the Letter to the Addressers." By the end of the year, it seemed as if all the Opposition booksellers were either dead, in prison, or in a state of bankruptcy.

The names of the booksellers singled out for prosecution had been collected in the main by the Treasury solicitors, William Chamberlayne and Joseph White, who had themselves got the names from lawyers. Although the lawyers had been encouraged to do the suing themselves, they had evidently declined, and the Government was compelled to act instead. On 12 July even the *Oracle* suggested that the Government would have been better advised to prosecute the reform societies: "With respect to the *publisher* of a LIBEL, it should [at least] be enquired, whether the man have waved his own judgment before the cogent conviction of the *purse* extended by some Secretary of Reform? If the case could be exactly sifted, we believe some compact of this sort is usually made—'YOU shall stand in the Law's danger, and WE will support you, and make your fortune.' The proof seems to be, that these publishers are for the most part needy adventurers; 'slaves that have set their life upon a cast/ To mend it, or be rid on't.'" Although no "enquiry" was made, the Government did offer to remove the various culprits from "the Law's danger" in return for their promises to support William Pitt in the future, and every one of them refused. The most obvious reason was not, however, the generosity of the reform societies, for an imprisoned bookseller was a hero to the populace, and, since the Government had no apparent objection to the continuation of his activities, his business prospered. No one was better aware of this fact than Ridgway and Symonds, who, having traded on their own martyrdom from the outset, were now trading on the martyrdom of others as well. The *Morning Post* of 4 July announced, for example, publication of *"These are the Times to Try Men's Souls. A Letter to John Frost, a Prisoner in Newgate. By Henry Yorke.* Printed for Ridgway and Symonds: 'First Year of Imprisonment in Newgate.'" As bookseller and editor of the Leicester *Herald*, Richard Phillips was also seeing to it that his imprisonment was well advertised, and notices of William Holland's publications were likely to include some reference to his own incarceration. The Government could still count on the services of J. S. Jordan, who had been frightened into defecting in July, 1792, and was therefore still at large, and it could still count on the services of John Almon. On 10 July *Lloyd's Evening Post* announced a new periodical, entitled *The History of France, from the Most Early Records, to the Death of Louis XVI: The Ancient Part by William Beckford, Esq. . . . the Modern Part by an English Gentleman, who has been Some Time Resident in Paris.* The periodical was to appear fortnightly, beginning on 1 August, it was to consist of thirty numbers in all, and each number was to include an "elegant copper plate print." The publisher was Jordan, and the unnamed "English Gentleman" was John Almon. Although Almon had probably never seen Paris, Beckford had found his stay there so illuminating that he had refused to complete the work on his return, and Almon was completing it for him.[56] Such men as Jordan and Almon were now, however, a rarity.

Although the Government lost more by these prosecutions than it gained, the prosecutions continued. By summer every bookseller who had published Paine's *Rights of Man,* Part II, or his *Letter Addressed to the Addressers* had been indicted, and the trials were under way. The cases which attracted most attention were those of Holt, the Robinsons, and Eaton. Daniel Holt, who was charged with selling "two very scandalous and atrocious Libels, *An Address to the Addressers* and *An Address to the Tradesmen, Mechanics and Labourers of Newark, on a Parliamentary Reform,*" was tried in the Nottingham Assizes in July; the Robinsons, who were charged with selling Paine's *Rights of Man,* Part II, were tried in the Bridgewater Assizes on 6 August, the witness against them being, according to *Lloyd's Evening Post* (14 Aug.), Alexander Pyle, a bookseller at Norton Fitzwarren, who testified to having purchased a copy of the work at their shop. Judgments in both instances were deferred. Daniel Isaac Eaton, who had already (3 June) been tried for publishing the *Rights of Man*, Part II, without decisive results, was tried in Guildhall on 10 July for having published on 1 February the *Letter Addressed to the Addressers*. Representing the Government on this occasion were the Attorney General, Sir John Scott, and the Treasury lawyers, Chamberlayne and White; representing Eaton were again Vaughan and Guerney. The results were the same as before. According to the *Star* of 12 July:

> [The jury] found the Defendant *Guilty of publishing*.
> Lord KENYON—Gentlemen, I am afraid the Court must expect a verdict of guilty or not guilty. The law has committed the business to you.
> FOREMAN—We have considered this business, my Lord, and this is the only verdict we can give—Guilty of publishing.
> Lord KENYON—I have no right to ask where your doubts are. If you have any doubts, I shall endeavour to remove them. If you have not, I do not wish to say any thing voluntarily.
> FOREMAN—My Lord, we have considered it as much as possible among ourselves, and we can give no other verdict.
> Lord KENYON—I do not know very well what it means, whether it implies guilty or not guilty. You are bound and sworn to try this issue—whether the Defendant is guilty or not guilty.
> Upon this the Gentlemen of the Jury retired again for nearly an hour, to reconsider of their verdict. They then found the Defendant *guilty of publishing the Pamphlet in question*.
> Lord KENYON—This is certainly the same verdict. If you persist in it, I cannot help it. It must be recorded.
> FOREMAN—My Lord, we have maturely investigated this business, and cannot agree on any other verdict—Guilty of publishing the Pamphlet in question.

"The Verdict given in the case of EATON—*Guilty of publishing the Pamphlet*, is considered by the Lawyers as a nullity," said the *Oracle* on 13 July. "If the Pamphlet was innocent, there could be no guilt in the publication, and on the merits of the Pamphlet nothing has been decided. It would perhaps be deemed too great a stretch of authority for the Judges to affix any definite meaning, or legal construction to the words; and there only remain two ways in which the affair must terminate, either to proceed no further, or to order a new trial." Although the Government chose "to proceed no further," it was not through with Eaton.

The Government could not win a case against a bookseller, for, when the jury convicted, the bookseller became a hero, and, when it acquitted or evaded the issue, the Government looked ridiculous. Booksellers, who had been previously regarded as rogues, were now, thanks to William Pitt, men of "independent spirit." Bankruptcy proceedings also had disadvantages, for the name of another Opposition bookseller on the list was likely to stimulate the legal reformers. The Government newspapers always blamed the lawyers for the excessive cost of such actions, Lord Kenyon continued to disbar them, and in late July he ruled generally that lawyers could no longer regard every member of a firm as a separate client: they could bill the firm only as an individual. Even when there were no booksellers on the list, the lists were embarrassing. William Pitt, said the *Morning Chronicle* on 5 July, "is the first Minister that ever saw fifty bankrupts in a week for many weeks together." But the embarrassment was in one respect an advantage, for it occurred to no Opposition newspaper that the Government might itself be adding to the lists. The fact that several actions had been instigated by Ministerial papers and that the names of Pitt's enemies were figuring rather prominently in the announcements aroused no suspicions, or at least the suspicions were not published. The result was that a bankrupt bookseller was not a hero, and, if he recovered from the bankruptcy, the Government was subjected to no ridicule.

Although a bankruptcy proceeding was likely to interest only those financially concerned, the *Oracle* always somehow acquainted its readers with the fortunes of John Bell. On 14 May all of Bell's property was turned over to assignees. By 10 June he had got permission to continue the British Theatre and hoped to get permission to continue *The Fugitive Poetry* as well. The *Oracle* was not mentioned, and on 1 July the paper was advertised:

SALES BY AUCTION.

By Mr. CHRISTIE,
At his GREAT ROOM in PALL-MALL, on Thursday, July 11, at
One o'clock,
By Order of the ASSIGNEES of JOHN BELL,
The PROPERTY of the VERY GENERALLY CIRCULATED and
WELL KNOWN NEWS-PAPER, called
THE ORACLE.
The PURCHASERS may be accommodated with the TYPES and PRINTING MATERIALS belonging to it, at a FAIR VALUATION. It will be sold in One Lot, or divided into Eight Shares, as the Company at the Time of Sale may prefer.
FURTHER PARTICULARS will be explained at the Time of the SALE, or in the MEAN TIME (to PRINCIPALS only) upon application to Mr. BELL, at the BRITISH LIBRARY in the STRAND.

The advertisement appeared in the *Oracle* of 1, 2, 10, and 11 July and in the *World* of 1, 3, 10, and 11 July. The advertisements of 10 July substituted "TOMORROW" for "JULY 11"; the advertisements of 11 July substituted "THIS DAY." The advertisement also appeared in the *Oracle* of 12 July with "YESTERDAY" substituted for "THIS DAY," but elsewhere the *Oracle* announced: "The Sale of this Paper, which was advertised for yesterday the 11th instant, by Mr. CHRISTIE, was postponed until farther notice, to be given hereafter by public advertisement." On 13 July the *Oracle* commented: "Mr. PITT has been very falsely accused of a dangerous ambition, which aims at the greatest dignities and at universal power. Be it, however, known, as an ingenious Writer remarks, that the object of all ambition is the power of doing good. Opinion, confidence, popularity, are as effectually the sources of this power as any office can be." Since "opinion, confidence, [and] popularity" were all on the side of Fox, the *Oracle* seemed to be warning Pitt that, whether he continued in office or not, he could not afford to lose its support. This warning would have come from Sheridan and his agent, Peter Stuart.

Throughout July the *Oracle* carried daily columns of advertisements for the British Library, and on 30 July the *Oracle* was advertised again, the sale now being scheduled for 1 August at one o'clock. The advertisement, identical in character with the earlier one, appeared in the *Oracle* of 30 and 31 July and 1 August and in the *Morning Post* of 1 August. On 8 August, according to Stanley Morison,[57] Bell's "quire stock [was sold] at the Doctors' Commons." Although the outcome of these sales was not reported until 9 December, the purchaser of the *Oracle* was James Bell, Jr., John Bell's nephew, who was presently printing the paper, and the purchasers of the remaining properties were "a number of [his] friends." Daniel Stuart was infuriated. "The Bankrupt Laws require to undergo a complete revision," the *Morning Post* declared on 9 August. "Two Bankruptcies, it is estimated, make a man's fortune, and the practices of many Assignees, call aloud for correction. There is too often a conspiracy formed between the petitioning creditor, the Assignees, and the Bankrupt, to plunder the other just creditors of their property, which is easily effected by such a junction." Peter Stuart, who may or may not have been one of the "just creditors," had evidently expected to get the *Oracle* for himself, but had been outwitted by John Bell. But Bell certainly had nothing to do with the management of the newspaper for the next few months, and on 19 August advertisements for his other enterprises disappeared. Stuart and Boaden continued to edit the *Oracle* during these months, and, although its political character remained unchanged, there were innovations. Most of them were literary, but there was a new interest in public service, the *Oracle* of 31 August listing, for example, all the penalties currently "inflicted" for violation of the game laws with a view to ameliorating them. On 24 August, too, the *Oracle* introduced the headline.

Except for the *Oracle*, the Government was as seemingly indifferent to English newspapers as it was to English reformers. In the provinces the Leicester *Herald* was thriving, and on 20 July Benjamin Flower began the Cambridge *Intelligencer*. Both papers were hard fighters for peace and reform. In London the Government suffered daily embarrassments from the four Opposition papers, at least two of which were now subsidized by Lord Lauderdale. The *Anti-Jacobin* later (9 April, 1798) stated that "the nostrums of Doctors LA-D-RD-LE and Co." were being applied to several newspapers during this period, notably the *Morning Post*, the *Courier*, and the *Gazetteer*, and even *The Times* thought they were being applied to more than one. Lord Lauderdale had in fact leased the *Morning Post*, and, since by July the *Morning Post* was obviously allied with the *Courier*, anyone would have supposed that he or one of his wealthy friends, possibly the Duke of Bedford, was assisting that newspaper as well. He was probably not assisting the *Gazetteer*, for the *Gazetteer* was now copying most of its material from the *Morning Chronicle*. The most effective newspaper of the group was as usual the *Chronicle*, which was filled with brilliant and telling political commentary from correspondents. One of them, "The Calm Observer," whose theme was the partition of Poland, provided such devastating accounts of the conduct of Britain's allies that the *True Briton* could only protest (5 July): "The Opposition Prints still persist in endeavouring to confound the Partition of Poland with the War against France. Of the former transaction His MAJESTY's Ministers have uniformly expressed the utmost abhorrence; but are we therefore to forego the advantages arising from an Alliance with Prussia and Russia, to assist us in crushing the common disturbers of the Peace of Europe?" By 29 July the *Gazetteer* understood that "Mr. JENKINSON is now writing a pamphlet to prove that the seizure of *Poland* by the Empress [of Russia] will only tend to establish and preserve the *balance of power!*" The identity of "The Calm Observer," like the identity of other such correspondents, was in dispute from June on. Although the *Chronicle* insisted that it did not know who he was itself, the *True Briton* insisted that he was either Lord Uxbridge or Lord Pomfret. "The *Jacobin Chronicle* disavows all knowledge of the *Calm Observer*," the *True Briton* noted with exasperation on 19 July. "This is only a little touch of that *Jesuitism* with which those *calm observations* abound, and for which their Noble Author is so happily distinguished." On 4 September the earlier essays were reprinted as a pamphlet, entitled *Letters on the Subject of the Concert of Princes and the Dismemberment of Poland and France [First Published in the Morning Chronicle between July 20, 1792, and June 25, 1793]. With Corrections and Additions. By A Calm Observer.* By this time all the Ministerial papers agreed that the author was Vicesimus Knox, and Knox did not deny the fact. The author was actually, however, the politician and political economist, Benjamin Vaughan, one of the Cambridge radicals, although currently resident in London.

Since, in addition to its other sins, the *Morning Chronicle* was ruining the reputation of the *True Briton* by its incessant ridicule of Burges and Rose, there was every reason for the Government to act. But, when the people were outraged by so slight a thing as the prosecution of a bookseller, the Government could not afford to prosecute the *Morning Chronicle*, especially for so slight an offense as the publication of an advertisement and especially at a time when it was fighting particularly hard for the interests of Fox. Hence, although the *Chronicle* was under indictment and the principals had even been brought to court, the trial was postponed, supposedly owing to difficulties finding a jury. But the Government was not entirely remiss, for on 19 June the *True Briton* had revealed that the *Chronicle* was getting much of its information from "an *inferior Clerk* in one of the Public Offices, who is in habits of intimacy with Mr. Fox," and by 23 July the clerk had been silenced. "The *Jacobin* Journal is become astonishingly dull of late," gloated the *Oracle*. "It was once wont to boast its priority of intelligence and activity of effort—but its *Office-oil* is withheld; and it flashes but a hopeless and malignant gleam of gloomy desolation." On 14 August the *Morning Post* further reported: "Mr. DUNDAS, consistent with the dignity of his situation, has issued orders that the *Under Clerks* in the service of Government shall be instantly dismissed, if detected *in future* betraying the confidence reposed in them, by giving information to the Newspapers. This notice has operated like an electric shock, from the highest to the lowest public Officer, particularly in the Treasury."

The Government was still buying propaganda. "The Treasury folks are . . . great *musical amateurs*," said the *Morning Post* on 10 August, "for it is evident that they have all the *ballad singers in pay!*" And on 15 August the *Gazetteer* stated that every one of the Ministerial papers was also "in pay." But, since in most cases the pay was inadequate, the Government had counted on the *True Briton* to punish possible defectors. The *True Briton* was in no position to do so, its own prestige having been destroyed by the *Morning Chronicle*. In addition, the point at issue in its battle with the *Chronicle* was a subscription for Fox, and Fox had admirers even among Treasury writers. *The Times* had supported the subscription from the outset, to the exasperation of the *Oracle*, which remarked on 14 June: "What the *Jacobin* Print [the *Chronicle*] means by the most respectable Print on the side of *Government*, is merely that which from the *Principles* about it is likely to go over to the *common file*." The *Morning Herald* remained silent until mid-July, when it also supported the subscription. "There are now great compliments passing between two *enlightened* Prints, the one *soi-disant* in favour of His MAJESTY's Ministers, the other against them and all good measures," said the *True Briton* on 31 July. "Like the *Times*, they turn about like weathercocks, and verify the adage, '*Tempora mutantur et nos mutamur in illis!*'" The *True Briton*'s distress at this development greatly amused the *Gazetteer*, which taunted on 22 August: "The *half-pay* Editor of a Treasury Journal [John Heriot] seems to have been put on the *Irish* establishment, if we may judge from his *happy knack* at a *Bull*. The *veering* Herald, he observes, is now in *decided* opposition!" The *Herald* was not reclaimed. It printed anything until approximately November, when it settled on political neutrality as a matter of general policy. The *True Briton* was similarly uneasy about the *World*, although with no immediate justification, for throughout July the paper was a foe of both Fox and Lord Lauderdale. On 15 August it notified its correspondents that the "PUFF direct, *on a coming pamphlet, 'will carry conviction with it' to the Stamp Office, and must, therefore, be paid for if inserted*." This was the first indication that it was out of favor with the Government, but the *World* compensated for the moment by filling its pages with such puffs.

In Scotland the Government was less cautious. On 18 May Daniel Stuart had transmitted to various societies a resolution of thanks from the London Friends of the People for their recent assistance in the cause of Parliamentary reform, and, although he continued to carry on a personal correspondence with William Skirving, it was not determined whether the London Friends of the People would send delegates to the British convention or not. This convention, organized by the Associated Friends of the People in Scotland, of which Skirving was Secretary, was now scheduled to be held in Edinburgh, possibly on 13 August. But on 13 August the *Morning Chronicle* reported that "William Skirving . . . was apprehended [on 7 August], brought before the Sheriff, and examined, respecting some seditious publications lately circulated in [that] city. He was committed to prison, and [on 8 August] re-examined, and again committed to prison, till liberated in due course of law." A similar report appeared in the *World*. On 15 August the *Star* further reported that, having finally returned from France, Thomas Muir, Vice-President of the previous convention, had presented a petition to the High Court of Justiciary on 10 August, "praying their Lordships to recal the sentence of outlawry, as he was desirous to stand trial. The Court ordered the Petition to be served upon the Lord Advocate [Robert Dundas], and that his Lordship give an answer thereto by Tuesday next." On 21 August there were two reports, both dealing with events of 15 August. According to the *Star*, the Court had granted Muir's petition and scheduled his trial for 30 August. According to the *World*, Skirving had "applied, by Petition, to the Sheriff of Edinburgh, to be admitted to bail, which was granted, and he having found security to the extent of 3000 Scotch merks, was liberated from prison." On 22 August there was a report of another sort. "On Monday last [18 Aug.]," said the *Oracle*, "Mr. Ross, publisher of a Paper called *The Edinburgh Gazette*, who some time since made his escape from Scotland, being charged with seditious practices, was taken into custody at a house in Exeter-street, Strand, by Jealous and Carpmeal, officers belonging to Bowe-street; and on Wednesday [21 Aug.] he underwent an examination before the Secretaries of State; the result of which was, that he was ordered to be conducted back to Scotland. . . ." Ross's opinion of the situation there was obviously different from Muir's.

The First Prorogation: Rewards

On 3 July, according to the newspapers, Oxford University conferred "the degree of Doctor of Civil Laws on the Duke of Devonshire, the Earl of Dalkeith, the Marquess of Titchfield, the Earl of Kinnoull, Bute, Oxford and Mortimer, Fitzwilliam, Spencer, Mansfield, Inchiquin, and Darnley, Lord George Henry Cavendish, Viscounts Grimston, Feilding, and Valletort, Lords Naas, William Russell, and Malmesbury, Frederick Montagu, and William Windham." Not all of those honored were as yet supporting the Government; and, while they were accepting their degrees, the Duke of Devonshire was losing the Lord High Treasurership of Ireland and Governorship of County Cork; the Earl of Bute was losing the Lord Lieutenancy of County Glamorgan. On 5 July the University conferred more such degrees, the list this time including the names of Edmund Malone, Sir Gilbert Elliot, and Frederick North. Again, said the *Morning Post* on 11 July, the "University of Oxford . . . very wisely confined their Honorary Degrees to Ministerial Members of Parliament, and Gentlemen Commoners who were supposed *best able to pay for them.*" On 4 July the Duke of Portland's installation as Chancellor was formally celebrated. According to the *Oracle* (6 July), the introductory eulogy had been written by George Canning and was delivered by Mr. Dawkins. "Mr. BURKE and Mr. WYNDHAM," the *Oracle* went on, "were . . . honoured with the most flattering marks of that public approbation which is conferred on virtue, goodness, and talents, and which disdains to stoop to party considerations." According to the *Morning Post* (17 July), poetry for the various eulogies had been supplied by a number of writers: "Poetic praise of the Chancellor came from the speeches of the Gentlemen of Christ Church, which were written by the DEAN [Cyril Jackson], Mr. HALL, and Mr. CANNING; from that of Mr. TWISLETON, which was written by himself, and from that of Mr. CLARKE, which was written by his brother of Trinity. The Gentlemen of New College, and Mr. LUKIN, of Magdalen, composed their own verses. Mr. [George] RICHARDS, of Oriel, wrote for Mr. STIBBART, of Trinity, and has published under the title of 'Modern France.' Mr. CLARKE's Verses are also published. No other compositions are yet published, nor are any more authors of them known." As to "the Duke of PORTLAND's Latin Speech," said the *True Briton* on 6 July, "We may fairly presume, that Mr. BURKE had some hand in the composition. . . . Where, indeed, could his Grace have had more able assistance?"

Although the Ministerial papers felt that the affair had gone off splendidly, the Opposition papers felt that the point was debatable. On 17 July the *Morning Post* reported: "At the time of the Installation, a pick-pocket is said to have taken, in the Theatre, a purse of about fifty guineas from the person of the Earl of MANSFIELD:/ 'Iliacos intra muros peccatur et extra.'/ Out of the Theatre, the Vice-Chancellor lost, immediately after the Entertainment, at Wadham, all his wine glasses, 15 dozen, and all the crockery pye dishes." The Duke of Richmond had avoided the ceremony from pique, since it seemed to him that he had a better claim to the Chancellorship than the Duke of Portland, who was as yet not even a defector. The *Oracle* of 12 July tried to explain the situation: "We are told that the Duke of RICHMOND felt offence at a preference of the Duke of PORTLAND. The Party certainly for active service might have been stronger *fortified* by the selection of his Grace; but that it may be presumed did not form the *only* motive for their choice—they thought also of their *credit.*/ 'The very heart and front of their offending/ Had this extent no more.'" There were also some odd developments respecting Burke, whose name had appeared on neither list. On the morning of 6 July, the *Oracle* reported: "It was intended by the Heads of Houses to compliment [Burke] with an honorary degree; but the Masters of Arts, who had on a former occasion been opposed in their wishes to present him with a diploma, induced him to wave the proffered honour. This evening, however, a requisition is signing by a respectable number of Members of Convocation, for the purpose of taking the necessary steps to confer upon him a diploma degree, by which all parties will now be gratified." The degree was not conferred. According to the *Star* of that afternoon, "Mr. BURKE was again in the Theatre [on 5 July], but would not be prevailed upon to sit again among the Doctors, a seat to which he had been unknowingly conveyed the former day. Every thing that he does here endears him to the lovers of virtue, as every thing that he says does to the lovers of wit and taste./ His Degree is still postponed. The list of 150 names, which was signed last night, produced an answer from the Heads of Houses, that there was not time this week for the regular preliminaries to a Diploma Degree, but that every thing would be prepared early in the next Term." On 10 July the *Oracle* indicated that the degree would not be conferred at all. "It is far from being certain," it said, "that Mr. BURKE will obtain a diplomatic degree in the University of Oxford. 'Tis said he has not solicited it, and 'tis probable he does not wish it. The truth is, that when one surveys the numbers decorated with a degree, and considers that it was refused to the Abbe RAYNAL he can scarcely conceive it to be always a certain testimony of the eminence in Literature arrived at by the persons who bear it."

On 11 July the *Diary* published a full column of "LINES,/ ADDRESSED TO THE *Right Hon.* EDMUND BURKE," which began with the pronouncement, "Edmund, thy well wrote book is all divine," and concluded with the signature, "CAUSIDICUS." But the *World* was meanwhile assuring its readers that publication of the *Reflections* had been more than offset by the prosecution of Hastings and that, until Burke came to terms with Pitt on that score, he would get nothing. "The best Friends of Mr. BURKE say, 'that on the subject of Mr. HASTINGS, they pity and turn away from him.' This same feeling, Mr. BURKE seems to have; for no man more frequently—*turns away from himself*," it observed typically on 13 July. The Opposition papers, long persuaded that Burke wanted money more than honors, expected the Government to give him a pension. When no pension was announced, the *Morning Chronicle* slyly reminded him (3 Aug.) of the handsome subscription for Fox: "A few days ago Mr. WALKER, of Manchester, passed Mr. BURKE. Mr. WALKER observed, that Mr. BURKE's coat pocket was turned inside out. Mr. WALKER accordingly informed Mr. BURKE of the circumstance. Mr. BURKE politely thanked Mr. WALKER for the information, but added, that he had *turned* it himself, in order to make his pocket agree with the rest of his coat."

The Government was proving, said the *Morning Chronicle* on 1 July, that sagacious men supported the war:

INCONTESTIBLE PROOFS

That the war against France is political, moral, just, wise, and unavoidable.

Lord LOUGHBOROUGH thought the war was a wise war and a good war; and he was made Lord Chancellor of England, and is to be created an Earl.

The Earl of CARLISLE had also a firm persuasion of its rectitude and policy, and he changed his *green ribband* into a *blue* one.

Lord BEAUCHAMP had the happiness to agree with so many noble persons, and he became an Earl, made his father a Marquis, and elevated his eldest son and all his brothers to the rank of Lords.

Lord PORCHESTER was also brought to think that the war was just and necessary—and he was created an Earl.

Mr. ANSTRUTHER found also on the most scrupulous enquiry that the war was not only called for by circumstances, but indispensible to our welfare and true interests—and he was appointed a Welch Judge, and Standing Counsel to the new India Board.

After such incontestible evidence, what plague do the people of this country murmur at? But should scruples still remain, every forthcoming Gazette shall produce to their confounded senses, more proofs of the same kind.

The *Chronicle* was mistaken about Lord Loughborough, who did not get an earldom. The *Oracle*, which announced on 8 August that the "eminent services of Mr. BURKE, in resisting and exposing the seditious projects meditated, and in supporting so ably and successfully the Constitution of his Country, are, we understand, to be rewarded with a Peerage," was similarly mistaken. But on 5 July Francis Seymour-Conway, since 1750 Viscount Beauchamp and Earl of Hertford, was created Earl of Yarmouth and Marquess of Hertford. Previously styled Viscount Beauchamp, his son was henceforth styled Earl of Yarmouth, although he did not actually succeed to the titles until the following year. By the end of 1793, he had been sent to Berlin as ambassador. Lord Porchester was created Earl of Carnarvon on 3 July, and on 5 July the newspapers also reported the elevation of Lord Auckland. "Lord AUCKLAND has been called up to the British House of Peers, for uniting with Lord HAWKESBURY, and a few others of the Ministry, to precipitate this Country into a ruinous, an absurd, and an unpopular War," said the *Morning Post*. "If such circumstances make the stream of man's existence run more pure than that of an honest Plebeian, well may the grand-children of such Worthies boast hereafter of the *noble blood* of their *illustrious* ancestors!" The previous title had been Irish.

There were other kinds of rewards. The Chancellorship of Marischal College having previously been presented to the Earl of Mansfield, the Chancellorship of King's College, Aberdeen, was presented to the Duke of Gordon, who held it until his death. The Duke of Gordon was also commissioned a colonel in the Army; the Earl of Eglinton was commissioned a general. The Earl of Mornington, already Custos Rotulorum of County Meath (1781–1842) and Lord of the Treasury (1786–1797), was on 21 June appointed a member of the Privy Council and Commissioner for Indian Affairs. By mid-July the newspapers had discovered that George Rose's son was Secretary to the British Legation at the Court of Berlin. The Opposition papers were disgusted. "Since the appointment of *Master* GEORGE HENRY ROSE..., the Westminster Boys are all on tiptoe," the *Gazetteer* observed on 17 July. The elder Rose was prevented by journalistic responsibilities from going along, the *Morning Post* announced on 19 July, and, "[as] soon as GEORGE ROSE can find time to relinquish his paragraphical pursuits, and his comments on *this* and other prints, in his *gasping* Journal, he intends to feel the pulse of the Hampshire folks, with respect to another trial in Parliament of his *celebrated Estate Bill.*" Although on 20 July the *World* protested that *"Master* ROSE" had quit the University of Cambridge two years earlier and had since been "educating in the *Diplomatic School* of Lord AUCKLAND," the Opposition papers continued to regard him as a schoolboy. Salaries in many instances were sharply increased. "Mr. BURKE himself sets down the salary of the Bishop of DURHAM at 10,000*l.* and yet there are curates in that neighbourhood who do all the drudgery of crape for 20*l.* a year each," the *Star* noted on 30 July. Since supporters of the war could apparently have anything for the asking, newspapers were filled with requests of one sort or another, all privately paid for and all directed to Pitt. Some of the applicants dealt with the matter directly. On 5 July, for example, the *World* stated that the Marquess of Salisbury ought to be Lord Lieutenant of Ireland, since he had spent "more private fortune to support the present Government than any nobleman in England." Other applicants inserted rumors of their appointments. This method was evidently preferred, for such rumors were rampant. Still other applicants contented themselves with puffs, either because Pitt already knew what they wanted or because they were willing to trust his judgment. One of these was John Wilkes, who, to the exasperation of the Opposition press, advertised his enthusiasm for the war from July on. What Wilkes evidently had in mind was one of the places relinquished by Brass Crosby. Crosby had died in February.

Deaths, like marriages, were likely to be reported only if the newspaper was personally interested or if the event was politically significant, and even then the report was not necessarily reliable. On 5 August, for example, the *Diary* reported the death of Dr. Charles Burney, the musicologist, who himself contradicted the report in the *Diary* of 7 August, and on 11 November the *Oracle* denied persistent reports of the death of Charles Fox. "THIS great Orator and Politician has been mentioned these few days back, as having joined in the Shades the companions given him here in *busto*—DEMOSTHENES and CICERO," it said. "In plain English he was said to have died on Friday [8 Nov.], at St. Anne's-Hill, or if not dead, near it./ However, as his friend SHERIDAN has it, if he [did die], 'he is the most imprudent man alive,' for he was in company with some living friends on Saturday. The rumour [probably] grew out of... the wish some enterprising geniuses might have of trying the influence of such an event upon the *political system* in the ALLEY." The denial was repeated on 12 November. Other notices seemed to be misplaced. The *Gazetteer* of 9 April reported, for example, the death on 5 April, "at James Mackintosh's Esq; Kensington-square, [of] Miss Ann Harper, daughter of the Late Col. Harper, many years in the service of the East-India company." One would have expected to find this notice in the *Oracle* or the *Morning Post*, if only because those papers were edited by Mackintosh's in-laws. But the *World*'s announcement (10 Dec.) of the death on 8 December of the elder Francis Const, "in Villars Street, Strand, aged 72," was hardly surprising, the younger Const having been long associated with the *World*, and neither was the *Morning Chronicle*'s announcement (10 Oct.) of the "sudden death" on 6 October of the Rev. William W. Hodson, "B. D., Vicemaster and one of the Senior Fellows of Trinity Hall, University of Cambridge, and Vicar of Hitchen, Herts." The *Chronicle* had been ridiculing Hodson since July, 1792.

The deaths of the botanist, William W. Hudson on 23 May, of the Earl of Buckinghamshire on 3 September, and of the Duke of Somerset on 15 December were passed over in silence. Hudson had no places, the Earl of Buckinghamshire, although once (1776–1780) Lord Lieutenant of Ireland, left behind him only the Deputy Lieutenancy for the County of Norfolk, and the Duke of Somerset left nothing except a Whiggish heir, who was still a student at Cambridge University. The death of the Earl of Exeter on 26 December was noticed only by the *World*, which observed on 30 December: "Another of Mr. HASTINGS's Judges has paid the debt of nature in the person of the Earl of EXETER—scarce a week passes but either by death or creation some changes transpire materially to affect the Impeachment. It will be the fortune of this Gentleman to be *tried* by one set of men, and to be *judged* by another. The different changes that have taken place in the High Court of Parliament since the Impeachment began, amount now to near 140 Members." In 1767 the Earl of Exeter had got a Fellowship in the Royal Society and a Fellowship in the Society of Antiquaries; he had got nothing since. But the death of Brass Crosby on 14 February was quite another matter. Not only was this one reported at length by all newspapers, but on 15 February the *Diary* scooped the rest by publishing a list of Crosby's positions: "Mr. Alderman Crosby," it announced, "was President of the Royal Hospitals of Bridewell and Bethlehem, Governor of the Irish Society, Vice President of the London Workhouse, and Chairman of the four principal City Committees, viz. 1. the City and Bridgehouse Estates; 2. the Thames Navigation; 3. the Control of Coal and Corn-meters; 4. the General Purposes." Some of the posts were evidently still vacant in July.

Although newspapermen did not become chancellors of universities, presidents of hospitals, or even deputy lieutenants of counties, they did sometimes become commissioners of bankrupts or commissioners of the Stamp Office. For this reason perhaps, all newspapers were alert to vacancies in those fields. The first such vacancy occurred on 11 July with the death of George Harris, "supervisor of the Stampers at the Stamp office," and was reported by all newspapers on 16 July. The second occurred in September with the death of "Mr. Stephen Stephens of the Stamp Office" and was announced by newspapers on 17

September. The third occurred on 2 November with the death of Richard Hargrave, "aged 82 years, one of the Commissioners of Bankrupts," and was announced by newspapers on 7 November. The fourth occurred on 4 November with the death of Richard Tickell and was announced the following day. The announcement was made by the *Oracle* in the form of a eulogy. The eulogy, which occupied two-thirds of a column, identified Tickell as "a Commissioner of the Stamp Office," a brother-in-law of Sheridan, and the author of *Casette Verte*, of *Anticipation*, and of an opera, entitled *The Carnival of Venice*. A similar eulogy appeared in the *World* of 6 November, this one identifying Tickell as "one of the Commissioners of the Stamp Office, which place is valued in the Red Book at 500*l*. per annum," as well as a man of many "colloquial and literary talents." He was thrice married, said the *World*, his second wife being Mary Linley, Sheridan's sister, by whom he had some children: these Sheridan, "with his usual benevolence, has taken under his protection." His third wife, "the beautiful Miss LEE, daughter to Counsellor LEE of Bedford-square," was still living. To the list of Tickell's writings, the *World* could add only "some lively Epilogues." The *Oracle* was meanwhile denying that Tickell was a suicide. "On Monday died at Hampton Court Palace, in consequence of a fall from the parapet of his apartments, Richard TICKELL, Esq.," it announced on 6 November. "The unhappy accident which occasioned his death at first gave rise to a report, which, we are authorized to assert, is wholly unfounded." On 7 November the *Oracle* again denied that Tickell had committed suicide, it denied that he was in financial straits, and it informed the *World* that he had been married only twice, his first wife being "Miss Sheridan," by whom he had three children. By 8 November it had learned with relief that a coroner's jury had on 5 November returned a verdict of accidental death, and on 14 November the *World* finally admitted that Tickell had had only two wives. The relationship between Sheridan and Tickell (the first wives of the two had been sisters) was never clarified. Tickell's case was extraordinary. The *Oracle* was concerned because of the connection with Sheridan and especially because of the manner of the death, which, it was obviously afraid, would be publicized by other papers to Sheridan's disadvantage. In the main, newspapers were interested in patronage, and the decedent's importance was therefore measured by his holdings. William Pitt seems to have had a similar view.

The war had been contrived to defeat the moderate reformers, especially the Friends of the People, and so to keep the present Government in office, and, although it was very unpopular throughout the country, it was strongly supported by Parliament. There had been numerous defections on account of it, and, since the Government could even rely on the votes of the Portland faction, the Opposition, now scathingly referred to (*Diary*, 16 July) as "Modern Patriots," was almost nonexistent. The unpopularity of the war did not trouble Pitt during the summer of 1793, for the obvious reason that he expected the war to be over shortly, the worst of it by the time Parliament convened on 13 August. What did trouble him was the possibility that, once France had been defeated, all the alarmists would defect back to their original positions, yield to *vox populi*, and, either by means of an election reforms bill or an immediate vote of no confidence, throw him and his friends out of office. The wholesale trials of booksellers and talkers and the lavish distribution of gifts were intended to guard against this development, and the Government was fortifying itself in other respects. On 1 July the *World* reported that Dundas had been "re-elected Member of Parliament for the city of Edinburgh, having relinquished his seat by accepting the office of President of the Board of Controul for East India Affairs." Now that George Rose's activities had been restricted to journalism, Dundas was the Achilles heel of the Administration, and the profusion of his rewards made the situation worse. The *Diary*, the *Oracle*, and even Rose's papers, the *Sun* and the *True Briton*, rose to his defense against bitter attacks from the Opposition press. On 20 July the *Gazetteer* replied to one such defense:

Mr. DUNDAS's POPULARITY:

A Morning Paper of yesterday has made a notable discovery of Mr. DUNDAS's popularity as a Minister, from his having received the thanks of the *Convention* of the Royal Burghs of Scotland for his publick services.

This Convention, as it is called, happens to be the *Junto*, who have, in conjunction with Mr. DUNDAS, Mr. [John] ANSTRUTHER, and other *patriotic* characters, hitherto opposed Mr. SHERIDAN's plan for a reform in the government of the Royal Burghs!

Of course, so favourable an occasion could not be lost, of reviling Mr. SHERIDAN, for having presumed to doubt the *Popularity* of Mr. DUNDAS in Scotland, at a time when he was burned in effigy in almost every town, of which the above celebrated Convention of Delegates are the *enlightened* Representations.

Dundas's places were still a scandal, and the announcement that he had refused one of them after all hardly helped. As the *Gazetteer* put it on 4 July: "Mr. DUNDAS's new appointment of *Custos Rotulorum* for the county of Middlesex, the ministerial papers say, is very compatible with the office of Secretary of State for the Home Department. It seems he and several other gentlemen have declined accepting the Lord Lieutenancy, as it is attended with considerable expence, and but little patronage! In general these offices have hitherto been united, as the patronage of the one has been thought a sufficient recompence for the expence of the other." The news that Dundas would get a peerage was greeted with jeers, and he remained a commoner, although he did add to his other titles "Elder Brother of Trinity House," as so did Lord Grenville. The problem had been solved as well as it could be, for Pitt needed Dundas to deal with the alarmists, and yet there was a limit to what he could do for him.

Another disappointed applicant was Lord Lonsdale, who had been denied, said the newspapers, a second title because he had done nothing to support the war. Lord Lonsdale retaliated, according to the *Morning Chronicle* of 2 July, by refusing to "bring in Mr. [John] ANSTRUTHER again for Cockermouth; in consequence of which, Mr. ANSTRUTHER's younger brother will yield to him the Scots Boroughs." Robert Anstruther had just been elected Member of Parliament for the Anstruther Easter Burghs. The Government struck back in turn. Many years earlier Lonsdale had contracted to purchase an estate from Lord Wemyss for £7,880. In 1786 he had changed his mind, but had been compelled by Lord Wemyss to complete the agreement. On 27 July, 1793, the case was again tried in the Court of Chancery, and this time Lord Loughborough ordered Lonsdale to pay the money in full, plus an interest of 4 per cent "from the time it should have been paid and do so by Michaelmas term next." "The verdict had against Lord LONSDALE . . . will prevent that Nobleman from finishing the long promised first-rate man of war, which he was to have given to his Country," observed the *Morning Post* on 3 August. "His Lordship must feel extremely unhappy that he is thus prevented from fulfilling his wishes." The *World* (16 Aug.) wanted the ship under any circumstances: "Lord LONSDALE.—This Nobleman, whose professions of zeal for his King and Country, induced most people to suppose him anxious for the prosperity of both, offered Government, more than *ten years* ago, with a generosity worthy a man of his immense fortune, to build, *at his own expence*, a 74 gun ship. The offer was accepted, and his public spirit was by every body applauded. Upon strict enquiry we do not find that this ship has been built. This *is not* worthy of imitation by other Peers." The Government did not get its ship, but John Anstruther was finally returned as Member for Cockermouth. The reason was perhaps suggested by the *Star*, which mentioned on 14 November that Lord Lonsdale had "so many suits in Chancery, that with all the expedition the forms of the Court will admit, they cannot possibly be decided in the course of the present century!" With all this litigation in progress, Lord Lonsdale could not afford to be at odds with the Government.

The Government further strengthened its Parliamentary hand by bringing in George Canning. The first announcement appeared in the *Gazetteer* of 3 July: "On Friday last [29 June] GEORGE CANNING, Esq. of the Inner Temple, was elected a Member for the Borough of Newton, in the Isle of Wight, in the room of the Right Hon. Sir RICHARD WORSLEY, Bart. who vacated his seat by accepting the Office of Steward of the Chiltern Hundreds." Despite Canning's supposed intimacy with Sheridan, the news seems to have taken the *Oracle* by surprise, and it was still uncertain what to make of it on 6 July:

> Young CANNING, of the Inner Temple, who has been within these few days returned for Newtown, Isle of Wight, will, it is believed, fight under the Opposition Banners.
>
> It is however, certain, that the particular party which may happen to influence his talents will find in him that degree of courage and capacity so essentially requisite to form the Public Speaker.

The best proof of Mr. CANNING's abilities are the praises of SHERIDAN, with whom he is in habits of intimacy.

Sir RICHARD WORSLEY's resignation in favour of Mr. CANNING is variously talked of. If it be true, as some time ago reported, that the Hon. Baronet is about succeeding Sir ROBERT AINSLIE at *Constantinople*, we may presume that his Parliamentary successor will join the Ministry.

Since his assistance in the Oxford installation was evidence enough that Canning would not "fight under the Opposition Banners," the *Oracle* could have been concerned only with saving Sheridan's face and incidentally reminding Canning not to forget an old friend. But the *World*, which enjoyed nothing more than a joke on Sheridan, was still implying on 11 July that Canning was his protégé: "*Young* CANNING, who has been under the tuition of SHERIDAN for some time past, is now elected to serve in Parliament," it announced, with the addendum on 25 July: "Mr. CANNING . . . is mentioned as of first rate literary and political talents." Canning's election was again announced by the *Oracle* of 15 October. Although no date was given, readers would have supposed that it had just occurred.

There was also an election in Scotland. On 31 July the *Morning Post* reported that "[on] Monday [29 July] the Dukes of QUEENSBURY and ROXBURGH, and the Earls of ENGLINTON and BREADALBANE, took the oaths of Allegiance, Supremacy, and Abjuration, before the Lord Chancellor, in Lincoln's Inn Hall, to qualify them to vote upon the approaching Election of a Peer, to complete the number of the Sixteen Peers for Scotland. We presume their Lordships propose sending their proxies upon the occasion." The purpose of the election was to decide upon a successor for Lord Stormont, now the second Earl of Mansfield, and the nominees were Lord Somerville and the Marquess of Tweeddale, the latter being Lord Lauderdale's brother-in-law. The election was held in Edinburgh on 8 August. Although Lord Somerville was elected "by a large majority," Lord Lauderdale delayed the proceedings, said *Lloyd's Evening Post* (14 Aug.), by urging "the meeting" not to accept the votes of British peers created since the Union, despite the recent ruling of the Lords. The *Star* later (20 Sept., 1796) stated that Lord Stormont "had been one of the Representatives of the Scots Peers in the higher House of Parliament ever since 1754, and . . . , what is singular, in the last Parliament he sat in a double capacity, and was entitled to two votes, as Viscount STORMONT representing the Scots Peers, and as a British Earl by the title of Earl MANSFIELD, and every time the roll was called he must have been named by both titles." The truth is that Lord Stormont was actually replaced by Lord Somerville, but, when Lord Elphinstone died, on 19 August, 1794, Lord Stormont in turn quietly replaced him and continued as his replacement until his own death. He was also voting as the Earl of Mansfield.

The First Prorogation:
State of the War

On 12 July the British Government signed a treaty with The Two Sicilies; on 14 July it signed a treaty with Prussia. The newspapers were informed of neither. On 10 July Condé fell to the Allies; on the same date, the Great Committee of Public Safety, which, together with the Committee of General Security, was to rule France until July, 1794, was formally established. As President of the previous committee, Danton had organized France's defense and dictated her foreign policy, but his power was now at an end. On 13 July Marat was stabbed in his bath by Charlotte Corday; on 23 July the French lost Mainz; and on 26 July they also lost Valenciennes, which was finally captured by the English after a siege which had begun on 23 May. By August the French were cashiering officers of noble birth. All of these events were appropriately reported. The fall of Condé was announced on 15 July. The Prince of Saxe-Coburg had occupied the city, it was then understood, on 13 July and would go on to take Maubeuge, Quesnoy, Cambrai, and Lille. The surrender of Mainz to the Prussians was announced by the *Oracle* on 29 July as having occurred on 22 July, and readers would have known something about the battle, since on 6 July the *Sun* and the *True Briton* had published a small map of Mainz and its environs, indicating the position of the various armies. A similar map of Valenciennes had been published earlier. The surrender of Valenciennes was announced by the *True Briton* on 31 July as having occurred on 27 July; it was announced by the *Oracle* on 1 August as having occurred on 28 July.

Readers would nevertheless have had a difficult time separating fact from fiction. Some of the fiction was unavoidable, for official bulletins during the 1793–1794 campaign were prepared by Sir James Murray, Adjutant General to the Duke of York, and these no one could understand. Having heard (2 Oct.) that Boswell was "translating" some of Murray's communiqués "into verse," the *Morning Post* could only observe fervently that, "[if] he translates them into any thing that can explain them to the Public, we shall be the first to applaud his ingenuity." But there was also an abundance of guessing, as well as an abundance of wilful misrepresentation for the usual reason of influencing the market. All victories were anticipated a dozen times, and many stories were simply manufactured in newspaper offices. "POLITICAL LIES," proclaimed the *World* on 20 July. "—Two only were yesterday propagated; that in the morning by a newspaper, which announced the Massacre of the Queen of France; and that in the afternoon in the City, by the Stock Jobbers, who reported with their usual industry, the defeat of the Allied Armies, and the destruction of the works erected before *Valenciennes*." The "newspaper" was the *Oracle*, which had stated specifically (19 July): "We have reason to believe, from private Correspondence communicated to us that the QUEEN of FRANCE has been massacred in *Paris*." The *Oracle* again published the story on 12 August, having by this time supposedly confirmed it. On 13 August the *Oracle* further announced that Danton had overthrown the French government and installed himself as dictator.

There were dissatisfactions. The lethargy of the Dutch was derided by most newspapers, and, except for the *Sun* and the *True Briton*, the newspapers had little confidence in Britain's other allies. Although on 23 July Russia concluded a treaty with Poland, the *Oracle* predicted on 24 July that Prussia and Austria would protest any settlement and that Poland was more important to either of them than France. Lord Howe, who had been looking for the French fleet since May, was beginning to appear ridiculous, and the *Oracle* was annoyed (8 Aug.) because the Duke of York's command was limited to the forces in the United Provinces. There was also some early concern about the popularity of the war, and on 3 July the *Oracle* suggested, with pointed reference to the *Morning Chronicle*:

> It might be as well, if a Party vehicle were guarded in its hints at *rising dissatisfaction* in the People of England at any measure of Government, and particularly at one so universally canvassed as the War against *France*. This has by no means been a War entered into upon the *will* of Prerogative, and supported upon its *power*—With the utmost candour Mr. PITT came to the House of Commons, and stated the reasons which led His MAJESTY to declare that with *France* this Country was at War—To those reasons a string of Jacobinical objections were made by two men [Fox and Sheridan], and supported only by *forty-three* of all the COMMONS of Great Britain.

But on 13 July the *Oracle* itself stated: "The progress of the War, it must be confessed, is not very rapid, and the proportion of success or miscarriage cannot be ascertained by either side.—So dreadful is the task of invasion upon territories which have many Fortresses,. and those defended with obstinate fidelity, and desperate valour." News of the victories dispelled the gloom, however, and by mid-July the Ministerial papers were again predicting that the end was in sight. "The expence of the present War to us is but very trifling, compared with former Wars," the *Oracle* observed on 8 August. "In the last we combated almost all Europe, and now we have all Europe with us carrying on hostilities at a joint expence. This circumstance brings it also to nearly a certainty, that the War will be of short duration." All that really remained, the *Oracle* added on 10 August, was the capture of Lille and Dunkirk, and this would be quick work.

The war had always been popular with the upper classes, and the Government was obviously determined to keep it so. For, as soon as Parliament was prorogued, the Ministerial papers announced that the Duke of Richmond was planning a camp at Waterdown, similar to the camp at Bagshot, which had proved so successful the previous year. Although the camp was accordingly organized, it turned out to be a fiasco. The Duke of Richmond, already regarded by the Opposition papers as a coward and an alarmist, demonstrated that he was a bungler and a meddler as well. On 18 July the papers reported that he had neglected to provide water for his soldiers; on 19 July the *Gazetteer* reported that he was personally supervising the kitchens and actually helping with the cooking. Presiding over individual pots were now, it appeared, the captains. "The DUKE of RICHMOND, the most attentive of all commanders, directs the Captains to mount guard over the kettles in which the men boil their victuals," the *Morning Chronicle* remarked on 19 July. "We do not hear that he gives them any thing to put into the kettles." Even the *World* was disgusted. The Duke of Richmond has ordered "*that a* CAPTAIN *shall attend the culinary Preparations for the Men,*" it announced with exasperation on 20 July. The camp had previously been much publicized by the Ministerial papers, but at this point they lost interest. The Opposition papers did not. Every day there were new reports, each of which put the Duke of Richmond in a worse light. The *Morning Chronicle* of 24 July announced, for example:

WATERDOWN CAMP.

The second important event, in this most famous of all military schools (the general order for Captains to mount guard on the *soup kettles* was a mere matter of *domestic* regulation) places the defects of the law, with respect to military discipline, in a stronger point of view than the first—a man who had engaged as suttler for one of the regiments, had the audacity to speak his sentiments of the Duke of RICHMOND in the presence of one of his Grace's servants. An Aid-de-camp was sent next day to acquaint the Colonel of the Regiment, and the offender was dismissed. As he had not entered upon his office before the offensive words were spoken, he was not deemed amenable to Martial Law—which shews clearly that all the followers of and spungers upon a camp, with all the venders of gin and gingerbread, ought to be included in the Mutiny Bill.

The *Morning Post* was simply sarcastic. "Should the siege of Valenciennes continue a fortnight longer, the Duke of RICHMOND will positively embark for Ostend," it notified its readers on 31 July. "Indeed, if the French were informed that his Grace had been embarked, it would instantly terrify them into a surrender of that Fortress!!" And on 5 August: "The Treasury Prints state, that the Duke of RICHMOND deserves well of his Country; for when the City was in danger from the machinations of English JACOBINS, he *slept* in the Tower!" By this time the camp was being moved to Brighton, where it would at least be ornamented by the presence of the Prince of Wales. The *World* celebrated the move (12 Aug.) with a two-column description of the Duke of Richmond's seat at Goodwood, punctuated with high praise of the Duke's patriotism, but omitting mention of his abilities. On the following day, "the whole body of troops" arrived, having marched sixteen miles and, according to the *World* (15 Aug.), having been accompanied every step of the way by the Duke himself.

But nothing, it appeared, could dampen the enthusiasm of the upper classes. Although Boswell was prevented from visiting the army by "the *villainous accident*" of 5 June,[58] everyone else made the pilgrimage as a matter of course and was personally conducted around the battlefields by the Duke of York. When the Opposition papers suggested that the Duke might prefer to be left alone, at least until he could capture Valenciennes, they were informed by the *Morning Herald* that the Duke welcomed the interruptions. "It is not true," the *Herald* stated positively on 17 July, "that the Duke of YORK, as has been said in some papers, disapproves the visits of English Gentlemen to his army. His Royal Highness is never more happy than in receiving his countrymen, and in shewing them every attention, which is consistent with his military duties." At home, the ladies, decked out in the "*Cap en Militaire*" or "*Valenciennes* Helmet," were still preparing for the care of the bereaved. In August the numerous charities instituted for this purpose were combined as The United Society for the Relief of Widows and Children of Seamen, Soldiers, Marines, and Militiamen Fallen in Action; and on 16 August the *Oracle* reported that, of the £17,500 thus far collected, £5,500 could be credited to the "Ladies' List."

The gallantry of the Duke of York was hardly more conspicuous than that of his brothers, Prince Ernest and Prince Adolphus. Prince Ernest was attached to the Hanoverian army as Lieutenant General; Prince Adolphus was a volunteer with the British forces. On 27 July the *World* further reported that Prince Edward, "with that spirit which has distinguished every branch of his August Family, has petitioned the War Office, and has obtained leave to remove from Canada to Jamaica." The Prince of Wales was a particular joy. As the *World* put it on 5 July:

HEIR APPARENT.

It must afford the utmost satisfaction to every sincere lover of his country, to learn that there is the *greatest* harmony and *union* of *sentiment* between our *patriotic* SOVEREIGN and the HEIR APPARENT.

The latter now, like HENRY V. has thrown off his former associates, being convinced that the greater part of them had the ambition only of being *Vice*-Roys over *him*.

His retirement proceeds more, perhaps, from *policy* then *penury*. As they embraced him with the cordiality of hollow friendship, he leaves them with the politeness of a well-bred Gentleman who has sat up all night with a set of sharpers, conscious that he has just been plundered!

Throughout early July the Prince was in frequent conference with Pitt, Dundas, his uncle, the Duke of Gloucester, and the King and Queen; and he was in attendance at all royal functions, usually arm-in-arm with the Duke of Gloucester. Although he did not move to Windsor, as the newspapers had expected, nor did he sever relations with Mrs. Fitzherbert, his sense of military responsibility left nothing to be desired. As soon as the conferences were concluded, he set out for Ashford, where on 18 July he reviewed his regiment and gave a dinner for the officers. On 29 July he set off to review the troops at Waterdown and would proceed from there, said *Lloyd's Evening Post* (31 July), to Brighton. Since his regiment would form part of the Duke of Richmond's Brighton camp, the expectation was that he would remain in Brighton for the next several weeks.

Preparations for the move were in fact already in progress. On 25 July Mrs. Fitzherbert closed her London house, and on 27 July the *Gazetteer* mentioned that she "and Miss B. PIGGOT are arrived at Brighton. Mrs. F— occupies this season the house adjoining to the Pavillion, belonging to Mr. WELTJIE." The *World* of 3 August reported a further development:

PRINCE OF WALES's CAMP BED.

A most superb Bed has just been finished for the PRINCE of WALES, and is to be fixed in his Royal Highness's Tent, previous to their MAJESTIES' visit to the Camp. The form of the Bed is square; the hangings of a very delicate chintz; a white ground, with a lilac and green cloud. The fringes, tassels, and other ornaments, are very rich and beautiful. The four corners are ornamented with the PRINCE's Feathers and Motto.

The rest of the furniture for the Tent is in corresponding elegance, and will, on the breaking up of the Camp, be removed to the Marine Pavillion, at Brighton.

Mrs. FITZHERBERT has a Tent, for her occasional visits to the Camp, furnished with splendour, very little inferior to the former.

According to *Lloyd's Evening Post* (5 Aug.), the Prince's regiment would "be encamped in a beautiful spot by the sea-side," and the Prince would "dine at the mess every day, and be in actual services, in all respects." The "State-Room" of his tent would be as elaborately furnished as the bedroom, the chairs alone to cost £1,000.

On 7 August *Lloyd's Evening Post* announced that, on the evening of 5 August, the Prince had met his regiment at the outskirts of Brighton and personally conducted the men to their new quarters. His own tent had already been pitched. The *World* of 9 August reported that all was going well: "The little Camp which is formed here is to become the fashionable lounge in the evening; the PRINCE's Tent is erected in the center; it is large, and fitted up in the most elegant stile./ The PRINCE has a very fine Charger here, which was sent to his Royal Highness by the Duke of YORK, from the Continent: it is remarkable for having had seven men shot on his back." "[Yesterday was] expected to be a joyful and busy day," the *World* added on 13 August, "—for besides its being the PRINCE of WALES's Birth-Day, one division of the troops that are to form the camp, [were] to come in./ The Ladies all sport a Bonnet *a la Militaire*, which has been invented by the fashionable milliner, Mrs. FITCH." Although the hope was that the fashionable elegance of the Prince's "little Camp" would outweigh the silliness of the Duke of Richmond's great one, the Government seemed to feel that the elegance was being overdone, for on 15 August the *Public Advertiser* declared: "When the Prince of Wales first beheld his magnificent Camp Bed, his Royal Highness, so far from feeling any satisfaction at the splendour of it, ordered all the costly and elegant parts of its furniture to be taken away, as positively contrary to his orders. Every unnecessarily expensive ornament was therefore taken down, and returned upon the hands of the furnisher. This is an absolute fact."

Prince Augustus and the Duke of Clarence were not participants. Although both of them opposed the war, Prince Augustus had not done so publicly, and his inactivity was excused in any event on the ground of ill health. The problem was the Duke of Clarence. Still smarting from the lashing it had suffered at his hands on 17 June, the Government devoted the early part of the summer to his conversion. The numerous conferences between the Prince of Wales and Dundas during June and early July were thought by the Opposition papers to have concerned the Duke, and it was generally understood that he was being subjected to constant lectures from his older brothers, his parents, and his uncle, the Duke of Gloucester. Nothing availed. Not only did he refuse to hoist his flag on the *London*, but on 5 July the *Morning Herald* reported that he had "hitherto made no further preparations for a voyage, than the ordering of his villa, at Petersham, to be sold. His *baggage* is not yet brought *within compass!*" At this point the Government turned the matter back to the newspapers, which, in the evident hope that the Duke loved his mistress more than he did his principles, resumed their abuse of Mrs. Jordan. Much of the abuse was general ridicule. "BON MOT OF THE DUKE OF C.—This very hot weather made his Highness remark that nothing could be *kept* long in it—'You can keep *Pickle* in all weathers,' replied the arch character to whom the observation was directed," reported the *World* typically on 18 July. Some of it was not. The *Morning Herald* of 11 July suggested, for example, that Mrs. Jordan's greed was ruining the Duke financially: "As the YOUNG GENTLEMAN who has incurred a debt of 80,000*l.* was lately known, by his payments, to live within his income, and has not since been distinguished for any extraordinary expenditure, there is some difficulty in accounting for the *dilapidation* of his finances. The only solution is by supposing, that his *fair* friend did not leave her *old course*, without ensuring a *profitable* voyage!" The Government was inordinately uneasy about the Duke of Clarence, but whether it was afraid that he would influence some of the recent defectors, whether it was afraid that he would incite popular demonstrations, or whether it was simply afraid that his speech of 17 June would be used to advantage by the Opposition papers was not clear. It was clear, however, that the speech would provide ammunition for the cannons of the *Morning Post*.

Probably because they never believed that victory would be swift, the Opposition papers completely misunderstood William Pitt. It seemed to them that, since the war was so evidently unpopular with the people, Pitt would like to get out of it and would get out of it if he could do so without losing face and office. It also seemed to them that the most obvious scapegoat was Edmund Burke, who had headed the war party and whose relationship with the Government had been uneasy anyway, owing to the prosecution of Hastings. By early July the Opposition papers were accordingly stating that Burke was solely responsible for the war, that Pitt had always secretly opposed it, and that Burke had been motivated, not by historical insight or by concern for the Constitution, but by an utter detestation of the "swinish multitude." On 4 July the "swinish multitude" spoke back through the medium of the *Morning Chronicle*:

> THE SWINISH HERD TO EDMUND BURKE.
> Be pleased, great Sir, to find us work.
> We make no insolent pretentions
> To feast on sinecures and pensions;
> We know our food must be the getting
> Of our own labour, pains and sweating;
> 'Twas so, they say, in ages past,
> And must be so while time shall last.
> But, Sir, tho' this is fit and meet,
> We cannot quite forget to eat,
> Nor miss our usual grains and water,
> Without just asking, What's the matter?
> You told us, and we hoped it true,
> With folks above we'd nought to do.
> We've nought to do, 'tis mighty plain,
> With any thing our betters gain;
> But when they meet with checks and crosses,
> We find a partnership of losses,
> And must be scotched in work and wages,
> Because crusading all the rage is.
> Now this we think not quite the thing,
> So please to hint it to the—.

The lines were reprinted by the *Morning Post* on 5 July, at which time the *Post* and the *Courier* announced that they were soliciting gifts for "the Spital-Field Weavers," who, in their opinion, needed help a great deal more than the soldiers. It was also understood that a petition for peace was being readied in Glasgow. On 12 July the *Morning Post* protested: "Mr. BURKE is not a Jew, he was bred at St. Omers; the idea which some people encourage of his being a Hebrew, proceeds, we presume, from his detestation of the *Swinish Multitude!*" Such items were now appearing in all Opposition papers and also in the *World*, which, as representative of Hastings, was more interested in ruining Burke than it was in continuing the war.

The *Star*, the *Diary*, and the *Oracle* had risen to Burke's defense by praising his patriotism and demonstrating, by quotations, mainly from the *Reflections*, that some of his predictions had been sound. The *Oracle* of 19 July noted, for example: "THE PROPHECIES OF MR. BURKE./ 'Nothing that I can say will hasten them by a single hour in the execution of a design which they have long since entertained. They will assassinate the KING, when his name will be no longer necessary to their designs; but not a moment sooner. Tyrants seldom want pretexts. Fraud is the ready Minister of Injustice.'/ All Europe has wept at the melancholy accomplishment of this vision." But such demonstrations only supported the thesis that Burke had been responsible for the war, leaving the question of Pitt's present attitude unanswered. The *Sun*, the *True Briton*, the *Public Advertiser*, and *The Times* had nothing to say on the subject, and, although the *Star*, the *Diary*, and the *Oracle* sometimes suggested that Pitt still regarded the war as "just and necessary," they were at a loss to explain why Burke was being passed by in the distribution of rewards. The war was certainly unpopular with the people, and, if the Opposition papers wanted to make Burke the whipping boy, the Government apparently had no objection.

Everything looked brighter in late July than it had for some time. The Allies had won three victories, and the economy seemed to be righting itself: at least, the number of bankruptcies was declining. But opposition to the war seemed to be growing. Notices of desertions from the Army and the Navy flooded the newspapers, and the Glasgow petition for peace was collecting signatures apace. On 18 July the *Morning Post* estimated that there were twenty thousand; on 31 July it estimated that there were sixty nine thousand. On 8 August the *Post* further reported that a petition was being prepared in Manchester and that similar petitions were expected from every manufacturing town in the country. Backing this information was unremitting abuse of Burke. "Mr. BURKE is the constant frequenter of Windsor Terrace; on Sunday he had a salute from His MAJESTY, which he seemed to feel exalted him considerably above the *Swinish multitude*," the *Post* mentioned on 30 July. And on 3 August: "Mr. BURKE, in the next edition of his pamphlet, intends to rob the Queen of France of his *amorous panegyric*, and apply it to Madame de CORDÉ. If not her pen, she certainly has brandished her *dagger* to more effect than the *desultory orator*." "Mr. BURKE is already studying praises to be delivered in Parliament on the valiant Mad. Cordé. To those he will oppose the *delicate* similes engendered in his brain, in consequence of the state of the corpse of that famous Knight of the *Dagger*, MARAT," it added on 15 August. On 9 August Burke was censured for his treatment of Priestley: "Mr. BURKE has made several assertions against Dr. PRIESTLEY, which the latter says, 'he has not the power to prove, nor the honour or decency to retract.' In this situation, it is cruel to place any individual, and there is no situation in life that ought to exempt a man from being obliged to explain his motives, or retract his words, who will wantonly traduce or asperse the character of another without any grounds of authority whatever." Everything Burke did or was thought to have done was subjected to ridicule. On 30 July the *Morning Post* attributed to him some verses, which it apparently regarded as particularly bad: "EPITAPH./ *The following Epitaph for the Tomb of Sir* JOSHUA/ REYNOLDS, *comes from the Pen of Mr.* BURKE.

> Beneath this tomb, in sacred sleep,
> The virtuous REYNOLDS lies;
> Ye passengers forbear to weep,
> A good man never dies."

The verses also appeared in the *Morning Chronicle* of 1 August, but the *Chronicle* revised the headnote to read: "The following, which has been ascribed to Mr. BURKE as an Epitaph for the tomb of Sir JOSHUA REYNOLDS, is a translation of a Greek epigram as old at least as the days of CALLIMACHUS." On 5 August the *Post* published an epitaph on Burke:

> To the EDITOR *of the* MORNING POST.
> SIR,
>   Having read in the *Post* [actually in the *Chronicle*] of Monday last, a curious Sternholdian Epitaph on Sir J. REYNOLDS, said to come from the pen of Mr. BURKE, and which he has translated from CALLIMACHUS: I send you an humble imitation of it, on Mr. BURKE himself, when it shall please Heaven to remove him from among the *Swinish Multitude*. Wishing well to your spirited Paper, I am, &c.
>
> A. B. C.
>
> Under this nettle-bearing sod,
> The furious EDMUND lies;
> But name not FRANCE—or else, by G—
> He'll burst his tomb, and rise!
>
> *August* 3.

On 7 August the *Morning Post* struck out against the war, citing as authority for its statements the Duke of Clarence. "So popular is the War among our Country BUMPKINS, who know just as much about the cause of it as His Majesty's Ministers, agreeable to the assertion of the DUKE of CLARENCE," it scoffed, "that they stand to be shot at for six-pence a day, in preference to receiving six times that sum in assisting to get in the harvest!" On 8 August it reiterated the theme of all Opposition papers that Pitt had been duped, adding the suggestion that the King was also opposed to the war: "Those who are in the confidence of the King declare that he is averse to the war, a circumstance long since strongly insinuated by the Duke of CLARENCE. The old friends of Mr. PITT it is well known, advised him against the measure. The fact is, Mr. PITT, to secure a large majority, hearkened alone to the advice of his new allies, and it is therefore not astonishing that the advice of such intemperate and wrong-headed men as EDMUND BURKE, and Messrs. POWIS and WYNDHAM, should have precipitated him into so un-popular a measure." But the Duke could not be cajoled into an alliance with Lord Lauderdale, and Pitt had as yet nothing to gain by ending the war.

The Second Prorogation:
On to Dunkirk!

The second prorogation of Parliament, from 13 August to 29 October, surprised most of the newspapers, since Pitt needed money and he could have asked for it then with minimum embarrassment. But he needed much more money than the newspapers, which were unaware of the treaties, realized. The news that England was obligating itself to finance the entire war would be a shock which, Pitt seems to have felt, nothing less than the capitulation of Dunkirk could cushion. On 30 August the Government concluded another such treaty with Austria. Dunkirk seemed, however, to be within easy grasp. On 18 August General Lake defeated the French at Lincelles, and on 21 August, according to the *Oracle* (24 Aug.), Field Marshal Freytag, commanding the Hanoverian forces, two thousand Austrian troops, ten squadrons of English and five of Hessian cavalry, and an undetermined number of "Emigrants," captured a half-dozen villages within sight of Dunkirk. The *Oracle* printed the story entirely in boldface and captioned it "IMPORTANT VICTORY OVER THE FRENCH." This was the first appearance of such a headline. On 2 September the *Oracle* announced that the siege of Dunkirk was under way, and on 6 September it stated that Pitt would ask for a loan of twelve million pounds. The *Oracle* expected trouble. Pitt would, it predicted, be subjected to "a considerable portion of public odium; and every Politician would express his astonishment, if Mr. PITT escaped the bitterness of party invective, or the spleen of disappointed projectors." Although the *Oracle* was anticipating as usual, all newspapers agreed that the Allies were making good progress, and the Ministerial papers were predicting a speedy end to the war. By the time Parliament convened, the Allies, they were sure, would be in Paris.

Opposition to the war was nevertheless growing. In mid-August there was a succession of riots against the crimps, and on 22 August the *Oracle* reported that "the fury of the populace does not appear to be yet abated. Their determination, they do not hesitate to avow, is to destroy every house that harbours the class of people which is the object of their revenge." The *Morning Post*, always sympathetic with the rioters, suggested on 24 August that they might also search the neighborhood of the Admiralty:

> There are every hour in the day two ruffianly crimps stationed near the Admiralty, who are guilty of the most abominable outrages against the Liberty of the Subject. Men, and even children do not escape these fellows, who are known in the neighbourhood by the name of *Skin Merchants*. There is not a

countryman or boy that arrives there, that they do not cajole by some frivolous pretext into a public-house, into whose pocket they convey a shilling, and then insist that he is enlisted. The number thus trepanned is really shocking, and the relations of these poor people in the country conceive they are murdered, as they are kept in a continual state of intoxication, and not suffered to write to their friends, nor apply to a Magistrate.

There was so much interest in the Glasgow petition for peace that the Ministerial papers felt obliged to say something about it. The *Oracle* dealt with the matter obliquely by attacking Lord Lauderdale, now known to have been responsible for the petition. "The activity of Lord LAUDERDALE is amazing, and his indisposition and his health leave him at equal *liberty*," it sneered on 14 August. "An exhausted frame sent him to FRANCE; he recruited at once his body by the *air*, and his mind by the philosophy of PARIS. . . ." The *World* dealt with it directly· "REAL GLASGOW PETITION," it announced on 31 August. "*May it please your Majesty,/* We, your Majesty's most *dutiful* and *loyal* subjects, the JACOBINS of Glasgow, not being people of property, nor willing to acquire property by any other industry than by *our equal rights of participating equally in all the property of your loyal people in common,* like our common ancestor ADAM, and his family, as it is written in the Book of Genesis, beg leave to approach your throne with all the *humility* of the most *loyal* Jacobins. . . ." And on 2 September: "Many *loyal* people wish to be informed who is to be the sturdy JACOBIN that shall *dare* to present the *Glasgow* Petition to his Majesty, 'against the *war* with *their friends,* the *French anarchists!*' Every well-wisher to *British freedom* and to a *worthy* MONARCH must consider the presenter as a *Cataline* of his country." By this time another such petition was being readied in London.

The British Convention, tentatively scheduled for 13 August, had been postponed until 29 October, but on 13 August the Corresponding Society did meet at the Globe Tavern to discuss the state of the nation, with a view to petitioning for peace. The speaker was Joseph Gerrald, and his indictment of the Government was evidently very effective, for one of his auditors suggested that the simplest way to solve the problem was to assassinate Pitt. Dundas later[59] mentioned that a plot was actually "formed" sometime during this period "to destroy Mr. Pitt, & the mode proposed was for a few men to place themselves upon Putney Bridge and to block up the passage in such a way as to prevent Mr. Pitt who usually went to Wimbledon at night with one servant only, & seize Him & throw *Him into the River*. This being known was guarded against." There was a similar plot, Dundas remembered, to "destroy" himself. But the suggestion at the meeting of 13 August was taken seriously only by the Ministerial newspapers. As the *Gazetteer* put it on 23 August: "The Treasury writers are under infinite obligations to the *hot-headed zealot,* who moved the *assassination* of Mr. PITT. It has furnished them with new themes of panegyric on that great statesman, while it gives them an opportunity of ringing the *changes* on their favourite *instrument* the *Jacobin tocsin*." Although Daniel Stuart was acquainted with

Gerrald at this time and was listening to him "describe his visits and harangues to those clubs,"[60] the *Morning Post* withheld comment. A few days later, the Corresponding Society advertised another meeting, this one to be held at the Globe Tavern, Fleet Street, on 2 September for the purpose of considering the petition. On the morning of 2 September, however, the Lord Mayor, Sir James Saunderson, notified "the house" that the meeting would not be "suffered," and the proprietor of the Globe Tavern accordingly refused to "suffer" it. The Society thereupon engaged Lewis's Auction Room in Oxford Road instead, and, at three-thirty that afternoon, six or seven hundred members assembled and, with John Noble presiding, heard and approved the petition. Someone then moved to censure Sir James Saunderson "for exercising a stretch of authority unknown to the Constitution," and someone else moved an amendment "that the conduct of Sir JAMES SAUNDERSON is unworthy the notice of [this] Society." The amendment was adopted "with incessant applause, and ordered to be printed in six London Papers." One of these was the *Oracle*, which explained (4 Sept.) to its readers: "The Lord MAYOR has sent orders, that the meetings of the London Corresponding Society shall not in future be held at the Globe Tavern." Another was the *Morning Post*, which added (3 Sept.) a full account of the proceedings.

The *Morning Post* was enraged. "It is highly creditable to the *noble, patriotic*, and *disinterested* Sir JAMES SAUNDERSON, that Government applauded his virtues, and have complimented him with a sinecure employment," it observed on 4 September. "The citizens must feel also their *dignity*, in having a Member thus distinguished to represent them, and will doubtless return *him* again, to *serve them* in Parliament." "On all occasions, Sir JAMES SAUNDERSON, is anxious to avow himself the supporter of all the measures of Mr. PITT," the *Post* said again on 6 September. "He even admires the Duke of RICHMOND, as a great military character, and a more profound politician. If so, how can he act so inconsistently not to say, unconstitutionally, as to prevent the London Corresponding Society from following up with steadiness and temperance those very measures first suggested by those IDOLS which he so much admires, but who abandoned them probably because other more *patriotic* avocations diverted them from their once first and great object, a Parliamentary Reform." The *Post* continued its attacks until 28 September, when the city elected as mayor for the ensuing year Paul Le Mesurier.

The Duke of Clarence had not changed his mind, although the Ministerial papers liked on occasion to pretend otherwise. The *World* of 16 August reported that his nineteen-year-old brother, Prince Adolphus, heading a squadron of "the Hanoverian Horse," had "so gallantly charged the enemy on the 6th instant, and put them to flight" that he himself almost lost his life: "one of the French cavalry made a stroke with his sabre at the Prince, and cut the corner of his hat entirely off; his Royal Highness instantly drew a pistol, with which he shot the French-man through the head." The report was followed by the meditation:

From the known spirit and courage of every branch of the Royal Family, the inactivity of the DUKE of CLARENCE must be to him very irksome, particularly when he daily hears of the services rendered to their country, and the laurels gained by his Royal Brothers, in whose honours he cannot but be anxious to participate; for whatever may be the Duke's political sentiments, we dare not doubt, but if ever called into action, he would prove, that a love of his country, and a thirst after glory, are as predominant in him as in any of his Royal Relatives.

A certain Admiral [it] is thought will not be entrusted with the command of any other *vessel* in the present disturbances than the *Jordan.*

According to the *Morning Post* (12 Sept.), Prince Adolphus was rewarded for his "gallantry" with the colonelcy of "a regiment of Hanoverian cavalry," and on 19 August the *World* announced that the recalcitrant Duke would "participate"in the "honours" after all: "The Duke of CLARENCE was yesterday with the Board of Admiralty, and had a long interview with the Lords. His Highness will shortly go to Portsmouth, to take upon him the command of the *Duke*, of 98 guns." On 24 August the *Oracle* further announced that he had "ordered a magnificent pair of colours for the Royal Surrey Regiment of Militia, which will cost him 120 guineas." But a few days later the Ministerial papers were again deploring the Duke's "inactivity." It looked, too, as if there would soon be more "inactivity" to deplore, for on 20 August the *Morning Post* reported that Prince Augustus Frederick, who had spent the last winter in Italy in a bad state of health, was now completely recovered and intended to return to England.

The camp at Brighton, which was intended to preserve whatever popularity the war enjoyed, seemed almost calculated to destroy it. The Prince of Wales had thrown himself into the project with great enthusiasm, but Mrs. Fitzherbert's presence was embarrassing to the Ministerial papers, and, although the Prince did have some fashionable friends, the camp seemed to attract only the disreputable ones. All he had supplied was therefore an atmosphere of debauchery for the Duke of Richmond's make-believe. The Opposition papers were vastly amused. On 19 August the *Morning Chronicle* reported with mock seriousness:

BRIGHTON CAMP,
AUGUST 15.

We are just returned from a desperate engagement we have been fighting this morning on a height near Brighton, assisted by all our cavalry. Victory at length crowned our valour. The last furious charge of the 10th dragoons routed the enemy; we came back with drums beating and colours flying; and as the fruits of our conquest, we are to rest on our arms till Monday next, when it is given out, that we are to storm the enemy in their redoubts and entrenchments.

Our loss in killed was nothing; but almost every man of us was severely wounded in the eyes, for which an abstersive application of cold water was prescribed.

Oh! that I had a pen to describe, or a pencil to delineate the daily labours of our great Commander—To paint the immortal Master-General toiling at forming a line, with camp colour-men, running footmen, aid-de-camps, Brigade Majors, Brigadier-Generals, &c. &c. and the line with invincible obstinacy, resisting his utmost efforts. I think I see him, as he appeared this morning, dismounted, with a theodolite in hand, the camp colour-men supplanted by two running footmen, who are dancing about in all directions; the aid-de-camps from the center to the extremities of the line, and from the extremities to the center; the Brigade-Majors in all points of the compass, and the Major-Generals lost in amazement— So have I seen some such imitators of the great Mr. FLOCKTON, cursing in all the vehemence of rage the awkwardness of his puppets, while he by pulling every string but the right one, served only to increase the confusion!

Last night we fired a *jeu-de-joy*, to the infinite delight of a numerous assembly; but, although the men bellowed themselves hoarse with the most loyal huzzas, not a drop of beer could they extract—In imitation of our General, we are all rigid oeconomists.

"PETER PINDAR," said the *Morning Post* on 23 August, "is employing his talents on a descriptive Poem, relating to the Wars of the Duke of RICHMOND. The hissing of mutton-chops, the frying of sausages, the flight of the poultry, and the desperate conflicts fought at the Suttler's, between some old geese and hungry militia-men, will afford ample scope to the amusement of his Muse!"

Among the Prince of Wales's friends was "a certain Baronet" (probably Sir John Lade) whose fights with his wife and certain other people "of fashion" had been faithfully chronicled by the *World*. On 23 August the *World* reported additional trouble. On Sunday, 18 August, the Rev. [Vicesimus] Knox, Head Master of Tunbridge School and Rector of Runwell and Ramsden-Crays, Essex, had preached a sermon at the parish church, Brighton, on the text, "Glory be to God in the highest, and on earth peace and good will towards men." Although it seemed to certain "military gentlemen" in the congregation that the Rev. Knox was impugning the war and hence the Constitution, they said nothing until 20 August, when Knox and his family had the audacity to visit the Brighton theater. The "military gentlemen" at once ordered them to leave, Knox tried to explain his remarks, the "officers" refused to listen, and there was a squabble. But, the "officers" having threatened to evict them bodily, the Knoxes quit the theater and, on the following morning, quit Brighton as well. It seemed to the *World* that the battle fought by these "gallant officers" eclipsed all the campaigns of the Duke of Richmond, but the *Morning Chronicle* purported to think otherwise. On 24 August it published an unsigned "Ode to the Duke of Richmond, By a Witness of the Military Ardour of His Grace at the Head of his Troops," which read in part:

> Oh! let me slink behind this gaping group,
>   Awe-struck and dazzled by that martial form—
> Say, is it MARS or RICHMOND heads the troop?—
> Hark! how they thunder—lo! all spirits droop
>   But RICHMOND's—how his soul enjoys the storm!

Well may you tremble, clod-hoppers, and stare!—
Fly—o'er your necks he'll urge his fiery course;
See how he gallops!—lo, now here—now there—
Stand back—away, ye dastards, have a care—
Away—make room for RICHMOND, and his horse!

Oh, could our foes—but ne'er must they behold
The Hero—Britain's safeguard and her boast!
Britain restrains his arm, let France be told,
Keeps *here* the Chief *in pity* to her host,
Rather than sweep from earth such rogues away,
She keeps the champion harmless—and in pay!

On 26 August the *World* again denied that the Prince of Wales was wallowing in luxury. That "very elegant bed, which was put up for him in his Marquee," had positively been "taken down, and one much more plain, and suitable to a camp, put up," it said. It also denied that Sir William Medows "has given up his command here in disgust." Sir William Medows, it assured its readers, was "in poor health." Other such denials followed. But even *Lloyd's Evening Post* was suggesting that it had perhaps been a mistake to move the camp to Brighton. As a case in point, it mentioned (2 Sept.) "a ball and supper" which the Prince had given on 27 August for "100 Gentlemen and 100 Ladies." Although the gentlemen had been ordered to be "out [the next] morning at seven," they were in no condition to comply, and, at the Prince's request, the Duke of Richmond had canceled the games. At no time, said *Lloyd's Evening Post*, did the Duke of Richmond know how many officers he could count on. The plan had in fact been to return the camp to Waterdown on 8 September, but on 31 August the *World* reported that the soldiers greatly preferred Brighton and had petitioned the Duke of Richmond to that effect. By 2 September the Duke of Richmond had consented to let them stay, on the ground, said the *World*, that the Brighton climate was probably "healthier."

As the *Morning Chronicle* indicated on 4 September, the Brighton climate was at least lustier:

THE SUSSEX CAMPAIGN.
What daring *Democrat* dare say
That RICHMOND's troops, at Brighton,
Are kept for mere parade and play?
And not—for *serious* fighting?

Behold, at least, *one* grand exploit!
('Tis true, upon my life, Sir!)
Six heroes bold have put to flight—
A *parson*—and his *wife*, Sir!

Nor is it only in the field
That they have feats perform'd, Sir!
Strong places they have forc'd to yield,
And *orchards* bravely storm'd, Sir!

O YORK! what prowess had they shown,
Had they been sent with YOU, Sir!
Dunkirk, ere now, had been our own!
And so had Cambray, too, Sir!

England! how happy is thy lot!
O! qualis, quae Letitia!
Since *Thou*, for thy defence, hast got
RICHMOND, and his MILITIA!

The *"parson"* was, of course, Knox; *"Letitia"* was Lady Letitia Lade. On 6 September the *Morning Chronicle* announced publication on Sunday, 8 September, of *The Substance of a Sermon, Preached in the Parish of Brighthelmstone by Dr. K. from St. Luke ii, 14. . . . With an Authentic Account of the Outrage Committed on that Gentleman and his Family at the Theatre of that town by the Officers of Militia.* An account of Knox's life and salient passages from the sermon would also appear, it said, in the *Sunday Reformer.* The publisher of the pamphlet was not named, but his address, No. 33, Ludgate Street, was identical with that of George Riley, printer of the *Sunday Reformer.* The *Chronicle* supplemented the announcement with additional sarcasm regarding the Duke of Richmond:

> No one can accuse his Grace of RICHMOND of obstinately adhering to any fixed plans. The orders issued in a morning from his Pavilion, are not unfrequently countermanded the next day, sometimes that very evening. This shews the fertility of his genius. His variety of military knowledge is so great, that unless some method like this were taken, the world might never be acquainted with half of it.
>
> It is to be regretted that so many of our brave countrymen should have fallen in battle, while a noble DUKE is so busily employed on land to show how it is possible to fight without the smallest personal danger.
>
> The Duke of RICHMOND has had a more serious alarm in his camp at Brighton, than when he fortified the Tower. A detachment of *sans-culottes* gin kegs contrived to effect a landing in the evening just in front of the camp, and before they were discovered by his Grace, had so completely *fraternized* a number of the privates as to make them treat all his manoeuvres that depend on marching in straight lines with the utmost contempt. These insidious invaders, we are happy to add, were all taken prisoners, and patroles established to guard against such attempts in future.

Although the Opposition newspapers conceded that the Allies would take Dunkirk, none of them expected the war to end as a result. Readers of the *Morning Chronicle* were given constantly to understand that the campaign was being bungled and that, as a military strategist, Pitt was in the same class as the

Duke of Richmond. "Former Ministers, when at war with France, chose to attack her in the most vulnerable part, her colonies," the *Chronicle* remarked on 17 August. "Mr. PITT pursues a more magnanimous and disinterested system; he scorns to attack France where France might lose and Britain gain; he assails her where conquests must be made with the greatest difficulty, and where, when made, they are worth nothing." This sentiment, like all sentiments expressed by the *Chronicle*, was echoed by the *Gazetteer*, which mentioned on 26 August: "The praise of all Europe, we are told, is to await on the exertions of the British army in the present campaign in the Netherlands. This eulogy is fairly earned. Our efforts are not only *disinterested*, but we pay dearly for the opportunity of shewing our *valeur!*" It seemed to the *Morning Chronicle* of 31 August that the country would pay dearly indeed:

> In every way the influence of the Crown is to be increased, and in none can it be so effectually done as by new levies. Every man taken from the mass of the people, dressed in red, and saddled upon the half-pay list after six months service is a point gained to the Crown; and for this reason, if Dunkirk should be kept only for the winter, and cost this country 100,000*l.* it would be ranked "among the cheap defence of nations."
>
> Ministers do not affect to disguise the truth that the attack on Dunkirk is their measure. One of them entertained a mixed company a few days ago with a dissertation on the advantages to be derived from its capture. The principal advantage is, that it will prevent smuggling; that is, at the expence of six or eight regiments, we are to save the clandestine importation occasionally of a few casks of brandy.

And what about the Dutch? asked the *Gazetteer* again on 26 August: "The primary cause assigned for the present war, in its commencement, was the danger which menaced our allies in Holland. It will be difficult to prove, however, that their gratitude or zeal has justified our interference in the Crusade. We have hitherto found their fleets *in* harbour, and their armies *out* of the field!" This question troubled even the *Oracle*. "While the exertions of our countrymen, both at home and abroad, demand the highest encomiums, the reluctant and frigid activity of the DUTCH, whom we snatched from the brink of destruction, calls aloud for censure . . . ," it declared on 6 September. "When the French menaced their political existence, . . . they were aroused to a sense of danger. But when, by the valour of Allies, the Invaders are repelled from the Dutch territories, the MYNHEERS immediately relapse into a state of shameless stupefaction and criminal indifference." The *Morning Chronicle* noted only (9 Sept.): "The Dutch, who are certainly not famed for the celerity of their motions, in their late retreat lost not even one man. This is a clear proof of their eagerness in the cause, where none were determined to be left behind." The *Chronicle* was equally disgusted with the coddling of Sardinia. "Among the happiest measures of the present campaign may be reckoned that of sending a fleet to the Mediterranean, where it could have no other object than that of defending our valuable ally the King of Sardinia," it observed on 2 September. "The whole expence of that fleet is to be added to the subsidy of 200,000*l.* a year which we pay for the defence of his territories, and which *we may be doomed to pay*, under the articles of the treaty, *for ever.*" No newspaper quite understood what Lord Howe was doing, and, to guard against sarcasms on that score, the *World* announced on 7 September that his recent "return to Torbay is merely for the purpose of obtaining a fresh supply of provisions, stores &c.—as soon as this is done, his Lordship will sail in quest of the French Fleet./ The Opposition Prints will no doubt find infinite fault with Lord HOWE for returning into Port, and will forget to inform their few readers, that the principal object for which his Lordship so soon left Port is attained—namely, the safe arrival of our valuable Fleets of merchantmen from *Jamaica* and *Oporto.*"

The Opposition papers were agreed that the capture of Dunkirk should be followed by immediate negotiations for peace, but they were no longer agreed on the means of achieving this object. The *Morning Chronicle*, which had previously subscribed to the *Morning Post*'s hypothesis that, if the war were identified exclusively with Burke, Pitt might open negotiations of his own accord, now felt otherwise. It was now obviously determined to identify the war with Pitt and to persuade its readers that Pitt had not only contrived it, but was presently conducting it, for the sole purpose of increasing the power of the Crown and thereby maintaining himself in office. The war, in short, was to be the issue which at long last would rid the country of Pitt. Readers were constantly reminded that the people were paying for the war and that Pitt's friends were profiting from it. "The *Red Book* was not amongst the patriotic publications of the REEVITES," the *Chronicle* observed on 2 September; and on 6 September: "A person asked a friend why the Court Calendar was frequently called the *red book*;—because, quoth the other, it *blushes* for a considerable portion of its contents."

The term, "The Red Book," served a very useful purpose during this period, although its meaning was becoming ambiguous. There were in fact two "Court Calendars," one for the scrutiny of a few Government officials, the other for publication. There was a vast difference between them, since the second was not only highly incomplete, but inaccurate, especially with respect to the emoluments involved. To the *Morning Chronicle*, the term usually meant the secret list of patronage; to the *Gazetteer*, it almost invariably meant the published one. Similarly, announcements of appointments might be based on either list, and, since hearsay was at least as reliable as the official *Gazette*, it probably made little difference where the newspaper got its information. The only real difference was that an announcement based on hearsay was likely to be repeated at intervals, as the rumor spread from one editorial office to another. The *Morning Chronicle* did not, however, publish rumors. Its tactic was to leave the contents of that mysterious *"Red Book"* to the imagination of its readers, and readers with poor imaginations could always consult the *Gazetteer*. The "leaders" of The Crown and Anchor Association, Reeves, Bowles, and Topham, were now, said the

Gazetteer on 23 August, "*Commissioners of Bankrupts*." "Mr. ROSE, it is said, has at length preferred a *promise* of the very lucrative place which he enjoys, as principal Clerk of the House of Lords, for his son. The emoluments of the office, for it cannot be called an *employment*, are nearly 4000*l.* a year," the *Gazetteer* added on 31 August. And on 5 September: "JAMES REYNOLD has been appointed new Surveyor of Stamps vice GEORGE HARRIS, deceased."

The *Morning Post* was adhering to its former strategy. Its readers were given to understand that this was a war of despots against peoples, caused in the first instance by Austria and Prussia and now involving England only because their ally, Burke, had misled William Pitt. On 19 August the *Oracle* reported that Marie Antoinette had on 2 August been moved from The Temple "to the prison of the Conciergerie." The *Morning Post* was profoundly disturbed. "We have reason to believe, that . . . this week will bring an account of the execution of the QUEEN," it said on 3 September. "How must every feeling mind lament, that last year the EMPEROR and his Ally did not treat with France, procure a peace, and save the lives of this unhappy family. How much more humane and praise-worthy would this have been, than prosecuting a War, either for the purposes of extermination, or through objects of aggrandizement." Such statements were backed by letters, paragraphs, and verses, indicating that the war was being kept alive by Burke, who was motivated by hatred of the people, idolatrous worship of kings, and sympathy with Roman Catholicism. "The *Arch Alarmist* has betaken himself to his Rosary, and is determined, by the aid of additional prayers, to secure a situation in the regions of bliss," the *Post* reported on 2 September. "The idea of meeting MARAT in the nether world has had a wonderful effect in exciting the Alarmist to acts of exemplary piety." The *Post* was assisted by other newspapers. On 4 September the *Morning Chronicle* contributed the verses:

MESSRS. P-TT *and* D--D-*s*
TO THE PEOPLE OF ENGLAND.

If noble blood 'mong swine may lurk,
    As MASTERS you must need indure us;
You're but the hogs of EDMUND BURKE,
    But we, the hogs of EPICURUS.

R. P. Q.

The most helpful support came perhaps from the *World*, which observed typically on 17 August: "EDMUND BURKE is preparing himself for another *Phillipic* against Mr. HASTINGS. It is to contain the *flower of invective*, but un-fortunately the scent is gone by." The *Morning Post*, which was now also defending Hastings, remarked on the same day: "Mr. BURKE has in vain searched after a precedent to discover, if the Impeachment could not be con-tinued after the decease of the prisoner. He cannot suppose, we hope, that the heirs of Mr. HASTINGS, were he to die, are subject to fine and imprisonment.

Mr. BURKE, on all occasions, affects to forget, that precedents are the bond and disgrace of Legislature. They are not wanted to justify right measures, and are absolutely insufficient to excuse wrong ones." To all of this, there was only one reply. "Mr. Burke, in his lofty and capacious mind, foresaw, three years since, the full consequences of the dreadful rebellion in France," said the *Public Advertiser* on 4 September.

The Second Prorogation:
Demise of the Diary

The Ministerial newspapers had never functioned as a team, and the high-handed tactics of the *Sun* and the *True Briton* had only aggravated the dissension. "The Conductors of the Treasury Clerks' Journal are bawling loudly for the ATTORNEY GENERAL to come to their aid," the *Morning Chronicle* noticed on 16 August. "Men of such *veracity* and such *courage* stand in need of an able second." The *True Briton* was currently engaged in a quarrel with *The Times* over the sources of its information. The quarrel was continued on 5 September, when William Walter accused Burges privately[61] of acquainting John Heriot with the content of the King's mail before the King himself even saw it. On the same day, he protested to Dundas:[62]

> It is notorious, & I could prove the fact, that scarce a Dispatch comes from the Armies, or is there a Paris Journal forwarded to any of the Public Offices, but what is immediately transmitted to the *Sun* office. This system is now become so general, that I foresee my property in particular must suffer, if it continues. Probably I may feel the more vexed at this circumstance, because I know my conduct deserves a different treatment from Government. My father was imprisoned sixteen months in Newgate for Paragraphs written by the Conductor of the two Papers in question [Heriot], & another person employed by Mr. Steele. . . . State Papers are published, Paris Gazettes are forwarded to the office, and in short, the Columns of these Newspapers are filled with writings from persons either paid by Government or Gentlemen in office. . . .
> I address this letter to you, Sir, from no motives of jealousy. I complain only of the system of sending every foreign Newspaper from the Public Offices to the *Sun* Office. . . .

Dundas seems to have responded by at least giving *The Times* priority in the Home Office.

The *Oracle*, now owned by James Bell, Jr., was still concerned for Sheridan's interests, but its support of Pitt remained otherwise firm. On 19 August Bell's advertisements disappeared, and on 22 August the paper announced that it would henceforth specialize in foreign news: "THIS PAPER WAS PUB-LISHED AT SIX IN THE MORNING./ The VERY VALUABLE SOURCES OF INTELLIGENCE, of which WE ARE EXCLUSIVELY IN POSSESSION, afford ample proofs of our anxiety to afford the EARLIEST INFORMATION at this IMPORTANT CRISIS. . . . Mr. [James] BELL has received BY EXPRESS/ THE PARIS PAPERS/ up to the 9th of August. . . ." It would also, it said, specialize in the arts, with a view to correcting certain unfortunate tendencies. On 23 August it accordingly introduced a column, entitled "COURT OF HUMBUG," which ridiculed modern music, literature, and drama. Although this column was short-lived, the *Oracle* was for a while more interested in literary titbits than in scurrility. "FRANKLIN the Philosopher originated the air *Ça ira*," it announced typically on 5 September. "When in the progress of the American Revolution any check was communicated to him, it was his custom to say, 'Je m'y attendois, mais cependant *Ça ira*.' SEDAINE the Dramatist seized it, and it has supplied *France* with perpetual enthusiasm." Bell's advertisements reappeared on 5 September and again on 13 and 14 September, but there was still no statement from John Bell himself.

Although the *Public Advertiser* also remained loyal to the Government, the second prorogation had its effect on the *Morning Herald*, the *World*, and the *Diary*. Since the owner of the *Morning Herald*, the Rev. Henry Bate Dudley, was himself a friend of the Opposition, the paper had already been supporting Fox's fund, and it now seemed inclined to desert Pitt altogether. In one respect, it did; but, with a daily sale of only eight hundred, it could not refuse any material which was paid for, and so it was still printing some Ministerial propaganda. The *World*, which had been relying on puffs to augment its own income from the Treasury, still regarded itself as Ministerial, but its owner, Edward Topham, was not accepting the cancellation of his subsidy quietly. Unlike Dudley, Topham had been rewarded for his labors, being now Deputy Lieutenant of the East Riding in Yorkshire and a Commissioner of Bankrupts; but, in considera-tion of his work for The Association, he seems to have felt that he could also expect a resumption of the subsidy. Other arguments having evidently failed, Topham tried blackmail. "CAPTAIN TOPHAM, we understand," the *World* mentioned casually on 2 September, "has been for some time past dedicating occasional leisure hours to a Biographical Sketch of his own Life. It is reasonable to suppose that the leading POLITICAL EVENTS of his time will constitute a large part of that history—which is intended to be published only after his death." Since Pitt did not like to be threatened, the subsidy was not renewed, and the "Biographical Sketch" was not written, but Topham evidently hoped for some adjustment, since the *World* did not defect until October. The *Diary* quit altogether.

William Woodfall, who was almost as fond of addresses to the public as John

Bell was, had obviously labored over his final communication, since it monopolized the issue of 26 August, being reprinted on 30 and 31 August:

THE
PRINTER *of the* DIARY
TO THE
PUBLICK.

It is now between Twenty-four and Twenty-five Years, since the PRINTER of this PAPER became the Servant of the Publick, and as he feels himself under the necessity of quitting their Service, decency requires that he should say a word or two of his kind Masters and Mistresses at parting, as other servants, under such circumstances, usually do when they seperate not in anger, nor part (as the vulgar phrase is) in ill-blood. Attacked last Winter with a nervous fever, which his Physician (the late worthy and skillful Dr. AUSTIN) ascribed to too great irritability of mind, the consequence of unremitted attention to business, he had a hard struggle for his life, and recovered so slowly, that it was not till the late warm weather set in, that he thought himself out of danger. Far from being surprized at his having been attacked in a manner so alarming, the Printer thinks he has abundant reason to be thankful, that he has been enabled for so many years together, to defy disease, and to sustain an incessant pressure of unexampled fatigue of mind and body, without feeling serious injury to his health before, or in any material degree impairing his constitution. As a Reporter of Parliamentary Debates, he has spent day and night, without rest from his labour, for several days together, in the severest seasons, for six, and sometimes eight months of each year; and he has been incited to these extraordinary exertions (for such, now they are nearly at an end, he may, without imputation of vanity, be permitted to term them) by the flattering encouragement he experienced from the first men in the kingdom, among those most competent to decide, how far his Reports did tolerable justice to the arguments of the very distinguished Orators that have taken part in the Debates in Parliament during as busy, interesting, and important a period of the British History, as any recorded in our annals. Increase of reputation in a path of literature untrodden before, in so public a manner during the present century, excited many rivals, and of late years he has found himself obliged to contest with an host of able Competitors, who, while he kept the field singly, came forward in chosen bands, avowedly to drive him from his post. It is his utmost ambition to have found, by the continuance of the Publick favour, that it has been the general opinion that against all his Opponents, he made at least no despicable stand. The stoutest Warriors have been worn out by long continued active service, and the Printer at length finds that it is proper for him to uncase, to lay aside his military accoutrements, and to sink into the less publick, but not less useful character of a private Citizen. While his indisposition continued, he was necessarily obliged to do most of that duty by others, which he had himself before been uniformly accustomed to discharge. During the last Session of Parliament, he was not able to attend either House more than three or four days; but he has no hesitation to declare that, in his judgement, those who acted for him as Reporters, did him ample justice. The Agency, however, was unavoidably attended with considerable expence, and as it had been very seriously hinted to him, that if he wished to preserve his existence, he ought not to venture again to encounter the extreme fatigue which is indispensibly connected with the conduct of a Newspaper during a busy Session of Parliament, he began to reflect deliberately on the subject. The value of his life to a large family, was too important a consideration not to make a due impression on his mind; he decided instantly to abandon what he was told from authority, not to be questioned, he could no longer personally perform, without incurring a risque that would be highly injurious to the interest of others, much dearer to him, than any addition of fame or fortune, or even than existence itself. His two eldest Sons having been intended and educated for a Profession [the law], if not more liberal, at least more profitable than his own, the question then became how far he could, with tolerable profit carry on his Paper by agents, superintended, and aided occasionally by himself. Upon an examination of the articles that constitute the expence and produce, he found that in consequence of the increased number of daily papers, which of course lessen the advantages of each other, there would remain a balance of so very moderate an amount in point of profit, that it would not be worth his while to continue the DIARY on that plan. When the Readers recollect that (exclusive of the extraordinary circumstances attending the conduct and printing of a Newspaper, a sort of exposure to the most abuseful waste of property, to incessant hurry, and call for attention, that belong scarcely to any other publick business whatever) by the insertion of five lines at a time, which, through the inadvertency of a second person, when the Editor was himself perhaps indispensibly absent, might have found their way into one of his pages, the Printer stood exposed to a tedious deprivation of liberty, an infamous punishment, intolerable to a feeling mind, or even absolute ruin, he will not surely think a *very moderate* profit an adequate compensation for what is constantly felt and risqued by those who are responsible for all the consequences which such a concern may render them liable to. Upon these considerations, the Printer was convinced that the most prudent step would be to dispose of his Paper, and let those who were circumstanced differently from himself, take the whole adventure upon their own shoulders, not doubting but that the DIARY might be increased considerably in its value as a property, in the hands of active spirits, fired with genius, and endowed with talents. He advertised it for sale, had several offers, and was for some time in treaty, but could not effectuate a bargain before the end of the last Session of Parliament, owing, in a great measure, to the prevalent and general scarcity of cash, and failure of credit. He need not waste many words to convince the Readers of this Address, that the summer season is not the most profitable one for the Proprietors of Newspapers; in proportion as the town thins, the number of each Paper daily sold diminishes, and Advertisers are well aware that it is less advantageous to them to become customers to the morning publications, than in winter, unless their object be to attract notice to matters of a nature immediately temporary. This circumstance, added to various other inconveniences, as well as the encreased expence of carrying on the printing business in the Newspaper line (which has of late been aggravated by demands on the part of the Journeymen, that the Printer cannot but consider as unreasonable and enormous, since their Employers can in no shape be remunerated) has decided him to retire at the end of the present month, from the publick service, and apply himself solely to BOOK-WORK, and the other branches of the Printing Business which are distinct from Newspaper Printing.

The consideration of his family will not permit him to look to that state of relaxation, which nearly Five and Twenty Years uncommonly hard duty, might reasonably have been imagined to entitle him to enjoy. He shall, however, withdraw with the heart-felt satisfaction of being conscious that he has not wilfully abused the powers of the important Office he has so long held. He is not aware that he has in any instance wittingly wounded the feelings of individuals, wantonly disturbed domestic peace, or done the least injury to the general morals of society. He pretends to no positive virtues, unless his having studiously avoided using his press either as a pillory or a pistol—sporting with the hopes of practising upon the fears of others, may, in this age of abuse of freedom, be deemed such; and Historians tell us, that times have existed, when a steady disdain of falling in with the prevalent vice of the day, has been sometimes honoured with being considered as a virtue.

In Politicks the Printer has been moderate, but decided; attached to Government from principle, as far as his limited powers would permit, he has uniformly endeavoured to support it, as the best means of preserving our enviable and excellent Constitution. At the same time he has manifested a due respect for the splendid talents of the leading Members of Opposition; in fact, he has neither vilified the one set of men, nor worshipped the other. Too proud to flatter, he has not condescended to abuse, conscious that the cause which could not be supported by fair reasoning with candid argument, was indefensible in itself, and incapable of being sustained.

As a Theatrical Critick, zealously ardent for the success of the Drama, from a thorough conviction that a well-regulated stage was the best possible succedaneum to the laws of a free country, the Printer early in life assumed the office, and is led to flatter himself that his constant attention to the productions and performances of each Play-house, has neither discouraged the efforts of Dramatic Writers, nor damped the exertions of the Comedians.

Having thus stated the principles on which he has acted, and explained his reasons for retiring as a Newspaper Printer, reasons which, from the nature of the subject, unavoidably carry the complexion of a string of *Egotisms*, the Printer has only to thank his Patrons for all past favours, to tell them honestly and fairly, that although he quits his Paper in possession of the wonted vigour of his mental faculties, neither his Health nor his Interest will let him continue it longer, and to bid his competitors for publick favour farewell, sincerely wishing them better success than he has experienced, and hoping, that when they make to port ultimately, they will return from their last Newspaper Voyage with full bills of health, and freights sufficiently valuable to complete their stores, so as to render them capable of enjoying all the comforts and happiness of life, for the remainder of their days!

Appended to the address on 30 August were the announcements:

After to-morrow, many of the materials used for the composition of the DIARY, with the Galleys, Chases, Brass Rules, &c. &c. will be sold, at a fair appraisement;

also the Office, with a Stone Front, hitherto appropriated to the reception of advertisements. The Office (which is well worth the attention of Wharfingers, Coal-Dealers, or any who want a small Accompting House near the Thames, or in their back-yard,) to be removed at the expence of the Purchaser.

The OFFICE CLERK, and PUBLISHER of this PAPER, wishes for an ENGAGEMENT for HIMSELF and SON. Where CONFIDENCE and ASSIDUITY are required, they flatter themselves they would be particularly useful. The Family will undertake any retale Business, either in town or country, on Commission; or take charge of a store in any of the United States; that of Virginia would have the preference. . . .

Please to enquire at the office of this Paper. Or a line, directed to A. B. No. 58, Upper Charlotte Street, Rathbone Place, will meet due attention.

Appended to the address on 31 August was only the advertisement for materials and house. The address had also appeared in the *Oracle* of 28 August, and on 29 August the *Morning Post* paid its own respects to the author:

MR. WILLIAM WOODFALL.

This Gentleman, so well known and so long admired for his abilities in laying before the Public *Parliamentary Reports*, has advertized his intention of retiring from that line of life.—We are sorry to add, that decline of health, and inadequacy of recompence, are the motives which have led to this determination.

Of that line of Literary Exertion, from which he has derived so much more fame than profit, he may be termed the Father; for he certainly was the first who ventured to aim at uniting that *expedition* with the *accuracy* of detail, to which the Debates in Parliament have been brought, by his exertions, and those who are now his successors. If therefore the striking into untrodden paths, wherein to display the talents and exertions of the human mind be, as heretofore, a solid claim to the character of *Genius*, Mr. WOODFALL must be said to possess that claim in a pre-eminent degree.

One advantage he certainly enjoys beyond the common lot of the Candidates for fame—although his labours in the pursuit of it have ceased, he yet happily lives to witness and enjoy it in the concurring admiration of a discerning Public, and the cordial esteem of a very extensive circle of friends.

The DIARY *expires* on the last day of the present month.

The *Diary* did expire on 31 August, and by early September the *Public Advertiser* had formed a liaison with the *World*, having evidently no news-gathering facilities of its own.

Woodfall's address had actually been intended for Pitt, who was being reminded of the author's long service for "the Publick" and for the Government. Insofar as the paper had wavered in its support of Pitt, Woodfall was saying, the fault lay with "agents," to whom he had entrusted the *Diary* during his illnesses, for he himself had always been "attached to Government from principle," and in fact the *Diary* had recently been nothing except an apologist for Dundas. The Government must understand that, broken in health and now deprived of the £400 subsidy, he could no longer continue the paper, and yet his financial situation was such that he needed an income. What he was therefore suggesting was some kind of reward, by way of pension or sinecure, which would provide for himself and his family during the years which remained. Other newspapers were very well aware of what Woodfall was saying, and, except for the *Sun*, the *True Briton*, and, oddly enough, the *Public Advertiser*, all of them were sympathetic with his predicament. The *Oracle* and the *Morning Post* had already spoken up on his behalf, and on 31 August the *World* reprinted his address with the headnote:

> The following is the ADDRESS of a GENTLEMAN, whose exertions, as a REPORTER of PARLIAMENTARY DEBATES, have justly claimed the admiration of the Public; but who, alas! has not been rewarded by them as his distinguished merits deserved. As the CONDUCTOR of a DAILY PAPER, he has proved himself a Man of Literature, and of great Genius; and those who have had the happiness to be personally acquainted with Mr. WILLIAM WOODFALL, can with us vouch for his being a Man of the most *strict Honour* and *Probity*. That such a Man should have spent *Five and Twenty Years* in the service of the Public unrewarded, is a reproach upon the Country!

Woodfall needed help, for, when he penned his address, he was certainly out of favor with the Government. Since at least 1789,[63] he had been closely associated with George Rose's intimate, Andrew Strahan, who had planned his political activities and shared, it appeared, some of his business interests. Strahan had undoubtedly arranged the subsidy for the *Diary* and may even have been a silent partner in the enterprise. When, at the end of 1792, the *Diary* ran into trouble with the Government, Strahan, one suspects, interceded, for the subsidy was continued, and Woodfall was soon sharing the appointment with Strahan of Law Printer to the King. But there had evidently been further trouble, for Woodfall was no longer Law Printer to the King, and the *World* was going out of its way to persuade Pitt that Woodfall was "a Man of the most *strict Honour* and *Probity*." Pitt, as it turned out, was not persuaded.

On 1 November *Lloyd's Evening Post* mentioned that Peter Roberts, who had long held the post of City Remembrancer, had died and that on 31 October the Board of Aldermen had appointed his son, Thomas Roberts, Remembrancer pro tempore, the election of a new Remembrancer having not yet been scheduled. On the same day, the *Morning Chronicle* announced the candidacy of William Woodfall:

> REMEMBRANCER
> OF THE
> CITY OF LONDON.
> It is with infinite pleasure that we see our valued friend and late compatriot, Mr. WOODFALL, a Candidate for the vacant office of City Remembrancer. If ever a man was endowed with accomplishments peculiarly requisite for the office

to which he aspires, Mr. WOODFALL, whose memory has been the wonder of his countrymen, is qualified for that of *Remembrancer*; and to doubt of his success would be a libel, not merely on the judgment, but the gratitude of the Citizens of London.

One duty of the Remembrancer of the City of London, is to attend the debates of the House of Commons, that he may report to his constituents such proceedings "as may affect the City of London, or the trade thereof:" for this purpose the Remembrancer has, by antient usage, been entitled to a seat below the Bar. In this essential part of the office, Mr. WOODFALL has for twenty years been in truth the Remembrancer, not merely of London, but of the kingdom at large; and if he has been induced, at last, to retire from so laborious a task, it is due to him in justice by his successors, to declare that *he established the school, in which they but feebly imitate their master.*

The office of City Remembrancer was evidently lucrative, for Brass Crosby had paid £3,600 for it in 1760 and had sold it at a profit in 1761; and Woodfall certainly had a unique claim to it, having served the city well during its quarrel with the Commons in 1770–1771. He had even, the aldermen might have recalled, spent several months in Newgate for printing the debates at their instigation and in contempt of Parliament.[64] But the situation had changed since 1771. City elections were now commonly decided by Pitt, and, since Pitt would not endorse Woodfall, Woodfall needed all the help he could get. The newspapers provided it. To begin with, every one of them supported him as the only possible candidate, and, although many of the eulogies were written in Woodfall's style, Woodfall had certainly not paid for their insertion. "WOODFALL the celebrated *Parliamentary Reporter*, is a candidate for the *City Remembrancer's* office. The people cannot have a more *faithful* MEMORY," the *Oracle* commented on 2 November. "Mr. WILLIAM WOODFALL, with the fairest character, and with claims indisputable, if we consider his *former* profession, is soliciting now to be made City—*Remembrancer!*" said the *Morning Post*. Supplementing the *Post's* statement was a long letter from "AN INDEPENDENT LIVERYMAN," who attested that his vote would not be influenced by Pitt. On 4 November the *World* announced that "Mr. WILLIAM WOODFALL, the late Editor of the Diary, is a candidate for the vacant Office of Remembrancer, in the gift of the City of London.—As a man of strict probity and integrity, every one must wish him success." And on 7 November the *Oracle* reprinted the *Morning Chronicle's* statement of 1 November. But opposition to Woodfall's candidacy was growing.

On 4 November the *Morning Post* had stated: "One of Mr. WOODFALL's adversaries says, that the office of Remembrancer requires nothing more in the person who fills the employment than a *common understanding*. If this is the case, honest WILLIAM stands no chance against the *other* candidates." But the *Sun*, which had previously supported Woodfall, now felt that, in addition to "common understanding," the Remembrancer ought to have legal training. The *Oracle* disagreed. Woodfall was not, it admitted on 7 November, "a professional man": "But when a competition arises, it may be fairly asked, who can presume to surpass Mr. WOODFALL either for talents as a reporter, or for virtues as a man? It is one part of the Remembrancer's business to attend to the political discussions in the House of Commons, and to report to his constituents such proceedings 'as may affect the City of LONDON, or trade thereof.' In the ensuing Sessions of Parliament, the most important perhaps which ever occurred in this country, no man is so admirably calculated for a situation which is highly interesting to his fellow-citizens." The *World* also disagreed. "Mr. WOODFALL is well aware of the propriety of his claim," it said on 8 November, "since the duties of the *Remembrancer* require nothing but a clear, comprehensive, and accurate memory, united with conciliating manners. Perhaps, since the days of THEMISTOCLES, no man has possessed a happier memory than Mr. WOODFALL; and without prostituting praise, we think the urbanity of his manners, (the result of his good temper) too striking to be unnoticed." On 7 November the *Morning Post* had denied "on authority" that "Mr. [Nathaniel] MIDDLETON, of *happy memory*, is a candidate for the office." Supposedly a witness against Hastings, Middleton was notorious for his lapses of "memory."

Woodfall's principal rival was Timothy Tyrrell. On 9 November the *Morning Chronicle* compared the qualifications of the two:

CITY REMEMBRANCER.

The strongest opposition to Mr. Woodfall, as a candidate for the office of City Remembrancer, is grounded on the capital and unpardonable crime of his not having been bred an *attorney*: a new species of obloquy! Such a fact, damning in itself to all who are not of that honourable profession, is enough to send any man to perdition, let the other points of his character be ever so good, respectable, and unexceptionable. As the cry has been raised on this dreadful defect in Mr. Woodfall, it may be worth while to ask, how far the most powerful opponent is his superior in *extensive legal knowledge*, or, to adopt his milder terms, *a well grounded knowledge of the law*, and what sort of legal education Mr. Woodfall and his opponent have severally had? The latter, as report says, and perhaps, in this instance, common fame is a common liar, was bred a jeweller, served his apprenticeship in Foster Lane, and set up in that trade for himself. He afterwards moved into the profession of the law, and having, *pro formâ*, articled himself to an attorney, at the expiration of the accustomed five years, became a practitioner in a profession which he has not disgraced, because truth requires that it should be declared, his manners have been uniformly those of a gentleman, and his conduct pure and upright. Mr. Woodfall for many years attended the Courts of Justice; has received personal compliments from the Bench, for his accuracy and knowledge of practice, on more than one occasion; and if the good opinion of the late Sir John Fielding can be entitled to any weight or consideration; in matters of criminal law, it may not be idle to state that Mr. Woodfall was consulted by him, with the utmost assiduity and confidence, in every difficult case, for the latter years of the valuable life of that most able and active magistrate.

The *Morning Post* could only add at this point (9 Nov.): "An Irish Gentleman observed, at the Turk's Head Coffee-house last night, that Mr. BURKE ought to be elected City *Remembrancer*, as there was no Gentleman who had so happy a knack of *remembering to forget* all his former patriotic positions and arguments." But Woodfall was now strongly supported by the *Public Advertiser*, which observed, for example, on 9 November: "CITY REMEMBRANCER./ We are pleased to find that the canvass goes on so successfully for a member whose pre-eminent qualifications lead us to believe that the scale of election will pre-ponderate in his favour. We are above any assertion, wearing the hue of com-pliment. We have not the happiness of knowing Mr. Woodfall; but his public services, private virtues, and exclusive elegibility, characterised by the concurrent testimony of public opinion, are so impressive, that we cannot resist the impulse of expressing our disinterested and most hearty wishes for his success."

Other newspapers remained at least hopeful. Letters in Woodfall's defense appeared frequently in the *Oracle*; and on 16 November the *Morning Chronicle* again spoke out: "Among the curious reasons assigned, why a certain office in the city should be filled by an Attorney, is, that though the salary is small, he has an opportunity of making it worth his while, by charging *fees for attendance* to his employers.—Pracy, in private life, would not a man prefer a steward or agent who would be content with the fair emolument of his situation, to one who professed an intention of making the most of him, by charging *fees* upon every occasion?" On 21 November the *Morning Chronicle* announced: "At this day's Court of Common Council, we understand, the vacancy of the office of City Remembrancer will be declared, and at a subsequent court the election will come on, by the event of which we shall be able to decide whether the Corpora-tion of London pays any regard to the merit of twenty-five years public service, in a situation the most laborious and difficult, that ever fell to the lot of an individual to fulfil." It seemed to readers, who were unacquainted with the situation, that the *Chronicle* was fighting on the wrong side. The *Chronicle*, which had no patience with such thinking, replied to one of them on 4 December with a bit of advice:

CITY REMEMBRANCER.

A correspondent observes that the Dissenters are justified in opposing Mr. WOODFALL, as a candidate for the office of City Remembrancer, because, however estimable in other respects, Mr. Woodfall, as the conductor of a newspaper, supported the present administration. To this, we answer that a great majority of the dissenters did long, and many of them do now, support the present adminis-tration; and therefore cannot honestly object to Mr. Woodfall's conduct similar to their own.

Mr. Woodfall's support of administration was always constitutional, liberal and manly—his exertions, whenever the repeal of the corporation and test acts was brought before parliament, as useful as they were extraordinary. Dissenters, in whose behalf he has so materially contributed to convince the public, that men ought not to be excluded from civil offices on account of their religious opinions, will act neither consistently nor gratefully, if they alledge his political opinions as a ground of exclusion from a civil office, the due execution of which, those opinions can neither promote nor impede.

Although the *Chronicle* could not say so, Woodfall's "political opinions" were actually those of the *Morning Chronicle*, and, in supporting his candidacy, it was only waging another battle against Pitt. The prospects were not very bright. On 5 December the *Chronicle* announced that fourteen members of the Company of Stationers were pledged to Woodfall, and on 9 December the *Oracle* indicated that success was assured: "Mr. WILLIAM WOODFALL, notwithstanding an opposition of the most bitter malignity, will undoubtedly be triumphant in his canvas for the office of *City-Remembrancer.*" The *Oracle* was always wrong.

On 12 December the Lord Mayor (Paul Le Mesurier), "21 Aldermen, almost the whole of the Commoners, the Recorder, and the Sheriffs" assembled at Guildhall, where they interviewed four candidates for the office of Remembrancer: "Mr. TYRREL, Mr. WOODFALL, Mr. ROBERTS, and Mr. NEWMAN." "Mr. NEWMAN resigned, Mr. TYRREL was silent, and Mr. WOODFALL," said the *Morning Post* (13 Dec.), "made a most beautiful and energetic speech, which rivetted the attention of the whole Court. He touched very pointedly upon the calumnies which had been circulated against him, under the pretext that he was not acquainted with legal proceedings; . . . he went through a variety of topics respecting Parliamentary custom and usage, in a most elegant and convincing stile./ Mr. ROBERTS made a very neat speech." The ballot for "Mr. TYRREL." was, however, 138, for Woodfall 95, and for Roberts 12. "It is with regret we state," the *Morning Post* added, "that Mr. WOODFALL has lost his Election for the Place of City Remembrancer. But he must feel some consolation in being convinced, that *merit* and *honourable conduct* are not always necessary toward the obtainment of City honours. Heretofore the place has been almost a sinecure; but Mr. WOODFALL has pointed out the duties of the Office to the City Sages, from which we hope that Mr. TYRREL will not depart." Woodfall's speech was printed by the *World* and the *Public Advertiser*, and the *Oracle* printed an additional speech, which he had delivered after the election. The *Oracle* also carried (13 Dec.) an advertisement in which Woodfall thanked everyone, especially the editors of newspapers, for their support and attributed his defeat to "Mr. TYRRELL's having long been a member of the Common Council and Chairman of the Committee of City Lands" and having heard of Roberts's death several hours before he did. Woodfall had perhaps expected to be defeated, for volumes of his Parliamentary debates had been advertised for some time.

Catastrophe at Dunkirk

On 28 August Lord Hood occupied Toulon, on 9 September the Duke of York was defeated at Dunkirk, and on 11 September the Austrians captured Quesnoy. On 25 September Poland came to terms with Prussia, on 26 September Britain signed a treaty with Portugal, and on 3 October the seventy-three imprisoned Girondists were proscribed by the French Convention. On 9 October France declared an embargo on British goods, on 13 October France issued a declaration of war against Genoa, and on 14 October Marie Antoinette was finally brought to trial. Readers learned of these developments slowly and imperfectly.

On 9 September the *Oracle* reported that the siege of Dunkirk had been abandoned; on 10 September it reported that it had not been abandoned; and on 12 September the earlier report was confirmed, the British having lost, it was estimated, three thousand men, the French six thousand. On 11 September the *True Briton* announced that the British had, however, occupied Toulon. The *Morning Chronicle* refused to believe it. "The wilful misrepresentation of the Treasury Prints on every subject," it said on 12 September,

> is matter of serious concern, for thus the public money is shamefully squandered, not in spreading the knowledge of useful truths, but in propagating the most pernicious falsehoods. They stated for instance, with the most unblushing effrontery, that the *Courier Universel* of the 1st September of which Lord ELGIN had transmitted an Extract to Ministers, had stated, "That the British fleet, under the command of Lord HOOD, upon an invitation from the inhabitants of Toulon, had sailed into that port, and taken possession of the town, as well as of all the ships of war in the harbour, amounting, besides frigates and other vessels, to *sixteen or eighteen sail of the line*." Now *we* had transmitted to us, by our vigilant and active Correspondents, the identical *Courier Universel* to which they ascribe this account, and no such article was contained in it: not a word was mentioned of Lord HOOD's fleet having entered the port of Toulon, much less of 16 or 18 sail of the line having fallen into his hands.

But this report was also confirmed. By 14 September the *Public Advertiser* had even calculated how much the capitulation would yield in prizes: "Lord Hood has already acquired . . . , by prize money, not less than seventy thousand pounds." On 17 September all newspapers published the proclamation of 26 August, in which Lord Hood promised that, inasmuch as "the Sections of Toulon have, by their Commissioners to me, made a solemn declaration in favour of Monarchy, have proclaimed Louis XVII. son of the late Louis XVI. their lawful King, and have sworn to acknowledge him, and no longer suffer the Despotism of the Tyrants which at this time govern France, but will do their utmost to establish Monarchy, as accepted by their late Sovereign in 1789," he would "take possession of Toulon, and hold it in trust only for Louis XVII. until Peace shall be re-established in France. . . ." On 20 September the *Sun* added, for the elucidation of its own readers, a "Plan of the Town and Harbour of Toulon," identifying the ships captured and their exact position at the time of the capture. On 17 September, too, the *World* scoffed at a report in *The Times*, which, "replete with rumours, yesterday stated the defeat of the Republican army in *La Vendée*, and that SANTERRE, the Paris Brewer, had been taken prisoner, and had been drawn to pieces by four *dray-horses*." In fact, however, news from La Vendée was encouraging. On 2 October the *Oracle* mentioned that the "principles of the Council" were "unmixed in favour of monarchy," the peasants also being "well effected to the cause of Royalty," and on 12 October it could report that the Royalists were "gaining advantages" daily.

Other news swung from extreme to extreme. On 13 September the *Oracle*, which purported to know more about the situation than any other paper, published a communication from "MILES," regretting that the British had not acted "in concert" with the Prince of Saxe-Coburg. Without replying to this observation, the *Oracle* stated that it was now impossible for the British to take Dunkirk before spring. The Prince of Saxe-Coburg could not help, and the Duke of York could not do it alone. The Duke was himself being called upon to help the Dutch, and he was "in no condition to afford" even that assistance. He had lost the whole *"batting train* of HEAVY CANNON" to the French, the 42nd and 57th regiments, which had been promised to him, had been "driven back to Portsmouth, and the 78th has not yet left Deal." In addition, said the *Oracle*, the *"damps* about this time begin to rise from the unwholesome soil of *Dunkirk*, and will render it impossible for any Army now to set down before it. The whole enterprise should seem badly concerted. Either the communications were not exact between Government and the DUKE of YORK, or the marine force intended to co-operate with his Royal Highness has been blamefully retarded." While the *Oracle* was pondering this situation, the *True Briton* announced (16 Sept.) that Stanislaus Augustus, King of Poland, had been assassinated by Poninski, one of the deputies, but the story was subsequently retracted. As the *World* put it on 17 September: "The TRUE BRITON apparently killed the King of Poland yesterday morning, without any other cause than that of giving the SUN an opportunity of reviving the unfortunate Monarch in the evening."

By this time the Duke of York had, said the *Oracle* (17 Sept.), retreated to Dixmude and would probably retreat further, since he was in danger of being cut off from the Prince of Saxe-Coburg. He had also requested that the cavalry be recalled and the infantry be sent in its place, the country being extremely swampy. On 19 September the *Oracle* reported an additional retreat; the army was now expected to go into winter quarters shortly, at which time the Duke of York would return to London. This report was revised on 20 September, when the *Oracle* announced that the Prince of Saxe-Coburg was joining the Duke of York after all, that the armies would be combined, and that this "formidable striking force" would again attack Dunkirk. Unfortunately, the *Oracle* added, it would get no assistance from "the Prussians or the Army of the Rhine," both being totally inactive. This report was itself revised on 21 September, when the *Oracle* announced excitedly that the Austrians had captured the whole of French Flanders and that Brest had offered to capitulate on the same terms as Toulon. Similar announcements had evidently appeared in other newspapers, for on 23 September the *Morning Post* noticed that the "Gazette in this day's paper falls far short of the stock-jobbing reports which have prevailed for the last week. As to the 1500 French said to have been drowned in the River Lys, the Gazette is totally silent. The whole affair seems nothing more than a trifling skirmish, though magnified by our Stock-jobbers, into an important contest, in which the Allies had had a decisive victory." By this time the *Oracle* was gloomy indeed, being even uncertain as to "the issue of the present War on the Continent." On 2 October the Duke of York's army was understood to be in Menin, but another retreat, said the *Oracle*, was in contemplation. There was also bad news from the West Indies, where soldiers were dying by the hundreds from the ravages of disease. These reports continued throughout October and November, and on 12 October the *True Briton* announced that "LA FAYETTE lately died in his Prison at *Magdeburg*." Although Lafayette was still a hero to the Opposition papers, he was no hero to the *Oracle*, which remarked on 14 October: "Many have expressed the most anxious solicite for the fate of LA FAYETTE, who yet are not in the practice of mourning the heroes of the FRENCH REVOLUTION.—His case is suspected to have had something peculiarly hard—and he falls a seeming Martyr to the jealousy of Sovereigns. It will one day be clearly manifest that this man was at the bottom of every cabal in the early stage of the Revolution, and that to him alone is owing the unhappy LOUIS, expired by the *guillotine*." Lafayette was in fact still alive.

At least as interesting as developments on the Continent were developments at home, for, having been assured that Dunkirk was so crucial that its capture would practically conclude the war, readers were not to be persuaded that the capitulation of Toulon was after all more important. Since, in addition to justifying the necessity of the war, he would now have to justify its conduct, Pitt, no newspaper doubted, was in trouble. Even before the Dunkirk disaster, the Ministerial papers were indicating that he might not after all ask for an increase in taxes, but might continue to finance the war by loans. The Opposition newspapers had responded by stressing the effects of the war on the economy. "EIGHT HUNDRED AND SEVENTY-THREE is the exact number of *Commissions of Bankruptcy* which have appeared in the London Gazette, from the first of January to the last day of July. Many of the firms consisted of from two to five partners," said the *Morning Chronicle* on 26 August. Although the number dropped during August and September, unemployment, which was the concern of the *Morning Post*, increased. More loans also meant a rise in the national debt, and on 10 September *The Times* replied to quibblings on this score with the pronouncement: "If the NATIONAL DEBT be an immense pyramid, whose shadow darkens the whole land, as Mr. SHERIDAN expressed himself in the House of Commons, it is a pyramid, whose substance is one of the greatest bulwarks to the existence of our present happy Constitution. It is a BOND, with *Warrant of Attorney, to confess judgment,* given by the People, to secure allegiance to Monarchy, and preservation to MAGNA CHARTA. And they well know, that wherever a rebellion shall prevent the State from paying the interest, the principal is lost for ever. We have an instance of it in France, and that country is of course ruined."

On 12 September the newspapers confirmed the defeat of the Duke of York, and on the same day the *Oracle* reported that "Lord LAUDERDALE yesterday presented to the KING a petition from the City of Glasgow, signed by upwards of 40,000 persons, intreating His MAJESTY to put an end to the War." The newspapers were too stunned by the news of Dunkirk to react to either report until 13 September, when the *Morning Post* at least commented on that subject. "TWELVE million is the sum Mr. PITT will ask of the Country next Session, to carry on a war suggested by Mr. BURKE, and espoused, for what reason we know not, by the Minister," it remarked grimly. But this time it also had something to say of "The Minister": "Mr. PITT is certainly establishing his claim to the title so long bestowed on him of a *Heav'n-born Minister*; for, from the commencement of this war, to the present moment, he has trusted the security of possessions, trade, &c. to Heaven alone; directing the whole of our force, both by land and sea, to the support of our Allies, in the prosecution of their just and equitable pursuits." Rumors of changes in the Administration were now rampant. The *Oracle* had understood that the person who was to be held "blamefully" responsible for "the whole enterprise" was the First Lord of the Admiralty, the Earl of Chatham; the *Gazetteer* had understood that responsibility would be diverted to Dundas. Hence Lord Chatham would not be dismissed, it said, but Sir Gilbert Elliot would probably "be called from the line of *Alarmists*" to replace Addington as Speaker, and Addington would then replace Dundas as Home Secretary. Both suppositions were wrong.

On 14 September the Ministerial *Public Advertiser* condemned, oddly enough, the treatment of soldiers, especially in Ireland, where the "horrid practice of houghing [hamstringing] is not yet banished. . . . At Bandon, in that kingdom, a soldier of the light dragoons, quartered there, has been lately houghed in a very shocking manner." The *Sun* was meanwhile advising its readers to ignore the Glasgow petition: "The *forty thousand names* appending to a Scotch petition lately presented by a *Patriotic* Earl . . . are not all of *Glasgow*—the greater part of them live in *Air.*" On 16 September the *Public Advertiser* mentioned that Prince Adolphus had returned on 12 September from "the British Camp before Dunkirk," having been wounded during the siege. This announcement was followed by high praise of him and a disparaging reference to one of his brothers. "The Duke of Clarence," said the *Advertiser*, "enjoys domestic happiness with all its charms at Petersham; Mrs. Jordan's daughters are with him, and live in such easy state of familiarity that when speaking to or of his Royal Highness, they call him papa, and papa Clarence." The *Morning Chronicle* was preoccupied with the cause of the Dunkirk debacle:

> It was reported on Saturday [14 Sept.], and generally believed, that the Duke of RICHMOND had resigned the office of Master General of the Ordnance. The formalities usual on such occasions may be gone through a day or two sooner or later, but since the news of the retreat from Dunkirk arrived, the event has been considered as certain.
>
> Respecting the cause of the failure of the expedition against Dunkirk, there is but one opinion: that it was solely owing to the want of proper support, from the Ordnance and Admiralty Departments.
>
> The Duke of RICHMOND is not a man to retire from office in quiet. He will endeavour to prove, that the fault lay not with him; and this he can hardly do, without proving that it lies with somebody else. He will conduct his own defense; but who is to conduct that of the Admiralty, is yet a secret. The discussion, if not very useful, will be entertaining. In the course of it, the public will expect information on various knotty points; particularly, why the ordnance, ammunition and gun-boats, known to be necessary for the siege of Dunkirk, never stirred from the river Thames, till the Duke of YORK encamped before the town.
>
> When the army retreated from Dunkirk there was not time to spike the heavy cannon, nor to throw the stores and ammunition into the canals. The whole was left to be taken possession of by the French, in a state fit for immediate service.
> . . .

Although the Duke of Richmond had not previously been mentioned, the *Chronicle*'s suggestion that he was at least as culpable as the Earl of Chatham and considerably more expendible, Lord Chatham being Pitt's brother, was eagerly seized upon by the *Oracle*. The infantry should indeed have been sent instead of the cavalry, it said on 17 September, the Duke of Richmond had been responsible for the blunder, and rumors of his resignation were therefore probably accurate. The *World* withheld judgment. "The Opposition wish much for the resignation of the Duke of RICHMOND, whilst he very naturally wishes to retain his official situation," it observed.

By 18 September the Duke of Richmond was regarded by all Ministerial papers as the perfect scapegoat. The possibility of a debate between him and a representative of Lord Chatham was no longer hinted at, the only question being whether he would resign or have to be dismissed. The *Public Advertiser* liked to think that he had already resigned:

> It was on Monday [16 Sept.] generally reported, that the Duke of Richmond had resigned his post as Master-General of the Ordnance, in which he is to be succeeded by Lord Amherst.

The Duke of Richmond, it may be remarked, has not been at any of the Cabinet Meetings for some time; but this may be accounted for by his necessary attention to his duty in camp. How far, therefore, the above report is well founded, we will not take upon ourselves to determine. . . .

To those who love to look on the dark side of affairs, the late motions of the Duke of YORK afford matter of lamentation; and it is whispered that a certain *Noble Duke* is about to resign his office, on account of the failures attributed to him in that department, and which, it is said, have distressed our troops on the Continent. This report is not however very probable. . . .

"Such it seems is the late unpopularity of the Duke of RICHMOND at Woolwich," said the *Oracle*, "that when his resignation was spoken of as certain there last Friday, most of the people employed in the Warren testified their gladness by shouting and other demonstrations of rejoicing." By this time (18 Sept.), the *Oracle* certainly understood that he had been dismissed and that there had been numerous other alterations:

CHANGE IN THE MINISTRY.

We do not attempt to pledge our credit for the truth of the reports which were yesterday circulated about the Court, but merely state them as the rumours of the day.

The Duke of RICHMOND had scarcely returned, it appears, to meditate upon his late cool reception at St. James's, when a formal notice was communicated, that his services could be dispensed with.

The Marquis CORNWALLIS upon his return from *India*, will, it is expected, be appointed Master General of the Ordnance, and Lord AMHERST in the mean time has been prevailed upon to occupy that important station.

The Marquis of STAFFORD, who has never been supposed to be reconciled to the Ministry since Lord Thurlow's resignation of the Seals, has also quitted the Board.

Lord CAMDEN, whose ill-health has for some time deprived him of his usual attendance at the Cabinet Councils, but who has earnestly wished to name his successor, has seceded without accomplishing his intention.

Lord CHATHAM, finding his station irksome also at the Board of Admiralty, during this important crisis, exchanges for one of the places vacated by Lord CAMDEN and the Marquis of STAFFORD.

Lord HOOD is to succeed Lord CHATHAM at the head of the Admiralty Board; so Opposition will no longer have to complain of inexperience or insufficiency for that peculiar trust.

Lord ELGIN is recalled from the Court of Vienna, and Lord AUCKLAND mentioned as his successor.

Sir GILBERT ELLIOTT and Lord MALMESBURY have constantly attended the conferences lately held at the house of Mr. DUNDAS. Mr. ADDINGTON, however, seems unwilling to vacate the Speaker's Chair for the troublesome charge of Secretary of State; and therefore Sir GILBERT ELLIOTT will be otherwise provided for.

The Oracle was correct in almost no particular. Whenever the Ministerial newspapers demanded anyone's resignation, his die was cast, or it had been cast on all previous occasions, but the Duke of Richmond was obviously a special case. In 1789 he had strongly supported the Queen and William Pitt against the Princes; and his nephew, Colonel Charles Lennox, had even fought a duel with the Duke of York before the matter was settled. He was no favorite, therefore, of the Duke of York, and the Duke of York had evidently won over the King, but he still had an ally of sorts in Pitt and the Queen. Pitt had no objection, it appeared, to demanding his resignation through the newspapers, but, if the Duke refused to comply with the demands, no one knew what Pitt would do. On 19 September the *World* stated that Pitt could not in any event face Parliament until Dunkirk was in British hands, and it is consequently "supposed," it said, that "the SESSION of PARLIAMENT will commence shortly after the close of the CAMPAIGN. . . . The Duke of RICHMOND," it added, "*certainly has not* resigned his situation." The *Public Advertiser* understood otherwise. "The Duke of Richmond has resigned the office of Master-General of the Ordnance, the business of which will be transacted by Lord Amherst, till the arrival of Marquis Cornwallis, when it will be offered to the latter Nobleman," it said. "His Grace's first offer of resignation was made on Wednesday last [11 Sept.], but was not then accepted; a second application, made in writing, on Saturday [14 Sept.], was more earnest, and his Grace is now preparing to leave his department, as soon as his papers can be ready for delivery to a successor." By 20 September the *Oracle* was inclined to shift responsibility to the Dutch, the situation respecting the Duke of Richmond having reached a stalemate. As it explained matters to its readers, a "private communication through the medium of PRINCE ADOLPHUS, from the Duke of YORK to His MAJESTY, concerning the late failure of the expedition against *Dunkirk*, caused the recent *cool* reception of the Duke of RICHMOND at St. James's"; but the Duke of Richmond had refused to take the hint: he was "determined to remain in power, and to enjoy the emoluments and influence annexed to the very active situation of Master General of the Ordnance." The *Morning Post*, which hated defectors, was still blaming the Duke of Richmond and in addition Lord Loughborough, who, it now understood, had planned the campaign in the first place. On 23 September it reported that the Duke of Richmond had at least quit: "The Duke of RICHMOND has given in his resignation, in writing, to the KING—so that he now ceases to be Master-General of the Ordnance; at the same time, that he will attend occasionally at the Board, until his successor is officially announced." But the Duke of Richmond was only one of the culprits, said the *Post*, and the "arrival of Sir JAMES MURRAY from the Duke of YORK's army, is for the purpose of giving his opinion as to the cause of the failure of the British forces ordered against Dunkirk. The Public call for a full and impartial investigation of the business, and on the information of Sir JAMES, will be founded such future proceedings as may be deemed necessary, against those who are accounted culpable."

Although there had been considerable disagreement as to what the Duke of Richmond had done or might do, there had been no disagreement as to what he ought to do, but on 21 September the Ministerial newspapers rose generally to his defense. It now seemed to them that he was completely innocent and that he had been simply the victim of an Opposition plot. As the *World* put it: "The Duke of RICHMOND will now perhaps experience a temporary suspension of hostilities from Opposition, but they will soon be renewed, when they find that his Grace, though retiring from Office, means still to give his warmest support to the present Administration." On 23 September the *World* amended this state-, ment, since it now appeared that the Duke of Richmond had not "retired": "The Duke of RICHMOND, who the ignorant prints have dismissed from the Ordnance Department, yesterday transacted official business of high importance with Mr. PITT, at his House in Downing-Street." The *Oracle*, always concerned for Dundas, was making it very clear that, if Dundas was replaced, as he probably would be, the replacement would have nothing to do with Dunkirk:

> Mr. ADDINGTON, in his high Office of SPEAKER of the House of Commons, has acquitted himself so satisfactorily to both sides of the House, that there is no likelihood of his being superseded under any Administration; whereas the Office of Secretary of State, with all its patronage, is at all times precarious.
>
> Sir GILBERT ELLIOT, if proposed as SPEAKER, will be unanimously elected. The *Phalanx* could not oppose the nomination, they having twice proposed him in opposition to Mr. ADDINGTON, and at each time Mr. FOX bestowed upon him the most boundless panegyrics.
>
> Lord MANSFIELD is amongst the number of Candidates spoken of to succeed Mr. DUNDAS as SECRETARY of STATE.
>
> Whoever may be the new SECRETARY of STATE, we understand it to be settled that Mr. DUNDAS is not to meet the Parliament in that capacity.
>
> The patronage of the Home SECRETARY of STATE, is far greater than that of any other Minister; but it is generally suspected, that another great Officer of State always makes a point of, at least, *going his halves.*

On 25 September the *Oracle* repeated that, although the salary of the Speaker was £6,000 a year, the Speaker had no patronage, whereas the patronage of the Home Secretary was enormous. As to Dunkirk, the *Oracle* added: "A Letter is said to have been received by a GREAT PERSONAGE, from the Continent, complaining in the most bitter terms of a certain PEER. If the relation we have some reason to credit be veritable, the feelings of an illustrious HERO are so wounded by disappointment, that a *personal* call is likely to be made for *explanation*, when he shall return to this Country." The *Oracle* would not say positively that the Duke of Richmond was at fault, for, in its own opinion, the Dutch might have saved the day and did not. The Duke was himself having trouble on another account, for on 24 September the *World* reported: "The *rear* of Brighton Camp has been attacked by a great body of Prostitutes from London, who have threatened to *consume* the whole force; the neighbouring Magistrates, however brought their *authority* in time to the assistance of the Men and Officers, and took about 25 prisoners, and ordered them to Horsham Strong House to *temper* hemp." *Lloyd's Evening Post* hastened to add (25 Sept.) that, when this particular attack occurred, the Prince of Wales was in London. On 25 September the *Morning Chronicle* again challenged the Duke of Richmond: "If you have the spirit of a man, step forward and explain the mystery [of Dunkirk], let us know where the fault lies; your silence will be interpreted as a mark of your guilt. . . . In justice to a gallant army which has been deceived, and to a generous people who have been injured, an investigation into this affair shall be made." The Duke of Richmond was silent.

On 26 September, according to the *Oracle* (27 Sept.), Lord Hood, Sir Gilbert Elliot, and Major Charles O'Hara were appointed Commissioners for the port of Toulon and would "superintend and manage its concerns" henceforth, in accordance with the promises made in Lord Hood's declaration of 26 August. The "concerns" had previously been managed by Baron Mulgrave, to whom Lord Hood had turned over command of the garrison in early September. Several newspapers understood that Sir Gilbert Elliot had also been appointed Clerk of the Privy Council vice "Mr. Fawkener, who retires on a pension," but this rumor was subsequently (30 Sept.) corrected by the *Morning Chronicle*. "Sir GILBERT ELLIOT is not appointed Clerk of the Privy Council," it told its readers. "He is sworn a Member of the Privy Council, and goes out Commissioner to Toulon; but the reward of his new lights, although undoubtedly settled, for Sir GILBERT is a prudent man, is not yet made public."

Although the Opposition papers had expressed horror at the way the war was being conducted, their real concern was to force the Government into negotiations, which would end it altogether. On 11 September Lord Lauderdale had presented to the King the Glasgow petition for peace. This fact had not been widely publicized at the time, but the *Morning Post* had supported it with further abuse of Burke. It was backed of course by the *World*, which could not forget that Burke was responsible for the prosecution of Hastings. "Mr. BURKE is preparing a closing Speech against Mr. HASTINGS," the *World* had observed characteristically on 28 August. "Will the common voice of the country keep him from being vulgar and violent!" The *Post* was also backed by the other Opposition papers, which could not forget that Burke was an apostate. "Mr. BURKE, speaking of his political sentiments, says, 'They come from one, who wishes to preserve *consistence*; but who would preserve consistence by varying means to secure *the Unity of his End*'—a pension," remarked the *Gazetteer* on 11 September. "A Dramatic Writer has offered, it is said, to purchase all Mr. BURKE's *Plots*; and a Country Tragedian is in treaty for his *Dagger*." But the *Morning Post*'s purpose was to hold Burke exclusively responsible for the war, thus exonerating Pitt, who would be free to negotiate a peace. From 12 September on, this purpose was the *Post*'s *raison d'être*. Every number of the paper hammered at

Burke, with special reference to his dagger and to his contempt for the "swinish multitude."

On 18 September the *Morning Chronicle* announced that, "Ministers" having not seen fit to print the text of the Glasgow petition in their *Gazette*, it was itself printing it at the request of Lord Lauderdale, and on 19 September the petition was also printed by the *Morning Post* and the *Oracle*. The *Morning Post* could further report that the King had reacted favorably, whereas, the *Post* added on 20 September: "Mr. BURKE does not feel that reception at Court which he expected. He has, by his exaggerations, and much foul language, precipitated this Country into the War, which can never terminate as long as his doctrines are approved of, that it is impossible for the People to negociate with the present men who hold the Reins of Government in France." Except for one or two outbursts, the Ministerial papers had ignored the petition, but on 21 September several of them opened fire on Lord Lauderdale. "Lord L. is now busy, not in drawing up *manufacturing petitions*, but in writing a PETITION of a more serious nature to the *French Convention*, not to include *his property* in their late *marauding decree!*" said the *World*. "Lord L. is gone into *deep mourning* at the Convention decree of the 7th instant, *which forfeits all English property . . . in France!*"

The King's feeling about the war had actually not been indicated, but it did seem clear that the Duke of York blamed the Duke of Richmond for the Dunkirk disaster and that, to the King's annoyance, Pitt was refusing to dismiss him. On 21 September the *Oracle* stated that the King was also uneasy about Pitt's treatment of the Duke of Clarence, and the "reason why his ROYAL HIGHNESS of CLARENCE is not now at sea," the *Oracle* went on, "is said to be his declaration in the House of Lords, that he considered the War no longer necessary." Pitt was making him pay for this "declaration." The *World* was meanwhile (21 Sept.) assuring its readers that the Duke of Clarence had been treated very well: "The Duke of CLARENCE, being elected a Member of the Board of Agriculture, is constantly humming the Ballad—/ 'I that once was a SAILOR a PLOUGHMAN am now.'" The *Morning Post* was still demanding to know why the country was fighting. "We are to have innumerable taxes next year, but what does this signify?" the *Post* asked on 24 September. "Mr. PITT will declare, that we are able to bear them again and again; and REEVES, and his Associators, will of course assure us, that it would be *treason* to deny his assertion." Reeves was himself no longer in the country, having gone "to *Lisbon*," said the *Oracle* on 21 September, "for the recovery of his health." On 24 September the *World* exploded. "The Opposition writers are perpetually calling upon the friends of Administration, to state the specific object of the present War," it said with exasperation. "If the war had been commenced by this country, perhaps the question might be properly asked; but when it is recollected that we are carrying on a defensive war, that is, one in which our adversaries were the aggressors, our only object must be, by our exertions to force the enemy into such a peace as may give us 'indemnity for the past and security for the future.'"

The *World* was also weary of the incessant talk about the economy. "Mr. WYNDHAM has been challenged to explain the meaning of his declamation, when he said, 'Perish the Commerce of this Country if it must perish, but let the Constitution live,'" it noted on 28 September. "We doubt not, but if Mr. WYNDHAM was pleased to satisfy these pamphleteering champions, he could very readily do it, and foil them with their own weapons." But "Mr. WYNDHAM" had indicated no inclination to do so.

Matters of this sort did not trouble William Pitt, but the defeat at Dunkirk was evidently telling, for on 28 September the *Morning Chronicle* reported that he was resorting to "a fresh POLITICAL INTRIGUE." For once, the intrigue did not involve Edmund Burke. As the *Chronicle* explained the situation, the alarms of the previous December had "produced, as it is well known, a schism in the party of Opposition. With some, the eagerness for places, exemplified in the instances of Lord LOUGHBOROUGH and those connected with him; with others an honest, although . . . mistaken apprehension of the prevalence of levelling doctrines, operated so powerfully, as in a great measure to destroy that combination of men. . . ." But the "consequences of this disunion" had "far from equalled Mr. PITT's expectations," for Fox had not been won over, and "others of the Rockingham party" had supported Government policies without supporting the Government. Pitt was therefore attempting "*to get a sanction to his own personal power, and those principles on which he obtained it, from the Members of the old* ROCKINGHAM PARTY, *by persuading them to quit* Mr. Fox *entirely, and accept of responsible situations under him*"; and the "means by which he is endeavouring to accomplish [this object]," the *Chronicle* went on, are

worthy of his education. Aware that upon the general principle of the war with France, as it stood at the time of its declaration by the Convention in February last, the Dukes of PORTLAND and DEVONSHIRE, Earl FITZWILLIAM, and others of the Rockingham Party, concurred in an opinion of its necessity, and consequently, in order to give it a fair support, suspended their concert against his administration, aware too, of the success of his ALARM of last year, he is now once more plotting a stratagem by which he hopes to extort from their terrors what it would be desperate to solicit from their approbation.

In order to effect this, certain persons who condescend to act as his agents, are commissioned to convey to those quarters where they hope it will have its effects, "Mr. PITT's *great reluctance* to go on with this war; the innumerable difficulties which daily rise up against the execution of any decisive and vigorous plan for its termination, his readiness to concur *in any plan* which those persons . . . may suggest, but that for this purpose it is absolutely necessary that they should act in concert with him, and add the sanction of their characters to that of their opinions." These *go-betweens* are then told to dwell upon "the little temptation which Mr. PITT has to continue the war upon other terms—that the Whig families are risquing the whole of the good their co-operation with him last year has effected, by a conduct which has the appearance of a sulky jealousy of his views, and which in the country at large has the effect of discrediting the conductors of the war, and through them the war itself." They are then instructed to paint in the strongest colours "the encreasing strength of Opposition by such an accession of public opinion;—the probability that in time large bodies of individuals may assemble to petition against the war,—that those bodies, influenced by *Jacobin emissaries*, may connect questions of domestick policy with these petitions—that they may think again of PARLIAMENTARY REFORM, and thus, all the mischief of French principles again be brought into a most dangerous activity. That in this event, those who from principles have always opposed Parliamentary Reform, will recollect that Mr. Pitt always on principle approved it; . . . that something is due to *his own* consistency and character, and that it cannot be expected he will continue separating himself more and more from his old friends, the mob, unless the remaining members of the Whig Party (Mr. Fox excepted) shall agree cordially to unite in the only way in which their union can be useful to him, . . . namely, by taking offices."

> Such, the public may depend upon it, is the language of the present day; and part of the plot is already commenced in the appointment of Sir GILBERT ELLIOTT. This Gentleman, although not an original connection of Lord ROCKINGHAM, was long very intimately confided in by the chiefs of the Whig Party. From Sir GILBERT to Mr. BURKE, from Mr. BURKE to Mr. WINDHAM, a similarity of views and wishes, arising from a similarity in their ways of thinking, is easily reciprocated. Mr. WINDHAM once caught in this snare, the rest, it is hoped by these hucksters in political morality, will follow of course. The line of defence will be broken, and Mr. PITT at the head of his barbarous invaders, trample down at once all that remains of public principle and private honour, to this distracted country.

In short, Pitt was threatening to support reform unless the "Constitutionalists" took office; he was threatening to negotiate a peace unless the warmongers took office.

First Alarm of an Invasion

Although only the *Morning Post* took Pitt's threats seriously, no newspaper knew what effect they would have on the Duke of Portland and his friends. The *Morning Chronicle* did what it could by impugning the principles of every new appointee. Since there were now constant changes in the diplomatic personnel and numerous promotions in the military services, much of its comment had to do with those matters; and, in the case of Dr. Samuel Horsley, it was anticipated (30 Sept.) by the *Public Advertiser*. Bishop Horsley, a long-time foe of Dr. Priestley and a zealous supporter of the war, was being transferred from the see of St. David's to the see of Rochester and the Deanery of Westminster. It was also assisted by other newspapers, the *World* and the *Gazetteer* reporting on 3 October that "Sir GILBERT ELLIOT, it is understood, is to have a salary of 5000*l.* a year, during his mission, at Toulon; besides all incidental expences," and the *Oracle* mentioning on 5 October that "Lord HOOD is expected to be created a British Peer, which must of course produce a new Election for Westminster. Mr. TOOKE is pledged to become a candidate. We have not heard any person yet mentioned to stand on the Ministerial interest." According to the *Public Advertiser* of 2 October, "the expences of the last Westminster election" had not yet been settled, the "trial between Lord Hood and Mr. Horne Tooke" being currently scheduled "to come on next Term." On 13 October the subject was Lord Hawkesbury, who, said the *Gazetteer*, "boasts of doing all the business of the Board of Trade *for nothing*, but, besides his emolument as Chancellor of the Dutchy of Lancaster, has a *snug* place in the customs, which produces him a *clear thousand* per quarter, though the salary is put down in the *Red Book* at 750*l.* per annum! The business is done by Deputy."

The *Morning Post* was convinced that Pitt would act on his threats, and, to enable him to do so, it redoubled its attacks on Burke, whose hysterics had supposedly been Pitt's undoing. "Mr. BURKE," it said on 28 September, "who, some sessions ago, was not able to find France upon the map, in the ensuing Session, will probably be much puzzled to point out the situation of Poland"; and on 30 September: "Mr. BURKE generally makes it a practice after dinner, to recite *Satan*'s Soliloquy to his guests—/ 'My voice is still for War,' &c." On this occasion it was supported by the *Morning Chronicle*, which observed (30 Sept.): "Mr. BURKE, the determined advocate of monarchy, is at present employed in drawing a comparison between the conduct of the French in Brabant, and that of the EMPRESS of RUSSIA in Poland, in order to prove the inseparable connection between the exercise of royalty and the possessors of every virtue, so that the same actions which in a Republic are stigmatized as oppressive and cruel, in a Sovereign assume the character of justice and clemency: *such is the influence of imbred royalty!*" On 2 October it was further supported by the *Gazetteer*, which told its readers: "Mr. Burke declared, that he thought French *opinions* ten times more dangerous than their *swords*: the Dutch troops seem to think quite the *reverse!*" On 5 October the *Oracle* protested that "Mr. BURKE is now deservedly a favourite with the *Sovereign*. It is our firm belief that to his BOOK the present *security* of our system may be attributed"; and on 8 October: "On Friday [4 Oct.] Sir GILBERT ELLIOT and Mr. BURKE dined with the MINISTER at Mr. DUNDAS's at Wimbledon. Mr. BURKE, we are told, was more than usually facetious after dinner. Every one knows his happy talent at description, and few men are so richly endowed with that fund of humour and genius, which are the charm of society." The *Morning Post* had not given up. "When Mr. BURKE, the Calumniator of the *Swinish* Multitude, hears that the Hessians all escaped in the last engagement, he will be apt to say, with the Prince of HESSE, that '*he has brought his pigs to a bad Market,*'" it observed on 7 October. "Mr. BURKE," it added on 11 October, "has been much complained of for his abusive language against Opposition; but Opposition considers that his tongue is no slander, for experience has taught the nation, that when he curses the one side, he means no ill; and when he blesses the other side, he means no good." On 18 October the *Post* remarked that "Mr. BURKE must feel happy, now that the Bishop of TOULON has been restored to his Functions, and is suffered to say HIGH MASS, without interruption from the *Sans Culottes*. . . . According to the doctrines of Mr. BURKE," it went on, "the Jews are the only people who alone should suggest any alteration in the Constitution; for when he abused the People of England, he could not have meant to include the Jews among *the Swinish Multitude*. . . . Mr. BURKE," it said finally, "was to have succeeded Lord HOBART, as Secretary to the LORD LIEUTENANT of Ireland, but that the trial of Mr. Hastings required his attendance in this kingdom. He was also, after his labours had been concluded there, to have been called up to the Irish House of Peers, by the title of Lord CONNAUGHT." The *World*, which still had strong feelings about this trial, had begun on 8 October a serialized account of it, based on paragraphs which it had itself published during the years; and on 17 October it advertised a two-volume work, entitled *The Trial of Warren Hastings, Esq. from February 1788, to June 1793, with a Preface.* On 12 October it had concluded a long account of the proceedings with a summary of the changes in the House of Lords since the trial began:

Total Peers dead, or Scots Peers in the last, but not in this Parliament   65
Total Creations, new Bishops, and new Scots Peers   31
Total Peers succeeding by descent   30

Total Changes since the Impeachment   126.

In addition to being represented as the archfoe of peace, Burke was also represented as the archfoe of reform; and reform, owing in part to the Government and The Association, was still a much-publicized issue. "Mr. BOWLES, in a late publication, declares without reserve, for the old Government of France; expecting no great difficulty to form, among his new emigrant friends, associations similar to that of the Crown and Anchor, of which, it is said, he was the original projector," the *Gazetteer* had remarked on 16 August. Talkers and booksellers were still being tried in the Provinces, although, as the *Morning Post* had protested on 26 August, the trials were becoming increasingly farcical:

> Nothing is a stronger proof of the contrariety of the sentiments of the People of England, than the result of the various trials in the different parts of the country for Libels. In one county, what is deemed a crime of the blackest nature, in another is not considered an offence. Men who have been tried for the publication of PAINE's book, have been acquitted, while others are pronounced guilty, and punished with fines, and others with confinement from three to twelve and eighteen months. The consequence of this is, that it has perverted the minds of Englishmen with regard to a trial by Jury, as the inference they draw from such proceedings is, that a retrospect is taken of a man's conduct, when put on his trial for a simple offence, and he is punished for other *reputed* crimes, without the power of calling Witnesses, that even with respect to these would establish his innocence.

There had been two new arrests in London. On 12 September the *Morning Post* had advertised *Treachery No Crime; or, The System of Courts. Exemplified in the Life of General Dumourier. By The Author of "The Jockey-Club,"* published by Symonds and Ridgway: "First Year of our Imprisonment." The author, although not identified, was Charles Pigott; and on 3 October the *Oracle* mentioned that "Mr. PIGGOTT, *commonly called* LOUSE, and a Mr. [William] HUDSON [actually Hodgson] were arrested Monday [30 Sept.] at the London Coffee-House, Ludgate Hill, for drinking seditious toasts" and had been examined at Guildhall the following day. On 5 October it noted that the two had been admitted to bail, each in the amount of £500, their sureties in the amount of £250; and on 8 October it reported that they "seem to think it hard that securities, which they think of a very considerable amount, should be demanded of them in consequence of their being *gentlemen*." Both of them were Irish, and, since the *Oracle* had never heard of "Hudson," he, it supposed, was a recent arrival.

All reformers could count on the support of the *Morning Post*. "The motto of the Treasury Print [the *True Briton*], *Nolumus Leges Angliae mutari*, is a direct censure upon the Legislature of this Country, who are every Session employed in endeavouring to amend, by *altering the Laws* of this Realm," it declared on 3 September; and on 27 September it had some words of advice for the mighty generally:

NECESSARY RECOLLECTIONS.

The insolent in office should *recollect*, that they were paid, and supported, by the very People they keep waiting unnecessarily, and treat rudely and disrespectfully.

The *Oppressor* should *recollect*, that he may one day lie at the mercy of the *Oppressed*.

The enemies of PAINE's writings should *recollect*, that they cannot *refute* them.

Mr. REEVES, and the Association Gentlemen, should *recollect*, it is easy to see that they want to support the system of corruption, which *supports them*, and that they cannot bear the truth.

People of title should *recollect*, that none but fools and knaves bow to them, and that all surreptitious distinctions, are derogatory to the dignity of human nature.

Placemen and Pensioners should *recollect*, that they are *Paupers upon the Public*, and that the blood and sweat of millions is expected to support their depravities.

Priests of all sorts should *recollect*, that true Religion wants neither flattery, mystery, nor ostentation.

Kings and Princes, on the Continent, should *recollect*, that the People pay and *maintain them*, to be their guardians and protectors, and not to *traffic* in their flesh and blood.

Prosecutors should *recollect*, that truth is none the *less so* for being prosecuted and persecuted, and that it will *spread* in proportion as these are exercised.

The People should *recollect* and *think* for themselves; and that when they do not, they are the worst of Slaves.

"The People" had not responded with as much enthusiasm as the *Morning Post* hoped. On 10 September the *Post* had announced: "The London Corresponding Society consists of about nine hundred Members, five hundred of whom are constant attendants. They are all men of property and respectability, and it is not a little flattering to the Duke of RICHMOND and Mr. PITT, that they so far approve of their measures formerly at the Thatched House, that they have adopted them, and will no doubt, for consistency's sake, expect to be supported by those two great leaders, when the Society shall petition the Senate for a Parliamentary Reform." On 20 September it had further announced: "The London Corresponding Society augment daily in numbers. No less than three hundred members offered themselves since their last Meeting, all of whom have been accepted. Their Petition for a Parliamentary Reform has now some thousand signatures." But such statements were probably intended as threats, for the *Post* was still infuriated with Saunderson for having barred the Corresponding Society from the Globe Tavern.

No other newspaper mentioned the petition or any other English reform activities during this period, and, although there were riots in Bristol, they had nothing to do with suffrage. The issue there was "the propriety of again letting the Bridge Toll." "The Proprietors" of the Bristol bridge had promised, said the *Star* (4 Oct.), that the toll would be discontinued as soon as the expenses of building the bridge had been defrayed, but, with the blessing of the Corporation, they decided instead to extend it. On the morning of 28 September, a mob assembled to "cut the tollgate to pieces and drive out the keepers." The gate was repaired, the keepers reinstated, and the mob, now consisting of several thousand people, burned the gate to the ground, swearing "vengeance" this time on anyone who attempted to interfere. According to the *Oracle* (3 Oct.), which was trying to minimize the gravity of the situation, the Riot Act was read, bells were rung, drums were beaten, and everything was done to persuade the mob to disperse. But there was no way of settling the matter peacefully, for "many people had been greatly hurt, and two of the Corporation had their heads broke, and the Mayor lost both his hat and wig, and narrowly escaped being wounded." The militia was therefore called out, and, before the battle was over, one man had been killed and three of the ringleaders arrested. On 29 September, the *Oracle* added, "Mr. BENGOUGH," the Mayor, himself collected the toll, having read the Riot Act first, and there was no further disturbance. *Lloyd's Evening Post* reported (4 Oct.) otherwise. On 28 September the mob had consisted, it said, of at least twelve thousand people, of whom the soldiers had that day killed fifteen and wounded over fifty, and there had been additional casualties on 1 October. The soldiers were still, it understood, unable to walk the streets singly, and Lord Bateman was under heavy guard. The riots in fact lasted throughout the year, with further increases in the number of casualties. The *Star* had expected something of the kind, for, as it explained on 5 October, the toll for use of the bridge, although the original cause of the violence, was only part of the grievance: "The TAX which is so obnoxious at Bristol, consists of a pound rate on all the houses, a toll on the bridge, and 2½*d.* per ton on all ships coming to Bristol, except certain vessels that pay per voyage." Otherwise everything seemed to be quiet. On 20 September the *Oracle* reported that Mackintosh's friend, Thomas Christie, "author of an answer to Burke," had "with great difficulty" adjusted matters with the French, had been released from prison, and would soon be returning to England. But this information was offset by news that in August Thomas Cooper had sailed for America with two sons of Dr. Priestley and that on 3 October Thomas Paine had been denounced by the French Convention. It looked as if those two would not be returning.

There had also been little reform activity in Scotland, but whereas the Government was extremely cautious in dealing with the English reformers, it had been rash indeed in dealing with the Scots. On 20 August the *Oracle* brought its readers up to date on those developments:

> William SKIRVING, who styles himself Secretary General for the Friends of the People in Scotland, has presented a Petition to the Court of Justiciary, wherein he declaims against the Sheriffs and Procurator Fiscal of the County of Edinburgh, for proceeding oppressively against him, and imprisoning him for a Paper not in the least improper, although they are pleased to call it libellous and seditious. He states that he in conjunction with others, had only exerted himself in support of the People and their rights, and to obtain a *proper Constitution* for the Country. Their Lordships replied, that they knew of no such office as he had assumed, and that his liberation only could be gained by offering legal and acceptable bail.
>
> Mr. MUIR has put aside his sentence of fugitation, but is detained upon the original charge, and has given bail for appearance.

Skirving subsequently furnished bail, and the trial of Thomas Muir began on 30 August, as scheduled, lasting two days. The newspapers still thought that Muir was being tried only for reading a letter to the Edinburgh Convention the previous December, but he was charged in addition with a variety of other "seditious" acts, supposedly performed during September, October, and November, 1792. The witnesses against him were informers, many of whom he had regarded as friends, and, although, being an advocate, Muir defended himself, the jury convicted. Having stated as his opinion that "the tendency here is plainly to overturn our present happy Constitution—the happiest, the best, and the most noble Constitution in the world, and I do not believe it possible to make a better," Lord Justice Clerk Braxfield thereupon sentenced him to fourteen years transportation.

Since the Government hated nothing so much as a repatriated reformer, there was nothing surprising about the outcome of Muir's trial, but the newspapers were nevertheless appalled. The news seems to have reached London on 3 September, for on 4 September *Lloyd's Evening Post* gave it a fourth column, the *Oracle* gave it one-half column, the *Morning Post* gave it one column, and the *Morning Chronicle* gave it two and one-half columns. On 5 September the *Oracle* gave it an additional column, but by this time it was the principal story in every newspaper, regardless of its politics. Among the witnesses at the trial had been William Skirving, who had testified, according to the newspapers, that "Mr. MUIR went to London [in January] to be present at a meeting of the Friends of the People; that he [Skirving] received a letter from Mr. MUIR at London, giving an account of what he did at the meeting; that it was the opinion of the society in London that he should go to France, in order to see if he could have any influence to prevent the execution of the King; that he received a letter from Mr. MUIR at Paris, informing him that he would return to his friends in Scotland immediately." The implication of the London Friends of the People was extremely welcome news to the Government; but, if Skirving actually did so testify, in the hope of thereby escaping prosecution himself, he had second thoughts, for on 6 September the *Morning Post* and the *Morning Chronicle* published a letter in which Skirving denied that he had said any such thing. The letter had been addressed to Daniel Stuart, and Stuart had also supplied the comment:

> The Editor of the MORNING POST [MORNING CHRONICLE] is requested to insert the following Letter, addressed to the Secretary of the Society of the Friends of the People, associated for the purpose of obtaining a Parliamentary Reform, Frith-street, London.
>
>   "Edinburgh, Sept. 2, 1793.
> Sir,
>   I ought to have wrote you on Saturday [31 Aug.], to give your Society the means of contradicting the aspersion, which you will see by the accounts of Mr.

Muir's trial, has been thrown upon them. I have not been able to command a settled thought since the alarming issue of that astonishing trial. I never had a higher opinion of any person's integrity, uprightness and philanthropy; nor is it diminished, but increased. The feelings which I must therefore have had, since that event, will plead my excuse with men of feeling.

In the evidence which I was called on to give, I stated the reason for his going to London, and that I had received a letter from Mr. Muir, when at London, explaining the cause of his proceeding to Paris, which letter I was very sorry that I could not produce, though I had preserved it carefully. Being desired to state, if I could recollect, the reason which Mr. Muir assigned in that letter for his journey to Paris, I said, that it was the opinion of FRIENDS, that if Mr. Muir would go to Paris, he might have great influence with many to mitigate the sentence of the French King. These FRIENDS were taken for your Society, and much freedom was used to reprobate both the Society of the Friends of the People in London, for presuming to send a missionary into another country, and Mr. Muir for accepting such commission. But I declare, upon my honour, that the thought of his being sent by the Society of the Friends of the People in London, never came into my mind: And if I expressed myself so, which is impossible I could do, I expressed a falsehood; and which I am bound in justice to the Society in this manner to contradict.

. . . . . .

W. SKIRVING."

In addition to the preceding letter, we have the very best authority for asserting, that when Mr. Muir was admitted to a Meeting of the Society of the Friends of the People last Winter, there was not a word uttered by him, or any Member of that Society, about the French King, or about French Affairs. The reason he assigned for desiring to be admitted, was, to state the oppressive and unjust steps then taking against the Friends of Reform in Scotland. He did so; and that was all. No Commission, instruction, or direction whatever, was given to him respecting the French King, French Affairs, or any other measure; either by the Society, or by particular Members,—or even by any single Member of the Society;—nor was it known, whether he was to remain in London, to return to Scotland, or to quit the kingdom. The slightest idea of his going to France was neither expressed, nor understood.

Whatever were the actual facts about Skirving's testimony, this letter certainly decided his fate.

The newspapers continued to be preoccupied with the case of Muir. "The trial of Mr. MUIR, and the sentence passed on him, is as much a topic of conversation as the War," the *Morning Post* said on 10 September. "When a Gentleman has been convicted on the evidence of his own servants, it must alarm the mind of every man in the Country, particularly when they contemplate the sentence that followed." By 19 September there was additional news: Thomas Fyshe Palmer, a Unitarian clergyman, hitherto unknown to the London papers, had on 12–13 September been tried in the Circuit Court of Justiciary in Perth, convicted, and sentenced to seven years transportation. The *Morning Post* gave this trial well over a column, as so did most other newspapers. On 26 September the *Morning Chronicle* added to its previous account another two-column summary and on 27 September another long report of the trial of Muir. The *Public Advertiser* was unexpectedly sympathetic with Palmer; the *Oracle* was sympathetic with Muir. On 27 September the *Oracle*, "by way of convincing . . . the PUBLIC at large, of our Impartiality," printed a long letter in his defense, signed "SCOTUS." On 1 October it hoped that the King would pardon him, and on 3 October it printed a second letter from "SCOTUS." On 4 October it itself defended Muir in a long editorial, insisting that the jury must have been "swept away by their feelings." Muir was thought to be on his way to London. "Mr. THOMAS MUIR, who was lately condemned to transportation for *fourteen years*, on account of his thinking that the British Constitution would be better for a reform of its abuses, was conveyed in the dead of the night on board a King's ship in Leith Roads, and he is expected to be landed safe in Newgate," the *Morning Post* had reported on 2 October.

Having gone to so much trouble to keep Muir in France, the Government would in any event have dealt with him severely, but the treatment of Palmer was gratuitous. The only possible motive was further to alarm the alarmists, and this stratagem could be practiced, the Government seems to have felt, only in Scotland. In England it could prosecute only the insignificant. News of Palmer's sentence was, however, followed by rumors of new conspiracies in various English cities, and on 11 October the *Oracle* announced triumphantly that "THOMAS WALKER, WILLIAM PAUL, OLIVER PEARSON, JOSEPH COLLIER, GEORGE M'CULLUM, SAMUEL JACKSON, BENJAMIN BOOTH, JOHN SMITH, JAMES CRESTHAM [Cheetham?], and HENRY YORK" had been arrested for conspiring in Manchester during the period, beginning 1 November, 1792, and ending 12 June, 1793, to overthrow the Constitution and assist the French and would be tried at the next Lancaster Assizes. The discovery of this plot was represented as a fine piece of detective work on the part of William Pitt, but, since there were no trials, the announcement may have been intended to divert interest from Fox's anniversary dinner. The Ministerial newspapers were apparently uneasy about the effect of this dinner, for, as soon as it was advertised, they resumed interest in Fox. "The *Popular Pauper* was a day or two since accosted in the street by a Beggar, by the very familiar stile of '*Brother Charley!*'" the *World* told its readers on 2 October. "The *great man* looked big, and d-d the fellow, who archly replied, 'Ah, *two of a trade* can never agree.'" On 8 October the *Oracle* observed that "OPPOSITION DINNERS are seldom heard of now, though the cessation can scarcely be thought to arise from any *want of appetite*"; and on 9 October it warned the celebrants that nothing they said could damage Pitt: "Imagination can scarcely conceive a greater triumph than that with which the MINISTER will meet Parliament. His opponents are so crushed, or dissevered, that it is folly to consider them as a Party. They sit opposite to HIM in all senses, who knows no interest but that of THIS country."

The dinner, which commemorated the thirteenth anniversary of Fox's first election as Member for Westminster, was held at the Shakespeare Tavern on 10 October and was reviewed at length by the Opposition papers. It was also reviewed by the *Oracle* and the *World*. The *Oracle* mentioned only that the "number present, we guess, might exceed Five Hundred," among them being Sheridan, Grey, Byng, Lord Lauderdale, "Lords J. and W. RUSSEL, Alderman COMBE, and Capt. MORRICE, who sang a number of songs." The account in the *World* began:

Mr. FOX's ANNIVERSARY.

Yesterday the partizans of Mr. Fox commemorated the Anniversary of his Election for Westminster with their usual riot and disorder at the Shakespeare.

Many of the hungry rogues gloated on the dishes as they came to table with such ravenous appetites that they will suffer for a week to come with the pain of repletion. They were ignorant how to conduct themselves, not having tasted any thing but a little salt and carrots, with some dry bread for a fortnight. . . .

Other newspapers ignored the affair.

The sentences imposed on Muir and Palmer were still very much in the news and likely to continue so, for on 11 October Charles Stuart, still *agent provocateur* for the Home Department, wrote to someone, probably Dundas: [65]

Sir,

I have learnt a good deal of the plan of the winter [Parliamentary] campaign and I shall do myself the honour of transmitting it to you occasionally—especially as, every day, I shall be gaining new lights as to the minutiae.

What I wish to apprise you of, at present, is, that it is determined to bring forward *Muir's* business in parliament—Adam is talked of for the Commons—Lauderdale for the Lords—& Thurlow, who is now at East Bourne, I understand from a certain quarter has expressed his sentiments about *Muir*, highly pleasing to the remnants of opposition—Mulgrave, you will be surprised to hear, has coincided in opinion with T.—he is there likewise—Every one concerned in Muir's prosecution, ought therefore to be early informed—that the Defence, in parliament, may be properly prepared.

[John?] Stewart, who went off [to France] with Muir, I heard on Monday, was in London last week, from whence he shipped himself off to Norway—he was in the metropolis for a fortnight. Sir, with gratitude and respectful regard, I remain your most devoted humble Servant.

C. Stuart.

Lord Mulgrave had returned from Toulon in a pique, having greatly resented the appointment of O'Hara. Stuart's information may have had something to do with the Government's decision to invent another alarm, although there were numerous reasons for it besides.

If the *Morning Chronicle* was correct, Pitt had threatened to negotiate with the French if the Rockingham Whigs did not accept office. They had shown no inclination to do so. News from the Continent continued to be bad, with the result that enthusiasm for the war was dwindling even among the upper classes. The Prince of Wales was still setting a fine patriotic example, as so was Prince Edward, who, according to *Lloyd's Evening Post* (7 Oct.), was now in Canada, where he had been "promoted to the rank of Major General in the Army." But Prince Adolphus, although "recovered from the wounds he had received in Flanders," would not, *Lloyd's Evening Post* thought (16 Oct.), return; the Duke of Clarence was as obstinately opposed to fighting as ever; and the Duke of York was, to say the least, disgruntled at the lack of support provided for him at Dunkirk. On 7 October the *World* had commented that the "Duke of RICH-MOND has acted apparently under the guidance of some malignant star during the present campaign. At one time he sends off ordnance too late, and at another forgets to send it at all." But such comments were rare, for the Duke of York was now, it appeared, blaming Lord Chatham for the disaster. There had been hints in the newspapers for some time that the Duke of Clarence was willing to do his duty if the duty assigned to him was commensurate with his rank, training, and ability, and it was becoming increasingly evident that what he had now in mind was the post of first Lord of the Admiralty, so that Lord Chatham's resignation was being urged from two sides. In short, Pitt had saved the Duke of Richmond only at the jeopardy of his brother.

The Ministerial papers had responded to this development with eulogies of Lord Chatham and vitriolic comments on the Duke of Clarence and Mrs. Jordan. "Perhaps," the *World* had remarked on 2 October, "there is no situation in life that affords more *variety*, or gives rise to more extraordinary changes of circumstances than that of the *Stage*. Mrs. JORDAN, who, a few years ago, was at best nothing more than the miserable heroine of many a miserable itinerant troop, and continually *working up against the stream*, is now *running right before the wind*, ycleped a *Dutchess*, and *privately* invested with all the *Royal* and *Ducal* Honours!" But a few days later the situation changed. Most of the newspapers were withholding comment, and *The Times* was evidently supporting the Duke of Clarence, for on 12 October the *True Briton* lashed out at Walter:

> The EDITOR of THE TIMES, having been compelled to acknowledge, in that Paper of yesterday, the falsehood of his calumnious assertion respecting certain paragraphs which had appeared in THE TRUE BRITON, has endeavoured to shelter himself from the contempt which awaits him, under a forced construction of the Article in question. That subterfuge shall not serve his turn. The EDITOR, impressed with the respect due those whose characters have so wantonly and shamefully been attacked, thus publicly gives the LYE to the assertions contained in THE TIMES of yesterday, respecting a Gentleman in Office and a certain Admiral; not one syllable of which . . . is true.
>
> With regard to the other ribaldry contained in the paragraph in question, the EDITOR has only to say, that if the success of THE TRUE BRITON, and his own consequent losses, provoke the EDITOR of THE TIMES to vent his spleen through

the medium of his Newspaper, he will do well to take care how he *dares* to level his shafts against those high and respectable Characters, whom he has, with so much virulence, presumed to calumniate.—With respect to the *rest*, if such a mode of attack is persisted in, a method, though perhaps unceremonious, yet effectual, may be found of putting a stop to it.

Walter was apparently going to be horsewhipped. But by 14 October the *Oracle* was also suggesting that the Duke of Clarence had been mistreated: "*A propos* of the Duke of CLARENCE—Mr. CONDUCTOR (in consequence of your late paragraph respecting him) whence can it come to pass that we behold him at this most important juncture unemployed in the profession to which it is well known he served a *regular*, and, by all accounts, honourable apprenticeship—as a *British Admiral*?/ We have claims to his services, and as the SON of OUR SOVEREIGN—not to say a word of his early proofs of valour—'Nothing can be rotten in the state of *Denmark*,' where his Honour is concerned—The Clue must be got at./ Yours, &c./ A BRITON." This communication was followed (16 Oct.) by an editorial on the subject of Dunkirk, the point of which was that the Duke of York had some very bitter feelings about Lord Chatham, who had failed to support the action by sea.

These problems and others the Government solved in its usual fashion. On 11 October *Lloyd's Evening Post* had reported that the camp at Brighton would be discontinued. The Light Dragoons would be broken up into segments, stationed at Brighton, Lewes, and Chester, respectively, and other regiments would be distributed throughout the country. By 15 October all newspapers understood that the dissolution was in progress and that the Prince of Wales had returned to Carlton House in anticipation. But on 16 October *Lloyd's Evening Post* announced that the regiments had been ordered to remain at Brighton and that the Prince of Wales was leaving for Brighton at once. The *Morning Chronicle* was exasperated. "Every year Mr. PITT brings forth a new bugbear. Last year we had an *insurrection* in disguise; this year we are to have an *invasion* incog," it observed (16 Oct.). "Whether this [new alarm] is done to procure the erection of barracks throughout England, or simply to prepare the public mind for a campaign, or for both we shall soon see. . . ." The erection of additional barracks turned out to be only part of the "bugbear." On 19 October the *World* announced that the camp at Brighton was being greatly augmented, since "the report" was that "the French are collecting great forces at *Cherbourg*, in order to make a descent upon England.—The park and horse artillery are ordered back to camp, and forage contracted for a fortnight longer. The quarters . . . will form a line of communication along the coast, and it is supposed that ten more Regiments will immediately reinforce the encampment." On 21 October *Lloyd's Evening Post* further announced that a "plan has lately been laid before his Royal Highness the Prince of Wales, and approved of, the design of which is, to raise two battalions of Highlanders, of 1000 men each, for the service of the ensuing campaign, the Prince to be Commander in Chief."

The Third Prorogation

Marie Antoinette was beheaded on 16 October. The *Oracle* of 23 October devoted a full page, heavily bordered in black, to an account of her trial and death, and more such accounts appeared in other newspapers the following day, when the report was officially confirmed. Proceedings of the trial with long editorial commentaries were published by several newspapers in late October, and the *Oracle* maintained interest in the case throughout November and December, publishing on 12 November a column of "anecdotes" of the late Queen and in mid-December Mrs. Robinson's long-awaited "Monody to the Memory of the Late Queen of France," which was much admired by all papers, especially (20 Dec.) by the *True Briton*. Although the death of the Queen attracted considerably more notice than the death of the King had attracted nine months earlier, it seems to have influenced no one's thinking about the war, and neither did the rumors of an impending invasion. As a war minister, Pitt had shown himself to be less than adequate; yet no newspaper believed that, in a period of actual crisis, he would entrust the defense of the country to the Duke of Richmond. The purpose of the camp at Brighton, it was still supposed, was to protect the seacoast, but this fact was no longer stressed by the Ministerial newspapers, and, had it not been for the Opposition papers, the Duke of Richmond's activities might have been ignored altogether. "His Grace of RICHMOND, it is now said, is to take upon him the command of the British troops under the Duke of YORK," the *Morning Post* commented on 17 October. "All who have noticed the Campaigns at Waterdown and Brighton, by which his Grace has rendered himself notorious this Summer, will agree, that he is very likely to gather those laurels which may adorn the brow of the Royal Duke." "The Duke of RICHMOND in his plans of fortifying has no doubt been guided by his own military ardour," the *Morning Chronicle* remarked on the same day. "His fortifications are by no means calculated to supersede the efforts of British valour; for it is remarked that exactly in proportion to the pains bestowed by his Grace in fortifying any particular situation, the less defencible it is." "The Duke of RICHMOND, since the report of an Invasion has constantly slept *in his boots*, and his horses are ready saddled, that in case of the French attempting to land, he may be the first to communicate the intelligence to his Majesty *in person*," said the *Gazetteer* on 24 October. The first indication that the camp might be discontinued was a mention in *Lloyd's Evening Post* (30 Oct.) that on 28 October "the Prince of Wales's regiment of Light Horse marched into winter quarters at Brighton."

Having failed to alarm anyone with the threat of an invasion, Pitt would not, the Opposition papers thought, face the Commons on 29 October. The *Morning Chronicle* thought he was making a mistake. As it put it on 17 October: "The Ministers feel some hesitation in meeting Parliament early, which is likely however rather to be increased than diminished by delay. Before they inform us what we have to pay in consequence of the present war, they wish if possible to find something to state that we have gained." The *Chronicle* itself could report only one such "gain": "The DEY of ALGIERS has declared war against the French, but in the most *voluntary* and *disinterested* manner. Whatever rumours may say to the contrary, he has neither been *bullied*, nor *subsidized* by the British Ministry!" On 21 October the *World* predicted that Parliament would not convene until after Christmas. The *Oracle* was still hopeful, since, according to its communiqués, the Prince of Saxe-Coburg was expected to attack Maubeuge hourly and success was assured, the Duke of York having joined him with three thousand of his best troops. But success, it turned out, had not been assured, the Austrians having been beaten on 17 October. The *Oracle* reported this fact on 22 October, implying at the same time that the British might under the circumstances withdraw from Toulon: "To keep possession of *Toulon* is by military men deemed impracticable against the forces with which it is now invested—but the destruction of the French Fleet there will be a blow of moment sufficient to make the enterprize be esteemed one of the most important in the present War." On 24 October the *Morning Post* repeated that Parliament could expect another prorogation. Nothing now, it told its readers, could offset the defeat at Dunkirk. Pitt could not ask for money unless he could boast of victories, and he could manage without further funds until early January. On 25 October the *Sun* announced that Pitt had negotiated a peace. In view of the *Morning Chronicle*'s statement (28 Sept.) that he had been threatening to do so unless the old Rockingham Whigs joined the Government, the announcement would have seemed plausible. It seemed particularly so now, when peace appeared to many to be the only solution to the problem.

"If we may believe the Treasury prints, the only *peaceable* subjects of his Majesty, are those that are advocates for a *continuance* of the war," the *Gazetteer* remarked on 26 October. But until 28 October, when it admitted that it had been the victim of a hoax, the *Sun* was in fact enthusiastic about peace, and there was no agreement as to the way the war was going. On 29 October the *Gazetteer* noticed disgustedly that "[some] of the Treasury papers are attempting to prove, that the defeat at Maubeuge was as good as a victory; because, say they, none of the subsidiary troops was engaged, and it was therefore a *cheap* day for England." But the *Oracle* took a very gloomy view. Although the Prince of Saxe-Coburg was planning another attack on Maubeuge, the *Oracle* did not (28 Oct.) expect it to succeed, the Duke of York, it understood, was inactive, and the French were rapidly occupying all of Maritime Flanders. On 29 October the *Oracle* further reported that Ostend had been lost and that Lord Howe's fleet had been encircled by the French. The only good news came from Scotland. "HIGH-LAND TROOPS," the *Oracle* announced on 28 October. "By Lieutenant [Francis] Mackenzie's desire a plan has been laid before Mr. DUNDAS, exhibiting upon what terms that Chieftain will raise ONE THOUSAND MORE of those excellent Soldiers, within one month from the present time, for his MAJESTY's service./ There is no doubt but that MINISTERS will accept the offer—Indeed the above Gentleman alone possesses the power of Clanship in any thing like the old degree. He has never once raised his rental by extortion, and is indeed adored by his vassals." There was no such enthusiasm on the part of Prince Augustus, whose arrival in England had been reported by the papers on 21 October, of Prince Adolphus, who, the *Gazetteer* repeated on 24 October, "does not return to the army in Flanders during the present campaign," or of the Duke of Clarence. On 17 October the *Morning Post* had mentioned that the "Duke of CLARENCE has discharged seventeen of his domestics. The Duke having the prospect of a young Family, is determined to retrench. Mrs. JORDAN has taken a house in town, and her *accouchement* is hourly expected." The Duke was evidently also "determined" to be First Lord of the Admiralty, for on 28 October the *Oracle* published a letter from "ONE OF THE PEOPLE," who said again that the Duke had somehow antagonized Pitt, that Pitt had retaliated with spite, and that he, the author, meant to investigate the matter personally.

On 29 October the King again prorogued Parliament, this time to 21 January. On the same day the *London Gazette* published a Royal declaration regarding the war. The declaration, subsequently referred to as "Pitt's Manifesto," was reprinted by the *Morning Chronicle* on 30 October, although the *Chronicle* frankly admitted that it had no notion what it meant. The King seemed to be calling on the French Royalists to do something, but whether he wanted them to give up or whether he wanted them to continue their struggles until France was again a monarchy, the *Chronicle* did not know. Other newspapers seemed to be similarly baffled, for the "Manifesto" was almost ignored. The Ministerial papers did, however, agree that the situation was presently hopeless. "AMERICA opening her friendly doors to the ARTS and SCIENCES! THEATRES rising, and WORKS of GENIUS patronized! These are thy blessed effects, O PEACE! How many ruined persons have not occasion to curse FRANCE!/ A Mr. RUTTER was unfortunate enough to take forty Guineas to return *two every day* till Dunkirk was taken. He has already offered 500 to get quit of his bargain," said the *World* on 30 October. The *Oracle* was inclined to "curse" Holland. "Never was courage so impetuous and ardent as that of the DUTCH TROOPS," it remarked sarcastically on 1 November. "The CAVALRY in order to retreat with expedition, plunged *glowing* hot into the river *Sambre*, and then a loud *hiss* followed of course." The *Morning Post* was "cursing" Lord Loughborough. Although it still blamed Burke for starting the war, it now held Lord Loughborough responsible for managing it; and it evidently regarded him as the arch-culprit, for, from 1 November on, readers heard little of Burke, but they were reminded every day that the campaign had been planned by a lawyer and that military strategy was being devised in the Court of Chancery. Readers of the *Gazetteer* were again being told (1 Nov.) that the "*patriotism* of Mr. ANSTRUTHER has just been rewarded by a new place; he is appointed standing Counsel to the Board of Controul, with a salary of 500*l*. a year!" The appointment was now evidently official.

On 1 November the *Oracle* had mentioned "rumours" that Menin and Ypres were again in the hands of the French, the British having lost in the process "two battalions of Hanoverian Grenadiers." On the same day, John Heriot, "Proprietor and Conductor of the *Sun*," announced that he was collecting flannel waistcoats for "our gallant Soldiers fighting in Flanders." On 2 November the *True Briton* announced a similar collection, John Heriot being named as agent. The response seems to have surprised everyone, for, although little was said of the projects to begin with, the *Sun* was soon talking of nothing else. On 6 November Heriot, as "Editor of the *Sun*," thanked, through the medium of the *True Briton*, the hundreds who had already contributed, and more contributions were obviously in the making. On 6 November *Lloyd's Evening Post* reported that "a subscription is set on foot in Birmingham, each subscriber to find six flannel waistcoats for our brave soldiers serving under the command of his Royal Highness the Duke of York," and by 8 November it had "[heard] that the Ladies of Leicester are diligently employed in preparing Waistcoats for the Soldiers. The present Chief Magistrate, Mr. Mansfield, has sanctioned the measure by subscribing 50. . . ." The camp at Brighton was being broken up, *Lloyd's Evening Post* added (6 Nov.) incidentally. The remaining six regiments would be distributed, and the Prince of Wales would live in London, visiting Brighton, where his own regiment was stationed, from time to time.

The inevitability of another prorogation was bound to affect several of the Ministerial newspapers. *The Times*, still subsidized by the Treasury, weathered the crisis with nothing more serious than a change of printer, Adam Anderson being replaced on 11 November by Charles Bell. The *True Briton*, owned, as it was, by members of Government, was secure, but Daniel Stuart was dubious about the *Sun*, since Heriot was now identifying himself as "Proprietor and Editor" of that newspaper and "Editor" only of the *True Briton*. Without Treasury support, the *Sun* was undone, and Stuart, who was always in the market for another newspaper, did what he could to hasten its demise. On 15 October the *Morning Post* included in a satiric list of "New Books": "Method of Extracting the luscious Juice of 'the Rose,' from the Rays of 'the Sun.' By the Editor of an Evening Paper." This aspersion was followed by a battery of aspersions, and on 25 October the *Sun* was the recipient of one of Stuart's forgeries. With stock-jobbing rampant and the reputation of the *Sun* at a very low ebb, the forgery would have provided Stuart with the money to buy that newspaper, but Heriot evidently declined to sell, for the *Sun* did not change hands. Stuart refused to give up. The *Sun* was again under attack on 9 November, when the *Morning Post* announced:

The Underlings of the Treasury, who set up a gross and Vulgar Print, for the purpose of attacking, like Assassins, those respectable Characters, from whose presence they shrink in Parliament, have *equivocally* disclaimed having any future connection with this foul Vehicle of Slander. To prove to Mr. DUNDAS, and other persons in Power, that they have abandoned this ungentlemanlike business, all official intelligence has been withdrawn from that quarter, though their intelligence in dull and vulgar personal paragraphs still convinces us, that the very *men* [Heriot and Steele] who were near bringing an innocent Printer [John Walter of *The Times*] to the pillory for their libel on an illustrious character, are still determined not to desist from their precious labours.

The *Morning Post* was especially indignant about the *Sun*'s collection of flannel waistcoats.

The *Star*, which had been more Ministerial than Opposition, was now tending to revert to the Opposition, the *Morning Herald* was at least neutral, and the *Public Advertiser* announced on 23 October that it was for sale:

To the PUBLIC.

Various circumstances having arisen to induce the Printer [Henry Sampson Woodfall] to quit the labours of his Profession in the *Newspaper Line*, he takes the opportunity of returning his most sincere and grateful thanks to his numerous Customers and Correspondents, for the Favours conferr'd on him during the last Half Century.

As he intends shortly to give up the Printing of the PUBLIC ADVERTISER, any persons inclined to treat for the same are desired to apply to the Printer.

N. B. Such persons may be accommodated with the Materials at a fair Valuation—and as a further accommodation, the Printer will permit the Publication to be continued at his House for a limited time on a proper consideration.

The PRINTING BUSINESS in *general* will be continued as usual; and private Gentlemen, as well as those immediately concerned in the Trade, may be assured that any Works entrusted to his Care, will be executed with Accuracy and Dispatch.

The announcement was repeated on 2 November, the second paragraph having been altered to read: "As he intends after this day to give up the Printing of the PUBLIC ADVERTISER, the Public are respectfully informed, that this Paper will be continued at this House until new arrangements, which are in contemplation, shall be completed. The particulars will be submitted to the public in a few days, though the present Printer has not any further concern in it."

On 4 November the *Public Advertiser* was printed by John Irving, the address being unchanged, and on 4, 5, and 6 November the paper advised its readers: "The parties to whom Mr. WOODFALL has transferred the property of this Paper, respectfully beg leave to recommend themselves to its Patrons and Correspondents./ At present they can only promise that every exertion shall be used for rendering the PUBLIC ADVERTISER an interesting source of general information; but, in a very short time, they propose submitting to the World a PROSPECTUS of the Plan they are forming for the future management of this Paper, upon a more extensive Scale than it has hitherto been conducted." Irving was an employee of the Treasury, and, although there was no Treasury propaganda in the issue of 4 November, there was an abundance of it thereafter, with fulsome praise of every Ministerial hanger-on. Henry Sampson Woodfall does seem to have quit the paper, for, in recommending his brother William for City Remembrancer, the *Public Advertiser* mentioned (9 Nov.) that it had "not the happiness of knowing [him]." But on 27 November the printing was turned over to another Treasury hireling, Nicholas Byrne, who, from 11 November, 1790, to perhaps 2 March, 1792, had been printer of the *Morning Herald*. The politics of the paper remained, of course, unchanged.

The *World* had also become unruly. The last indication that Topham was interested in the paper was an item published on 18 October: "There is at this time in the Garden of Capt. TOPHAM . . . in Essex, an apple-tree in full blossom." Although the *World* had thus far remained Ministerial, it had had great trouble filling its pages, and by 26 October Charles Stuart had been sent over to assist. Stuart brought with him "Grey's Beggar's Opera," in which he had lampooned Paine, Frost, Horne Tooke, and every member of the Whig Club. The piece was very tiresome. It had probably already been rejected for the stage, and the *Diary* and the *Public Advertiser*, which had once consented to print it, had changed their minds after a few installments. But Swan was desperate, and so on 26 October the *World* presented the first part, promising not to quit until it had presented the whole. On 27 October Stuart, who was understandably delighted, sent a copy of the newspaper to Dundas along with some suggestions. "Sir," he wrote:[66]

> I have the honour to transmit you the first Number of the *Parody*—I am afraid that government are proceeding upon a wrong plan—They do not consider that by *monopolizing* Intelligence to a Morning and an Evening Paper [the *True Briton* and the *Sun*], they render the other papers hostile to them—papers, too, that are really devoted to them—They do not consider, with Louis XIV. that by managing the Literate, which he did I believe, at the expence of 5000 a year, he in a great degree managed all Europe, & managed his fame to posterity.—They do not consider, that altho' every paper were to be annihilated but the Morning Chronicle and the True Briton—the Sun and the Star—that there is an *under current* of *Jacobin Pamphlets* that deluge the land by thousands, and perhaps they know nothing, or very little about them, or their circulation.
>
> They do not consider that while Government is pleased and most highly flattered by an article of Intelligence which is in no other of the Morning Papers but one—that at the same time thousands of pamphlets are circulated on that day, primed with lasting materials that totally destroy that ephemera of the day. —They do not consider that while they circulate *News*, the others circulate *Sentiments*.—While government circulates an evanescent cloud, the others circulate a shower that falls, and nourishes, and brings forth fruit.

The truth is, every thing is to be managed by managing the press.—The artillery of the French could not be managed a month, without they managed the artillery of the Press.—I look upon the press as flint to a gun, or potfire to a cannon.—Whenever I hear of a French victory, I in general ascribe it to their artful circulation of Journals and Bulletins throughout every municipality in every department.—What has convulsed the mind, here, of late, but the press? —What can do it away, but by taking every advantage of destroying, and multiplying the same engines?—I say to government, that you must either lead it, or I am afraid it will destroy you.—When I hear of the French casting *cannon*, I think nothing of them at all, provided you can only prevent them from casting *types*!—at least to direct their pressure to your views.

I firmly believe, without any vanity, that I know as much in the engineering of the press, as any press engineer in Britain.—The system, I am afraid, that government is proceeding on is wrong.—If you, or Mr. Nepean entertained an idea that such a declaration of mine is not altogether preposterous or wrong, your commands are enough for me to give in an immediate Plan, which I am now turning in my mind.

. . . . . .

As you were so kind as [to] say I might draw the half quarter—would you mention it to Mr. Nepean to morrow, as I shall on Tuesday draw the 1/2 quarter, the whole of which is due on December 9th. Sir, with grateful respect I remain your ever devoted ser^t C. Stuart.

On 28 October Stuart wrote to Nepean:

Sir,

In consequence of Mr. Dundas allowing me to draw at half quarter, I have taken the liberty of drawing on you for 25£ for Wednesday—being the one half of the current quarter, due on Dec 9—which I hope you will be so kind as honour.

. . . I mean, in a few days, to trouble you with my ideas as to the management of the press in its utmost latitude, at the present moment, and the management of other matters,—the public mind.

My parody of the Beggar's Opera, I have begun inserting in the World. The first Number was in, on Saturday, the second to-day. [The second actually appeared on 29 October.] I have taken considerable pains in revising and altering many of the speeches—but I have kept my Dramatic *Time* a year backwards, as I really think that the atrocious scenes that have been acting since December last, are too vivid for Satires—I mean in February, to publish it as a pamphlet, after the whole has been inserted in the World. I am busy in other respects, with matters of a political nature, which I hope will please Mr. Dundas and you, and every other real friend to the happiness of the country.

. . . . . .

Sir, I am with the most heart-felt gratitude

Your ever-devoted humble Servt.

C. Stuart.

A similar letter was sent to Dundas. Since both letters were endorsed "Windsor, Street-Street," Charles was evidently having further trouble with creditors. The parody appeared in half-page installments at the rate of approximately two a week, concluding at last on 7 January, 1794. Although Swan seemed to like it, mentioning on 4 November, "The Parody of Gay's Beggar's Opera, which appears occasionally in our Paper, it is allowed, keeps the closest to the text of any ever read," it must have cost the *World* whatever subscribers remained. In addition, all of Stuart's knowledge "in the engineering of the press" failed to keep the paper in line. The Government could not count on its support during November, and by December only the relentless installments of Stuart's drama indicated that the *World* had ever been connected with the Treasury.

The Opposition newspapers were less affected by the prorogation. The *Morning Chronicle* was flourishing. Coleridge was now a contributor, as so was "Thomas Fool," "Peter Pindar," and numerous unidentified correspondents, and on 21 November Porson contributed the first of his "Orgies of Bacchus," the second appearing on 27 December. There was a change in the *Courier*, but this was owing most likely to the political situation. The *Courier* had been edited by the Rev. Charles Este, who understood that he would be rewarded with a good living when Fox came into office. Since there was little possibility of Fox's coming into office, Este's departure was not surprising. It is datable, however, only on the basis of his *A Journey in the Year 1793, through Flanders, Brabant, and Germany, to Switzerland* (London, 1794), which indicates that he was on the Continent from early November to late December. Although Este may have been traveling as foreign correspondent for the *Courier*, he probably was not, since the paper said nothing about "New Arrangements"; nor did it have any original news from the Continent during the period of his absence. His successor as editor was most likely Thomas George Street. On 20 August, 1800, Street stated in the *Courier* that he had been "Editor of [that newspaper] almost from its commencement to its establishment; from its infancy to its manhood; from the year 1793 to the spring of the year 1797." He made approximately the same statement, again in the *Courier*, on 11 January, 1811, the difference being that this time he made it negatively and with certain qualifications. He "was not," he said, "the Editor at [the *Courier*'s] birth nor for a long time after, a celebrated Clergyman [Este] having been its first Editor; nor was he the Editor at the time he joined in purchasing it in June 1799, nor for a long time before; it having had several Editors about that time, one of whom was Mr. [John] THELWALL. And at no time, till he became a Proprietor in 1799, had he any influence in the direction of the politics of the Paper, he having till then been a mere servant on a salary, under the control of the Proprietors, some of whom were at all times extremely forward in dictating what the politics should be."

The only clue to the identification of those proprietors in late 1793 was a list of subscribers to the newspaper's charity, the Spitalfield Weavers, published on 27 November. Since the charity was primarily a piece of propaganda, one may suppose that it was supported principally by the *Courier* itself. The first and largest donation was a gift of £6 6s. from the "Proprietors and editor." This was followed by a gift of one guinea from an individual proprietor, John Parry, by a gift of 10s. 6d. from "J. Williamson," and by a gift of one guinea from "Jordan, bookseller." Captain John Williamson had edited the *Morning Post* in 1783–1784 and in 1787–1788 had been connected with the *World*, resigning from that newspaper because he was "otherwise engaged." [67] He had always supported Fox, and by 1793 he had evidently run into some trouble on that account, for on 22 November the *Morning Post* protested: "Captain WILLIAMSON, who is as great an enemy to the present French Oligarchy as any man living, and as good a Sailor as any in the Navy, has been refused a ship, because he was heard to say, that he admired the brilliant abilities of Mr. Fox. What can shew the meanness and contemptibility of certain wretched men more than this?" J. S. Jordan, still under indictment for publishing Paine's *Rights of Man*, had, when last heard of, been allied with John Almon in a publishing project for the Government. The list was reprinted on 12 December with a few additions. Joseph Cottle of Bristol had donated one guinea, George Dyer 5s., and the "Proprietors" another £5 5s. Cottle was handling collections in the Bristol area, of which there were thus far none. But the proprietors may have had far less to do with "dictating what the politics should be" than Lord Lauderdale, for, from July on, the *Courier* was intimately linked with the *Morning Post*, and, as Daniel Stuart testified in connection with the State trials of late 1794, he was personally associated with Street at this time.

"Pitt's Manifesto"

By early November news was arriving of new executions in France. The Marquis de Sillery, included in the proscription of 2 June, had been guillotined on 21 October, and on 24 October the Girondists had been brought to trial. Accounts of their trials appeared in the newspapers of early November, with the addendum in the *Oracle* of 5 November: "ROBESPIERRE, there can be no doubt, aims at, and even now possesses, the Sovereign authority. . . ." The execution of Brissot and twenty other deputies was reported on 12 November as having occurred on 2 November, although it seems actually to have occurred on 31 October, and on 15 November the *Oracle* reported the execution of "*L'Égalité*, ci-devant Duke of ORLEANS." The Duke of Orleans was mourned by no newspaper. On 13 October France had, it appeared, declared war on Genoa, although the country was now, the *Oracle* understood (12 Nov.), in a state of insurrection: "Last night it was confidently reported, that the friends of the *guillotined* BRISSOT, after his execution, had declared themselves in a state of insurrection, and massacred an incredible number of the Convention. We mention this merely as a report, though STOCKS rose *one per cent.* on the supposed facts." This rumor was subsequently corrected, but it did seem certain that the terror was spreading from Paris to Lyons, and by 17 November readers had learned of the worship of the Goddess of Reason seven days earlier. At home there was violence in Bristol, where the riots had resulted in more casualties. On 23 October the *Morning Chronicle* listed eleven killed and forty-five wounded in recent uprisings, and on 6 November it predicted that these might be only the beginning: "A servant of Mr. SMITH, of Stapleton, died on Tuesday last, in consequence of a wound he received in the thigh, during the riots. The Coroner's Jury on the following day brought in a verdict—*Wilful Murder* against the person or persons who ordered the Military to fire!/ This verdict, it is feared, will be productive of very unpleasant consequences." A meeting had been scheduled for 2 November to ascertain the cause of the disturbances, but the *Chronicle* did not know the results.

The political situation remained unchanged. No gains were reported for the Government, and only one was reported for the Opposition, the *Oracle* mentioning on 2 November that "Mr. Serjeant ADAIR being returned to Parliament, is expected in the ensuing Session to act with the Opposition *Phalanx.*" Adair was thought to have instituted the fund for payment of Fox's debts. But the "intrigues" were evidently continuing. On 5 November the Whigs held the first meeting of the season at the Crown and Anchor, with Fox presiding and Adam, Byng, and the Earl of Derby making speeches, and the *Public Advertiser* took advantage of the occasion to deny positively that Pitt was threatening to negotiate a peace unless the Rockingham Whigs took office, as the *Morning Chronicle* had once reported. The *Morning Chronicle* replied on 11 November with the assertion that, not only had every word it said on 28 September been correct, but that the "Earls Spencer and Fitzwilliam have been applied to, through indirect channels, to give, by their acceptance of responsible offices, a sanction to the principle on which Mr. PITT obtained his power; namely, *the secret favour of a Court faction, in defiance of the Representatives of the People.* Before many days are over," the *Chronicle* continued:

> a similar application will be made to a noble Duke [the Duke of Portland], whose name was used without his authority, last year, by an honourable Baronet [Sir Gilbert Elliot] lately gone Commissioner to Toulon. It was stated [by the *Chronicle* on 28 September], that the method taken by Mr. PITT to effect his purpose, was by again having recourse to that ready disposition to ALARM which had so strongly manifested itself on a former occasion among the description of persons to whom his present applications were to be made, and that the ground on which he meant to revive apprehensions which had so well answered his views, was by manifesting on his part a disposition *to make peace with France,* and leave the original supporters of the war in the lurch.

. . . [The] DECLARATION lately published in the London Gazette, and which is the sole composition of Mr. PITT himself (of whose flimsy style of speaking, and Machiavelian mind, it bears, indeed, the most indisputable marks), is principally put forth in order to promote the view [that he means to treat for peace]: and it must be acknowledged that the language of those immediately connected with him, as well as of his newspapers, appears most exactly to correspond with this [impression]. The *Manifesto*, not improperly called Mr. PITT's LAMENTATION, is every where imagined to be *the token of approaching peace*; an opinion generally and industriously propagated in most of the chief manufacturing and country towns in Great Britain. Wherever the meaning of such a document is doubtful, and worded, as this one is, so as to suit any emergency, the disposition of unthinking people . . . is rather to take that explanation which the agents of Administration put upon it, than to believe that it either means nothing, or means deceit. The consequences are plain: this Declaration, so interpreted, is every where considered as a *signal of distress* held out even to the present Executive Government of France, earnestly desiring peace, and searching for some pretence to treat. The words made use of by the best of the Government papers [the *London Gazette* in the declaration of 29 October], are too remarkable not to be once again copied by us.—

"It cannot be doubted, that if the French Nation, convened by a due and regular representation, SHOULD DETERMINE THAT THE REPUBLICAN FORM OF GOVERNMENT IS BETTER ADAPTED TO IT THAN ANY OTHER; if, by the dignity and consistency of its proceedings, it could make itself respected at home, and guarantee its engagements, foreign powers would in that case consider things IN A MORE FAVORABLE LIGHT, and would readily ASSENT TO THAT SOLEMN DETERMINATION which in a state of serious and manly deliberation, should appear to be the sense of the French nation."

The use to be made of this opinion in those quarters to which we have alluded, it is no longer possible to mistake. Mr. PITT's design being to get either Lord FITZWILLIAM, or Lord SPENCER, or the Duke of PORTLAND, to come into office under him, we may easily conceive the following to be the language by which he will endeavour to effect it.—"I have made no promise in my Manifesto, not to negociate with the present Executive Government of France. I *will* negociate with them, unless you join me, and put an end at once to every future hope you may have of acting with Mr. Fox. Mark the mischief I shall do you by such conduct. If Mr. Fox had been suffered to negociate *before* we tried to give a Government to France by force, whether he had succeeded or not, the country would not have been disgraced; but if *I* negociate, in the present state of things, *after* having tried the question with France, and experienced nothing but calamity, disaster, and defeat, there is no possible mischief which may not be expected to follow. But what is that to me? among friends, you know, that in politics I am a *mere adventurer*; that I got my place by exciting, in the year 1784, a clamour against ARISTOCRACY, and against all of you; and that if I am turned out, I have nothing to do but to join my old friends and revive it. Who will be the sufferers by this—you or I? On the other hand, if you consent to join me, and thus cut off your retreat to popular opinion for ever, I will, on my part, try another campaign, on any principle you yourselves shall desire."

To readers of London newspapers, the evidence in support of the *Chronicle*'s thesis would have been largely negative. The Ministerial papers were pre-occupied with the collection of flannel waistcoats. "A Subscription was on Thursday opened at the Stock Exchange, for the very liberal purpose of furnishing Flannel Waistcoats for those brave fellows employed in defence of their country under his Royal Highness the Duke of York. It is with pleasure we understand, that upwards of 40*l.* were immediately subscribed," the *Oracle* reported on 9 November. On 11 November the *Sun* thanked contributors to its fund, and on 12 November the *True Briton* announced that it also had a fund, the contributors to which included "Geo. Aust, Under Sec. of State, 20*l.*; John Heriot, 20*l.*; Mrs. Heriot 20*l.*; James Bland Burges, Under Sec. 100*l.*; Francis Freeling, General P. O., 15*l.*; Mrs. Freeling, 15*l.*; Thomas Harris 50*l.*" John Bowles was collecting for Hampstead, the *True Briton* added. The *Sun* and the *True Briton* were now crammed with letters of encouragement, although it was beginning to seem to other newspapers that some diversion might be in order. "It is suggested," said *Lloyd's Evening Post* on 13 November, ". . . that nearly a sufficient quantity of [flannel waistcoats] being already provided or actually making up, . . . further benevolence may be most advantageously applied in the furnishing of flannel caps, yarn stockings, socks, trowzers, and strong shoes." As an example of what it had in mind, *Lloyd's Evening Post* had mentioned (11 Nov.) that the "Female orphans of the Asylum, which is patronized by her Majesty, and those of the charity supported by the Philanthropic Society, under the patronage of his Grace the Duke of Leeds" were "busily making flannel caps for soldiers to be worn under their hats." But nothing had quite the appeal of flannel waistcoats. The subscriptions were ridiculed by the Opposition press and by the *World*, which remarked on 11 November: "A ludicrous attempt has been made by the Editor of an Evening Paper, by purchasing flannel waistcoats for the army abroad. The effect may be innocent, but the design is as clear as the Sun." The rage, however, continued. By 15 November, according to the *Oracle*, there was hardly a village without a collecting agency for flannel waistcoats. The war was otherwise almost forgotten. On 7 November the Duke of York's army had gone into winter quarters at Tournai, but there was no mention of a spring campaign; and, although on 7 November the *Oracle* had announced new treaties with Austria and Prussia, who agreed to fight on until the Republican faction was "annihilated," other Ministerial papers stoutly denied that they had done anything of the sort. Also denied was a rumor that Britain was interfering with the commerce of America. Most newspapers had strong feelings on this subject. As readers of *Lloyd's Evening Post* knew, the United States was having a war of its own. "The Cherokees of the five lost towns upon the *Tennessee* have declared war against the United States of America, and have begun some predatory incursions with a body of 600 men," it had reported on 7 January; and on 1 February: "Recent advices from Philadelphia bring intelligence, that the war with the Indians continues with unabated fury. Northern and southern

Indians have, it is feared, formed an alliance to attack the American frontiers from the North and the South." "The Americans still continue to be much harassed by the Indians on their frontiers, particularly on the side of Kentucky, but such measures are taking [*sic*] by them, both for resistance and negociation, as . . . will shortly put an end to this evil," it said again on 4 October. By November this war was beginning to interest the *Morning Post* and the *Courier*, which wondered frankly if the Indians were being encouraged by the British.

Other evidence in support of the *Morning Chronicle*'s statements was similarly negative. There were no new pamphlets on the war, but on 9 November the *Morning Chronicle* announced that Henry Mackenzie had again attacked the Opposition: "The *Man of Feeling* has, a second time, in order to gratify his Patrons, employed his pen in the scurrilous abuse of Opposition; for this repeated prostitution of his talents, he has the double consolation of a place under Government and a pension.—Which makes all doctrines plain and clear, &c." The *Chronicle* was probably referring to *Additional Letters to Brutus*, collected from the Edinburgh *Herald*. Mackenzie had published his *Letters to Brutus* the previous year, and earlier in 1793 he had published an abridgment of George Chalmers's *Life of Thomas Paine, by Francis Oldys, A. M., of the University of Pennsylvania*. Another of the Government's writers had, the *Morning Post* understood (12 Nov.), quit: "TOM STEELE, it is said by the Government Scribblers, is as capital a hand at a long winded paragraph, as any Gentleman about town. Since the absence of the Duke of YORK, and the departure of the armies, he is officially employed, and has, much to his credit we believe, desisted from such literary labours." Steele was Paymaster General of the Forces. But, now that Stuart's parody was being printed by the *World*, readers did not lack for "scurrilous abuse of Opposition" in the newspapers. Of the state of political negotiations, nothing further was said until 13 November, when the *Public Advertiser* announced: "Earl Spencer, and the Earl of Moira have joined their virtues and their talents to the support of Administration, and a more valuable accession could not have been selected from the catalogue of noble and illustrious characters." That afternoon the *Sun* added another "valuable accession" in the person of Earl Fitzwilliam, and by 14 November the Duke of Richmond seemed to be fighting desperately to retain his place in the Ordnance. The *Star* spoke up strongly in his defense and of course at his expense:

. . . One of the Duke of RICHMOND's first measures on coming into office, was increasing the salaries of the civil branch, at the same time that he utterly abolished all perquisites or fees whatever in the Ordnance. In consequence of which, those who had business to transact, or accounts to pass, were relieved from that galling procrastination, which attended every step in many of the public offices, unless they were content to submit to the most exorbitant fees and impositions. Every creditor to the Ordnance was regularly paid without deductions or delay—and immense sums were by this means saved to government, as the contractors were now obliged to supply every species of stores at the lowest rate; whereas before, they were under the necessity of charging an exorbitant price to recompence them for the loss they sustained by delay in payment and the fees of office. All the former complaints against our military stores were immediately done away, as they are now procured of the best quality, and our gunpowder, the constant theme of execration in the navy and army, become the first in Europe, from its being manufactured under his Grace's inspection, in works belonging to Government.—His time is solely dedicated to the important office he holds. Business seems his pleasure. And from the greatest to the most minute affairs, every thing within the sphere of the Ordnance has felt the beneficent influence of his comprehensive and penetrating genius.

Most frequently mentioned as Richmond's successor had been Lord Cornwallis, who had resigned as Governor General of India on 13 August and on 10 October had left for England. The pro tempore replacement was to have been the Commander in Chief of the Army, Lord Amherst. Although it looked now as if the post was being offered to one of the recent converts, the offer was refused, as so, said the *Morning Post*, were all offers of the sort.

The *Morning Post* made its statement on the morning of 14 November:

> The Coalition proposed by Mr. PITT, and so confidently stated as having been agreed to by EARL FITZWILLIAM on the part of his friends, was yesterday rejected on the part of the OPPOSITION. The object of Mr. PITT was to have strengthened Administration by the acquisition of that part of the Aristocracy which has reprobated the War, and suggested measures diametrically opposite to those he has pursued. Among the principal Members which he wishes to gain over, are the Dukes of PORTLAND and BEDFORD, Earl FITZWILLIAM, Earl MOIRA, Lord WYCOMBE, &c. and their adherents. But these Noblemen, in the most unequivocal terms, refused to coalesce with the strange and heterogeneous party in Power.
>
> After a Minister has plunged himself headlong into a predicament foretold by those very people whom he solicits now to join his Administration, it is absurd to suppose, when public matters wear still a worse aspect, that they would forfeit their honour and consistency to cover his errors. The defection of the Alarmists of the Opposition last year, has only served to expose their timidity and weakness, for if their *imbecility* was not manifest, what need had a Minister of a more numerous or better support?

Pitt's only enemy was the people. Thanks to his management of elections and creations, Pitt always had the support of Parliament, and the *Morning Post* could very well ask why he needed further support. Since the only possible reason was vanity, no reader could have thought that he would go so far with this particular "*alarm*" as actually to commence negotiations for peace. He did not. It was in fact already clear from the Ministerial papers that he would prosecute the war to the end. The *Gazetteer* of 16 November observed sadly: "We are gravely told by a certain description of men, that if French principles were introduced into other countries there would be an end to all *law* and *religion*; but they never think of telling us, that there would be an end to all placemen and pensioners. The latter assertion, however, would be by far the most easy to prove. . . ." The *Gazetteer* was perhaps reacting to the report (*World*, 12 Nov.) that the "Presentation" of Dr. Horsley to the Bishopric of Rochester and the Deanery of Westminster had "passed the Great Seal" on 9 November. The *Morning Chronicle* was concerned with another development. "A Treasury Paper has the audacity to propose, that, as a test of those who are attached to the constitution, a subscription shall be set on foot for the purpose of defraying the expenses of the war," it noticed on 16 November. "What is the object of this proposal, but to render the Minister independent of Parliament, by furnishing him with money to carry on the present destructive war, without a necessity for their concurrence? Should such a measure be carried into effect, what becomes of the constitution, which guards as its most sacred principle, the right of the representatives of the people to provide for every public expence? But it is thus that the advocates of ministers . . . , under the pretence of zeal for the fabric of the constitution, are aiming a blow at its very foundation." On 18 November *Lloyd's Evening Post* mentioned that Prince Adolphus would return to the Continent after all, leaving on 21 November; on the same day, the *Oracle* announced that "Major-General O'HARA" had been appointed Commander in Chief of the British forces at Toulon; and on 19 November the *Morning Chronicle*, which had again been examining the "Manifesto" of 29 October, demanded that Pitt "come forward with a candid, explicit declaration as to the extent which [he means] to engage us for the restoration of Monarchy in France. Either the Dutch have misunderstood this Manifesto, which well they may, or they do not concur in its views; and whether the one, or the other be the case, further explanations on our part, or on theirs, are indispensable." Replies had already been arranged.

On 20 November the new Commissioners for Toulon issued in the King's name another declaration, promising to hold and defend that city until "monarchy shall be re-established in France." Although the King "by no means desires . . . to prescribe the form of its government," Article IV read, France, in its present state of "anarchy," was so "[threatening] the tranquillity of his own subjects" that the King did not "hesitate to declare that the re-establishment of monarchy, in the person of Louis 17th, and the lawful heirs of the crown, [appeared] to him the best mode of accomplishing [the] just and salutary views [he had in mind]." The justification of the war, it again appeared evident, was not the independence of Holland, but the security of the British Constitution. Opposition papers were well enough acquainted with Pitt's methods to know that talk of peril to the Constitution was always backed by "proof" of such peril. But, since the Toulon declaration was not released to the press, they were unwary. Knowing only that peace did not figure in Pitt's plans, they concentrated on the evils of war. Now that winter had set in, the hysterical concern for the soldiers was affecting even the Opposition, the *Oracle* mentioning on 22 November that that "brightest ornament of exalted life," the Duchess of Devonshire, "is *literally* employed in

MAKING FLANNEL SHIRTS for the brave fellows in *Flanders*." On 20 November the *Morning Post* reminded its readers that the soldiers were not the only victims of the war: "The silk-weavers in Spital-fields to the number of thousands, are in want of bread, to procure which, many of them have been obliged to sell or pawn their looms, and other implements of industry:/ The parish of Lambeth has given public notice, that the distresses of the weavers and other poor manufacturers are such, and their daily wants so pressing, that the ordinary parochial taxes can no longer supply them. Is there a man so dull of understanding, or so hard of heart, as to say that the distresses of these people are not occasioned by war . . . ?" On 21 November the *Post* again announced that the "Gentleman who has the Commercial Department in the MORNING POST" was soliciting donations for the Spitalfields weavers and other "INDIGENT AND LATE WORKING MANUFACTURERS." The *Post* did not deny that the Army needed warm clothes, but it did not believe that the people should be called on to supply them: "Let those to whom the business of cloathing the Army is entrusted, explain why a necessity arises, to render it incumbent on the Public . . . to furnish Cloaths for an English Army." On 22 November the *Post* reported that donations were coming in: "As the object of THIS Subscription is not of an OSTENTATIOUS nature, any Sum, however trifling, will be chearfully received." The first list of "SUBSCRIPTIONS RECEIVED," printed on 23 November, indicated that this statement had been taken seriously. The largest contributions were gifts of £3 3s. from "The Proprietors of the Morning Post" and £2 6s. from Martin Van Butchell. Among the other contributors were "The Editor 1/1/0; C. D. H. 1/1/0; J. Norris 0/5/0; Mr. Legge 1/1/0." Although the list was re-printed daily, the additions were so few that the total on 28 November was still less than £25, and the *Courier*, which had been conducting a drive of its own, was having even less success. On 30 November the *Morning Post* complained bitterly that no one was interested in "pure Charity," but that everyone was goaded by "ignorance, Fear, or base ostentation" to support any political scheme devised by the Government. There were now, the *Post* and *Courier* estimated, six thousand unemployed weavers. The soldiers were well supplied with at least one item, for, according to the Ministerial papers, boatloads of flannel waistcoats, along with a few flannel caps, were being delivered to the Continent daily. On 4 December *Lloyd's Evening Post* again appealed for diversification: the soldiers also, it said, needed shoes. Another such appeal followed in the *World*. "FLANNEL WAISTCOATS," it remarked on 9 December. "After all the quantities that have been sent, it has been discovered, the Soldiers could not get them on under their regimentals. *Trowsers* and *Great Coats* are really useful; and these the COMMITTEE at the CROWN and ANCHOR have very properly adopted."

The *Morning Chronicle* and the *Gazetteer* were as usual more concerned about the beneficiaries of the war than about the victims. The *Morning Chronicle* of 21 November had a good deal to say on this subject:

THE FRUITS OF CONVICTION.

The expences of the war are not to be estimated by the sums necessary to maintain our fleets and armies; nor yet by the subsidies which we so wisely paid to foreign princes. Our home alliances—our domestic subsidies—and the amount of the new places, pensions, and appointments, which we have been obliged, in *pure patriotism*, to create and bestow on proselytes, merely for the sake of carrying on the war, are all to be added to the account. In short, the *expence of Convicts* [*sic*] is to be taken into the estimate; and, it will be a cheering consolation to the starving poor of England, to see what a bountiful harvest this war has proved to the men who took it into their hearts zealously to support it.

Lord LOUGHBOROUGH was the first man in England *to be convinced*, and therefore, with the utmost propriety of gratitude, an arrangement was made to elevate him to the highest lay station, next to the Princes of the Blood, in England. What pecuniary refuge was also made for his retirement, when the dangers of the war shall allow [him] to retire, he has not thought it necessary to state to the public.

The Earl of YARMOUTH followed this *grand* example, and *was also convinced*. The first fruits of his convictions were the dignity of a Marquis for his father [the Earl of Hertford], and that in this war against Jacobinism, a Jacobin plan was followed of creating a new place expressly for him. It was found that we must, like the Jacobins, have *Commissioners of the Armies*, and he was accordingly sent Commissioner to the Army of the King of PRUSSIA, at an expence of six thousand pounds a year to this country.

Lord GEORGE CONWAY, the noble Earl's brother, *was also convinced*, and he was appointed *Confidential Secretary*, and *Occasional Courier*, at the expence of five hundred guineas a trip.

Lord MALMSBURY was *convinced*, and after being fruitlessly employed in some confidential and friendly embassies at home, he is now to be sent on a special commission to the Court of Berlin, at an expence of five or six thousand pounds a year.

Sir GILBERT ELLIOT had also the good fortune *to be convinced*, and one of the Jacobin places was created for him. He was sent Commissioner to Toulon at the expence of 7500*l.* a year.

JOHN ERSKINE, Esq. nephew to Lord LOUGHBOROUGH, and a barrister at law, *was also convinced*, and he was not only made Purse-bearer to the Chancellor, worth not less, through the bankruptcies of the war, than 1500*l.* this year, but he was also appointed Commissary General at Toulon, a place of which the profits are not to be calculated; and if Toulon should be evacuated before his arrival, his noble and learned uncle bargained that he should have forty shillings per day or half pay for life.

JOHN ANSTRUTHER, Esq. had also the honour of being *convinced*, and of seeing the expediency of going to war with France, and Mr. HAYES, a Welch Judge was prevailed on to resign on a pension of 500*l.* a year; and Mr. ANSTRUTHER was appointed in his room. But this was not enough, a new place was also created for Mr. ANSTRUTHER, viz. that of *standing Council* to the *Board of Controul*, with a salary of 800*l.* a year, to be made up by fees, 1,200*l.* a year; so that with his Judgeship, the fruits of his conviction are 2000*l.* a year. The East India Company is authorized by Act of Parliament to pay the expences of the Board of Controul, a *sum not exceeding* 16,000*l.* a year. The Board calls upon the Company for 4000*l.* each quarter. Out of this are to be paid, to the first Commissioner, 2000*l.*; to the other two Commissioners, 1500*l.* each, making, with Mr. ANSTRUTHER's 1200*l.* 6200*l.* The remaining 9800*l.* a year, being neither accounted for to the Company nor in Parliament, is supposed to be absorbed in the ordinary expences of the office.

Sir GREY COOPER has had also a *seasonable conviction* come upon him, and his Majesty was graciously pleased to bestow pensions of 200*l.* a year on each of his daughters.

Sir PETER BURRELL was also *convinced* of the propriety and wisdom of the war, and he succeeded in procuring an increased term in the most beneficial lease upon the Crown, of "the chains for mooring of ships in the River Thames from London Bridge to Bugby Hole, with all fees, duties and profits thereto belonging," and which lease is worth an immense sum per annum.

To these we might add the *honours* that have sprung from *conviction.* The Earl of CARLISLE, for instance, was convinced, and he was invested with the blue ribband instead of the green. Lord PORCHESTER was convinced, and he was created Earl of CARNARVON. General [John] VAUGHAN was convinced, and he was made a Knight of the Bath.

We refer without acrimony or observation, these facts to the *disinterested* part of the public, and shall simply demand whether it is not very natural for these noble and honourable persons to continue in the belief that the war ought to be persevered in.

On 16 December the *Gazetteer* stated again: "An effectual plan for the prevention of unnecessary wars:—Lay a tax of 90 *per cent.* on all places and pensions above 500*l.* a year, and of 50 *per cent.* on all below that sum, during the continuance of war.—*Probatum est.*"

Other newspapers were listing other "Fruits of Conviction." On 22 November the *Oracle* reported that "Sir GILBERT ELLIOT is allowed 15,000*l.* equipage money, as Commissioner for managing the Civil Affairs of *Toulon.*" The announcement was repeated by the *Morning Post* on the following day and by the *World* on 23 November, and on 28 November the *Post* remarked: "As TOULON has been taken in the name of LOUIS XVII. of course Sir GILBERT ELLIOT will look to him for the payment of the *immense* salary annexed to his recent employment." On 12 October General Conway had, it appeared, been promoted to Field Marshal, and on 6 December the Lord Chancellor of Ireland, Baron Fitzgibbon, was created Viscount Fitzgibbon. On 2 December the papers reported that that archalarmist, Sir Joseph Banks, had on 30 November been elected President of the Royal Society. Banks had evidently wanted this post very much, for, from mid-November on, he inserted puffs of himself in the *World* and the *Oracle,* the *World* of 16 November mentioning, for example: "Sir JOSEPH BANKS has renewed his Conversaziones in Soho, where most of the celebrated literary characters of this metropolis will as usual assemble." After the election the puffs disappeared. On 30 November the *Morning Post* explained the presence in London of another member of The Association. Having remarked that the principal beneficiaries of the war were Pitt, Rose, Dundas, and Reeves, the *Post* went on to say that "Mr. Chairman REEVES, the Chief Justice of Newfoundland, has not yet set off for that place, but still remains in town, in case the Cabinet or Mr. PITT should want his assistance in any intricate affair, relating either to their domestic or foreign concerns." Although Dundas was the most vulnerable of the quartet, he was not lacking in admirers. "The good-humoured, open frankness of Mr. DUNDAS, in executing the duties of his Office endears him to every man that has occasion to transact business with him," the *True Briton* commented on 27 November. "Mr. DUNDAS's laudable affability has lately exercised the merry malignity of the *Jacobin* Writers," the *Oracle* remarked on 9 December. "They have very foolishly assailed him, because he possesses all the integrity and patriotism which the OPPOSITION GENTLEMEN want; and because, forsooth, he discharges the duties belonging to the Secretary of State for the Home Department without fee or reward. These virtues are in the *jaundiced* eye of the feeble *phalanx* the most culpable of all moral acts!"

There was continuing interest in the new Bishop of Rochester, Dr. Horsley, who on 6 December was installed as Dean of Westminster; and the appearance on 4 December of *The Conduct of France since the Year 1789, towards Great Britain, Examined, with Appendix and Notes. By Mr. Miles* revived interest in his pensions. Some juggling had occurred in the Stamp Office. On 2 November the *World* reported that Thomas Linley had succeeded John Reynal as Deputy Supervisor of Stamps, and on 30 November the *Morning Post* mentioned that "Mr. MEADOWS" had replaced Francis Fownes Luttrell as Commissioner of the Stamp Office. Luttrell, readers understood from the *Oracle* (2 Dec.), had been appointed Commissioner of Customs. On 2 December the *Public Advertiser* further announced that "Mr. Burke the younger, has been appointed a Receiver of the Crown Rents, in the city of London, and counties of Middlesex, Essex, Hertford, Norfolk, and Huntingdon." When the announcement appeared in the *World* (3 Dec.), "the son of the *Declaimer*" had been substituted for "the younger." The *World* was greatly upset. On 27 November it had published a long diatribe on Burke, signed "A FRIEND *to the* FREEDOM *of the* PRESS" and probably written by Major Scott. On 4 December it published another. The author was now terrified that Pitt would sacrifice Hastings as a favor to Burke. By 12 December the *World* had evidently been reassured. "Mr. BURKE is preparing a *furious Philippic* against Mr. HASTINGS," it remarked placidly. "It has been the fate of good and great Men in all Ages to suffer for a time,—but the Public does them justice at last." The *Morning Post*, which had lost interest in Burke as soon as it realized that Pitt meant to continue the war, was now lambasting him again, this time in support of the *World*. "A German Critic on Mr. BURKE's Book [the *Reflections*], calls it '*Insigne plane, sed insanum opus.*'—'*a work of splendid insanity*,'" it said on 13 December; and on 14 December: "Wages have been laid, that the Trial of Mr. HASTINGS will outlive his Judges."

Some of the alarmists fared worse than they expected. On 23 November, according to the *Morning Post* (26 Nov.), Lord Mulgrave returned from Toulon to stay, having been "replaced as Commander in Chief of British forces serving in the South of France by General O'HARA," and Lord Howe, who was expecting the richest reward of all, got nothing. On 28 November all newspapers reported that he had captured the entire French fleet, "consisting of 7 sail of the line, 5 frigates, 2 brigs, and more than 30 sail of transports with troops on board, headed for the West Indies." The report was not contradicted "with certainty" until 10 December, when it turned out that he had not captured a ship, the fleet having escaped under cover of night. The *Morning Post* still purported to believe it. "Lord HOWE's Prize Money, in consequence of his late capture of the French fleet, will amount to, at least £10,000,000!" it calculated on 13 December. The posts which now most interested the newspapers, those of Viceroy and Chief Secretary of Ireland, did not change hands. Most frequently mentioned as successor to the Earl of Westmorland as Viceroy had lately been the Earl of Moira; and on 9 December the *Morning Post* reported that "Mr. COOKE is spoken of as the successor to Lord HOBART [as Chief Secretary]. This man, with a few obscure literary adventurers, visited Ireland when Lord CARLISLE was the Viceroy of that country [1780–1782]. In a few years he became Parliamentary Clerk to the [Irish] House of Commons, where the Members did not suffer him to hold any conversation with them, except what was of an official nature. From this situation he was raised to an M.P. and at the time of the Regency he succeeded Mr. [Charles Francis] SHERIDAN as Secretary at War. If he should now be made Secretary to the LORD LIEUTENANT, we shall have those men '*booing and booing*' [*sic*] to him, who during the Administration of the Duke of RUTLAND [1784–1787], treated him with so much indifference and hauteur." Edward Cooke was the third son of Dr. William Cooke, Provost of King's College, Cambridge. Lord Hobart had been appointed Governor of the Presidency of Madras in October, with provisional succession to the Governor Generalship of India. He resigned as Chief Secretary on 15 December and was succeeded on 16 December by Sylvester Douglas, as the newspapers learned later.

Legal and Prison Reforms; The Death of Lord George Gordon

The Duke of Portland, Earl Fitzwilliam, and Earl Spencer had declined offices by 14 November, and, instead of negotiating a peace, as he had threatened, Pitt had made it clear, not only in the Toulon declaration of 20 November, which readers would not yet have seen, but also in the Ministerial newspapers, that he would prosecute the war until the Bourbons were back on the French throne, in order thus to preserve the British Constitution. Talk of the Constitution was always followed by another alarm, and, the alarm of an invasion having failed rather miserably, the Government would attribute the danger to the local "Jacobins." That it was contemplating such a maneuver as early as October is evident from Charles Stuart's letters to the Home Office.

On 26 October the *Oracle* reported that Thomas Christie had returned from Paris, that he had not "sacrificed a large sum of money to enable him to escape," as some newspapers had said, but that he had "left Paris with a regular passport, obtained in the ordinary way, without costing him a farthing." Also, it reported:

LONDON CORRESPONDING SOCIETY.

The Members of this Society, to the amount of 700, met on Thursday [24 Oct.] in a house and paddock near Hackney, for the purpose of electing two Delegates to represent them in the Convention which is to be held at *Edinburgh*, for the purpose of concerting the necessary measures to obtain an EQUAL REPRESENTATION of THE PEOPLE.

There were about 2000 present.

In order to convince the people of the erroneous sentiments which they entertained of the designs of the meeting, Mr. GERALD, Mr. MARGAROTT, and Mr. JENNINGS, harangued them from the windows of the house, with such effect, that they declared, by universal acclamations their approbation of the views of the Society.

The Members now proceeded to the Election of the two Delegates: JOSEPH GERALD and MAURICE MARGAROT, were unanimously elected.

What the Government wanted, it is clear from Stuart's correspondence, was evidence of treasonable or at least seditious activities on the part of some reformers, and, since it seemed to Stuart that the British Convention or perhaps Christie might supply it, one reason for his letter of 27 October was to urge Dundas to watch developments in those areas:

How are the London Corresponding Society, as I have heard, to pay for their Scotch Delegates?—By the Press.—By the sale of "The Political Progress" now circulating as I've heard by them, throughout the three kingdoms—the profits of that, are to pay their expences—Have you seen it?—I have got a copy of it within these few days—it is said to be written by the late Lord Fordenstoun [*sic*] —but I dont believe it—I have read it with attention, and I see nothing particular in it but much dogmatical derision from the superficial view of things— besides, being borrowed and gleaned from "Burgh's Political Disquisitions," "Doddington's Diary"—"Macpherson's History," & "State Papers,"—and one anecdote from Lord Chatham's "Life."

I mean to take the liberty of sending it this week to Mr. Nepean, as I suppose you must have seen it.—Kay's name, opposite Somerset House, is at the bottom of it, along with two Edinburgh booksellers.

You cannot be too vigilant about the Scotch meeting—Gerald, one of the banditti delegates, is a man, I believe, that is very, very violent—he is an American and Jacobin, too—well educated at Dr. Parr's, and fluent in speech, and well primed in "sense half-mad."

How did Christie leave Paris, as he says, with a regular passport without costing him a farthing?—What is his business here?—Why was he so peculiarly favoured by the Convention?—I believe you will find him at the head of the Dissenters here—and I don't understand his coming over at such a time as this.

Joseph Gerrald had practiced law in America from 1784 to 1788, but he had been born in the West Indies of British parents.

On 28 October Stuart transmitted to Nepean his copy of *The Political Progress of Great Britain; or, an Impartial Account of the Principal Abuses in the Government of this Country, from the Revolution in 1688. The Whole Tending to Prove the Ruinous Consequences of the Popular System of War and Conquest* (Edinburgh: Printed for Robertson and Berry, No. 39, South-Bridge and T. Kay, 332, Strand, London). The pamphlet was first published in 1792, and the actual author was James Thomson Callender, who had already been indicted for conspiring with James Robertson and Walter Berry to publish the "sedition," as Nepean would have known. In his covering letter Stuart said again that the "pamphlet is now circulating everywhere by the London Corresponding Society. . . . In the meantime, permit me to add, that 'the L. Corresp. Society' are worse than the worst of the Jacobins," Stuart went on. "—Their pretexts at Reform, you will find, are all a farce.—In my simple opinion, you will find them of the same kidney as the Conventicles of the last century in Scotland or the most hideous of the most hideous Jacobins of the present—and you see they are sending their *Ambassadors* to the Scotch Meeting of to-morrow, I believe— You cannot have too horrid an opinion of them—and you cannot be too vigilant. —I should rather think that you will soon hear of some [invitations?] to overt acts." Although the "meeting" was well riddled with spies, the spies had nothing to report, and the Government was not ready to act in any event, Parliament having been prorogued to 21 January.

The opening of the British Convention had been scheduled to coincide with the opening of Parliament. When it became evident that Parliament would again be prorogued, there was apparently some discussion about postponing it, for Daniel Stuart was not notified until mid-October that it would be held as planned. By this time, he said,[69] it was too late to consult the London Friends of the People, and he wrote Skirving to that effect, adding that, although the society would send no formal delegates, "it was highly probable some members . . . , then in Scotland, would be present, and that whatever they agreed to, I had no doubt the society would confirm. I said Lord Lauderdale might perhaps attend." On 4 and 5 November, respectively, the *Morning Post* and the *Morning Chronicle* reported that "a numerous and respectable Delegation from all the Societies in Scotland, associated for the purpose of promoting a Parliamentary Reform, assembled in the Masons' Lodge, Blackfriars Wynd, [at twelve o'clock on the morning of 29 October,] when they made choice of Mr. [John] M'Intyre, of Edinburgh, President, and re-elected William Skirving, of Strathrudie, Secretary. . . . The Society meets to-morrow, for the dispatch of business. . . . Delegates from all parts of England are expected to attend." This was the last mention of the Convention in the London papers. The Convention was in fact circumspect. Particularly in evidence were David Downie, a goldsmith from Edinburgh, James Robertson and Walter Berry, who had completed their terms in prison, the Ross brothers, William and George, who described themselves as "clerks" in the office of the Edinburgh *Gazetteer* and transmitted accounts of the proceedings to their newspaper, and Alexander Callander, an Edinburgh reformer. Henry Yorke was present as representative of the London Constitutional Society, as so was Matthew Campbell Brown as representative of the Sheffield Society. The Convention lasted seven days, adjourning on 6 November. But, a few hours before it adjourned, Archibald Hamilton Rowan and Simon Butler from Ireland, Margarot and Gerrald from the London Corresponding Society, and Charles Sinclair from the London Constitutional Society were introduced. The London delegates had just arrived; Rowan, as the London papers learned later, had arrived on 4 November, had been arrested within the hour, and had just been admitted to bail. In view of these developments, a second Convention was subsequently scheduled for 19 November.

In England the Government was still punishing printers and booksellers, but only under the cloak of bankruptcy laws. On 26 October the *Oracle* mentioned that John Bell finally had his "certificate," but, included in the list of new bankrupts, were "John Jarvis, of . . . Lincoln's Inn-Fields, printer," and "John Strachan, of the Strand, bookseller." The worst of it was, the *Oracle* added on 29 October, that the "certificate" was often meaningless, for "[one] of the most important *points* determined in the Court of King's Bench during the last Term [is that a] person against whom a second COMMISSION OF BANKRUPT has been issued who has not paid 15*s*. in the pound, is liable to an action by any of his

Creditors, notwithstanding they have signed his Certificate." On 12 November "William Locke, Red-Lion Street, Holborne, printer," was added to the group. But the trials of provincial talkers and booksellers was petering out, and there were no new trials in London. On 2 November, according to the *Oracle* (5 Nov.), "the Bill preferred against Mr. PIGOTT, on a charge of having uttered seditious words in the London Coffee-house, Ludgate-hall, was thrown out by the Grand Jury./ A true bill, at the same time, was found by the Grand Jury against Dr. HUDSON [Hodgson], on a similar charge. The Doctor, who had been out on bail, was ordered to find fresh securities, and committed to Newgate till he found the same." The *Morning Post* was not pleased. "Mr. PIGGOT," it said on 7 November, had been "confined more than three weeks in the prison, immured during six-teen hours in a damp stone dungeon, at the risque of his life, and at considerable expence." On 13 November the *Oracle* reported that the verdict in the case of "King *vs.* Eaton," "found GUILTY *of publishing the Pamphlet in question*," had been debated on 9 November, but the judges had reached no decision as to its interpretation.

Although by mid-November there was every indication of another major alarm, the newspapers were too concerned with other matters to be aware of it. There was continuing interest in the sentences of Muir and Palmer, and the death of Lord George Gordon revived demands for various legalistic reforms. The public had always been curious about the prisons. According to *Lloyd's Evening Post* (25 July), such a "mob" had assembled to watch the transfer of eighteen prisoners from Newgate and Clerkenwell to "the New gaol in Cold-Bath Fields" that the transfer was finally conducted before dawn on the morning of 18 July. The fact that no one knew who was in the prisons intensified the curiosity. "A person last week died in the gaol at Chester, where he had been confined twenty years, for a debt originally amounting to twenty pounds," said the *Public Advertiser* on 10 September. Newgate was especially fascinating, since it was the worst prison and therefore housed those the Government particularly disliked. One year in Newgate was considered the equivalent of two years in King's Bench. On 24 October the *Gazetteer* reported that one of the inmates, Lord George Gordon, "is very much indisposed. It is thought his Lordship has caught the gaol distemper." On 25 October the *Morning Post* repeated that "Lord GEORGE GORDON lies dangerously ill of the Gaol distemper"; and by 1 November there were rumors of an epidemic. The *Oracle* assured its readers that the rumors were ridiculous: "NEWGATE./ The report of an epidemic disorder having broke out in this Prison, is totally void of foundation./ And the PUBLIC may be assured, that, from the best Authority, (except Lord GEORGE GORDON and THOMAS TOWNLY M'CAN, one of the persons convicted of a conspiracy in the King's Bench Prison), there are no other prisoners dangerously ill./ In the Mens sick ward there are three only; and this time twelve months, upwards of *thirty* were dangerously ill of a fever." On 1 November Lord George Gordon died. The

Oracle (2 Nov.) gave him an obituary of one and one-half columns, protesting in passing the severe and unreasonable securities demanded of him and also the state of the prisons.

Most newspapers responded similarly. The *Morning Post* announced (2 Nov.):

LORD GEORGE GORDON.

This unfortunate Nobleman died yesterday morning of a malignant fever, in Newgate. It is now six years since Lord GEORGE has been confined for a Libel on the late Queen of France, and it is rather remarkable, that the exit of that ill-fated Nobleman and the Queen, should have happened much about the same period. His Lordship, during his confinement, was for many months a solitary prisoner at the State side of the Jail, and during his confinement, demeaned himself with much propriety, even contributing, in a liberal manner, to the distresses of the wretched culprits in Newgate. It is about five years since he became a convert to the Jewish religion, to the tenets of which, he strictly adhered. He seemed extremely sincere in his conversion, and argued ingeniously with others, to become proselytes to his opinions. This day the body of Lord GEORGE is to be delivered to his relations for interment.

The report of the Jail Distemper raging in Newgate, has been contradicted by authority; of course we presume that the illness of Lord George GORDON and Mr. MACAN, was nothing more than a common fever. We are happy to be assured of this circumstance, as the afflictions of the unhappy people confined in Newgate are sufficiently poignant, not to require any additional misfortunes. With respect to Mr. GILLESPY, the Surgeon of Newgate, our former statements had no reference to the Hospitals which he attends, and which are at present in a very healthy state.

Mr. KIRBY, Keeper of Newgate, yesterday informed the Prisoners on the State Side, That if any symptoms of the dreadful fever, now raging there, appeared in any of those not yet afflicted with it, he had received orders to remove them to the Hospital amongst the Felons!

The *World*'s obituary included some preachments:

LORD GEORGE GORDON

Yesterday morning died in Newgate, in the sixth year of his imprisonment for publishing a libel on MARIE ANTOINETTE, the late unhappy QUEEN of France.

In the year 1780, he rendered himself extremely popular, by making long and violent declamations in the house of Commons, against Popery; and soon after distinguished himself in St. George's Fields, as President of the Protestant Association, by assembling together the largest concourse of people that had ever been convoked on any occasion.

When he had assembled the mob, however, he knew not how to conduct them, and afforded a fatal example of the rash folly of heating the minds of a multitude, whose ideas are confused and indeterminate, whose passions violent and ungovernable, and whose prejudices are intemperate and rash.

Enflamed and agitated, they knew not why, nor wherefore, the people thronged to the Houses of Parliament, and there attacked the Members of each according to their own vague opinions of retribution for suppositious injuries.

After this followed those terrible and sad events, which might have been checked in their commotion, but for a misguided consideration.

In 1787, he produced his libel against the QUEEN of France, for which he was tried, found guilty, and sentenced to five years imprisonment, a considerable fine, and security for his good behaviour. In Newgate he changed his religious principles, and became as warm an advocate for Judaism, and the Laws of Moses, as he had formerly been for the Protestant Reformation, and the doctrines of CALVIN.

At the expiration of his sentence of imprisonment, he was brought up to the Court of King's Bench to proffer his security. Here he made a ludicrous and lunatic appearance, and his bail were rejected as insufficient. He was, therefore, again remanded to Newgate.

Though related to the noble family of GORDON, neither his brother, nor other relatives ever attempted to effect his liberation from confinement, as his brain was supposed to be disarranged; and his habits, and opinions, too rude and violent for refined behaviour, or domestic peace.

It is rather remarkable, that his death should so speedily follow that of the miserable Princess whose reputation he had so openly insulted.

His remains were yesterday removed from Newgate by his friends.

This seems to have been the only hostile obituary, for the *Sun* and the *True Briton* said nothing, and, although the *Public Advertiser* did not hear of the death until 4 November, its obituary was even more sympathetic than those in the Opposition papers:

LORD GEORGE GORDON.

Lord George having been long remarkable for the eccentricities of his conduct, and singularities of opinion, we think it our duty to gratify the public curiosity with a few biographical remarks upon a character so emphatically striking.

On Friday morning [1 Nov.], about two o'clock, his Lordship expired of a fever, which baffled the skill of Dr. Lettsom, who attended him; he was delirious for three days previous to his death; the last ten hours of which he was speechless.

Lord George was the third son of Cosmo George, Duke of Gordon, by Catherine, daughter of William, Earl of Aberdeen. He was born in London, and his late Majesty George II. stood as his godfather.

At an early period he entered the Navy, which he quitted during the American War, in consequence of some altercation with Lord Sandwich relative to promotion.

His Lordship represented the borough of Luggershall in Parliament, during several Sessions [1774–1780]; and, as he animadverted with great freedom, and often with great wit, on the proceedings of both sides of the House, it was usual at that period to say, that there were three parties in Parliament—the Ministry, the Opposition, and Lord George Gordon.

The dreary hours of his confinement were devoted to reading and the study of ancient and modern history. Several of his publications upon miscellaneous subjects are characterized by sound arguments, and illumined by flashes of genuine humour; his language was animated, and his diction correct and classical. His conduct to his fellow prisoners was beneficent, and his heart alive to the impressions of sensibility.

Such is a brief sketch of an individual, who ended his days in a prison. With respect to the alledged cause of his confinement, a recent melancholy event induces us to be silent. With respect to the severity of his sentence, and the bail demanded for his liberation, we are also silent. Those, however, in whose memory the riots of the year 1780 are yet fresh, when they consider the present state of political speculation, and weigh the character, genius, and talents of Lord George, must in candour admit; that such a person could not well be at large without some degree of hazard to the good order of society.

His Lordship has left one niece [Lady Charlotte Gordon] married to the heir of the Duke of Richmond [Charles Lennox], and another [Lady Susan Gordon] upon the point of giving her hand to the Duke of Manchester.

This obituary may have been Henry Sampson Woodfall's last contribution to the *Public Advertiser*.

The paragraph, denying the "report of an epidemic disorder having broke out in Newgate," was reprinted by all Ministerial papers on 2 November, but on 3 November Thomas Townley Macan, serving a three-year sentence for trying to blow up King's Bench Prison, died of a fever very similar to that which had killed Lord George Gordon; and on 4 November the *Morning Post* demanded to know what was going on: "The Physician who attended the unfortunate Lord GEORGE GORDON, should state to Government, whether or not that alarming complaint, the Jail Distemper, has, or has not been the cause of his Lordship's death. If so, respect at least for the Public, and the safety of the metropolis, should oblige Government to have the unfortunate Prisoners at the State Side of Newgate properly aired either on the battlements of the prison, or in coaches, which may be guarded, otherwise the distemper, if such it be, is likely to [sweep?] through the prison, and consequently reach many parts of the Metropolis." The *Post* also published a letter from John Frost, stating that Gordon and Macan had, to his certain knowledge, died "of a putrid fever of the most malignant kind." Frost had sent a modified version of this letter to the *Oracle*, which published it on 5 November:

> Felon Side, Newgate, Sunday,
> Nov. 3,
> (*20th Week of my Imprisonment.*)

SIR:

In the ORACLE of Friday [1 Nov.] is a paragraph asserting that the Gaol of Newgate is free from any infectious disease. How such an assertion crept into your paper it is not for me to determine! But from melancholy experience, and the duty I owe the numerous friends who have visited me since my confinement, and who may be misled by the above paragraph, I feel myself obliged to state, on the authority of Dr. LETTSOM, that Lord GEORGE GORDON died on Friday last of a putrid fever of the most malignant kind; and that, at seven o'clock this evening,

THOMAS TOWNLEY MACAN died of the same disease; that THOMAS LLOYD, a prisoner, has recovered from it, of whom Lord GEORGE GORDON during his last illness said he had caught the infection. That T. W. HOLLAND's Apprentice was removed with a fever upon him; and that a friend of mine, who visited Lord GEO. GORDON this day s'nnight, has been indisposed from the day after. With respect to myself, such has been the precarious state of my health, that notwithstanding every precaution of bark, and other remedies, my medical friends are daily fearful of finding me attacked with the disease.

JOHN FROST.

Although Frost did not know it, there had already been an inquest on the death of Lord George Gordon, which, so far as the coroner was concerned, ended the matter. The newspapers did not know it either until 5 November, when an account of the proceedings appeared in the *Morning Post*.

According to the *Morning Post*, the inquest had been held at Newgate on 2 November, and it was immediately established that Lord George Gordon had taken ill on 19 October and had grown steadily worse until he died at two o'clock on the morning of 1 November. "The Apothecary, Mr. Lloyd, of Snow-hill, who attended during his illness, declared the disorder to be a putrid fever." Another prisoner, Thomas Lloyd, an American citizen, "confined in Newgate for a libel," thereupon testified that he had known Gordon since the previous December, that he had understood, "as so, he supposed, did everyone else," that he was mad, and that he had found him instead to be "quite sane and intelligent." Having satisfied "the *punishing justice*," Gordon, said Lloyd, had gone to Court on 28 January to satisfy "the *preventive justice*," and he had not been depressed by the results, which he had in fact anticipated. However, Lloyd went on, Gordon hoped, "*by obtaining a liberation from prison*," finally

to overcome . . . all that influence, which he used to say he knew was operating against him, from the Monarch on the Throne, down to the wretch who lives on the veriest dregs of office.

The deponent . . . saw him contract the expences of his table, and other domestic necessaries, in order to lay by a sum sufficient to hire bail, as he had been advised by an Attorney; he saw these endeavours were vain, for the Attorney, instead of encouraging such as offered themselves under the proposed reward, in several cases absolutely prevented them. Some Gentlemen of respectability generously volunteered to bail him, but afterward, on being given to understand that such a step would disoblige some elevated characters, who were not the friends of the deceased, they declined any further interference in his behalf. In short, after innumerable attempts to effect this purpose, and finding himself forsaken and deceived, not only by others, but by men whom he was to pay for their good offices, he sunk into an involuntary Apathy. He discontinued the exercise which he had been accustomed to take, and a friend, who really possessed property sufficient to qualify as one of the bail, was no longer invited to visit him. Great debility was apparent, and at length his constitution was incapable of resisting even the slightest degree of infection. The Deponent was taken ill about three weeks ago with a violent pain in the region of the heart, and on the third day was covered with purple spots, which he shewed to his friends, they agreed it was of a putrid nature; the spots lasted some time, but were attended with no other symptoms. When the deceased had been ill a few days the like purple spots appeared on him. Then the deceased declared publicly, that he judged he had caught the distemper of the Deponent. The Deponent's physician however said, the complaint which he had had must have been slight indeed, if it was of a putrid nature. The Deponent only states the circumstance respecting himself, to shew that Lord George Gordon's debility, arising from a confinement which the deceased believed would be perpetual, and which he considered as in the highest degree cruel, might be eventually the cause of his death, although in contradiction of this opinion, the deceased had told the Deponent but a few days before his death, that he was confident a just Providence would yet permit him to see an end of all his enemies, in like manner as he had seen that of the Sieur de LAUNEY, who was some time since hanged in Paris, and of MARIE ANTOINETTE, who lately expired on the scaffold.

The Inquest heard no other evidence, and after consideration brought in their verdict, "By the visitation of God."

"It is estimated, that the number of debtors confined in the different prisons of this kingdom, at present amount to 30,000 persons. . . ," the *Morning Post* added.

By this time the *Morning Post* was obviously fighting for the reform of penal laws, especially those involving imprisonment for debt and very especially those involving imprisonment for nonpayment of those "securities for good behavior" of which the Government was so fond. The *World* had been fighting for legislation regulating the practices of the legal profession, but, since Lord George Gordon was a victim of the machinations of lawyers, as well as a victim of the machinations of the Government, the *World* had hardly delivered its preachments, when it became an ally of the *Morning Post*. What the two papers had in mind was a comprehensive reform bill, covering all aspects of the situation, and, since only Lord Moira had thus far indicated any interest in such a bill, it was of awful consequence to them. that he remain in England. On 7 November the *Morning Post* mentioned sadly: "There is no truth in the rumour, we trust, that Earl MOIRA, is to succeed Lord WESTMORELAND, as the Viceroy of Ireland. There is no man, however good his intentions, who condescends to be entrammelled by the Minister, who can be popular in that country. Earl MOIRA has too much pride to submit to such trammels, and if he does not, there is no probability of his being appointed to such a situation." "Amongst the prisoners in the Fleet Prison at present, there are a noble Lord, a Baronet, two Generals, an Admiral, and several sons, brothers, nephews, &c. of Members of Both Houses of Parliament," the *World* told its readers on 11 November. On 12 November the *Morning Post* stated that the Earl of Moira had probably accepted: "It is confidently asserted, that [he] will succeed Lord WESTMORELAND as Viceroy of

Ireland; and that Major DOYLE will be the Secretary to his Lordship." By 14 November it was evident that he had not accepted. Both newspapers were ecstatic. "It is [now] hoped," said the *Morning Post*, "that Earl MOIRA will not leave the country before the Meeting of Parliament, that he may accomplish his wish of relieving the various Prisoners confined throughout the kingdom for debt. Mr. GREY is also pledged to the same laudable purpose, and as a matter of great Humanity, and a measure that must ultimately prove advantageous to the Country, we hope that no party considerations will stop its progress." "The PHILOSOPHER and the MORALIST might wonder why ENGLAND could be engaged in a War to rectify the errors of other States, and at the same time, groan under the miseries created by the *Abuse of her own Laws*," said the *World*. "Can the REVOLUTIONARY TRIBUNAL of FRANCE be a greater Disgrace to that Country, than the *lower* ATTORNIES are to ENGLAND?—Certainly NOT." This statement was followed by more exposés of the profession, and on 15 November the *Morning Post* assured its readers that "Earl MOIRA has certainly been pressed by His MAJESTY to accept of some civil employment, which the Noble Earl has declined. He said, as a soldier, it was his duty to serve his country and His MAJESTY, but that he could not think of joining the Administration, whose measure, he foresaw, must bring ruin on the country. Earl MOIRA stands high in the opinion of all partizans, and will not easily forfeit the Popularity which he has so justly earned, to gratify Mr. PITT, and that Gentleman's political friends." "Popularity" seems to have meant a great deal to the Earl of Moira, for the *Oracle* was now insisting that he was the most "popular" man in the British Isles. Lord Moira was also a purchaser of puffs.

The death of Lord George Gordon had provided an incentive for the various reforms; in addition, it was an embarrassment to the Government and its friends, and the newspapers' continued preoccupation with the case seems to have had more to do with the latter than the former. Lord George had asked to be buried in the Jewish cemetery, but, since the cemetery would not, as it turned out, admit converts, there had been considerable question as to what to do with the body. The Gordons had finally and, the newspapers thought, grudgingly consented to inter it with the family. The Gordons, who were not loved by the newspapers anyway, had hardly endeared themselves in this instance, and much of what the press had to say subsequently was intended to disparage them. Having admitted on 9 November that there was "no Fever at present on the State Side of Newgate," the *Morning Post* went on to say: "Lord GEORGE GORDON was allowed five hundred a year by his family. He lived frugally but not inhospitably. He was never intoxicated, as he seldom drank any thing but porter, which, with his pipe, were his chief solace. The money he saved yearly out of his annuity, was appropriated to the relief of the unfortunate in Prison. From the lowest Jewish old clothes-man to the Royal Brothers, he had been visited in his Prison, and was always courteous to strangers, but boasted that he never uncovered in the presence of his Royal Friends, who visited him in jail, because one of them kept on his hat in his chamber." "HASTE," announced the *Morning Post* on 14 November. "—Within a fortnight after the death of LORD GEORGE GORDON, his niece, LADY SUSAN GORDON, was married to the DUKE of MANCHESTER." This marriage is presently dated 7 October, hence before his death. The circumstances of Lord George Gordon's death were also not forgotten, and the Government was evidently uneasy, for on 11 November the *Oracle* published a letter, which Dundas had written to the Lord Mayor, James Saunderson, on 6 November, advising him that reports of a malignant disease in Newgate had been sent to the King and that the King had ordered an investigation. Saunderson's reply was included. Writing on 8 November, Saunderson said that he had at once asked Dr. Carmichael Smyth and Dr. David Pitcairn to look into the matter and that they had found no evidence of infectious fever in either the men's "Felons section, the Infirmary, the State side, the women's Felon section, or the debtors' section." There were 190 debtors in the prison at the time; there had been between "500 and 600 prisoners" in all during the last six months; and there had been only 9 deaths. The prison was in a good condition, bright and airy, and the inmates were in a presently healthy state. The report was dated "Newgate, 7 Nov." On 14 November *The Times* denied "on high authority" that there had been any "fever" in Newgate. The *Morning Post* had evidence to the contrary. "Doctor LETSOM reported, we are assured, to the late Lord MAYOR [Saunderson], that the fever of which Lord GEORGE GORDON, and Mr. MACAN died, was of the most malignant kind," it said on 15 November. "Why this report is with-held from the Public, rests with Sir JAMES SANDERSON to explain. If the fever was of a putrid kind, it should be mentioned for this reason: because though the unfortunate prisoners, by using the necessary precautions, avoided the distemper, yet strangers who visited them, and used none, might have fallen victim to the contagion." The *Gazetteer* thought so too. On 16 November it published a letter from James Ridgway and Henry D. Symonds, stating that "Dr. LETTSOME" had investigated the prison on 7 November at the request of Sir James Saunderson and had told them then that Gordon and Macan had died of "an infectious gaol fever of the worst kind, that it was of the same class, with the *yellow fever*, and nearly related to it." It also published a letter from Thomas Lloyd, who stated that "Dr. LETTSOME" told him and Frost on 31 October that Gordon and Macan were dying of "a putrid fever, and that of the most malignant kind," and that he had "mentioned to the turnkeys, the necessity of ventilating the jail . . .; he particularly recommended the burning of some combustibles, sprinkling boiled vinegar, and exploding gunpowder, as the most likely mode of getting rid of the infection." The account concluded with another letter from John Frost, dated 14 November, by which time Frost was himself confined to bed. Frost repeated that he had been told by "Dr. LETTSOME," who attended Gordon and Macan, that there was "a malignant fever" in the prison and that Dr. Lettsom had recommended that "every effort" be made to "destroy the contagion, by burning tar-barrels, pitch, assafedita, brimstone, camphor, and canimomile flowers, by sprinkling about tar-water and vinegar, in which had been boiled rue, spice, &c. and by frequent explosions of Gunpowder." But none of these measures was taken until 6 November and then only in anticipation of the visits of Dr. Pitcairn and Dr. Smyth.

Prosecution of the Morning Chronicle

By 29 November the lists of bankrupts had swollen to include the name of "George Smith, late of King street, victualler." Smith had made the mistake of suing George Rose. By this time the lists also included the name of Thomas Cooper, who was being thus discouraged from returning to England, and on 24 December the *Oracle* mentioned that "John Fraser, late of Chelsea, Middlesex, Nurseryman," was being similarly ordered to surrender to his creditors. Fraser, a relation of Mackintosh, had financially assisted the Government's archenemy, the old spurious *Star*. The Government was paying off some very old debts. By mid-November it was also preparing a new alarm. On 15 November the *Public Advertiser* reported that Archibald Hamilton Rowan had been arrested in Edinburgh, but that Colonel Macleod had provided bail for his release. The report was repeated by the *Oracle* of 20 November, the *Oracle* adding that Rowan had been arrested "as a seditious person" and that the bail had amounted to "166*l*. and over." The arrest had occurred on 4 November. On 26 November the Government struck again. G. G. J. and J. Robinson, who had been convicted on 6 August of publishing Part II of Paine's *Rights of Man*, were brought into court for sentencing. The Robinsons fared remarkably well, John being fined £100, the other three £50 each. The reason was, said the *Oracle* (27 Nov.), that the pamphlet was not regarded as libelous at the time they published it, and only John knew it was being published at all. Holt and Winterbotham, who were summoned to the Court of King's Bench on 27 November, fared worse. Daniel Holt, who had been awaiting sentence since July for selling "two very scandalous and atrocious Libels," was fined £50 and sentenced to two years in Newgate Prison for the first offense and fined an additional £50 and sentenced to an additional two years in Newgate for the second. He was also ordered to find securities for good behavior for another five years, himself in the amount of £200 and two others in the amount of £150 each. The dissenter, William Winterbotham, convicted in July of preaching seditious sermons the previous November, was fined £200 and sentenced to four years in New Prison, Clerkenwell. The securities in his case were £500 for himself and £250 for each of two others. On 29 November *The Times* ordered all reformers to cease and desist:

"*O Reformers of England*! take warning by what you hear and see! Remember the Epitaph of an Italian:—'I was well—I would be better—and here I am!'"

Although these were harbingers of what was to come, most newspapers ignored them. There was some interest in the case of William Locke, recently (16 Nov.) declared a bankrupt and now, it appeared, being prosecuted for libel besides. The first mention of the litigation was an item in the *Oracle* of 19 November, indicating that on 18 November Locke, as publisher of "The Bon Ton Magazine or Microscope of Fashion and Folly," had appeared in the Court of King's Bench to be criminally indicted for a libel "of an indecent nature" on "Mrs. MIDDLETON." She was already, said the *Oracle*, suing him in a private action in Doctors' Commons. The criminal action was again mentioned by the *Oracle* on 30 November, the first hearing having occurred on 28 November. Locke had published during the course of the year *The Confessions of the Countess of Strathmore; written by Herself. Carefully Copied from the Original Lodged in Doctors' Commons*; but no "Mrs. Middleton" was connected with this work. A "Mr. MIDDLETON, of *happy memory*," had, however, figured in the trial of Hastings. For a while there was also great interest in Salisbury's attempts to find a mayor. The last mention of this case was on 22 November, when *Lloyd's Evening Post* reported that the city had just elected the seventh candidate, who, like the six previously elected, had paid the £100 fee and declined the honor. As the newspapers understood it, the former mayor had entertained so lavishly that no one could afford to succeed him. But the major concerns were still the various legalistic reforms and, now involved with them, the sentences of Muir and Palmer.

On 4 October the newspapers understood that Muir had been put on a ship in the dead of night and would be lodged in Newgate until arrangements were made to transport him. By 15 November the *Oracle* was expecting his arrival within a few days, although it was certain the King would pardon him, Muir being "a Gentleman," who had already suffered quite enough for his "youthful follies." But on 19 November the *Oracle* reported that he had not left Edinburgh until 14 November and that he was traveling with "four common Felons." In addition, said the *Oracle* on 23 November, he had been prevented from seeing his friends: "EDINBURGH, NOV. 15./ On Friday last [probably 1 Nov.], a Deputation from the Convention of Delegates for Reform in Parliament waited upon the LORD PROVOST [Thomas Elder], wishing that six of their number might be allowed to dine with Mr. MUIR, now on his passage to Newgate, London. His Lordship required a list of their names to be given him, and ordered the inner turnkey to admit them when they came to the gaol—When they proceeded to the gaol, the gaoler refused to admit them without a written order." When they asked the Lord Provost to supply one, he said that he had changed his mind, but finally reconsidered the matter and allowed two of the group to visit him. By 27 November the *World* was expressing great concern about both Muir and Palmer, who, it had been informed, had finally sailed "from Leith Roads" on 22 November; and so were the Opposition papers, although, as the *Morning Post* said on 29 November, an English prison was not a pleasant place either: "Several people have commented not a little on the severity of the sentence passed against Mr. MUIR and Mr. F. PALMER, which transports them for seven years; but surely this is preferable to being locked up in a dreary prison for four years, with an eternal scene of profligacy before the prisoner's eyes, besides being subject to the stench and diseases peculiar to a loathsome prison." On 4 December *Lloyd's Evening Post* announced that Muir and Palmer had arrived:

> Last week Mr. Thomas Muir and the Rev. Fyshe Palmer arrived in the [Thames] River from Leith on board a revenue-cutter. Orders were sent down for delivering them into the custody of Duncan Campbell, the contractor for the hulks at Woolwich; and on Saturday [30 Nov.] they were put on board the hulks. On Sunday [1 Dec.] a second order was sent down to separate them; and they were placed in different hulks at Woolwich; the former in the Prudenna, and the latter in the Stanislaus. They are in irons among the convicts, and were ordered yesterday to assist them in the common labour, on the banks of the River. Mr. Muir is associated with about 300 Convicts, among whom he and Palmer slept last Friday evening, after their arrival. Mr. Muir is rather depressed in spirits; but Mr. Palmer appears to sustain his misfortune with greater fortitude.

The *World* was sickened. These two, it reminded its readers on 7 December, were "Gentlemen," Palmer having been "a Senior Fellow of Queen's College, Cambridge."

The *World* was still complaining loudly about the lawyers, who were boasting, it said on 29 November, that they could not be touched because "*the* COURTS *were all linked in their Chain.*" The *World* called upon "*the* COURTS" to vindicate themselves, and "*the* COURTS" responded by resuming disbarments of lawyers proved to have accepted bribes or forged documents. On 21 November the *Star* reported that a "person whose claim to a peerage, together with a large estate, is said to be proved, beyond all doubt of controversy [probably Walter Howard, who was contesting the Norfolk title], was a few days since appointed to the office of Deputy Cook in the public kitchen in the King's Bench Prison"; and on 23 November the *Oracle* announced that "the American lawyer, Mr. LLOYD," had been moved "from the State to the Felon side of Newgate" because "the Sheriffs, or the Keeper of the prison [Mr. Kirby], are offended with the letters which appeared, stating that Dr. LETTSOME called the fever malignant." On 2 December *Lloyd's Evening Post* mentioned that the Attorney General, Sir John Scott, had requested that Winterbotham be moved from the New Prison, Clerkenwell to Clerkenwell, Bridewell, the former being a prison for felons, and that the request had been granted; and by 5 December John Frost was again in the news. This was the day he was scheduled to appear in the pillory, and hand-bills were distributed announcing the fact,[70] but he did not appear. Because of "his severe illness," said *Lloyd's Evening Post* on 6 December, "the ceremony was put off to a future day." By 9 December another investigation of Newgate had been completed with the usual generally happy results. According to the *Morning Post*:

STATE OF NEWGATE.

The Grand Jury for the City of London presented to the Court their return of the state in which they found His Majesty's gaol of Newgate, and state that they found the prisoners perfectly satisfied with the treatment they experienced from Mr. KIRBY, the Keeper, whose humanity and care entitled him to their best thanks; that the felons' ward was not in so clean a state as they could wish, which on enquiry they understood to be owing to the great number of female convicts now in the prison, not any having been transported for a considerable time. They therefore recommended it to the Court, to represent to Government the necessity of immediately sending those off who are under sentence of transportation.

On the Debtors' side they found the windows without any glass casements; and recommended, that for the comfort and health of the unfortunate Debtors, at this inclement season of the year, that directions should be given for immediately putting up glass casements.

The Lord Mayor [Paul Le Mesurier] informed the Jury, that a representation of the crouded state of the Felons' side of Newgate, owing to the number of Female Convicts, had been made to Government; and they had in consequence taken up a vessel for the purpose of transporting those people, which would sail, at the farthest period, within six weeks.

Although Lord Moira was still thought to be interested in legalistic reform, it looked as if he would be absent during the next Parliamentary session. "The expedition, on which the Earl of MOIRA has lent his arm to a drooping Government, is to be directed to the interior of France . . . ," the *Morning Post* had reported sadly on 19 November. "The noble Earl in undertaking this expedition makes a material distinction between his civil and military duties. As a Soldier he holds himself bound to obey the demand which the King makes of his service, but in his civil character of hereditary Councillor of the Crown, he maintains his opinion, that the war was undertaken without necessity, against prudence and policy, and that it has been conducted without wisdom, alacrity, or vigour." On 22 November the *Post* mentioned that the Earl of Moira was leaving for Portsmouth at once and would be Commander in Chief of the forces "destined to descend on the coast of France," and by 6 December it understood that the exact "destination" was Saint-Malo. According to the *Oracle*, he was now in Jersey, his army with him.

The *Morning Post*'s interest in legalistic reform had, however, been diverted by the second British Convention. The Convention had begun on 19 November, and, although it was completely Jacobinistic in organization and tone, the *Morning Post* published long accounts of its proceedings from 2 December on. Other papers commented from time to time. "*Disappointment* is the *hot-bed* of *patriotism*," observed the *Public Advertiser* on 3 December; "a noble Lord [Lord

Tweeddale], whose pretensions to become a *legislator* have been resisted by the decree of a *Great Assembly*, is now become an active member of a *Scotch Convention*, which openly solicits the assistance of *certain classes* of men, to overturn that system which so cruelly *excludes* his Lordship. . . ." "The eyes of ADMINISTRATION are no doubt directed to the very strange proceedings of the EDINBURGH CONVENTION," said the *Oracle* on 4 December. "—We think it might not be amiss to enquire a little into the nature of the promised UNION of two countries, to be accomplished, (WE hope NOT) without the interference of Government. . . . The modesty of Lord DAER in declining the Chair of the above Convention will be no doubt properly remembered by the CALLENDER in the fulness of time." Alexander Callender had taken the chair instead. By the following day the country was in a state of general alarm, and the Government was therefore ready to deal with the *Morning Chronicle*. Since a prosecution of the *Chronicle* was almost equivalent to a prosecution of Fox, the jury had been very carefully selected. The trial had originally been scheduled for Trinity term, but had been postponed, supposedly for want of a full jury, and on 15 November the court had selected another jury altogether. Erskine had protested this irregularity without success, and on 9 December Lambert, Perry, and Gray appeared in the Court of King's Bench to answer for a libel published almost one year earlier. All three were acquitted.

The verdict was a major setback for the Government, but the Government's management of the trial was also a major blunder. Popular feeling about the *Morning Chronicle* was quite different from popular feeling about Thomas Paine, and the case against the *Chronicle* happened to be particularly weak, amounting to nothing more than publishing an advertisement for a reform society in Derby. No jury would regard this publication as seditious libel unless it was in a state of panic about reform societies, and this jury was not. Although the Government had prepared the ground for such panic by breaking up the British Convention, apprehending another fifty talkers and booksellers in the provinces, and instituting certain actions in London, the news failed to arrive in time, or the events were not publicized. On the morning of 9 December, the *Morning Post* summarized the proceedings of the Convention for the period beginning 25 November and ending 2 December. Nothing extraordinary had happened. That afternoon *Lloyd's Evening Post* mentioned that "James Eaton" had been arrested again and had appeared at the Old Bailey on 6 December to plead guilty or not guilty to a charge of having published "Pig's Meat." The indictment had been "held over," and he had been committed to Newgate until he found bail of £500 for himself and £250 for each of two sureties. The *Post* seems to have confused two different actions. Daniel Isaac Eaton was charged with publishing a periodical, begun on 9 September, under the title, *Hog's Wash; or A Salmagundy for Swine*, later (2 Nov.) retitled *Hog Wash; or Politics for the People*, and still later (7 Nov.) retitled *Politics for the People*. The journal, although classified as a weekly, appeared irregularly, concluding finally on 30 January, 1795. The editor, according to the colophon, was "D. I. Eaton." *Pig's Meat; or Lessons for the Swinish Multitude*, also a weekly and also lasting from 1793 to 1795, was the work of Thomas Spence, who was named in the colophon as publisher. In addition, said *Lloyd's Evening Post*, warrants had on 5 December been issued for the arrest of Gerrald, Margarot, Sinclair, and Callander, described as delegates from the London Corresponding and Constitutional Societies, for the arrest of Matthew C. Brown, delegate from Sheffield, and for the arrest of Alexander Scott, William Skirving, and the Ross brothers, the latter being "Conductors" of the Edinburgh *Gazetteer*. All papers had been seized, and the nine were supposedly still in prison. The report was accurate only in part. On 5 December the Convention was informed that Gerrald, Margarot, Alexander Callender, Alexander Scott, William and George Ross were in prison and their papers seized and that William Skirving had been arrested, but was now at liberty. A committee was immediately appointed to find bail for the others, but, before it could leave the hall, the Lord Provost, Thomas Elder, and other magistrates burst in and ordered the Convention dissolved. Skirving and Brown refused to dissolve it, Brown was pulled from the chair by Elder, and the Convention thereupon quit the Masons' Lodge to meet that night at Canongate Lodge. But the report was accurate enough for the purpose if only it had been published in time for the jury, deliberating the guilt of Perry, Gray, and Lambart, to see it.

It is ironic that the Government, which finally had some justification for an alarm, should have failed so dismally with this one. As no one knew better than Pitt and Dundas, alarms depended for their success on newspaper hysteria, but the hysteria had not been arranged in advance, and even the Ministerial newspapers happened to have something else on their minds. The *Sun*, the *True Briton*, *The Times*, the *Public Advertiser*, and the *Oracle*, from which hysteria might certainly have been expected, were having problems of their own. The *Sun* and the *True Briton* were engaged in another all-out battle with *The Times* over the matter of priority. Heriot had been informed by Evan Nepean that Dundas had forbid his giving further information to newspapers, but he had since seen stories in *The Times* which could have come only from Nepean's office. On 10 December he told Nepean so,[71] adding that he felt "much hurt that by you so decided a preference should be given to a man [John Walter] whom all who know him view with contempt & distrust." Heriot intended to take this matter up with Dundas. The *Public Advertiser* was still in a state of transition. On 2 December "the Proprietors" had another word for "THE PUBLIC": "The increased circulation of this Paper, within the space of a few weeks, is a circumstance highly flattering to the Proprietors, as it evinces that their endeavours at improvement have not passed entirely unnoticed./ This mark of public favour, while it demands an immediate and most grateful acknowledgement, will also powerfully stimulate their exertions to complete the very extensive arrangements now making to render the *Public Advertiser* more deserving the approbation of its generous patrons." On the night of 5 December, the

Public Advertiser had a fire. The *Advertiser* itself indicated that the damage had been slight. "The Proprietors of this Paper, availing themselves of the impression which the assistance of their Friends (afforded in a moment of imminent peril) has made in their breasts—beg they will accept of their most unfeigned acknowledgements for the generous aid they contributed in the preservation of their property, the destruction of which for some time appeared inevitable, by the sudden ravages of the accidental Fire which last night broke out in their Printing-House," it said on 6 December. But other newspapers indicated that the damage was extensive. According to *The Times* (6 Dec.) and the *True Briton* (7 Dec.), "the whole inside of the premises" of "Mr. Sampson Woodfall's printing-office" had been "consumed"; according to the *Morning Post* (7 Dec.), the fire not only "nearly consumed [the printing-house, but] damaged the adjoining houses. Some of the Printing Materials were saved, but the greater part of them were destroyed." By 14 December the *Public Advertiser* had made a recovery of sorts.

The *Oracle* was experimenting. On 2 December the *Oracle* had announced that "next month" John Bell would print "The Asiatic Jockey Club"; on 7 November the *True Briton* published a list of his advertisements, giving his address as No. 148, Oxford Street; and on 7 December the *Oracle* promised its readers the "First copper-plate Map of France and Part of Germany, showing the Seat of the War." The map, occupying a full page and labeled "Engraved for the *Oracle*; Printed for J. Bell," appeared on 9 December, and with it came a long explanatory statement from John Bell himself:

JOHN BELL,
OF THE BRITISH LIBRARY, STRAND,
TO THE PUBLIC,
ON HIS BEGINNING THE WORLD AGAIN.

MY CERTIFICATE *has been honourably confirmed.*

The ORACLE, and the Printing Materials belonging to that Property, have been purchased of my ASSIGNEES, by my NEPHEW [James Bell], and consequently that NEWSPAPER will continue under our joint direction.

The BRITISH LIBRARY has been purchased of my ASSIGNEES, by a number of my Friends, who admit me as the Renter thereof, at a stipulated Sum.

The BOOK and COPPERPLATE UTENSILS have been purchased for my use at the Public Sale of part of my Late Property, by particular Friends, who entitle me to the free use of them, on conditions which are mutually agreeable. *It is therefore that I am enabled thus*

TO SOLICIT THE
PATRONAGE OF THE PUBLIC.

The first and material object which will call forth my exertion is
THE ORACLE.

Which is at present universally known—it has been well received—but from my late perplexed situation, it has not had those attentions which it will be now in my power to bestow. Henceforth The ORACLE *shall be*, in every respect, *what a*

Newspaper should be—INTELLIGENT, IMPROVING, AND GENERALLY USEFUL—*well printed and published early every morning*: but as the most transcendent merit may be buried in oblivion, unless it have a fair opportunity of being scrutinized, I now address myself to those in particular who individually wish me well, and to the PEOPLE who will protect and encourage such persons as laudably aspire to their favour; entreating that they will take The ORACLE to their protection, and recommend it to universal judgment, wherever they go, during the course of Two Months; the expence of the Paper will be but *Two Shillings per Week*.

The CONSEQUENCES will shew the fullest effects of an industrious and experienced man's efforts, they will give him an opportunity of proving his pretensions to public favour, and the Purchasers will at least receive as valuable a Morning Print, in every respect, as the Press produces.

The ORACLE will therefore thus claim peculiar distinction from Monday the ninth day of December, 1793; and on that day it will assume an *eccentric* appearance of uncommon and extraordinary value.

I will again repeat my earnest entreaties that The ORACLE *may be received and recommended by* ALL FAMILIES, *in order that a fair trial may be given to the professional pretensions of*

JOHN BELL.

Bell's notion of *"what a Newspaper should be"* was the same as Stuart's and Boaden's, except that Bell had no interest in "Literature" and he did have an interest in maps, which had probably been suggested by the *Sun*. His maps were certainly popular, for on 10 December he announced:

THE ORACLE.

The Demands for our PAPER of YESTERDAY exceeded all Precedent for any PUBLICATION whatever. TEN THOUSAND might have been sold before Six o'Clock in the Morning; and TWENTY THOUSAND before the Evening, had it been possible to print them. This Demand exceeded my most sanguine Calculation; for I had provided only FIVE THOUSAND STAMPS as my Estimate of the Day's Sale. The Process of Copper-plate Printing being at least in a Twentyfold Degree slower than that of Letter-press, it will require a long Time to fulfil the Commissions already received for the ORACLE of yesterday. The Public, however, shall not be disappointed of it at the usual Price of FOURPENCE. I will keep the Types in Arrangement, and work the Presses Night and Day until they are fully supplied, should it be a Fortnight to come.

This Representation being the Fact, and having been honoured with the personal and epistolary Congratulations of many Persons of Fashion and Consequence, and of still many more humble, though equally respectable Friends, on my presenting myself to the Public again, I must intrude on the Space usually allotted for more important Matter, to attempt, though most feebly, to express my humble and most sensible Acknowledgments.

My Gratitude will best be demonstrated by my future Efforts; and those shall be unremittedly exerted to the best of my Abilities, to produce what shall approach as nearly as possible to Perfection, in whatever I presume hereafter to undertake.

The ORACLE is my first Object; and the Patronage of it to the Extent that I will endeavour to preserve, will place me in a Condition to render ample Justice to every Man—it is, therefore, that I again solicit.

JOHN BELL.

This statement was reprinted on 11 December, with the addendum: "*I sold nearly* THREE TIMES *the* NUMBER *of* PAPERS *Yesterday, that I did on any day of the preceding week.*/ J. BELL." But Bell had failed to realize that, although the *Sun* could publish its maps for almost nothing, he was losing money on every map he sold. On 14 December the *Oracle* announced a revision of policy:

GEOGRAPHY, AND THE ORACLE.

In order to facilitate and encourage the pleasing and very useful study of GEOGRAPHY, we shall comply with the WISHES of THOUSANDS, and frequently treat the READERS of the ORACLE with such

MAPS AND CHARTS

as may be necessary to elucidate the various COUNTRIES and different situations, which, commercially or politically, may engage the attention of the SUBJECTS of GREAT BRITAIN. In doing this we shall become the DAILY EXPOUNDERS of NEWSPAPERS in general, and be referred to as EXPOSITORS, when all our CONTEMPORARIES are forgotten.

IT IS THEREFORE

ONE PART of OUR EXTENDED and IMPROVED PLAN, to give at least One Valuable

COPPER-PLATE MAP
OR CHART,

In the Course of every Month, to the

REGULAR DAILY PURCHASERS
of
THE ORACLE,
GRATIS.

After the First Day's Publication, which will be confined to THEM, THE ORACLE, containing such MAPS or CHARTS, will be sold at an *advanced Price.*

WE NOW ANNOUNCE,

That, on the FIRST of JANUARY NEXT, a Valuable COPPERPLATE PRINT of a MOST INTERESTING SCENE, will be delivered, *gratis*, as a TRIBUTE of GRATITUDE and RESPECT for the very flattering encouragement which THIS PRINT is now experiencing from the PUBLIC AT LARGE.

This announcement was reprinted on 17 and 19 December.

The Opposition papers also had problems. From 10 December on, the *Courier* reported trouble with the Post Office, and on 12 December it informed its readers:

We have received several letters from different parts of the Country, particularly from Bristol, Nottingham, and Portsmouth, complaining of the irregular delivery of the COURIER. We are convinced that this sometimes arises from partiality, and a shameful abuse of official authority, which we are determined to have fully investigated, and properly controuled. At the same time, we must acknowledge, that it has more than once happened from the late hour of our publication; for which we hope that the great quantity of our original information, and the very late and interesting intelligence, which the COURIER conveys, will apologize as far as regards the past. For the future, we shall endeavour, by extraordinary means, to get the COURIER as early to press as those publications which are mere repetitions of what has been printed in the morning. The Public, we trust, will give us credit for this exertion, when they find all the other papers, as might be observed on Tuesday and yesterday morning, merely echoes of the preceding day's COURIER.

The *Morning Post* had at last severed connections with Carlton House and was finally free, as it told its readers on 9, 10, and 12 December, to be truly liberal:

TO THE PUBLIC.

The recent encouragement this Paper has received demands our sincere Acknowledgments. The confessed importance of the Affairs which are now on the eve of discussion, will furnish us with an opportunity of which we shall be happy to avail ourselves, to manifest our Gratitude by adequate Exertions.

A Change which has taken place in the Property of this Paper, has opened the way for Communications at once ample, liberal, and intelligent. On this head it is only necessary to add, that the Proprietor who during the last Winter interfered in the conduct of the Paper [probably Louis Weltje], *has no longer any Connection with the* MORNING POST.

The Arrangements which have been made in consequence, are such as, we trust, require only to be announced. The Public will soon be convinced of their superior value.

The *"arrangements,"* to which the *Post* referred, seem to have involved the *World*, since the two newspapers were now intimately related. The *World*, which was still publishing Charles Stuart's parody, had announced on 6 December that, "[in] compliance with the request of several of our Correspondents," it would "collect" and "reprint" the "whole of this Burlesque" as a pamphlet sometime in January. The *Morning Chronicle*'s problems had been solved, although certainly not without suspense.

Perry, Gray, and Lambert had been charged with "wickedly, seditiously, and maliciously" publishing on 25 December, 1792, an advertisement, which tended "to infuse distrust into the minds of the people, and to render them discontented with His Majesty's Government." They were defended by Erskine. The jury retired at two o'clock in the afternoon, reappearing five hours later with the verdict, *"Guilty of publishing, but with no malicious intent."* Lord Kenyon stated that this verdict would not do and effectively ordered the jury to return a verdict of guilty. At seven-thirty the jury again retired, first to Lord Kenyon's home, where it remained until nine o'clock, and then to a room in Westminster Hall, where it was locked up without a fire. At two o'clock in the morning, the members asked for fire and refreshments, which were provided by lawyers for the Crown and the defense; and at five o'clock they agreed on a verdict of not guilty.

The Alarm Postponed

Not only did the newspapers fail to anticipate the alarm; they also failed to recognize it. The papers of 9 and 10 December should have been filled with stories of the British Convention, but those which were not filled with long addresses to the public were more interested in John Frost, in Muir and Palmer, in conditions at Newgate, in the practices of lawyers, and in the trial of the *Morning Chronicle* than they were in the witch hunts. The *Morning Post* of 10 December did mention that the arrested delegates had, it understood, been released on bail, but it wanted to "conduct an examination of the legality of the action" before it revealed the whole story. The *Oracle* knew only that Gerrald, Sinclair, Margarot, Brown, Hastie, and probably other delegates "to a Convention in Edinburgh for promoting reform" had been arrested "in consequence of the active part which they had taken in pursuit of the object for which they were delegated." In addition, it said, "WILLIAM HOGDSON" had been tried at the Old Bailey on 9 December for "[using] seditious words, toasting the French Republic, calling the King 'a *German* hog-butcher,' &c." He had been sentenced to two years in Newgate and fined £200 with securities of £400 for another two years. By 6 December Margarot, Gerrald, Callander, Scott, and the Rosses had in fact been released and had appeared at the Convention to describe the indignities they had suffered. The meeting was again interrupted, there were more arguments, and the Convention was dissolved by the magistrates once and for all, not, however, before Gerrald had appealed eloquently and lengthily to God to help the members and their cause. The adjournment of the Convention, which was achieved only by a show of force, was followed by more arrests. William Hodgson was a medical doctor, evidently little known, for the newspapers had previously called him "Mr. HUDSON" or "Dr. HUDSON." The triweekly papers mentioned only the arrests in the provinces.

The *Morning Post* had otherwise a word of commendation for Lord Kenyon: "The conduct of the Court of King's Bench is extremely laudable, in restraining from practice those Attornies who bring an absolute disgrace upon every part of the profession." It was also happy to report that, although "Mr. MUIR continues ill, his irons have been lightened; he is permitted to walk the deck if he chuses."

But the big news in all papers, daily and nondaily alike, was the trial of the *Morning Chronicle*. The *Chronicle* was particularly disliked by the *Oracle*; yet even the *Oracle* gave the story major coverage, reprinting the advertisement, although it misdated it 16 July, 1792, on which the action had been based. Interest in this case continued through 16 December, many newspapers supplementing their original accounts on subsequent days. *Lloyd's Evening Post*, for example, published three accounts, one on 11 December, another on 13 December, a third on 16 December, the last including names of the jurors; and, although the *Chronicle* itself published only one account, it devoted the entire issue of 12 December to it. Almost all papers, too, applauded the jurors. "The verdict of *Not Guilty* upon the cause of LAMBERT, PERRY, and GRAY, reflects the highest honour upon the Jury, and the Jurisprudence of this country," the *World* commented on 12 December. "Had it been given otherwise, Mr. FOX's Bill would have been deprived of its energy, and the Liberty of the Press shackled for ever. Every Publisher of a Journal must have studied the law to know what is politically wrong; or the repetition of opinions that have been established for centuries, might provoke an exorbitant fine, and a rigorous imprisonment." A similar statement appeared on the same day in *The Times*.

The "apprehension" of Eaton on 9 December "for selling a Seditious Libel, contained in a Work entitled *Politicks for the People, or a Salmagundy for Swine*," was reported by the *Morning Post* of 11 December and the *Oracle* of 12 December; and on 12 December the *Post* remarked: "It will appear strange to hear that a man [Thomas Spence] has been indicted for a libel, for selling *pigs' meat*. Surely even Mr. BURKE will say, that it is cruel to starve the *Swinish Multitude*." Although the *Post* discontinued the minutes of the Convention after 9 December, it noticed on 11 December that the Government had issued another "lot of indictments," and on 12 December it announced that those already arrested had been released:

> EDINBURGH, DEC. 6.
>
> After being examined on Thursday last [5 Dec.], by the Sheriff [John Pringle], the persons who call themselves Members of the British Convention were admitted to bail. They again met in the evening at the usual place (a Mason Lodge,) where the Lord PROVOST [Thomas Elder] attended, and after pointing out the impropriety of such assemblies, requested they would dismiss, which with some slight murmuring was complied with. They last night again met at a place in the suburbs, from which they were also removed by the Lord Provost and other Magistrates; and this day a Proclamation was issued from the Council Chamber, signifying the determination of the Magistrates to suppress all such meetings in future.

The "Proclamation," signed by Elder and Pringle, the latter as "Sheriff depute," was itself printed by the *Oracle*. The two had, said the *Oracle* (12 Dec.), determined to end the Convention, "because of [its] seditious tendency"; Elder and other magistrates had "dispersed the meetings" on 5 December and again on 6 December; on 6 December Pringle had informed the members that they could not meet "in the country" at all; and on 7 December he and Elder had issued a proclamation, stating that, if they attempted to meet again, they would be "apprehended as disorderly." The proclamation had been widely circulated.

Since the *True Briton* had finally indicated some concern about the Convention, the *Morning Post* also (12 Dec.) had a comment on that newspaper: "Mr. ROSE has, with MERLIN, invented a machine for *grinding paragraphs*, which he uses . . . for the use of the Government prints. The misfortune is, that this piece of Mechanism can send forth nothing but idle and vulgar declamation. Several specimens may be seen in one of the Treasury Papers of this morning, and they may be known by the words *Jacobins* and *Levellers*, indiscriminately applied to all those who call for Reformation, or a Renovation of the Constitution." Merlin, a steady advertiser in newspapers, sold various mechanical contrivances in a shop at No. 11, Prince Street. A suggestion that the Convention had been bent on revolution moved the *Morning Post* to sarcasm: "All the *fond* parents in England are making interest to have their *dear children* entered on board Lord HOWE's fleet, as they know that they must remain safe under the care of that judicious sailor and gallant commander." Lord Howe was still looking for the French navy and had still not seen a single French ship. The *Courier* was meanwhile reviving its fund for the Spitalfields weavers, whom it represented as the real victims of war and "Constitutionalism"; but this maneuver was anticipated by the London aldermen, who, according to the *Morning Post* (13 Dec.), met on 12 December "with 128 commoners" to consider the weavers' "distressing circumstances." The result of this meeting was that £500 was subscribed for their immediate relief and a fund was established for further donations. On 14 December the *Morning Post* "applauded" the Prince of Wales for "patronizing" a concert given for the benefit of the weavers at the London Tavern on 12 December. "We may expect to see His Royal Highness libelled . . . by the underlings of the Treasury, for supporting a charity which they have insinuated is of a Political nature, in opposition to Government, and which ought not to have been countenanced," the *Post* added hopefully. But the *Sun* and the *True Briton* were similarly gratified. The *Courier* saw no reason under the circumstances to continue its own fund after 12 December. The *Morning Post* felt otherwise. Every day it reprinted the full list of subscribers, and, although by 25 December there had been only three additions, Sir Edward Hughes having given 2s., "Martin Van Butchell, his Wife and Children" having given 5s. 6d., and "G." having given one guinea, the *Post* boasted that, meager as the gifts were, they were at least "voluntary." The *True Briton*, which was still printing columns of donations to its fund "to furnish extra-clothing for the Army," was sufficiently galled to protest on 26 December that these donations were also "given voluntarily, [and not] through fear of seeming *disaffected.*"

The newspapers fought for the remainder of the year, principally about the war, the *Morning Post* leading the attacks on the Ministerial press and its principal target being the *True Briton*. "The underling of the Treasury [John Heriot], who wrote the licentious and wicked libel against the Duke of YORK, for which an innocent and obscure Printer [John Walter] was near losing his ears, is now employing his *brilliant* talents in a manner diametrically opposite," it proclaimed on 16 December. "Such is the *accommodating* disposition of this sniveling genius, that he is now bespattering his Royal Highness with ill-judged compliments, which are as fulsome and unnecessary, as his former attacks were base, cruel, and cowardly." On 23 December, having restated its opinion of "one of the public, or rather *private* Prints, which we now understand is the property of *several* of the lowest Clerks of the Treasury," the *Post* went on to observe: "We are assured, in [this] nonsensical Ministerial print, that the Summer Campaign has been the most *brilliant* and successful for this Country ever remembered. We have gained about fourteen miles of *territory*, for which we have paid Twelve Millions of money. Our accessions in France could be covered with the British Guineas expended in the absurd project of conquering the Republic."

The war had in fact gone from bad to worse. On 12 December the insurgents in La Vendée had been defeated at Le Mans and at Savenay, on 18 December the British, after two solemn promises to the contrary, had evacuated Toulon, and on 26 December the Austrian general, Wurmser, was defeated at Weissenburg. News of this defeat, along with news of the arrest of Thomas Paine on 27 December, had of course not yet arrived; rumors of the evacuation of Toulon were first mentioned by the *Oracle* on 21 December. Also Lord Howe had returned to port, having not sighted a single French ship during his seven-month search. "JOHN BULL seems much mortified to think that Lord HOWE, during his last expedition, *took nothing, but cold*," the *Morning Post* observed on 17 December. This observation was followed by some verses:

LORD HOWE's EXPEDITION.
With hostile pomp to chase th' insulting foe,
And lay great Gallia's glittering glories low,
Lo! Howe's tall Navy ploughs the briny plain,
While his proud pendants sweep th' indignant main!

But ah! soon vanish'd from the Hero's sight,
The faithless Prize, and veil'd in mists of Night,
The laurels faded on the brows of fame,
Gloomy he measures back the way he came.

Thus Philip once, with sixty thousand men,
March'd up the hill, and then march'd down again.

There were more such verses in subsequent numbers, those on 19 December reading, for example:

LULLABY. A PARODY.
Peaceful, *slumb'ring* o'er the Ocean,
Lord Howe fears no Frenchmen nigh;
The winds and waves in *dangling* motion,
Rock him with their Lullaby.
CHORUS.
Lullaby, lullaby, lullaby, now they fly,
Lord Howe fears no Frenchmen nigh.

Is the wind *North East* yet blowing?
Still no Frenchmen he'll descry;
The *lucky fog* its boon bestowing,
Puts its finger in his eye.
CHORUS.
Lullaby, lullaby, lullaby, in his eye,
Lord Howe sees no Frenchmen nigh.

The *Morning Post* had no monopoly on this sport, for most of the Opposition papers participated, the *World* of 31 December contributing the quatrain:

ON A LATE NAVAL RETURN.
Lord! How he goes out to encounter the Foe;
Lord! How he returns from his Victories past;
Lord! How many Ships has he *taken*, do you know?
Lord! How he has *taken* himself home at last.
HOW *and* ABOUT IT.

Nor was Lord Howe the only butt.

Windham was evidently again under attack, for on 21 December the *Oracle* noticed indignantly: "In the *Guillotine Chronicle* of Tuesday last [17 Dec.] is the following passage: 'A Member of the British Senate could say, "PERISH COMMERCE! *if our National Honour is at stake, and can be preserved by the sacrifice.*"' —/ The person to whom this passage evidently alludes is Mr. GEORGE HARDINGE, who certainly made use of the two first words, but added these—/ '*If it is by that sacrifice alone that we can save* THE CONSTITUTION. *Let us even at that price, if it must be paid, have a* GOVERNMENT *that will ensure to us our property, and life!*'" While other Opposition papers were holding placemen and pensioners largely responsible for the war, the *Morning Post* had no doubt (16 Dec.) that the real reason for the war was the preservation of corruptions: that "[any] thing like Reformation in this country, particularly of an oeconomical nature, must ruin thousands. But these would be *placemen* and pensioners!" On 19 December the *Post* estimated that "Mr. GEORGE ROSE, in *sinecure* places and others, enjoys situations to the amount of 13,000*l.* per annum, and yet there are those who would chearfully do his business for 1,000*l.* a-year." Although no one knew how "Lord MOUNTMORRES" was being rewarded, the *Post* of 24 December mentioned that he "still remains in this Town" and that "His Lordship is one of the most industrious Authors of the age. There is no subject on which he will not write, despising, as usual, the dull trammels of *Grammar* and *Orthography.*" "The Duke of RICHMOND," the *Post* added on 31 December, "is at present employing his pen in writing the History of the Summer Campaign in this Country, which, while it renders him immortal as a HERO, must establish his character as a great Literary Genius. . . ." The *Morning Chronicle* was meanwhile (31 Dec.) mentioning that "Mr. SYLVESTER DOUGLAS is appointed Secretary to the Lord Lieutenant of Ireland, in the room of Lord HOBART; and thus another of the Gentlemen who had the honour of being convinced of the wisdom and propriety of the war, receives this important office, as the fruits of his conviction . . .; a pension of 3000*l.* a year on the Irish establishment is given to Lord HOBART to induce him to become *Governor General of India*, worth 20,000*l.* a year!" Lord Hobart had resigned as Chief Secretary of Ireland on 15 December, and Douglas had succeeded him the following day. Lord Hobart's appointment as Governor of the Presidency of Madras and provisional successor to the Governor Generalship of India had been made in October. Lord Hobart sailed for Madras in early 1794. Sir Gilbert Elliot was now in Florence, trying to stiffen Italian resistance to France.

The Princes were not presently involved in these controversies. Except for an occasional dinner with Mrs. Fitzherbert (*Lloyd's Evening Post*, 25 Dec.), the Prince of Wales was now an exemplary son, and it even looked as if he was finally severing relations with her. According to the *Morning Herald* (29 Nov.), Mrs. Fitzherbert spent the final months of the year at Brighton, making occasional visits to London: "Mrs. FITZHERBERT's hotel has undergone several decorations, preparatory to her occasional visits during the winter; but her chief residence will continue to be in the neighbourhood of the *Pavillion*, Brighthelmstone." The Prince spent the final months in London, with occasional visits to Brighton. He visited Brighton on 2 December, according to *Lloyd's Evening Post* (4 Dec.), only, however, for the purpose of giving "a dinner to several of the Nobility, Military Officers, &c. at his pavilion"; and in London, said *Lloyd's Evening Post* (23 Dec.), he was an intimate of that arch-Tory, the Duchess of Gordon, who "often" gave dinners for him and his friends. Prince Augustus was still living quietly at Windsor, and so, contrary to earlier reports, was Prince Adolphus. The Duke of Clarence was still at Petersham. Readers heard nothing of him, but on 3 December they were notified by the *Morning Post* that "Mrs. JORDAN nearly approaches the term of her *accouchement*; but until that takes place, we cannot tell whether the infant is to be a *Bishop*, an *Admiral*, a *General*, or a *Maid of Honour.*" The "*accouchement*" did not occur until January. On 12 December the *Post* reported that "Mrs. JORDAN has commenced the Editor of a public print, and has sent letters to those she knows, and those she does not know, to make a trial of her paper for a few days. The name of it we have not yet learned, but we suppose that it will be called '*Little Pickle's Gazette.*'" On 13 December it further announced that "LITTLE PICKLE's eldest daughter who was born in Ireland, has been put apprentice to a Milliner. She assumes the name of *Smith*, and is to be kept unknown to the NOBLE offspring of this celebrated Lady." Prince Edward, said *Lloyd's Evening Post* (23 Dec.), would be created Duke of Cumberland on his return. The King had already bought Cumberland House for his use as a town residence.

Also seemingly uninvolved in the controversies over the war were the Edinburgh arrests. Except for the *Oracle*, the Ministerial papers indicated no interest in the British Convention after 12 December. This was hardly surprising, for, now that the *Morning Chronicle* was acquitted, the alarm would serve no useful purpose until the following year, the opening of Parliament having been delayed to 21 January. But the Opposition papers seemed generally unaware of this fact, or they did not know what to do about it, for only the *Morning Post* showed any deep concern. On 14 December the *Post* insisted that the arrests had been made on evidence invented by spies and that the meetings had actually been innocent. It repeated this statement on 16 December, adding that it was still investigating the "legality" of the arrests. It also understood, however, that the Convention was continuing its meetings despite the "Proclamation" against them: *"We have received further particulars respecting the Sittings of the People, calling themselves the Convention of Delegates in Scotland; but as the legality of their Assembling is questioned, we shall not lay their Proceedings before our Readers, it not being our wish to publish any article that may give offence to the existing Government of this Country."* The *Morning Post* was certainly not sympathetic with this action, for on 17 December it announced: "EDINBURGH, Dec. 8./ This day, notwithstanding the avowed determination of the Civil Power to suppress all illegal and unconstitutional meetings, an attempt was made by the persons who stile themselves 'The British Convention,' to assemble at the Cockpit in the Grasmarket. Two of the Magistrates, supported by the Constables, and City Guard, attended to resist this insult to their authority, and in consequence WILLIAM SKIRVING, and C. BROWN were taken into custody, as disturbers of the peace, and are now under examination."

There had been considerable disagreement as to who was under arrest and who was not. On 16 December the *Oracle* reported the arrest on 5 December of Margarot, Gerrald, Sinclair, Callander, Skirving, Scott, and the Rosses, all of whom, it thought, were delegates from London societies, of Brown from Sheffield, and of "W. MOFFAT" from Edinburgh. On the same day *Lloyd's Evening Post* printed a letter from Edinburgh, stating that by 10 December all the English delegates, plus "the Secretary of the Convention" and "the Printer of the Gazetteer," that is, Skirving and one of the Rosses, had "received their indictments to stand trial." On 17 December the *Morning Post* announced that "Mr. HORNE TOOKE is to plead the cause of the Members of the Convention, to be tried before the Court of Justiciary, and for that purpose he intends . . . to set out for Scotland in . . . a few days." By 18 December the *Post* had some reliable information:

EDINBURGH, Dec. 12.

We formerly mentioned that several persons belonging to the Societies of the Friends of the People, had been apprehended in consequence of a warrant from the Sheriff. Their names are,

W. Margarot, of London,	A. Callander, Edinburgh,
J. Gerald, ditto,	W. Skirving, ditto,
C. Sinclair, ditto,	A. Scott, ditto,
M. C. Brown, Sheffield,	W. Ross, ditto,
W. Moffat, Edinburgh,	G. Ross, ditto.

After undergoing an examination, they were all admitted to bail.

The Public already know, that the Magistrates and Sheriff issued a proclamation, prohibiting the persons stiling themselves the *British Convention* from holding any meeting in future. Notwithstanding this intimation, however, an advertisement was circulated on Tuesday [10 Dec.], signed W. SKIRVING, calling a meeting of the General Committee of the People, to be held at twelve o'clock, on Thursday (this day,) at the Cock Pit, Grasmarket. When this advertisement appeared, a warrant was granted for apprehending W. Skirving; and yesterday he underwent an examination before the Magistrates, in which he said, that he held a lease of the Cock pit till Whitsunday next, and that he did not think the meeting which he had called was illegal. The Magistrates informed him, that no such meeting would be permitted, and ordered him not to attempt to convene it. He was afterwards dismissed.

This day, at twelve o'clock, a vast croud of people assembled near the Cock-pit, anxious to know the event. Previous to this, however, the Constables and other Peace Officers were ordered to attend, and the Magistrates were in waiting. [When Skirving and Brown arrived, shortly after twelve o'clock, they were barred from entering. Skirving thereupon gave Brown a paper, asking him to read it.] It stated the orders issued by the Magistrates prohibiting this Meeting; it contained a Remonstrance against this prohibition, as illegal; and concluded, that . . . the Meeting was necessarily adjourned to a future day. But, while Brown was reading the paper, one of the officers took it from him; and immediately he and Skirving were both apprehended, and carried to the Council Chamber.

The question of whether anyone had actually been indicted or not remained unanswered, as so did many other questions. According to the *Morning Chronicle* (19 Dec.), Skirving and Brown had been dismissed by at least 14 December "after an examination before the magistrates . . .; they having, previous to this, been under bail upon another charge." According to *Lloyd's Evening Post* (20 Dec.), the bail of Gerrald and Margarot had been fixed at 2,000 merks after an examination by the Sheriff. The *Post* did not know whether the bail had been provided or not, but it did know that the two were still complaining loudly about the seizure of their papers. Another mystery was the status of Lord Daer, who had also taken "an active part in the business of the British Convention." The *Morning Post* understood on 14 December that a warrant "had been issued by the Provost of Edinburgh" for his "apprehension," and it was the later (20 Dec.) understanding of *Lloyd's Evening Post* that a similar warrant had been issued by the Court of Justiciary; but he was not reported to be under arrest. The *True Briton* had been silent throughout.

Except for the *Oracle*, the Ministerial papers had also been silent on the subject of the lawyers, Muir and Palmer, Frost, and legalistic reform generally. But the *World* always felt strongly about lawyers, and all Opposition papers were distressed about Muir and Palmer. "It is said that nothing can equal the insolence of the servants of Edinburgh, since the severe sentence passed upon Mr. MUIR," said the *Morning Post* on 13 December. "He was treacherously informed against by his own servants, to whom he was a kind and humane master; in consequence of which, every servant in Edinburgh conceives that their masters are at their mercy, and that they can . . . have them transported whenever they please." "Mr. MUIR is still detained on board the hulks at Woolwich," the *Post* added on 14 December. "This unfortunate young Gentleman bears his melancholy situation with firmness and fortitude. He is silent as to the severity of the Scottish verdict, and it would reflect no discredit on His Majesty's Ministers, were they to interest themselves in his favour. The punishment he has undergone . . . must be adequate to any crime he could have committed, short of murder." By 16 December the *Post* could announce that "[on] Wednesday last [11 Dec.] we understand Lord LAUDERDALE, Mr. SHERIDAN, and Mr. GREY, waited on Mr. Secretary DUNDAS, and stated to him the grounds on which they were convinced of the illegality of the sentences by which Mr. MUIR and Mr. PALMER are now on board the hulks at Woolwich, previous to their being transported to Botany-Bay, and of their intention to bring the matter before Parliament, on which account they urged the propriety of deferring the execution of the sentence.—It gives us satisfaction to learn that the application was received with proper attention; and we are hopeful that Messrs. MUIR and PALMER's fate will be decided by the mild spirit of English jurisprudence." The *Gazetteer* understood that the matter was settled: the cases would positively be retried in English courts. By 17 December Fox had also become interested. Lord Lauderdale, said the *Morning Post*, had already visited Muir in his "Gloomy Recess," and Fox would visit him shortly. Although on 18 December *Lloyd's Evening Post* repeated that "the sentence passed on Mr. Muir and Mr. Palmer . . . is for the present suspended from being carried into action," the focus of attention was now John Frost.

Frost was supposed to have stood in the pillory on 5 December, and someone had distributed handbills advertising the fact. On 11 December the *Morning Post* denied that these had been distributed by friends of Frost: "It has been insinuated, that Mr. JOHN FROST or his friends had a bill circulated, stating that he was to have stood in the Pillory, at a certain hour one day last week, for the purpose of collecting a multitude. How infamous to attribute such an act to the prisoner, who certainly in such a disagreeable situation would willingly dispense with company. The fact is, we should apprehend, quite the reverse; and, in our opinion, there was something so cruel and infamous in the circulation of that hand bill, that we trust the authors, however loyal or patriotic they might be, will be brought to exemplary punishment." Frost was prevented from appearing that day by a severe illness, and, according to the *Star*, he was still ill on 13 December: "Mr. FROST's imprisonment in Newgate expires on the 19th instant; his state of health is very precarious; he is daily attended by two physicians, who report, which report is transmitted to the Sheriffs; yesterday they reported his fever had left him, but he continued very weak." By 16 December, according to the *Gazetteer*, he was even worse: "Mr. FROST's imprisonment expires on the 19th instant; but it is doubtful whether he can then return to his expecting family, he being so ill that Doctors PITCAIRNE and SOMERS, who attend him, by order of the Secretary of State, have thought it necessary to call in the assistance of Mr. HOWARD, Surgeon to the Middlesex Hospital." Since his sentence required that he spend one hour in the pillory, the supposition was that he would appear on 18 December, and handbills were again issued stating that he would do so, dead or alive. Again a crowd assembled, and again he failed to appear. As the *Morning Post* put it on 19 December:

Mr. FROST.

Yesterday the PILLORY was brought a second time to Charing Cross, on which it was thought that Mr. FROST would have been obliged to stand, in consequence of his sentence. All the Constables in Westminster assembled between twelve and one o'clock, who, of course, dispersed, an intimation being given by the Sheriffs, that Mr. FROST was too ill to attend. He was attended by Doctors HOWARD and PITTCAIRN, by direction of Government, who make their report of his indisposition accordingly.

The MOB, which was immense, did not seem in the least disappointed, but waved their hats in the air, and cheered the departure of the Pillory from Charing Cross. The term of Mr. FROST's confinement expired yesterday, and this day he will be enlarged from Newgate.

The *Oracle*'s account differed somewhat. The public was informed about noon, it said, that the sheriffs had got a report from Dr. Edmund Somers and G. Howard, stating that it would endanger Frost's life to stand in the pillory. Dr. Pitcairn, who had already visited Frost on behalf of the sheriffs, was sent for, but could not come. This situation having been anticipated, "a council" had been held at Dundas's home on 17 December, where it had been resolved that, if Frost was too ill to stand in the pillory, he "should be deprived of all the usual immunities of a British subject." Since "the said *John Frost*" had not stood in the pillory, he "*has now no longer claims to the privileges of a Subject of Great Britain.* ... Mr. MUIR and Mr. PALMER are to be removed from the *Hulks* to *Newgate*, as an act of mercy," the *Oracle* added. "Mr. FROST's apartments are prepared for their reception, of which they will take possession this day."

There were numerous accounts of Frost's liberation. According to *Lloyd's Evening Post* (20 Dec.):

Mr. John Frost was brought out of Newgate [between eleven and twelve o'clock], and placed in a coach, apparently very feeble, and rolled in blankets; Mr. Kirby, the keeper accompanied him to the house of Mr. Justice Grose, in Bloomsbury-square, where he, with two sureties, entered into the recognizance required by his judgment for keeping the peace. He was then discharged out of custody. As soon as he was at liberty the multitude took the horses out of the carriage, and drew him along the streets, stopping at every marked place, particularly St. James's Palace, Carlton-House, Charing-cross, &c. to shout and express their joy; and in this state they conducted him to his own house in Spring-Gardens, where Mr. Thelwall made a speech, and intreated them to separate peaceably, which they accordingly did.

According to the *Morning Post*:

Mr. FROST.

The indisposition of this Gentleman having caused that part of his sentence, the standing on the Pillory, to be dispensed with, he was yesterday liberated from his confinement, but not before a detainer was lodged against him for some of the expences attending the election of Lord Hood at Westminster. But the money being immediately placed in the hands of the Sheriff, the difficulty arising from the detainer was soon removed.

At a quarter past twelve o'clock, his carriage drew up to the Felons' door, into which he was assisted by some intimate friends. A great crowd of people were assembled on the occasion, who saluted him with repeated huzzas! Then they proceeded to unharness the horses; but, at the urgent request of some Gentlemen who rode with Mr. Frost in the carriage, they at length reluctantly desisted. But the numbers increasing as he proceeded to Judge Grose's house in Bloomsbury-square, it was impossible to restrain their impetuosity, while the Clerk was taking the recognizance.

Having got possession of their object, they drew the coach, without horses, along Holborn, Compton and Prince's-street, and instead of proceeding the nearest way down Hedge-lane, they took a circuit along Piccadilly to St. James's-street; at the bottom of which they expressed their loyalty by stopping at the Palace and giving three cheers. This was repeated at Carlton House, and at York House. When they arrived at Charing-Cross, the coach was drawn round the rails, exactly to the spot where the Pillory was yesterday erected, and the people gave three loud and expressive huzzas!

They then proceeded without interruption to Spring Gardens. When Mr. Frost was safely lodged, being too ill to address the populace, one of his friends expressed his gratitude to them, and requested them to disperse, lest they would give umbrage to the Civil Power. This was instantly complied with.

The last thing belonging to Mr. Frost, put into the cart which contained his furniture, was a small *laurel*, which the porter finding some difficulty to place at the tail of the cart, the populace cried out, "Fix it in the front;" the man not choosing to give himself the trouble, put it on his head, and was walking away with it, when the Keeper of Newgate [Mr. Kirby] followed him, snatched it away, and entered the prison with it in his hand, amid the hisses of the multitude.

According to the *Oracle*:

JOHN FROST.

Yesterday morning this *worthy* was dismissed from *Newgate*.

A vast concourse of people were assembled at the prison doors to receive him —apparently with tumultuous dispositions.

Their *hero* was wrapped up in flannel. He was accompanied by his solicitor ADAMS, and attended by the SHERIFFS and their deputies.

An *Artificial Tree* had been prepared by the *Monster Williams*, which was designed to inspire the MOB as the Tree of LIBERTY!!!

Mr. KIRBY, however, frustrated the attempt, by seizing the *emblem*, and destroying it.

Mr. ADAMS, with his head out of the coach, *affectedly* desired the mob not to take the horses. This sinister design was also defeated by Mr. KIRBY, who declared he would take the first man into custody who should interrupt the *course* of Justice.

They afterwards proceeded to Judge GROSE's Chambers in Bloomsbury-square. He entered into a recognizance for *his good behaviour* for five years—himself in 500*l.*—*Citizen* WILLIAM SHARP, the Engraver, and *Citizen* BRAND, Serjeant's Inn, 250*l.* each. The latter gentleman was one of the assignees under his commission of bankruptcy!

"In the course of Wednesday morning some thousands of the following malevolent printed hand-bills were distributed in the several parts of London and Westminster—'This day JOHN FROST will be put in the pillory *dead* or *alive*,'" the *Oracle* added. "HORNE TOOKE a few days since, going to see Mr. FROST in Newgate, gave in the following description of himself to the Turnkey, as a passport for his being admitted into the prison:—'Citizen TOOKE, next door neighbour to Citizen DUNDAS, at Wimbledon, desires to visit Citizen FROST in Newgate,'" the *Oracle* said again on 21 December.

"KING'*s* BENCH PRISON," remarked the *World* on 21 December: "About fifteen hundred persons are lost to Society in this place./ It has been calculated, that five eights of these unfortunate people are imprisoned for debts under 50*l.* and that a considerable portion of the remainder are confined for the *Costs* of Attornies." The *Morning Post* was more interested in Newgate. "Neither Mr. MUIR nor Mr. PALMER had reached Newgate yesterday, though they have been for days hourly expected from the Hulks," it told its readers on 23 December. "The State side of the Prison is now so full, that there is not room for another Prisoner. Should Government persevere in prosecuting Booksellers, and poor *Devils* for selling such stuff as *Pig's Meat* [a reference to Thomas Spence], it would be well if they directed some clever Architect, to build a new wing to the prison." Or, the *Post* added in another paragraph, let the English courts transport their felons to Edinburgh. The *Post* was similarly exasperated about the registration of visitors: "The stupid regulation of every person inserting his name in a book, who visits the State Side of Newgate, is still continued. The list is regularly sent every day to the Sheriffs and the Secretary of State [Dundas]. The immaculate Lord HAWKESBURY cons them over with the aid of spectacles, and what is the consequence of their discoveries?—Nothing. For the fact is the names are all fictitious, and the Parties, to their surprise, often see their own names actually inserted as visitors, to the best Patriots in Prison."

The First Preparations for the Opening of Parliament

The *Public Advertiser* said nothing about its "new Arrangements" until 14 December, when it published a lengthy prospectus, republishing it on 16 and again on 21 December:

THE
PUBLIC ADVERTISER,
OR,
POLITICAL AND LITERARY DIARY.
PRO REGE ET LEGE.

THIS PAPER having passed into new hands, the present Proprietors respectfully lay before the Public the system which they intend to pursue in the future management of it, and the grounds on which they rest their hopes of success in an undertaking as arduous as it is expensive.

To see at once what in the new conduct of the Paper they ought to adopt, and what to avoid, they had but to consider the causes which produced, at different periods, the extraordinary rise and declension of THE PUBLIC ADVERTISER. They found, that when great exertions are made, and the aid of great literary abilities was called forth into action, this Paper took the lead of all the daily publications in the kingdom; and, as a proof of the high estimation in which it was held by a Public no less judicious in appreciating merit, than liberal in rewarding it, that its circulation was beyond all precedent extensive. It was on this account that the celebrated JUNIUS distinguished it by his communications.

They found also, paradoxical as it may appear, that its astonishing success was, in a great measure, the cause of its decline. Proud of the glory which it had acquired, it seemed to think it might relax its exertions, and sit down quietly under the shade of its laurels, in the fond security that its prosperity would be as lasting as the fame of JUNIUS, with whose name it had been coupled. It was not then aware, that exertion was necessary to preserve what exertion had raised, and that a reduced or invalid establishment must be inadequate to a great, active, literary, and political warfare. The consequences were such as might naturally have been expected.

The present Proprietors, learning wisdom from the errors of others, are determined not to spare either labour or expence to recover the respectability of this Paper, to recommend it more especially to the *Literary World*, and to render it worthy of a revival of that extensive patronage which it once so conspicuously enjoyed.

The Proprietors feel themselves called upon at the present juncture to state fairly and unequivocally the line they mean to pursue in the POLITICAL Department of their Paper; they therefore, without hesitation, declare themselves inviolably attached to the inestimable Constitution of Great Britain; to the person of His Majesty; and to the illustrious House of Hanover, to whom that Constitution has wisely delegated the guardianship of the rights and liberties of these realms, in Church and State—and that the sentiments of duty which they feel towards their amiable Sovereign, are heightened when they reflect on the exemplary pattern of every excellence, religious, moral, and domestic, which he exhibits to the imitation of his people.

They likewise pledge themselves to conduct the Paper on principles of INDEPENDENCE; to support Ministers only when they find them deserving of support; and for this reason they will always look to *measures*, not *men*. They at the same time feel it an act of justice to acknowledge, that his Majesty's *present* Ministers are fully entitled to, and possess their confidence at this momentous period, when the nation is engaged in a war, not of aggrandizement or ambition, but of necessity and self-defence; a war carried on against those, whose principles, if unrestrained, could overturn not only the British Constitution, but even civil society itself.

In thus availing themselves of that *Freedom* of the Press, which they consider as the grand bulwark of all the privileges of Englishmen, they shall ever hold it to be their indispensable duty, cautiously to shun its *perversion* and *abuse*. They profess a respectful submission to the authority of the Laws: but they should deem themselves deserving of the severest penalties which laws can inflict, were they to make the Press an engine of licentiousness—were they to use it for the purpose of inflaming or deluding the Public mind—or convert it into an instrument, open or disguised, for the destruction of that admirable system which it should endeavour to preserve and perpetuate.

The PROCEEDINGS in both HOUSES of PARLIAMENT, at all times interesting, are more peculiarly so at a juncture like the present; the Proprietors of THE PUBLIC ADVERTISER have, therefore, regardless of expence, engaged the assistance of GENTLEMEN of the FIRST ABILITIES as PARLIAMEN-TARY REPORTERS:—the speeches will be given upon such a scale, as to be ample, yet not prolix, and with that accuracy which marks the principal features of debate, but with due attention to necessary brevity.

The system adopted by the French Convention, for breaking off all communication with surrounding nations, renders it extremely difficult to procure *early* intelligence of what is passing in France. The Proprietors of this Paper have, nevertheless, succeeded in forming such a correspondence, though at a heavy expence, as will secure to them a DECIDED AND ENVIABLE PRIORITY OF CONTINENTAL INFORMATION.

It has long been matter of surprise and regret, that, amidst the variety of diurnal publications, not one has appropriated a portion of its pages to the reception of LITERARY COMMUNICATIONS. To supply this deficiency, and to offer to Men of Letters a respectable medium for the circulation of the many valuable productions of genius, which there is reason to fear are now withheld from the World, a few columns of THE PUBLIC ADVERTISER will be frequently devoted:—an arrangement which the Proprietors presume to hope will tend to the promotion of science, and the more general diffusion of elegant information; and entitle the Paper to the additional appellation it is intended to assume of THE LITERARY DIARY.

Without interfering with the periodical productions of those gentlemen, whose elaborate criticisms are so advantageous to Literature, it is proposed occasionally to extract from the numerous publications daily issuing from the Press, the most striking and important passages, with the addition of a few illustrative remarks.—THE PUBLIC ADVERTISER will also be enriched, from the Foreign Literary Journals, with the most important results of Academic and Professional labours.

To the lovers of Literature, circumstances trivial in themselves become strongly interesting as they relate to or are connected with genius and ability— the Authentic Anecdote, the Biographic Sketch, are sought for with avidity, and cherished with fondness—these will occasionally enter into the plan of the Literary Department.

CASES of importance adjudged in the different Courts of Law, will be reported with that clearness and precision, which are indispensable in the statement of judicial determinations.

Observations on the DRAMA will be directed to that improvement which is the end and aim of genuine criticism.

The happiest efforts of the Painter, the Sculptor, and the Architect, will be recorded with that honest national pride, which delights to dwell on the progressive excellence of Arts protected by Royal munificence, and cultivated by public favour.

ADVERTISEMENTS will be inserted as early as possible, and in the order they are received, carefully excluding such as may offend the eye of delicacy.

On this extended plan and with all the modern improvements in the department of the PRESS, THE PUBLIC ADVERTISER, OR POLITICAL AND LITERARY DIARY, will be submitted to the public on the 1st of January 1794; and as the expence attending so enlarged an arrangement must necessarily be very great, the Proprietors flatter themselves they will appear justified in raising the price of their paper to FOUR PENCE: as it is absolutely impossible that a Newspaper really entitled to public favour, can, without a ruinous loss, be sold for less. [The paper was now priced at $3\frac{1}{2}d$.]

To the Learned World in general, and more particularly to those respectable literary characters who have already honoured THE PUBLIC ADVERTISER with their valuable communications, the present Proprietors address themselves with respect and confidence; earnestly soliciting their support and assistance in the perfection of a plan, which so obviously tends to the general circulation of useful knowledge.

———

N. B. This Paper will be published at so early an hour, as to admit of its being sent the same day by the Morning Coaches to the distant parts of the kingdom.

Until 1 January, 1794, the *Public Advertiser* retained its old title, it had little to say about anything, and it had no advertisements whatever. It was also still printed by the Treasury printer, Nicholas Byrne. It was not clear from the prospectus whether the paper had again changed hands or not, but it did seem evident that there would be a change in the conductor after the first of the year. The author of the prospectus was obviously not the man who on 6 December had thanked his "Friends" for extinguishing the fire at the "Printing-house." But he was also not John Bell or Peter Stuart. This fact is of consequence because one of the several depositories for "Advertisements, and other communications" was the office of John Bell, "No. 148, opposite Bond-street, in Oxford-street," because by March, 1794, the *Public Advertiser* had been amalgamated with the *Oracle*, because Stuart was in the market for a newspaper, having tried to buy the *Oracle* earlier, and because the renovated *Public Advertiser* sounded very much like the old spurious *Star*, conducted by Peter and Charles Stuart and James Mackintosh in 1789, the only difference being that the *Public Advertiser* was to champion the King and William Pitt, whereas the spurious *Star* had championed the Prince of Wales against both.

The prospectus was in any event an indictment of the British Convention, it indicated very clearly that the issues during the ensuing session of Parliament would be the King and the Constitution, and it seemed to suggest that the *Public Advertiser*, subsidized perhaps by the Home Office, would supplant the *True Briton* as the principal Ministerial paper. Although he had been using *The Times* and the *Oracle*, Dundas had no paper of his own, and the Government needed another newspaper anyway. It had lost the *World*, which, except for the columns of excerpts from Charles Stuart's parody, was supporting the Opposition; it had failed to silence the *Morning Chronicle*; and it was facing a very militant and, by the end of the year, a very radical *Morning Post*. The *Chronicle* would be assisted in its tactics by the *Gazetteer*, the *Post* by the *Courier*. The *Courier* was now at least lacking Este, for Este inserted the announcement of his return in the *Oracle*. "The Rev. C. ESTE is at present busied upon a work, from which much information and amusement may be expected,—'a Journal of his late Travels over the Continent.' *Italy* has principally occupied his attention," remarked that newspaper on 21 December. Since Italy was now "principally [occupying]" the "attention" of the Government, Este was evidently hoping to become a pamphleteer for the Treasury.

One month before Parliament convened, Ridgway and Symonds published anonymously Daniel Stuart's *Peace and Reform, against War and Corruption. In Answer to a Pamphlet, Written by Arthur Young, Esq., Entitled "The Example of France, a Warning to Britain."* Although excerpts had been appearing in the *Morning Post* since August, the work was evidently completed in October, for it was aware of the sentences of Muir and Palmer, but not of the British Conventions. The first excerpt to be identified as such was a long defense of Fox, published by the *Morning Chronicle* on 20 December. The defense had been taken, said the

Chronicle, from a pamphlet, called *Peace and Reform*, which had "just appeared." On 21 December the work was advertised by the *Oracle*, which was also advertising another pamphlet for Ridgway and Symonds, entitled *The Errors of Mr. Pitt's Present Administration, Many Recent, Unfortunate, and Dangerous. By a Gentleman Unconnected with Foreign Interests or Internal Parties. Veluti in Speculum.* This "*Gentleman*" was later thought to be Dennis O'Bryen. The pamphlets were readvertised by the *Oracle* on 24 December, and on 23 December *Peace and Reform* was advertised by the *Morning Post*.

The Errors of Mr. Pitt's Present Administration was, as the name implied, an account of Pitt's blunders; *Peace and Reform* was concerned with his cunning. The pamphlet dealt ruthlessly with Reeves, Sir Joseph Banks, John Heriot, John Bowles, Judge Braxfield, Burke, and the numerous others who had connived to keep Pitt in office in contempt of the will of the people. It argued vehemently for immediate negotiations with France and for the only kind of reform which the Friends of the People, the Whigs, the populace, and even the majority of the radicals ever wanted, namely, "to make the House of commons independent of the executive power, or of a small number of wealthy men, and to make it act upon an identity of interest with the people." And it concluded with an extravagant eulogy of Fox, which began with the declaration:

> The many wicked aspersions thrown on the character and conduct of [Mr. Fox], may . . . be justly construed as eulogiums on his public virtue; for, if ever there was a man, who conscious of acting with rectitude, maintained the true interests of his country with firmness, consistency, and moderation, against all that could deject and terrify, he is the man: If ever private interest and public fame; if ever the sweets of social life, and the prospects of state elevation were sacrificed to the national welfare, and to the liberties and happiness of mankind, they were sacrificed by Mr. Fox last winter. He stood forward, almost alone, and with gigantic power arrested the Government in its wanton intoxicated career. Sedition and insurrection had been declared to exist, the Attorney-General's table was said to be loaded with hundreds of indictments, and thousands were recorded as disaffected persons, upon the authority of anonymous letters, and the veracity of common informers. The suspension of the Habeas Corpus Act was announced in the House of Commons. . . . But Mr. Fox stood forward with truth and energy. The Government was awed:—It paused:—and, finding the proofs of insurrection and sedition vague and trifling, it refrained from [carrying its measures into effect]. He undauntedly struggled to avert the calamities of War; he did not succeed: But he succeeded in what was of much more immediate importance perhaps, in shielding the remaining Liberties of the English people.

There was much more.

Since both pamphlets were dated 1794, they had evidently been intended for release early in January and had been released at this time because of the Edinburgh arrests, Lord Lauderdale and his friends being afraid that the trials would begin shortly and that the Government would attempt as usual to blame

Fox and the Friends of the People for everything which had happened at the British Convention. As it turned out, the pamphlets appeared none too soon. By 21 December the *Oracle* was calling Burke's *Reflections* the greatest work in the English language. "From Mr. BURKE we may yet look for one more immortal work," it added, "a View of the BRITISH CONSTITUTION, progressively analytical, and which may more conduce to the . . . confusion of our turbulent innovators, than any publication that ever issued from the press, since that Constitution 'was first put upon its hinges.'" The *Morning Post* agreed that some clear-cut statements about the nature of the British Constitution were overdue, but Burke, it thought (25 Dec.), was the last man in the world to make them:

MR. BURKE.

When Mr. BURKE, in his celebrated love-paroxism, exclaimed, "The Age of Chivalry is no more," how justly might he have proceeded to shed his tears of eloquence on the ashes of Truth, of Shame, of common Honesty, and common Reason! How pathetically might his creative Genius have deplored that spirit of Independence, which is the only incentive to every thing great and good, and which, once surrendered, degrades Man into a being the most abject and pitiable! That creatures, who have so prostituted themselves to venality, should, in their servile state, defend and panegerize the acts of their Masters, ought not to be wondered at, because it is natural; but that men of liberal and enlightened Minds; Men, who neither have bartered their Principles nor their will, should be so absurd, as not only not to see through the intrigues of Ministers, but even to vindicate their measures, is an instance of perversion in the human mind, so strange, and uncommon, as to demand a rank among those eccentricities of life, which it is in vain to endeavour to develope.

All Opposition papers were now being flailed by the *Oracle*. "The *Conductors* of the Jacobin Prints may well be called *Guillotine* Conductors; for they daily murder common sense and common honesty!" it snarled on 24 December; and on 25 December it reported happily: "*Certain* SEDITIOUS PAPERS having long been driven out of all *genteel* circulation, now begin to be scouted from the *tap-room*. The honest MECHANIC, made *wiser* by our means, rejects the ill-digested fallacies imposed upon him. The ORACLE has the honour to receive the daily abuse of every thing *low*, *illiterate*, and *factious* in the Country. Does any Man need to be told why? Alas! they who *suffer* may be allowed, if GENTLEMEN, to *complain*, if otherwise, to *abuse*." The *Oracle* was referring to a new advertising tactic, probably contrived by John Bell.

One of the papers thus "scouted from the *tap-room*" was the *World*, which on 24 December published an address on the subject:

To CORRESPONDENTS.
We have been informed by some FRIENDS, *that attempts have been made, by a certain* HIGH CONSTABLE [Robert Jones], *in some respectable Coffee Houses in London, to obtrude another* PRINT [the *Oracle*] *on the Public taste.—By such low and* disgrace-

ful *measures, we should disdain to be recommended;—but if our Cotemporaries think differently, it becomes us only to say, that our numerous Friends in the Public line, need not fear this Fellow's menaces—he has not the power to Billet Soldiers* partially *—and should any instances occur, of improper conduct in the execution of his Office, if our Friends will furnish us with the proofs necessary, we will bring him to punishment.—We are happy to announce, by respectable authority, that a Bill will be brought the ensuing Session into Parliament, vesting the authority of giving Billets to Soldiers in the neighbouring Magistrates.—A public Newspaper must want patronage indeed, when it descends to be benefitted by any influence which a Parish Officer may prostitute his authority to carry into effect.*

If this Officer (whose name we shall not long withhold) paid as much attention to the duties of his situation, in ridding his neighbourhood of the numerous prostitutes and pickpockets, he would not, perhaps, have the contempt which his ignorance, and the abuses of his Office, have so justly entailed upon him.

The *World* of 26 December was more specific:

HIGH CONSTABLE.

We before hinted, that a certain High Constable, *by virtue of his Authority*, had endeavoured to obtrude a particular newspaper upon several Coffee-houses within his District.—Since this report we are enabled to prove, that such improper influence has been used by the High Constable for Westminster.

The following is a Copy of a Letter which has been circulated very industriously among the Coffee-houses, Brothels, &c.—but (as we understand) with little effect:

"SIR,

The daily Newspaper, entitled The [*Oracle*], will now be conducted in the most spirited and intelligent manner: on that account I have taken an interest in its welfare, and therefore presume to request the favour of you to give it a trial in your House, at least for two or three Months. By your so doing *I shall consider myself as particularly obliged*, and shall be happy TO RETURN THE COMPLIMENT BY ANY MEANS IN MY POWER.

"I am, SIR,
"Your most obedient humble Servant,
(Signed)   ROBERT JONES,
High Constable for Westminster."

The High Constable for Westminster, keeps an Office for providing SUBSTITUTES, for those on whom the lot may fall, to serve in the Militia; he is also a Coal Merchant, Snuff Manufacturer, Collector of Taxes, &c. &c.!—by this it should appear he is a man of *great industry*.

On 26 December the *Oracle* assured its readers that Colonel Macleod had had nothing to do with the later "commotion" in Edinburgh, having positively quit the Convention on 5 December; on 27 December the *Morning Post* reprinted the eulogy of Fox from Stuart's *Peace and Reform*, the same one which had appeared in the *Morning Chronicle* one week earlier; and on 30 December the *Post* published part of Skirving's indictment, concluding it on the following day. Joseph Gerrald of the London Corresponding Society had also, it said, been indicted, and many other indictments were expected to follow. "Subscriptions, to a very large amount, have been privately made for the support of the Delegates assembled at Edinburgh," the *Post* added hopefully on 31 December. "The prosecutions instituted against them will be resisted by the first legal characters in the Country. Besides, Jurymen will be more cautious in bringing in a Verdict . . . , when they reflect on the Sentence passed on Mr. PALMER and Mr. MUIR." Although the opening of Parliament was still three weeks away, preparations were obviously in progress. Pitt finally had what he had so long wanted: evidence of actual sedition. No newspaper doubted that he would exploit it to the fullest.

Notes for Part III

1. Arthur Aspinall, *Politics and the Press c. 1780–1850* (London: Ernest Benn Ltd., 1949), pp. 451, 452–453.

2. For Burns's contributions during 1793–1795, see Lucyle Werkmeister, "Robert Burns and the London Daily Press," *Modern Philology*, LXIII (1966), 322–335. For Coleridge's and Porson's contributions, see Werkmeister, *Coleridge and the London Newspapers 1790–1797*, forthcoming.

3. See Werkmeister, *The London Daily Press, 1772–1792* (Lincoln: University of Nebraska Press, 1963), p. 255.

4. *The Farington Diary by Joseph Farington, R. A.*, ed. James Greig (London: Hutchinson and Co., 1922–1928), I, 28.

5. Robert L. Haig, *The Gazetteer 1735–1797* (Carbondale: Southern Illinois University Press, 1960), pp. 230–233, 236, 238.

6. *Politics and the Press*, p. 165.

7. PRO 30/ GD 8/ 333–334, 355–357.

8. PRO 30/ GD 8/ 333–334.

9. PRO 30/ GD 8/ 270–271, 302, 314, 333–334.

10. *The Newspaper Press, in Part of the Last Century, and Up to the Present Period of 1860. The Recollections of James Amphlett* (London, 1860), p. 10.

11. See [Stanley Morison,], *The History of The Times 1785–1841* (London: The Times, 1935), p. 68.

12. Vansittart Papers, B. M. Add. MS. 31,230, ff. 128–130. I am indebted to Professor W. A. Moffett for calling this letter to my attention.

13. PRO 30/ GD 8/ 292, 333–334.

14. PRO 30/ GD 8/ 214, 333–334.

15. *History of The Times*, pp. 61–62.

16. *History of The Times*, pp. 34–35.

17. *The Farington Diary*, I, 156.

18. *The Farington Diary*, I, 28.

19. *Public Characters of 1806*, ed. Richard Phillips (London, 1806).

20. PRO 30/ GD 8/ 333–334.

21. PRO 30/ GD 8/ 148.

22. PRO 30/ GD 8/ 301, 333–334.

23. PRO 30/ GD 8/ 301, 333–334.

24. For the whole of which, see *The Parliamentary History of England* (London, 1817), XXX, 239–270.

25. See Daniel Stuart, "The Newspaper Writings of the Poet Coleridge," *Gentleman's Magazine*, n.s., IX (1838), 570; Daniel Stuart, "The Late Mr. Coleridge, the Poet," *Gentleman's Magazine*, n.s., X (1838), 125; *Specimens of the Table Talk of Samuel Taylor Coleridge*, 1 May, 1832. But in all instances substitute *the Corresponding Society* for *the Friends of the People*. As Daniel Stuart said and Coleridge very well knew, there was no mystery about the size of the Society of the Friends of the People, the list of members having been several times published.

26. See *London Daily Press*, pp. 111–112.

27. See *London Daily Press*, pp. 141–142, 146. He was still deceiving his clients in 1809. See *The Farington Diary*, V, 176.

28. *Memoirs of the Whig Party during My Time. By Henry Richard Lord Holland*, ed. Henry Edward Lord Holland (London, 1852), I, 39, 41, 44, 45.

29. *Collected Letters of Samuel Taylor Coleridge*, ed. Earl Leslie Griggs (Oxford: Oxford University Press, 1956), I, 51.

30. *The Correspondence of William Augustus Miles on the French Revolution 1789–1817*, ed. Rev. Charles Popham Miles (London, 1850), II, 64.

31. Daniel Stuart, *Peace and Reform, against War and Corruption* (London, 1794), p. 67.

32. *London Daily Press*, p. 209.

33. See Roland Bartel, "The Story of Public Fast Days in England," *Anglican Theological Review*, XXXVIII (1955), 1–11.

34. *Peace and Reform*, p. 13.

35. *London Daily Press*, pp. 146–147.

36. *Gentleman's Magazine*, n.s., X, 125.

37. HO 42/27.

38. Cyrus Redding, *Fifty Years' Recollections, Literary and Personal, with Observations on Men and Things* (London, 1858), I, 64.

39. See *London Daily Press*, pp. 327, 329.

40. See *London Daily Press*, pp. 3–4.

41. See *Politics and the Press*, p. 280.

42. See *London Daily Press*, p. 107.

43. See [James Maitland, 8th Earl of Lauderdale,] *Letters to the Peers of Scotland* (London, 1794), pp. 6–8.

44. Haig, p. 238.

45. See *London Daily Press*, pp. 67–68.

46. See, for example, Redding, I, 94–95; "Editors and Newspaper Writers of the Last Generation. By an Old Apprentice of the Law," *Fraser's Magazine*, LXV (1862), 174.

47. *Gentleman's Magazine*, n.s., X, 26.

48. *Gentleman's Magazine*, n.s., X, 26.

49. *Gentleman's Magazine*, n.s., X, 26.

50. Obituary of Daniel Stuart, *Gentleman's Magazine*, n.s., XXVIII (1847), 323.

51. *Biographica Literaria.... By Samuel Taylor Coleridge*, eds. H. N. Coleridge and Sara Coleridge (New York, 1847), p. 759.

52. *Gentleman's Magazine*, n.s., X, 24.

53. *Gentleman's Magazine*, n.s., X, 25.

54. *Letters from the Lake Poets ... to Daniel Stuart*, ed. Mary Stuart (London, 1889), p. x.

55. See *London Daily Press*, pp. 207, 208, 214.

56. For Almon's letter on the subject, see *London Daily Press*, p. 145.

57. Stanley Morison, *John Bell, 1745-1831* (Cambridge: privately printed, 1930), p.31.

58. Lucyle Werkmeister, *Jemmie Boswell and the London Daily Press, 1785-1795* (New York: New York Public Library, 1963), p. 52, note.

59. *The Farington Diary*, V, 163.

60. *Gentleman's Magazine*, n.s., X, 125.

61. HO 42/26.

62. *History of The Times*, pp. 69-70.

63. See *London Daily Press*, pp. 280-282.

64. See *London Daily Press*, pp. 3-4, 280.

65. HO 42/26.

66. HO 42/26.

67. *London Daily Press*, pp. 78-79, 156.

68. HO 42/26.

69. *The Parliamentary History of England*, XXXI, 866-867.

70. The British Museum has a copy of this handbill.

71. HO 42/27.

CHRONOLOGICAL TABLE,
BIBLIOGRAPHICAL NOTE, AND INDEX

Chronological Table

1792

5 January	Grand Jury quashes Mrs. Billington's suit against Ridgway.
14 January	Opera House burns.
25 January	Thomas Hardy organizes Corresponding Society.
31 January	Opening of Parliament.
1 February	Mrs. Billington moves Court of King's Bench for prosecution of Ridgway.
2 February	Pitt ridiculed by Merry in *The Magician No Conjuror* at Covent Garden.
18 February	Prince of Wales ridiculed by Holcroft in *Road to Ruin* at Covent Garden.
? March	Surrender and imprisonment of John Almon.
1 March	Thompson announces intention of moving for investigation of 1788 election.
7 March	Fox introduces problem of Prince of Wales's debts.
10 March	Death of third Earl of Bute.
12 March	First sale of Prince of Wales's stud.
13 March	Thompson moves for investigation of 1788 Westminster election.
14 March	Rose files action for libel against *Morning Post*.
18 March	Dibdin files suits for trespass against Swan and Locke of the *Observer*.
20 March	Westminster electors sign petition for investigation of Rose's activities in 1788 Westminster election.
4 April	Fox presents petition from Westminster electors.
5 April	Duke of York's Establishment Bill and Bill for Reducing the National Debt signed by the King.
11 April	Founding of the Society of the Friends of the People.
15 April	First conference on payment of Prince of Wales's debts.
20 April	France declares war against Austria and Hungary.
26 April	Friends of the People resolve to move for reform.
30 April	Death of fourth Earl of Sandwich.
30 April	Grey announces intention of moving for election reforms on behalf of Friends of the People.
8 May	Fox moves for consideration of Westminster petition.
11 May	Fox moves for repeal of statutes against the dissenters.
21 May	Proclamation against Seditious Writings.
21 May	Ministerial papers open fire on Lord Thurlow.
23 May	Passage of Middlesex Justices Act.

25 May	Proclamation against Seditious Writings supported in Commons by Windham and friends of the Earl of Guilford.
31 May	Proclamation against Seditious Writings supported in Lords by Prince of Wales, Lord Rawdon, Lord Porchester, Earl Spencer, and Duke of Portland.
2 June	Covent Garden closed for repairs; Mrs. Merry dismissed.
6 June	John Taylor arrested in Edinburgh for inciting riots against Government.
11 June	Passage of Fox's Libel Bill.
15 June	Parliament prorogued to 30 August.
15 June	Resignation of Lord Thurlow as Lord Chancellor.
1 July	Duel between Lord Lauderdale and General Arnold.
4 July	Mackintosh's *Letter to . . . Pitt.*
7 July	Plot to blow up King's Bench Prison foiled.
9 July	Sampson Perry of *Argus* completes prison term. John Bell of *Oracle* convicted of libels on the Guards. Tattersall of *Morning Post* convicted of libels on Lady Elizabeth Lambart; damages fixed at £4,000. Tattersall and William Williams of *Morning Post* convicted of libel on Rose; damages fixed at £100.
10 July	Tattersall of *Morning Post* indicted for libel on the King; action diverted to William Williams. Sampson Perry of *Argus* indicted for libel on the Commons.
12 July	John Taylor tried in Edinburgh for inciting riots against the Government; acquitted on evidence that he was agent of the Government.
16 July	Jordan pleads guilty to publishing Paine's *Rights of Man*, Part II.
17 July	Marplay apprehended; £10,000 recovered.
24 July	Prussia declares war on France.
25 July	Colman's allowance adjusted.
27 July	Duke of Brunswick's manifesto against the French Revolution.
30 July	Duke of Richmond begins military camp at Bagshot.
1 August	Lord Mansfield created Earl of Mansfield, County of Middlesex, with special remainder to Viscount Stormont.
1 August	Strengthening of Westminster police force.
4 August	Death of General Burgoyne.
5 August	Death of second Earl of Guilford.
6 August	Still-born child born to Mrs. Jordan and Duke of Clarence.
7 August	Military camp at Bagshot concludes with Grand Review.
9 August	Pitt appropriates Wardenship of Cinque Ports and Governorship of Dover Castle.
10 August	Riots in Paris; Tuileries stormed; Swiss Guard murdered; monarchy suspended; Royal Family under guard. British resolve to recall French ambassador, Earl Gower.
19 August	Revolutionary Tribunal established in France.
26 August	French decree against priests.
27 August	Covent Garden opens for winter season.

30 August	Prince of Wales ridiculed by Mrs. Inchbald's *Young Men and Old Women* at the Haymarket.
30 August	Parliament prorogued to 15 November.
2 September	French massacres.
13 September	Paine, Frost, and others leave for Paris.
20 September	French defeat Prussians at Valmy.
21 September	France declared a republic.
22 September	Beginning of Opposition *Courier*, second evening daily.
27 September	Duke of Portland elected Chancellor of Oxford University.
1 October	Beginning of Ministerial *Sun*, third afternoon daily.
10 October	Death of second Baron Mulgrave.
10 October	Duke of Portland installed as Chancellor of Oxford University.
17 October	Dibdin files suit for libel against Swan and Bostock of the *World*; fight between Dibdin and Scott. Beginning of the Holman scandal.
1 November	Richard Porson elected Regius Professor of Greek at Cambridge University.
6 November	Austrians defeated at Jemappes.
6 November	Reeves publishes prospectus for The Association.
14 November	French capture Brussels.
15 November	Parliament prorogued to 3 January.
16 November	Lord Auckland's Declaration.
16 November	French Executive Council declares the Meuse and the Scheldt open to the sea.
19 November	France pledges support for all liberation movements.
20 November	First meeting of The Association.
22 November	Rumors of augmentation of forces.
23 November	Lady Lambart collects £4,000 from Tattersall; George Rose collects £100.
28 November	Ridgway and six other printers indicted for seditious libel.
29 November	First retrenchments of the Prince of Wales.
30 November	First purgings; the King cashiers Lord Sempill and Lord Edward Fitzgerald.
? December	Arrest of Rowan in Ireland.
1 December	Phantom uprising; militia called out; the Tower and the Bank under guard.
3 December	Dalrymple and Macleod cashiered.
4 December	Bounties for enlistments announced; construction of barracks begun.
?5 December	*Argus* seized by the Treasury.
8 December	Frost indicted for seditious utterances; outlawed; £100 offered for apprehension. Sampson Perry convicted of libel; outlawed; £100 offered for apprehension.
10 December	Inspection of fortifications of the Tower.
11 December	Convention of Associated Friends of the People in Scotland begins; adjourns 13 December.
11 December	Three-day riots against the reformers begin in Manchester.
12 December	Rumors of augmentation of the Army confirmed.

12 December	*Morning Herald* publishes John King's speech at Egham.
13 December	Convocation of Parliament; King announces augmentation of the forces and end of the war in India; Fox moves for investigation of the insurrection of 1 December; Attorney General boasts of two hundred indictments in process; Duke of Clarence strongly supports the war.
13 December	Two-day riots against reformers and dissenters begin in Cambridge.
14 December	Fox moves for negotiations to avert war.
15 December	Fox moves to send Minister to France to negotiate peace; Burke deserts Opposition.
15 December	Cambridge under martial law.
17 December	Ridgway and Holland indicted for sedition; Grey moves to indict Reeves for sedition.
18 December	Pitt unanimously re-elected as Member for Cambridge University.
18 December	Paine convicted *in absentia* for publishing a seditious libel; outlawed; defended by Erskine.
19 December	Beginning of newspaper attacks on Erskine.
19 December	Alien Bill introduced by Lord Grenville.
20 December	French declare all Bourbons banished except those in The Temple.
26 December	Alien Bill passed by Lords.
28 December	Alien Bill submitted to the Commons; Elliot announces defection of the Duke of Portland; Burke's dagger scene.
31 December	Elliot retracts his statement regarding the Duke of Portland's defection.
31 December	French ambassador, M. Chauvelin, notified that he has had no diplomatic status since 10 August.

1793

? January	Macan sentenced to three years in Newgate for trying to blow up King's Bench Prison.
1 January	*Argus* recommenced as Ministerial *True Briton*, a morning daily, owned by members of Government.
3 January	Muir arrested in Edinburgh; released with apologies.
4 January	Alien Bill passes the Commons; supported by right wing of the Opposition.
5 January	Creditors of Prince of Wales asked to submit accounts.
7 January	M. Chauvelin protests Alien Bill.
7 January	Carter, a "bill-sticker," sentenced to six months in prison; Tytler tried for sedition in Edinburgh; outlawed.
8 January	Ministerial papers begin attacks on M. Chauvelin.
8 January	Frost declared a bankrupt.
8 January	Morton, Anderson, and Craig tried in Edinburgh for sedition; trial ends 11 January; all agents for Dundas.
10 January	Elder and Steward tried for sedition in Edinburgh.
10 January	Ministerial papers begin campaign for enlistments.
13 January	M. Chauvelin submits letter from M. Le Brun, pleading for peace.
13 January	Thomas Spence arrested.

17 January	M. Chauvelin begs for permission to present new credentials.
19 January	Public dinner of the Friends of the Liberty of the Press.
20 January	M. Chauvelin's petition to present credentials rejected.
21 January	Execution of Louis XVI.
22 January	Alien Act becomes effective.
22 January	Reduction of the Prince of Wales's household.
23 January	Second partition of Poland.
24 January	*Morning Chronicle* publishes Thomas Law's exposé of The Association.
25 January	M. Chauvelin arrested for debt, freed, and flees to France.
25 January	Lord Auckland's Memorial.
26 January	Muir's trial scheduled for 11 February.
28 January	Lord George Gordon returned to Newgate, having failed to furnish securities.
28 January	Berry and Robertson go on trial in Scotland; Callender outlawed, having absconded.
28 January	Death of Jeremiah Hargrave, proprietor of the *Morning Post.*
28 January	Newspapers publish Prince of Wales's letter to the Duke of Portland; Rumors of Erskine's dismissal as Attorney General to the Prince of Wales; Prince of Wales commissioned Colonel of 10th Regiment of Light Dragoons.
28 January	Announcement of strengthening of King's legal counsel.
28 January	Report of Lord Loughborough's acceptance of the Chancellorship.
28 January	Fox's *Letter . . . to the . . . [Westminster] Electors.*
28 January	King asks for augmentation of the forces; debates on the message postponed.
29 January	Erskine's dismissal verified.
29 January	Mrs. Inchbald's comedy, *Every Man Has His Fault,* with many references to the Prince of Wales, produced at Covent Garden.
29 January	Mrs. Jordan demands that Drury Lane produce *Anna* or release her from her contract.
30 January	*Oracle* announces reconciliation of the King and the Prince of Wales.
30 January	Arrival of French ambassador, M. Maret.
31 January	Advertisements for Wordsworth's *Descriptive Sketches.*
1 February	Replies to Fox's *Letter . . . to the . . . [Westminster] Electors.*
1 February	Debates on King's message; war supported by right wing of Opposition.
1 February	France declares war on England.
4 February	Smith and Mennons tried in Scotland.
5 February	John Bell fails to appear for sentencing; arrest ordered.
9 February	Eyre replaces Loughborough as Lord Chief Justice of Common Pleas.
9 February	Friends of the People hear Report on the State of the Representation and resolve that Tierney will prepare petition for election reforms.
9 February	Newspapers announce declaration of war.
11 February	Maitland moves to expedite trial of Hastings.
11 February	King's message respecting declaration of war.

12 February	Debates on King's message; Fox moves for amendments; war supported by right wing of Opposition.
12 February	Macdonald named Lord Chief Baron of Exchequer vice Eyre.
13 February	Scott named Attorney General vice Macdonald; Mitford named Solicitor General.
14 February	Death of Brass Crosby.
15 February	Frost pleads not guilty.
18 February	First reports of presses of seamen.
18 February	Advertisements for Godwin's *Political Justice*.
18 February	Young's *The Example of France* published by The Association.
18 February	Fox moves resolutions to end the war.
?20 February	Lord Rawdon introduces the Debtor and Creditor Bill.
21 February	Grey moves for peace.
21 February	Nottingham petition for election reforms rejected; Pitt questions right to petition.
22 February	Commons reviews Stockbridge election; unseats Major Scott, but exonerates him from charges of bribery.
22 February	Taylor moves against the housing of soldiers in barracks.
22 February	*Morning Herald* publishes Paine's letter to John King and John King's reply.
23 February	Duke of York commissioned Commander in Chief of the forces in the United Provinces.
23 February	Spence acquitted; Symonds convicted; Holland sentenced to one year in prison.
23 February	Advertisements for *The State of the Representation*, published by the Friends of the People.
25 February	Muir outlawed in Scotland.
25 February	Mrs. Jordan makes seasonal debut at Drury Lane in *Anna*.
26 February	Locke convicted of trespass in action brought by Dibdin.
26 February	French capture Breda.
28 February	Burke complains of contrived delays in trial of Hastings.
1 March	French capture Gertruydenberg.
2 March	Brook Watson appointed Commissary General to the Army.
2 March	King announces pardon of all deserters surrendering by 30 April.
4 March	Cambridge court resolves to prosecute Frend.
4 March	Phillips sentenced to eighteen months in Leicester jail.
4 March	Sheridan moves for investigation of supposed uprising of 1 December, 1792.
5 March	Forty-five resignations from the Whig Club, collected by Windham.
5 March	John Bell apologizes to the Guards.
6 March	Anderson elected M.P. for London vice Watson.
6 March	King asks for employment of 12,000 Hanoverian troops to assist the Dutch.
7 March	France declares war on Spain.
7 March	Boaden's *Ozmyn and Daraxa* at Drury Lane.
9 March	Public dinner of Friends of the Liberty of the Press.

11 March	Debate on the budget; Pitt appeals to Fox to support the Administration.
12 March	Scott announces intention of introducing the Traitorous Correspondence Act.
13 March	Beginning of the quarrel between Harrison and the Maras.
14 March	First uprisings in La Vendée.
15 March	Scott introduces Traitorous Correspondence Bill.
18 March	Austrians defeat French at Neerwinden.
18 March	Berry and Robertson sentenced in Scotland, despite ambiguity of verdict.
18 March	Murphy's *The Rival Sisters* at Drury Lane.
20 March	Death of the first Earl of Mansfield; Lord Stormont succeeds.
20 March	Introduction of Stockbridge Election Bribery Bill.
25 March	British sign treaty with Russia.
25 March	Pitt arranges a loan of £6,000,000.
25 March	General Dumouriez signs secret treaty with Austrians.
27 March	Lord Rawdon's Debtor and Creditor Bill passes second reading in the Lords.
1 April	Debates on the loan.
4 April	Cumberland's comic opera, *The Armourer*, at Covent Garden.
5 April	Lord Auckland's Memorial.
6 April	French government establishes first Committee of Public Safety.
9 April	*Morning Herald* publishes John King's letter to Paine.
9 April	Traitorous Correspondence Bill passed by the Commons.
10 April	Stockbridge Electors Incapacitating Bill introduced.
10 April	British sign treaty with Hesse-Cassel.
11 April	Further consideration of Stockbridge Election Bribery Bill postponed indefinitely.
?12 April	Drury Lane patent cleared.
15 April	Second reading in Lords of Traitorous Correspondence Bill.
18 April	Reynolds's comedy, *How to Grow Rich*, performed at Covent Garden.
19 April	National fast.
20 April	Public dinner of the Friends of the Liberty of the Press.
22 April	Traitorous Correspondence Bill passes the Lords.
25 April	British sign treaty with Sardinia.
25 April	Sheridan moves for censure of Auckland's Memorial of 5 April.
26 April	Outlawry of Almon reversed.
1 May	Lord Lauderdale submits petition from Robertson and Berry, protesting their sentence.
2 May	Symonds and Ridgway plead guilty to publishing sedition.
3 May	Stockbridge Electors Incapacitating Bill shelved for three months.
3 May	Frend's trial begins.
3 May	Almon released on bail.
6 May	Lord Thurlow opposes Lord Rawdon's Debtor and Creditor Bill.
6 May	Grey presents petition for election reforms from Friends of the People.

7 May	Grey's motion for election reforms defeated.
8 May	Passage of Commercial Credit Bill.
8 May	British take St. Amand.
8 May	Ridgway sentenced to four years in Newgate, Symonds, already serving two, to an additional two.
10 May	Holland again indicted for sedition.
11 May	Bell announces his bankruptcy.
18 May	Swan convicted of trespass; Dibdin awarded £100 damages; also awarded £100 damages from Locke.
24 May	Renewal of charter of East India Company, this time with salaried board.
25 May	Friends of the People resolve to continue fight for election reforms.
25 May	Burke's treatment of Hastings censured by Archbishop of York.
25 May	British sign treaty with Spain.
27 May	Woodbridge's farce, *The Pad*, performed at Covent Garden.
27 May	Frost convicted of seditious utterances.
27 May	Defeat of Stockbridge Election Bribery Bill.
28 May	Baker moves to denounce Archbishop of York's statement as libel on the Commons.
30 May	Burke moves for preparation of history of Hastings's trial to exonerate Managers from responsibility for delays.
30 May	Frend banished from the University of Cambridge.
31 May	Frend appeals to the University authorities.
31 May	Wharton moves for an investigation regarding the rights of the people.
31 May	Lambton gives notice of a motion regarding interference of peers in elections.
31 May	Lord Rawdon's Debtor and Creditor Bill defeated.
31 May	Beginning of Reign of Terror.
2 June	Girondists overthrown.
3 June	Eaton tried for libel; verdict indecisive.
5 June	Advertisement of subscription for payment of Fox's debts.
6 June	Grey moves to postpone trial of Hastings to next session; Commons votes to continue it on 12 June.
7 June	Grey and Burke protest continuation of trial of Hastings on 12 June; trial postponed to next session.
7 June	Lambton withdraws motion regarding interference of peers in elections.
8 June	Rowan indicted in Ireland.
10 June	Covent Garden closes for the summer.
10 June	Bell announces suspension of British Library.
21 June	Whitbread moves for prosecution of the *World* for publishing statement of the Archbishop of York; motion defeated.
15 June	General Dumouriez arrives.
17 June	General Dumouriez ordered to leave the country.
17 June	Fox moves for peace.

17 June	Earl Stanhope moves to denounce Auckland's Memorial of 5 April; motion strongly supported by the Duke of Clarence, who castigates the Government for beginning the war.
17 June	Frost sentenced to six months in Newgate with one hour in the pillory.
19 June	Mrs. Bateman assails Sheridan for refusing to employ her as an actress.
20 June	Lord Rawdon succeeds as second Earl Moira.
21 June	Parliament prorogued to 13 August.
25 June	Swan and Bostock convicted of libel; Dibdin awarded 1s. damages.
27–28 June	Board of Delegates upholds Frend's banishment from the University of Cambridge.
29 June	Canning elected Member of Parliament for Newton.
? July	Holt convicted of publishing sedition; trials of talkers and booksellers in provinces begin.
1 July	Christie advertises auction of the *Oracle*.
3 July	Expiration of Tattersall-Weltje lease on *Morning Post*; paper probably leased by Daniel Stuart as agent of Lord Lauderdale.
3–5 July	Oxford confers honorary degrees on all the politically favored.
4 July	Grand celebration of Duke of Portland's installation as Chancellor of University of Oxford.
5 July	First fashion column.
10 July	Eaton tried for another libel; verdict again indecisive.
10 July	Austrians capture Condé.
10 July	French establish Great Committee of General Security.
12 July	British sign treaty with The Two Sicilies.
13 July	Assassination of Marat.
14 July	British sign treaty with Prussia.
20 July	Benjamin Flower begins the Cambridge *Intelligencer*.
23 July	Prussians capture Mainz.
25–26 July	Winterbotham convicted of preaching seditious sermons.
26 July	English capture Valenciennes after long siege.
?1 August	*Oracle* purchased by James Bell, Jr.; other property of John Bell purchased by friends.
2 August	Marie Antoinette transferred to prison.
6 August	Robinsons convicted of publishing sedition.
7 August	Skirving arrested in Scotland.
8 August	Lord Somerville elected Representative Peer.
10 August	Muir petitions for trial.
13 August	Corresponding Society meets to prepare petition for peace; someone moves the assassination of Pitt.
13 August	Parliament prorogued to 29 October.
13 August	Duke of Richmond's summer camp moved from Waterdown to Brighton.
15 August	Skirving released on bail; Muir's petition for trial granted.
15 August	First reports of riots against the crimps.

18 August	Ross, editor of Edinburgh *Gazetteer*, arrested in London and returned to Scotland.
18 August	British defeat French at Lincelles.
26 August	Lord Hood promises to hold Toulon in trust for Louis XVII.
28 August	Lord Hood occupies Toulon.
30 August	British treaty with Austria.
30–31 August	Trial of Muir; Muir sentenced to fourteen years transportation.
31 August	*Diary* discontinued.
2 September	Corresponding Society evicted from Globe Tavern by order of Saunderson as Mayor.
9 September	British defeated at Dunkirk.
11 September	Austrians capture Quesnoy.
11 September	Lord Lauderdale presents to the King the Glasgow petition for peace.
12–13 September	Trial of Palmer in Scotland; Palmer sentenced to seven years' transportation.
16 September	Covent Garden reopens for winter season; further renovations.
19 September	Colman opens the Haymarket under the Drury Lane patent.
26 September	Treaty with Portugal.
28 September	Beginning of Bristol riots.
28 September	Le Mesurier elected Lord Mayor of London, succeeding Saunderson.
28 September	*Morning Chronicle* charges that Pitt is privately threatening to negotiate a peace and support reform unless the Rockingham Whigs take office.
28 September	Pigott and Hodgson arrested for proposing seditious toasts.
3 October	Girondists proscribed by French Convention; Paine denounced.
9 October	France declares embargo on British goods.
10 October	Anniversary of Fox's election celebrated at public dinner.
13 October	France declares war on Genoa.
14 October	Trial of Marie Antoinette.
15 October	First alarms of an invasion; Richmond fortifies the coast.
16 October	Marie Antoinette beheaded.
17 October	Austrians defeated at Maubeuge.
23 October	*Public Advertiser* advertised by H. S. Woodfall.
24 October	Trial of the Girondists.
24 October	Corresponding Society elects Margarot and Gerrald delegates to the British Convention.
25 October	Daniel Stuart forges French document; delivers it to the *Sun*.
29 October	Parliament prorogued to 21 January.
29 October	"Pitt's Manifesto" regarding the war published in the *Gazette*.
29 October	Beginning of the first British Convention in Edinburgh.
30 October	Raising ceremony for the new Drury Lane theater.
31 October	Execution of Brissot and twenty other deputies.
1 November	W. Woodfall announces candidacy for office of City Remembrancer.
1 November	Death of Lord George Gordon; rumors of epidemic in Newgate Prison.

2 November	Inquest on death of Lord George Gordon.
2 November	H. S. Woodfall quits the *Public Advertiser*.
2 November	Pigott released; true bill found against Hodgson.
3 November	Death of Macan.
4 November	Richard Tickell commits suicide.
4 November	Rowan arrested in Edinburgh.
6 November	First British Convention adjourns.
6 November	Death of John Mac Murray.
6 November	Brighton camp breaking up; end of invasion alarm.
6 November	King demands an investigation of Newgate Prison.
7 November	Drs. Smyth and Pitcairn return favorable report of Newgate; Dr. Lettsom reports an infectious fever.
7 November	Duke of York's army goes into winter quarters at Tournai.
10 November	French worship of the Goddess of Reason.
10 November	Lady Lambart marries Captain Ricketts of the Navy.
13 November	Jerningham's tragedy, *The Siege of Berwick*, at Covent Garden.
14 November	*Morning Post* announces that the Rockingham Whigs have refused to take office.
19 November	Beginning of second British Convention.
20 November	The British again promise to hold Toulon for Louis XVII.
23 November	O'Keeffe's comedy, *The World in a Village*, at Covent Garden.
26 November	Robinsons fined for publishing sedition.
27 November	Holt sentenced to four years in Newgate; Winterbotham to four years in New Prison, but later transferred to Clerkenwell.
30 November	Muir and Palmer arrive; transferred to hulks in The Thames.
30 November	Banks elected President of the Royal Society.
1 December	Death of William Owen.
5 December	*Public Advertiser* office destroyed by fire.
5 December	Frost adjudged too ill to appear in the pillory.
5 December	Gerrald, Margarot, and others arrested in Edinburgh; Skirving also arrested, but released on previous bail; Lord Provost orders the Convention dissolved; Skirving and Brown protest.
6 December	British Convention dissolved by magistrates; Margarot, Gerrald, and others released on bail.
6 December	Ashley sues Harrison for Madame Mara's failure to perform; Madame Mara sues Harrison for vilifying her character.
7 December	Edinburgh magistrates issue proclamation, forbidding further meetings of the Convention.
9 December	*Morning Post* announces that Weltje is no longer a proprietor; *Morning Post* publishes report of grand jury on the state of Newgate Prison.
9 December	First copper-plate map in the *Oracle*; Bell announces he will help his nephew manage the paper and that he has rented the British Library from the purchasers.
9 December	Eaton again arrested; Hodgson convicted and sentenced to two years in Newgate; Perry, Gray, and Lambert of *Morning Chronicle* acquitted.

10 December	Skirving advertises another meeting of British Convention for 12 December; arrested, examined, and dismissed.
11 December	Lauderdale, Sheridan, and Grey petition Dundas to delay transportation of Muir and Palmer, pending a motion in Parliament.
12 December	Skirving and Brown prevented from continuing British Convention; arrested, examined, and dismissed.
12 December	Tyrrell elected City Remembrancer; Woodfall defeated.
12 December	Royalists defeated in La Vendée.
14 December	Prospectus for new *Public Advertiser*, to commence 1 January.
15 December	Lord Hobart resigns as Chief Secretary of Ireland; succeeded by Douglas.
16 December	Prince Hoare's operative farce, *My Grandmother*, at the Haymarket.
18 December	British evacuate Toulon, leaving half the French ships intact.
18 December	Frost again prevented by illness from standing in the pillory.
19 December	Frost released on payment of securities, but stripped of all rights as British citizen.
19 December	Toulon retaken by the French.
21 December	Daniel Stuart's *Peace and Reform* published.
26 December	Austrians defeated at Weissenburg.
27 December	Paine arrested in Paris.

Bibliographical Note

Despite the multitude of books on the subject, scholars still know remarkably little about eighteenth-century newspapers. The principal reason is that historians have been misled by the journalists themselves into accepting as the truth, the whole truth, and nothing but the truth what is actually evasion, extenuation, rumor, and falsehood. The trouble began in the late eighteenth century, when the first journalists felt called upon to publish their apologies, for, since other journalists followed suit, there was soon a spate of such publications: *Memoirs of John Almon, Bookseller of Piccadilly* (London, 1790); memoirs of Sampson Perry, affixed to *An Historical Sketch of the French Revolution Commencing with Its Predisposing Causes, and Carried on to the Acceptation of the Constitution in 1795* (London, 1796), 2 vols.; John Benjafield, *Statement of Facts* (Bury St. Edmunds, 1813); "Memoir of James Perry, Esq.," *European Magazine and London Review*, LXXIV (1818), 187–90; John Taylor, *Records of My Life* (London, 1832), 2 vols.; "John Heriot" in *The Annual Biography and Obituary for the Years 1817–1836*, XVIII (1834), 44–49; Daniel Stuart's various apologies and accusations in the *Gentleman's Magazine*, n.s. IX (1838), 485–92, 577–90, and X (1838), 22–27, 124–28, and George Lane's reply in the *Gentleman's Magazine*, n.s. X (1838), 274–76; William Jerdan, *Autobiography* (London, 1852–53), 4 vols.; Cyrus Redding, *Fifty Years' Recollections, Literary and Personal, with Observations on Men and Things* (London,

1858), 3 vols.; James Amphlett, *The Newspaper Press, in Part of the Last Century, and up to the Present Period of 1860: The Recollections of [the Author]* (London, 1860); "Editors and Newspaper Writers of the Last Generation, by an Old Apprentice of the Law," *Fraser's Magazine*, LXV (1862), 169–83; and John Payne Collier, *An Old Man's Diary, Forty Years Ago* (London, 1871–72), 4 Pts. To these were added other biographies and collections of anecdotes, based primarily upon hearsay and yet also purporting to be factual: *Public Characters of 1801–1806*, publ. Richard Phillips (London, 1801–6); John Nichols, *Literary Anecdotes of the Eighteenth Century* (London, 1812–16), 9 vols; *A Biographical Dictionary of Living Authors* (London, 1816); and C. H. Timperley, *A Dictionary of Printers and Printing* (London, 1839), reissued in 1842 as *An Encyclopaedia of Literary and Typographical Anecdote*.

In 1850 this material became the basis for the first general survey of the press, and today there are many such surveys, the most important being F. Knight Hunt, *The Fourth Estate: Contributions towards a History of Newspapers, and of the Liberty of the Press* (London, 1850), 2 vols.; Alexander Andrews, *The History of British Journalism, from the Foundation of the Newspaper Press in England, to the Repeal of the Stamp Act in 1855* (London, 1859), 2 vols.; James Grant, *The Newspaper Press: Its Origin—Progress —and Present Position* (London, 1871), 3 vols.; Henry Richard Fox Bourne, *English Newspapers: Chapters in the History of Journalism* (London, 1887), 2 vols.; and Harold Herd, *The March of Journalism: The Story of the British Press from 1622 to the Present Day* (London, 1952). However impressive these works appear, they have done the cause of scholarship little good. Not only have they discouraged caution with respect to the memoirs and anecdotes, but they have introduced new material with the same reckless disregard for source. In almost any other field, works so slightly documented as these would have had no stature whatever, but in this particular field they have been and still are regarded as standard for the simple reason that there has been no alternative. Moreover, they do have a value of sorts, for, however vague and erroneous they are in detail, they are sometimes correct in substance, and hence they occasionally supply a clue which might otherwise be forever lacking. This is particularly true with respect to the earlier histories, namely, those of Hunt, Andrews, and Grant. All one can do, therefore, is to attempt to discover the source of the material and, when such discovery is impossible, to apply the yardstick of plausibility. But one must be wary; for the source of a great deal of the material was the journalists themselves, and no self-respecting eighteenth-century writer boasted of his connection with the newspapers. He admitted the connection only when it was already common knowledge, and he wrote or talked only for the sake of glossing over his own crimes and the crimes of his various employers and associates. From such a man writing and talking for such a purpose, we cannot expect the whole truth.

Although there has been no real attempt to correct or even evaluate the memoirs, anecdotes, and histories, there has been some valuable supplementation. John Trusler, *The London Advertiser and Guide* (London, 1790) and James Savage, *An Account of the London Daily Newspapers, and the Manner in Which They Are Conducted* (London, 1811) seem to be sound; and *Catalogue of an Exhibition Illustrating the History of the English Newspaper. . . . from the Library of The Press Club, London* (London, 1932) and Stanley Morison, *The English Newspaper: Some Account of the Physical Development of Journals Printed in London between 1622 & the Present Day* (Cambridge, 1932) are at least noteworthy, although they lean too heavily upon Bourne to be altogether reliable. Far more reliable are three accounts of individual newspapers: Wilfrid Hindle, *The Morning Post 1772–1937: Portrait of a Newspaper* (London, 1937); *History of "The Times,"* Vol. I (London, 1935); and Robert L. Haig, *The Gazetteer, 1735–1797: A Study in the Eighteenth-Century English Newspaper* (Carbondale, 1960). All three of these accounts are based upon primary sources, including, in the last two cases, examinations of the newspapers. But the most significant of the supplementary works is, of course, Arthur Aspinall, *Politics and the Press c. 1780–1850* (London, 1949), which ended (or should have ended) once and for all any naive thinking with respect to the late eighteenth- and early nineteenth-century press.

It is too much to expect that any study of late eighteenth-century newspapers will be entirely adequate or completely accurate, for the field is new, and the subject is enormously complex: the best any scholar can hope is that his work will make some kind of contribution. Contributions are usually assessed in terms of bibliography, but in this instance I am inclined to think that bibliography is less important than methodology. How, in short, does one study the newspapers? It is my opinion that he should begin by reading them, not one of them, but all of them together, and that he should supplement this reading with a reading of pamphlets, Parliamentary debates, Court records, and plays. For the newspaper press was primarily an arena for the waging of political wars, and the same wars were being fought in the pages of pamphlets, on the floor of Parliament and the various Courts, and on the stages of theaters. Having put the newspapers into context, one is in a position to begin the search for evidence. Here his problems are manifold, for the evidence is scant, it is widely distributed, and very little of it can be taken at face value.

In the main this evidence will come from four sources: letters and diaries, litigations and semi-litigious actions, financial records, and the memoirs, anecdotes, and early histories, to which reference has already been made. The first source is almost inexhaustible, for, since newspapers were themselves news, almost everyone had something to say about them, the only questions being how much the sayer was likely to know and how much he was likely to reveal. This source is perhaps also the most important, for diarists and letter-writers are notoriously less discreet than keepers of formal documents. Considerable research has already been done in this field, a number of letters relating to the journalistic involvements of the Whigs, the Prince of Wales, the Home Department, and the Treasury being included in the *History of "The Times," Politics and the Press*, and Aspinall's three-volume edition of *The Letters of King George IV, 1812–1830* (Cambridge, 1938); but there is still considerable research to do. The second source is disappointing, for, even when the testimony and the various affidavits are available, they add little to what one might already have learned from the newspapers, which is itself little. In the case of most ex officio actions, the printers were paid to be scapegoats, and they stood their trials without unduly embarrassing anyone. Even in the case of private actions, everyone was circumspect: there were certainly no exposés of politicians or the press generally. The fact remains that some of the intra-newspaper litigations, especially those reported by Haig, provide concrete information about the business of running a newspaper, which is not only significant in itself, but significant also, I suspect, in political context.

The third source is in most respects also disappointing. What one would most like to find is a straightforward account of the financial transactions of a newspaper, but this he will probably never find, for the reason that it probably never existed. What he may find and what Hindle and Haig have, in fact, found are newspaper ledgers and minutes of meetings, which identify personnel, list salaries, and record the legitimate operations of the paper. But, for an account of those extra-legitimate operations upon which every newspaper depended for much of its income, he must look elsewhere, and he will often look in vain. The ledgers of Buckingham House, Carlton House, the Home Department, the Whig Party, and the reform societies are, so far as anyone knows, lacking, so that what remains are some fragmentary Treasury records, dealing with the disbursement of Secret Service funds. These records, discovered by Aspinall and first printed in *Politics and the Press*, are therefore the only financial records presently available, but they are enormously helpful, especially when they are combined with the information derived from diaries, letters, and the newspapers themselves. In fact, by this time one knows enough about the political workings of the press to examine the final source, the memoirs, anecdotes, and early histories, judiciously. He may not, of course, be able to prove or disprove all the statements, but at least he can deal with them on the basis of probabilities.

All of this has entailed a great deal of labor, and it is only the beginning, for it has concerned itself with only the political aspect of the problem. There are numerous other aspects, for, although newspapers derived most of their extra-legitimate income from politicians, they derived some from the theaters, some from societies of various sorts, some from individuals, some from businesses, and some, even before 1792, from stock-jobbers. Since there has been no investigation of any one of these aspects, a great deal of work remains to be done before anyone can write a definitive history of the press. I should myself doubt that a really definitive history will ever be written.

Index

Abercorn, John James Hamilton, 1st Marquess of (suc. as 9th Earl [S] 1789; cr. Marquess [GB] 1790), 284, 285
Aberdeen, William Gordon, 2nd Earl of [S] (1679–1745; suc. 1720), 437
Adair, James (c. 1743–1798), lawyer and politician (MP Cockermouth 1775–1780; MP Higham Ferrers 1793–1798; King's Sergeant 1782), 300, 317, 421
Adair, Robert (1763–1855), friend of Fox, 116
Adam, William (1751–1839), barrister and politician, friend of 2nd Earl of Guilford, later of Fox (manager for impeachment of Hastings; MP Ross-shire 1790–1794; treasurer for management of Opposition press), assists Duke of Clarence against libelists, 87; approves *Courier*'s support of Fox, 116–117; refuses to subsidize *Observer*, 135–136; supports Proclamation against Seditious Writings, 81; opposes Grey's motion for reform, 274; supports Opposition, 149, 155, 157, 221, 223; scheduled to protest Muir's sentence, 409; addresses Whigs, 421; mentioned, 10, 31, 105–106, 166
Adams, Mr., solicitor to Frost, 464
Addington, Henry (1757–1844), statesman (MP Devizes 1784–1805; Speaker 1789–1801), 292, 392, 394, 396
Address of Thanks, debates on, 147–149
Administration, *see* Pitt Government
Admiralty, Department of the, 371, 393
Admiralty, First Lord of the, 410, 414
Adolphus Frederick, Prince (1774–1850), 10th child and 7th son of George III (KG 1786; Col. in Hanoverian army

1793; Col. of Hanoverian regiment 1793), wounded at Dunkirk, 370, 392; commissioned Col. of Hanoverian regiment, 371; returns to England, 392, 410, 414, 426, 458; mentioned, 362
Advertisements, interest in, 19; charges for, 20; definition of, 20; tax on, 20; importance of, 30; location of, 165–166; mentioned 170–171
Agriculture, Board of, 289, 294, 398
Ailesbury, Caroline Campbell Bruce, Countess of (1721–1803; m. Gen. Conway 1747), 52
Ailesbury, Thomas Bruce, 4th Earl of [GB] (1729–1814; cr. [*sic*] 1776; KT 1786), intimate of George III, 240
Ainslie, Sir Robert (1730?–1812; cr. Baronet 1775), diplomat (ambassador to Turkey 1775–1793) and numismatist, 358
Albemarle, William Charles Keppel, 4th Earl of [GB] (1772–1849; suc. 1772), 244
"Albert" *see* Armstrong, John
Aldgate, 271
Algiers, Dey of, *see* Baba Hassan
Alien Bill, introduction of, 153; stipulations of, 153–154, 248, 249; debates on, 154–157, 179, 182–184, 214; supported by Lord Stormont, Earl Spencer, the Duke of Portland, 155; supported by Lord Tichfield, 157; supported by Lord Mulgrave, 200; preparations for final debates, 179–182; protested by M. Chauvelain, 186; attempts to justify, 184–185, 253; Burke thanked for, 189–190; applied to M. Chauvelin, 189–190; applied to General Dumouriez, 303

Allerton Estate, 57
Allibone (or Allibond), Sir Richard (1636–1688), Judge of King's Bench (presided at the trial of the seven Bishops), 237
Allies, defeats, 134; conduct deplored, 189, 223, 360; victories, 359, 366, 368; see also Austria and Prussia
Almon, John (1737–1805), bookseller and journalist, background, 38, 207; publishes apology and life of Earl of Chatham, 38, 112, 433; surrenders, 60, 197; assigns errors to outlawry, 135; newspapers' concern for, 197; Wilkes's interest in, 197, 268; outlawry reversed, 268; released, 268, 275–276; pamphleteer for Government, 265, 343; completes History of France, 343, 420; owed £900 by Whigs, 38, 112
Alvensleben, Johann Frederich Karl von (1719–1795), Hanoverian minister at German embassy in London, 303
"Amanda," 69
America, United States of, war with Cherokees, 423–424; eulogized by World, 414; Gerrald's residence in, 433; rumored migration of Erskine and Mingay to, 253; advertisement for position in, 383; Cooper's migration to, 405
American war, opposed by Burke, 7; ship for promised by Lonsdale, 226; mentioned, 17, 18, 379, 437
Amherst, Jeffrey, 1st Baron [GB] (1717–1797; cr. Baron Amherst of Holmesdale 1776; cr. Baron Amherst of Montreal with sp. rem. to nephew 1788), army general (Commander in Chief 1793–1795; Governor of Guernsey 1770–1797), 395, 425
Amphlett, James (1775–1860), journalist, 171
Anderson, Adam (fl. 1787–1793), printer, 24, 173, 415
Anderson, James (1739–1808), agitator and informer, 195–196
Anderson, John William (1736–1813), politician (Sheriff of London, 1791–1792; MP London 1793–1806), 245

Anderson's Coffee House, 281
Andrews, Miles Peter (c. 1742–1814), poet, dramatist, politician, 19, 25, 26, 177, 312
Angerstein, John Julius (1735–1823), merchant, 255, 257
Anna, 315–316
"Anna Matilda," see Cowley, Mrs. Hannah
Annual Register, 27
Anspach, Margrave of, see Brandenburg-Anspach, Christian, Margrave of
Anstruther, John (1753–1811), lawyer and politician (manager for impeachment of Hastings; MP Cockermouth 1790–1796; KC 1793; Solicitor General to Prince of Wales 1793–1795; Welsh judge 1793–?; standing counsel to Board of Control, 1793–?), friend of Fox, 207; secedes from Opposition, 146; supports Government on Address of Thanks, 149, 207; cr. KC, 207; Solicitor General to Prince of Wales, 207; supports augmentation of forces, 210; opposes motion for reform, 273; opposes reform of Royal Burghs of Scotland, 356; returned for Cockermouth by Lonsdale, 357; standing counsel to Board of Control, 415, 428, 429; Welsh judge, 428, 429
Anstruther, Robert (1757–c. 1810), politician (MP Anstruther Easter Burghs 1793–1794), 357
Anstruther Easter Burghs, 271
Anti-Jacobin, 346
Anti-Jacobin Review, 116
Antiquaries, Society of, 264, 296
Antwerp, 145, 258
"Aprées, Shonny," 70
Argus, character, history, title, printer, address, 32–33; personnel, 32, 33, 41, 74, 84, 146, 151; organ of Corresponding Society, 31, 35, 38, 72, 103; defender of Thomas Paine, 72, 80; rumored subsidy by French, 113; protests treatment of John "Jew" King, 115; prosecuted for libel, 143; demise

of, 24, 143, 151, 154, 171; rumored continuation in Paris, 197; continuation in England as *True Briton*, 143

Ariosto, Ludovico (1474–1533), Italian poet, 335

Armstrong, John (1771–1797), poet and journalist, 19

Army, reduction of, 54, 137; augmentation of, 137, 140, 142, 146, 147; dispersal through country, 139; housing in barracks, 140; purges, 140–141; budget, 153; purges denounced by Fox, defended by Burke, 155; bounties for enlistments, 180; reason for augmentation demanded by Fox, 183; augmentation by independent companies, 187, 188; pay increased without authorization of Parliament, 224; further augmentation asked by the King, 190, 204; Fox pleads for delay in considering augmentation, 193; said by Fox dependent on Crown, 224; augmentation moved by Pitt, 209–210; scramble for commissions, 225; ineffectiveness of bounties, 226–227, 243; desertions, 227, 336; impossibility of conscription, 227; reliance on independent companies, 227; reliance on Hanoverian mercenaries, 243, 247; treatment of soldiers in Ireland, 392; *see also* Barracks, Crimps, *and* Independent companies

Army, Duke of York's, Commissary General to, 245, 246; composition of, 298, 303; visitors to, 225, 362; defeated at Dunkirk, 389; communiqués from, 395; retreat to Menin, 391; collection of flannel waistcoats for, 423; retires to winter quarters, 423; *see also* War charities *and* York, Frederick, Duke of

Army of the Rhine, 391

"Arno," *see* Andrews, Miles Peter

Arnold, Benedict (1741–1801), American, later British general, 82, 85

Ashford, 363

Ashley, John (1734?–1805), musician, impresario, agent, 312–313

Ashton, Samuel, reformer, 78, 83

Asiatic Jockey Club, 449

Associated Friends of the People, plans for Scottish convention, 135, 141; Scottish convention, 145; Muir's connection with, 195; Muir's letter to, 233; plan British convention, 275, 349; Skirving secretary of, 405; arrest of members, 460; *see also* British conventions; Scottish convention; *and* Skirving, William

Association for Protecting Liberty and Property against Republicans and Levellers, The (The Association), alternate names, 154; prospectus, 134–135; Reeves's connection with, 136, 376; Topham's connection with, 136, 174, 376, 379; Bowles's connection with, 137, 376, 403; rewards to heads of, 376–377; co-operation with Government, 136–137, 216; effect of, 137, 144; circulates works of Paine and Pigott, 137, 236, 402–403; solicits anonymous informations, 138, 201, 208, 233; sponsors home visits, 141, 252; demands loyalty oaths, 141, 142; foments Manchester riots, 146, 152; foments Cambridge riots, 152; denounced by Lord Lansdowne, 147; revives doctrine of rights of kings, 148; animates Friends of the Liberty of the Press, 155, 208; harasses Opposition newspapers, 167; propagandized by *World*, 176; instigates burnings of Paine's effigy, 180; denounced by *Morning Chronicle*, 181, 182, 237, 253; assists Government with alarms, 199; denounced by Erskine, 200; practices exposed by Law, 201; practices defended by *Oracle*, 208, 215; deterioration of, 200, 233; publishes works by John "Jew" King and Young, 223; refers informations to Government, 233, 236, 341–342; aided by Windham, 236; praised by *Public Advertiser*, 237; supports national fast, 264; places spies in taverns, 341; publishes abuse of

496

Association, The (con't).
George III, 341; defines "seditious words," 341–342; calls contradiction of Pitt treason, 398; supports corruption, 404
Asylum, 105, 423
Attorney General, *see* Macdonald, Sir Archibald *and* Scott, Sir John
Attorneys, *see* Lawyers
Attwood, Thomas, 287
Auckland, William Eden, 1st Baron (1744–1814; cr. Baron Auckland [I] 1789; cr. Baron Auckland [GB] 1793; FRS 1786), politician and diplomat (Auditor and Director of Greenwich Hospital 1771–1814; MP Heytesbury 1784–1793; Ambassador to The Netherlands 1789–1793), background and character, 6; early friendship with Sheridan, 266; Declaration and first Memorial, 216, 217; approached by Dumouriez regarding negotiations, 217; Declaration and first Memorial presented to Parliament, 218; credited with defection of Dumouriez, 259; second Memorial, 264, 266; dismissal demanded by *Oracle*, 264; conduct censured by Sheridan, 266; Memorial protested by Sheridan, 264, 265–266; Memorial defended by Pitt, 266; Memorial praised by *True Briton*, 266, 267; recalled, 266, 294; considered as Home Secretary, 294–295, 296; pensioned, 295; created British peer, 294, 352; second Memorial denounced by Stanhope, 304; rumored to be Ambassador to Vienna, 304; mentioned, 172, 264, 353
Augustus Frederick, Prince (1773–1843), 9th child and 6th son of George III (m. Lady Augusta Murray), opposed to war, 363; marriage announced by *Oracle*, 299–300; returns to England, 371, 414, 458
Aust, George (fl. 1786–1808), politician (Foreign Under Secretary 1789–1796), 118, 125, 174, 423

Austen, William (1754–1793), medical doctor on staff of St. Bartholomew's Hospital, 380
Austria, France declares war on, 76, 217; preparation for invasion of France, 85; invasion of Poland, 85, 104; conduct denounced by Fox, 149, 210, 211, 219; partition of Poland, 189, 223, 266, 360; treaty with, 368, 423
Austria, Emperor of, *see* Leopold II *and* Francis II
Austrian Netherlands, 156, 210, 258
Austrians, commanded by Prince of Saxe-Coburg, 156; defeated at Jemappes, 134; detention of Lafayette, 189; bested by French, 156, 212; rumored occupation of Holland, 258; rumored capture of Breda and Gertruydenberg, 258; rumored defeat by Dumouriez, 258; negotiations with Dumouriez, 258, 266, 302–303; capture of Quesnoy, 389; rumored capture of French Flanders, 391; defeated at Maubeuge, 413; defeated at Weissenburg, 456; *see also* Allies *and* Saxe-Coburg, Friedrich Josias, Prince of
Ayre, Richard (fl. 1783–1794), printer, 37
Ayre's Sunday London Gazette, 37, 169

Baba Hassan, Dey of Algiers, 127, 413
Bagshot, military camp at, 82, 103–104, 130, 361
Bahamas, 287
Baker, William (1743–1824), politician and lawyer (MP Herts. 1790–1802), 73, 84, 291
Balance of power, 179, 347
Baldwin, Henry (d. 1813), printer and bookseller, 26
Ballad singers, 348
Bandon, 392
Bank of England, 139, 246
Bank of Scotland, Governor of, 254
Bankruptcies, number of, 103, 144, 231, 255, 269, 270, 285, 345, 366, 391, 443; called sign of prosperity by *Public Advertiser*, 264, 269; called sign of

prosperity by Dundas, 270; costs of, 285; legal fees respecting, 344–345; Lord Loughborough's profits from, 269, 307; instigated by Ministerial papers, 345; instigated by Government, 231, 344–345, 434–435; demands for reforms respecting, 285, 346, 434–435

Bankrupts, Commissioners of, 231, 285, 354, 376–377, 379

Banks, Sir Joseph (1743–1820; cr. Baronet 1781; DCL Oxford 1771; President of Royal Society 1793–1820), natural scientist, early liberal sympathies, 40–41; expected to subsidize The Association, 136; inquisitor for The Association, 141, 252, 469; elected President of Royal Society, 429; purchaser of puffs, 200, 429

Bannister, Charles (1738?–1804), actor at Covent Garden, 42

Barham, Joseph (1759–1823), politician (MP Stockbridge 1793–1799), 242

Barker, James (fl. 1779–1798), printer and bookseller, 26

Barlow, Joel (1743–1812), American poet and reformer, 149, 196, 219, 233

Barracks, first construction of, 139, 140, 411; protested by *Morning Chronicle*, 140; Taylor's motion against, 224; Fox's arguments against, 224; defended by *Sun*, 224; demonstrations against, 227; *see also* Army

Barry, Richard, clerk in the Stamp Office, 98

Barrymore, Henry Barry, 11th Earl of [I] (1770–1823; suc. 1793), 225

Barrymore, Richard Barry, 10th Earl of [I] (1769–1793; suc. 1773), 225, 279

Bateman, Mrs. Eliza Charlotte, actress, 216–217

Bateman, John, 2nd Viscount [I] (1721–1802; suc. 1744), politician (Lord Lieutenant of Co. Hereford 1747–1802), 405

Bath, 94

Bath, Thomas Thynne, 1st Marquess of [GB] (1734–1796; cr. 1789; FRS 1764; Elder Brother of Trinity House 1770–1796; KG 1778, but not installed; Groom of the Stole 1782–1796; FSA 1784), 240

Bath theater, 61

Bathie, the Rev. George, 27

Bathing machines, 330

Bearcroft, Edward (c. 1737–1796), lawyer and politician (Bencher of Inner Temple, 1772; MP Saltash 1790–1796), 215, 231

Beauchamp, Viscount, *see* Yarmouth, Earl of

Beaufort, Henry Somerset, 5th Duke of [GB] (1744–1803; suc. 1756; Lord Lieutenant of Co. Monmouth and Co. Brecknock, 1787–1803; Lord Lieutenant of Co. Leicester 1787–1799; inv. KG 1786 and inst. by dispensation 1801), promised Chancellorship of Oxford, 105, 106–107, 107–108, 111; fails to get Chancellorship of Oxford, 108, 132; sinecures and honors, 132; influence, 240

Beaumarchais, pseudonym for Pierre Augustin Caron (1732–1799), French dramatist and politician, 116

Beckford, William (d. 1799), historian, 275, 343

Bedford, Francis Russell, 5th Duke of [GB] (1765–1802; suc. 1771), politics, 10; interest in horses, 58; opposed to Friends of the People, 79; patron of Covent Garden, 92; returns four members to Commons, 240; donates to payment of Fox's debts, 301; patron of opera, 322; patron of Drury Lane, 323; possible contributor to *Courier*, 347; refuses to join Government, 425

"Beef-eaters," 117

Beef-steak Club, 92–93

Belgic provinces, 258

Bell, Charles (fl. 1793–1817), printer, 173, 415

Bell, James (fl. 1792–1794), printer, nephew of John Bell, background, 117; printer and publisher of *Oracle*, 117,

Bell, James (con't).
166, 176, 346; steward for dinner of
Friends of the Liberty of the Press, 237;
proprietor of *Oracle*, 346, 378, 379,
449
Bell, John (1745–1831), printer and bookseller, co-founder of *World*, dismissed
as printer of *World*, founder of *Oracle*,
23, 25; proprietor and publisher of
Oracle, 23, 25, 176; influenced by
Sheridan, 50; quarrel with Heriot, 29,
118–119; sued by Lord Lonsdale, 55,
60, 61, 66, 135, 231; indicted for libels
on Guards, 56, 60; convicted of libels
on Guards, 96, 97, 176; outlawed, 215,
231; attempts to adjust matters with
Government, 230; apologizes to
Guards, 232; financial difficulties, 176,
231–232; attempts to divorce himself
from *Oracle*, 280; announces bankruptcy, 280–281, 434; regains control of
British Library, 281–282, 345, 449;
publishes poems of Lady Manners,
311; loses *Oracle*, 346; advertises in
Oracle, 379; advertises in *True Briton*,
449; publishes *Asiatic Jockey Club*, 400;
address to the public, 449–450; possible
two-month lease on *Oracle*, 449, 450;
certificate as bankrupt confirmed, 449;
first copper-plate map, 165, 449, 450–
451; possible connection with *Public
Advertiser*, 468; forces publicans to
accept *Oracle*, 470, 471; mentioned,
345; *see also* British Library, British
Theatre, *and Oracle*
Belvidere, George Rochfort, 2nd Earl of
[I] (1738–1814; suc. 1774; Governor of
Westmeath 1772–1814; Irish pension
of £800 a year 1776–1814), 33
Bengal, 289
Bengough, Mr., Mayor of Bristol, 405
Benjafield, John (fl. 1783–1813), soldier
and journalist, blackmails Carlton
House into buying *Morning Post*, 15,
36; threatens suit against Weltje for
collection of annuity, 36; collects
annuity from Tattersall, 68, 333

Bentley, Richard (1748–1831), pamphle-
teer, 205, 383
Berkeley, George Cranfield (1753–1818),
Naval officer and politician (MP
Gloucestershire 1783–1810), 306
Berlin, Court of, George Rose, Jr. Sec-
retary of delegation to, 296, 352–353;
Earl of Yarmouth Ambassador to, 352;
Lord Malmesbury's mission to, 428
Berry, Walter, pamphleteer and book-
seller, 214–215, 233, 286, 433, 434
Bethlehem, President of Royal Hospital
of, 354
Beverley, John (1743–1827), Esquire
Bedell of Cambridge University, 277
Bew, John (d. 1793), printer and book-
seller, 342
Bickerstaffe, Isaac (fl. 1735–1812), play-
wright, 88, 317
Bicknell, Charles (fl. 1788–1793), solicitor
to Prince of Wales, 67, 68
Billington, Mrs. Elizabeth (1768–1818),
singer and actress, professional reputa-
tion, 43; mistress of Prince of Wales,
17, 86; sues Ridgway, 85–87, 88; quits
England, 87
Birmingham, riots in, 122–123; threatened
with economic retaliations, 271; ad-
dress to residents of, 282–283; collects
flannel waistcoats, 415
Bland, Mrs. Hester (1759–1848), 15
Bland, Mrs. Maria Theresa (1769–1838),
actress at Drury Lane, 42
Boaden, James (1762–1839), playwright,
journalist, biographer, associated with
Sheridan on spurious *Star*, 23; editor
of *Oracle*, 23, 176, 346; *Ozmyn and
Daraxa*, 314; mentioned, 450
Board of Control, *see* East India Affairs,
Board of Control for
Board of Trade, *see* Trade, Board of
Bond, George (1750–1796), lawyer, 117
Bond, Nicholas, magistrate at Bow Street
police station, 89, 115, 325
Bonham, John, 237
Bonnor, Charles (fl. 1777–1829), actor,
playwright, employee of Post Office

(Deputy Comptroller General 1788–1792; Comptroller General 1792–1795), 61–63, 92

Bon Ton Magazine, 444

Booksellers, deaths of, 342; punished by bankruptcies, 344–345, 434–435; prosecutions of, 341, 342–344, 356, 403, 435, 447; changing reputation of, 342, 343, 344, 347

Booth, Benjamin, Manchester laborer and reformer, 408

Bostock, Robert (fl. 1789–1794), printer, printer of *World*, 26, 174; early prosecutions for libels on Burke, 292; sued by Dibdin, 89, 174, 317, 317–318

Boswell, James (1740–1795), biographer and journalist, contributor to *Public Advertiser*, 24, 178; probable defender of Rose in *World*, 64; spy at British Convention, 145; hopes to visit Army, 362; quoted, 26; mentioned, 359

Bourbons, restoration of, demanded by Windham, 210; said by Fox actual reason for war, 183, 211; favored by Burke, 223; not mentioned by King, 205–206; implied in declaration to Toulonese, 426, 432

Bourne, Frederick, journalist, 37, 168, 317

Bourne, William S., employee of the Post Office, 37, 135–136

Bowles, John (fl. 1790–1809), pamphleteer for Government (Receiver General of South District of Wiltshire 1792–?; Commissioner of Bankrupts 1793–?), pamphlets keyed to debates, 27; denounces reformers, 49; opposes Fox's Libel Bill, 49, 82; Receiver General of South District of Wiltshire, 132; "projector" of The Association, 137, 403; replies to Paine's *Rights of Man*, 137; castigates Friends of the Liberty of the Press, 235; justifies war, 249; Commissioner of Bankrupts, 376–377; collects flannel waistcoats in Hampstead, 423; assailed by Daniel Stuart, 469

Bowles, the Rev. William Lisle (1762–1850), poet, 167

Boxers, 164

Boxing, 25, 164

Brabant, 302, 402

Brand, Mr., lawyer, 464

Brandenburg-Anspach, Christian, Margrave of (1736–1806), 52

Braxfield, Robert Macqueen, Lord (1722–1799; assumed title 1776), judge (Lord Justice Clerk of High Court of Justiciary, Scotland 1788–1799), called "The Hanging Judge," 195; tries Berry and Robertson, 233, 286; tries Muir, 233, 406; newspapers unconcerned with, 286; flailed by Daniel Stuart, 469

Breadalbane, John Campbell, 4th Earl of [S] (1762–1834; suc. 1782; FRS 1784; Representative Peer 1784–1806), 358

Brecknock, Lord Lieutenant of, 132

Breda, 225, 243, 257, 258

Brest, 391

Breteuil, Louis Auguste le Tonnelier (1730–1807), French diplomat and politician, 120

Breton, William, 237

Brett, Mr., 22

Bridewell, President of Royal Hospital of, 354

Bridgewater, 343

Brighton, Prince of Wales's first visit to, 13; residence of Duke of Orleans, 18; Prince of Wales's pavilion, 13, 14, 17, 126, 129, 260, 363, 458; Prince of Wales's debts in, 214; Prince of Wales's arrival in, 363; military camp at, 361–362, 363–364, 371–374, 396–397, 411, 412, 415; troops stationed in, 411; mentioned, 100, 330, 415

Brighton theater, 61, 90–91, 94, 372

Brissot, de Warville, Jean Pierre (1754–1793), French revolutionist, regarded by Opposition press as man of peace, 76; friend of Lord Lauderdale, 212; Fox unacquainted with, 223–224; executed, 420; mentioned, 54, 212, 218, 420–421

Bristol, riots in, 404–405, 421; collections for Spitalfields weavers, 420; mentioned, 187, 451

Britain, cannot afford war, 212; France declares war on, 217; sends ships to defend Holland, 217; treaties with Prussia and Two Sicilies, 359

British, capture Valenciennes, 359, 360; *see also* Army, Duke of York's *and* York, Duke of

British Convention (first), Daniel Stuart's correspondence regarding, 336; Friends of the People not participators, 349; postponement of, 369; Corresponding Society elects delegates to, 432; Charles Stuart's cautions respecting, 433; attended by Lord Lauderdale, 336; riddled with spies, 433; harmlessness of, 434; *Morning Post* publishes minutes of, 335

British Convention (second), reason for, 434; tone of, 446; dissolved by magistrates, 447; arrest of delegates to, 448; again dissolved, 453, 454–455; attempts to reconvene, 459, 460; preparations for trials of delegates to, 469, 472; Friends of the People to be blamed for, 469–470; newspaper reports of, 446–447, 453, 454–455, 459–460, 468

British Critic, 283

British Gazette, see E. Johnson's British Gazette

British Library, *Oracle* advertising medium for, 23; advertised in *Oracle*, 231–232; advertised in *Morning Chronicle*, 280; involved in bankruptcy proceedings, 280–281; rented to John Bell by friends, 449; advertised in *Oracle*, 281, 282; *see also* Bell, John

British Museum, 105

British Press, 338

British Theatre, 281, 282, 345

Brittany, 259

Broome, Ralph (d. 1817), satirist and versifier, 26, 70

Brown, H. (fl. 1793–1798), printer, 174

Brown, Matthew Campbell, Sheffield reformer, delegate to first British Convention, 434; refuses to dissolve second British Convention, 448; attempts to resume meetings, 459, 460; arrested, 448, 453, 459, 460; released on bail, 460

Brunswick, Prince Ferdinand of (1721–1792), 6, 104

Brunswick-Wolfenbuttel, Amelia Elizabeth Caroline, Princess of (1768–1821), 16–17

Brunswick-Wolfenbuttel, Charles William Ferdinand, Duke of (1735–1806), general (commander of Austro-Prussian army 1792–1794): Manifesto, 102, 104, 110, 120; defeated at Valmy, 119, 121; crimes denounced by Fox, 149, 210

Brunton, Elizabeth, see Merry, Elizabeth

Brussels, 134, 258

Bryant, Mary, 276

Buckingham, George Nugent-Temple-Grenville, 1st Marquess of [GB] (1753–1813; cr. 1784; nom. KG 1786; Teller of Exchequer [I] 1764–1813; Lord Lieutenant of Ireland 1782–1783, 1787–1789; Lord Lieutenant of Buckinghamshire 1782–1813), 239

Buckinghamshire, John Hobart, 2nd Earl of [GB] (1723–1793; suc. 1756; FSA 1784; FRS 1785), 354

Budget, presented, 245; debates on, 245, 246–247, 255; reactions to, 247–248; effect on market, 255; complaints about inclusion of income from East India Company, 287–288

Buller, Sir Francis (1746–1800; cr. Baronet 1790), judge (KC 1777; puisne judge of King's Bench 1778–1794), 276

Bullock, John, informer, 135, 276

Bunbury, Henry William (1750–1811), caricaturist, 181, 182

Bunbury, Thomas Charles, 6th Baronet (1740–1821; suc. 1764), sportsman and politician (MP Suffolk 1790–1812), 17, 286

Burges, James Bland (1752–1824), politician and journalist (Foreign Under Secretary 1789–1795), contributor to *Diary*, 22; writer for Government, 27; original proprietor of *Sun*, 118; principal contributor to *Sun*, 118; censured by *Star*, 120–121; distorter of news, 120; amused by *The Times*'s complaints about the *Sun*, 125; assists with demise of *Argus*, 143; founder of *True Briton*, 171; proud of *Sun* and *True Briton*, 172; responsible for "lie" regarding M. Maret, 217; reissues "Alfred's Letters," 258; befriended by Fox, 302; opposes fund for paying Fox's debts, 302; accused of "ingratitude" by *Morning Chronicle*, 305, 309; threatened with exposure, 306; assailed by *Morning Chronicle*, 302, 306, 307–308, 309, 310, 347; assailed by *Gazetteer*, 306; accused by William Walter of giving priority to Heriot, 378; subscribes to war charity, 423

Burgess, J., the "pickle-man," 302, 307–308, 310–311

Burgh, James (1714–1775), political writer, author of *Political Disquisitions* (3 vols., London, 1774–1775), 433

Burgoyne, John (1722–1792), dramatist and general (MP Preston, 1768–1792), 91–92

Burke, Edmund (1729–1797), statesman (MP Malton 1780–1794; Paymaster General of Forces 1782, 1783; principal Manager for prosecution of Hastings), character and political background, 6–9; friendship with Fox, 6; early concern with affairs of East India Company, 7, 8; principal prosecutor of Hastings, 7; supports Sheridan and "New Whigs" during King's illness, 14; publishes *Reflections*, supports war with France, 7–8; thought to be managed by Pitt, 7–8; answered by Mackintosh, 40; fears newspapers, 27; continued association with Whigs, 8–9; publishes *Appeal . . .* to the New Whigs, 8–9, 106; abused by all newspapers, 49; ridiculed by *World* for prosecution of Hastings, 25–26, 49; silent regarding war, 54; victim of Treasury intrigues, 70; condemns moderate reform and "theory," 77–78; abuses English radicals, 77; denounces reformers, 79, 149; accuses Cooper of corresponding with Jacobins, 84; blamed for Portland's election as Chancellor of Oxford, 111; said responsible for founding of *Sun*, 118; denounces Unitarians as Jacobins, 123; effigy burned at Cambridge, 123; said to have accepted pension from Rockingham Whigs, 133; said to have negotiated with Pitt regarding trial of Hastings, 134, 181, 186; opposes negotiations with France, 149, 150; regrets Fox won't join Government, 149; denies being bribed by Pitt, 150; moves to Treasury bench, 150; enraged by Erskine's defense of Paine, 150; not loved by populace, feared by press, 150–151; assails Sheridan, 154, 155, 192; abused by *Oracle* for treatment of Sheridan, 154–155, 176; temper, 154–155; despairs of conversion of Fox, 155; accuses Fox of impertinence, 155; denounces "phalanx," 157; accuses Fox of calling Jemappes "a glorious victory," 157; brandishes dagger, 157; flailed by Opposition papers as warmonger, 180–182, 185–186, 188, 190; abused by Ministerial papers as prosecutor of Hastings, 185; censured as warmonger by Courtenay, 187; thanked for Alien Act, 190; blamed for murder of Louis XVI, 190; rareness of newspaper commendations, 190; audience of Prince of Wales, 202; eulogized by *Oracle*, 202–204; credited with Prince of Wales's conversion, 203–204; rumored to become Home Secretary, 204; assists in dismissal of Erskine, 204; scapegoat for Government's negotiations with Sheridan, 202; dislikes

Burke, Edmund (con't).

Sheridan, 204; opinions echoed by Windham, 210, 400; accuses Fox of corresponding with French, 211; will be answered by Cooper, 215; calls Fox, Mackintosh, and Sheridan heroes to Jacobins, 219; calls Fox agent of Brissot, 223; denunciations of French echoed by John "Jew" King, 224; slates Lord George Gordon, 229; denounces Fox, Mackintosh, and Sheridan as enemies to Constitution, 233; opposes Sheridan's inquiry respecting seditious activities, 236–237; hopes Friends of the People will dissolve, 239; insistent regarding trial of Hastings, 241; exonerated by Dundas for prolonging trial, 241; assailed by *Oracle* for persecution of Hastings, 242; complains about conduct of Lords, 242; approves desertions of Fox, 244; resigns from Whig Club, 244; economy bill disregarded by Pitt, 246, 287; defines "Whig" and "Tory", 251; attacks Fox on Traitorous Correspondence Bill, 251; says "sleep" necessary for body politic, 251; answered by Sheridan, 251–252; asserts Priestley corresponding with Jacobins, 253; insults Fox and Erskine, 261; assailed by Opposition papers for speeches on Traitorous Correspondence Bill, 253, 261–262; addressed by Parkinson, 262; addressed by author of *The Gallic Lion*, 262; challenges petition of Friends of the People, 272; censured by Opposition papers, 283; praised by Murphy for alerting country, 283; humiliated by Pitt, 287; quarrel with Speaker, 289; earlier condemnation of East India charter, 288, 289–290; fear of offending Dundas, 290; silent on including East India revenues in budget, 288; absent from debates on renewal of East India charter, 289–290; censured for absence by Fox and Sheridan, 289, 290; denounced for treatment of Hastings by Archbishop of York, 290–291; asks Baker to ignore comment of Archbishop of York, 291; quarrel with Government regarding resumption of Hastings's trial, 291–293; praised by Francis, 292; censured by Ministerial papers for treatment of Hastings, 299; praised by Ministerial papers for condemnation of French Revolution, 299; regarded as principal enthusiast for war, 299; criticized for contributing nothing to Fox's fund, 303; opposes Fox's motion for reform, 304; detested by *Morning Post*, 335; helps write Portland's Latin speech, 350; praised at Portland's inauguration, 350; gets no Oxford degree, 351, 366; punished for prosecution of Hastings, says *World*, 351; thought to prefer pension, 351; rumored to be created peer, 352; eulogized by *Diary*, 351; attempts of Opposition papers to make scapegoat for war, 365–366; censured for treatment of Priestley, 366; represented by *Morning Post* as duping Pitt into war, 367, 376, 377, 392, 397, 398, 401, 402, 414; censured by Opposition press for apostasy, 386–387, 397, 430; represented as archfoe of reform, 402; attacked by *Morning Chronicle* and *Gazetteer*, 401–402; assailed by *World* for persecution of Hastings, 377, 397, 430; assailed by *Morning Post* for persecution of Hastings, 377–378; slated by Daniel Stuart, 469; warmongering defended by Ministerial papers and *Star*, 365–366, 378, 402; epitaph on Reynolds, 366; visits Windsor, 366; rumored to become Lord Lieutenant of Ireland, 402; rumored to be created Irish peer, 402; dines with Pitt, Dundas, and Elliot, 402; urged to define British Constitution, 470; quoted, 353; mentioned, 116, 399; *see also* "Chivalry, days of"; Dagger scene, Burke's; "Sleep," Burke's simile respecting; *and* "Swinish multitude"

Burke, Richard (1758–1794), son of Edmund Burke (Receiver of Crown rents in City of London and Counties of Middlesex, Essex, Hertford, Norfolk, and Huntingdon, 1793–1794), 430

Burney, Dr. Charles (1726–1814), musicologist, 353

Burns, Robert (1759–1796), 167, 311

Burrell, Sir Peter (1754–1820; knighted 1781; suc. 1787 as 2nd Baronet), lawyer and politician (MP Boston 1782–1796; Deputy Great Chamberlain to House of Lords 1781–1820; grantee of chains and moorings on Westminster side of Thames 1793–1820), 429

Bute, John Stuart, 3rd Earl of [S] (1713–1792; suc. 1723; KG 1762; President Society of Antiquaries 1780–1792; Chancellor of Marischal College 1761–1792; Ranger of Richmond Park 1761–1792; Prime Minister 1762–1763; Trustee of British Museum 1765–1792), death of, 104, 263; honors and emoluments, 104–105

Bute, John Stuart, 4th Earl of [S] (1744–1814; suc. 1792; FSA 1776; DCL Oxford 1793; Lord Lieutenant of Co. Glamorgan 1772–1793; pension of £7,000 a year 1782–1814), 105, 349, 350

Bute Government (1762–1763), 28

Butler, Simon (1757–1797), lawyer and reformer (first president of United Irishmen of Dublin), 434

Byng, George (1764–1847), politician (MP Middlesex 1790–1847), 200, 244, 300, 409, 421

Byrne, Nicholas (d. 1833), printer and journalist, 417, 468

Cabinet, 31, 33, 34

Cadell, Thomas, the younger (1773–1836), bookseller and publisher, 201

"Ça Ira," 137, 397

Calamy, Edmund (1743–1816), barrister of Lincoln's Inn, 237

Callaway, Betty, domestic servant, 128–129

Callender, Alexander, Edinburgh reformer, delegate to first British Convention, 434; presides at second British Convention, 447; arrested, 448, 459, 460; released on bail, 453

Callender, James Thomson (1758–1803), Edinburgh bookseller and publisher, 214–215, 433

"Calm Observer, The," *see* Vaughan, Benjamin

Cambrai, 374

Cambridge, hostility to Pitt, 122; riots, 151–152; martial law, 152

Cambridge, University of, Mrs. Billington's concerts at, 17; Unitarian tradition at, 122–123; hostility to Pitt and Burke, 123; popularity of Fox, 123, 213; incident involving Lord Loughborough, 106; student indignation regarding Porson, 123; Porson elected Regius Professor of Greek, 123–124, 152; Pitt re-elected MP for, 107, 109–110, 122–124, 151–152; refuses to sponsor Wakefield's publications, 289; tries and banishes Frend, 235, 277–278; George Rose, Jr., an alumnus of, 353; Duke of Somerset student at, 354; mentioned, 347, 354

Cambridge Intelligencer, 169, 346

Camden, Charles Pratt, 1st Earl of [GB] (1714–1794; knighted 1761; cr. Baron Camden [GB] 1765; cr. Viscount Bayham and Earl Camden 1786; FRS 1742; KC 1755; Lord President of Council 1784–1794), 394

Camelford, Thomas Pitt, 1st Baron [GB] (1737–1793; cr. 1784), 80

Campbell, Duncan, contractor for hulks at Woolwich, 445

Campbell, John, 1st Baron (1779–1861; cr. 1841), 35

Canada, 362

Canning, George (1770–1827), statesman (MP Newton 1793–1796), expected to be brought into Parliament by Opposition, 53; election to Commons, expected to be protégé of Sheridan, 357–358;

Canning, George (con't).
writes introductory eulogy and poetry
for Portland's installation as Oxford
Chancellor, 350; quoted, 170
Canongate Lodge, Edinburgh, 448
Carlisle, Frederick Howard, 5th Earl of
[GB] (1748–1825; suc. 1758; KT 1757–
1793; KG 1793; Lord Lieutenant of
Ireland 1780–1782), follower of 2nd
Earl of Guilford, 10; free to defect,
105; pledges support to Government,
156; secession from Opposition announced, 180; supports augmentation
of forces, 211; nominated KG, 295,
352, 429; mentioned, 431
Carlton House, donated to Prince of
Wales by King, 12; first renovations,
12; closed, 13; renovations resumed,
13; entertainments at, 55; further
renovations, 60; Thurlow visits, 127;
Prince expected to vacate, 128, 129;
reductions of staff, 130, 202, 214; Prince
will reserve suite in, 130; still resident
of, 202; Sheridan's visits to said
unwelcome, 207; Lord Rawdon visits,
254; Pitt visits, 260; cheered by Frost's
friends, 463
Carlton House coterie, personnel, 13,
17–18; coerced into supporting World,
14; coerced into buying Morning
Post, 15, 36, 68; newspaper interests
managed by Sheridan, 15; frequents
faro parlors, 164, 330; sells interests
in Post, 334, 452; see also Wales,
George Augustus Frederick, Prince
of
Carnarvon, Henry Herbert, 1st Earl of
[GB] (1741–1811; cr. Lord Porchester
[GB] 1780; cr. Earl of Carnarvon 1793;
LL.D. Cambridge 1769), urges founding of Friends of the People, 79; refuses
to join Friends of the People, 79;
supports Proclamation against Seditious
Writings, 82; supports Address of
Thanks, 147; supports augmentation of
forces, 211; created Earl, 79, 352, 429
Caroline, Princess, see Brunswick-Wolfen-

buttel, Amelia Elizabeth Caroline,
Princess of
Carpmeal, Thomas, officer of Bow Street
police station, 349
Carter, Mr., poster of bills, 198–199, 252
Cartwright, John (1740–1824), political
writer and reformer, permanent chair-
man of Constitutional Society, 76,
78; original member of Friends of
the People, 76; ignored by Minis-
terial papers, 84; admits correspond-
ing with Jacobins, 84, 102; thinks
Constitution guarantees universal suffrage, 234
Casino, 164
Caswall, Timothy (d. 1802), friend of
Pitt (Commissioner of Excise 1790–
1802), 110
Catherine II, Empress of Russia (1729–
1796; suc. 1762), 305, 347, 401
Cator, John (1728–1806), politician, 241
Catwater, 227
Caulfield, Susan, mistress of General
Burgoyne, 91
"Causidicus," 351
Cavan, Elizabeth Davies Lambart, Dowager Countess of (d. 1811), sues Tattersall for libels on daughter, 65–66, 97,
98–99; newspapers' hostility toward,
99; collects damages, 138; demands
apology from Morning Post, 331–332;
mentioned, 333; see also Lambart, Lady
Elizabeth
Cavan, Richard Ford Lambart, 7th Earl
of [I] (1763–1837; suc. 1778; £300
pension 1778–1836), 98, 332
Cavendish, George Augustus Henry,
styled Lord (1754–1834; DCL Oxford
1793), politician (MP Derby borough
1780–1796), 300, 349
Cawthorne, Joseph (fl. 1762–1796),
political writer (£100 pension 1782–
death), 27, 283
Chalmers, Alexander (1759–1834), biographer, editor, journalist, 24, 26, 177
Chalmers, George (1742–1825), antiquary,
historian, journalist, 424

Chamberlayne, William (c. 1761–1829), solicitor to Treasury, 236, 279, 280, 342, 344

Chambre, Alan (1739–1823), lawyer, 268

Chambre, Thomas, solicitor in Chancery, 331

Charing Cross, 462, 463

Charles I, 279

Charles II, 178

Charlotte Sophia, Queen (1744–1818; m. George III 1761), character of, 3, 4; conduct during King's illness, 4, 14, 18, 362, 395; dislikes Mrs. Fitzherbert, 13, 16; approves of Mrs. Jordan, 15–16; friend of Pitt, 107; newspapers' opinion of, 4; newspapers' interest in, 164; attitude toward fashions, 164, 165; confers with Prince of Wales, 362

Charter House, Governor of, 105

Chatham, John Pitt, 2nd Earl of [GB] (1756–1835; suc. 1778; FSA 1784; KG 1790), politician (1st Lord of the Admiralty 1788–1794; Elder Brother of Trinity House 1792–1835; Lt. Col. 3rd Foot Guards 1792; Col. in the Army 1793), accepts bounties for enlistments in Navy, 188; commissioned Colonel, 225; responsible for Dunkirk, 392, 393, 410; resignation expected, 392, 394; resignation urged, 410; defended by Ministerial papers, 410

Chatham, William Pitt, 1st Earl of [GB] (1708–1778; cr. 1766), statesman, 38

Chauvelin, François Bernard, Marquis de (1766–1852), French ambassador to Court of St. James, remains as ambassador, 110; suspected of subsidizing *Argus* and *Morning Chronicle*, 113; has no diplomatic status, 186; accused of managing *Morning Chronicle*, 186; protests detention of vessels bound for France, 186; insulted by Ministerial papers, 186, 187, 188, 191; presents letter from M. Le Brun, 188–189; credentials refused, 189; request for immunity refused, 190; departs, 190, 191, 204; correspondence submitted to Commons, 204; correspondence reviewed by Pitt, 210; denounced as spy by Lord Beauchamp, 210; correspondence reviewed by Fox, 211; correspondence examined by *Oracle*, 216; accused of absconding, 217

Cheetham, James, Manchester reformer, 408

Cherbourg, 411

Cherokees, 423

Chester, 411, 435

Chesterfield, Philip Stanhope, 5th Earl of [GB] (1755–1815; suc. 1773; FSA and FRS 1776), Post Office official (Joint Postmaster General 1790–1798), 61–62

"Chicken, The," *see* Taylor, Michael Angelo

Chifney, Samuel (1753?–1807), jockey, 17

Chiltern Hundreds, Steward of, 357

"Chivalry, days of," 182

Christie, James (1730–1805), auctioneer, 35–36, 68, 334, 340, 345–346

Christie, Thomas (1761–1796), reformer, 76, 405, 433

Christ's Hospital, 28

"Cincinnatus," *see* Cawthorne, Joseph

Cinque Ports, Wardenship of, vacated by death of 2nd Earl of Guilford, 105; promised to Duke of Dorset, 105, 106, 132; appropriated by Pitt, 107–109, 112–113, 131, 294; emoluments of, 108–109, 110

Clairfait, François Sebastien Charles Joseph de Croix, Count de (1773–1798), Austrian general, 259

Clarence, William, Earl of Munster and Duke of (1765–1837; cr. 1789; KT 1770; KG 1782), 3rd child and 3rd son of George III; naval officer (Rear Admiral 1790; member of Board of Agriculture, 1793), early attachments to older brothers, 3–4, 11; sent to sea, 12; conduct during King's illness, 14; partner to Dutch loan, 15; liaison with Mrs. Jordan, 14–15; concern for libels on Mrs. Jordan, 87; father of premature child, 87; financial situation, 16, 132;

Clarence, William (con't).
not the author of *Anna*, 315; strongly supports war, 147–148, 225; reluctance to act, 225; hoists flag on *London*, 262; expected to join Grand Fleet, 262, 300, 304; wants to command Grand Fleet, 305; denounces purpose and conduct of war, 304–305, 364, 370–371, 390; Government's attempts to convert, 304, 364, 410; refuses to join Whigs, 367; provides aid and comfort for *Morning Post*, 367, 414; in debt, 364; will sell Petersham, 364; censured by Ministerial papers, 370–371, 392–393, 410; defended by *The Times*, 410; supposedly mistreated by Pitt, 398; defended by *Oracle*, 411; expected to command *Duke*, 371; named member of Board of Agriculture, 398; wants to be 1st Lord of the Admiralty, 410, 414; lives quietly at Petersham, 458

Clarke, Mr., of Christ Church, Oxford, 350

Clarke, Mr., of Trinity College, Oxford, 350

Clerkenwell, 435

Clermont, William Henry Fortescue, 1st Earl of [I] (1772–1806; cr. Baron [I] 1770; cr. Viscount and Baron [I] with sp. rem. to brother 1776; cr. Earl [I] 1777), friend of Prince of Wales (Governor and Custos Rotulorum of Co. Monaghin 1775–1806; Customer and Collector of Port of Dublin 1784–1806), 59, 60, 133

Coburg, Prince of, *see* Saxe-Coburg, Friedrich Josias, Prince of

Cockpit, Grasmarket, Edinburgh, 459, 460

Coinage and the Mint, Comptroller of, 132

Coke, Thomas William (1754–1842), politician (MP Norfolk 1790–1807), 300

Cold Bath Fields, 435

Coldstream Guards, 50–51, 56, 60, 96, 97, 132, 176, 225, 232

Coleridge, Samuel Taylor (1772–1834), 41, 167, 419

Collier, Joseph, Manchester surgeon and reformer, 408

Colman, George, the elder (1732–1794), dramatist and theater manager, 42, 43, 93–94

Colman, George, the younger (1762–1836), dramatist and theater manager, manager of Haymarket, 42; victimized by Government, 43; concern about allowances, 92; presents case in *World*, 94, 95; affairs adjusted, 93–94; rents Haymarket to Drury Lane Company, 95, 313; *The Mountaineers*, 318; relations with Sheridan, 322; negotiations with Sheridan, 323, 324, 325; opens Haymarket under Drury Lane patent, 318, 323, 324; puffed by *Oracle* and *World*, 318; praised by Ministerial papers, 324; *The Battle of Hexham* quoted, 329

Combe, Harvey Christian, *see* Coombe, Harvey Christian

Combe, William (1741–1823), satirist and political writer, 24, 27, 28

Commercial Credit Bill, 269, 270

Commissary General to Duke of York's Army, 245, 246

Committee of General Security, 359

Committee of Public Safety, 190, 264, 359

Common Pleas, Lord Chief Justice of the Court of, 216, 231, 248

Commons, George III's battle with, 4; constitution of, 239–240; not a representative body, 285; *see also* Petition, right to

Condé, 359

Const, Francis, the elder (1721–1793), lawyer, 354

Const, Francis, the younger (1751–1839), lawyer, 230, 317, 354

Constantinople, ambassador to, 358

Constitution, British, Burke says war essential for preservation of, 8; Friends of the People dedicated to preserving, 75, 76–77, 79, 83–84; pronounced perfect by Pitt, 77, 80; Friends of People said bent on changing, 78, 80; Fox says changes in sometimes necessary, 77, 79; alarms regarding safety of, 80; *Star* denounces "abuses" of, 135; dangers to urged by The Association, 136–137; riots against sponsored by Home Department and The Association, 137; Lauderdale, Erskine declared threats to, 141; loyalty oaths to demanded by The Association, 141; defended by John "Jew" King, 146; threatened, says George III, 146, 147; Manchester citizens meet to defend, 146; supported by Stormont, 147; popular feeling regarding, 150; Elliot says support of essential, 156; Opposition papers hostile to, says The Association, 167; *Morning Chronicle* indicted for libel on, 168, 208; *True Briton* dedicated to preservation of, 171–172; dispute as to which paper is most devoted to, 175, 199–200; defense of as pretext for war, 179, 194, 206–207, 214, 218, 426; clubs formed to protect, 180; Fox says needs to be changed, 183; Fox says in danger from above, 183; rumors of insulting toasts to, 185; not imperiled, says Fox, 193–194; not supported by Irish Catholics, 194–195; endorsed by Duke of Portland, 203; to be defended by new batch of lawyers, 207; endorsed by Prince of Wales, 208; extolled by Pitt, 209–210; regarded by people as secure, 226–227, 228; Fox, Mackintosh, and Sheridan called enemies of, 233; does not guarantee universal suffrage, 234; dangers to "proved" by remedies, 248; Government said to be subverting, 251, 274; Burke's "sleep" simile applied to, 253; Burke's lecture on nature of, 261; corruptions said necessary to, 272; triumph of expedience, says Pitt, 274; called "most perfect" by Milner, 277; national debt called bulwark of, 392; eulogized by Braxfield, 406; subverted by private financing of war, 426; talk

of dangers to followed by alarms, 432; security of requires restoration of Bourbons, 432; Burke urged to define, 470; *see also* "Constitutionalists"; Petition, right to; *and* Reform, moderate

"Constitutionalists" versus reformers, 80, 275, 400

Constitutional Society, London, history, politics, reputation, 34, 72; probable subsidizer of *Gazetteer*, 34, 38; Mackintosh's connection with, 40, 73; Cartwright permanent chairman of, 76, 78; meeting disrupted by constables, 77; not influenced by Friends of the People, 78; breaks with Friends of the People, 78, 84; corresponds with Jacobins, 84; Tooke active in, 102; denounced by Jenkinson, 182; denounced by Mulgrave, 182–183; annual dinner, 267–268; communicates with Daniel Stuart, 268; petitions for election reform, 269; said to be linked with Friends of the Liberty of the Press, 273; sends Yorke and Sinclair to British Convention, 434; delegates to British Convention arrested, 448

Constitutional Society, Sheffield, 78, 84; *see also* Brown, Matthew Campbell

"Contradiction fee," 21

Conway, Lord George, 428

Conway, Henry Seymour (1721–1795), politician and army officer (Field Marshal 1793; Governor and Captain of the Isle of Jersey 1772–1795), 52, 60, 128, 130, 429

Cook, William, lawyer, biographer, dramatist, and journalist, 28

Cooke, Edward (1755–1820), politician (Clerk to Irish Commons 1786–1789; MP Lifford [I] 1789–1790; MP old Leighlin borough [I] 1790–1801; Under Secretary to Military Department [I] 1789–1795), 431

Cooke, William, Jr. (1749–1824), clergyman and classical scholar (Regius Professor of Greek at Cambridge 1780–

Cooke, William, Jr. (con't).
    1792; rector of Hempstead with
    Lessingham, Norfolk 1785–1824), 124
Cooke, William, Sr. (1711–1797), clergy-
    man (Provost of King's College, Cam-
    bridge 1772; Vice Chancellor of
    University 1773; Dean of Ely 1780),
    124, 431
Coombe, Harvey Christian (c. 1752–
    1818), politician, 76, 244, 300, 409
Cooper, Sir Grey (c. 1726–1801; suc. as
    3rd Baronet 1775), politician, 429
Cooper, Thomas (1759–1840), natural
    philosopher, lawyer, and Manchester
    reformer, denounced by Burke, 77, 84;
    member of Manchester Constitutional
    Society, 84; ignored by Ministerial
    papers, 84; refused membership in
    Friends of the People, 84; replies to
    Burke, 102, 181, 215; corresponds with
    Jacobins, 102; house burned, 146;
    threatened by Ministerial papers, 215;
    loses interest in reform, 237; again
    denounced by Burke, 237; arrest
    represented as imminent, 276; sails for
    America, 405; declared bankrupt, 443;
    mentioned, 80
Corday d'Armont, Marie Charlotte
    (1768–1793), assassin of Marat, 359,
    366
"Coriolanus," see Cawthorne, Joseph
Cork, Governor of County, 350
Cornwall, Duchy of, 11, 12, 18
Cornwallis, Charles, 1st Marquess [GB]
    (1738–1805; suc. as 2nd Earl, Viscount
    Brome and Baron Cornwallis of Eye
    [GB] 1762; cr. Marquess 1793; nom.
    KG 1786), army officer and politician
    (Constable of The Tower 1784–1805;
    Governor General of Bengal and
    Commander in Chief in East Indies
    1786–1793), expected to end war in
    India shortly, 53; created Marquess,
    146; concludes war in India, 147;
    returns two members to Commons,
    240; rumored to become Home
    Secretary, 296; rumored to become

Master General of Ordnance, 394, 395,
    425; returning to England, 425
Corresponding Society, organization of,
    33; politics of, 34; probable subsidizer
    of Argus, 33, 38; advertises existence,
    72; character and objectives, 72; dues,
    75; not influenced by Friends of the
    People, 90, 273; purports to be growing
    apace, 84; Tooke active in, 84, 102;
    Hardy perpetual secretary, 84, 193;
    Margarot and Gerrald prominent in,
    135; membership of, 193; actual
    strength of, 193–194, 404; helps
    Friends of the People petition for
    election reform, 268; petitions for
    annual parliaments and universal suf-
    frage, 273; insistent upon radical
    reform, 273; prepares petition for
    peace, 369, 370; evicted from Globe
    Tavern, 370; petitions for reform, 404;
    elects Gerrald and Margarot delegates
    to British Convention, 432; finances
    delegation to British Convention by sale
    of pamphlet, 433; Charles Stuart's
    cautions respecting, 433; delegates
    arrested, 448; delegates indicted 472;
    mentioned, 74
Corruptions, Pitt's dependence on preser-
    vation of, 8; early efforts to divert
    attention from, 8; Burke's changing
    attitude toward, 8; essential to Constitu-
    tion, says Windham, 272
Cottle, Joseph (1770–1853), Bristol book-
    seller, 420
Courier, continuation of Cabinet, 34;
    founding of, 116–117; financing, title,
    printer, address, 116–117, 168; pro-
    prietors, 116–117, 419–420; personnel,
    116–117, 168, 169, 419; character and
    politics of, 116–117, 166, 167, 168, 419,
    420; critical of Sun, 120; silent on Fox-
    Pitt coalition, 125; detests Burke, 150,
    181–182, 190; dependence on Post
    Office, 167; pleads for release of Lafay-
    ette, 189; protests arrest of Rowan,
    194; on fashions, 330; allied with
    Morning Post, 346–347, 420, 468;

Lauderdale possible subsidizer, 346–347; collects for Spitalfields weavers, 365, 419–420, 427, 455; concerned about Cherokees, 423; loses Este as editor, 468; harassed by Post Office, 451–452; quoted, 37, 330, 419; mentioned, 118, 119, 310, 336

Courier de l'Europe, 143

Courier Universel, 389

Courtenay, John (1738–1816), politician (MP Tamworth 1780–1796; manager for impeachment of Hastings), member of Friends of the People, 76; resigns from Friends of the People, 84; publishes pamphlet on French Revolution, 188; active in Friends of the Liberty of the Press, 200, 237; said to have called Jemappes a "glorious victory," 303

Courtenay, William, 3rd Viscount [GB] (1768–1835; suc. 1788), 320

Covent Garden, politics, management, actors, playwrights, 27, 42, 324; difficulties with Opposition press, 43, 61; renovations of theater, 43; Mrs. Wells's connection with, 26, 89, 90, 91, 94, 320; Holman scandal, 88, 312; presents Holcroft's *Road to Ruin*, 92; presents Merry's *The Magician No Conjuror*, 92, 93; Mrs. Merry dismissed, 93; theater closed for renovations, 90, 92–93, 94; renovations not subsidized by Opposition, 92; opens for 1792–1793 season, 94; refuses to engage Mrs. Merry, 94; King's preference for denounced by *Morning Chronicle*, 137; audience calls for "God Save the King," 138; productions, 312; Mara scandal, 312–313; closes for summer, 312, 313; complications regarding patent, 313; opens for 1793–1794 season, 318; account of renovations, 318–319, 327; productions, 320, 328; modernized version of *Hamlet* controversial, 319–320; refuses to engage Mrs. Merry, 321, 335; embarrassed by Mrs. Esten, 321–322; mentioned, 28, 163, 328

Cowley, Mrs. Hannah (1743–1809), poetess and playwright, 19, 25

Cowper, George Nassau Clavering-Cowper, 3rd Earl [GB] (1738–1789; suc. 1764), 25

Cowper, Hannah Anne, dowager Countess (d. 1826), 54–55

"Cowslip," *see* Wells, Mrs. Mary

Craftsman, 37, 169

Craig, Malcolm, agitator and informer, 195–196

Crewe, John (1742–1829), agriculturist and politician (MP Cheshire 1768–1802), 300

Crimps, 164, 368–369

Cromie, Sir Michael (1745–1824; knighted 1772; cr. Baronet 1776), banker in Liverpool, 33

Crosby, Brass (1725–1793), city politician (*see text for list of places*), 140, 353, 354, 385

Crossley, Mr., lawyer, 71

Crouch, Mrs. Anna Maria (1763–1805), novelist and actress at Drury Lane, 42

Crowder, John (d. 1830), printer and journalist, 24, 26, 177

Crown, influence of, denounced by Commons, 4; defended by Pitt and Burke, 8; means of preserving, 8; enhanced by charter of East India Company, 289; enhanced by war, 375, 376

Crown and Anchor, 30, 234, 300, 307, 421

Crown and Anchor Association, *see* Association for Protecting Liberty and Property . . . , The

Crown Inn, Peckham, 143

Crown lawyers, 143, 207; *see also* King's Counsel

Crown Rents, Receiver of, 430

Cumberland, Henry Frederick, Duke of (1745–1790; cr. 1766), brother of George III, 38, 100

Cumberland, Richard (1732–1811), playwright, 312

Cunninghame, William, 73

Curwen, John Christian (c. 1756–1828), politician (MP Carlisle 1791–1812), 76, 84, 249, 250

Customs, Commissioner of, 430; Comptroller of, 109; Printer to, 174

Cuthbertson, C., 316

Cyner, Mr., 300

Daer, Basil William Douglas, styled Lord (1763–1794), reformer, 447, 460

Dagger scene, Burke's, references to, 181, 182, 185, 397, 398; see also Marat, Jean Paul

Daily Advertiser, 30, 31, 69, 165–166, 172

Dalkeith, Charles William Henry Scott, styled Earl of (1772–1819; DCL Oxford 1793), politician (MP Marlborough 1793–1796), 349

Dalrymple, Alexander (1737–1808), hygrographer to the Admiralty, 253

Dalrymple, William (c. 1735–1807), reformer and Army officer, 140, 145, 146

Daly, Richard (d. 1813), manager of Dublin theater, 15, 87

Danton, George Jacques (1759–1794), French revolutionist, 224, 359, 360

Danzig, 223

Darnley, John Bligh, 4th Baron Clifton [GB] and 2nd Earl of [I] (1767–1831; suc. 1781; DCL Oxford 1793), 263, 349

Davis, Mr., proprietor of Morning Post, 35, 36, 68, 334, 340

Davis, Charles, proprietor of London Packet, 26

Davis, Lockyer (1719–1791), bookseller, 26, 342

Dawkins, Mr., orator at Oxford, 350

Deal, 390

Deaths, newspaper interest in, 353, 355

Debates, Parliamentary, see Parliamentary debates

Debrett, John (d. 1822), bookseller, 74

Debrett's, 34

Debt, laws respecting imprisonment for, revision demanded by papers, 179, 228, 230, 285, 440, 441, 464; exploited by

lawyers, 228; exploited by Government, 228, 230, 287; revision opposed by Government, 230; revision advocated by Moira, 446; see also Insolvent Debtors Bill

Debtor and Creditor Bill, see Insolvent Debtors Bill

Debtors, "enlargement" opposed by Lord Thurlow, 287; number in London prisons, 440; number in Newgate, 442; living conditions in Newgate, 446; number in King's Bench, 464

"Della Crusca," see Merry, Robert

Della Cruscan poetry, 19–20, 23, 25, 69, 163, 177

Derby, 208, 447

Derby, Edward Smith Stanley, 12th Earl of [GB] (1752–1834; suc. 1776; Lord Lieutenant of Lancaster 1776–1834), 79, 91, 133, 211, 421

Devaynes, William (1730?–1809), banker (Director of East India Company 1784–1796), 255

Devonshire, Georgiana Cavendish, Duchess of (1757–1806), hostess for Whigs, 426–427

Devonshire, William Cavendish, 5th Duke of [GB] (1748–1811; suc. 1764; KG 1782; DCL Oxford 1793; Lord High Treasurer of Ireland and Governor of Co. York 1766–1793; Lord Lieutenant of Co. Derby 1782–1811), 35, 166, 240, 349, 399

Diary, title, address, proprietor, editor, personnel, 22, 125, 172, 384; subsidized by Treasury, 22, 170, 173; character, 22, 163, 172, 173; champion of Dibdin, 22, 88–89, 317; shares news with Public Advertiser, 23, 173, 178; concerned about Lady Cavan's action against Morning Post, 66, 98, 99, 138; complains of being sued by lawyers, 70; puzzled by Pitt's indifference to radicals, 72; publishes advertisements for Friends of the People, 76; publicizes charges against Holman, 88; publicizes conduct of Mrs. Wells, 90, 164;

obituary of Burgoyne, 90; obituary of Guilford, 105; denies subversion of Covent Garden, 92; reports on building of Drury Lane theater, 95, 314; lists salaries of actors, 96; reports Pitt's seizure of Cinque Ports, 107, 111, 125; expects Pitt to be re-elected, 107; concerned for Almon, 112, 197; reports flight of Paine, 112; uneasy about *Sun*, 120, 125; approves election of Porson, 124; on economies of Prince of Wales, 101, 127, 128, 129–130, 208; apologizes for Weltje, 129; defends Malone's *Shakespeare*, 130; sobered by phantom insurrection, 142; alarmed by Burke, 150–151; shifts to moderate reform, 125, 383; respected by *True Briton*, 172; advertised for sale, 173, 380; new type, 173; prints excerpts from Fox's *Letter*, 205; supports Anderson for MP, 245; prints excerpts from Charles Stuart's parody, 282, 283, 417; eulogizes Burke, 283, 351, 365; eulogizes Dundas, 294–295, 356, 383; publicizes Mara scandal, 312; condemns fashions, 328–329; succumbs, 178, 179, 333, 379–383; quoted, 113, 115, 131, 136, 138, 139, 140, 173, 215, 239, 287, 303, 353, 354, 355; mentioned, 317, 331, 342, 366, 385; *see also* Woodfall, William

Dibdin, Charles (1745–1814), dramatist and performer, defended by *Diary*, 22, 88–89, 317; defended by *Public Advertiser*, 24, 317; sues 'Swan and Locke of *Observer*, 88, 317; sues Swan and Bostock of *World*, 88–89, 179; fights with Scott, 89; settles suits, 317, 318

Dignum, Charles (1765?–1827), actor at Drury Lane, 42

Dilly, Charles (1739–1807), publisher, 26

Dixmude, 390

Dodd, James William (1740?–1796), actor at Drury Lane, 96

Doddington, George Bubb (1691–1762), politician, author of *Diary*, ed. H. P. Wyndham (Salisbury, 1784), 433

Dominica, 287

Dorset, John Frederick Sackville, 3rd Duke of [GB] (1745–1799; suc. 1769; nom. KG 1788; Lord Lieutenant of Kent 1769–1797; Lord Steward of the Household 1789–1799), wrecker of marriages, 91; promised Wardenship of Cinque Ports, 105, 106, 108, 132; returns two members to Commons, 240

Douglas, Sylvester (1743–1823), barrister and politician (FSA 1781; KC 1793; Bencher 1793; Chief Secretary of Ireland 1793–1795), son-in-law of 2nd Earl of Guilford, 207; defects, 207; King's Counsel, 207; appointed Chief Secretary of Ireland, 431, 458

Dover Castle, 105, 110

Downie, David, Edinburgh goldsmith, 434

Drury Lane, Sheridan principle proprietor of, 11; politics, management, actors, 42; building condemned, 43; cost of new building, 43; harassments by Government, 43; difficulties with Ministerial press, 43, 313, 323; problems respecting housing, 92, 322; company thought to be dissolved, 95; building expected to be ready by Christmas, 1792, 95; leases Haymarket for 1792–1793 season, 95–96; King's avoidance of denounced by *Morning Chronicle*, 137; near-riot at, 137; inquiry into harassments demanded by *Morning Chronicle*, 137; attended by Royal Family, 147; problems respecting patent, 313, 314; moves to Opera House, 313; productions, 314–315; presentation of *Anna*, 315–316; Mrs. Bateman's complaints respecting, 316–317; loses money on operas, 314; construction of new building to be completed by 1793, 314; leases patent to Haymarket, 318; said deserted by Sheridan, 324; progress of new building, 318, 319, 322–323, 325–327; raising dinner for new building, 325–327; mentioned, 163; *see also* Kemble, John Philip *and* Sheridan, Richard Brinsley

Drury Lane Haymarket, *see* Drury Lane

Dublin, Customer and Collector of the Port of, 133

Dublin, United Irishmen of, *see* United Irishmen of Dublin

Dublin, University of, Vice Chancellor of, 132

Dublin theater, 87, 323

Dudley, the Rev. Henry Bate (1745–1824), clergyman, journalist, dramatist, founder of *Morning Post*, 338; founder of *Morning Herald*, 22, 379; leases *Morning Herald* to Government, 22–23; collections from Treasury, 23, 175; moves to country, 23, 174, 175; livings, 174; negotiates with Covent Garden for production of *Witch of the Alps*, 92, 320; mentioned, 172; *see also Morning Herald*

Duke, 371

Dumouriez, Charles François (1739–1823), French Foreign Minister and General, admired by Opposition papers, 76; expected to attack Holland, 145; threatens invasion of England, 206; attempts negotiations with Auckland, 217; takes Breda and Gertruydenberg, 225, 243; denounced by Burke, 251; defects to Austria, 258, 259, 266, 297, 330; rumors respecting, 302–303; visits England, 303, 330; commended by Burke, 304; friendship with Lady Wallace, 330; mentioned, 120, 403

Dundas, Henry (1742–1811), politician (Keeper of the Signet [S] 1779–1800; PC 1782–1785; Treasurer of the Navy 1783–1800; Commissioner of the Board for East India affairs 1784–1793; Chancellor of the University of St. Andrews 1788–1802; LL.D. Edinburgh, 1789; MP Edinburgh 1790–1802; Home Secretary 1791–1794; Governor of the Bank of Scotland 1790–1802; President of Board of Control for East India affairs 1793–1801; Elder Brother of Trinity House 1793–1802; Custos Rotulorum of

Middlesex 1793–?), intimate of Pitt, 5, 6, 294; character of, 5–6; "frankness" of, 288, 430; regarded as a fool, 116; "popularity" of, 6, 180, 356; effigy burned in Scotland, 116, 145, 180, 356; buys puffs, 20; contributes to newspapers, 27; opposes motion to reform Royal Burghs of Scotland, 76; strengthens London police, 81, 115; supports Proclamation against Seditious Writings, 81; moves to abolish slave trade "gradually," 85; accompanies Pitt on visits to castles, 110, 121; Paine's letter to published, 112; puffed by *Oracle*, 115, 116, 117; changes personnel in Home Office, 115; sends Taylor to Edinburgh as agitator, 116; taunted by *Morning Chronicle*, 116; employs Watt as spy in Edinburgh, 116; expected to be Irish Secretary, 131; places and emoluments protested by Opposition papers, 132; co-operates with The Association, 136, 233; sponsors publications, 137; employs spies, informers, and agitators, 137, 170, 196, 228; reports to George III on Scottish Convention, 145; supports Address of Thanks, 149; opposes negotiations with France, 149; flailed by Opposition papers, 180; appealed to for release of Lafayette, 189; reads King's message for augmentation of forces, 190, 204; accuses Lauderdale of being a Jacobin, 218; manages affairs in Scotland, 195; ignores unrest in Ireland, 196; confers with Prince of Wales respecting Erskine, 202, 204, 214; expected to be replaced by Burke, 204; supports augmentation of forces, 219; expected to be replaced by Windham, 221; supports motion to expedite trial of Hastings, 241, 242; should contribute salary as Treasurer of Navy to financing of war, says *Morning Chronicle*, 248; marries, 253–254, 331; appointed Governor of Bank of Scotland, 254; supports Commercial Credit Bill, 270; says bankruptcies sign of prosperity, 270; supports improved treatment of convicts, 286; moves for renewal of charter of East India Company, 288; controls East India patronage, 288; once assailed by Burke because of charter, 289–290; Burke's present fear of, 290; supports postponement of Hastings's trial, 291–292; opposes prosecution of *World*, 292; reconciliation with Burke, 293; collects money from Treasury, 294; responsible for defection of Loughborough, 294; relinquishes salary as Home Secretary, 294, 295, 430; accused by Opposition papers of monopolizing places, 293–294, 300; accused by Sheridan of monopolizing places, 294; reputation sullied, 294; resignation expected, 294–295, 295, 296, 396; defended by *Diary*, 294–295, 383; expected to be created peer, 294, 356; appointed Custos Rotulorum and Lord Lieutenant of Middlesex, 296; refuses Lord Lieutenancy of Middlesex, 356; named President of Board of Control, 295, 296, 356; confers with Portland, 297; orders Dumouriez to leave the country, 303; submits treaties, 304; confers with Prince of Wales regarding Duke of Clarence, 304, 362, 364; provides names of seditious talkers for prosecution, 341; forbids Government employees to give information to papers, 347; named Elder Brother of Trinity House, 356; attacked by Opposition papers, 356; assassination plotted, 369; gives priority to *The Times*, 378, 448; puffed by *The Times*, 468; confers with Elliot and Malmesbury, 394; defended by *Oracle*, 396, 430, 468; responsible for Dunkirk, 392, 396; expected to be replaced by Mansfield, 396; entertains Elliot, Burke, and Pitt, 402; advised by Charles Stuart of plans respecting Muir, 409; offered troops by Mackenzie, 414; advised by Charles Stuart respecting management of press, 417–

418; puffed by *True Briton*, 430; major beneficiary of war, 430; urged by Charles Stuart to watch British Convention, 432–433; asks for report on Newgate, 442; relies for success on hysteria of press, 448; promises detention of Muir and Palmer, 461; strips Frost of privileges as British citizen, 462; ridiculed by visitors to Newgate, 464, 465; quoted, 369; mentioned, 284, 377, 416; *see also* Home Office

Dundas, Sir Lawrence (c. 1710–1781; cr. Baronet 1762), politician (Commissary General and Contractor to the Army 1748–1759), 246

Dundas, Robert (1758–1819), nephew of Henry Dundas, lawyer and politician (Lord Advocate of Scotland 1789–1799; MP Edinburghshire 1790–1801), 145, 349

Dundas, Robert (1771–1851), son of Henry Dundas, 131, 132, 349

Dundee, 271

Dunfermline, 271

Dunkirk, capture of represented as crucial, 360, 391; capture of seemingly assured, 368, 374; Pitt's dependence on capture of, 368; Opposition papers on importance of, 374–375; defeat at, 389, 390, 410; second attack on rumored, 391; responsibility for defeat at, 392, 393, 394, 395, 396, 397, 398, 410; significance of defeat of, 399, 413; mentioned, 374

Dunmore, John Murray, 4th Earl of [S] (1730–1809; suc. 1756; Governor of Bahama Islands 1787–1796), 300

Durham, Chancellor of, 216

Durham, Shute Barrington, Bishop of (1734–1826; Bishop of Durham 1791–1826), 353

Durham, Thomas Thurlow, Bishop of, *see* Thurlow, Thomas

Dutch, guaranteed navigation of Scheldt, 183; Auckland's Declaration to, 216–217; Auckland's Memorial to, 217; not

Dutch (con't).
coerced into war, 222; Auckland's
second Memorial to, 265, 266; lethargy
of, 360, 375, 402; ask Duke of York for
help, 390; blamed for defeat at Dunkirk, 395, 396; protest continuation of
war, 426; *see also* Holland
Dutch loan, 14, 16, 52, 56
Dyer, George (1755–1841), poet, pamphleteer, journalist, 122, 167, 264, 311,
420
Dyke, Mr., auctioneer, 334

East India Affairs, Board of Control for,
Lord Grenville President of, 6, 132;
Dundas Commissioner of, 132; Dundas
moves to salary members of, 288;
Dundas named President of, 294, 295,
296, 356; Edward George Eliot
appointed to, 294; Jenkinson appointed
to, 295, 296, 297; Anstruther standing
counsel to, 352, 415, 428; salaries
allotted to members of, 428–429;
budget for, 428–429
East India Company, Burke's preoccupation with, 7; purchaser of puffs, 21;
charter previously denounced by Burke,
288; expiration of charter of, 288;
revenues from improperly included in
budget, 288; renewal of charter moved
by Dundas, 288; debates on renewal of
charter, 288, 289; newspaper reactions
to renewal of charter, 289–290;
patronage controlled by Dundas, 288;
amount of patronage, 288–289; tool of
Pitt, 289; renewal of charter a mockery
of trial of Hastings, 290; mentioned,
294, 354; *see also* India
East Bourne, 409
East Retford, High Steward of, 109
East Riding, Co. York, Deputy Lieutenant
of, 174, 200, 379
Eaton, Daniel Isaac (d. 1814), bookseller, publishes petition for Friends of
the People, 279; tried for publishing
Paine's *Rights of Man*, 279–280, 286,
344; tried for publishing Paine's *Letter*

Addressed to the Addressers, 343, 344,
435; arrested for publishing *Hog's
Wash*, 447–448, 454
Edgcumbe, George, 1st Earl (Mount)
[GB] (1720–1795; cr. 1789; Lord
Lieutenant of Cornwall 1761–1795;
Joint Vice Treasurer of Ireland 1784–
1793; DCL Oxford 1773; FSA 1775;
FRS 1784), 239
Edinburgh, Watt employed as spy in,
116; Taylor incites riots in, 116;
Dundas re-elected MP for, 356; men-
tioned, 135, 271
Edinburgh Convention, *see* Scottish
Convention
Edinburgh *Gazetteer*, 434, 448
Edinburgh *Herald*, 424
Edinburgh theater, 95, 321
Editorial, 167
Edward, Prince (1767–1820), 5th child
and 4th son of George III, Army
officer (Major General 1793), 362, 410,
459
"Edwin," 20
Egham, John "Jew" King's speech at,
146, 196, 222
Eglinton, Archibald Montgomerie, 11th
Earl of [S] (1726–1796; suc. 1769),
politician and Army officer (Col. of
51st Foot 1767–1795; Representative
Peer 1776–1796; Governor of Edin-
burgh Castle 1782–1796; General
1793), 321–322, 358
Egremont, George O'Brien, 3rd Earl of
[GB] (1751–1837; suc. 1763), 240
E. Johnson's British Gazette, 37, 169
Elder, John, Edinburgh bookseller, sta-
tioner, and reformer, 195–196
Elder, Thomas (1737–1799), Scottish
magistrate (Lord Provost of Edinburgh
1788–1790, 1792–1794), 444, 448,
455
Election, Shaftesbury, 279
Election, Stockbridge, 241, 267; *see also*
Stockbridge Election Bribery Bill *and*
Stockbridge Electors Incapacitating Bill
Election, Thetford, 184, 221

Election, Westminster, of 1788, Government's management of exposed by spurious *Star*, 50; inquiry into Government's management of demanded by *Morning Post*, 49, 63; case of Smith vs. Rose publicizes Government's interference in, 49–50, 63; Thompson's motion for investigation of, 63–64, 98; debate on Thompson's motion for investigation of, 64–65, 75; effect of scandals respecting, 72, 246; Frost's suits against Hood in consequence of, 278, 463; Hood's suit against Tooke in consequence of, 401; *see also* Westminster electors

Election, Westminster, special, 401

Election, Woebley, 221

Election reforms, goal of Friends of the People, 75; would remove Pitt from office, 75; opposed by Duke of Portland, 81, 157; *State of Parliamentary Representation* prepares ground for, 99; Lord Lauderdale champion of, 140; supported by Fox, 157; Government confronted with demands for, 207; identified by Pitt with opponents to war, 242; demanded by Francis, 267; opposed by Commons, 268; supported by Corresponding Society, 268; petitions for, 268–269, 270; Grey's motion for, 284; Pitt's *bête noire*, 285, 356; urged by Stuart's *Peace and Reform*, 469; *see also* Nottingham petition *and* Reform, moderate

Elections, Rose's management of, 5, 8; Friends of the People devoted to eradication of abuses, 75, 76; Grey's motion for eradication of abuses, 76–77; managed by Government, 184; settled by Commons in favor of Government, 221; corrupt state of, 240–241; abuses exposed in *Letters to the People of North Briton*, 267; abuses urged by Francis as general, 267; abuses urged by Sheridan as general, 274; Lambton protests interference of peers in, 284; *see also* Representative Peers

Elgin, Thomas Bruce, 7th Earl of [S] (1766–1841; suc. 1771), diplomat (Representative Peer 1790–1807; British envoy at Brussels 1792–1795), 120, 258

Eliot, Edward Craggs-Eliot, 1st Baron [GB] (1727–1804; cr. 1784), 239

Eliot, Edward George (1758–1797), politician (MP Liskeard 1784–1797; Lord of the Treasury 1782–1793; member of Board of Control 1793–1797), 295

"Ellen," 69

Elliot, Mr., Army private, 51

Elliot, Sir Gilbert (1751–1814; suc. as 4th Baronet 1777; DCL Oxford 1793), politician and diplomat (MP Helston 1790–1795; PC 1793; Commissioner for Toulon with lifetime retirement at half pay 1793; Minister to Italian States 1793–1794), friend of 2nd Earl of Guilford, 10, 105; announces Portland's defection, 156, 421; retracts, 157; DCL Oxford, 350; confers with Dundas, 394; rumored to become Speaker, 392, 394, 396; once admired by Fox, 396; Commissioner for Toulon, 397, 400, 421; salary and other emoluments as Commissioner for Toulon, 401, 428, 429; Privy Council, 397; rumored to be made Clerk of Privy Council, 397; dines with Burke, Dundas, and Pitt, 402; on diplomatic mission in Florence, 458

Elphinstone, John, 11th Baron [S] (1737–1794; suc. 1781), politician (Lieutenant Governor of Edinburgh Castle 1781–1794; Representative Peer 1784–1794), 358

Elwes, John (d. 1789), 86

Ely, Dean of, *see* Cooke, William, Sr.

"Emma," 19

England, Church of, 264, 283

English Chronicle, 37, 169, 334

English Revolution Society, 253

Ernest Augustus, Prince (1771–1851), 8th child and 5th son of George III; Army officer (KG 1786; Lieutenant General 1793), 299, 362

Erskine, John (Purse Bearer to Lord Chancellor 1793; Commissioner of Toulon with lifetime pension of £750 thereafter 1793), 428

Erskine, Thomas (1750–1823), barrister and politician (KC 1783; Attorney General to Prince of Wales 1783–1793; FRS 1787; MP Portsmouth 1790–1806), politics, 10; functions, 11; Attorney General to Prince of Wales, 11, 18, 87; pamphleteer and contributor to newspapers, 38; wit, 97, 98; defends Charles Stuart in Mackintosh vs. Stuart, 67; scheduled to second Grey's motion for reform, 76; represents Mrs. Billington in Billington vs. Ridgway, 87; defends Tattersall, 97, 99; fee for defense of Tattersall, 99; champion of freedom of press, 140; expected to defend new indictees, 140; denounced by True Briton for exorbitant fees, 141; supports Fox's amendment to Address of Thanks, 149; denounced by Burke for defense of Paine, 150; supports Fox's motion for negotiations, 150; defends Paine, 150, 152–153; assailed by Ministerial papers for defense of Paine, 153; to be punished for defense of Paine, 153; thanked by Fox, 183; censured by Mulgrave, 183, 214, 264; champions law against subversions of Government, 198; honored by Friends of the Liberty of the Press, 198; flailed by Ministerial papers, 200; speech at dinner of Friends of the Liberty of the Press published as pamphlet, 200, 201; dismissed as Attorney General to Prince of Wales, 204, 207–208, 213; interpretation of dismissal, 208; attempts to see Prince of Wales, 207; derided by Ministerial papers, 212; assailed by Public Advertiser for defense of Paine, 213; scoffed at by World, 221; defends Frost, 231, 276; effect of dismissal on Friends of the Liberty of the Press, 233; absent from dinner of Friends of the Liberty of the Press, 237; opposes Traitorous Correspondence Bill, 249–250; rumored to be emigrating to America, 253; identified with Friends of the Liberty of the Press, 253, 339; insulted by Burke, 261; defends Ridgway and Symonds, 268; seconds Grey's motion for reform, 272; represents Ashley and Mara, 312; represents Swan and Dibdin, 318; defends Morning Chronicle, 447, 452

"Escape," 17, 59, 97, 182

Este, the Rev. Charles (1752–1829), clergyman and journalist, early history, 25; edits Cabinet, 33; sues Topham for collection of pension, 113, 174; first editor of Courier, 116, 168; offers to support Fox, 116–117; quits Courier, 419; advertises for sponsor for book, 468

Esten, Mrs. Harriet Pye (Bennet) (c. 1768–1868 [sic]), actress at Covent Garden, engaged by Covent Garden, 42, 322; background, 321, 322; liaison with Duke of Hamilton, 321–322; assailed by World, 322, 323–324

Esten, James, 321

Evans, James, bookseller, 55, 61, 135

Evening Mail, data regarding, 24, 26, 178; Treasury payments to, 26, 170, 173, 178; quoted, 186, 221–222, 268, 297

Exchequer, Auditor of, 109; Lord Chief Baron of, 216; Teller of, 18, 82

Excise, Commissioner of, 110

Executive Council, French, 186, 298

Exeter, 342

Exeter, Brownlow Cecil, 9th Earl of [GB] (1725–1793; suc. 1754; FRS and FSA 1767), 354

Eyre, Sir James (1734–1799; knighted 1772), judge (Lord Chief Baron of Court of Exchequer 1767–1793; Chief Justice of Court of Common Pleas 1793–1799), manages affairs of Colman, 43–44, 94; succeeds Thurlow as Chancellor pro tempore, 83; named

Chief Justice of Court of Common Pleas, 216; dismisses Frost's action against Hood, 231

Falkland, Henry Thomas Cary, 8th Viscount [S] (1776–1796; suc. 1785), 33

Farington, Joseph (1747–1821), painter, 167, 174

Faro, 33, 128, 164, 309, 330–331; see also Gambling

Farren, Elizabeth (1759?–1829), actress at Drury Lane, 42, 91–92, 96

Farren, William (d. 1795), actor at Drury Lane, 42, 96

Fashions, 164–165, 328–329, 330; see also "Pad"

Fast, national, 243, 264

Fawcitt, Sir William (1728–1804; KB 1786), military officer (Lieutenant General 1782; Colonel of 3rd Dragoon Guards 1792), 214

Fawkener, William Augustus (1747–1811) diplomat (Clerk of Privy Council), 397

Feilde, the Rev. Matthew (1749–1796), educator (Master of Lower Grammar School, Christ's Hospital 1776–1796), 27, 28

Fielding, William Robert, styled Viscount (1760–1799), politician and military officer (MP Newport 1790–1796; DCL Oxford 1793), 349

Fennell, James (1766–1816), actor and playwright, 94

Ferdinand, Prince, of Brunswick, see Brunswick, Prince Ferdinand of

Fielding, Sir John (d. 1780), blind magistrate, 386

Finey, William (fl. 1781–1797), journalist, 24, 173

Fitch, Mrs., milliner, 363

"Fitz-Alan," 69

Fitzgerald, Edward, styled Lord (1763–1798), military officer and reformer, member of Friends of the People, 76, 140; cashiered from the Army, 140, 155–156; cousin of Fox and brother of

Duke of Leinster, 180; member of Constitutional Society, 268

Fitzgibbon, Anne, Lady, 32

Fitzgibbon, John, 1st Viscount [I] (1748–1802; cr. 1793; cr. Baron Fitzgibbon [I] 1789), politician (Lord Chancellor of Ireland 1789–1802), 32, 132, 429

Fitzherbert, Maria Anne (Smythe) (1756–1837), wife of Prince of Wales (m. Edward Weld 1775; m. Thomas Fitzherbert 1778; m. Prince of Wales 1785), status of marriage, 12–13; disliked by Queen, 13, 16; accompanies Prince of Wales to Brighton, 13; breaks with Fox, forms alliance with Sheridan, 13; houses in London and Brighton, 13, 14; blackmailed by World, 14; proposed settlement with, 16; member of Carlton House coterie, 18; buys puffs in newspapers, 20; responsible for Carlton House's purchase of Morning Post, 36; blackmailed by Ridgway, 86; insulted by Oracle, 100; Prince of Wales's support of condemned by newspapers, 126, 128; frequents faro parlors, 164; defended by Oracle, 202–203; assists in Sheridan's intrigues, 202–203; alarmed by Prince's negotiations with Pitt, 260; moves to Brighton, 363, 371, 458

Fitzpatrick, Richard (1747–1813), soldier, politician, and man of fashion (MP [I] Kildare 1790–c. 1797; MP [GB] Tavistock 1774–1807; manager for impeachment of Hastings; Major General 1793), 79

Fitzroy Crofties, Miss, 331

Fitzwilliam, William, Viscount Milton [GB] and 2nd Earl [I] (1748–1833; suc. 1756; DCL Oxford 1793), follower of Duke of Portland, 10; subsidizer of Opposition press, 31, 32; rumored to become First Lord of the Treasury, 131; discontinues aid to newspapers, 166; returns five members to Commons, 239–240; DCL Oxford, 349; supports war, 399; threatened by Pitt, 421, 422;

Fitzwilliam (con't).
defection announced, 424; defection denied, 425; refuses office, 432

Flanders, 391

Fleet Prison, 285, 440

Flockton, Mr., puppeteer, 372

Florence, 458

Flower, Benjamin (1755–1829), Cambridge liberal, 122, 169, 346

Ford, Richard (1759?–1806), politician and magistrate, 15

Fordenstoun (?), Lord, 433

Foster, John (1740–1828), lawyer and politician (MP [I] Co. Louth 1768–1800; PC [I] 1779; Bencher King's Inn, Dublin 1784; Speaker of Commons [I] 1785–1800), 214, 232

"Fool, Thomas," 419

Forces, Paymaster General of the, 424

Forgeries, 340

Foundling Hospital, 105, 156

Fox, Charles James (1749–1806), statesman (MP Westminster 1780–1806; Foreign Secretary 1782, 1783; manager for impeachment of Hastings), character and abilities, 9; as leader of the Whigs, 9, 10; "Man of the People," 9, 77, 242; popularity, 9, 242, 346; politics, 9; break with Burke, 7, 8; Lauderdale's attachment to, 10; confidence in Sheridan, 11; relationship with Prince of Wales, 12, 13; Sheridan's intrigues against, 14; supported by Skinner, 35; lack of interest in newspapers, 37–38; represented by *Morning Chronicle*, 22, 35, 38, 126, 166; early friend of Canning, 53; censures George III for failure to pay Prince of Wales's debts, 56, 57; presents petition of Westminster electors, 65, 66, 75, 78; receives information from Daniel Stuart, 74, 194; excluded from Friends of the People, 75, 79; advocates change in Constitution, 77; defends Grey's motion for reform, 77; subverts object of Friends of the People, 77, 78, 79–80; splits Opposition, 77; friendship with

Portland, 81; opposes Proclamation against Seditious Writings, 81; Government's attempts to separate from Friends of the People, 81, 149, 153; ignored by press, 82; exasperates *World*, 83; wooed by Pitt with passage of Libel Bill, 100, 111; accepts credit for passage of Libel Bill, 83; acts as Lauderdale's second in duel with Arnold, 85; admired by Lord Derby, 91; wooed by Ministerial papers, 100; wooed by Prince of Wales, 100–101; possible reaction to Portland's defection, 106; supported by *Courier*, 116–117; entreated to join Government, 121–122, 125; moves for repeal of laws discriminating against dissenters, 123; worshiped at Cambridge, 123; ignored by *Oracle*, 126; defection expected, 131, 135; rumored to become Home Secretary, 131; lambasted by Paine and Pigott, 133; Portland's attachment to, 139; moves for information regarding insurrection, 149, 399; refuses to join Government, 149; denounces spies and informers, 149; moves for negotiations to avoid war, 149; moves to send Minister to Paris, 149–150; effect of motions on people, 150; Burke's despair of converting, 150, 155; supported by *Diary*, 151; ignored by Ministerial papers, 151; denounces arrest of booksellers as illegal, 152; assailed by *Sun*, 153; uninfluenced by Sheridan, 154; defends Sheridan against Burke, 154; accused by Burke of impertinence, 155; unaware of Sheridan's intrigues, 155; expected to defect with Portland, 155; flattered by Ministerial papers, 155; censures Army purges, 155; feared by Carlisle, 156; nature of political differences from Portland, 156–157, 157; duped by Elliot regarding Portland's defection, 156–157; opposes Alien Bill, 157; supported by Adam, 157; said by Burke to have called Jemappes a "glorious victory," 157;

relationship to Leinster and Lord Edward Fitzgerald, 180; flailed by *Oracle*, 176; eulogized by Opposition papers, 180; lambasted by Ministerial press, 180; apologized to by Thomas Grenville, 183; moves for delay in consideration of Alien Bill, 183–184; deserted by friends, 183–184, 209; blamed for execution of Louis XVI, 190; defended by *Morning Chronicle*, 190; publishes *Letter ... to [Westminster] Electors*, 191–192; content of *Letter*, 192–193; purpose of *Letter*, 193–194; consults with Sheridan regarding size of Corresponding Society, 193–194; Portland said too trusting of, 203; censured by Prince of Wales's letter to Portland, 204; reactions of newspapers to *Letter*, 191–192, 205; effect of *Letter* on Pitt, 204; *Letter* replied to by Bentley, 205; once patron of Anstruther and Garrow, 207; opposes motion for augmentation of forces, 204, 210–211; derided by Ministerial papers, 212, 213; reaction to *Letter* at Cambridge, 213; opposes Address on King's announcement of war, 219, 360; assailed by Burke as hero to Jacobins, 219; moves for negotiations to stop war, 219, 220, 221; jeered at by *World*, 222; editions and sale of *Letter*, 222; accused by Burke of friendship with Brissot, 223; moves resolutions for conduct of war, 223–224; unacquainted with Brissot, 223–224; supports motion against barracks, 224; Government's uneasiness regarding *Letter*, 226; thinks war popular, 226; said by Burke enemy to Constitution, 233; victim of anonymous defamations, 233; urges acceptance of Nottingham petition, 234; supports Sheridan's motion regarding seditious activities, 236; *Letter* answered by Young, 238; represented by Government as agent of French, 238; censured in *Address to Friends of the People*, 239; hated by Pitt, 242, 243; supports war,

242; accused by Ministerial papers of high treason, 243; embarrassed by resignations from Whig Club, 244; spied upon, 244–245; ridiculed by Ministerial papers, 245; supports budget, 247; lectured to by Pitt, 247; criticized for quibbling by *The Times*, 248; accused of corresponding with French, 249; Traitorous Correspondence Bill intended to discredit, 249, 253, 260, 266–267; opposes Traitorous Correspondence Bill, 249, 250, 251, 252–253, 261; *Letter* replied to by Alexander Dalrymple, 253; clash with Pitt over matter of loan, 257; protests King's proclamation barring return of British citizens, 260; said by *The Times* to be deserted by Portland, 263; supports censure of Auckland's Memorial, 266; ignored by Ministerial papers, 268; objects to Commercial Credit Bill, 270; ridiculed by Charles Stuart, 271; supports Grey's motion for reform, 274; *Letter* again answered by Bentley, 283; *Letter* answered by Charles Stuart in *A Short Review*, 283; lectured by *World*, 283; protests inclusion of revenues from East India Company in budget, 288; opposes renewal of East India Company charter, 289; censures Burke for avoiding debates on East India Company charter, 290; heads peace party, 299; censured for "glorying" in Jemappes, 299; beginning of subscription for payment of debts, 300; subscription instituted by Adair, 421; subscription supported by *Morning Chronicle*, 300; accused of selling Clerkship of Pells, 300–301; contributions to payment of debts, 300, 301; subscription supported by *The Times*, 302; motion for peace endorsed by *Morning Chronicle*, 302; Burke fails to contribute to subscription, 303; motion for peace defeated, 303–304; fund ridiculed by *True Briton*, 305; friend in Government office gives information to

Fox, Charles James (con't).
Morning Chronicle, 306; battle between *Morning Chronicle* and *True Briton* over subscription for payment of debts, 306–311; Loughborough fails to contribute to subscription, 307; serialized eulogy in *Morning Chronicle*, 308; progress of subscription, 310; losses at faro, 331; eulogized by *Morning Post*, 337; subscription supported by *Morning Herald*, 347, 349; subscription supported by most Ministerial papers, 348; subscription opposed by *World*, 348; envied by Burke, 351; death of reported, 353; earlier supporter of Elliot, 395; anniversary dinner, 408–409; supported by *Courier*, 419; hope of taking office, 419; cost of Williamson's admiration of, 420; presides at Whig meeting, 421; Pitt's attempts to separate Rockingham Whigs from, 422; will visit Muir, 461; eulogy from *Peace and Reform* printed by *Morning Chronicle*, 468–469, 471; to be blamed for British Convention, 469–470; eulogy from *Peace and Reform* printed by *Morning Post*, 471; mentioned, 10, 447; *see also* Fox's Libel Bill *and* Jemappes

Fox-North coalition, *see* Portland Government

Fox's Libel Bill, progress of, 49; denounced by Bowles, 49, 82; passed, 82–83; celebration of passage, 83; supposedly favored by George III, 83, 85; effect on trial of reformers, 84; effective in trial of *Morning Chronicle*, 454

France, earlier developments in, 54; declares war on Austria and Bohemia, 76; threatened invasion by Prussia and Austria, 85; declares war on Prussia, 104; declares herself a republic, 110; political developments late 1792, 110; declares Scheldt and Meuse open to sea, 134; declares support of all liberation movements, 134; rumors of war against, 144; George III's anxiety regarding, 146–147; fulminations regarding conduct of, 147; Fox moves to send Minister to, 149–150; rouge et noir imported from, 164; pretended negotiations with, 187, 189; George III alarmed by ambitions of, 204; sends M. Maret to England to avert war, 209; conduct of denounced by Pitt, 209–210; Holland needed as barrier against, 210; interference in affairs of condemned by Fox, 210, 211, 223; almost bankrupt, 212, 247; aggressions of confused by Pitt with demands of moderate reformers, 214; fighting Austria, Prussia, and Sardinia, 217; declares war on Holland and Britain, 217, 218; declaration of war said unjustified, 218; encourages sedition in Britain, 219; Pitt refuses to negotiate with, 219; Holland indifferent to conduct of, 243; declares war on Spain, 249; Lauderdale's supposed holdings in, 250, 261; old and new regimes alike detested by Sheridan, 252; British subjects free to return from, 260; Grenville's treaties with potential enemies of, 297; state of during summer, 1793, 297, 298; outraged by Austria and Prussia, 377; declares embargo on British goods, 289; declares war on Genoa, 389, 420; economic collapse thought imminent, 392; impossibility of negotiating with, 398; British property confiscated in, 398; Algiers declares war on, 413; blamed by *World* for war, 414; executions in, 420; Pitt threatens a peace with, 421–422; negotiations with urged by Daniel Stuart's *Peace and Reform*, 469; *see also* Committee of General Security; Committee of Public Safety; Executive Council; France, war against; French; National Assembly; National Convention; *and* Paris

France, war against, advocated by Burke, 8; seemingly forgotten, 54; regarded as inevitable, 145; essential for protection of patronage, 147; reason for phantom uprising, 147, 149; supported by Duke of Clarence, 147–148; opposed by Fox, 148–149; Fox moves for negotiations to avert, 149; already commenced, according to Burke, 149; supported by Parliament, 150; Government determined to foment, 153; implied in Alien Bill, 153; supported by Sheridan, 154; opposed by *Star*, 166; not supported by *Diary*, 163; supported by *Oracle*, 176; *Public Advertiser*'s confusion regarding, 178; purpose of, 179; preparations for, 179; Grey demands Government's intentions respecting, 182; Fox demands to know purpose of, 182; uncertainty as to Pitt's plans regarding, 185–186, 187–188, 189, 217; pretended negotiations to avert, 188, 189; execution of Louis XVI as possible pretext for, 190–191, 210–211; Fox pleads for avoidance of, 193; threat to Constitution as pretext for, 194, 206–207, 214, 426; not supported by Irish, 195; fomented by The Association, 201; resolved on, 205–206; barring French "metaphysics" as pretext for, 206; declaration of urged by Beauchamp, 201, 211; thought to be popular, 211; expected by Fox to be endless, 211; expected by Stormont to be brief, 211–212; Britain cannot afford, 212; announcement of, 216, 217; reasons given by French preposterous, says Pitt, 218, 360; support of urged by Pitt, 218; Fox moves for negotiations to stop, 219; Fox pledges support to, 219, 223, 242, 247, 251; Stanhope demands to know object of, 220; supported by Duke of Portland, 220, 263, 399; animates King's friends, 221; caused by French, 222, 226, 258; Fox urges end of, 223; first reactions to, 224–227; early optimism respecting, 225; rumors of French victories, 225; people's attitude toward, 226–227; creates new problems for Pitt, 228; results in bankruptcies, 231; phantom insurrection as

preparation for, 235–236; opponents of identified with moderate reformers, 242; Pitt afraid to reveal setbacks, 243; defense of Holland as pretext for, 243; excuse to increase patronage, 246, 247; justified by Pitt, 246, 247, 266; financed by loans, 247, 255, 391, 392; expected duration of, 247, 297, 355, 360, 368; to be fought largely by mercenaries, 247; defended by Alexander Dalrymple, 253; provides justification for Traitorous Correspondence Bill, 259; reason for demanded by Sheridan, 265–266; end of rumored, 295; newspaper ignorance of state of, 298; Burke principal enthusiast for, 299; unpopularity of, 244, 299, 303–304, 355, 366; denounced by Clarence, 304; influences fashions, 330; Pitt's problems respecting, 332; supporters rewarded by Government, 351–352, 353; Pitt's reason for, 355, 398; progress of, 359–360, 413, 423; *Oracle* apologizes for, 360; opposed by Prince Augustus, 363; misunderstanding of Pitt's attitude toward, 364–365, 366; opposition to, 366, 368; Burke as scapegoat for, 365, 366, 367, 376, 377, 402; financed by Britain, 368; popularity to be established by military camps, 371; increases influence of Crown, 375; Pitt responsible for, 365; conduct bungled by Pitt, 391, 397; reason for demanded by *Morning Post*, 398; end threatened by Pitt, 400; dwindling interest in, 410; unaffected by execution of Marie Antoinette, 412; restoration of Bourbons as object of, 426; possible financing by private contributions, 426; Pitt's intention of continuing, 431; preservation of corruptions as reason for, 457; *see also* French *and* War charities

Francis, Philip (1740–1818), politician (MP Bletchingley 1790–1796), member of liberal wing of Opposition, 10; pamphleteer and contributor to

Francis, Philip (con't).
newspapers, 38; founder of Friends of the People, 72, 79; on first secretarial committee of Friends of the People, 73; supports Grey's motion for reform, 272; lectured to by the *World*, 283; opposes renewing charter of East India Company, 288; supports motion for prosecution of *World*, 292; advises Burke to return to Opposition, 292, 293; on committee for payment of Fox's debts, 300

Francis II, Emperor of Austria (1768–1835; suc. 1792), 76, 377

Franklin, Benjamin (1706–1790), 379

Fraser, John (fl. 1788–1793), nurseryman, 67, 443

Frederick William II, King of Prussia and Bohemia (1744–1797; suc. 1786), marries eldest daughter to Duke of York, 16, 53; France declares war on, 76; declaration to Poland, 216; mentioned, 52

Frederick William III, King of Prussia and Bohemia (1770–1840; suc. 1797), 331

Freedom of the press, *see* Press, freedom of the

Freeling, Francis (1764–1836), Post Office official (Deputy Comptroller General 1792–1795), appointed to Post Office, 63; thought to be proprietor of *Sun*, 118; impedes delivery of Opposition papers, 167, 170; delivers copies of *Sun* and *True Briton* gratis, 172; subscriber to *True Briton*'s charity, 423

Freemasons Tavern, 73

French, rumored landings of, 80; defeat Prussians at Valmy, 119; annex Savoy, 148; banish Bourbons, 155; occupy Austrian Netherlands, 156; insulted by *London Gazette*, 188; possible invasion by, 206; willing to negotiate, 211; denounced by Auckland, 217; refuse to negotiate, 217; constantly insulted by British Government, 219, 227; mer-

cenaries no match for, 212; Burke's tirade against, 223; flailed in sermons, 243; called savages and madmen, 188, 245; Fox accused of corresponding with, 249; capture Breda, Klundert, and Gertruydenberg, 257; evacuate Holland, 258; denounced by Dr. Milner, 277; annex Mainz, 298; cashier officers of noble birth, 359; lose Mainz, 359; lose Lincelles, 368; defeat Duke of York, 390; conduct in Brabant, 401; Pitt's threat to negotiate with, 409; mass troops on coast, 411; occupy Maritime Flanders, 413

French fleet, Lord Howe's search for, 297, 360, 376, 431, 455; presented to British at Toulon, 413

French immigrants, 153, 185, 186, 189, 235, 248, 249

French "liberty," 149

French "opinions," reason for war, 179, 206, 210, 228; impossibility of combatting with force, 192; George III's anxiety regarding, 204; cause death of Louis XVI, 209–210

French Reign of Terror, 297

French Revolution, detested by Burke, 7, 80, 150, 292, 299; Paine's defense of, 7; British enthusiasm for, 7; Orleans's rôle in, 18; Merry's enthusiasm for, 39; celebration of anniversary of, 39; charged by Burke to "theory," 77–78; denounced by Wilde, 80; blamed for unrest in Britain, 182; defended by Courtenay, 188; Windham's preoccupation with, 272; Hardy sympathetic with, 273; mentioned, 391

French Royal Family, 110, 145, 154, 206

French Royalists, 414

French West Indies, 297

Frend, William (1757–1841), reformer, heads Cambridge radicals, 122; prosecuted by University, 235, 236; banished from University, 277–278; appeals sentence, 278; mentioned, 123

Freytag, William von (1711–1798), Hanoverian Field Marshal, 368

Friends of the Liberty of the Press, Society of the, organization of, 39, 40; celebrates passage of Fox's Libel Bill, 83; members of, 117, 244, 339; revived as antidote to The Association, 155; censures jury for convicting Paine, 183; lambasted by Mulgrave, 173, 200, 214; honors Erskine, 198; addressed by Erskine and Sheridan, 200–201, 204; denounced by *Public Advertiser*, 201, 237; impedes activities of Government, 208; censured by Prince of Wales, 208; undaunted by censure of Prince of Wales, 233; denounced by Bowles, 235; holds public dinner, 234, 235, 237–238; resignations from, 237; Erskine and Mingay identified with, 253; holds additional public dinner, 264–265; called composition of Constitutional Society and Friends of the People, 273; assailed by Charles Stuart, 283; *see also* Press, freedom of the

Friends of the People, Associated, *see* Associated Friends of the People

Friends of the People, Society of the, original sponsors, 72, 79; bylaws, 73; first secretarial committee, 73; first treasurers, 73; Mackintosh's connection with, 73; Daniel Stuart's connection with, 73–74, 268, 336; reason for organization of, 74–75; organization of, 72–73, 75–76, 79; objects of, 75, 76, 469; dues, 75; constitution of, 75; weakness of, 75; original members of, 76, 79; condemned by Fox's friends, 79; Declaration of, 74–75, 76, 79; later members of, 76, 117, 140, 168; publication of Declaration, 74, 78; final dissolution of, 74, 78; Address of, 76; publication of Address, 76, 78; resolves to move for eradication of election abuses, 76; submits Declaration and Address to Commons, 76; motion regarding election reforms announced by Grey, 76–77; undone by Fox, 78, 79–80; consequent misunderstanding of, 78; failure to influence radical societies, 78, 273; refuses correspondence with Constitutional Society, 78, 84; refuses to sponsor British Convention, 78–79; represented as enemy to Constitution, 81; target of Proclamation against Seditious Writings, 81, 83, 149; reluctance to participate in British Convention, 83–84, 349, 434; resignations from, 84, 93; Mackintosh's *Letter to . . . Pitt* apology for, 99; ignored by newspapers, 99; Government's attempts to separate from Fox, 100, 122, 149; Pitt's fear of, 111; defended by *Oracle*, 117; supported by *Diary*, 125; credited for Prince of Wales's economies, 126; readying campaign for reform, 99, 131; denounced by Paine, 133; does not control *Star*, 135, 166; publishers for, 138, 279; receives minutes of Scottish Convention, 145; blamed for sedition, 147; Government's attempts to discredit, 153; supported by *Morning Post*, 166; represented as candidate by Mingay, 174; assailed by *World*, 184; defended by Sheridan against Burke, 219, 220, 239; objects impugned by rumors, 238; resolves to petition for reform, 237; publishes *State of the Representation*, 99, 239–241, 267; censured by Young, 239; censured in *Address to the Friends of the People*, 239; target of Traitorous Correspondence Bill, 244, 249, 253, 260, 266–267; Francis protests election abuses on behalf of, 267; relies on petitions, 268; supported by radical societies, 268–269; accused of plotting rebellion, 268; attacked by Charles Stuart, 270–271; submits petition for reform, 272; "sneers" at protested, 273; held responsible for Friends of the Liberty of the Press, 273; advised by Pitt to "disband," 273–274; resolves to continue, 274, 278, 284; new attacks on, 279; supported by *Oracle*, 280; lectured by *World*, 283; publishes petition, 284; publishes new

Friends of the People (con't).
  Address, 284; thanks other societies, 348; war contrived to defeat, 355; implicated by Skirving in trial of Muir, 406; Skirving's letter to, 406–407; to be blamed for British Convention, 469–470; see also Reform, moderate
Frost, Eliza (Mrs. John Terrence), 198
Frost, John Terrence (1750–1842), lawyer and reformer, sues Hood, 50, 65; flailed by World for publication of pamphlet, 112; goes to Paris, 112; utters seditious words during visit to London, 135, 142; indicted and outlawed, 142–143, 196; castigated by Burke, 149, 150; assailed by Ministerial papers, 151, 153; denounced by John "Jew" King, 196; writes insulting letter to Pitt, 197–198; declared bankrupt, 198, 464; insolvency denied, 198; returns and surrenders, 231; sues Hood, 231; released on bail, 234, 252; Government's reluctance to prosecute, 236; functions at dinner of Constitutional Society, 268; tried, convicted, and sentenced, 276, 278; actual crimes, 276, 278; Henry Yorke's Letter to, 343; lampooned by Charles Stuart, 417; letters on state of Newgate, 437, 442; precarious health, 439, 442; appearance in pillory postponed, 445–446, 461–462; public interest in 453, 461–464; appearance in pillory canceled, 462; stripped of rights as British citizen, 462; released, 462–464; billed for expense respecting Hood, 463
Fugitive Poetry, 345
Fuller, John, later owner of Morning Post, 334, 339, 340
Furlonger, Mr., proprietor of Morning Post, 35, 68

Gallic Lion, The, 262
Galloway, John Stewart, 7th Earl of [S] (1735–1806; suc. 1773; Representative Peer 1774–1790; KT 1775; Lord of the Bedchamber 1784–1806), 285

Galston, 271
Gambling, 331
Game laws, 346
Garrow, William (1760–1840), lawyer (KC 1793; Bencher of Lincoln's Inn 1793), 128, 129, 207, 230
Garroway's Coffee House, 31
Garter, Knight of the, 295
Gazetteer, title, history, editor, printer, address, circulation, 34, 168; personnel, 28, 34, 39, 41; connection with Craftsman and General Evening Post, 37; character of, 163, 167; politics of, 31, 35; supports Paine, 72, 80; organ of Constitutional Society, 38; ignored by Government, 72; sued by lawyer, 71; denounced as subversive by Oracle, 102; on Prince of Wales, 127; changes of editor, 168; shifts to moderate reform, 166; on Poland, 189, 347; on Burke, 190, 283, 290, 397, 402; on Muir, 215, 333, 461; on ship promised by Lonsdale, 226; on Auckland's Memorial, 266; defends Maitland, 283–284; on Lord George Gordon, 287, 442; supports Insolvent Debtors Bill, 287; on Dundas, 295, 356; on placemen and pensioners, 296, 296–297, 376–377, 401, 415, 425–426, 427, 429; on Jenkinson, 296; on Rose, 296–297; on True Briton, 298, 306, 307; defends Fox, 303; on treaties, 305; on Burges, 306; on Loughborough, 307; advertises Dyer's Poems, 311; on Drury Lane, 314; on Mrs. Jordan, 315; on "pad," 329; later search for Radcliffe, 336; Owen proprietor of, 342; probably not assisted by Lauderdale, 346, 347; copies material from Morning Chronicle, 347, 375, 468; on George Rose, Jr., 353; on Richmond, 361, 412; on motion to assassinate Pitt, 369; on Dutch, 375, 402; on conduct of war, 375; on Dunkirk, 392; on state of the war, 413; on taxing placemen and pensioners, 429; on Palmer, 461; on Frost, 462; quoted, 28, 137, 143, 195, 231, 239, 244, 285,

294, 295, 296, 298, 321, 348, 353–354, 357, 363, 414, 435; mentioned, 125, 336

Genoa, 389, 420

General Advertiser, 28, 34, 38, 60

General Evening Post, 37, 169

George III, King (1738–1820; suc. 1760), character of, 3, 4, 164; early conflicts with Prince of Wales, 11–12; settlement with Mrs. Robinson, 12; early autocratic activities, 7; censured by Commons for undue influence, 4; struggle with Commons, 4; patronizes Lansdowne Government, 9; overrides Commons to appoint Pitt First Minister, 4, 9; opposes impeachment of Hastings, 7; increases income of Prince of Wales, 13; illness of, 4, 14–15, 24, 246; patronizes Thurlow, 18, 118; insists on marriage of oldest Princes, 16; firm supporter of Pitt, 4; comparison with Pitt, 4–5; supposed retirement from politics, 4; Pitt's dependence upon, 14; activities reported by papers, 164; newspapers' opinion of, 4, 5; people's opinion of, 142; exploits Burke, 7–8; Almon convicted of publishing libel on, 38; said by *Oracle* to disapprove of Pitt, 52–53, 55, 56; opens Parliament, 53; favors adequate establishment for Duke and Duchess of York, 53, 55; silent respecting war with France, 54, 85, 102; censured by Fox for failure to pay debts of Prince of Wales, 57; defended by Pitt, 57; signs Establishment Bill for Duke and Duchess of York, 59; signs bill for reduction of national debt, 59; expected to review Prince of Wales's debts, 60; attitude toward Fox's Libel Bill, 83, 85; issues Proclamation against Seditious Writings, 80, 101–102; thanks Parliament, 85; Tattersall and Williams indicted for libel on, 97–98; rewards friends, 104; appoints Pitt Warden of Cinque Ports, 107; hates Fox, 118; recalls ambassador from Paris, 110;

reconciliation with Prince of Wales, planned by Sheridan and Thurlow, 127; Wolcot in pay of, 137; avoidance of Drury Lane denounced by *Morning Chronicle*, 137; Williams imprisoned for libel on, 138; calls out militia, 139; offers bounties for Navy enlistments, 140; conducts Army purges, 140; eulogized, 143; receives report on Scottish Convention, 145; convokes Parliament, 146–147; censured by Fox, 148; rumored payment of Prince of Wales's debts, 153, 202, 213–214; purges defended by Burke, 155; rumors of insulting toasts to, 185; refuses to review Chauvelin's credentials, 189; orders Chauvelin to leave, 191; castigated by Fox for summoning militia, 192; not in danger, 194; promises aid to Irish Catholics, 195, 232; asks for augmentation of forces, 190, 193, 204, 205, 209; debates on message regarding augmentation of forces, 209–213, 214; reconciliation with Prince of Wales, 203, 254–255, 362; announces declaration of war, 218–221; friends animated by declaration of war, 221; promises pardon to deserters, 227; justification for summoning of militia demanded by Sheridan, 235; policy of proving existence of disease by producing remedy, 248; proclaims national fast, 243, 264; asks Hanoverians to help Holland, 243; bars British subjects from returning from France, 260; right to issue proclamations debated, 260; pardons Mary Bryant, 276; favors Auckland as Home Secretary, 295; prorogues Parliament, 304; abused by The Association, 341; recognizes Burke, 366; attitude toward war doubtful, 367, 398; receives Glasgow petition for peace, 392, 397, 398; blames Richmond for Dunkirk, 395, 396, 398; supposedly uneasy about Pitt's treatment of Duke of Clarence, 398; expected to pardon Muir, 408, 444;

George III (con't).

prorogues Parliament, 414; promises to hold Toulon for Louis XVII, 426; urges Moira to accept office, 441; orders investigation of Newgate, 442; lauded by *Public Advertiser*, 468; mentioned, 154

Gerrald, Joseph (1763–1796), lawyer and reformer, active in Corresponding Society, 135, 369; toasted by Friends of the Liberty of the Press, 237; member of Constitutional Society, 267; acquainted with Daniel Stuart, 268, 336, 369–370; escapes arrest, 276; harangues Corresponding Society, 369; elected delegate of Corresponding Society to British Convention, 432; Charles Stuart's cautions respecting, 433; reaches Edinburgh, 434; arrested, 448, 453, 459, 460; released on bail, 453, 460; indicted, 472

Gertruydenberg, 243, 257, 258

Gifford, William (1756–1826), miscellaneous writer, 20

Gillespy, Mr., surgeon at Newgate, 436

Gillray, James (1757–1815), caricaturist and journalist, 181

Girondists, 54, 297, 389, 420

Glamorgan, Lord Lieutenant of Co., 105, 350

Glasgow Association, President of, 140

Glasgow petition, 335, 366, 369, 392, 398

Glasgow theater, 318

Globe, 338

Globe Tavern, 369, 370

Gloucester, Recorder of, 105

Gloucester, William Henry, Duke of (1743–1805; cr. 1764), brother of George III (Keeper of Cranbourne Chase 1767–1805; Colonel of 1st Foot Guards 1770–1805; Warden of New Forest 1771–1805; Chancellor of University of Dublin, 1771–1805; FRS 1780; LLD Cambridge 1787; Field Marshal 1793; President of London Infirmy?), 14, 362, 364

Gloucester Bastille, 279

Godfrey, David, 237

Godfrey, John (1763–1841), 73

Godmanchester, Recorder of, 105

"God Save the King," 136, 138, 146

Godwin, William (1756–1836), political philosopher, novelist, playwright, 42, 223, 275

Goodall, Mrs. Charlotte (fl. 1784–1813), actress at Drury Lane, 42

Gordon, Alexander, 4th Duke of [S] (1743–1827; suc. 1752; KT 1775; FRS 1784; cr. Baron Gordon and Earl of Norwich [GB] 1784; Chancellor King's College Aberdeen 1793–1827; Colonel in the Army 1793), brother of Lord George Gordon, 228; refuses to provide securities for Lord George Gordon, 229, 437; commissioned Colonel in the Army, elected Chancellor of King's College Aberdeen, 352; harassed by newspapers, 441–442

Gordon, Catherine, Duchess of (1718–1799), mother of Lord George Gordon, 437

Gordon, Lady Charlotte (Mrs. Charles Lennox) (1768–1842; m. Charles Lennox 1789), 438

Gordon, Cosmo George, 3rd Duke of [S] (c. 1721–1752; suc. 1728), father of Lord George Gordon, 437

Gordon, George, styled Lord (1751–1793), early career, 228–229, 436, 437, 438; appears in court with securities, 229; slated by Burke, 229; newspaper reactions to hearing, 229–230; despondency of, 287; treatment protested by newspapers, 287; death of, 435–440; newspapers' interest in, 441–442; burial, 441; *Morning Post* on death of, 442; *Gazetteer* on death of, 442

Gordon, Jane, Duchess of (1748–1812; m. 4th Duke of Gordon 1767), hostess for Tories, buys puffs in newspapers, 20; blackmailed by *The Times*, 299; entertains Prince of Wales, 299, 458; sister of Lady Wallace, 330

Gordon, Lady Susan, Duchess of Manchester (1774–1828; m. Duke of Manchester 1793), 438, 442

Gordon riots, 228, 436–437, 438

Goring, Charles (c. 1744–1829), 237

Gould, Sir Henry (1710–1794), judge (Justice of Common Pleas 1763–1794), 98

Gower, George Granville Leveson-Gower, styled Earl (1758–1833), diplomat (MP Stafford 1787–1799; ambassador to Paris 1790–1792), 110, 186

Grand Fleet, 297, 298, 305

Grant, Rev. Dr. (1737–1809), writer for Government in Scotland, 30

Grant, William (1752–1832), politician and judge (MP Shaftesbury 1790–1793; KC 1793; Joint Justice of Carmarthen Great Sessions 1793), 207, 278–279

Graham, Robert (1744–1836), lawyer (KC 1793; Attorney General to Prince of Wales 1793–?), 207

Grattan, Major John, Army officer, 33

Grattan, Mrs. Lucia (m. 1783), 33

Gray, James (d. 1796), journalist, proprietor, conductor, and principal writer for Morning Chronicle, 34, 167; indicted for libel, 215; member of Whig Club, 244; tried for libel, 446, 452–453, 454

Grenville, Thomas (1755–1846), book collector and politician (MP Aldborough 1790–1796), 183

Grenville, William Windham, 1st Baron [GB] (1759–1834; cr. 1790), politician (Home Secretary 1789–1791; President of Board of Control 1790–1793; Foreign Secretary 1791–1801; Ranger of St. James's and Hyde Parks 1791–1794; Elder Brother of Trinity House 1793–1834), character of, 6; member of Pitt's intimate circle, 6; sent to Lords to deal with Thurlow, 18; purchaser of newspaper puffs, 20; refers Fox's Libel Bill to judges, 82; has reversion of Auditorship of Exchequer, 109; places and sinecures, 132; blames Grey for phantom insurrection, 147; silent regarding nature of insurrection, 148; introduces Alien Bill, 153, 156; dismisses Chauvelin, 186; gives Chauvelin's correspondence to newspapers, 186; receives letter from Le Brun, 188–189; appealed to for release of Lafayette, 189; refuses immunity to Chauvelin, 190; receives credentials from Maret, 209; correspondence with Chauvelin reviewed by Pitt, 210; Fox's comments on correspondence with Chauvelin, 211; introduces motion for augmentation of forces, 211; correspondence with Chauvelin reviewed by Oracle, 216; Chauvelin's refusal to talk to denounced by True Briton, 217; moves Address on King's message, 220; relinquishment of emoluments suggested by Morning Chronicle, 248; supports Traitorous Correspondence Bill, 263; signs treaties, 297; amount of patronage, 300; defends Auckland's Memorial, 304; named Elder Brother of Trinity House, 356

Grey, Charles (1764–1845), politician (MP Northumberland 1786–1807; manager of trial of Hastings), member of Opposition, 10; moves for investigation of Nootka Sound, 134; sponsors organization of Friends of the People, 72, 79; member of secretarial committee of Friends of the People, 73; announces intention of moving for election reforms, 76–77, 78, 79, 80, 99, 111, 267, 268; denounced by Ministerial papers, 80; defends Friends of the People, 81; Lauderdale's second in near-duel with Richmond, 82; temporizes regarding British Convention, 83; lambasted by Paine and Pigott, 133; blamed for phantom insurrection, 147; supports Fox's amendment to Address of Thanks, 149; accuses The Association of instigating Manchester riots, 152; moves for indictment of Reeves, 152; assails Pitt's policy of secrecy, 182;

Grey, Charles (con't).
  steward of dinner for Friends of the Liberty of the Press, 200; supports Fox's resolutions on conduct of war, 223; moves for negotiations for peace, 224; supports Taylor's motion against barracks, 224; represented by Government as agent of French, 238; ridiculed by Ministerial papers, 245; target of Traitorous Correspondence Bill, 249, 266; opposes Traitorous Correspondence Bill, 251; officiates at dinner of Friends of the Liberty of the Press, 264; presents petition of Friends of the People, 272, 279, 284; moves for election reforms, 271, 272, 279, 284; debates on motion for election reforms, 272–274; moves for postponement of Hastings's trial, 291–292; intercedes on behalf of Mrs. Bateman, 317; attends Fox's anniversary dinner, 409; promises penal reform bill, 441; requests detention of Muir and Palmer, 461; mentioned, 216

Griffin, Mrs. William (fl. 1774–1792), printer, 69

Grimston, James Bucknall, 3rd Viscount [I] (1747–1808; suc. 1773; FSA, FRS 1786; cr. Baron Verulam [GB] 1790; DCL 1793), 349

Grose, Sir Nash (1740–1814; knighted 1787), judge (Judge of King's Bench 1787–1813), 463, 464

Grosvenor, Richard, 1st Earl [GB] (1731–1802; cr. 1784; cr. Baron Grosvenor [GB] 1761; FRS 1771), 58

Guerney, John (1768–1845), lawyer, 279, 280, 344

Guilford, Frederick North, 2nd Earl of [GB] (1732–1792; suc. 1790), early career, 4, 9; politics, 9–10; friends of, 6, 10, 83, 221, 263; no journalistic writings, 37; friends support Proclamation against Seditious Writings, 81; death of, 104, 105; places and honors, 105, 106, 108, 110–111, 295; mentioned, 106, 156, 301

Guilford, George Augustus North, 3rd Earl of [GB] (1757–1802; suc. 1792; styled Lord North 1790–1792; manager for impeachment of Hastings; FRS 1782; Captain of Deal Castle 1790–1802), follower of 2nd Earl of Guilford, 10, 105; supports Proclamation against Seditious Writings, 81, 105; refuses Governor Generalship of India, 105; votes with Opposition, 155, 221; opposes Traitorous Correspondence Bill, 263

Guilford, High Steward of, 132

Gustavus III, King of Sweden (1746–1792; suc. 1771), 55

H., C. D., 334, 427

H., J., see Haslewood, Joseph

Habeas Corpus Act, 156, 182, 469

Hackney, 432

Hague, The, 294, 297

Hale, Sir Matthew (1609–1676), English judge, 249, 249–250

Hall, Charles Henry (1763–1827), educator (tutor and censor of Christ Church, Oxford 1792–1797), 350

Hall, John (1739–1797), engraver, 37

Hamilton, Douglas, 8th Duke of [S] (1756–1799; suc. 1769; cr. Duke of Brandon [GB] 1782; KT 1785), tastes, habits, and background, 164, 321; liaison with Mrs. Esten, 321, 322; attacked by World and Morning Post, 322, 323–324

Hamilton, Lady Elizabeth (1753–1797; m. 12th Earl of Derby 1774), 91, 92

Hamilton, Elizabeth Anne, Duchess of (1757–1837; m. 8th Duke of Hamilton 1778), 322

Hamoaze, 227

Hampstead, 423

Handel (1685–1769), 3

Hanoverians, 243, 247, 298, 303, 362, 370, 371, 415

Hanover Square Rooms, 43, 321

Hardinge, George (1743–1816), lawyer and politician (Queen's Solicitor

General 1782–1794; MP Old Sarum 1784–1802), 252, 457

Hardy, Thomas (1752–1832), shoemaker and reformer, organizes Corresponding Society, 72; confers with Daniel Stuart, 74, 336; perpetual Secretary of Corresponding Society, 84, 193, 273; friend of Lord George Gordon, 228; petitions for election reforms, 268; 273; functions at dinner of Constitutional Society, 268; plans British Convention, 275; escapes arrest, 276

Hare, Mr., nurseryman, 67

Hare, James (1749–1804), 79

Hargrave, J., lawyer, 168–169, 313

Hargrave, Jeremiah (d. 1793), publican, 35, 36, 68, 168, 334

Hargrave, Richard (c. 1711–1793), Commissioner of Bankrupts, 355

Harper, Colonel, 354

Harper, Ann (d. 1793), 354

Harris, George (d. 1793), Surveyor of Stamps, 354, 377

Harris, R. (fl. 1792–1795), printer, 116

Harris, Thomas (d. 1820), manager of Covent Garden, paymaster for Treasury, 27; friend of Rose, 42; attitude toward playwrights, 42; finances renovations, 92; provides room for "Beef-Steak Club," 92–93; fearful of Dudley's opera, 93; attacked by Merry, 94; encourages Mrs. Merry, 321; involved in patent snarl, 313; subscribes to True Briton's charity, 423; mentioned, 324

Harrison, James, 312, 312–313

Hartman, Isaac (fl. 1790–1808), banker in Liverpool, 33

Haslewood, Joseph (1769–1833), antiquarian and poet, 169, 334

Hastie, Archibald, reformer from Paisley, 453

Hastings, 90

Hastings, Warren (1732–1818), administrator (Governor General of India 1772–1784), impeachment of, 7; defended by Ministerial papers, 49, 291; pitied by World, 49, 365, 377, 397, 430; pitied by Oracle, 155, 242; Burke abused for persecution of, 186, 299; Plumer counsel for, 207; counsel for rewarded by Government, 290; testifies, 290, 291; Burke's attack on, 292; defended by Morning Post, 377–378, 430; see also Scott, Major John

Hastings, trial of, begun, 7; inevitable outcome, 7; damaging to George III, 7; presided over by Thurlow, 18; Burke's negotiations respecting, 8, 181, 186; unpopularity of, 7, 241; protested by World, 26, 291, 402; protested by Oracle, 181; regretted by St. James's Chronicle, 221; embarrassing to Government, 241; Pitt's inability to end, 241; prolongation not chargeable to Burke, 241; inquiry into means of expediting, 242; sessions begun before Burke arrives, 242; attended by Burke, 289; mocked by renewal of charter of East India Company, 290; ridiculed by Ministerial papers, 290; inquiry into cause of prolongation moved for by Burke, 291; of interest only to Burke, 291; debates on resumption of hearings, 291, 291–292, 292; changes in Lords since beginning of, 354, 402; testimony of Middleton, 386, 444; prevents Burke from accepting post in Ireland, 402

Hawke, Martin Bladen, 2nd Baron [GB] (1744–1805; suc. 1781), 85

Hawkesbury, Charles Jenkinson, 1st Baron [GB] (1729–1808; cr. 1786; DCL Oxford 1773; Clerk of the Pells [I] 1775–1808; President of the Board of Trade 1786–1804; Chancellor of the Duchy of Lancaster 1786–1803; Collector of Island customs), list of places, 132; supports war, 221; supports Traitorous Correspondence Bill, 263; influence in Cabinet resented by Pitt, 295; aided by Jenkinson, 296; responsible for war, 352; emoluments, 401; examines lists of visitors to Newgate, 465

Haydn (1732–1809), 43

Hayes, Mr., Welsh judge, 428

Haymarket, nature of patent, 42; management, 42; politics of, 42, 43, 93, 324; earlier difficulties with press, 43; Mrs. Wells a performer at, 90; adjustment of Colman's salary, 92, 93–94; produces Mrs. Inchbald's *Young Men and Old Women*, 93; refuses to employ Mrs. Merry, 93; building leased to Sheridan, 95; Colman's scruples regarding, 95–96; produces Colman's *The Mountaineers*, 318; opens under Drury Lane patent, 318, 322, 323; productions, 324–325, 328; mentioned, 100

Headline, 346, 368

Hearne and Pearce, lawyers, 281

Hendy, Mr., a workman, 325

Henry V, King of England (1387–1422; suc. 1413), 362

Henry IV, King of France (1553–1610; suc. 1589), 181

Hereford, High Steward of, 105

Heriot, John (1760–1833), novelist and journalist, early career, 27–28; helps Government imprison John Walter, 29, 378, 416, 456; quarrels with John Bell, 29, 118–119; writes for *World*, 26, 29, 69, 118, 119; publishes work on Gibraltar, 69; disliked, 118–119; edits *Sun*, 118, 119, 170; Treasury payments to, 170–171; edits *True Briton*, 171; invents stories, 298; has priority of news, 378; owns *Sun*, 415; refuses to sell *Sun* to Stuart, 415; attacked by *Morning Post*, 416; subscribes to *True Briton*'s charity, 423; complains to Nepean about coddling of *The Times*, 448; flailed by Daniel Stuart in *Peace and Reform*, 469; quoted, 118, 119

Heriot, Mrs. John (d. 1833), 423

Hertford, Francis Seymour-Conway, Earl of Yarmouth and 1st Marquess of [GB] (1718–1794; cr. 1793; cr. Earl of Hertford 1750; KG 1757; Lord Lieutenant of County Warwick 1757–1794), 352, 428

Hesse-Cassel, 297, 304

Hesse-Cassel, Landgrave of, *see* William IX

Hessians, 298, 402

Hewardine, William, journalist, 27, 29

Hicks, Mr., proprietor of *Morning Post*, 35, 68

Hoare, Prince (1755–1834), playwright and painter, 325

Hobart, Robert (1760–1816; styled Lord 1793–1804; Chief Secretary to Lord Lieutenant of Ireland 1789–1793; MP Lincoln 1790–1796; PC [GB] 1793; Governor of Madras 1793–1797), added to Privy Council, 293; expected to resign as Chief Secretary in favor of Burke, 402; appointed Governor of Presidency of Madras, 431, 458; pensioned as Chief Secretary, 458

Hodgson, William (1745–1851), medical doctor, writer, and reformer, 403, 435, 453

Hodson, Mr., lawyer, 138

Hodson, the Rev. William W. (1743–1793), educator and playwright (Vice Master, Trinity College, Cambridge 1789–1793), 106, 354

Hog's Wash, 447–448

Holcroft, Thomas (1745–1809), dramatist, novelist, reformer, 42, 93

Holland, Dumouriez expected to attack, 145; French designs on, 148; defense of opposed by Fox, 148–149, 183, 211; guaranteed navigation of the Scheldt, 173; indifferent to violation of treaty, 173; essential to balance of power, 210; Britain obligated to protect, 210; will fight for independence, 210; mention of surprising to newspapers, 214; France declares war on, 217, 218; Britain sends ships to, 217; not forced into war, 222; Duke of York's departure for, 225, 232; Hanoverians dispatched to, 243; defended by Prussians, 243; refuses to fight, 243; overrun by French, 258; rumored evacuation by French, 258; occupied by British, 298; invaded by

Dumouriez, 302; lethargy denounced by newspapers, 375; blamed for state of the war, 414; *see also* Dutch

Holland, Henry (1746?–1806), architect, architect for Carlton House, 12; architect for Brighton pavilion, 14; increases estimated cost of Drury Lane theater, 94, 313; completes plans for Drury Lane, 322; settles quarrel with workmen, 325; promises completion of Drury Lane by 1794, 325, 326, 327

Holland, Henry Richard Fox, 3rd Baron [GB] (1773–1840; suc. 1774), 10, 79, 212–213

Holland, William, bookseller, 152, 234, 279, 342, 343, 439

Holland, Mrs. William (d. 1793), 342

Holman, Joseph George (1764–1817), actor at Covent Garden, 42, 88, 96, 312

Holt, Daniel, bookseller, 343, 443

Home Office, changes in personnel, 115–116; employs Watt as spy, 116; employs Charles Stuart, 116; cooperates with The Association, 136; controls newspapers, 170; gives priority of news to *The Times*, 378; patronage of, 396; Stuart's letters to, 432–433; probable subsidizer of *Public Advertiser*, 468; mentioned, 293; *see also* Dundas, Henry

Home Secretary, rumored to be Burke, 204; rumored to be Windham, 221, 295–296; rumored to be Auckland, 294–295; rumored to be Carlisle, 295; rumored to be Cornwallis, 296; rumored to be Addington, 392, 394, 396; rumored to be Mansfield, 396

Home visits, 136, 141, 251, 252

Hood, Samuel, 1st Baron [I] (1724–1816; cr. 1782), politician and naval officer (MP Westminster 1784–1788; MP Reigate 1789–1790; MP Westminster 1790–1796; Vice Admiral 1787; Lord of the Admiralty 1788–1795; Commander in Chief at Portsmouth 1791–1793; Commander of Channel Fleet 1793; Commissioner for Toulon 1793; Commander in Chief in the Mediterranean 1793–1794), sued by Frost for expenses incurred in 1788 election, 50, 64, 65, 231, 276, 278; embarrassments regarding 1788 election, 64; occupies Toulon, 389; declaration to Toulonese, 389–390, 397; rumored to become First Lord of the Admiralty, 394; Commissioner for Toulon, 397; rumored to be created British peer, 401: sues Tooke for expenses in 1790 election, 401; Frost charged with further expense for 1788 election, 463

Hopetoun, James Hope, 3rd Earl of [S] (1741–1816; suc. 1781; Representative Peer 1784–1790; commanded Hopetoun Fencibles 1793), 254, 285

Horse racing, 163–164

Horsham Strong House, 397

Horsley, Samuel, *see* Rochester, Bishop of

Horton, Lady, operator of faro table, 331

"Houghing," 392

House, Harry, 237

Howard, G., surgeon at Middlesex Hospital, 462

Howard, Henry (1757–1843), genealogist, 237

Howard, Walter (1759–1830?), contestant for Norfolk title, 445

Howe, Richard, 1st Viscount [GB] (1726–1799; cr. 1782), naval officer (Elder Brother of Trinity House 1787–1796; cr. Baron Howe and Earl Howe [GB] 1788 with sp. rem. of Baronage to daughters; Vice Admiral of Great Britain 1792–1796; Commander in Chief of Grand Fleet 1793–1797), assumes command of Grand Fleet, 209, 226, 297, 305; searches for French fleet, 360, 376; rumored capture of French fleet, 413–414, 431, 455; returns to port, 456–457; ridiculed by Opposition papers, 455, 456–457

Huddersfield, 271

Hudson, William, *see* Hodgson, William

Hudson, William W. (1730?–1793), botanist, 354

Hughes, Miss, common-law wife of Joseph Holman, 88, 312

Hughes, Sir Edward (1720?–1794), naval officer and philanthropist, 455

Hughes, John (1677–1720), dramatist, 281

Hulse, Samuel, 3rd Baronet (1747–1837; suc. 1759), military officer (Major c. 1785; Treasurer and Receiver General for Prince of Wales 1787–1806; Major General 1793), general background, 18; functions as Treasurer to Prince of Wales, 60, 130, 202; leaves for Holland, 225

Huntingdon, Recorder of, 105

Hurlstone, Thomas Y. (fl. 1790–1795), playwright and journalist, 23, 312

"Hush money," 21, 179

Hyde Park, Ranger and Keeper of, 132

Ideson, Luke, 252

Inchbald, Mrs. Elizabeth (1753–1821), playwright, 93, 100, 312

Inchiquin, Murrough O'Brien, 5th Earl of [I] (1726–1808; suc. 1777; KT 1783; DCL Oxford 1793), 289, 349

Independent companies, 187, 188, 224, 227

India, Burke's early protests regarding management of, 289–290; Governor General of, 105, 431, 458; war in, 53, 147; mentioned, 241, 291, 292, 394; see also East India Affairs and East India Company

Insolvent Debtors Bill, introduced by Rawdon, 231, 254, 264; said unnecessary, 254; provisions of, 254; debates on, 254; unwelcome to Pitt, 254, 255; progress of, 286; newspaper reactions to, 286–287; defeated, 287

Insurrection, phantom, rumors regarding, 138–140, 142–144; inquiry into demanded, 147; intended as preparation for war, 147, 149, 235–236; denounced as trick, 148–149; intended to separate Fox from Friends of the People, 149; obfuscated by Alien Bill, 153; Paine and Perry tried in wake of, 197; invented by Government, 235, 236; proved by

summoning militia, 248; splits Opposition, 399; mentioned, 219, 411, 421

"Intention" as factor in libel, 280, 286

Invasion, alarm of, 411, 412, 413, 432

Ireland, Prince of Wales's popularity in, 15; Treasury writers in, 30; commotions, 144; rumors of arrests, 179; Government's blundering in, 194; as liability in event of war, 194–195, 196, 232; spared Dundas's agitators, 195; new indictments in, 214; situation in, 232–233; Traitorous Correspondence Bill not applicable to, 260; fresh trouble in, 275; rumored invasion of, 298; "houghing" of soldiers in, 392; unpopularity of Pitt's toadies in, 440; mentioned, 434

Ireland, Chief Secretary of, 431, 458

Ireland, Lord Chancellor of, 132, 429

Ireland, Lord High Treasurer of, 350

Ireland, Lord Lieutenant of, 296, 297, 353, 354, 402, 431, 440–441

Irish, 194, 195

Irish Attorney General, 214

Irish Catholics, 194–195, 232

Irish Defenders, 277

Irish Government, 276

Irish Parliament, 15, 180, 214

Irish Society, Governor of, 354

Irish Volunteers, 276, 277

Irvine, 271

Island Customs, Collector of, 132, 401

Italy, 210, 468

Jackson, Cyril (1746–1819), educator (Dean of Christ Church, Oxford 1783–1809), 350

Jackson, Samuel, Manchester chapman and reformer, 408

Jackson, the Rev. William (1737?–1795), journalist and bon vivant, 23, 165, 176

"Jacobin," as synonym for reformer, 141

Jamaica, 115, 284, 362, 376

J'Anson, W. (fl. 1787), 114

Jarvis, John (fl. 1783–1793), printer, 434

Jealous, Mr., officer of Bow Street police station, 349

Jekyll, Joseph (1754–1837), wit, lawyer, politician (MP Calnes 1787–1816; FRS, FSA 1790), 222, 223, 245

Jemappes, Austrians defeated at, 134; called "glorious victory," 157, 211, 299, 301, 303, 305, 306, 310

Jenkinson, Robert Banks (1770–1828), politician (MP Rye 1790–1803; Commissioner for Indian Affairs 1793–1799), buys newspaper puffs, 20; maiden speech praised, 53–54; supports Alien Bill, 182; opposes Fox's resolutions on conduct of war, 223; opposes Grey's motion for reform, 272; assists Hawkesbury, 296; appointed to Board of Control, 295, 296, 297; supposed author of pamphlet on Poland, 347

Jennings, Henry Constantine (1731–1819), art collector and reformer, 432

Jenour, Joshua (1755–1853), printer, journalist, and pamphleteer, 31, 165

Jerdan, William (1782–1869), journalist and miscellaneous writer, 116, 118

Jerningham, Edward (1727–1812), poet and playwright, 282, 311, 320

Jersey, 446

Jockey Club, 17, 36, 187

Johnson (or Johnston), Mr., banker, 255, 256

Johnson, Mrs. Elizabeth (fl. 1787–1798), printer and editor, 37

Johnson, Joseph (1738–1809), bookseller, 102, 276, 311

Johnson, Dr. Samuel (1709–1784), 150

Jones, Inigo (1573–1652), architect, 323

Jones, Robert, constable, 470, 471

Jordan, Mrs. Dorothy (1761–1816), actress at Drury Lane and mistress of Duke of Clarence, background, 15, 16, 42; preyed on by extortionists, 87; called "Little Pickle," 87; delivers premature child, 87; Clarence's concern for, 300; quarrels with Kemble, 314–315; appeals to Sheridan, 314–315; championed by Oracle, 315; makes seasonal debut in Anna, 315–316; abused by Ministerial papers, 364, 370,

393, 410; pregnant, 414, 458; supposed editor of newspaper, 458; apprentices daughter to milliner, 458–459

Jordan, J. S., bookseller, publishes trial of Smith vs. Rose, 63; publishes volumes of state papers, 74; indicted for publishing Rights of Man, 81, 420; trial of postponed, 74; pleads guilty, 99; supports Government, 343; publishes History of France, 343, 420; possible proprietor of Courier, 420

Journalists, see Newspapermen

"Julia," 177

"Junius," 465

Juries, "packed," 200

Jury, trial by, 403

Kay, T., publisher, 433

Kearsley, George (d. 1790), bookseller, 342

Keats, Richard Goodwin (1757–1834), naval officer, 262

Kemble, John Philip (1757–1823), actor and theatrical manager, manages Drury Lane, 42; at Edinburgh theater, 95; salary, 96; Colman's distrust of, 95–96; quoted on Burke's dagger scene, 182; quarrels with Mrs. Jordan, 314–315; conduct at production of Anna, 315–316; assailed by Oracle over production of Mrs. Robinson's opera, 316; assailed by Oracle over treatment of Mrs. Bateman, 316–317; performs in Colman's The Mountaineers, 318; inspects Drury Lane theater, 322; mentioned, 324

Kempshot, 128, 129, 260

Kentucky, 423

Kenyon, Lloyd, 1st Baron [GB] (1732–1802; cr. 1788), judge (Chief Justice of King's Bench 1788–1802), presides at trial of Mackintosh vs. Stuart, 67; disbars lawyers, 71, 228, 230, 254, 345, 453; apologizes to Tattersall, 97–98; orders jury to find for Rose in Rose vs. Tattersall and Williams, 98; gives furious instructions to jury in case of

Kenyon, Lloyd (con't).
Cavan vs. Tattersall, 98; not admired
by papers, 99; presides at trial of Paine,
152; later supporter of *True Briton*,
171; called "the moral Judge," 230;
considers sentences of Symonds and
Ridgway, 268; releases Almon on
probation, 276; nonsuits Ashley in
Ashley vs. Harrison, 312; presides at
trial of Eaton, 344; orders jury to find
Morning Chronicle guilty, 452–453;
mentioned, 229
Kilmarnock, 271
King, John (1760–1830), politician
(Under Secretary of State for Home
Department 1792–1806), 115–116
King, John, called "Jew" (fl. 1775–1798),
banker and journalist, background, 33,
196; politics, 33, 196; edits *Argus*, 32,
33, 84; sues Walter, 24, 32; cautious
respecting Pitt, 96; later publications,
113–114; persecutions, 113–115;
defects, 146; letters to Paine, 196, 222–
223, 224, 260–261
King's Bench Prison, plot to blow up,
101, 198, 225, 435, 438; loyalty address
by inmates of, 225; conditions in, 285,
435; debtors in, 464
King's College, Aberdeen, Chancellor of,
352
King's Counsel, 278, 290; *see also* Crown
Lawyers
King's Haymarket, *see* Opera House
Kingston-on-Thames, High Steward of,
132
Kinnaird, George, 7th Baron [S] (1754–
1805; suc. 1767; FSA 1784), banker and
Chairman of British Fire Office, 73,
285
Kinnoull, Robert Auriol Hay-Drum-
mond, Baron Hay of Pedwardine [GB]
and 10th Earl of [S] (1751–1804; suc.
1787; DCL Oxford 1793), 211, 263,
285, 349
Kipling, Thomas (d. 1822), divine
(deputy Regius Professor of Divinity,
Cambridge University), 278

Kirby, Mr., Keeper of Newgate, 436, 445,
446, 464
Kirkcaldy, 271
Klunert, 257
Knight, Robert (1768–1855), 237
Knox, the Rev. Vicesimus (1752–1821),
preacher, educator, and miscellaneous
writer (Head Master Tunbridge
School), 347, 372, 373, 374
Kosciusko, Thaddeus (1746–1817), Polish
general, 189

"L.," *see* More, Mrs. Hannah
Lade, Sir John (1759–1838; suc. as 2nd
Baronet 1759), roué, 17, 57, 225, 372
Lade, Lady Letitia Darby (d. 1825; m.
Sir John Lade c. 1789), 17, 374
Lafayette (1757–1834), held by Austrians
189; *Courier* pleads for release of, 189;
said to have betrayed French Royal
Family, 206; contrasted with Du-
mouriez, 302; blamed for death of
Louis XVI, 391; rumored death of,
391; hero to Opposition papers, 391
Lake, Gerard (1744–1808), army officer
(First Equerry to Prince of Wales
1787–1808; MP Aylesbury 1790–1802;
Major General 1790; Deputy Governor
of Berwick 1793–1794), 18, 60, 225, 368
Lake, Warwick (c. 1743–1821), manager of
Prince of Wales's stables, 18
Lamb, Charles (1775–1834), 28
Lambart, Lady Elizabeth, 65–66, 97, 99,
331–332; *see also* Cavan, Elizabeth
Davies Lambart, Dowager Countess of
Lambert, John (fl. 1791–1810), printer,
34, 215, 447, 452–453, 454
Lambeth, 427
Lambton, William Henry (1764–1797),
politician (MP Durham 1787–1797),
adheres to left wing of Opposition, 10;
on first secretarial committee of Friends
of the People, 73; founder of Friends of
the People, 79; supports Fox's resolutions on conduct of the war, 223;
supports inquiry into seditious activities, 236; postpones motion regarding

peers' interference in elections, 284; intercedes on behalf of Mrs. Bateman, 317

Lancaster, Chancellor of Duchy of, 132, 401; Lord Lieutenant of, 133; mentioned, 408

Lane, George (fl. 1793–1838), journalist, 335, 338, 338–339, 339

Lane, William (1745?–1814), publisher, 37

Lanesborough, Brinsley Butler, 2nd Earl of [I] (1728–1797; suc. 1768), 33

Lanesborough, Lady Jane Isabella (1737–1828), 33

Lansdowne, William Petty, 1st Marquess of [GB] (1737–1805; cr. 1784; suc. as 3rd Earl Shelburne [I] 1753; KG 1782; First Lord of the Treasury 1782–1783), Government ousted by Fox-North coalition, 9; political affiliations, 10, 209; early patron of William Cook, 28; opposes Address of Thanks, 147; opposes augmentation of forces, 211; character and interest of newspapers in, 212–213; disliked by Whigs, 213; intimacy with Lauderdale, 213; opposes Address on declaration of war, 221; shaken by Portland's support of war, 222; returns four members to Parliament, 240; opposes Traitorous Correspondence Bill, 263, 265; early patron of Pitt, 309; slurred by True Briton, 309

Lara, Deborah, 33

"Large Ox, The," 104

Larkens (or Larkins), William (d. 1800), army officer with East India Company, 28

Lauderdale, James Maitland, 8th Earl of [S] (1759–1839; suc. 1789; manager of trial of Hastings; Representative Peer 1790–1796), character and background, 10; political position, 10; incessantly abused by Ministerial papers, 49, 80, 84, 101, 180, 263–264, 348, 369, 398; no purchaser of puffs, 60; returns from France, 49; finances Oracle, 60; possible connection with volumes of state papers, 74; original sponsor of Friends of the People, 72, 79; finances Daniel Stuart's services for Friends of the People, 74, 336; moderating influence on Friends of the People, 75, 80; quarrels with Duke of Richmond, 82; sneers at Arnold, 82; opposes Proclamation against Seditious Writings, 82; fights duel with Arnold, 85; denounces camp at Bagshot, 103; departs for France, 101, 117; puffed by Oracle, 117; returns from Continent, 130; cancels support of Oracle, 130, 166; champions election reforms, 140; blamed for murder of Louis XVI, 190; said to have dined with Dumouriez, 206; opposes augmentation of forces, 211, 212; quarrels with Loughborough, 212; derided as friend of Brissot, 212, 218; defends friendship with Brissot, 212; applauded by Morning Chronicle, 213; intimate with Lansdowne, 213; called Jacobin by Dundas, 218; opposes Address on declaration of war, 220–221; weeps at Portland's support of the war, 220, 221–222; moves amendment to end the war, 221; says people duped into war, 226; called agent of French, 238; supposed holdings in France jeopardized by Traitorous Correspondence Bill, 250, 261, 398; opposes Traitorous Correspondence Bill, 263; submits petitions from Berry and Robertson, 286; disturbed by abuse in Sun and True Briton, 335; near-duel with Richmond, 335; interests represented by Morning Post, 335–336; said to control Morning Post, 336; evidence of involvement in Morning Post, 335–336, 339, 340; tenure of lease on Morning Post, 339, 346; assists Courier, 346–347; protests votes of British peers in Scots election, 358; Clarence refuses alliance with, 367; prepares Glasgow petition, 369; presents Glasgow petition, 392, 397; expected to protest Muir's sentence, 409; attends Fox's

Lauderdale, James Maitland (con't). anniversary dinner, 409; attends British Convention, 336, 434; visits Muir, 461; requests detention of Muir and Palmer, 461; uneasy respecting trials of delegates to British Convention, 469; mentioned, 244, 285, 358

"Laura" and "Laura Maria," see Robinson, Mrs. Mary

La Vendée, 258, 297, 390, 456

Law, Edward (1750–1818), lawyer and politician (KC 1787; principal counsel for Warren Hastings; King's Attorney and Sergeant for County of Palantine 1793–1802), 290

Law, Thomas (1759–1834), economist, 201, 208, 215, 233, 233–234, 236

Lawyers, practices of, 70–71; suits against newspapers, 70–71; suits for publication of illegal lottery schemes declared illegal, 71; disbarments of, 71, 228, 230, 254, 345, 445; castigated by newspapers, 179, 287, 453; exploitation of laws regarding debtors, 228; saddled with costs for suing on frivolous grounds, 230; practices in London, 230; lambasted by World, 230, 254, 286–287, 440, 445, 461, 464; urged by Treasury to sue booksellers, 236; increase in number of, 269, 285; accused of charging excessive fees in bankruptcy proceedings, 285, 344–345; denounced by Reynolds in How to Grow Rich, 312; provide Treasury with names of booksellers for prosecution, 342; disbarred for forgeries and briberies, 445; mentioned, 386, 461; see also Debt, laws respecting imprisonment for

"Learned Pig, The," 104

Le Brun, Pierre Henri Marie Tondu, called (1754–1793), French Foreign Minister, 189

Lee, Mr., lawyer, 355

Lee, Sophia (1750–1824), playwright, 91

Leeds, Francis Godolphin Osborne, 5th Duke of [GB] (1751–1799; suc. 1789; FRS 1773; FSA 1776; Lord Lieu-

tenant of East Riding, Yorkshire 1782–1799; Governor of Scilly Isles 1785–1799; Governor of the Lévant Company 1792–1799), 221, 423

Legal reforms, see Lawyers and Debt, laws respecting imprisonment for

Legge, Mr., 334, 427

Leicester, city of, 342, 415; Lord Lieutenant of, 132

Leicester Herald, 235, 346

Leinster, William Robert Fitzgerald, Viscount [GB] and 2nd Duke of [I] (1749–1804; suc. 1773; KP 1783), 180

Lemaitre, J. G. (fl. 1793–1803), reformer, 237

Le Mans, 456

Le Mesurier, Paul (1755–1805), merchant (MP Southwark 1784–1796; Lord Mayor of London 1793–1794), 370, 388, 446

Lennox, Charles (1764–1819), military officer and politician (secretary to Duke of Richmond 1784–1795; Colonel of Coldstream Guards 1788–1789; Lieutenant Colonel 35th Foot 1789–1803; MP Chichester 1790–1806), 4, 132, 395, 438

Leopold II, Emperor of Austria (1747–1792; suc. 1790), 54–55, 377

Letters to the People of North Briton, 267

Lettsom, John Coakley (1744–1815), physician and medical writer, 437, 442, 445

Lewis, William Thomas (1748?–1811), actor at Covent Garden, 42, 96, 312, 328

Lewis's Auction Room, 370

Leycester, Hugh (1750–1836), lawyer, 207

Libel Act, see Fox's Libel Bill

Lille, 359, 360

Lincelles, 368

Linley, Thomas, the elder (1732–1795), musical composer (Deputy Supervisor of Stamps 1793–1795), 430

Linlithgow, 271

Lisbon, 398

Little Haymarket, *see* Haymarket
"Little Pickle," *see* Jordan, Mrs. Dorothy
Liverpool, 187
Lloyd, Mr., apothecary, 439
Lloyd, Thomas, American lawyer, 439, 439–440, 445
Lloyd's Evening Post, title, colophon, politics, 26, 178; cancellation of Treasury subsidy, 178; on flannel waistcoats, 427; on trial of *Morning Chronicle*, 454; on Frost, 462–463; quoted, 187, 199, 202, 209, 214, 225, 227, 230, 231, 234, 242, 249, 258, 262, 263, 270, 289, 291, 297, 299, 312, 313, 343, 358, 363, 373, 384, 397, 405, 410, 411, 412, 415, 423–424, 426, 435, 444, 445, 447–448, 459, 460, 461; mentioned, 317, 331, 406
Loans, as means of financing the war, 246, 255; debates on, 257; negotiations for, 255–257; amounts of, 368
Locke, William, printer, first printer of *Observer*, 37, 317; sued by Dibdin, 88, 317; bankrupt, 435, 444; publishes *Bon Ton*, 444; sued by Mrs. Middleton, 444
Logan, Mr., a compositor, 317
Logographic Press, 24
London, 262, 364
London, City of, Opposition interests represented by Skinner, 35; as musical center, 42–43; police force controlled by Dundas, 81, 296; Comptroller of Customs of, 109; major crime in, 180; offers bounties for Navy enlistments, 187, 188, 227; Chamberlain of, 197; practices of lawyers in, 230; Le Mesurier elected Lord Mayor of, 370; holds elections for Remembrancer, 384–388, 417; elections influenced by Pitt, 385; sets up subscription for Spitalfields weavers, 455
London Chronicle, 37, 169
London Coffee House, 403, 435
London Constitutional Society, *see* Constitutional Society, London
London Corresponding Society, *see* Corresponding Society, London

London Courant, 86
London Evening Post, 26, 178
London Gazette, 27, 188, 198, 281, 294, 376, 391, 398, 414, 422
London Mercury, 26
London Packet, 26, 168, 178, 191, 209
London Recorder, 37, 169
London Tavern, 61, 244, 455
London Workhouse, Vice President of, 354
Long, Charles (1760–1838), politician (MP Rye 1789–1796; Joint Secretary of the Treasury 1791–1801; FRS 1792), supervises *The Times*, 24, 173; sends Combe to *The Times*, 28; patron of Miles, 29; unconcerned about France's subsidy of newspapers, 113; original proprietor of *Sun*, 118; has no sinecures, 132; handles monetary transactions for Treasury, 170; arranges free distribution of newspapers by Post Office, 172; mentioned, 5, 27
Longman and Co., 22
Lonsdale, James Lowther, 1st Earl of [GB] (1736–1802; cr. 1784; Colonel of Cumberland Militia, 1792), sues Evans, Bell, Wolcot, and Peter Stuart, 39, 55–56, 60–61, 66, 137, 231; employs Mingay as counsel, 135; commissioned Colonel of Cumberland militia, 141; got title for bringing Pitt into Parliament, 226; got title for promising ship during American war, 226; ship demanded by newspapers, 226, 357; disliked by press, 226; returns seven members to Parliament, 239; wants second title, 356–357; quarrels with Pitt over return of Anstruther, 357; sued by Wemyss, 357; litigations pending, 357
"Lorenzo," 20
Losh, James (1763–1833), lawyer, politician, and miscellaneous writer, 237
Loughborough, Alexander Wedderburn, 1st Baron [GB] (1733–1805; cr. 1780), lawyer and politician (Lord Chief Justice of Common Pleas 1780–1793;

Loughborough, Alexander (con't).
LL.D Dublin 1781; FRS, FSA 1787;
Lord Chancellor 1793–1801), supported
Sheridan and "New Whigs" during
Regency crisis, 14; threat to Lord
Thurlow during Regency crisis, 18;
early patron of Arthur Murphy, 29;
follower of Guilford, 10, 83, 105; ambitious to be Chancellor, 83, 399; offered
Chancellorship, 106; temporizes about
Chancellorship, 106; supports Proclamation against Seditious Writings, 106;
incident at Cambridge, 106; expected to
accept Chancellorship, 131; expected to
defect, 139; defection announced, 146,
180; strong supporter of Government,
155; accepts Chancellorship, 191, 204;
supposed conditions of acceptance, 191;
supports augmentation of forces, 211,
212; attacks Lauderdale, 212; ought to
relinquish salary for duration of war,
248; profits from bankruptcies, 269,
285, 307; on state of the prisons, 285–
286; opposes Insolvent Debtors Bill,
287; said won over by Dundas, 295;
ignores Fox's fund, 307; expected to
get earldom, 352; finds against
Lonsdale, 357; blamed for conduct
of war, 414–415; rewarded for support
of war, 428; gets sinecure for nephew,
428
Louis XIV, King of France (1638–1715;
suc. 1643), 417
Louis XVI, King of France (1754–1793;
suc. 1774), subscribes to new Constitution, 54; execution feared, 145; contrasted with Paine, 153; Sheridan's
concern for, 154; Burke blamed for
situation of, 155; contrasted with
Hastings, 155; imprisoned, 186; Chauvelin as representative of, 186; executed,
190, 204, 412; reactions to execution of,
190–191; execution expected to be
pretext for war, 190–191, 206; execution no proper reason for war, 192, 194,
210–211, 219; Sheridan as defender of,
192; defended by Marquis de Sillery,
192; execution not cited as reason for
war, 205, 206; execution as argument
for reform, 206; execution forgotten,
206; Nares's pamphlet on reign of,
206; execution result of French
"notions," 209, 210; execution caused
by Austria and Prussia, 210; French
resent grief over, 218; aftermath of
execution, 243; execution predicted by
Burke, 366; execution caused by
Lafayette, 391; Muir tried to prevent
execution, 406, 407; mentioned, 389
Louis XVII, King of France (1785–1795;
suc. nom. 1793), 259, 389, 390, 426,
429
Lovett, John, miscellaneous writer, 285
Lowndes, William, bookseller, 26
Loyalty addresses, 141, 180, 224–225
Loyalty oaths, 136, 141, 142, 180
Lukin, Robert (fl. 1773–1831), 350
Luttrell, Francis Fownes (1756–1823),
politician, 430
Lyons, 258, 421
Lys, 391

Macan, Thomas Townley (d. 1793), con-
vict, 198, 435, 438, 439, 442
McBride, John (d. 1800), naval officer
(Rear Admiral 1793), 259
M'Cullum, George, Manchester laborer
and reformer, 408
Macdonald, Sir Archibald (1747–1826;
knighted 1788), lawyer and politician
(MP Newcastle-under-Lyme 1780–
1793; Attorney General 1788–1793;
KC 1788; Lord Chief Baron of the
Exchequer 1793–1813; PC 1793), sends
notices of prosecution to Jordan and
Paine, 81; apologizes to Tattersall, 97;
co-operates with The Association, 136;
prepares seven indictments of printers
and publishers, 138; prepares two
hundred informations for prosecution,
149, 152, 198, 199, 236; supports
Address of Thanks, 149; prosecutes
Paine, 153; antagonizes newspapers,
179; prosecutes a "bill-sticker," 198;

activities impeded by Friends of the Liberty of the Press, 208; appointed Lord Chief Baron of Exchequer, 216; appointed to Privy Council, 216; mentioned, 98, 135, 198

M'Donnell, D. E. (fl. 1791–1808), journalist, 37, 76, 168, 169

M'Donnell, Thomas, Irish printer, 214

M'Intyre, John, Edinburgh schoolteacher and reformer, 434

Mackenzie, Francis Humberston (1754–1816), 414

Mackenzie, Henry (1745–1831), novelist and journalist, 424

Mackintosh, Catherine (Stuart), Mrs. James, 39

Mackintosh, James (1765–1832), pamphleteer, politician, journalist, lawyer, publishes *Vindiciae Gallicae*, 7, 40; supported by *Oracle*, 23, 111–112; contributor to *Morning Post*, 36, 339, 354; friend of Sheridan, 39; background, 39–40; character, politics, 40; relationship to Stuarts, 39; sues Charles Stuart, 67; connection with Friends of the People, 73, 76; honorary member of Constitutional Society, 73; *Letter to . . . Pitt*, 73, 99, 111; supposed author of Declaration for Friends of the People, 75; frightened by Proclamation against Seditious Writings, 99; travels in France, 111–112; possible aid in silencing *Argus*, 143; active in Friends of the Liberty of the Press, 155, 200, 237, 399; attacked by Burke, 219, 233; *Vindiciae* anticipates Godwin's *Political Justice*, 223; probably helped Daniel Stuart with *Peace and Reform*, 338; probable writer for *Oracle*, 339, 354; friend of Miss Harper, 354; friend of Thomas Christie, 405; related to Fraser, 67, 443; conducted old spurious *Star*, 468

Macleish, H. (fl. 1780–1794), printer, 37

Macleod, Norman (1754–1801), army officer and reformer (MP for Inverness-shire 1790–1796), member of Friends of the People, 140; cashiered from the Army, 140–141; castigated by the *World*, 146; supports inquiry into seditious practices, 236; provides bail for Rowan, 443; quits British Convention, 471

Mac Murray, John (1745–1793), publisher, 37, 166, 342

Macpherson, James (1736–1796), historian and miscellaneous writer, author of *A History of Great Britain* (London, 1775) (MP Camelford 1780–1796), 433

Macrae, C., printer, 33

M'Swyny, Bryan (d. 1819), printer, 116

Madras, Governor of the Presidency of, 431, 458

Magdeburg, 391

Mainz, 297, 298, 359, 391

Maitland, Thomas (1759–1824), politician (MP Haddington Burghs 1790–1796), returns from France, 49; member of first secretarial committee of Friends of the People, 73; leaves for France with Lauderdale and Moore, 101; opposes Alien Bill, 182; defends Lauderdale against Dundas, 218; supports Fox's motions on conduct of war, 223; supports inquiry into seditious practices, 236; moves for expediting Hastings's trial, 241, 242; opposes Traitorous Correspondence Bill, 250; en route to Jamaica, 283–284; defended by *Gazetteer*, 283–284

Malmesbury, James Harris, 1st Baron [GB] (1746–1820; cr. 1788; KB 1779; DCL 1793), diplomat (envoy to Berlin 1793), 294, 349, 394, 428

Malone, Edmund (1741–1812), Shakespeare scholar, 130, 177, 350

Manchester, riots, 146, 152; reformers, 276, 408; petition for peace, 366

Manchester, William Montagu, 5th Duke of [GB] (1771–1843; suc. 1788), army officer (Lord Lieutenant of Hunts 1793–1841), 438, 442

Manchester Constitutional Society, 84

Manchester *Herald*, 235

Mann, Horatio, 2nd Baronet (1744–1814; suc. 1786), politician (MP Sandwich 1790–1807), 260, 262

Manners, Lady Catherine Rebecca (c. 1767–1852), poetess, 281, 311

Manners, William, 1st Baronet (1766–1833; cr. 1793), 311

Mansfield, Mr., Mayor of Leicester, 415

Mansfield, David Murray, 7th Viscount Stormont [S] and 2nd Earl of [GB] (1727–1796; suc. as Viscount 1748; suc. as Earl 1793; KT 1768; DCL Oxford 1793), diplomat (Representative Peer 1754–1793, 1794–1796; Lord Justice General of Scotland 1778–1794; Keeper of the Scoon 1778–1796; Chancellor of Marischal College, 1793–1796; Joint Chief Clerk of Pleas in Court of King's Bench 1793–1796), follower of 2nd Earl of Guilford, 10, 105; bribed by Pitt, 106; supports Proclamation against Seditious Writings, 106; list of places and sinecures, 133, 263; supports Address of Thanks, 147; supports Alien Bill, 155; strong defender of Government, 155, 263; supports augmentation of forces, 211–212; supports Address of Thanks on declaration of war, 220; succeeds as Earl Mansfield, 262–263; votes twice, 262, 263, 358; appointed Joint Chief Clerk of the Pleas, 263; elected Chancellor of Marischal College, 263, 352; DCL Oxford, 349; robbed, 350; considered for Home Secretary, 396

Mansfield, Louisa, Countess of (1758–1843; suc. 1793), 262–263

Mansfield, William Murray, 1st Earl of [GB] (1705–1793; cr. 1776, 1792; LL.D. Glasgow 1754), 106, 262, 263

"Mansfield's Ghost," 269

Maps, 165, 359, 450–451

Mara, Madame Gertrude Elizabeth (1749–1833), German singer in England, 43, 96, 312, 312–313, 313

Mara, John, cellist, 312

Marat, Jean Paul (1744–1793), French revolutionist, 290, 359, 366, 377; see also Dagger scene

Marchmont, Hugh Hume-Campbell, 3rd Earl of [S] (1708–1794; suc. 1740; FRS 1753; Keeper of Great Seal of Scotland 1764–1794), 191

Maret, Hugues-Bernard, Duc de Bassano (1763–1827), French diplomat, 209, 217

Margarot, Maurice (d. 1816), French reformer in England, delivers opening address to Corresponding Society, 72; active in Corresponding Society, 135; steward for dinner of Constitutional Society, 268; helps to plan British Convention, 268; escapes arrest, 276; harangues Corresponding Society, 432; delegate from Corresponding Society to British Convention, 432; reaches Edinburgh, 434; arrested, 448, 453, 459, 460; released on bail, 453, 460

Margate, 99, 112, 330

Marie Antoinette, Queen of France (1755–1793), tries to escape, 54; diamond earrings, 126–127; libeled by Lord George Gordon, 229, 436, 437; rumors of execution, 258, 298, 359–360; Burke's eulogy of, 366; moved to prison, 377; tried, 389; executed, 412

Marischal College, Aberdeen, 104–105, 263, 352

Marlborough, George Spencer, 4th Duke of [GB] (1739–1817; suc. 1758; DCL Oxford 1763; FRS 1768; KG 1768; Lord Lieutenant of Oxon 1760–1817), 239–240

Marplay, John, stockbroker, 103

Marriages, newspaper interest in, 353

Marseille, 259

Masons' Lodge, Edinburgh, 434, 448

Mathews, Mr., journalist, 26

Maubege, 359, 413

Mayne, John (1759–1836), poet and journalist, 37, 166

Mazarin, Jules (1602–1661), French Cardinal and Prime Minister, 178

Mead, William (1628–1713), Quaker reformer, 280

Meadows, Mr., Commissioner of Stamp Office, 430

Meath, Custos Rotulorum of, 352

Mecklenburg-Strelitz, Princess Louise of (1776–1810; m. Frederick William III of Prussia 1793), 16, 331

Medows, Sir William (1738–1813), military officer (Lieutenant General 1793), 373

Melbourne, Peniston Lamb, 1st Viscount [I] (1744–1828; cr. 1781; MP Newport, Isle of Wight 1790–1793; Gentleman of Bedchamber to Prince of Wales 1783–1796), 59, 60

Menin, 391, 415

Mennons, John, Irish reformer, 215

Merlin, Mr., manufacturer of novelties, 455

Merry, Mrs. Elizabeth Brunton (1769–1808), actress, marriage to Robert Merry, 39; actress at Covent Garden, 42; dismissed from Covent Garden, 93; dropped as member of "Beef-steak Club," 93; applies to Haymarket, 93; travels on Continent, 93, 94; visits Covent Garden, 94; applies to Covent Garden, 94; moves to Bath, 94–95; thought to be pregnant, 164; encouraged by Harris, 321; performs in Norwich, 321; thought to have retired to Switzerland, 321; moves to Scarborough, 321

Merry, Robert (1755–1798), poet, journalist, early publications as "Della Crusca," 19, 25; contributor to Morning Post, 36, 93, 94, 169, 275, 334; background, politics, character, 39; early member of Friends of the People, 76, 93; The Magician No Conjuror performed at Covent Garden, 92; dropped as playwright by Covent Garden, 93; dropped as member of "Beef-steak Club," 93; travels on Continent, 93, 94; visits Covent Garden, 94; attacks Harris on behalf of his wife, 94; moves to Bath,

94; returns to Continent, 94–95; settles near Norwich, 275, 321; rumored retirement to Switzerland, 321; moves to Scarborough, 321; friendship with Topham, 321; politics, 321; author of letter signed "Philo-Pitti," in Morning Post, 334; starts for Continent with Pigott, 335

Meuse, 134

Microcosm, 54

Middlesex, Custos Rotulorum of, 296, 356; Lord Lieutenant of, 296, 356

Middlesex Hospital, 327, 462

Middlesex Justices Act, 72, 81, 115, 180

Middleton, Mrs., 386

Middleton, Nathaniel (d. 1807), employee of East India Company, 444

"Miles," 250

Miles, William Augustus (1753?–1817), political writer and minor diplomat, contributor to The Times, 24; Treasury writer, 27; early career and salary, 29; informs Long of Treasury subsidies to newspapers, 113; contributor to Sun, 118; adjustment of salary, 132, 430; payments by Treasury, 170; confers with M. Maret, 209; invents stories for True Briton, 298; publishes The Conduct of France, 430; quoted, 118, 217

Millan, Buchanan (fl. 1788–1795), printer, 23, 117, 118, 170

Milner, Isaac (1750–1820), mathematician and divine (Vice Chancellor of Cambridge University and Dean of Carlisle), 235, 277, 278

Minden, battle of, 6, 104

Mingay, James (1752–1812), lawyer, represents Mackintosh in Mackintosh vs. Stuart, 67; represents Lonsdale in Lonsdale vs. Bell, Stuart, Evans, and Wolcot, 135; attorney for World, 135; joins Whig Club, 135; member of Friends of the People, 184; defeated as MP for Thetford, 184, 221; identified with Friends of the Liberty of the Press, 253; rumored to be emigrating to America, 253; represents Harrison in

Mingay, James (con't).
Ashley and Mara vs. Harrison, 312;
represents Dibdin in Dibdin vs. Swan
and Bostock, 318
Mitchell, Rob, lawyer (fl. 1776–1794), 35,
36
Mitford, Sir John (1748–1830; knighted
1793), lawyer (MP Beeralston 1788–
1799; KC 1789; Solicitor General
1793–1799), 216
Modern Patriotism, 239
Moira, Francis Rawdon-Hastings, 1st
Baron Rawdon [GB] and 2nd Earl of
[I] (1754–1826; cr. Baron Rawdon
1783; suc. as Earl of Moira 1793;
FRS 1787; FSA 1793), army officer
(ADC to George III 1782–1793; Major
General 1793), intimate of Prince of
Wales, 18, 209; supports Proclamation
against Seditious Writings, 82; member
of *ad hoc* committee for payment of
Prince of Wales's debts, 126; urges
Prince to economize, 127; supports
Opposition on Address of Thanks, 148;
confers with Prince of Wales, 207;
defection announced, 209, 424; not
converted by Prince of Wales, 213, 254;
concerned about debtors, 230; warned
by *Oracle*, 230; elected FSA, 264;
sponsors Insolvent Debtors Bill, 264,
287; trusted by newspapers, 286, 287;
succeeds to earldom, 287; refuses to
join Government, 425; mentioned as
Lord Lieutenant of Ireland, 431, 440–
441; exhorted by newspapers to continue legal reforms, 440, 441; urged by
George III to take office, 441; concerned for popularity, 441; rumored to
have left for the Continent, 446; *see
also* Insolvent Debtors Bill
Mollenir, C., printer, 37
Monaghin, Governor and Custos Rotulorum of, 133
Moniteur, 219
Monmouth, Lord Lieutenant of, 132
Montagu, Frederick (1733–1800), lawyer
and politician (DCL Oxford 1793), 349

Monthly Communications, 178
Montrose, 271
Moore, Dr. John (1729–1802), medical
doctor and man of letters, 101, 117
More, Mrs. Hannah (1745–1833), dramatist, novelist, philanthropist, 167
Morning Chronicle, history, 34; proprietors and conductors, 34, 167, 169, 338;
printer, 34, 167; address, 34, 167;
personnel, 23, 39, 163, 167, 264, 419;
character, 35, 163, 167, 338, 347, 376;
politics, 35, 80, 126, 166; subsidy, 34,
38, 166; Government's cautions regarding, 22, 35, 377, 447; influence of, 167;
financial state of, 167, 419; attitude
toward, 447; inventor of editorial, 167;
connection with *Star*, 120, 166, 167;
echoed by *Gazetteer*, 347, 468; attitude
toward George III, 4; on *Baviad*, 20;
champion of peace, 54; on death of
Leopold II, 55; on sale of Prince of
Wales's stud, 58; on removal of Rose,
65; on Middlesex Justices Act, 72; on
taxes and the national debt, 103; on
Pitt's seizure of Cinque Ports, 108,
108–109; said to be paid by French,
113; on Dundas, 116, 180, 270; on the
Sun, 118, 120, 378; on Government's
indifference to developments, 121; on
Porson, 123; opposes Fox-Pitt coalition, 126; on Prince of Wales's economies, 127; on corruptive use of patronage, 131–133, 187–188; on harassments
of Drury Lane, 137; on phantom insurrection, 149; attacked by *Sun*, 153;
on Portland's possible defection, 156,
297; supports Friends of the People,
166; indicted for libel, 168, 208, 215;
denounced as seditious, 167–168, 175,
180, 186, 199; on possibility of war,
179, 185, 186, 187–188, 188, 189, 190,
205–206; on Burke, 181, 182, 185, 253,
261–262, 283, 365, 366, 401–402;
blames Government for murder of
Louis XVI, 190; on Fox's *Letter*, 191,
205; on Loughborough's acceptance of
Chancellorship, 191; on George III's

interference in Irish affairs, 195; publishes Frost's letter to Pitt, 197–198; on Government's indictments, 199; on sale of Opposition papers, 199–200; on Topham's greed, 200; on Friends of the Liberty of the Press, 201, 237; publishes Law's letter to Reeves, 201, 208; on execution of Louis XVI as reason for war, 206; on Prince of Wales's colonelcy, 204, 208; on Garrow, 207; defends Lauderdale, 213; on Government's policy of insulting the French, 227; on vulnerability of trade, 227; publishes Muir's letter to Associated Friends of the People, 233; on Frend, 236, 277, 278; publicans warned to avoid, 236; on activities of The Association, 237, 341; denounced by Burke, 237; on emoluments of members of Government, 248; on financing the war, 255, 426; on Pitt's economics, 255; on bankruptcies, 255, 264, 269, 270, 285, 345, 391; on the loan, 255–257; on state of the war, 258, 259; on spies and informers, 263, 341–342; on actual sedition, 263; on petitions for election reforms, 270; on Eaton, 280; advertises British Library, 280; on prisons, 285; on Burke's absence from debates on East India Company charter, 289–290; on Duke of Richmond, 299, 361, 393, 412; on fund for paying Fox's debts, 300, 301, 306–311, 347, 348; on Fox's motion for peace, 302–303; on Dumouriez, 303; assaults on Rose and Burges, 302, 305, 347; assaults on *True Briton*, 306–311, 347, 348, 378; sources of information, 306, 347–348; on Clarence's repudiation of the war, 304–305; advertises Wordsworth's *Descriptive Sketches*, 311; on Madame Mara, 312; on Holman scandal, 312; on Drury Lane, 313, 314, 325–326, 327; on Jordan-Kemble quarrel, 316; on the "pad," 328; on gambling, 309, 331; on the Glasgow petition for peace, 335, 398; publishes Skirving's letter regarding Muir, 336, 406–407; publishes excerpts from *Peace and Reform*, 337, 471; on trials of talkers and booksellers, 341–342; publishes "The Calm Observer," 347; ridicules Hodson, 354; censured by *Oracle*, 360, 454; on crimping, 367–369; on camp at Brighton, 371–372, 372–373, 373–374; advertises Knox's sermon, 374; on Sardinia, 375; on lethargy of the Dutch, 375; on conduct of the war, 374–375, 375–376; on The Red Book, 376; on responsibility for the war, 376; supports Woodfall for City Remembrancer, 384–385, 387–388; on Toulon, 389; on responsibility for Dunkirk, 393, 397; on "fruits of conviction," 397, 401, 427–429, 458; on Pitt's ultimatum, 399–400, 409, 413, 421, 421–422; on Muir, 407, 408; on Palmer, 408; on alarms of invasion, 411; on prorogation of Parliament, 413; on "Pitt's Manifesto," 414, 421–422, 423, 424, 426; on financing war by private contributions, 426; tried for libel, 447, 452, 453, 454, 468; on British Convention, 460, 472; quoted, 49, 50, 74, 81, 99, 139, 168, 169, 171, 180, 187, 194, 216, 225, 226, 262, 270, 294, 295, 349, 421, 457; mentioned, 74, 331, 406, 417

Morning Herald, history, 22–23, 338; early experiment with maps, 165; proprietor, 22; Dudley's connection with, 174; editor and other personnel, 23, 41, 163; printers, 23, 174, 417; address, 22, 174; circulation, 23, 174, 379; character, 23, 163; publishes first fashion column, 165, 329; politics, 22, 333, 348, 379, 416; subsidized by Treasury, 22–23, 170, 174, 175, 333; patronized by Palmer of the Post Office, 61, 62, 87; involvement in Billington scandal, 86; attempts to blackmail Mrs. Jordan, 87, 364; criticizes *Sun*, 120; publishes John "Jew" King's Egham speech, 146, 196; scored by *True Briton*, 175; publishes John "Jew" King's correspondence

Morning Herald (con't).

with Paine, 196, 223, 224, 260; protests treatment of Lord George Gordon, 287; supports fund for paying Fox's debts, 348; quoted, 60, 66, 318, 362, 458

Morning Post, history, 15, 29, 35, 36, 114, 336, 338, 420; proprietors, 35–36, 68, 168–169, 334, 340, 452; editors, 37, 168, 169, 354; printers and address, 37, 66, 97–98, 168; personnel, 36, 39, 40, 41, 74, 93, 94, 169, 275, 334, 335, 336, 338–339; connection with *English Chronicle*, 37, 334; character, 163, 334, 338–339, 340; politics, 31, 36, 80, 335–336, 336–337, 468; evident security against prosecutions, 36; influence, 167; preoccupation with Westminster election under Sheridan's management, 49, 49–50, 50, 63, 64–65, 166; defends Prince of Wales, 52; charges Frost still unpaid, 64; sued by Rose, 65, 66, 72, 98; sued by Lady Cavan 65–66, 72; loses Charles Stuart, 66; advertised for sale, 66; financial affairs, 67–68; probable cost of indemnifying proprietors, 68–69, 333; conditions of indemnification, 69, 169, 333; attacks Harris on behalf of Mrs. Merry, 94; punished by Pitt, 96; pays Lady Lambart, 137–138; pays Rose, 138; prints excerpts from Erskine's defense of Paine, 152; assails *True Briton*, 171, 175, 310, 348, 455; on spies and informers, 179; on Burke, 181, 365, 366–367, 377, 386–387, 402, 430, 454, 470; appeals for aid to Poland, 189; on Prince of Wales, 214; publicans warned to avoid, 236; defends Scott in election briberies, 242; on Rose, 297, 353, 455, 457; admires Mrs. Robinson, 311, 312; on Dudley's opera, 320; champion of Mrs. Wells, 320–321, 321; assails Mrs. Esten, 322; on Drury Lane, 323, 324, 325, 326, 327; on faro tables, 331; apologizes to Lady Cavan and Lady Elizabeth Lambart, 331–332; institutes fund for "Indigent Manu-

facturers," 334; expiration of lease, 333, 339; later history of, 334, 340; changes in proprietary, 334; boasts of new arrangements, 335, 338; evidence of Daniel Stuart's management of, 336–339, 340–341; said to be owned by Lauderdale, 336; taunts *Sun*, 337, 415–416; acquaintance with radical activities, 336; publishes minutes of British Convention, 336, 434, 446, 447, 453, 454, 455, 459, 460–461; prints excerpts from Stuart's *Peace and Reform*, 336–337, 468, 471; advertises *Peace and Reform*, 337, 469; profits from stockjobbing, 337–338; Lauderdale's lease on, 335–336, 339, 340, 346; conjectures as to date of Stuart's purchase of, 339–341; publishes Skirving's letter, 336, 406–407; personnel after expiration of lease, 338–339; advertises sale of *Oracle*, 346; demands revision of bankrupt laws, 346; loose alliance with *Courier*, 346–347, 420, 468; on Oxford ceremonies, 350; on Lonsdale's promised ship, 357; on Murray's communiqués, 359; on Richmond, 361, 395, 412, 458; on Duke of Clarence, 364, 371, 414; subscription for Spitalfields weavers, 365, 427, 455; on Glasgow petition for peace, 366, 398; on eviction of Corresponding Society, 370, 404; on camp at Brighton, 362; holds Burke singly responsible for the war, 376, 377, 392, 397, 398, 401, 402, 414; on execution of Marie Antoinette, 377; defends Hastings, 377–378, 430; supports Woodfall, 383, 384, 385, 388; on state of the war, 391, 392, 414–415, 456; on unemployment, 391–392; on the prospective loan, 392; on responsibility for Dunkirk, 395, 414–415; on the reason for the war, 398, 457; expects Pitt to make peace, 401; supports reformers, 403–404; on nature of the trials, 403; on Muir, 407, 453, 461; on Palmer, 407–408, 461; on prorogation of Parliament, 413; on

Mrs. Jordan, 414, 458–459; protests treatment of Williamson, 420; blames Loughborough for conduct of war, 414–415; on the Cherokees' war against the United States, 423; on possible Pitt-Portland coalition, 425; on "fruits of conviction," 429, 457; on Reeves, 429–430; on first British Convention, 434; protests treatment of Pigott, 435; on Lord George Gordon and conditions at Newgate, 435, 436, 438, 439–440, 441, 441–442, 442, 446, 464; on imprisonment for debt, 440, 441; on probable departure of Lord Moira, 446; announces separation from Carlton House, 452; related to the *World*, 452; on lawyers, 453; on prisons, 445; on Lord Howe, 455, 456–457; on Frost, 461–462, 463, 464; publishes indictment of Skirving, 471–472; quoted, 38, 95, 164, 168, 214, 226, 231, 328, 334, 343, 350, 358, 371, 403, 424, 431, 449, 454; mentioned, 320, 406

Mornington, Richard Wellesley, 3rd Baron of [I] (1760–1842; suc. 1781; KP 1783), politician (MP Windsor 1787–1796; Custos Rotulorum Co. Meath 1781–1842; Lord of the Treasury 1786–1797; PC 1793; Commissioner for East India Affairs 1793–1797), 272–273, 352

Morris, Charles (1745–1838), song writer, 200, 237, 409

Mortimer, Earl, *see* Oxford, Edward Harley, 5th Earl of

Morton, John, agitator and informer, 195, 195–196

Morton, Thomas (1764?–1838), playwright, 325

Mountmorres, Hervey Redmond Morres, 2nd Viscount [I] (c. 1743–1797; suc. 1766; cr. MA Oxford 1766; DCL Oxford 1773; FRS 1793), 20, 27, 132–133, 232, 255, 269, 457–458

Mozart (1756–1791), 43

Muir, Thomas (1765–1798), lawyer and reformer, Vice President of Scottish Convention, 145, 349; prominent in Associated Friends of the People, 195; reputation, 195; arrested, released, 195; nature of charge, 195; leaves for Paris, 194; scheduling of trial, 215; outlawed, 233; *Gazetteer*'s interest in, 233; petitions Court to stand trial, 349; rescheduling of trial, 349; released on bail, 405; *Morning Post*'s interest in trial, 335–336; general interest in trial, 406–408, 409, 453; Daniel Stuart's interest in trial, 336; Skirving's testimony at trial, 406; concern regarding sentence, 435, 444–445, 461; moved to London, 408, 445; treatment of, 444–445, 453; sentence to become Parliamentary issue, 409; visited by Lauderdale, 461; to be visited by Fox, 461; detention promised by Dundas, 461; mentioned, 468, 472

Mulgrave, Constantine John Phipps, 2nd Baron [I] (1744–1792; suc. 1790), 104, 105

Mulgrave, Henry Phipps, 3rd Baron [I] (1755–1831; suc. 1792; FSA 1793), politician and army officer (MP Scarborough 1790–1794; Colonel of 31st Foot 1793–1831; commander at Toulon 1793), Richmond's second in near-duel with Lauderdale, 82; succeeds to Baronage, 104, 105; quits Opposition, 182; supports Alien Bill, 182–183, 200, 214; specializes in attacks on Erskine, 214, 264; FSA, 264; commander at Toulon, 397; resents replacement by O'Hara, 409, 431; returns to England, 431; expected to protest Muir's sentence, 409

Murphy, Arthur (1727–1805), dramatist and miscellaneous writer, 27, 29, 283, 285, 314

Murray, Lady Augusta (c. 1762–1818), wife of Prince Augustus, 299–300

Murray, James, 7th Baronet (1755?–1811; suc. 1771), army officer (MP Weymouth and Melcombe Regis 1790–1811; Major General 1790; Adjutant

Murray, James (con't).
General to Duke of York 1793–1794), 359, 395
Murray, John, the elder, *see* Mac Murray, John
Murray, John, the younger (1778–1843), publisher, 166
Music, 42–43
"Myra," 69

Naas, John Bourke, styled Lord (1766–1849; DCL Oxford 1793), politician (MP Naas 1790–1794), 349
Nares, the Rev. Robert (1753–1829), divine and miscellaneous writer, 27, 29, 80, 206, 253, 283
National Assembly, French, 93, 94, 110
National Convention, French, 112, 145, 176, 190, 192, 243, 258, 259, 266
National debt, passage of bill for reducing, 53, 54, 59, 85, 101; regarded as evil, 101; regarded as blessing, 101–102; reduction postponed, 147; funding continued, 246; fund for reducing to be borrowed by Pitt, 247; fund not borrowed by Pitt, 256, 257; defended by Edward King, 303; called bulwark of Constitution, 392
Navy, plans for reducing, 54; augmentation of, 137, 142, 147; bounties offered for enlistments, 140, 180, 187, 188, 217, 227, 243; press warrants expected, 145; debate on budget, 153, 154; reason for augmentation demanded by Fox, 183; further augmentation to be asked, 190, 204; Fox pleads for delay in considering augmentation, 193; Pitt moves for augmentation of, 209–210; conscription unenforceable, 227; desertions from, 227, 366; presses, 227, 258; increases pay of sailors, 247; mistreats Williamson, 420; Treasurer of, 132, 248, 294
Neerwinden, 258
Neild and Bush, lawyers, 86
Nemplish bonnet, 329
Nepean, Evan (1751–1822), politician (Under Secretary for Home Office

1782–1794), accepts Clerkship of Supreme Council in Jamaica, 115; resumes position as Under Secretary, 115; paymaster for Home Office, 116; employs Charles Stuart, 116; visits Portugal, 121; refuses to finance Stuart's *Short Review*, 283; Stuart's letters to, 418, 433; Heriot's complaints to, 448
"Neptune," *see* Miles, William Augustus
Netherlands, The, 146–147, 375
Newark, 343
Newcastle, 51, 59, 100, 139, 258
Newcastle, Henry Pelham-Clinton, 2nd Duke of [GB] (1720–1794; suc. 1768; FRS 1747; Joint Comptroller of the Customs of London 1749–1794; LL.D. Cambridge 1749; Auditor of the Exchequer 1751–1794; KG 1752; High Steward of Westminster 1759–1794; Lord Lieutenant of Nottinghamshire 1768–1794), 109, 239
New Forest, Verderer of, 132
Newfoundland, Chief Justice in Court of Civil Jurisdiction of, 135, 430
Newgate, crowded state of, 285; newspaper interest in, 435, 453; conditions in 435, 464; Keeper of, 436; investigations of epidemic in, 435–439, 441, 442–443, 446; registration of visitors to, 464–465
Newman, Mr., candidate for City Remembrancer, 388
Newmarket, 17, 128, 305
Newmilns, 271
Newnham, Nathaniel (1742–1809), banker and alderman (Lord Mayor of London 1783; MP London 1780–1790; MP Ludgershall 1793–1796), 237, 244–245
News, Continental, problems respecting, 165
Newspapermen, status of, 27, 244; places available to, 354
Newspapers, opinion of King and Queen, 4; ignore Stanhope, 10; blackmail Prince of Wales, 13; number of, 19, 22,

163; character of, 19–20, 163–165; expenses, taxes, and average sale, 20; sources of revenue, 20–22; circulation of nondailies, 26; links between dailies and nondailies, 26; feared by Burke, 27; laws regarding licensing of presses, 31; laws preventing rentals, 31; legitimate income of, 31; average value of, 31; relation to theaters, 42; negotiations with Stamp Office, 70; harassed by lawyers, 70–71; demand legal reforms, 70–71, 228; indemnified against publishing advertisements of illegal lottery schemes, 71; respect Lord Derby, 91; protest damages awarded to Lady Lambart, 99, 332; interest in patronage, 105–106, 131; reactions to Pitt's appropriation of Cinque Ports, 107–109; puzzled by Pitt's indifference to developments, 110; expect Pitt's resignation, 111; Pitt's lack of reliance upon, 112–113; filled with loyalty addresses, 141; filled with rumors of witch hunts, 142; duped by phantom insurrection, 142; practice stock-jobbing, 144–145, 165, 298; increase in sale of, 163; interest in faro tables, 164; disapprove of "pad," 164–165; distrust Government's releases, 165; problems respecting foreign correspondence, 165; experiment with format, 165–166; introduce editorial, 167; revision of Government's policy respecting, 169; at mercy of Post Office, 170; combine on matters of common interest, 179; concerned for Almon, 197; united on freedom of the press, 201; unenthusiastic about Erskine's dismissal, 208; become interested in Lansdowne, 213; dislike Lonsdale, 226; opposed to imprisonment for debt, 230; opposed to trial of Hastings, 241, 291; Hastings's investment in, 241; silent regarding *State of the Representation*, 241; applaud Insolvent Debtors Bill, 254, 286, 287; unaware of treaties, 258–259, 368; publish Auckland's Declaration and

Memorial, 264; silent on passage of Traitorous Correspondence Bill, 265; confidence in Rawdon, 285, 287; protest treatment of Lord George Gordon, 287; taxes, 288; applaud Hastings's address, 290; sympathize with Archbishop of York against Burke, 290–291; reporting of debates as "privilege" or "right," 293; on state of the war, 298, 359–360, 374–375, 376; proper victims for extortion, 299; reactions to Clarence's denunciation of the war, 304–305; respect Duchess of York, 311; admire Mrs. Robinson, 311; employed by Mrs. Jordan against Kemble, 315–316; interest in marriages, 331, 353; affected by prorogations of Parliament, 332–333, 380; introduce the headline, 346, 368; public officers forbidden to give information to, 348; publish appeals to Pitt for sinecures and places, 353; interest in deaths, 353, 355; alert to vacancies at lower levels, 354; deplore lethargy of Dutch, 360; lack confidence in Allies, 360; support Woodfall for City Remembrancer, 385–388; interested in Muir and Palmer, 406–408, 453, 454; interested in death of Lord George Gordon, 441; dislike the Duke of Gordon, 441; interested in conditions in Newgate, 453; fail to support Government's alarm, 448, 453; interested in trial of *Morning Chronicle*, 452–453, 454; interested in lawyers, 453; *see also* Advertisements, Poetry, "Paragraphs," *and* Puffs

Newspapers, Ministerial, financed and protected by Government, 21; lack of co-operation among, 22, 378; number of, 19, 22, 170, 178; character of, 22–26, 170–178; source of material, 26, 178; protected by laws, 31; oppose trial of Hastings, 7, 186, 290; eager for war, 8, 54, 102, 103; suggest brides for Prince of Wales, 16; alarmed about Prince of Wales's popularity in Ireland, 15;

Newspapers, Ministerial (con't).
applaud Pitt's treatment of Sampson Perry, 32; refuse to support the elder Colman, 42; tolerate Holcroft, 42; attack Drury Lane, 43, 95, 323–324, 327; impugn loyalty of Lauderdale, 49, 101, 141; prepare for opening of Parliament, 49; praise Jenkinson, 53; silent respecting death of King of Sweden, 55; concerned about Post Office scandals, 61; denounce Friends of the People, 76, 78, 80, 81, 84, 238, 268; publish rumors of French landings, 80; praise speech of Prince of Wales, 82; praise Covent Garden renovations, 94; entreat Fox to join Government, 100, 121, 125; lambaste Tierney, 101; praise Richmond, 103–104; flounder, 112–113; hate *Sun*, 118–119; praise Thurlow for economies of Prince of Wales, 128; ignore radicals, 135; flail Erskine, 141, 153, 200, 208; ignore Scottish Convention, 145; praise Prince of Wales, 153; compliment Fox, 155; apologize for the Queen, 165; denounce *Morning Chronicle*, 167–168; affected by cancellation of subsidies, 178–179; prepare for debates on Alien Bill, 180, 181; placate Portland, 184; argue necessity of Alien Bill, 184–185, 187; insult Chauvelin, 186, 187; talk of peace, 188, 189; celebrate flights of radicals, 197; publicize Frost's debts, 198; Government's dependence on for alarms, 199; flail Friends of the Liberty of the Press, 200, 201; reply to Fox's *Letter*, 205; preoccupied with execution of Louis XVI, 206; rejoice over debates on augmentation of forces, 212; interested in Lansdowne, 213; alarmed by Fox's resolutions against war, 222; unaware of Godwin's *Inquiry*, 223; represent war as defensive, 226, 258; urge Clarence to participate, 226, 364, 370–371, 410; attempt to spur enlistments, 227; attack Fox, 243, 245, 408; support Anderson for MP, 245; mis-

interpret Traitorous Correspondence Bill, 249; hope for execution of Orleans, 264; publish sermons, 264; hint at arrest of Manchester reformers, 276; enthusiastic about military games, 299; divided over fund for paying Fox's debts, 300, 348; puff Haymarket, 324–325; defend faro games, 330–331; paid piecemeal by Treasury, 333; concerned about lawyers, 334, 461; instigate bankruptcies, 345; on Oxford installation, 350; on Waterdown camp, 360–361; denounce Glasgow petition, 369, 398; alarmed at motion to assassinate Pitt, 369; embarrassed by Mrs. Fitzherbert, 371; on Richmond's responsibility for Dunkirk, 393, 396; prepare public for dismissal of public servants, 395; defend Lord Chatham, 410; drop threat of invasion, 412; regard war as hopeless, 414; effect of prorogation on, 415–417; collect flannel waistcoats, 423; deny epidemic in Newgate, 438; fail to alarm the public, 448; indifferent to British Convention, 459; on Frost, 461; on Muir and Palmer, 461
Newspapers, Opposition, managed by Sheridan, 13, 63; financing of, 31, 37–38, 60; principal subsidizers, 31; harassed by Government, 21–22, 31; number of, 31, 166; character of, 31–37, 166–169; writers for, 37–39; suspicious of Pitt's pacificism, 8, 54–55; regard Burke as dupe of Pitt, 8; suspect negotiations regarding trial of Hastings, 8; apologize for Prince of Wales, 16; did not support elder Colman, 42; attack Covent Garden, 43; abuse Burke, 49, 283; blame Lady Cowper for death of Leopold II, 54–55; ignore Post Office scandals, 63; concerned with 1788 Westminster election, 63; urge removal of Rose, 65; advertise meetings of Corresponding Society, 72; explain France's declarations of war, 76; admire Dumouriez, 76; support Friends of the People, 76, 239; publish rumors

of Pitt's dismissal, 80; think Fox's Libel Bill doomed to defeat, 82; applaud Merry's *The Magician No Conjuror*, 92; defend Drury Lane, 95, 137; suspicious of Lady Cavan's suit, 98; protest manner of Rose's action, 98; regard national debt as evil, 103; harassed by Post Office, 117, 167; publicize corruptive use of patronage, 132, 133–134; protest construction of barracks, 140; protest Army purges, 140; sobered by phantom insurrection, 142; concerned about Manchester riots, 146; alarmed by Burke's speeches, 150; object to Alien Bill, 153; ridicule Burke's dagger scene, 157; harassed by The Association, 167, 199; beset by financial problems, 167, 170; act in unity, 167, 310; more powerful than Opposition, 167, 200; prepare for debates on Alien Bill, 180–181; expect war, 186; surprised by Pitt's mention of Holland, 214; outraged by conduct of Duke of Gordon, 229; remember Pitt's speech on Nottingham petition, 234; unenthusiastic about dinner of Friends of the Liberty of the Press, 238; refuse to support Newnham, 245; on Burke's speech defending Traitorous Correspondence Bill, 253; ignore national fast, 264; quote Fox on Auckland's Memorial, 266; amused by Windham's "metaphysics," 272; interested in trial of Frend, 277, 278; protest inclusion in budget of revenues from East India Company, 288; interested in Dundas's appointments, 294, 295, 356; assail the *True Briton*, 310; tire of Miss Hughes, 312; concerned about imprisonment for debt, 344; Pitt's indifference to, 346–347; on Portland's installation at Oxford, 350–351; on Burke's desire for a pension, 351; ridicule George Rose, Jr., 353; on Duke of Richmond, 361; on Duke of Clarence, 364; misunderstand Pitt, 364–365; make Burke scapegoat for war, 365–366, 367; ridicule

Brighton camp, 371–374; Lafayette hero to, 391; stress effect of war on economy, 391; try to force negotiations for peace, 397; effect of prorogation on, 419–420; ridicule collection of flannel waistcoats, 423; concerned for Muir and Palmer, 445

Nice, 217

Noble, John, reformer, 370

Nootka Sound, 134

Norfolk, Charles Howard, 11th Duke of [GB] (1746–1815; suc. 1786; Lord Lieutenant of West Riding 1782–1798; High Steward of Hereford 1782–1798; Recorder of Gloucester 1792–?; President of the Society of Antiquaries 1793–1815), politics and character of, 10; provides house for *Morning Chronicle*, 34; gets Recordership of Gloucester, 105; opposes Address of Thanks, 147; returns one member to Commons, 240; opposes Traitorous Correspondence Bill, 263; elected President of Society of Antiquaries, 264

Norfolk, Deputy Lieutenant of, 354

Normandy, 258

Norris, J. (fl. 1792–1794), printer, 98, 168, 258, 331–332, 427

North, Dudley (1749–1829), politician (MP Great Grimsby 1784–1796; manager for impeachment of Hastings; DCL Oxford 1793), 249, 250, 350

North, Frederick (1766–1827), politician (Chamberlain of the Exchequer 1779–1826; MP Banbury 1792–1794; DCL Oxford 1793), 76, 84

North, Frederick, Lord, *see* Guilford, 2nd Earl of

North, George Augustus, Lord, *see* Guilford, 3rd Earl of

North Government, 28

Northumberland, Hugh Percy, 1st Duke of [GB] (1714–1786; cr. 1766), 296

Northumberland, Hugh Percy, 2nd Duke of [GB] (1742–1817; suc. 1786; FSA 1787; FRS 1788; nom. KG 1788),

Northumberland, 2nd Duke of (con't).
army officer (Lord Lieutenant and
Vice Admiral of Northumberland
1786–1799; General 1793), 240
Norton Fitzwarren, 343
Norway, 409
Norwich, 271, 275
Norwich petition, 269
Norwich theater, 321
Nottingham, 271, 343, 451
Nottingham petition, 234, 269
Nottinghamshire, Lord Lieutenant and
Custos Rotulorum of, 109
"Novice John," see Lane, George

O'Beirne, the Rev. Thomas Lewis
(1748?–1823), divine and political
journalist, 38–39
O'Bryen, Dennis (1755–1832), surgeon,
journalist, politician, friend of Sheridan,
39; writer for Morning Post, 39, 169;
member of Friends of the People, 76;
active in Friends of the Liberty of the
Press, 155, 339; possible author of The
Errors of Mr. Pitt's Present Administration, 469
Observer, 26, 33, 37, 88, 135–136, 169,
317, 318
O'Hara, Charles (1740?–1802), army
officer (Lieutenant Governor of Gibraltar 1792; Lieutenant General in the
army 1793; Commissioner of Toulon
1793), 397, 409, 426, 431
O'Keeffe, John (1747–1833), dramatist,
89, 90, 91, 320
"Old Hubert," see Parkinson, James
"Old Kent," see Wells, Mrs. Mary
"Old Woman, The," see The Times
Oldys, Francis, see Chalmers, George
Oliver, Mr., friend of Thomas Paine,
196
One Pennyworth of Truth, 148, 152
Onslow, George, 4th Baron [GB] (1731–
1814; suc. 1776; cr. Baron Cranley
1776; DCL Oxford 1773; High
Steward of Kingston-on-Thames 1768–
1814; Lord Lieutenant of Surrey and

High Steward of Guilford 1776–1814;
Lord of the Bedchamber 1780–1814),
132
Opera, Italian, 42, 43
Opera company, 42, 43, 95
Opera House, renovated, 42–43; rented
by Drury Lane company, 43, 95, 313,
314; Taylor resumes management of,
314, 322; renovated, 324
Opie, John (1761–1807), portrait painter,
55
Oporto, 376
Opposition, character of, 9–11, 75; back-
ground of, 9; supported Prince of
Wales in Regency battle, 14; manage-
ment of the press, 21–22, 31–32; news-
paper's controlled by, 31, 37, 166, 169;
interests supported in London Government by Skinner, 35; ridiculed by
Holcroft, 42; protests interference in
Russian affairs, 53; plans for Canning,
53–54; attempts to alienate Pitt from
George III, 56; obligated to protest
Prince of Wales's provisions, 56; assists
Duke of York, 59; ignores scandals in
Post Office, 61; concerned with Rose's
interference in elections, 64, 66;
Wolcot ceases to write for, 61; moves
to abolish slave trade, 85; subversion of
Covent Garden denied, 92; supported
by people, 96; Burke's attempt to
split, 106; charges Pitt with holding
office illegally, 106; cautioned by
Ministerial papers, 109–110; indebted-
ness to Almon, 112; lambasted by
Paine and Pigott, 133; supported by
Rawdon, 148; right wing supports
Government, 155; scoffed at by Burke,
157; payments to newspapers, 166–167;
less powerful than newspapers, 167;
state of, 180, 184, 187, 209, 212, 222,
252, 355, 408; deserted by Portland,
203; said to be deserted by Rawdon,
209; urged to support the war, 218;
united, 219–220; supported by Adam
and Guilford, 221; keeps trial of
Hastings an issue, 241; conduct

denounced by Burke, 251; averted war with Russia, 269; attempts to reclaim Burke, 292–293; frequents faro parlors, 330–331; split by phantom insurrection, 399; brings Adair into Parliament, 421; scourged by Stuart's parody, 424; assailed by Mackenzie, 424; supported by *World*, 468; *see also* Rockingham Whigs

Oracle, history, 23, 25; titles, 23, 117; proprietors, 23, 176, 346, 378; editors, 23, 176; printers, 23, 117, 176, 346; subsidized by Treasury, 23, 176; influenced by Sheridan, 23, 143, 325, 339; Government's difficulties with, 23; character, 19–20, 23, 24, 86, 117, 163, 176–177, 346, 379, 450; politics, 22, 126–127, 154, 176, 281, 346, 378–379; personnel, 19–20, 23, 29, 70, 165; circulation, 150; lambastes *Baviad*, 20; feuds with *World*, 23, 126, 181, 470; attempts to extort money from Duke of York, 50, 59; thanks Sheridan, 51; on sale of Prince of Wales's stud, 52, 56, 57–58, 59, 100; used by Sheridan to force payment of Prince of Wales's debts, 50, 52–53, 56, 57, 63; extorts money from Prince of Wales, 55, 87; sued by Lord Lonsdale, 55, 56, 66; subsidized by Lauderdale, 60, 117, 130; puffs Lauderdale, 60; puffs Burke, 66; advertises sale of *Morning Post*, 69; announces leasing of *World*, 69; advertises meeting of Corresponding Society, 72; indicted for libels on the Guards, 72, 232; carries advertisements for Friends of the People, 76; involved in Billington scandal, 86, 87; on Mrs. Wells, 89; on Burgoyne, 91; on Merry, 93, 94, 95, 275, 321; on Drury Lane, 95, 313, 314, 315, 322–323, 325, 327; concerned about damages awarded Lady Lambart, 99, 332; disturbed by possible liaison between Fox and Prince of Wales, 100, 101; insults Mrs. Fitzherbert, 100; denounces *Gazetteer*, 102; reports Taylor's activities in Edin-

burgh, 102; on national debt, 103; on death of Earl of Guilford, 105; on Pitt's appropriation of Cinque Ports, 107, 110; on Pitt's re-election as MP for Cambridge University, 109–110; on Portland's election to Chancellorship of Oxford, 111, 350, 351; concerned for Mackintosh, 111–112, 354; puffs Dundas, 116, 117, 295, 296, 356, 396, 430, 468; harassed by the Post Office, 117; plots to make Sheridan Minister, 117–118, 126–128, 131; hates *Sun*, 118–119; on Porson, 124; puffs Thurlow, 126; on Prince of Wales's economies, 128, 130, 214; puffs Banks, 136, 429; gloats over demise of *Argus*, 143; anxious regarding Scottish Convention, 144, 145; concentration on stockjobbing, 144–145, 176, 298, 337, 360; concern for debates, 150, 212; assails Burke for attacks on Sheridan, 154–155, 182, 190; assailed by *True Briton*, 175, 215; puffs Mrs. Robinson, 177, 311, 312, 314, 316, 412; critical of Pye, 176–177; on trial of Hastings, 181, 242; puffs Portland, 184; vindicates Sheridan, 191–192; concerned for Almon, 197, 275–276; defends Pitt against Frost, 198; puffs Reeves, 200; on Friends of the Liberty of the Press, 201, 265; eulogizes Burke, 202–203, 203–204, 351, 352, 402, 470; praises Mrs. Fitzherbert, 202–203; on Prince of Wales's defection, 202, 203, 204, 260; on Prince of Wales's letter to Portland, 203, 204; denounces Lafayette, 206, 391; defends Reeves against Law, 208; on size of Opposition, 209, 408; on Chauvelin's correspondence, 216; on Prince of Wales's military ardor, 225; opposes revision of laws respecting debtors, 230; advertises Bell's projects, 231–232, 280, 346; on state of the war, 243, 257–258, 259, 359, 360, 368, 389, 390, 391, 413, 414, 415; condemns Holland's apathy, 243, 375, 414; on "fruits of conviction,"

Oracle (con't).

245–246, 247, 401, 429; assails Nares, 253; publishes Priestley's letter to Burke, 253; on bankruptcies, 255, 434–435; on terms of the loan, 256, 257, 368; demands removal of Auckland, 264; on Frend, 277, 278; announces Bell's bankruptcy, 280–281; considers reporting of debates a "privilege," 293; on Archbishop of York's comment on Burke, 293; announces marriage of Prince Augustus, 299–300; on payment of Fox's debts, 301, 310; interested in Dumouriez, 302–303; on Clarence's repudiation of the war, 305, 371, 398, 411; puffs Lady Manners, 311; on Madame Mara, 312; accuses Murphy of plagiarism, 314; champions Mrs. Jordan, 315, 316; champions Mrs. Bateman, 316–317; puffs Colman, 318; defends production of *Hamlet*, 319–320; applauds Sheridan's generosity to Colman, 324; puffs Reynolds, 324–325; attacks Lady Wallace, 330; interested in faro tables, 331; prints Glasgow petition, 335, 369, 398; advertises Daniel Stuart's *Peace and Reform*, 337, 469; later owned by Peter Stuart, 339–340; wants Government to prosecute reformers, 342–343; on trial of Eaton, 344; advertised for sale, 345, 346; warns Pitt of need for newspaper support, 345–346; purchased by James Bell, 346, 378, 449; Peter Stuart's hope of acquiring, 346, 468; annoyed with *The Times*, 348; assails *Morning Chronicle*, 347–348, 360, 454; reports death of Fox, 353; interested in death of Tickell, 355; on election of Canning, 357–358; wants Duke of York's command extended, 360; on riots against crimps, 368; on Marie Antoinette, 377, 412; supports Woodfall for City Remembrancer, 383, 384, 385–386, 387, 388; on responsibility for Dunkirk, 392, 393, 395, 396; on resignation of Richmond, 394, 395; on possible changes in Government, 394, 395; on Muir and Palmer, 408, 444; on Fox's anniversary dinner, 409; mentions possibility of evacuating Toulon, 413; charges Clarence is mistreated by Pitt, 414; on affairs in France, 320–321; on the death of Lord George Gordon and conditions in Newgate, 435, 436, 438–439, 442; puffs Moira, 441; on the British Convention, 447, 453, 459; publishes Bell's address, 449–450; publishes map, 448, 449, 450, 451; promises future maps, 451; possible lease by Bell, 450; on trial of *Morning Chronicle*, 454; defends Windham, 457; on Frost, 464; later amalgamation with *Public Advertiser*, 468; attempts to preempt coffee houses, 470; defends Macleod, 471; quoted, 31, 62, 69, 73, 85, 92, 103, 105, 115, 131, 152, 168, 190, 202, 215, 254, 268, 270, 276, 284, 290, 294, 295, 299, 300, 308, 317, 320, 322, 349, 350, 362, 370, 392, 397, 403, 405, 406, 408, 421, 423, 432, 435, 443, 444, 446, 454; mentioned, 118, 215, 248, 317, 406, 456, 461

Ordnance Department, 393, 394, 424–425

Orleans, 259

Orleans, Louis-Philippe Joseph, Duke of (1747–1793; suc. 1785), French revolutionist, 18, 51, 149, 190, 264, 420

Osnaburgh, Bishopric of, 59

Ostend, 303, 361, 413

Owen, William (d. 1793), bookseller, 342

Oxford, Edward Harley, 7th Earl of Mortimer [GB] and 5th Earl of [GB] (1773–1841; suc. 1790; MA Oxford 1792; DCL Oxford 1793), 349

Oxford University, Chancellorship vacated by death of Guilford, 105; Chancellorship promised to Beaufort, 105, 106–107, 107–108, 111, 132; Chancellorship given to Portland, 111, 112–113; Madame Mara's concerts at, 312; confers honorary degrees, 349, 350; installs Portland as Chancellor, 350–351

"Pad," 164–165, 312, 328–330
Paine, Thomas (1737–1809), pamphleteer; publishes *Rights of Man*, Pt. I, 7, 33; early acquaintance with John "Jew" King, 33, 196; influence of, 40; represented by *Argus*, 32, 33; defended by *Morning Chronicle*, 34; worshiped by Frost, 50; publishes *Rights of Man*, Pt. II, 72; denounced by Burke, 77; arrested, 77; defended by Opposition papers, 80; indicted, 81, 84; ignored by Ministerial papers, 84; continues activities, 84; circulates pamphlets, 102; elected member of National Convention, 112; leaves for France, 112, 196; publishes letter to Dundas, 112; scheduled for trial, 112; publishes *Letter Addressed to the Addressers*, 133–134, 135, 150; charges Burke and Pitt in negotiation on trial of Hastings, 134, 150, 181, 186; *Rights of Man* quietly circulated by The Association, 137, 236; effigies burned, 142, 145, 180, 199; employs Erskine as counsel, 150, 183, 196–197; assailed by Burke, 150, 219, 233; *Diary* uneasy about, 151; indictment of illegal, 152; tried, 152–153, 196–197, 198; jury censured by Friends of the Liberty of the Press, 183, 198; Erskine denounced for defending, 213; Muir charged with lending works of, 195, 215, 233; prosecutions of publishers of, 152, 199, 234, 235, 236, 268, 279–280, 342, 343, 344, 420, 443; correspondence with John "Jew" King published, 222–223, 224, 260–261; defended by *Morning Post*, 404; denounced by French Convention, 405; lampooned in Stuart's parody, 417; Chalmers's life of, 424; arrested in Paris, 456; mentioned, 10, 80, 117, 172, 183, 215, 447
Paisley, 271
Palmer, John (1742?–1798), actor at Drury Lane, 42, 96
Palmer, John (1742–1818), Post Office official, appointed Comptroller General, 61; quarrels with Postmasters General, 61–62; quarrels with Deputy Comptroller, 62–63; suspended, 62; influences *Morning Herald*, 61, 87; appealed to by Duke of Clarence, 87; lends Brighton theater to Mrs. Wells, 90; retires on pension, 254
Palmer, the Rev. Thomas Fyshe (1747–1802), Unitarian clergyman, tried and sentenced, 407; newspaper interest in, 407–408, 409, 435, 444–445, 453; arrives in London, 445; treatment of, 445; detention promised, 461; mentioned, 468, 472
Pamphlets, importance of, 417
Pantheon, 43, 95, 224
"Paragraphs," 19, 20, 337
Paris, 85, 110, 111, 112, 259, 297, 368, 421
Parkinson, James (d. 1824), surgeon, paleontologist, pamphleteer, 262, 279
Parliament, dislikes Pitt, 5; preparations for opening of, 49–53; prorogations of, 85, 94, 110, 121; convoked, 146–147; King's speech on opening of, 146–147; dictated to by Pitt, 150; consensus differs from that of people, 174; prorogued, 304, 332, 341, 367, 413, 414, 433, 434, 459; conjectures as to reasons for prorogations, 332, 413; Pitt's inability to face, 413; effect of prorogations on newspapers, 415–417
Parliamentary debates, coverage by newspapers, 19; stressed by *Diary*, 22; preceded by a Bowles pamphlet, 27; accounts of supplied to Ministerial papers, 30, 170; stressed by *Morning Chronicle*, 35, 167; garbled by *Sun*, 135–136; to be stressed by *True Briton*, 171, 172; reporting of as "right," 293; reporting of as "privilege," 293; *see also specific bills*
Parliaments, Clerk of the, 132, 248, 377
Parr, Samuel (1747–1825), pedagogue, 433
Parry, John, 116, 420
Parsons, J., bookseller, 283

Parsons, William (1736–1795), actor at
Drury Lane, 42, 181

Party, The, *see* Opposition *and* Whigs

"Pasquin, Anthony," *see* Williams, John

Patriot, 169

Patriote François, 220

Patronage, corruptive use of, 105; proper
and improper use of, 131; Lansdowne
moves to abolish, 147; Government's
effort to preserve, 153; as reason for
Alien Bill, 156; lavished on supporters
of war, 351–352, 353, 396, 428, 429;
appeals for a share of, 353; Home
Secretary's control of, 396; increased
by war, 425–426; *see also* Crown, power
of the *and* Red Book, The

Paul, William, Manchester paper-stainer
and reformer, 408

Paymasters General, 246

Payne, John Willett (1752–1803), naval
officer (MP Huntington 1787–1796;
Auditor and Secretary of the Duchy of
Cornwall 1791–?), 17–18, 53

Pearson, Oliver, Manchester laborer and
reformer, 408

Peck, Mr., 214

Pelham, Thomas (1756–1826), politician
(MP Sussex 1780–1801; manager of
impeachment of Hastings), 300

Pells, Clerk of the, 132, 300

Penn, William (1644–1718), 280

People, trust Fox, 9, 242; represented by
Fox, 9, 242; not included in Friends of
the People, 75, 78; support Opposition,
96; duped by phantom insurrection,
142–143; George III's speech called
calumny on, 148; possible effect of
Fox's motions on, 150; Alien Bill
meant to alarm, 153, 184–185; uninfluenced by Sheridan, 154; consensus
of differs from consensus of Parliament,
184–185; to be taxed to support corruptions, 191; distrust Pitt, 5, 194, 425;
informed by Fox as to reason for war,
194, 219; sensitive to harassments of
the press, 198, 199, 343, 347; effect of
Fox's *Letter* on, 205; will defend Con-

stitution, 206; propagandized into war,
220–221, 226; refuse to enlist, 226–227;
regard war as unnecessary, 228; think
Constitution safe, 228; not appealed to
by Fox, 242; not to be "inconvenienced"
by war, 246; will not pay taxes, 247,
255; Traitorous Correspondence Bill
protested on behalf of, 250; Traitorous
Correspondence Bill "calumny" on,
250; right to petition, 269, 273, 275;
French Revolution the result of ignoring, 272; will demand free elections,
273; Commons not representative of,
273; voice drowned out by Pitt, 275;
Fox sacrifices patronage for, 300;
opposed to war, 303–304, 366; opinion
called irrelevant, 304

Percy Coffee House, 142

"Perish Commerce," 252, 399, 457

Perry, James (1756–1821), journalist,
character and early career, 34–35; connection with *Morning Chronicle*, 34,
167, 338; Pitt's tolerance of, 35; gets
subsidy for conduct of *Chronicle*, 38;
member of Friends of the People, 76;
indicted for libel, 215; member of
Whig Club, 244; tried for libel, 447,
452–453, 454

Perry, Sampson (1747–1823), surgeon
and journalist, connection with *Argus*,
32; prosecutions of, 32, 35, 38; critic of
Pitt, 96; freed from prison and indicted
for libel on Commons, 96–97, 143; account of demise of *Argus*, 143; flees to
France, 143, 196, 252; circumstances of
trial and outlawry, 196–197; flight
celebrated by *The Times*, 252

"Personalities," 338

Perth, 271, 407

Peterborough House Press, 40, 41, 74

Petersham, 364, 393, 458

Petition, right to, 234, 239, 269, 273, 275,
278; *see also* Nottingham petition

Petre, Robert Edward, 9th Baron [GB]
(1741–1801; suc. 1742; FRS, FSA
1780), 300

"Phalanx, The," *see* Opposition *and* Whigs

Philadelphia, 423

Philanthropic Society, 423

Phillips, Richard (1767–1840), writer, publisher, bookseller, 235, 342, 343

"Philo-Pitti," *see* Merry, Robert

Phipps, Henry, *see* Mulgrave, Henry Phipps, 3rd Baron

Pigott, Arthur Leary (1749–1819), lawyer (Solicitor General to Prince of Wales 1783–1793; counsel for prosecution of Hastings), 207, 268

Piggot, Miss B., companion of Mrs. Fitzherbert, 363

Pigott, Charles (d. 1794), pamphleteer, author of *The Jockey Club*, 56–57, 133, 134; attacks Burke, 150; author of *Persecution*, 225; publishers of *The Jockey Club* prosecuted, 234, 236, 268, 279; assisted in circulating *The Jockey Club* by Government and The Association, 236; starts to Switzerland, 321; returns, 321; arrested and bailed, 403; freed by Grand Jury, 435; author of *Treachery No Crime*, 403

Pig's Meat, 448

"Pindar, Peter," *see* Wolcot, John

Pitcairn, David (1749–1809), medical doctor (physician in St. Bartholomew's Hospital 1780–1793), 442, 443, 462

Pitt, William (1759–1806), Prime Minister (MP Appleby 1781–1784; First Lord of the Treasury 1783–1801; MP Cambridge University 1784–1806; Lord Warden of the Cinque Ports and Governor of Dover Castle 1792–1806), detested for manner of acquiring office, 4, 9, 10, 106, 155, 157, 184, 421, 422; character, 4–5, 8–9; distrust of, 4, 53, 105, 123, 142, 194, 219, 272, 425; early difficulties with the press, 5; management of elections, 5, 8, 9, 41, 50, 221, 274; early followers of, 6; inner cabinet, 5; fondness for Dundas, 6, 294; manages Burke, 7–9; purports to approve impeachment of Hastings, 7; negotiates with Burke regarding trial of Hastings, 8, 134, 181, 186, 430; attitude toward

reformers, 8; reliance on corruptions, 8; earlier attempts to involve country in war, 8; hated by Opposition, 9, 10; relationship to Stanhope, 10; conduct during illness of George III, 14, 24; distrust of Thurlow, 18; buys puffs, 20; means of silencing critics, 21–22, 32, 233, 443; attitude toward ex officio indictments, 21–22, 198–199; sends Walter to prison, 24, 29, 32; writes for newspapers, 27; patronizes *The Times*, 28, 173; employs Cawthorne, 28; employs Miles, 29; punishes *Argus*, 32, 143; punishes Sampson Perry, 35, 38, 96–97, 143; tolerates *Gazetteer*, 34; distrusted by *Morning Chronicle*, 35; prosecutes Almon, 38, 60, 197; early patron of O'Beirne, 38; exposed by spurious *Star*, 41, 50; embarrassed by Rose, 50, 67; accused by *Oracle* of militating against Prince of Wales, 52–53, 55, 56, 57, 63; defended by Jenkinson, 53; establishes "sinking fund," 54; purports to favor peace, 54; silences *Oracle*, 55–56; absolved by Fox of mistreating Prince of Wales, 57; proposes settlement for Duke of York, 59; settles problems in the Post Office, 61, 254; *World* paid to support, 70; condemns all reformers, 77, 79; defends Constitution as perfect, 77; dismissal rumored, 80; hopes for defection of Fox, 81; supports Proclamation against Seditious Writings, 81; fails to convert Fox, 83, 111; punishes Merry, 92, 93; congratulated on national debt, 103; luck of, 105; distributes patronage of 2nd Earl of Guilford, 105–106; tries to get rid of 3rd Earl of Guilford, 105; possible advantage in splitting Opposition, 106, 425; appropriates Cinque Ports, 107–109, 125, 131, 294; visits castles, 107, 110–111, 121; thought to have reversion of Auditorship of Exchequer, 109; distributes patronage as Warden of Cinque Ports, 110–111; expected to resign, 108, 111–113,

Pitt, William, (1759–1806) (con't).

115–116, 119, 131; indifferent to state affairs, 110, 111, 112; afraid of Grey and the Friends of the People, 111, 121, 278; fails to win over Portland, 111; *Oracle*'s opinion of, 117, 126, 154, 176, 209, 379, 408; opposed by *Courier*, 117; *Sun* established by friends of, 118; entreats Fox to join Government, 121–122, 125, 131; re-elected as Member for Cambridge University, 107, 109–110, 122–124, 148, 151–152; coalition with Fox opposed by *Morning Chronicle*, 126; expected to resign as First Lord of Treasury, 131; possibility of ousting, 131, 131–133; coalition with Fox regarded as likely, 131, 135; uses patronage for purposes of bribery, 131–133; neglects Mountmorres, 132–133; friend of Reeves, 135; assailed by Ridgway, 138; castigated for apostasy, 141, 197–198, 370, 404, 421; accused of stockjobbing, 144, 257; admired by John "Jew" King, 146; Lansdowne moves to deprive of patronage, 147, 148; absent from debates on Address of Thanks, 148; Burke denies being bribed by, 150; *Diary* uneasy about, 151, 172, 173; dependence on alarms, 153, 195, 411, 421, 426, 448; negotiations with Sheridan, 154, 182, 216, 219, 260; censured by Portland, 155, 157; employs trickery respecting Fox, 155, 156–157; confines Rose's activities to journalism, 170; policy of secrecy denounced by Grey, 182; opposes delay in considering Alien Bill, 183–184; sneers at size of Opposition, 184; defended by *Sun* as to manner of getting office, 184; policy regarding moderate reformers, 185; intentions regarding war conjecturable, 185–186, 187–188; reason for creating independent companies, 187; appealed to for release of Lafayette, 189; mode of punishing enemies of state, 196–197, 233, 250; castigated by Frost, 197–198,

276; afraid of Fox's opposition to augmenting forces, 204, 209–210; negotiations with Prince of Wales, 130, 202, 204; supported by Douglas, 207; size of opposition to, 209; compromises with Portland, 209; moves for augmentation of forces, 209–210; supported by Eyre, 216; moves address on King's message regarding declaration of war, 218, 220, 360; conduct said responsible for war, 219; supported by Powys, 219; supported by Guilford's friends, 221; defends construction of barracks, 224; duped people into war, 226; unable to conscript, 227; mode of dealing with reformers generally, 228; mode of dealing with abolitionists, 228; continues imprisonment of Lord George Gordon, 229; faces trouble in Ireland, 232–233; encourages radical reformers, 234, 346; re-interprets right to petition, 234, 239, 278; responsibility for trial of Frend, 235, 277; presents budget, 245; supported by Ryder, 246; apologizes for war, 246–247; blunders respecting Traitorous Correspondence Bill, 250, 253, 255, 267; misuse of powers excused by Burke, 251; effects reconciliation between Prince of Wales and George III, 254; opposed to Insolvent Debtors Bill, 254, 255; negotiates for loan, 255–257; defends proclamation barring British citizens from returning, 260; bribes Stormont, 263; censured for neglect of Poland, 265; ordered to state object of war, 265–266; defends Auckland's Memorial, 266; appealed to by merchants, 269, 270; praised for Commercial Credit Bill, 270; applauded by *Public Advertiser*, 270, 282, 468; opposes Grey's motion for reform, 273–274; called untrustworthy, 272; controls Commons, 273, 274, 425; decides elections and appointments, 274; illness of, 284; battles election reformers, 285; humiliates Burke, 387; includes revenues from East India

Company in budget, 287–288; accused by Burke of mismanaging Indian affairs, 289; opposes inquiry into cause of delay in Hastings's trial, 291; reconciliation with Burke, 292–293; rewards all supporters, 293, 297–298, 300, 353; rumored resignation of, 295; refuses to have Auckland as Home Secretary, 295; resents Hawkesbury's influence in Cabinet, 295; intimate with Windham, 296; conferences with Portland denied, 297; not regarded as enthusiast for war, 299; opposes Fox's motion for reform, 304; once patronized by Lansdowne, 309; needs victories, 332, 368, 395; appealed to by Lauderdale regarding newspaper abuse, 335; hated by *Morning Post*, 335; errs in prosecuting booksellers, 344; embarrassed by bankruptcies, 345; warned of need of newspaper support, 345–346; refuses to reward Burke, 351; attempts to consolidate gains, 355–356; confers with Prince of Wales, 362; misunderstood by Opposition press, 364, 365, 366, 367; needs money, 367; will ask for additional loan, 368; move to assassinate by member of Corresponding Society, 369; supported by Saunderson, 370; bungles conduct of war, 374–375, 391, 392, 412; blamed for beginning war, 376; said by *Morning Post* to have been duped into war by Burke, 377, 392, 397–398, 401; refuses to be blackmailed by *World*, 379; loses support of *Morning Herald*, 379; appealed to by Woodfall, 383–384; influences City elections, 385; unable to increase taxes, 391; supports war by loans, 391, 392; defends Richmond, 395, 396, 398, 410; accused of mistreating Duke of Clarence, 398, 414; affect of Dunkirk on, 399; ultimatum to Rockingham Whigs, 399–400, 401, 409, 413, 421, 425; intimate with Elliot, 402; acts against Manchester reformers, 408; unable to meet Parliament, 413; issues

"Manifesto," 414, 421–422, 426; determined to prosecute war, 425, 432; asked by *Morning Chronicle* to state object of war, 426; may finance war by private contributions, 426; major beneficiary of war, 430; toadies unpopular in Ireland, 440; depends on newspaper hysteria for alarms, 448; slashed by Daniel Stuart, 469; expected to exploit British Convention, 472; mentioned, 178, 244, 377; *see also* Cinque Ports *and* Pitt Government

Pitt, Sir William Augustus (1728–1809; KB 1792), military officer (Colonel of 3rd Irish Horse 1775–1796; Lieutenant General 1777; General 1793), 209, 214

Pitt Government, embarrassed by elections of 1788, 5; opposed to impeachment of Hastings, 7, 241; negotiates with Burke regarding impeachment of Hastings, 8; attempts to get rid of Taylor, 11; supported by Queen in Regency battle, 14; opposed by Thurlow in Regency battle, 18; appealed to by puffs in newspapers, 21; advantages and disadvantages as manager of newspapers, 21–22; modes of rewarding and punishing newspapers, 21–22; subsidizes newspapers, 22–26; leases *Morning Herald*, 23; embarrassed by *Oracle*, 23; embarrassed by *The Times*, 24, 32; intrigues against Burke, 25–26; extent of propagandistic activities, 27, 348; journalistic contributions to newspapers, 27; principal writers for, 27–30; laws intended to penalize Opposition papers, 31; tolerates *Gazetteer*, 34; cautious respecting *Morning Chronicle*, 35, 347; reluctant to sue newspapers patronized by Prince of Wales, 36; influences proprietors of *Star*, 37; punishes Almon, 38, 135, 197, 268; silenced spurious *Star*, 41; harasses Drury Lane, 43–44, 137; coerces Colman, 44, 93; resists inquiry into 1788 Westminster election, 49, 63–64, 72, 75, 98; expected to kill Fox's Libel

Pitt Government (con't).

Bill, 49; interfered in affairs of Russia, 53, 221; cautious respecting *Oracle*, 60; employs Charles Stuart, 67; held responsible for fines by *World*, 70, 71; evident unconcern for enemies of state, 72, 74, 77, 84, 101–102, 135, 275, 276, 341, 342–343; punishes own enemies, 72, 344–345; augments London police, 72; supported on issue of reform by Portland faction, 75; attitude toward Friends of the People, 75, 80; inability to survive election reforms, 75; overawes reformers with camp at Bagshot, 82; attempts to beguile Fox by passing Libel Bill, 82–83; attempts to win Loughborough with Chancellorship, 83; reluctant to try Jordan and Paine, 84; unable to dictate to juries, 84; punishes *Morning Post*, 97; controls Drury Lane performances, 95–96; afraid of Opposition's influence on people, 96; punishes Bell, 97, 176, 215, 216, 230, 231–232; terrified of Parliamentary reforms, 100; attempts to discredit Friends of the People, 101; foments sedition in Edinburgh, 102; glorified by Bagshot camp, 103–104; recalls ambassador from Paris, 110, 186; loses interest in newspapers, 112–113, 346; suppresses investigation of affairs of *World*, 113; protects Walter against judgment demanded by John "Jew" King, 113–115; employs Watt as spy, 116; experiments with *Sun*, 119; misrepresents facts to *Sun*, 120, 165; antagonizes Unitarians at Cambridge University, 122–123; supports statutes discriminating against Unitarians, 123; negotiates with Sheridan, 130, 154–155, 202; lambasted by Paine and Pigott, 133; unconcerned with affairs on Continent, 134; disclaims connection with The Association, 135; finances The Association, 136; arranges near-riot at Drury Lane, 137; pretends to discover insurrection, 139, 142, 148; attempts to foment insurrections, 142, 402–403; offers rewards for apprehension of Frost and Perry, 142–143; silences *Argus*, 143; tries Sampson Perry, 143; accused of stockjobbing, 144; infiltrates Scottish Convention with spies, 145; charged with subverting freedom of press, 148; accused of inventing insurrection, 148, 149; Fox refuses to join, 149; always supported by Parliament, 150; not helped by Burke, 150; charged with illegal arrest in case of Paine's publishers, 152; actual defendant in trial of Paine, 152–153; relies on alarms, 153, 248, 249; supported on issue of war by right wing of Opposition, 155; defended by Burke for cashiering officers, 155; attempts to win over Fox by duplicity, 155, 156–157; supported by Carlisle on principle, 156; denounced for holding office illegally, 156, 182; employs boxers as crimps, 164; corruptive practices not supported by *Star*, 166; alters policy regarding press, 169–170; supported by newspapers, 170, 173, 176; owns newspapers, 172; discontinues subsidy of *Morning Herald*, 175; provides material for newspapers, 178; searches for traitors, 179–180; criticized by Windham, 183; challenged by Fox respecting preparations for war, 183; adds to ranks through by-elections, 184; thanked by *Public Advertiser* for Alien Act, 185; insults and dismisses Chauvelin, 186; offers bounties for enlistments in Navy, 187; augments Army by independent companies, 187; indicates war averted, 188, 189; blamed for death of Louis XVI, 190; accused of using war as excuse for increasing corruptions, 191; conducts trials in Scotland, 194, 348–349; opposition to reform represented as defense of Constitution, 194; justifies war as defense of Constitution, 194, 206–207; blunders in Ireland, 194–195, 196; thrives on unrest in Scotland and England, 195; blunders in Scotland, 195; apologizes to Muir, 195; John "Jew" King warned against by Paine, 196; prosecutes radicals, 196; agitated by return of Frost, 197; difficulties respecting Friends of the Liberty of the Press, 198; errs in trying Paine, 198; censured by Friends of the Liberty of the Press, 198; assailed by Spence, 199; relies on newspapers and The Association, 199; punishes Erskine for defending Paine, 201, 208; co-operates with The Association, 201, 236; uneasy about effect of Fox's *Letter*, 205, 226; postpones debates on King's message, 204, 205; never loses cases to Garrow, 207; to be aided by new batch of lawyers, 207; indicts *Morning Chronicle*, 208; intends to restore Bourbons, 211; obtains Portland's silence on augmentation of forces, 212; fulfills agreement with Prince of Wales, 213, 214; "sapped" by *Oracle*, 215; tries to intimidate reformers, 215; releases Auckland's communications, 216; reshuffles legal personnel, 216; said by Fox to be responsible for the war, 219; accused of duping the people, 220–221, 223; delays settling election of Scottish peers, 221, 263; reason for building of barracks, 224; uneasy about popular reaction to war, 226–227; problems respecting enlistments, 227; refuses to release Lord George Gordon, 229, 440; exploits laws regarding debtors, 228, 230, 287, 440; opposes revision of laws for imprisonment of debtors, 230; exploits laws regarding bankruptcies, 231, 344–345, 434–435; punishes Frost, 231, 278; contemns Friends of the Liberty of the Press, 235; tries to avoid trouble in Ireland, 232; challenged by Sheridan regarding phantom insurrection, 236; circulates works of Paine and Pigott, 236; accused of tampering with the press, 236; reluctant to try traitors,

236; activities defended by Burke, 236; frightened by Friends of the People, 238, 268; defends Scott in Stockbridge briberies, 242, 267; attitude toward Fox, 242, 243; suppresses news of defeats, 243; arranges embarrassment of Fox, 244; hints at Fox's correspondence with French, 244–245; influences London elections, 245; defeats Newnham, 245; "proves" existence of disease by producing remedy, 248, 249; accused of hypocrisy and deception, 250; accused of subverting Constitution, 251; accused of adopting worst of both French regimes, 252; accused of frightening Perry into flight, 252; signs treaty with Russia, 258–259; silent respecting progress of war, 259; yields on Traitorous Correspondence Bill, 260; encourages informers, 263; supported by Stormont, 263; regulates elections of Society of Antiquaries, 264; afraid of Grey's motion for reform, 268; stifles popular complaints, 269; threatens citizens of Birmingham, 271; Almon turns pamphleteer for, 276, 420; not responsible for trial of Frend, 277; cannot prosecute moderate reformers, 278; accepts defeat of Grant, 279; tries Eaton, 280, 344; controls elections of Scottish peers, 284; mismanages Indian affairs, 289; makes mockery of trial of Hastings, 290; opposes inquiry into causes of delay in Hastings's trial, 291; placates Burke, 292–293; rewards converts by padding expenses, 297; *True Briton* spokesman for, 298; provides military entertainments, 299, 360–361; orders Dumouriez to leave, 303; attempts negotiations with Duke of Clarence, 304, 364; faro tables owned by friends of, 331; prosecutes talkers and booksellers, 341–344, 434–435; urged by *Oracle* to prosecute reformers, 342–343; rewards supporters of war, 351–352; supported by Portland on issue of war, 355;

Pitt Government (con't).
accused of starting war to retain office, 355; Dundas vulnerable member of, 356; brings in Canning, 357; punishes Lonsdale, 357; plans Waterdown camp, 360–361; disapproves of Prince of Wales's elegance, 363; signs treaty with Austria, 368; indicted by Gerrald, 369; annoyed with Woodfall, 384, 385, 388; lacks communication with Duke of York, 390; rumored changes in, 392; denounced for conduct of war, 397; not approved by Portland, 399; hates repatriated reformers, 406; tries to involve Friends of the People in Muir's trial, 406; prosecutes Muir, 408; prosecutes Palmer, 408; prepares invasion alarm, 409, 413; not accused of bullying Algiers, 413; supported by Jordan, 420; suspected of instigating Cherokees, 423; looks for evidence of sedition, 432; sends archenemies to Newgate, 435; embarrassed by death of Lord George Gordon, 441; uneasy regarding conditions in Newgate, 442; dissolves British Convention, 447; humiliated by acquittal of Morning Chronicle, 447, 448; outlook respecting the press, 468; expected to exploit the British Convention, 469–470; see also Britain, Crown lawyers, and Treasury

"Placid, Secretary," see Burges, James Bland

Pleas, Clerks of, 263; Master of, 132

Plumer, Thomas (1753–1824), lawyer (counsel for Hastings; KC 1793; Bencher of Lincoln's Inn 1793), 207, 290

Plymouth, 179, 227

Poetry, character of, 19, 163; popularized by World, 25; Morning Chronicle's interest in, 35, 167; World's interest in, 69; Oracle's interest in, 177

Poland, invasion of, 85, 104; second partition of, 189, 223, 266; struggles for independence, 189; Allies' conduct toward denounced by Fox, 211, 223;

Morning Chronicle's essays on, 347; dismissed by True Briton as irrelevant, 347; treatment extenuated by Jenkinson, 347; treaty with Russia, 360; Prussia's and Russia's quarrel over, 360; treaty with Prussia, 389; Russia's conduct toward, 401–402; mentioned, 401

Pomfret, George Fermor, 3rd Earl of [GB] (1768–1830; suc. 1785), 347

Poole, 271

Pope, Alexander (1763–1835), actor at Covent Garden, 96

Pope, Mrs. Elizabeth (1744?–1797), actress at Drury Lane, 42

Porchester, Lord, see Carnarvon, Henry Herbert, 1st Earl of

Porson, Richard (1749–1808), classical scholar, background, 122; awarded "dividend" by Cambridge University and elected Regius Professor of Greek, 123–124, 152; contributes to Morning Chronicle, 167, 419

Porter, George (c. 1761–1828), politician (MP Stockbridge 1793–1820), 242

Portland, William Henry Cavendish Bentinck, 3rd Duke of [GB] (1738–1809; suc. 1762; Harleian Trustee of British Museum 1764–1809; FRS 1766; FSA 1775), statesman (Lord Lieutenant of Ireland 1782; Prime Minister 1783; Chancellor of Oxford University 1792–1809; President of Foundling Hospital 1792–?), headed coalition government, 9; political position, 9–10; followers of, 10; buys puffs in newspapers, 20, 184; subsidizes Opposition papers, 31; writes nothing for newspapers, 37; patron of O'Beirne, 38, 39; opposes election reforms, 81, 207; supports Proclamation against Seditious Writings, 81, 82; defection proclaimed by World, 82; attempts to convert Fox, 101; elected Chancellor of Oxford University, 106–107, 107–108, 111; rumor of willingness to join Government denied, 111; proposed as head of Fox-Pitt coalition, 121–122; expected to become Lord Lieutenant of Ireland, 131; desertion by Loughborough expected, 139; defection again proclaimed by *World*, 146; expected to convert Fox, 155; supports Alien Bill, but censors Pitt, 155; accepts Presidency of Foundling Hospital, 156; said by Elliot to have quit Fox, 156, 421; Fox's devotion to, 156–157; censors Pitt's manner of getting office, 157; stops payments to newspapers, 166; puffed by Ministerial papers, 184; criticism of Pitt protested by *True Briton*, 184; appealed to by Fox to delay consideration of augmentation of forces, 193–194; expected to defect, 203; Prince of Wales's letter to, 203, 204, 208, 209, 213, 355, 399; supports war, 207, 220, 222; silent respecting augmentation of forces, 209, 212; commended by Stormont, 220; grieves Lauderdale and Lansdowne, 221–222; refuses to take office, 221; returns one member to Commons, 240; continues as member of Whig Club, 244; fails to oppose Traitorous Correspondence Bill, 262, 263; said by *The Times* to have deserted Fox, 263; supports Government's policies, but not Government, 292, 355; conferences with Pitt and Dundas denied, 297; donates to fund for paying Fox's debts, 301; installed as Chancellor of Oxford, 350–351; unaffected by Pitt's ultimatum, 401, 421, 422, 425, 432

Portland Government, 12, 38
Portsmouth, 371, 390, 451
Portugal, 219, 389
Posen, 223
Postlethwaite, Dr. Thomas (1731–1798), educator (Master Trinity College, Cambridge University 1789–1798), 123, 124, 235
Postmasters General, *see* Chesterfield, Philip Stanhope, 5th Earl of *and* Walsingham, Thomas de Grey 2nd Baron

Post Office, corruptions of, 61, 62; quarrels in, 61–63, 254; delays delivery of newspapers, 117, 125, 166, 167, 170, 451–452; impedes delivery of foreign correspondence, 165; searches mail, 236, 244–245; puts employees in uniform, 329; mentioned, 37, 118, 136
Post Office, Secretary of the General, *see* Todd, Anthony
Powell, Mrs. (1761?–1831), actress at Drury Lane, 42
Powell, J., 32
Pownoll, Philemon (fl. 1790–1802), Liverpool banker, 33
Powys, Thomas (1743–1800), politician (MP Northamptonshire 1774–1797), 218, 219, 272, 367
Press, "Engineering" of, 417–418, 419
Press, freedom of the, extortion a "concomitant" of, 21; championed by Erskine, 141; subverted by Government, 148, 152, 236; defended by Erskine in trial of Paine, 152–153; matter of concern to newspapers, 201; condemned by Prince of Wales, 308; defended by Friends of the Liberty of the Press, 238, 265; triumphs in trial of *Morning Chronicle*, 454
Preston, T., 37
Priestley, Dr. Joseph (1733–1804), scientist, Unitarian preacher, writer, principal target of Birmingham rioters, 122–123; patron saint of Cambridge students, 122–123; denounced by Burke, 237; replies to Burke's charges, 253; Burke censored for treatment of, 366; hated by new Bishop of Rochester, 401; sons sail for America, 405
Princesses, 3, 164, 165
Pringle, John, Sheriff of Edinburgh, 454, 455
Printers, 434–435
Prisons, demand for reforms of, 179, 285, 435–440; reforms advocated by Lord George Gordon, 229; crowded conditions of, 269, 285; interest in, 435; *see also individual prisons*

Privy Council, Clerk of, 397

Proclamation against Seditious Writings, text of, 80–81; purpose of, 81, 149; debates on, 81–82; unenforced, 84; frightens Mackintosh, 99; supported by Prince of Wales, 100; protested by radical reformers, 101–102; affects stock market, 103; supported by Guilford, 105; supported by Stormont and Loughborough, 106; Paine's reply to, 133; supposed effect of, 146

Prussia, prepares for invasion of France, 85; invades Poland, 85, 104; declares war on France, 104, 217; defeated at Valmy, 119, 121; castigated by Fox for treatment of Poland, 194, 210, 211; partitions Poland, 189, 223; will fight to recover prestige, 210; beaten by France, 212; castigated by Fox for despotic treatment of France, 219; undertakes defense of Holland, 243; signs treaty with Britain, 258, 259, 423; signs treaty with Poland, 266, 347, 389; takes Mainz, 297, 359; more interested in Poland than France, 360; fights war of despots, 377; inactive, 391; Commissioner of the Army of, 428; see also Allies

Prussia, King of, see Frederick William II

Public Advertiser, titles, 467, 468; background, 23, 133, 229; proprietors, 23, 468; printers, 23, 177–178, 416, 417, 468; address, 23, 177–178, 416; price, 178, 467; connection with Diary, 23–24, 173, 178; politics, 22, 23–24, 178, 359; subsidized by Treasury, 23; subsidized by Dibdin, 88–89, 317; character, 23–24, 178, 468; personnel, 24, 39, 133, 178, 229, 269, 282, 455, 468; on Prince of Wales's economies, 51, 58, 60, 101, 127, 128, 153; on damages awarded Lady Lambart, 66, 98; publishes obituary of Burgoyne, 91; sneers at Mrs. Merry, 94; on death of Guilford, 105; on Pitt's appropriation of Cinque Ports, 107; on Portland's election to Chancellorship of Oxford

University, 111; on Paine's flight, 112; troubled by Government's indifference to developments, 121; entreats Fox to join Pitt, 122; on Weltje's domestic squabbles, 128–129; loses Treasury subsidy, 177–178; shares news with World, 178, 383; later demise of, 179; announces defections of Carlisle and Loughborough, 180; supports Alien Bill, 185, 190; reports Burke's negotiations with Pitt regarding trial of Hastings, 186; credits Burke with Alien Bill, 190; prints excerpts from Fox's Letter, 191; denounces Friends of the Liberty of the Press, 201, 237; gloats over dismissal of Erskine, 208, 213; gloats over reduction of Opposition, 212; sneers at motions of Opposition, 222; praises The Association, 222; strikes at Fox and Lauderdale, 238; lambastes Sheridan, 247–248, 250; supports Traitorous Correspondence Bill, 250; defends loan, 255, 257; supports national fast, 264; agrees bankruptcies sign of prosperity, 264, 269; on Commercial Credit Bill, 270; prints excerpts from Stuart's parody, 271, 282, 417; eulogizes Pitt, 282; lectures moderate reformers, 282, 283; opposes legal and penal reforms, 285, 435; supports Hastings, 291; expects Pitt's resignation, 295; opposes payment of Fox's debts, 300, 301, 305; on Clarence's repudiation of the war, 304, 392–393; on renovations of Covent Garden, 318–319; on Merry, 321; on Prince of Wales's camp bed, 363; defends Burke's warmongering, 378; on Hood's prizes, 389; on resignation of Duke of Richmond, 393–394, 395; on Palmer, 408; on death of Lord George Gordon, 437–438; sold, 333, 387, 416–417; supports Woodfall for City Remembrancer, 384, 387, 388, 417; character after sale, 417; on Pitt's ultimatum, 421; loses printing shop in fire, 448–449, 468; promises new

"arrangements," 416–417, 448, 465–467, 468; to become principal organ of Government, 468; later amalgamation with *Oracle*, 468; quoted, 28, 36, 60, 61, 85, 179–180, 197, 215, 216, 227, 276, 279, 285, 303, 324, 401, 424, 430, 443; mentioned, 24, 317; *see also* Woodfall, Henry Sampson
Public Ledger, 22, 24, 26, 163, 177
Public Safety, Committee of, *see* Committee of Public Safety
Puffs, 20–21
"Punctilio," 182
Pye, Henry James (1745–1813), poet (Poet Laureate 1790–1813), 176–177
Pyle, Alexander, bookseller, 343–344

Quakers, 228
Queensberry, William Douglas, Baron Douglas [GB] and 4th Duke of [S] (1725–1810; suc. 1778; cr. Baron Douglas 1786; KT 1753), 284, 285, 358
Quesnoy, 359, 389
Quick, John (1748–1831), actor at Covent Garden, 42

R., J. T., *see* Rutt, John Towill
Racing Calendar, 36
Radcliffe, William (fl. 1785–1826), journalist, 34, 102, 168, 169, 333, 336
Radnor, Jacob Pleydell-Bouverie, 2nd Earl of [GB] (1749–1828; suc. 1776; FSA 1779; Lord Lieutenant of Berkshire 1791–1819; Colonel of Berkshire Militia 1791–1800), 240
Raimbach, Abraham (1776–1843), engraver, 37
Rainbow Coffee-House, 36, 168
Rann, John, highwayman, 17
Rathband, Charles (d. 1795), journalist, 37
Rawdon, Baron, *see* Moira, Francis Rawdon-Hastings, 2nd Earl of
Raynal, Abbé Guillaume Thomas François (1711–1793), French historian and philosopher, 351

Raynsford, Nicolls, 237
Reader, Mr., lawyer, 317
Reason, Goddess of, 421
Red Book, The, 132, 376, 401; *see also* Crown, power of the *and* Patronage
Redding, Cyrus (1785–1870), journalist, 5, 119
Reed, Isaac (1742–1807), Shakespeare editor, 311
Reeves, John (1752?–1829), classical scholar, lawyer, pamphleteer, politician (Chief Justice in Court of Civil Jurisdiction in Newfoundland 1791–?; permanent chairman of The Association; Commissioner of Bankrupts 1793–?), background, 135; places and emoluments, 136; heads The Association, 134–135, 136; sponsors publications, 137; employs spies, informers, and agitators, 137, 228; demands loyalty oaths, 141; accused of publishing malicious libel, 152; praised by *Oracle*, 176; loses reputation, 200; Law's letter to, 201, 208; accused of duping people into war, 236; insists on home visits, 252; finds no sedition, 253; Peter Stuart's pamphlet dedicated to, 283; appointed Commissioner of Bankrupts, 376–377; goes to Lisbon, 398; supports increase in taxes, 398; supports corruptions, 404; chief beneficiary of war, 430; assailed by Daniel Stuart, 469
Reeves's Association, *see* Association for Protecting Liberty and Property . . . , The
Reevites, *see* Association for Protecting Liberty and Property . . . , The
Reform, Parliamentary attitude toward, 10, 75; denounced by Bowles, 49; converted to popular and Party issue by Fox, 77; types confused by Pitt, 77; opposed by *True Briton*, 171, 234–235; called "treasonable" by *Oracle*, 176; called menace to Constitution by Pitt, 194; denounced by John "Jew" King, 196, 261; execution of Louis XVI presented as argument for, 206; Pitt's

Reform (con't).
means of defeating, 228; opposed by
Mornington, 273; Burke archfoe of,
402–403; supported by *Morning Post*,
403–404
Reformers, moderate, defined, 8; enthusiastic about Mackintosh's *Vindiciae*,
40; represented by Friends of the
People, 75; confused by Pitt with
radical reformers, 77; supported by
Diary, 125, 151; supported by *Star*,
135; supported by Fox, 149; supported
by *Gazetteer*, 166, 168; defeated in
Thetford election, 184; overawed by
alarms, 185; confused by Pitt with
French aggressors, 214; impossibility
of prosecuting, 278; attacked by
Ministerial papers, 282; pursue lost
cause, 273–274; said unpopular with
people, 274; war contrived to defeat,
355; Pitt's threat to support, 400; *see
also* Election reforms
Reformers, radical, enthusiastic about
Paine's *Rights of Man*, 40; encouraged
by election scandals, 72; Government's
indifference to, 74, 81, 101, 111–113,
135, 341, 346; Friends of the People's
hope of redirecting, 76–77; expected by
Burke to dominate moderates, 78;
supported by Opposition papers, 80;
not objects of Proclamation against
Seditious Writings, 84; activities a
service to Pitt, 101–102, 153; called
agents of French, 151; represented by
Courier, 166, 168; represented by
Gazetteer, 168; Pitt's policy regarding,
196; want actual representation, 275;
lose faith in petitions, 275; *Morning
Post*'s acquaintance with, 336
Reformers versus "Constitutionalists,"
275
Regency crisis, 14–15, 18, 29, 32, 82, 132–
133, 246, 301
Reid, William Hamilton (d. 1826), poet
and journalist, 39
Representative Peers, 221, 263, 284–285,
285, 358

Reynal, John, employee in Stamp office,
430
Reynolds, Frederick (1764–1841), play-
wright, liaison with Mrs. Wells, 25;
Notoriety, 89, 90; flees to France with
Mrs. Wells, 90; *The Dramatist*, 138;
How to Grow Rich, 312; puffed by
Oracle, 324–325
Reynold, James, Surveyor of Stamps, 377
Reynolds, Sir Joseph (1723–1792), por-
trait painter, 366
Richards, George (1767–1837), clergyman
and miscellaneous writer (Fellow of
Oriel College, Oxford 1790–1796;
Vicar of Bampton and Rector of
Lillingstone Lovel 1792–1824), 350
Richardson, Joseph (1755–1803), jour-
nalist, politician, dramatist, 76, 237,
311
Richmond, Charles Lennox, 3rd Duke of
[GB] (1735–1806; suc. 1750; Vice
President RSA 1754–1806; FRS 1755;
KG 1782; FSA 1793), military officer
and politician (Lord Lieutenant of
Sussex 1763–1806; Master General of
Ordnance 1782–1783, 1783–1795; Field
Marshal 1792), character, abilities,
politics, 6; buys puffs in newspapers,
20; patronized William Cook, 28;
accused of apostasy, 82, 141, 370, 404;
quarrels with Lauderdale, 85, 335;
manages camp at Bagshot, 82, 103–104;
promoted to Field Marshal, 103; list
of places, 132; stands guard at Tower,
139; fortifies parks, 140; constructs
barracks, 140; presents Tower fortifications for public inspection, 143; quit
Opposition to save post in Ordnance,
182; breaks legs, 187; ridiculed by
Morning Chronicle, 248, 299, 303, 361;
returns two members to Commons, 240;
elected Fellow of the Society of Antiquaries, 296; puffed by *True Briton*,
308; piqued at losing Chancellorship of
Oxford, 350–351; manages Waterdown
camp, 360–361, 410; military bungler,
361, 375, 410, 411; ridiculed by

Morning Post, 361, 458; disgusts *World*, 361, 411; manages Brighton camp, 361-362, 371-374, 412; admired by Saunderson, 370; blamed for Dunkirk, 393, 396, 397, 398; resignation expected, 393, 394, 395, 396, 424, 425; treated coolly by George III, 395, 398; defended by Pitt, 410; ridiculed by Opposition papers, 412; services for Ordnance, 424-425; mentioned, 438

Richmond Park, Ranger of, 105

Richmond theater, 90

Ricketts, Captain, 332

Rickman, Thomas "Clio" (1761-1834), bookseller, 135

Riddell, Mr., 36

Ridgway, James (fl. 1782-1817), bookseller, earlier activities, 39, 85, 86; publisher for Friends of the People, 74, 138, 239, 268, 279; attempts to blackmail Mrs. Billington, 85-87; enemy of Pitt, 138; indicted for publishing libel, 138; rearrested, 152; publishes pamphlet by Courtenay, 188; publishes *Letters to the People of North Briton*, 267; pleads guilty to three indictments, 268; sentenced to Newgate, 279; combines publishing business with Symonds's, 279; *see also* Ridgway and Symonds

Ridgway and Symonds, 279, 337, 343, 442, 468, 469

Rigby, Richard (c. 1722-1788), politician (Paymaster General 1768-1782), 246

"Rights," 274

Riley, George (fl. 1792-1794), journalist, 169, 374

Rivington, Charles (1754-1831), bookseller, 331

Roaf, H., printer, 23, 174

Robbins, Henry (1753-1821), auctioneer, 31

Roberts, Peter (d. 1793), City Remembrancer, 384, 388

Roberts, Thomas, 384, 388

Robertson, James, bookseller, 214-215, 233, 286, 433, 434

Robespierre, Maximilien Marie Isidore de (1758-1794), French Revolutionist, 84, 224, 290, 420

Robinson, G. G. J. and J., booksellers, 139, 343-344, 443

Robinson, John (1753-1813), 443

Robinson, Mrs. Mary (1758-1800), poetess, dramatist, courtesan, ex-mistress of Prince of Wales, 11, 33; settles with Prince of Wales and George III, 12; early mistress of John "Jew" King, 33; correspondence published by King, 33; occasional writer for *Oracle*, 19-20, 177; buys newspaper puffs, 20; adulated by newspapers, 163, 177, 311-312, 412; employs newspapers to urge production of *Kate of Aberdeen*, 95, 314, 316; goes to Continent, 95; publishes *Three Poems*, 311; author of *Modern Manners*, 311; idolized by Daniel Stuart, 338; publishes *Monody to the . . . Late Queen of France*, 412

Rochester, Samuel Horsley, Bishop of (1733-1806; FRS 1767; DCL Oxford 1774), divine (Bishop of St. David's 1788-1793; Bishop of Rochester and Dean of Westminster 1793), 401, 426, 430

Rockingham Government, 38, 133

Rockingham Whigs, made Richmond a general, 6; Burke's early attachment to, 7; alarmed respecting activities of George III, 7; wooed by Pitt, 399; support war, 399; Pitt's ultimatum, 409-410, 413, 421; mentioned, 400

Rogers, Samuel (1763-1855), poet and journalist, 76

Rogers, Thomas (1735-1793), 237

Roscoe, William (1753-1831), historian, poet, miscellaneous writer, 276

Rose, George, Sr. (1744-1818), statesman and journalist (Secretary of the Treasury 1782-1783, 1783-1801; Master of Pleas in Court of Exchequer c. 1784-1818; Verderer of New Forest 1788-?; Clerk of the Parliaments 1788-1818; MP Christchurch 1790-1818),

Rose, George, Sr. (con't).
early association with Pitt, 5; managed
press and elections, 5, 22; embarrassment to Government, 5, 67, 113;
sponsors and subsidizes *Diary*, 22;
uses *World* for intrigues against Burke,
25–26; friend of Thomas Harris, 27,
42; contributes to newspapers, 27;
exposed by spurious *Star*, 41, 50;
exposed by *Morning Post*, 41, 166; sued
by Smith, 49, 50, 63, 443; quarrels with
Sheridan, 63; defended by *World*, 63–
64, 69, 98; defended by himself, 64;
protected by Pitt, 65; Westminster
electors petition for removal, 65, 66;
sues *Morning Post*, 65, 66, 97, 138;
protests leasing of *World*, 69–70;
refuses to defend *World* against lawyers,
70; conduct encourages reformers, 72;
suppresses investigation of *World*, 113;
persuades Burke of inability to manage
newspapers, 118; principal writer for
Sun, 118, 307; patronizes *Sun*, 125;
places, sinecures, and pensions, 132;
functions restricted to journalism, 170,
356; founds *True Briton*, 171; principal
writer for *True Briton*, 171; dislikes
The Times, 173; arranged subsidy of
World, 174; arranged subsidy of
Morning Herald, 164; castigates Dudley
and Topham, 174, 175; taunted about
emoluments, 247, 296–297, 300, 377,
450, 457; assailed by *Morning Chronicle*,
247, 302, 306, 307, 308, 309, 347;
assailed by *Morning Post*, 297, 455;
moves for postponement of Stockbridge
Electors Incapacitating Bill, 267; owns
True Briton, 307, 310, 356; assailed by
Gazetteer, 310; friend of Strahan, 384;
mentioned, 246
Rose, George Henry, Jr. (1771–1855),
diplomat (Secretary to British Embassy
at The Hague 1792–1793; Secretary to
British Embassy at Berlin 1793–1794),
296, 352–353, 377
Ross, George, publisher of Edinburgh
Gazetteer, 349, 434, 448, 453, 460

Ross, William, conductor of Edinburgh
Gazetteer, 434, 448, 453, 459, 460
Rouge et noir, 164
Rous, George (c. 1744–1802), 63, 200, 201
Rowan, Archibald Hamilton (1751–1834),
Irish reformer, member of United
Irishmen, 135; reputation, 194, 195;
arrested, released, 194; sends address
to Scottish Convention, 233; functions
at dinner of Constitutional Society,
268; indicted in Ireland, 276; freed on
bail, 276; candidate to British Conven-
tion, 434; arrested in Edinburgh, 434,
443; freed on bail, 434
Roxburgh, 271
Roxburghe, John Ker, Earl Ker [GB] and
3rd Duke of [S] (1740–1804; suc. 1775;
Lord of the Bedchamber 1767–1796),
358
Royal Academy, 21
Royal Burghs of Scotland, *see* Scotland,
Royal Burghs of
Royal Family, reputation and character
of, 3; activities reported by newspapers,
19; Government's unwillingness to
embarrass, 36; expected to be non-
partisan respecting theaters, 42; attend
Bagshot, 104; attend Drury Lane, 147;
Madame Mara's disrespect for, 312;
abused by The Association, 341
Royalists, 259
Royal Society, President of, 429
Rundel and Bridge, silversmiths and
jewelers, 127
"Rural Bard, The," 69
Russell, John, styled Lord (1766–1839),
politician (MP Tavistock 1788–1802),
finances attacks on Rose, 63, 166;
member of Friends of the People, 76;
resigns from Friends of the People, 84;
discontinues financing of newspapers,
166; supports motion for augmentation
of forces, 210; attends Fox's anniversary
dinner, 409
Russell, William, styled Lord (1767–
1840), politician (MP Surrey 1789–
1807; DCL Oxford 1793), 349, 409

Russia, near-war with, 8, 53, 221, 269; invades Poland, 85; partitions Poland, 104, 189, 223; assailed for treatment of Poland, 266, 347; treaty with, 258–259, 297, 304, 305, 360

Russia, Empress of, see Catherine II

Rutland, Charles Manners, 4th Duke of [GB] (1754–1787; suc. 1779; Lord Lieutenant of Ireland 1784–1787), 431

Rutland, John Henry Manners, 5th Duke of [GB] (1778–1857; suc. 1787), 240

Rutt, John Towill (1760–1841), drug merchant and poet, 35, 167

Rutter, Mr., 414

Ryder, Dudley (1762–1847), politician (MP Tiverton 1784–1803; Under Secretary in Foreign Office 1789–1790; Vice President of Board of Trade 1790–1801; Paymaster General of the Forces 1791–1800), 246

Sagar, Sergeant, 227

St. Albans, High Steward of, 133

St. Alban's Tavern, 314

St. Amand, 298

St. Foy, Mr., journalist, 143

St. George's Fields, 436

St. James's Chronicle, title, colophon, politics, 26, 178; subsidized by Treasury, 26, 178; on Lauderdale, 221; on trial of Hastings, 241; quoted, 168, 216, 253, 254–255

St. James's Palace, 394, 395, 463

St. James's Park, Ranger and Keeper of, 132

Saint Malo, 446

Salisbury, 444

Salisbury, James Cecil, 1st Marquess and 7th Earl of [GB] (1748–1823; suc. 1780 cr. 1789; DCL Oxford 1773; FRS, FSA 1784; KG 1793; Lord Lieutenant of Hertfordshire 1771–1823; Colonel of Hertfordshire militia 1773–1815; Lord Chamberlain of the Household 1783–1804), 353

Salomon, Johann Peter (1745–1815), violinist and musical director, 43

Saltram, 58

Sambre, 414

Samuel, Emanuel, journalist, 26, 90

Sanderson, Sir James, see Saunderson, Sir James

Sandwich, John Montagu, 5th Earl of [GB] (1743–1814; suc. 1792), politician (Master of the Buckhounds 1783–1806; MP Huntingdon 1768–1792; Recorder of Huntingdon and Godmanchester 1792–1814), 105, 240

Sandwich, John Montagu, 4th Earl of [GB] (1718–1792; suc. 1729), 33, 104, 105, 437

Sans Souci, 88, 89, 317

Santerre, Antoine Joseph (1752–1809), French revolutionary politician and general, 390

Sardinia, 217, 297, 304, 305, 375–376

Sardinia, King of, see Victor Amadeus III

Saunders, Mr., contractor, 325

Saunderson, Sir James (1741–1798; knighted 1786), banker and politician (Lord Mayor of London 1792–1793; MP Malmesbury 1792–1796), moves Address of Thanks, 148; seizes firearms, 139; opposes Sheridan's motion regarding seditious activities, 236; evicts Corresponding Society from Globe Tavern, 370, 404; voted contemptuous by Corresponding Society, 370; lambasted by Morning Post, 370; requests report on condition of Newgate, 442

Savenay, 456

Savignac, Paul, informer, 135, 276

Savoy, 148, 210, 217

Sawbridge, John (1732?–1795), politician (MP London 1774–1795; Lord Mayor of London 1775–1776), 76, 237

Saxe-Coburg, Friedrich Josias, Prince of (1737–1815), Austrian general, commands Austrian forces, 258; defeated at Neerwinden, 258; negotiates with Dumouriez, 258; proclamation of, 302; distrusts Dumouriez, 303; captures Condé, 359; fails to join British at

Saxe-Coburg (con't).
Dunkirk, 390, 391; attacks Maubeuge, 413; mentioned, 390
Say, Mary (1738–1831), printer, 34, 37
Sayers, James (1748–1823), lawyer, poet, caricaturist, 27, 29
Scheldt, 134, 145, 183, 210, 211, 222
Schwellenberg, Madame (d. 1797), companion of the Queen, 3, 4, 20
Scoon, Keeper of the, 133, 263
Scotland, Treasury writers in, 30; Lord Justice General of, 133, 263; Dundas's effigies burned in, 145, 180; anticipated uprisings in, 144, 145; Lord Advocate of, 145; prosecutions in, 179, 195–196, 214–215, 233, 248–249, 405–408; Keeper of Great Seal of, 191; Government's blunders in, 195; *Morning Post*'s interest in, 335; Royal Burghs of, 76, 356
Scotland, Bank of, *see* Bank of Scotland
Scotland, Representative Peers of, *see* Representative Peers
Scott, Mr., wine merchant, 89
Scott, Alexander, spy, 145, 448, 453, 459, 460
Scott, Sir John (1751–1838; knighted 1788; FSA 1792; FRS 1793), lawyer (Bencher of Middle Temple 1783; MP Woebley 1783–1796; Chancellor of Durham 1787–?; Solicitor General 1788–1793; Attorney General 1793–1799), persuaded by Thurlow to withdraw resignation as Solicitor General, 83; co-operates with The Association, 136, 201, 216; appointed Attorney General, 216, 221; re-elected Member for Woebley, 221; sneers at Fox, 250; introduces Traitorous Correspondence Bill, 248, 249, 260; challenged by Erskine, Fox, and Sheridan, 251–252; challenged by *Morning Chronicle*, 253; releases Almon, 275, 276; appealed to by Lauderdale, 335; prosecutes Eaton, 344; transfers Winterbotham to state prison, 445
Scott, Major John (1747–1819), agent of Warren Hastings, invests in news-

papers, 7, 241; writes for *World*, 26, 70, 430; attends Hastings's trial, 181; lost seat as Member for West Looe, 241; loses Stockbridge election, 241–242; responsibility for briberies diverted to electors, 242, 267; *see also* Hastings, Warren
Scottish Convention, 141, 144, 145–146, 233, 406
"Scotus," 408
Scrope, Bernard (fl. 1789–1792), politician, 115–116
Second editions, 165
Sedaine, Michel Jean (1719–1797), French dramatist, 379
Sempill, Hugh, 14th Baron [S] (1758–1830; suc. 1782), 140, 149, 155
Shakespeare, 130, 177, 319–320, 327
Shakespeare Tavern, 326, 409
Sharp, William (1749–1824), engraver, 464
Sheffield, 269, 282–283, 448, 459
Sheffield, John Baker-Holroyd, 1st Baron [I] (1735–1821; cr. 1781, 1783; FRS 1783), politician (Colonel of Sussex Regiment 1777–1821; MP Bristol 1790–1802), 244
Sheffield Constitutional Society, *see* Constitutional Society, Sheffield
Shelburne, Earl, *see* Lansdowne, William Petty, 1st Marquess of
Sheridan, Charles Francis, (1750–1806), politician (Irish Secretary at War 1782–1789), 431
Sheridan, Richard Brinsley (1751–1816), politician, dramatist, proprietor of Drury Lane (MP Stafford Borough 1780–1806; Under Secretary for Foreign Affairs 1782; Secretary of the Treasury 1783; manager for impeachment of Hastings), politics, 10; character, 11, 18; activities, 11, 13, 32, 42, 63; intimacy with Prince of Wales, 11, 13, 14, 86; background, 9, 14, 15, 23, 86; friendships and associations, 35, 39, 40, 53; manages political department of *Oracle*, 23, 176, 325; influences politics

of *Morning Post*, 36; journalist and pamphleteer, 38; contracts for Opera House for Drury Lane Company, 43; attacks Rose in *Morning Post*, 41, 49, 50, 63; attacks Pitt on behalf of Prince of Wales in *Oracle*, 50, 52–53, 55, 63; blackmails Duke of York, 50, 51; author of libel on Guards, 56; persuades Lauderdale to subsidize *Oracle*, 60; supports inquiry into 1788 Westminster election, 63; quarrels with Rose, 63–64; defended by *Morning Post*, 64; on first secretarial committee of Friends of the People, 73; moves for reform of Royal Burghs of Scotland, 76, 356; advises Duke of Clarence, 87; finances building of Drury Lane theater, 95; said to have accepted Mrs. Robinson's opera, 95; death of wife, 95; leases Haymarket, 95, 96; alarmed at friendship between Prince of Wales and Fox, 100, 117; praised by *Oracle*, 117, 126, 176, 378–379; plots through *Oracle* to replace Pitt, 117–118, 126–128; plots with Thurlow and Rawdon to reconcile Prince of Wales and George III, 126–128; attempts coalition with Pitt, 130–131, 154–155; helps Government destroy *Argus*, 143, 154; supports Fox's amendment to Address of Thanks, 149; supports negotiations to end war, 149; expresses concern for French Royal Family, 154; exasperates Burke, 154, 155; defended by Fox, 154; lacks influence, 154; helps revive Friends of the Liberty of the Press, 155; says *True Briton* paid by Government, 172; reopens negotiations with Pitt, 176, 182, 219; wrote paper defending Louis XVI, 192, 244; accused by Burke of speaking for National Convention, 192; ascertains strength of Corresponding Society from Daniel Stuart, 193–194; active in Friends of the Liberty of the Press, 200, 201, 204, 330; attempts to negotiate with Pitt through Prince of Wales, 202–203, 204,

207, 213, 216; disliked by Burke, 204; derided by Ministerial papers, 212, 216, 222, 235, 245, 266; silent regarding augmentation of forces, 210, 219; loses confidence in Pitt, 216; insulted by Burke, 219; defines "phalanx," 219–220; defends Fox against charge of Jacobinism, 219, 220; supports Fox's resolutions on conduct of war, 223; called traitor by Burke, 233; replies to Burke, 233; moves for inquiry into seditious practices, 235–237; defends Friends of the People, 239; letters opened by Post Office, 244; informs Fox of plan to embarrass him, 244; exposes war profiteering, 246, 247; supports budget, 247; accused by newspapers of obstructing war, 247–248; original target of Traitorous Correspondence Bill, 249, 253; warned by *True Briton*, 250; replies to Burke, 251–252; further dickerings with Pitt, 260; silent on Traitorous Correspondence Bill, 260; supports Fox, 260; protests Auckland's Memorial, 264, 266; supports Grey's motion for reform, 274; promises Friends of the People will persist, 278; not supported by Bell, 280; admonished by the *World*, 283; censures Burke for silence on renewal of East India Company charter, 290; supports prosecution of *World*, 293; calls reporting of debates a "right," 293; denounces Pitt's and Dundas's monopolizing places, 294; subscribes to fund for paying Fox's debts, 308, 309, 310; encounters difficulties respecting Drury Lane, 313; expected to sell Drury Lane holdings, 313; rents Opera House, 314, 322; appealed to by Mrs. Jordan, 314–315; appealed to by Mrs. Bateman, 317; supervises building of Drury Lane, 319, 322, 323, 325; difficulties with Colman, 322; negotiations with Colman, 323, 324, 325; accused of deserting Drury Lane company, 324;

Sheridan, Richard (con't).
attends raising dinner, 326; warns Pitt
of need for newspapers' support, 346;
quips on reported death of Fox, 353;
early relationship to Tickell, 355;
intimacy with Canning, 357, 358; on
national debt, 391; attends Fox's
anniversary dinner, 409; requests
detention of Muir and Palmer, 461;
mentioned, 216, 317
Sheridan, Thomas (1775–1817), army
officer and versifier, 117
Shield, William (1748–1829), musical
composer, 92
Shields, 250
Siddons, Mrs. Sarah (1755–1831), actress
at Drury Lane, 42, 96, 314, 323
Signet, Clerk of the, 294
Signet, Keeper of the, 131, 132
Sillery, Alexis Brulart de Genlis, Marquis
de (1737–1793), French soldier and
politician, 192, 244, 420
Sillery, Stéphanie Félicité Ducrest, Marquise de (1746–1830), miscellaneous
writer, 192
"Simkin," see Broome, Ralph
Simolin, Ivan (fl. 1781), Russian am-
bassador, 144
Sinclair, Charles, reformer, 448, 453,
459, 460
"Skin merchants," see Crimps
Skinner, Thomas (1737–1806), auctioneer
and London alderman, proprietor of
Morning Post, 35, 68; supports Opposi-
tion's interests in London government,
35; present politics, 35, 245; praised by
World, 245; on committee for payment
of Fox's debts, 300; advertises in
Morning Post, 334; mentioned, 244
Skirving, William, Scottish reformer,
Secretary of Scottish Convention, 145,
275; Secretary of Associated Friends of
the People, 275, 349, 405; plans British
Convention, 275; acquainted with
Daniel Stuart, 336; corresponds with
Stuart, 348, 434; arrested, 349, 405;
apologizes to Friends of the People for

testimony at Muir's trial, 406–407;
President of British Convention, 434;
arrested and freed, 448; refuses to dis-
solve Convention, 448; attempts to
resume Convention, 459, 460; arrested,
459, 460; released, 460; indictment
printed by Morning Post, 471–472
Slave trade, abolition of, 85, 228
"Sleep," Burke's simile respecting, 251,
252, 253
"Slow, Jonathan," see Waller, Major
Henry
Smith, Mr., of Stapleton, 421
Smith, Mrs. Charlotte (1749–1806),
poetess and novelist, 35
Smith, George (fl. 1788–1793), publican,
49, 50, 63, 443
Smith, James, Scottish reformer, 215
Smith, John, Manchester laborer and
reformer, 408
Smith, Joseph (1757–1822), Pitt's con-
fidential secretary (Comptroller of
Coinage and the Mint 1786–?; Secre-
tary of the Cinque Ports 1792–?;
Receiver of Stamp Duties 1792–?), 111,
132
Smuggling, 375
Smyth, James Carmichael (1741–1821),
physician and medical writer, 442,
443
Society column, 164
Society for Constitutional Information,
see Constitutional Society
Society of the Friends of the People, see
Friends of the People
Society of United Irishmen, see United
Irishmen
Somers, Edmund Sigismund (1759?–
1824), medical doctor, 462
Somerset, Charles Henry, styled Lord
(1767–1831; cr. MA Oxford 1786), 59,
60
Somerset, Edward Adolphus Seymour,
11th Duke of [GB] (1755–1833; suc.
1793), 354
Somerset, Lord Lieutenant and Custos
Rotulorum of, 105

Somerset, Webb Seymour, 10th Duke of [GB] (1718–1793; suc. 1793), 354

Somerville, James 13th Baron [S] (1727–1796; suc. 1765; Representative Peer 1793–1796), 358

Sonnet, 163

Sotheby, John (1740–1807), auctioneer, 102

Southampton, Charles Fitzroy, 1st Baron [GB] (1737–1797; cr. 1780), military officer (Colonel of 3rd Dragoons 1772–1797; General 1793; Groom of the Stole to Prince of Wales 1780–1797), 60

Spain, near-war with, 8, 22; Beauchamp on, 210; France declares war on, 249; treaty with, 297, 304

Speaker, 392, 394, 396

Speed, Henry (1766–1820), banker and politician (MP Huntingdon 1790–1796), 33

Spence, Thomas (1750–1814), author and bookseller, publisher for Friends of the People, 199, 279; indicted for selling Rights of Man, 199; publishes The Case of Thomas Spence, 199; acquitted, 234; arrested for publishing Pig's Meat, 447, 448; indicted, 454, 464

Spencer, George John, 2nd Earl [GB] (1758–1834; suc. 1783; FRS 1780; FSA 1785; DCL Oxford 1793), politician (High Steward of St. Albans 1783–1807), political affiliation, 10; buys puffs in newspapers, 20; supports Proclamation against Seditious Writings, 82; supports Alien Bill, 155; declines Lord Lieutenancy of Ireland, 297; DCL Oxford 349; threatened by Pitt, 421, 422; defection announced, 424; refuses office, 432; mentioned, 133

Spencer, Henry John, styled Lord (1770–1795), diplomat (MP Woodstock 1790–1795; Secretary of the embassy at The Hague 1790–1793; envoy to Sweden 1793–1794), 297

Spencer, Robert, called Lord (1747–1831), politician (MP Wareham 1790–

1799), political affiliation, 10; subsidizes newspapers, 31, 38; disapproves of Friends of the People, 79; discontinues aid to the press, 167

Spies and informers, denounced by Fox, 148; employed by Dundas, 170; denounced by Morning Chronicle, 263, 341–342; testify against Muir, 406; riddle British Convention, 433; mentioned, 179–180, 228

Spilsbury, Thomas (1733–1795), printer and journalist, 26

Spitalfields weavers, 365, 419–420, 427, 455

Sports, 163–164

Stafford, Granville Leveson-Gower, 1st Marquess of [GB] (1721–1803; cr. 1786; KG 1771; FSA 1784), politician (Lord Lieutenant of Staffordshire 1755–1800; Lord Privy Seal 1784–1794), 240, 394

Stamp Duties, Receiver of, 132

Stamp Office, refuses credit to newspapers, 70; silences Argus, 143; aids in financing True Briton, 171; collects from Morning Post, 338; collects from World, 348; appointments in, 430; mentioned, 98, 150

Stamp Office, Commissioners of, 354, 355, 430

Stamp Office, Supervisor of, 354

Stamps, Deputy Supervisor of, 430

Stamps, Surveyor of, 377

Stanhope, Charles, 3rd Earl [GB] (1753–1816; suc. 1786; FRS 1772), politics, 10; author of Rights of Juries Defended, 82; opposes augmentation of forces, 211; opposes the war, 220; moves to end the war, 220; moves for disapproval of Auckland's Memorial, 304

Stanislaus Augustus Poniatowsky II (1732–1798; suc. 1764), 390

Stapleton, 421

Star, history, 30, 37; title, printer, editor, address, 37, 166; proprietors, 37, 135, 342; personnel, 39, 41; politics, 31, 37, 416; defends Prince of Wales, 52; on

Star (con't).

sale of Prince of Wales's stud, 58; publicizes Mackintosh's suit against Stuart, 67; on Mrs. Wells, 90–91; on death of Burgoyne, 91; on damages awarded Lady Lambart, 98; on death of Guilford, 105; on Pitt's appropriation of Cinque Ports, 107, 108, 110; on Pitt's re-election, 109; combines news-gathering facilities with *Morning Chronicle*, 120, 166, 167; censures *Sun*, 120; harassed by Post Office, 125; engrossed with Dr. Waite's worm medicine, 125–126; concerned with distribution of patronage, 132; supports moderate reform, 135; denies control by Friends of the People, 135; reports augmentation of Army, 137; concerned about Army purges, 140; protests treatment of Almon, 197; protests "pad," 328, 329; on Burke's Oxford degree, 351; defends Burke's war-mongering, 365; puffs Richmond, 424–425; on debtors, 445; quoted, 3, 28, 60, 61, 62, 95, 101, 104, 121, 135, 138, 163, 195, 200, 209, 215, 232, 254, 263, 265, 284, 285, 287, 288–289, 293, 294, 295, 296, 297, 300, 303, 315–316, 344, 349, 353, 358, 404, 405, 445, 462; mentioned, 74, 116, 118, 119, 125, 281, 317, 366, 417

Star, spurious, personnel of, 39, 41, 468; politics of, 15, 468; ridiculed personnel of *World*, 25; exposed Pitt's and Rose's management of Westminster election, 41, 49, 50; financial transactions regarding, 66–67, 443; affairs publicized by victimized newspapers, 67, 140; began editorial, 167; *Public Advertiser's* resemblance to, 468; quoted, 6

Steele, Thomas (1753–1823), politician (MP Chichester 1780–1807; Joint Secretary of the Treasury 1784–1791; Joint Paymaster General of the Forces 1791–?), 246, 378, 416, 424

Steevens, George (1736–1800), Shakespeare editor, 130, 177, 311

Stephens, Stephen (d. 1793), employee of the Stamp Office, 354

Stevenson, James (fl. 1782–1789), printer and journalist, 41

Stewart, John (1749–1822), journalist and walker, 409

Stewart, William, Scottish reformer, 195–196

Stibbert, Robert (b. 1774), 350

Stock exchange, 423

Stock market, 80, 103, 144, 145, 187, 249, 255, 298

Stockbridge Election Bribery Bill, 267, 279

Stockbridge Electors Incapacitating Bill, 267

Stockbridge House, 100

Stockjobbing, on Pitt's resignation, 131; *Star* accused of, 137; Stuarts' mode of, 144, 337; history of, 144; news invented for purposes of, 165; practiced by *The Times*, 174; specialty of the *Oracle*, 176; growing reliance on, 179, 298, 337; on Fox's death, 353; on state of the war, 359–360; mentioned, 206, 225, 391, 415

Storace, Anna Selina (1766–1817), singer and actress, 43, 96

Stormont, Viscount, *see* Mansfield, David Murray, 2nd Earl of

Strachan, John, bookseller, 434

Strahan, Andrew (1749–1831), printer, 173, 374

Strathaven, 271

Strathmore, Mary Eleanor Bowes, Countess of (1749–1800), 444

Strathrudie, 434

Street, Thomas George (fl. 1788–1828), historian, journalist, 116, 419

Stuart, Charles (c. 1750–c. 1800), related to Mackintosh, 39; Opposition journalist, 39; early activities, 40–41, 50, 66–67, 86, 144, 337, 468; character of, 41, 140; assails Rose in *Morning Post*, 49–50; assails Rose in pamphlet, 63; sued by Mackintosh, 66–67; employed as spy and journalist by Home Office, 67, 116; arrested for attacking watchman,

140; author of *A Short Review*, 283; author of *S'yerg's Beggar's Opera*, 271–272, 282, 417; publishes extracts from *Opera* in *Diary*, 271–272, 282, 417; publishes extracts from *Opera* in *Public Advertiser*, 282, 417; contributes to *World*, 283; warns Dundas about Muir, 409; publishes *Opera* in *World*, 417–418, 419, 424, 452, 467; advises Dundas on "engineering" of press, 417–418, 419; draws advance on salary, 418; lives in Windsor, 418; warns Home Office of dangers from reformers, 432–433; cautions Nepean regarding Corresponding Society, 433

Stuart, Daniel (1766–1846), journalist, contributes to *Argus*, 33, 74; contributes to *Morning Post*, 36, 74, 169, 336; Opposition journalist, 39; related to Mackintosh, 39; character, 40–41, 339; early career, 40–41, 144, 337; connection with Friends of the People, 73–74, 76, 336; compiles volumes of state papers, 74; connection with Lauderdale, 74, 336; stockjobbing techniques, 144, 337–338; meets Fox, 194; publishes for Friends of the People, 239; acquainted with Gerrald, 268, 336, 369–370; later owner of *Morning Post*, 334; acquainted with Skirving, 336, 348, 434; acquainted with Hardy and Tooke, 336; probable manager of *Morning Post*, 336–339, 340–341; author of *Peace and Reform*, 336, 337, 468–469; forges documents, 337, 340; sends forged document to *Sun*, 337, 415; writes boasts and paragraphs for *Morning Post*, 338; style, 338; opinion of successful newspaper, 338; date of purchase of *Morning Post*, 339–341; annoyed at brother's failure to acquire *Oracle*, 346; thanks societies on behalf of Friends of the People, 348; tries to acquire *Sun*, 415–416; associated with Street, 420; eulogizes Fox, 371; quoted, 30–31, 74–75, 78, 118, 136, 141, 193–194, 224, 264, 268, 339–340

Stuart, Duncan, *see* Stuart, Charles

Stuart, Mathew, *see* Stuart, Charles

Stuart, Peter (c. 1758–1807), journalist, defends Mackintosh, 23, 39; associated with Sheridan, 23, 50; edits *Oracle*, 23, 176, 346; background, 39, 41, 86, 114, 144, 176, 337, 468; sued by Lonsdale, 55–56, 60, 135; author of libel on Guards, 56; not a member of Friends of the People, 76; attacks John "Jew" King, 113–115; puffs Dundas, 116; literary enthusiast, 117, 176, 177; early interest in stockjobbing, 144, 176, 337; *modus operandi* as stockjobber, 337; later purchase of *Oracle*, 339–340; forgeries, 337, 340; attempts to get *Oracle*, 346, 468; warns Pitt of need for newspaper support, 346; possible connection with *Public Advertiser*, 468; quoted, 30; mentioned, 450

Sturt, Charles (1763–1812), politician, 237

Suffolk, 271

Sun, founded, 118–119; proprietors, 118, 236, 307, 356, 415; financing of, 118; editor, 118, 170, 415; printer, 118, 170; address, 118, 170; contributors, 118; character, 118–119, 135, 172, 176; detested by other Ministerial papers, 118–119, 125, 378; circulation, 119; coddled by Government, 119, 136; mutilates and suppresses news, 119–120, 121, 165; assailed by *Star*, 125; alarms *Diary*, 125; on state of the war, 134, 135; extols Banks, 136; used by The Association, 136; denies augmentation of Army, 137; engages in witch hunts, 143; appendage of *True Briton*, 143, 172; attacks *Morning Chronicle*, 153, 199; attacks Erskine, 153, 208; attacks Fox, 153, 180, 190, 303; regarded as experiment, 169–170; delivered to country papers, 172; chides Portland, 184; insults Chauvelin, 186, 187; calls for bounties for enlistments, 187; approves treatment of Almon, 197; quarrels with *World* and

Sun (con't).

The *Times* over degree of loyalty, 199; defends construction of barracks, 224; opposes legal reforms, 230, 285; attacked by Sheridan, 236; reprints Burges's *Letters*, 258; controlled by Treasury, 270; denounced by *Morning Chronicle*, 270; announces Bell's bankruptcy, 280–281; lectures to reformers, 283; on trial of Hastings, 291; on Portland's negotiations with Pitt and Dundas, 297; assails Lauderdale, 335; hated by *Morning Post*, 335, 415, 416; publishes Stuart's forgery, 337, 415; defends Dundas, 356; publishes maps, 359, 390, 450; has priority of news, 378; on election of City Remembrancer, 384, 385; reports assassination of King of Poland, 390; on Glasgow petition, 392; announces peace, 413; collects flannel waistcoats, 415, 416, 423; battles for priority with *The Times*, 448; quoted, 121, 424; mentioned, 74, 201, 290, 360, 366, 417, 437, 455

Sunday Reformer, 169, 374

Sunderland, 258

"Suppression fee," 21

Surrey, Lord Lieutenant of, 132

Sussex, Lord Lieutenant of, 132

Swan, Isaac (fl. 1790–1795), lawyer and journalist, writer for *Observer* and *World*, 26, 37; leases *World*, 69, 71, 174, 318, 417; sued by Dibdin for libel in *Observer*, 88, 174, 317; sued by Dibdin for libels in *World*, 89, 174, 317–318; prints Charles Stuart's parody, 419

"Swinish multitude," 181, 262, 279, 365, 366, 367, 377, 398, 402, 447, 448, 454

Switzerland, 303

Sydney, Thomas Townshend, 1st Viscount [GB] (1733–1800; cr. 1789; cr. Baron Sydney [GB] 1783; FSA 1784), judge (Chief Justice in Eyre 1789–1800), 240

Symonds, Henry Delahy, bookseller, publisher for Friends of the People, 74,

239, 268, 279; indictments and sentences, 135, 234, 268, 279; combines business with Ridgway's, 279; publishes *Treachery No Crime*, 403; on death of Gordon and Macan, 442; *see also* Ridgway and Symonds

Taitt, John, informer, 276

Tattersall, Richard (1724–1795), horse auctioneer, proprietor and lessee of *Morning Post*, 35, 36, 68, 334; financial situation respecting Benjafield, 36, 333; financial situation respecting Prince of Wales, 36, 68, 333; sued by Rose, 65, 97, 138; sued by Lady Cavan, 66, 97, 98, 99, 138; financial situation respecting *Morning Post*, 67–68, 333; indicted for libel on George III, 97–98; shares in *Morning Post*, 333; expiration of lease on *Morning Post*, 333, 339; advertises in *Morning Post*, 334; quits *English Chronicle*, 334

Taunton, Recorder of, 105

Taxes, on newspapers and advertisements, 20; expected reduction of, 53, 54, 85; called blessing, 101, 102; reduction impossible, 147; increase impossible, 246, 247, 255; collection of, 274; increase threatened by Pitt, 304; increase impossible for Pitt, 332, 391; increase predicted by *Morning Post*, 398; cause riots in Bristol, 405

Taylor, Mr., once Commissary General, 246

Taylor, John (1757–1832), journalist, miscellaneous writer, agitator, author of pamphlet on Drury Lane, 43; employment by Treasury, 27; character, 29–30; salary, 29–30; tried as agitator in Edinburgh, 102, 116; drama critic for *World*, 320; probably paid by Dundas, 170; writes prologue for *The World in a Village*, 320; quoted, 28, 29, 33, 34, 94

Taylor, Michael Angelo (1757–1834), politician and lawyer (MP Poole 1791–1796; manager for impeachment of

Hastings), politics, 10; abused by Ministerial papers, 11, 49, 180, 222; pamphleteer and writer for newspapers, 38; opposes Alien Bill, 182; moves against construction of barracks, 224; mentioned, 337

Taylor, William (c. 1754–1825), manager of Opera House, leases Opera House, 42, 95; will manage Opera House, 314, 322; Sheridan's associations with, 322

Telegraph, 20, 80

Tennessee, 423

Thatched House, 404

Theaters, purchasers of puffs, 21; relation to the press, 42; political allegiances of, 42, 92; description of, 42–44; scandals involving, 85–91; *see also* Covent Garden, Drury Lane, Haymarket, Opera House

Thellusson, Peter (1737–1797), merchant, 127

Thelwall, John (1764–1834), lecturer and reformer, attends dinner of the Friends of the Liberty of the Press, 237; edits *Courier*, 419; functions at Frost's release, 463

"Themira," 177

"Themistocles," *see* Mountmorres, Hervey Redmond Morres, 2nd Viscount

"Theory," 77–78

Thirlwind, Thomas (fl. 1781–1794), printer, 150

Thompson, Thomas (c. 1768–1818), politician (MP Evesham 1790–1802), 63, 64, 65, 75, 98

Thorn, 223

Thurlow, Edward, 1st Baron [GB] (1731–1806; cr. 1778, 1792), lawyer (Bencher Inner Temple 1762; KC 1762; Lord Chancellor 1778–1783, 1783–1792; Teller of the Exchequer 1786–1806), background, 18, 38, 92; friendship with Prince of Wales, 18, 286; relations with Pitt, 82; opposes Fox's Libel Bill, 82–83; denounced by *World*, 82–83; resigns as Lord Chancellor, 83, 106; cr. Baron Thurlow of Thurlow, 83; gets

Tellership of Exchequer for life, 83; would protest Pitt's appropriation of Cinque Ports, 108; plots with Sheridan and Rawdon to regain Chancellorship, 117–118, 126–128; praised by *Oracle*, 117–118, 126; favored by George III, 118; urges Prince of Wales to economize, 127–128; fees charged as Chancellor, 141; opposes Insolvent Debtors Bill, 286, 287; opposes "enlargement" of debtors, 287; Stafford disappointed by resignation of, 394; expected to protest Muir's sentence, 409

Thurlow, Thomas (1737–1791), divine (Bishop of Durham 1787–1791), 18

Tickell, Richard (1751–1793), wit, pamphleteer (Commissioner of Stamp Office 1781–1793), 311, 355

Tierney, George (1761–1830), politician and journalist, pamphleteer and writer for newspapers, 38; Treasurer of Friends of the People, 73; founder of Friends of the People, 79; assailed by Ministerial papers, 80, 84, 101; author of *State of the Representation*, 99, 101, 238; helps revive Friends of the Liberty of the Press, 155; author of petition for reform of Friends of the People, 238, 272; author of Address of Friends of the People, 284

Times, The, history during Regency battle, 14, 24, 29; conductors and editors, 24, 173; printers, 24, 150, 173, 415; personnel, 24, 28; character, 21, 24, 163; politics, 22; circulation, 24–25, 150, 174; Long's patronage of, 28, 118, 173; subsidized by Treasury, 24, 170, 173, 415; early priorities of, 24; connection with *Evening Mail*, 24, 26; quarrel with John "Jew" King, 32, 113–115; on quarrels in Post Office, 61; asserts some newspapers in pay of French, 113; quarrels with *World*, 118, 199; quarrels with *Sun*, 119; complains of coddling of *Sun*, 125; gets foreign news from Aust, 125; engages in witch-hunting, 138, 143; supports *The*

Times (con't).

Association, 144; flays Erskine for defense of Paine, 153; disliked by Rose, 173; favored by Pitt, 173; quarrels with *True Briton*, 173, 175, 398–399, 410–411; sources of information, 174; flails Lauderdale, 180, 190, 346; supports Alien Bill, 185; urges necessity for war, 186, 226; on flight of Sampson Perry, 197; purports to be loyalest of newspapers, 199; demands ship from Lonsdale, 226; on Sheridan and Fox, 248; on Portland, 263; reports release of Almon, 276; opposes moderate reform, 283, 443–444; attacks Duchess of Gordon, 299; supports fund for paying Fox's debts, 302, 348; on Duke of Clarence, 305, 410; interested in faro parlors, 331; gets priority from Home Office, 378, 448; on progress of the war, 390; on national debt, 392; on conditions at Newgate, 442; on trial of *Morning Chronicle*, 454; puffs Dundas, 468; quoted, 31, 283, 334, 449; mentioned, 181, 366, 416; *see also* Walter, John *and* Walter, William

Timperley, Charles H. (1794–1846?), writer on typography, 116

Tirlemont, 258

Titchfield, William Henry Cavendish-Scott-Bentinck, styled Lord (1768–1809), politician (MP Buckinghamshire 1791–1809; DCL Oxford 1793), 10, 157, 183, 349

"Toby," 181

Todd, Anthony (d. 1797), Post Office official (Secretary of General Post Office 1762–1797), 10, 60

Tolwood Park, Steward, Keeper, and Guardian of, 109

"Tom Ego," *see* Erskine, Thomas

Tone, Theobald Wolfe (1763–1798), organizer of Society of United Irishmen, 135

Tooke, John Horne (1736–1812), philologist, miscellaneous writer, politician, probable contributor to *Argus*, 33, 84,

151; uses moderate reformers, 78; active in Corresponding Society, 84; moves to Constitutional Society, 102; character, 151; attends dinners of Friends of the Liberty of the Press, 200–201, 237, 264–265; assailed by *True Briton*, 215, 264–265; thought to be frightened into retirement, 215; friend of Merry, 275; ignored by Government, 276; Daniel Stuart's acquaintance with, 336; sued by Hood for expenses in Westminster election, 401; candidate for next Westminster election, 401; lampooned by Charles Stuart, 417; expected to defend reformers in Scotland, 459; registers at Newgate, 464; quoted, 193

Topham, Edward (1751–1820), journalist, playwright, biographer, bon vivant, background, 14–15, 25, 86; early friendship with Sheridan, 14, 15; founds *World*, 25; sued by Este, 25, 113, 174; friendship with Merry, 39, 321; leases *World* to Swan, 69, 70, 71; gets position for Samuel, 90; rescues Mrs. Wells, 90; first Secretary of The Association, 136; handles The Association's affairs in Yorkshire, 174, 379; attacked by *True Briton*, 174; appointed Deputy Lieutenant of East Riding, 174, 200, 379; quits *World*, 174, 175; collects from Treasury, 175; attends Hastings's trial, 191; censured for greed, 200; sends approved list of newspapers to provinces, 200; entertains Reynolds and Morton, 325; sells *World*, 340; appointed Commissioner of Bankrupts, 376–377, 379; attempts to blackmail Government, 379; fights for restoration of Treasury subsidy, 379; interest in the *World*, 417; mentioned, 119

Torbay, 376

Tornai, 423

"Tory," 251

Toulon, occupied by Hood, 389, 391; rumors regarding, 389; Hood's proclamation on occupation of, 389–390;

map of, 390; importance of, 391; Commissioners' declaration of, 413, 426, 431; possible withdrawal from, 413; promises regarding, 426; evacuation of, 456

Toulon, Commander in Chief at, 426

Toulon, Commissary General at, 428

Toulon, Commissioners for, 401, 421, 429, 397

Tower, The, supposed attacks on, 139; inspection of, 143; guarded by Richmond, 303, 361

Townshend, John Thomas (1764–1831), politician (Lord of the Admiralty 1789–1793; MP Whitchurch 1790–1800; Lord of the Treasury 1793–1800), 293, 295

Trade, Board of, 132, 246, 401

Traitorous Correspondence Bill, purpose of, 243–244, 248–249, 250, 260, 266; provisions of, 249, 260; introduced, 249; debates on, 249–253, 260, 261, 262, 263, 264; unpopularity of, 250, 253; newspaper commentary on, 253, 260, 261, 262, 263–264; bungled by Pitt, 255, 259, 267, 268; revisions of, 260, 265; supposed necessity for, 261; Portland's reaction to, 262; mentioned, 235

"Traveller," 59

Travis, George (1741–1797), divine (Archdeacon of Chester 1786–1797), 123

Treasury, payments to newspapers, 14, 15, 22, 23, 24, 25, 26, 170–171, 173, 174, 175, 177, 293, 415, 419; payments to writers, 27–30, 41, 50, 118, 170; slow paymaster, 49, 56; intrigues regarding Burke, 70, 118; fails to instruct writers, 113; finances founding of *Sun*, 118, 169–170; offers reward for apprehension of Frost, 143, 197; offers reward for apprehension of Sampson Perry, 143; subsidizing of press shifted to Home Office, 170; payments to press handled by Long, 170; finances founding of *True Briton*, 171; instigates

prosecutions of booksellers, 236, 342; returns seven members to Commons, 239; Steele's earlier connection with, 246; lends money to merchants, 269; controls *Sun* and *True Briton*, 270; transfers money to Dundas, 294; owns *True Briton*, 306; pays ballad singers, 348; employs printers, 417; appealed to by Este, 468; *see also* Pitt Government

Treasury, Lords of the, 293, 295, 352

Treaties, force of, 183

Trinity House, 187

Trinity House, Elder Brothers of, 105, 356

True Briton, founding of, 170, 171–172; continuation of *Argus*, 143, 171; sponsorship, 170, 270; proprietors, 170, 171, 306, 307, 356, 415; conductors, 171, 307, 310, 356; financing, 171, 306; editor, 171; printer, 171; address, 171; character and politics, 171–172, 176; personnel and contributors, 171, 172, 320; used by The Association, 136, 233–234; scourges other Ministerial papers, 172, 175; circulated free, 172; attacks *The Times*, 173, 299; flays Topham and Dudley, 174–175; quarrels with *World* over respective loyalty, 175; approves treatment of Almon, 197; attacks Fox, 190, 213, 224, 238, 299; attacks *Morning Chronicle*, 199, 347; on Friends of the Liberty of the Press, 201; on Erskine's dismissal, 204, 207, 208; reviews Prince of Wales's letter to Portland, 204; proclaims Prince of Wales's disapproval of Sheridan, 207, 216; insults Lauderdale, 212, 218, 221, 238, 263–264, 335; gloats over Prince of Wales's defection, 213–214; lies about Prince of Wales's debts, 213–214; attacks *Oracle*, 215; lies about Maret's credentials, 217; insults Chauvelin, 217; enraged at Dumouriez for attempting negotiations, 217; on possibility of war, 217; attacks Opposition, 222, 261; on Duke of Clarence, 225–226, 300, 304; opposes revision of laws respecting debtors, 230, 285, 286;

True Briton (con't).
cautions reformers, 234–235, 283; sneers at Sheridan's motion respecting seditious practices, 235; explains reason for war, 243; scoffs at Whig Club, 244; impugns motives of Friends of the People, 249; warns Sheridan, 250; supports Traitorous Correspondence Bill, 249, 250, 261; applauds Burke, 261; threatens Tooke, 265; attacked by *Morning Chronicle*, 270; on trial of Hastings, 291; defends appointment of Jenkinson, 296; implies Portland's defection imminent, 297; on the prospect of peace, 298; accused of willful misrepresentation, 298; speaks for Government, 298; attacked by *The Times*, 298–299; ridicules fund for paying Fox's debts, 300, 301, 302, 303, 305, 308, 309, 310; defends source of information, 305–306; battered by *Morning Chronicle*, 306–311, 347, 348; puffs Richmond, 308; puffs Mrs. Robinson, 311, 312, 412; on Drury Lane, 313, 315, 324; puffs Taylor's prologue, 320; denounces gambling, 331; carries advertisements for Christie, 334; hated by *Morning Post*, 335, 456; on "The Calm Observer," 347; on Poland, 347; unable to manage other papers, 348; on Portland's speech at Oxford, 350; defends Dundas, 356, 430; publishes map, 359; on state of the war, 359, 389; quarrels with *The Times* over priorities, 378, 448; hated by Ministerial papers, 378; on election for City Remembrancer, 384; announces assassination of King of Poland, 390; announces death of Lafayette, 391; attacks Walter, 410–411; collects flannel waistcoats, 415, 423, 455; carries advertisements for Bell, 449; on British Convention, 461; expected to be supplanted by *Public Advertiser*, 468; quoted, 206, 207, 227, 295, 296, 449; mentioned, 118, 215, 290, 334, 360, 366, 417, 437, 455

Trusler, John (1735–1820), divine, literary compiler, journalist, medical empiric, 178
Tunbridge School, 372
Turban, 329
Turkey Company, Governor of the, 105
Turk's Coffee House, 29
Tweeddale, George Hay, 7th Marquess of [S] (1753–1804; suc. 1787), 285, 358, 446–447
Twisleton, Mr., 350
Two Sicilies, The, 359
Tyrrell, Timothy, City Remembrancer, 386, 388
Tyrwhitt, Robert (1735–1817), 122
Tytler, James (1747?–1805), chemist and miscellaneous writer, 195

Unemployment, 255, 391–392
Unitarianism, defended by Rutt, 35; history of at Cambridge University, 122–123
Unitarians, 236
United Irishmen of Dublin, Society of, 135, 194, 233
Uxbridge, Henry Paget, 1st Earl of [GB] (1744–1812; cr. 1784), 347

Valenciennes, 298, 332, 359, 360, 361, 362
Valenciennes helmet, 330, 362, 363
Valletort, Richard Edgcumbe, styled Viscount (1764–1839; DCL Oxford 1793), politician (MP Fowey 1791–1795), 349
Valmy, 119
Van Butchell, Martin (1735–1812?), empiric and eccentric, 427, 455
Vaughan, Benjamin (1751–1835), political economist and politician (MP Calne 1792–1796), 347
Vaughan, Felix, lawyer, 279, 280, 344
Vaughan, Sir John (1748?–1795; KB 1793), general and politician (MP Berwick 1774–1795; Governor of Berwick 1780–1795), 429
Vaughan, Thomas (fl. 1761–1820), playwright, 20, 314

Vavasour, Thomas (c. 1746–1826), politician, 200

Verdun, 120

"Verus," see Burges, James Bland

Victor Amadeus III, King of Sardinia and Savoy (1726–1796; suc. 1773), 210, 305, 376

Vienna, 303, 394

Vint, John (1754–1814), printer and journalist, 37

Virginia, 383

Visites domiciliares, see Home visits

Waite, Dr., 125–126

Wakefield, Gilbert (1756–1801), miscellaneous writer, 122, 278

Wales, George Augustus Frederick, Prince of (1762–1830; cr. 1762; KG 1765), 1st child and 1st son of George III, military officer (Colonel 10th Regiment of Light Dragoons 1793): early life, 3–4, 11; character of, 11, 12; liaison with Mrs. Robinson, 11, 20, 33; first financial settlement, 12; fails to support Whigs in elections of 1784, 12; renovations of Carlton House, 12; marriage to Mrs. Fitzherbert, 12–13; blackmailed by newspapers, 12–13; harassed by debts, 13; second financial settlement, 13; breaks with Fox, 13; involved in Sheridan's intrigues, 11, 13; further renovations of Carlton House, 13; commencement of Brighton pavilion, 13–14; reunion with Duke of York, 14; again harassed by debts, 14; negotiates for Dutch loan, 14; fights for unfettered Regency against the Queen and the Government, 14; supported in Regency battle by Sheridan's "New Whigs," 14–15; supported in Regency battle by The Times, 24, 29, 32; supported in Regency battle by Thurlow, 82; supported in Regency battle by spurious Star, 468; popularity in Ireland, 15; estranged from parents, 16; possible brides for, 16–17, 331; refuses to marry daughter of King of

Prussia, 16; Newmarket scandal, 17, 182; pursues Mrs. Billington, 17, 86; politics, 17–18; friends, 11, 17–18, 22, 35, 67, 209, 225, 230, 286; buys controlling interest in Morning Post, 35–36, 66, 97; subsidizes newspapers, 38; ridiculed by Holcroft, 42; defended by Public Advertiser, 51; defended by Morning Post, 52; blackmailed by Oracle, 51, 53; plots with Sheridan to avoid sale of stud, 51–52, 55, 56; buys Conway's house, 52, 60; attends debates, 55, 59; debts referred by Fox to George III, 57; castigated by Pigott, 56–57; lax paymaster, 56; first sale of stud, 56, 56–59, 60, 127; second sale of stud postponed, 59–60; resumes renovations of Carlton House, 60; meeting of advisors to consider payment of debts, 60, 66, 67; subsidizes Oracle, 60, 87; attempts to sell Morning Post, 66, 67; loss on Morning Post, 67–68; account with Tattersall, 68, 99, 138; Opposition's dependence on, 81; supports Proclamation against Seditious Writings, 81–82, 100; assists Mrs. Billington against Ridgway, 86; ridiculed by Inchbald's Young Men and Old Women, 93; ridiculed by Holcroft's Road to Ruin, 93; praised by Oracle, 100, 117, 126, 202, 203; said to have bought Stockbridge House, 100; begs Fox to join Government, 100–101; economizes, 101, 127–128, 130; rents Brighton pavilion from Weltje, 126; continues association with Mrs. Fitzherbert, 126, 202, 203, 458; figures in new plot of Sheridan and Thurlow, 126–128; advised by Sheridan, Thurlow, and Rawdon regarding payment of debts, 126, 127–128; dissipations, 128; plans for winter, 129–130; negotiates with Pitt, 130; inspects fortifications of Tower, 143; defended by Ministerial papers, 144, 153; urged to dismiss Erskine, 153, 201; said to lose interest in horses, 163; no innovator of fashions,

Wales, Prince of (con't).
164; frequents faro parlors, 164, 330; appealed to for release of Lafayette, 189; creditors asked to submit accounts, 202; reduces staff at Carlton House, 202, 214; reunited with family, 203, 254, 299, 362; George III rumored to be paying debts, 202, 213–214, 255; defects to Government, 202, 203; confers with Burke, 202; confers with Pitt and Dundas, 202, 204; deceives Sheridan, 202, 204; rumors of repudiation of Sheridan, 207, 213, 216; writes letter to Portland, 203, 204, 208; dismisses Erskine, 204, 207, 208, 213; rewarded with Colonelcy of 10th Regiment of Light Dragoons, 204, 208–209, 213; gets newspaper help with payment of debts, 204, 213; appoints Graham and Anstruther Attorney and Solicitor Generals, 207, 210; fails to influence Portland, 209, 213; degree of defection questionable, 213–214; pays debts at Brighton, 214; confers with Dundas and Fawcitt, 214; preoccupied with regiment, 225, 299, 362–363, 410; asked to influence Rawdon regarding Insolvent Debtors Bill, 254; negotiates with Pitt, 260; fails to support Traitorous Correspondence Bill, 262; plans for summer, 260, 262, 299; intimate of Duchess of Gordon, 299, 458; confers with Dundas regarding Clarence's repudiation of the war, 304, 364; sells interest in *Morning Post*, 333, 334; confers with Pitt, Dundas, Gloucester, King, and Queen, 362; rides charger sent by Duke of York, 363; officiates at military camp at Brighton, 363, 363–364, 371, 372, 373, 397, 411, 412; expected to command battalions of Highlanders, 411; plans to live in London, 415; patronizes concert for Spitalfields weavers, 455; dutiful son, 458; mentioned, 147; *see also* Carlton House

Walker, Thomas (1749–1817), cotton merchant and reformer (founder of Manchester Constitutional Society), denounced by Burke, 77; heads Manchester Constitutional Society, 84; corresponds with Jacobins, 102; house burned, 146; threatened by Ministerial papers, 215; officiates at dinner of London Constitutional Society, 268; arrest predicted, 276; indicted, 408; mentioned, 351

Wallace, Lady Eglantine (d. 1803), 330

Waller, Major Henry (fl. 1784–1793), journalist, 239

Walsingham, Thomas de Grey, 2nd Baron [GB] (1748–1818; suc. 1781; FRS, FSA 1778), Post Office official (Joint Postmaster General 1787–1794), 61, 62, 117

Walter, John the elder (1739–1812), printer and journalist, founder and conductor of *The Times*, 24, 173; Printer to the Customs, 24, 174; earlier career, 24, 32; imprisoned during Regency battle, 24, 29, 32, 119, 173, 378, 416, 445, 456; sued by John "Jew" King, 24, 32, 113–115; collects from the Treasury, 24, 26, 173; pensioned, 173–174; attacked by *True Briton*, 410–411; Heriot's complaints respecting, 448

Walter, William (c. 1763–1822), 24, 118, 125, 173, 378

War charities, commenced by ladies, 225, 226–227; concentrated on collection of flannel waistcoats, 415, 416, 423, 426–427, 455; mentioned, 362, 365

War Office, 187, 188

Ward, Mrs., actress at Drury Lane, 42

Warton, Thomas (1728–1790), poet (Poet Laureate 1785–1790), 177

Warwick, 271

Waterdown, military camp at, 360–361, 363, 373, 412

Watson, Brook (1735–1807), merchant and politician (MP London 1784–1793; Director of Bank of England 1784–1807; Commissary General to Duke of York's army 1793–?), 245, 246

Watt, James (1769–1848), reformer, denounced by Burke, 77, 237; member of Manchester Constitutional Society, 84; travels on Continent, 146; arrest predicted, 276; mentioned, 80

Watt, Robert (d. 1794), spy, informer, agitator, 116, 136

Weatherby, Mr., proprietor of *Morning Post*, 35, 36, 68

Weatherby, James, journalist and clerk of Jockey Club, 35, 36

Weddings, newspaper interest in, 331

Weissenburg, 456

Weld, Richard, 237

Wells, Juliet (b. 1781), actress, 320

Wells, Mrs. Mary (fl. 1781–1812), actress at Covent Garden, background, 25, 89–90; convalescing from illness, 26; resumes work at Covent Garden, 42, 89–90; adventures reported by *World*, 89–90; puffs self in *World*, 90; writes drama commentary for *World*, 90; *Diary*'s comments on, 90, 164; performs at Brighton theater, 90–91, 94; attends trial of Hastings, 181; in Fleet Prison, 320–321

Weltje, Amelia Louisa, Mrs. Louis, 128–129

Weltje, Louis (d. 1800), maître d'hôtel to Prince of Wales, character and financial situation, 17; connection with *Morning Post*, 35–36, 68, 97; Benjafield threatens to sue, 36; owns Brighton pavilion, 126, 363; association with Prince of Wales embarrassment to newspapers, 128; domestic squabbles, 128–129; quits *Morning Post*, 334, 452

Wemyss, Francis Charteris, styled Earl of (1723–1808), 357

West Indies, 391

West Riding, Lord Lieutenant of, 105

Westley, James, publisher, 74

Westley, R. H., publisher, 239

Westminster, Dean of, *see* Rochester, Samuel Horsley, Bishop of

Westminster, High Constable of, 471

Westminster, High Steward of, 109

Westminster election, *see* Election, Westminster

"Westminster Elector, A," *see* Stuart, Charles

Westminster electors, petition for removal of Rose, 65, 66, 75, 78; Fox's *Letter* to, 191, 192–194; petition for election reforms, 271

Westminster Hospital, President of, 109

Westminster Journal, 37, 169

Westminster police, 296

Westmorland, John Fane, 10th Earl of [GB] (1759–1841; suc. 1774; KG 1793), politician (Lord Lieutenant of Ireland 1785–1795), 195, 240, 296, 431, 440–441

Wharton, John (1765–1843), politician (MP Beverley 1790–1826), 73, 237, 284

Whieldon, Mr. (d. 1793), printer and publisher, 173, 342

Whieldon and Butterworth, publishers, 173

"Whig," as defined by Burke, 251

Whig Club, Burke a member of, 8; gives financial aid to newspapers, 38; joined by Mingay, 135; Fox presented with resignations from, 244; bars further membership of journalists, 244; Newnham's resignation from, 245; expected to contribute to fund for paying Fox's debts, 300; lampooned by Charles Stuart, 417

Whigs, Burke's alliance with, 8–9; character of, 9; interests defended by Erskine, 11; submit Prince of Wales's debts to Parliament, 13; not aided by Prince of Wales, 17; respect James Perry, 34, 35; owe Almon £900, 38; defended by Reid, 39; enthusiastic about Mackintosh's *Vindiciae*, 40; opposed by *Oracle*, 51; assail Rose, 63; rely on Prince of Wales, 81; no augmentation of, 184; run Mingay at Thetford, 184; supported by Newnham, 244; called upon to oppose Traitorous Correspondence Bill, 250; temporarily deserted by Adam, 274;

Whigs (con't).
frequent faro parlors, 330; support
Elliot as Speaker, 396; meeting of, 421;
support election reforms, 469; mentioned, 98; see also Opposition and
Rockingham Whigs
"Whigs, New," 14, 15
Whitbread, Samuel (1758–1815), brewer
and politician (MP Bedford Borough
1790–1815), politics, 10; founder of
Friends of the People, 79; on first
secretarial committee of Friends of the
People, 73; opposes augmentation of
forces, 210; protests proclamation
barring British citizens from returning,
260; supports Grey's motion for reform,
273; promises that Friends of the
People will continue the fight, 278; asks
for indictment of Archbishop of York,
292; asks for indictment of World,
292–293
White, Joseph, Treasury solicitor, 229,
236, 279, 280, 342, 344
Whitehall Evening Post, 26, 178
Whitehead, William (1715–1785), poet
(Poet Laureate 1758–1785), 177
Wilberforce, William (1759–1833), politician and philanthropist (MP Yorkshire
1784–1812), 228
Wilde, John, professor of civil law at the
University of Edinburgh, 80
Wilkes, John (1727–1797), politician and
London official (MP Middlesex 1774–
1790; City Chamberlain 1779–1797),
20, 197, 268, 353
Wilkie, T., publisher, 37
William IX, Landgrave of Hesse-Cassel
(1741–1821; suc. 1785), 305
Williams, Mr., reformer, 464
Williams, John (1761–1818), satirist and
miscellaneous writer, 89, 241, 279,
318
Williams, William, printer, prints Morning Post, 36–37; sued for libel on Rose,
65, 97, 138; responsible for content of
Morning Post, 98; sentenced for libel
on George III, 97–98, 138

Williamson, John (fl. 1783–1793), journalist and naval officer, 420
Williamstadt, 258
Wilson, Mr., actor at Covent Garden, 42
Wilson, A., printer, 171
Wiltshire, Receiver General of South
District of, 132
Wimbledon, 215, 369, 464
Windham, William (1750–1810), politician (DCL Oxford 1793; MP Norwich
1784–1802; manager for impeachment
of Hastings), political affiliations, 10,
81; early supporter of "New Whigs,"
14; buys puffs, 20; supports Proclamation against Seditious Writings, 71;
expected to become Foreign Secretary,
131; supports Address of Thanks, 149;
strong spokesman for Government,
155; supports Alien Bill, 183; supports
augmentation of forces, 210; fights for
restoration of Bourbons, 210; accuses
Fox of corresponding with French, 211;
expected to become Home Secretary,
221, 295–296; opposes inquiry into
seditious activities, 236; called an
alarmist, 236; solicits resignations from
Whig Club, 244; credited with saying
"Perish Commerce," 252, 399, 457;
preoccupied with French Revolution,
272; opposes Grey's motion for reform,
272; argues from "metaphysics," 272;
intimate of Pitt, 296; opposes Fox's
motion for reform, 304; appealed to by
Mrs. Bateman, 317; created DCL, 349;
praised at Portland's installation, 350;
said to have duped Pitt into war, 367;
declines office, 400
Windsor Castle, 254, 262, 458
Winterbotham, the Rev. William (1763–
1829), Baptist minister, 342, 443, 445
Witch-hunting, 143
Wolcot, Dr. John (1738–1819), satirical
poet, journalist, medical doctor, writes
for newspapers as "Peter Pindar," 39;
sued by Lonsdale, 39, 44–45, 60–61,
135, 137; quits newspapers, 61, 137;
said to be in pay of George III, 137;

resumes writing for Opposition papers, 334, 419; quoted 119, mentioned, 372
Wolfe, Arthur (1739–1803), lawyer and politician (Irish Attorney General 1789–1798), 214
Wolfe, L., reporter of debates, 30, 170, 172
Wolkenstein, Countess of, 55
Woodbridge, Robert, playwright, 328
Woodfall, Henry Sampson (1739–1805), printer and journalist, prints and conducts *Public Advertiser*, 23, 177–178; loses Treasury subsidy, 178; length of public service, 416; farewell address, 416, 417; quits *Public Advertiser*, 438; loses printing office in fire, 449
Woodfall, William, the elder, conductor of *Diary*, 22, 125, 172; patronized by Rose, 22; illness of, 125, 172–173, 380, 381; supports existing governments, 172, 173; collects from Treasury, 173; tries to sell *Diary*, 173; appointed Law Printer to George III, 173, 384; friend of Strahan, 173, 384; testifies for Dibdin, 317; publishes farewell address, 379–383; as reporter of Parliamentary debates, 380, 383, 384, 385; "principles" of, 382, 383, 387; length of public service, 380, 382, 384, 385, 387; *Morning Post's* tribute to, 383; appeals to Pitt, 383–384; supported City against Parliament, 385; candidate for City Remembrancer, 384–388, 417; character of, 383, 384, 386; eulogized by *World*, 384; difficulties with Government, 384, 385, 388; knowledge of law, 386; advertises volumes of Parliamentary debates, 388
Woodfall, William, the younger, lawyer and journalist, 22, 173
Woolwich, 394, 445, 461
Words, seditious, defined by The Association, 341–342; prosecutions for uttering, 341–342, 356, 403, 435, 448, 453
Wordsworth, William (1770–1850), 311
World, history, 14–15, 16, 23, 25, 29, 54,

306; subsidized by Treasury, 14–15, 25, 70, 170, 174, 175; patronized by Rose, 25, 118; character, 19, 24, 25–26, 69, 70, 175–176, 417, 419; printer, 26, 174; address, 26, 174; proprietor, 26, 174; personnel, 26, 29, 37, 39, 69, 70, 90, 118, 119, 283, 420; politics, 22, 175–176, 318, 348, 379, 418, 419, 468; represents Colman, 45, 94, 95, 318; defends Hastings, 49, 70, 291, 351, 354, 365, 377, 397, 402, 430; blames Lady Cowper for death of Leopold II, 54–55; defends Pitt against *Oracle*, 65; taunts Duke of York and Prince of Wales, 57; tries to blackmail Duke of York, 58–59; on sale of Prince of Wales's stud, 57, 58–59; concerned about quarrels in Post Office, 61, 62; defends Rose, 65, 98, 138; on Frost's claims against Hood, 65; publicizes Mackintosh's action against Stuart, 67; leased to Swan, 69, 71, 318, 417; demands reforms of legal profession, 70–71, 228, 230, 286–287, 440, 441, 445, 461, 464; proclaims defection of Portland faction, 82; demands Thurlow's resignation, 82–83; exasperated with Fox, 83; interest in Billington scandal, 86; sued by Dibdin, 88–89; continues to abuse Dibdin, 89; on Mrs. Wells, 89–90; concern for Burgoyne's family, 91; on Mrs. Merry's dismissal, 93; on Covent Garden, 92–93, 318–319; on Merry, 93, 94, 95; on Drury Lane, 95, 313, 315, 326–327, 327; condemns Opposition, 96, 222; taunts Erskine for defending Tattersall, 97; concerned about damages awarded Lady Lambart, 99; sneers at Lauderdale, 101, 206; applauds high taxes and large national debt, 101–102; praises Richmond, 104; on Pitt's appropriation of Cinque Ports, 106, 107; on Portland's election to Chancellorship of Oxford, 106, 107–108, 111; on Frost, 112; on Paine, 112; on Porson, 124; quarrels with *The Times*, 118; detests *Sun*, 119; attacks *Oracle*,

World (con't).

126; on Prince of Wales's economies, 126, 144; on Duke of York's dissipations, 128; on phantom insurrection, 139, 140; publicizes arrest of Charles Stuart, 140; on Army purges, 140–141; announces demise of *Argus*, 143, 151; applauds the times, 143; on Scottish Convention, 145–146; on augmentation of forces, 146; demands Erskine's dismissal, 153, 221; Topham loses interest in, 174; litigations pending against, 174; demise predicted, 175; describes itself as loyalest to Constitution, 175, 199–200; shares news with *Public Advertiser*, 178, 383; assailed by *Oracle*, 181; scoffs at Friends of the People, 184; wants *Morning Chronicle* burned, 199; sympathizes with Friends of the Liberty of the Press, 201; sneers at Opposition, 222; opposed to imprisonment for debt, 230, 440, 441, 464; praises Const, 230, 354; supports Anderson as MP for London, 245; commends Skinner, 245; on Frend, 277; advises Fox, Sheridan, and Francis, 283; on state of prisons, 286; endorses Insolvent Debtors Bill, 286–287; earlier indictments for attacks on Burke, 292; threatened prosecution for libel on Burke, 292, 293; loses Treasury subsidy, 293, 333; on fund for payment of Fox's debts, 300, 303, 305, 308, 310; on Duke of Clarence, 304, 370–371, 398; announces edition of Shakespeare, 311; on conduct of Madame Mara, 312; sued by Dibdin, 317–318; on Mrs. Esten and Duke of Hamilton, 322, 323–324; on Mrs. Siddons, 323; puffs Reynolds, 324–325; on fashions, 330; denounces gambling, 331; on Lauderdale's control of *Morning Post*, 336; later consolidation with *Morning Post*, 340; carries advertisement for sale of *Oracle*, 345; out of favor with Government, 348; defends younger Rose, 353; represents Salisbury, 353; on Tickell, 355; on Lonsdale's promised ship, 357; on Canning's election, 358; on stockjobbing, 359–360; on Brighton camp, 361–362, 363, 396–397; on Richmond, 361, 372, 393, 395, 396, 410; on "spirit" of Royal Family, 362; on Mrs. Jordan, 364, 370, 410; on Burke, 365, 377, 397, 430; on Glasgow petition for peace, 369; on Adolphus, 370; on the Rev. Knox, 372; on Howe, 376, 457; attempts to blackmail Government, 379; on progress of the war, 390; supports Woodfall, 384, 386, 388; on significance of Dunkirk, 395; on reason for the war, 398; defends Windham, 399; on recipients of patronage, 401, 429; abuses Fox, 408; on Fox's anniversary dinner, 409; on possible invasion, 411; on prorogation of Parliament, 413; eulogizes America, 414; publishes Charles Stuart's parody, 417, 418–419, 424, 452, 468; on collection of flannel waistcoats, 423; puffs Banks, 429; on Lord George Gordon, 436–437; on Muir and Palmer, 444, 445; related to *Morning Post*, 452; on trial of *Morning Chronicle*, 454; fights with *Oracle*, 470–471; quoted, 11, 53–54, 62–63, 85, 87, 97, 115, 130, 138, 151, 152, 168, 174, 200, 206, 275, 276, 300, 318, 321, 349, 356, 390, 426, 430

Worsley, Richard, 7th Baronet (1751–1805; suc. 1768), antiquary, traveler, politician (MP Newtown 1790–1793; Steward of Chiltern Hundreds 1793), 357, 358

Wren, Sir Christopher (1632–1723), architect, 323

Wright, Mrs., milliner, 322

Wright, Thomas (d. 1797), bookseller, 330

Wrightson, William (1752–1827), politician, 300

Wurmser, Dagobert Siegmund, Count von (1724–1797), Austrian general, 456

Wycombe, John Henry Petty, styled Earl of (1765–1809), politician (MP Chipping Wycombe 1786–1802), 425

Wynne, Sir William, Doctor of Laws in Ecclesiastical Court at Canterbury, 278

Yarmouth, Francis Seymour-Conway, styled (1750–1793) Viscount Beauchamp and (1793–1794) Earl of (1742–1822), politician and diplomat (MP Oxford 1768–1794; Commissioner to Prussian Army 1793; ambassador to Berlin and Vienna 1793–1794), frightened by Burke's dagger, 181; accuses Fox of corresponding with French, 210, 211; supports augmentation of forces, 210, 211; changes titles, 352; ambassador to Berlin, 352; rewards and emoluments, 428

Yatman, Matthew, informer, 135, 276

York, 324

York, Frederica Charlotte Ulrica Catherine, Duchess of (1767–1820), expected to marry Prince of Wales, 16; marries Duke of York, 16; character and background, 18; not intimate of Carlton House, 18; financial settlement, 53, 55, 57, 59; respected by newspapers, 16, 311; estranged from husband, 311

York, Frederick, Duke of (1763–1827; cr. 1784; KB 1767; KG 1771; FRS 1789), 2nd child and 2nd son of George III; military officer (Lieutenant General 1784; Colonel of Coldstream Guards 1784–1805; General 1793; Commander in Chief of Forces in United Provinces 1793–1795), early relationship with parents, 3–4; early alliance with Prince of Wales, 11; education, 12; supports Prince of Wales in Regency battle, 14; dissipations, 14, 17, 128; debts, 14; negotiates for Dutch loan, 14; marriage, 16; associations, 18; buys puffs in newspapers, 20; blackmailed by Oracle, 50–51; Establishment Bill, 16, 53, 55, 57, 59; Oracle's libels on, 50–51; attends debates on Establishment Bill, 55; blackmailed by World, 57; witnesses passage of Establishment Bill, 59;

financial settlement, 59; pays newspapers for silence regarding sale of Prince of Wales's stud, 60; agrees to provide security for payment of Prince of Wales's debts, 127; earlier duel with Lennox, 132, 395; loses interest in horses, 139, 143, 163; inspects fortifications of The Tower, 143; frequents faro parlors, 164; commands brigade of foot guards, 208–209; commands British army, 225; accepts Bell's apology, 232; leaves for Holland, 225, 232; contrasted with Duke of Clarence, 304; estranged from Duchess, 311; Murray as Adjutant General to, 359; command limited to United Provinces, 360; conducts visitors around battlefields, 362; sends charger to Prince of Wales, 363; fails to take Dunkirk, 390, 392, 393; losses, 390; lack of communication with Government, 390; retreats, 390; expected to join Austrians, 391; blames Richmond for defeat, 395, 396, 398; angered by lack of support, 410; blames Chatham, 410, 411; expected to take Maubeuge, 413; inactive, 413; mentioned, 147, 374, 412, 415, 424, 456; see also Army, Duke of York's

York, William Markham, Archbishop of (1719–1807), divine (Archbishop of York 1777–1807), 290–291, 292, 293

Yorke, Henry Redhead (1772–1813), reformer, 343, 408, 434, 463

York House, 463

Young, Arthur (1741–1820), agriculturist, journalist, politician (Secretary of Board of Agriculture 1793–1820), The Example of France sponsored by The Association, 223, 238, 297; lambastes Friends of the People, 239; answered by Stuart's Peace and Reform, 336–337, 468; appointed Secretary of Agriculture, 297

Ypres, 415

Zouch, the Rev. Henry (1725?–1795), antiquary and social reformer, 286